CW00816482

BAHRAM & THE AGA KHAN III

Bahram at stud in Newmarket; 1937

© Lionel Edwards Estate by courtesy of Felix Rosenstiel's Widow & Son, London

BAHRAM & THE AGA KHAN III

By Peter Corbett

Published in 2016 by Rinaldo Publishing Stowmarket IP14 3QX

© Peter Corbett

The right of Peter Corbett to be identified as the author of this work has been asserted in accordance with the Copyright, Designs and Patents Act 1988

All rights reserved. No part of this publication may be reproduced, stored in a retrieval system, or transmitted in any form or by any means, electronic, mechanical, photocopying, or otherwise without prior permission of the publisher.

A catalogue record of this book is available from the British Library.

ISBN 978–0–9566642–1–1

Typeset by RefineCatch Limited, Bungay, Suffolk, NR35 1EF

Printed and bound by CPI Group (UK) Ltd, Croydon, CR0 4YY

Also by Peter Corbett

Bayardo, the Life Times & Legacy of an Edwardian Champion

"They say the Lion and the Lizard keep
The Courts where Jamshyd gloried and drank deep:
And Bahram, that great hunter—the Wild Ass
Stamps o'er his Head, but cannot break his sleep.

Edward FitzGerald: The Rubaiyat of Omar Khayyam

Acknowledgments

I would like to thank Nigel Pullen for compiling the Appendices; without Nigel's indefatigable research in discovering all the winners sired by Bahram a complete record would not have been possible. Nigel was helped in tracing Bahram's winners and those of his descendants abroad by Manuel de Luque, John Prather, Rosana Rivera and Anne Visser.

Nigel, together with Alistair Nicolson, provided vital facts, information and advice in helping to write the chapter on the Aga Khan's breeding methods. This should not be taken as an indication that either shares all my views on breeding methods. However, although there are serious areas of disagreement both have provided essential information and opinion that have provided guidance in certain areas. Alistair may not agree with some of my conclusions but he will recognise where he has been of influence. I am particularly grateful for their help and enthusiasm.

Nigel also helped in the chapters on Blandford and Friar's Daughter. The list of winning descendants of Friar's Daughter was compiled by Nigel.

Particular thanks are extended to Mark Burkhardt, Lissa Oliver and Geraldine Childs for reading the texts. Mark was ever vigilant in correcting some of my occasionally eccentric punctuation and offering help and advice on all matters. This book has been enhanced by Mark's conscientious, objective, and when necessary critical observations. Lissa brought a different angle and her help in many areas helped bring clarity and provide ideas. Geraldine helped to provide perspective from the point of view of the racing enthusiast and to make sure the book remained largely readable. Their help and support are greatly appreciated.

Tim Cox was always available to cheerfully supply any obscure fact from his prodigious library. In addition he supplied some most informative letters written to and by the late Peter Willett with all manner of interesting recollections. Before his death Peter kindly gave his permission to quote from the correspondence. Tony Morris supplied books and newspaper cuttings. Greg Way supplied books, patiently allowing me to make use of those that I could not afford to buy and willing assembling periodicals and publications for those that I could.

The Jockey Club were kind enough to allow their copy of the painting of Bahram and Frank Butters which appears on the front cover to be reproduced. William Jarvis, who also has a copy of the painting, has kindly allowed me to make use of his copy.

William was also kind enough to allow me to photograph items in his possession and direct me in researching aspects of Frank Butters life. He also scrutinised the first few pages of the first chapter on Butters to check that I had not made any genealogical errors. William also put me in contact with his uncle: John Waugh who was generous with his time and provided many reminiscences which added much colour and insight to the chapters on Butters.

Tricia and Geoff Wragg were kind and very entertaining with their memories of the time Harry Wragg trained the Aga's horses that ran in the colours of the Aga's fourth wife Yvette.

Julian Muscat kindly provided transcripts of interviews with the Aga Khan IV: Karim. These provided a fascinating insight into His Highness's views on breeding and racing.

Geraldine MacCann's father assisted Colonel Peacocke in saving Bahram's life as a foal. At a memorable dinner hosted by Dick Brabazon, Geraldine related the story. The Aga was so delighted he presented her father with a signed photograph of Bahram!

Geraldine Childs displayed considerable diligence in discovering what might be the only photograph of Friar's Daughter. She also supplied the photograph of Bahram taken at Ascot. Geraldine was also kind enough to provide copies of the race cards reproduced.

Grateful thanks are extended to David Roe for arranging permission to reproduce the drawings and paintings by Lionel Edwards.

Finally, to my wife Brenda I owe so much; for her help with the photographs, designing the jacket and unfailing support, particularly when I wondered if this project would ever be completed.

Picture acknowledgments

The author and publisher are grateful to the following for providing the majority of the illustrations in this book and for allowing their copyrighted photographs to be reproduced:-
Rouch Wilmot Thoroughbred Library
Mary Evans Picture Library
Getty Images
The painting on the front cover by Alfred Haigh is reproduced courtesy of Jockey Club Estates.
The colour painting of Bahram by Alfred Haigh and the photograph of the artist at work are both reproduced courtesy of The National Horseracing Museum, Newmarket.
The drawings and paintings by the late Lionel Edwards appear by kind permission of his family.
Whilst every effort has been made to trace the copyright holders of all the illustrations for this book, it has not been possible in every case. The publishers will be pleased to rectify any omissions whenever possible.

Ratings

The ratings given throughout this book are either *Timeform* annual ratings from 1948, A century of Champions prior to that date, or the author's calculated with reference to the ratings supplied in the both of those publications. Not all the ratings are the same and where they differ those concerned are indicated. The individual ratings for each of Bahram's races are the author's. All ratings are calculated using the same principals used by those publications: they are designed to be comparable with any horse that ran since the beginning of the Twentieth Century. For example a horse rated 130 in Bahram's time is considered the equal of a horse rated 130 at any time in the Twentieth Century and up to the present day.

The value of money

Wherever a sum of money is quoted the approximate present day value is given in brackets. For example a pound in 1900 is worth about 99 pounds today, in 1920 about 33 pounds and in 1935 about 53 pounds today. It should be remembered that any true comparison is impossible because the retail prices index is not measured in the same way today as in Bahram's time. Money was not spent in the same way or on the same products in the past as today. Inaccurate it may be but it is the only method available to compare the value of money today with the past.

Foreword

The original idea for this book was to record the life and times of Bahram together with his legacy. Such a book would inevitably cover the lives of the people involved in his production and care: his owner and breeder, trainer and jockey. It was during the research on the lives of these three: the Aga Khan III, Frank Butters and Freddie Fox, that it became clear that no suitable biographical works of any length exist about Butters and Fox and that there was nothing about the Aga Khan III that satisfactorily covered all aspects of his life.

During the early 1950's two biographies of the Aga Khan; by Stanley Jackson and Harry Greenwall, appeared which are of only limited use in fully understanding his life. Both biographies, while they are interesting and provide much useful information, are not always light reading. On occasions they become mired in difficult to follow and hard to comprehend minutia with regard to the Aga's political and religious activities. However, on the credit side both Jackson and Greenwall enjoyed the advantage of being able to talk to their subject. The Aga Khan's own memoirs followed soon afterwards but were disappointing in many ways and failed to correct the errors he claimed were inherent in both books.

Therefore at the time of the Aga Khan's death all that existed were two hagiographies and a book of self-serving memoirs which were clearly inadequate in understanding the life of this extraordinary man who was a God to millions and an avuncular and, usually, a popular figure in the West. A further biography; by Willi Frischauer, followed in 1970 which added more without revealing enough of the Aga to satisfy the more demanding students. However, in the last thirty years two books by Mihir Bose and Anne Edwards went much further in helping those interested in better understanding the life of the Aga Khan III.

However, neither covered his life as a racehorse owner and breeder to any extent. In these important areas of the Aga Khan's life the books by Greenwall, Jackson, Bose, Edwards and Frischauer were short on understanding and detail. Somewhat surprisingly all five books displayed something approaching indifference and sometimes astonishing ignorance to the whole subject of thoroughbred breeding and racing. For example Frischauer described Pearl Diver and My Love as half-brothers because they were both products of the same sire! Greenwall misspelt Mumtaz Mahal and described the Ascot Gold Cup as a handicap! These were by no means isolated errors where the Aga Khan's racing activities were concerned.

It therefore seemed clear that a book covering both the Aga Khan's private life, his time as a world figure and God to millions of his followers, together with his influence and achievements in the area of thoroughbred breeding and racing would fill a gap.

Unfortunately such a book would be on an enormous scale and would leave little room for the original subject Bahram! Instead, while this book covers the Aga Khan III's life in all aspects, his private, political and religious activities are covered in précis form only. The space and scope of such a book as this does not allow for any searching insight into many areas of the Aga's life.

Where the Aga Khan III is concerned this book is essentially an overview of his life with only his career on the turf and as a breeder dealt with in any detail. Readers interested in seeking a greater insight into family history, political and religious activities are directed to the biographies by Frischauer, Bose and Edwards; and to a slightly lesser extent, the ones by Jackson and Greenwall.

The standpoint adopted on the majority of issues concerning the personal, sporting and racing life of the Aga Khan III is a critical one. The time has passed when biographies of prominent individuals are of any use to students and researchers if they fail to be objective and address the more sensitive areas of the subject's life. On this basis, sycophancy should have no part in any biography that seeks to discuss a life in a detached and impartial manner. However, achieving a satisfactory balance between recording events and interpreting them requires a fine balance. It is hoped that the reader will not feel that objectivity and fairness have been forsaken.

Plashwood
May 2016

Contents

Prologue   xv

1 The Life of the Aga Khan III; Part I   1
2 The Life of the Aga Khan III; Part II   37
3 The Aga Khan III; his life in racing Part I   83
4 The Aga Khan III; his life in racing Part II   135
5 The Aga Khan III; his and other breeding methods   185
6 Frank Butters; Part I   219
7 Frank Butters; Part II   235
8 Freddie Fox   285
9 Blandford   317
10 Friar's Daughter   333
11 Sandown Surprise   343
12 Glorious Goodwood and York   355
13 Middle Park Stakes   361
14 Champion Juvenile   369
15 Two Thousand Guineas   379
16 Derby and Ascot   395
17 Triple Crown Champion   421
18 Bahram the Great   439
19 Turkhan, Big Game & Persian Gulf   465

Statistics   485
Appendix I   Bahram at Stud   515
Appendix II   Big Game, Turkhan and Persian Gulf at Stud   535
Appendix III Other sons at stud   549
Appendix IV   Daughters as Broodmares   565
Sources   597
General Index   601
Index of Horses   609
Index of Races   617

Prologue

1904 Tully Ireland. A future peer of the realm is in earnest conversation with one of the world's religious leaders. The former is attempting to persuade the latter to enter the world of thoroughbred racing. Although it will be another 17 years before any positive steps are taken, this is the genesis of the greatest racing and breeding dynasty of the twentieth century.

1919 Co. Kildare Ireland. A colt foal is attacked in his paddock by carthorses that had broken in. It looked doubtful if he could survive the ordeal but he recovered to become a top-class racehorse but an even better sire.

1923 Alexandra Park. A smallish juvenile filly wins on her debut. It was to be her only success during a modest racing career. However, it is as a brood-mare that she will gain fame and her place in history.

1930 Newmarket. The flat season has concluded and as a result of the international financial crisis Britain's leading trainer has lost his position with a top owner. At the worst possible time, and aged over fifty, he sets up as a public trainer without owners or horses. However, his courage is to be rewarded and he progresses to even greater heights.

1931 Epsom Downs. A popular veteran jockey has ridden the winner of the Derby and probably believes that the pinnacle of his career has been reached. However, the following year a colt will be foaled that is destined to be greater than any horse he has ridden or could ever have dreamt of riding.

1934 Sandown Park. The most valuable juvenile race of the year is about to be run. A debutant colt, considered slightly backward and an outsider at 20–1, is taking his place in the line-up. The race is run and as the horses pass the post the large Saturday crowd is stunned and largely silent, seemingly unable to comprehend exactly what they had seen.

1 The Life of the Aga Khan III; Part I

A young Indian man is standing on the deck of a boat which is sailing slowly away from a British port. He is dressed immaculately from head to toe as an English gentleman and gazes wistfully at the gradually disappearing shoreline. He does not move until the last vestige of land has disappeared from view and then sighs as he turns and walks towards his cabin. When he reaches his final destination he will be attired in traditional Oriental dress and the disembarking port will be his home in India. However, he is determined that it will not be too long before he can again wear the clothes of fashionable London and return to enjoy all the delights of the metropolis.

*   *   *

The Aga Khan III was born Sultan Mohamed Shah at Karachi (then part of India under British colonial rule) on 2nd November 1877. From 1885 he was styled His Highness Aga Sultan Mohamed Shah, Aga Khan III. After many honours bestowed by the British at his death he was styled His Highness the Rt. Hon. Aga Sultan Sir Mohamed Shah, G.C.S.I. G.C.I.E. G.C.V.O. G.C.M.G. However, for the purposes of this book from now on he will generally be referred to as "The Aga". This is purely for reasons of simplicity and not to be regarded as any lack of respect.

At the age of eight, on the death of his father: the Aga Khan II Ali Shah, from pneumonia after getting wet while out shooting, he succeeded to the title of Aga Khan, first bestowed on his Persian-born grandfather by the British Government.

The Aga Khan III is the 48th in direct descent from the prophet Mohamed but the Aga owes his eminence to the arrival in Afghanistan in 1841 of Aga Khan Mehalatee, the refugee rebel chief of a Persian province, who was adopted by the British to further the cause of

Empire. Since that time the family of the Aga Khan has risen from Asian obscurity to the heights of political and social power together with great wealth.

The Aga Khan Mehalatee: the Aga Khan I was governor-general of the province of Kerman in Persia. He was a man of great military flair but little judgment and following some indiscreet involvement in an attempt to force his claims to the throne he fled. During the unrest his safety was threatened, he was defeated in battle and lucky to escape with his life.

The Aga Khan Mehalatee travelled through Afghanistan during the first Afghan war and was able to render assistance to the British army. He made for India, intending to settle in Bombay, and was again useful to the British government during the Sind campaign.

After an unhappy time in Calcutta he settled in Bombay, under British protection, and was duly rewarded. The title of His Highness was conferred upon him, his position as a religious leader recognised and, just as importantly, this was accompanied by a large pension. From then until his death in 1881 he acted as a peaceful religious leader. He was succeeded by his son: Ali Shah, who ruled for only four years.

*   *   *

The Aga Khan III descended in direct line from Fatima, daughter of the prophet Mohamed, of the Beni-Fatimite Caliphs, one time rulers of Egypt and of the Kwaja dynasty of Persia. He was thus the 48th Imam (spiritual head) of part of the Ishmaili sect of the Shia Muslims scattered over Asia and Africa and estimated to number in excess of ten million people. There are several Ismaili sects and the Aga Khan's followers are descendants of Nizari Ismailis known as Khojas. The Aga Khan is not the leader of the Ismailis, but of a sect within the Ismailis called the Khojas.

The followers of the Aga Khan pay a *dasong* (a tithe, which would normally be of ten per cent) to him each year of one eighth of their income. It is impossible to know how much money in total the *dasong* raises. In any event the Aga Khan III was wealthy in his own right with a fortune, astutely managed by his mother, estimated at twenty million pounds (1,980,000,000), although as will be shown later this may be on the high side.

*   *   *

Ali Shah had not wanted his son to be aware of his divine status however, this changed with his early death and from the age of eight the young Aga was trained to be conscious of his inheritance and the magnitude of its responsibilities. Although the Aga Khan III claims a heritage as a descendent of the prophet his followers: the Khojas, actually pray to him as a God. In other words he is accorded a status higher than the prophet Mohamed, something the other Muslims might consider blasphemous. Ismailis consider themselves to be superior to other Muslims: more sophisticated and different from the rest of the Islamic fraternity.

The Aga's early years were difficult, even harsh. This may have been because he was the only surviving heir, his two full brothers had both died in infancy and his two half-brothers in their young manhood. He was delicate and, rather morbidly, a succession of English doctors had forecast that he would not live to age twenty-five. In consequence he was watched over vigilantly and with some trepidation, nurses fussed over him, particularly after his father died, when the young Aga was just four-years-old. Never again would he be totally carefree as his responsibilities were immediately made clear.

The Aga's father's death was not the disaster for his mother that it might have been. The ritual of suttee: a widow being sacrificed on her husband's funeral pyre was commonplace in India at that time. Although it was a Hindu rather than a Muslim practice some Khojas practised it. However, with Lady Shah her husband's death liberated her and she took control of the young Aga's financial affairs, with considerable success.

*   *   *

From the age of his succession at the age of eight until he was eighteen the young Aga's life was largely unchanging: November to April was spent in Bombay, and then as it grew hotter around May the family moved to a hill station about 100 miles away called Mahabaleshwar. When the rains duly arrived the family moved down to Poona which was still cooler than Bombay and it was not until November that the weather permitted a return to Bombay.

As a youngster the Aga was often unhappy, because not only was he weighed down by the prospect of his future responsibilities but also by his largely solitary existence. His routine was boring and puritanical not helped by his being extremely short-sighted; something his family refused to acknowledge in the belief that he was being self-indulgent! At this time the Aga was gradually being made aware of the extent of his divine status and he occasionally received followers who came to pay homage and respects. The Dowager Countess of Jersey visited India in 1888 and recalled the young Aga as a stout youth with dark eyes and hair and a very composed manner. The Dowager was told that he sometimes had a milk bath and that his followers were then allowed to drink the milk in which he had bathed.

The Aga's early moral and educational instruction came mainly from his mother, Lady Ali Shah, a truly remarkable and accomplished woman, who, in addition to understanding finance and investment, was deeply religious and extremely well read in Persian and Arabic literature. She was conscious of the need to maintain discipline and frequently ordered his bottom to be spanked; on one occasion the beating he received from an Islamic tutor was so severe a servant pleaded with Lady Shah to intervene. "No" she replied. "It is better that he should be punished than grow up ignorant. He must learn to fulfil his destiny." There seems to be only one portrait of her which was taken in middle age and unfortunately gives her rather the appearance of the sort of woman that tells fortunes at a fair! The Aga once admitted that his mother was the only person of whom he was ever afraid.

For all matters Islamic the Aga was mainly tutored by an individual who was a "bigoted sectarian" whose mind was "one of the darkest and narrowest" he was ever to encounter. "It was saddening and in a sense frightening to listen to him talk. He gave one the feeling that God had created men solely to send them to hell and eternal damnation".

In his memoirs the Aga wrote "The vast majority of Muslim believers all over the world are charitable and gently disposed to those who hold other faiths, and they pray for divine forgiveness and compassion for all. There developed, however, in Iran and Iraq a school of doctors of religious law whose outlook and temper – intolerance bigotry and spiritual aggressiveness – resembled my old teachers, and…. who ardently and ostentatiously sing the praises of the Lord, and yet are eager to send to hell and eternal damnation all except those who hold precisely their own set of opinions".

The Aga was also tutored by three Europeans: Messrs. Gallagher, Lawrence and Kenny. However, it was not until Mr. Kenny took over the Aga's education that his short-sightedness was diagnosed! Kenny had once worked as an optician and immediately noticed the problem and was able to convince the Aga's family that he really was short sighted.

His tutors must have had some effect as by the age of thirteen the young Aga could read and write tolerable English and French, good Russian and fair Arabic. In addition he had a sound knowledge of Roman and Islamic history; was grounded in the elements of science and chemistry, physics, botany, biology and zoology. The Aga was not content with simple theory; each of his houses had a small laboratory where he conducted experiments. Despite this he never sat an examination in his life; the result of which was that his intellectual capacity was never tested. This may account for his letters and writings being unstructured, often lacking stops, commas and possessing poor grammar and syntax.

The Aga's early passion though was reading; so much so that when he needed books he resorted to stealing! He had no allowance and organized with his cousin to take books. The bookshop proprietor noticed and told his mother and uncle who ensured that the books were paid for; but it was decided to teach the boys a lesson. Nothing was said and when they again stole books – by hiding them under an *abba* (a wide all-enveloping cloak) – his uncle was waiting and the subsequent humiliation ensured that kleptomania would never be one of the Aga's life-long hobbies!

The Aga's education continued under Mr. Kenny's direction until the age of eighteen; however, his mother's influence, control and guidance were always close at hand. In future the Aga was to travel far and wide, not always with his mother's approval and often against her wishes, as he pursued a Western lifestyle. However he never lost touch with Lady Shah until her death and they remained close until the end.

*   *   *

In 1893 the Aga was just fifteen when he initially revealed to the British, who were ever on the alert for ways to maintain their authority in India, how he might be of beneficial influence to them in future. During the Bombay riots the Aga issued instructions to his followers to avoid any participation in the disturbance.

*   *   *

In the summer of 1896 when the Aga was only 18 a strange and always unexplained event took place. The Aga later claimed he had fallen in love with a beautiful girl: Shahzadi and had persuaded his mother to arrange a marriage. Shahzadi's father was the Aga's uncle: Aga Jangishah who in company with his son Abbas; a friend of the Aga's, went on a pilgrimage to Mecca. On their return, when they stopped at Jeddah, they were ambushed and stabbed to death.

The culprits were apprehended and imprisoned but they never stood trial as they were found dead in their cells the following morning; poisoned. No proof of a plot has ever emerged but there was a suspicion that Jangi was proposing to usurp the Aga either in favour of himself or his son Abbas. The inference was that the Aga had arranged for the culprits to be poisoned in order to avoid his family being implicated in the original murders.

Whatever the truth the effect on the Aga was dramatic: his health was affected badly with various fevers and rheumatic complaints. Despite this the marriage went ahead on his nineteenth birthday. There has always been a suspicion that Lady Shah ensured that the nuptials took place in order to silence the rumours that either she or the Aga was responsible for the death of the bride's father.

The marriage was a complete failure; the problem could have been sexual; possibly non-consummation. In any event the marriage was effectively over within two years and they had separated; although they stayed married and the Aga provided his wife with every conceivable luxury. Shahzadi, however, remained bitter until the end of her life; she died in middle age fat, neglected, largely forgotten and scorned by the Aga's family. However, she was never formally, and more importantly legally, divorced from the Aga while she was still alive; something that caused him considerable problems later.

*   *   *

The young Aga did not lack courage which he demonstrated again in the late summer of 1897 when bubonic plague swept through Bombay. Professor Haffkine was working on an inoculation following Pasteur's work in this field. However, this was regarded with scepticism and the Aga allowed Haffkine to use a bungalow to carry on his work and was himself inoculated to demonstrate to his superstitious followers that this was not harmful.

*   *   *

Despite his youth at the age of nineteen he was chosen to present the address on the occasion of Queen Victoria's Diamond Jubilee. This was not only on behalf of Muslims but "on behalf of a representative assemblage of the citizens of Bombay and Poona". His address contained praise for the magnificent reign of Victoria and an assurance of his loyalty to the British throne. Lord Elgin, Viceroy at that time, was impressed by the easy grace the young Aga brought to the occasion.

*   *   *

It had taken some time but by early 1898 the Aga's health was restored and he was ready to embark on a visit to Europe which he commenced in February of that year. Accompanied by two of his household servants, the Aga set off from Bombay on a ship bound for Marseilles. He was intending to visit first the Riviera and then England. Apart from his servants the Aga was initially largely alone as he did not know anybody. However, he barely noticed as he spent most of the time mesmerized by the glamour and splendour of all the prominent individuals he observed.

The Aga sent a note to Queen Victoria requesting an audience. This was acknowledged and a short while later a summons arrived to dine with her. At last! The Aga was dazzled by the world's most powerful monarch and apart from the Aga treating the Queen's Indian secretary, the despised Munshi, with discourtesy, something that affronted her; she seems to have liked him.

The Aga loved the Riviera but realized that if he was to make his mark he had to make an impression in London. He would be better noticed there but although he was to achieve celebrity later, *The Times* made no mention of his visit, the first time the name of the Aga Khan III appeared was in1906, and in 1898 he was not considered a prominent enough individual. However, Queen Victoria's invitation to Windsor effectively opened all doors to him. The Queen received him privately; extended her hand to be kissed and told him she was going to Knight him. However, as he was a prince The Queen considerately did not ask him to kneel; she simply handed the order to him. In addition the Aga formed a lasting friendship with the Prince of Wales; later Edward VII, this was despite the difference in years as Edward was 36 years the Aga's senior.

*   *   *

The Aga took full advantage of the opportunities England offered: embracing a European lifestyle and wearing fashionable stylish clothes. He was fitted with a complete wardrobe: frock and morning coats, stiff collars, silk hats, patent leather shoes and gloves, country attire for visits to stately homes and country houses. His wardrobe was complete with all that was *de rigueur* for a modern gentleman about to be caught up in the social whirl of activities offered by *fin de siècle* London.

The Aga's hectic schedule took in balls, garden parties at ducal mansions, country house weekends, dining at the finest tables in London, the opera, and, of course thoroughbred racing. On at least one occasion there was dancing and he would have much enjoyed accompanying the many attractive women available; unfortunately he could not dance. This omission was corrected immediately on his return to India when he hired a young Englishman to teach him.

European women made an immediate impact on the Aga and he found he preferred them to Asian women. However, he would need to learn some European manners! At one dinner party he was introduced to Florence Nightingale who observed that he was "a most interesting man, but one is never likely to teach him sanitation". Apparently during the course of dinner he had used the corner of the tablecloth to wipe his mouth and belched loudly as he left the table!

Probably unaware of the mixed impression the Aga had made he was euphoric; he liked the role women played in European society and he enjoyed their company. His exotic background and generous behaviour was attractive to all sorts of women: actresses, ballet dancers and young socialites. He particularly liked them slim and dark-eyed, however, he was discreet in his relationships; he was never seen alone with a woman in public and private dinners were held in rooms or hotel suites.

The Prince of Wales made him a member of the Marlborough Club and, as the Aga was a successful owner and breeder in India, Queen Victoria presented him with a Royal Household badge for the enclosure at Ascot. He never forgot this gesture and he was immensely proud of the courtesy which was extended to him by each succeeding monarch throughout his life.

Marlborough Club membership was rarely given to those outside Britain's aristocracy and to Indians of the Aga's generation it was quite an honour. The club was the most coveted of all offering as it did immediate entrée into royal circles. The Aga and the Prince became good friends and probably disagreed over only on issue: tobacco. When offered a cigarette the Aga took one puff and laid it aside with an apology. He never touched a cigarette again.

Over the years the Aga wrote letters from all over the world to friends and political associates; generally from hotels in the South of France. However, communications to the Palace or British officials in London were always written from the Marlborough Club.

The Aga visited the Prince of Wales's stud at Sandringham and he attended the Derby where backed the winner Jeddah. He told the

Duke of Connaught that he hoped to win the Derby one day. Whether this was just a conversational remark or, he was so captivated by the world's premier horse race that he resolved that he must win it, is not known.

*   *   *

Effectively India had been under British rule and part of the Empire since the famous defeat of the Nawab of Bengal in the battle of Plassey by Robert Clive in 1757. The battle was fought to protect the trading posts of Calcutta. The British version of the history of acquisition in India is largely a myth: the steady advance, absorbing Indian states and replacing corrupt Indian rule with good honest British administration. However, the British originally went to India for trade and never forgot it. For one hundred years it was governed by the East India Company until the Mutiny in 1857 by soldiers employed by the Company rebelling against their rule. The outcome was that all power was transferred from the East India Company to the British Crown who then administered most of India until independence in 1947.

The British did not view it as inequitable that a few of its appointed administrators should govern so vast and populous a country. Britain viewed Indians with a mixture of paternalism and arrogance, exploiting the caste system as a means of maintaining power. India was to all intents and purposes a conquered land with even the wealthy and titled viewed as an inferior and subordinate race.

The Aga Khan was in a different position: he was not just rich but as an Imam had jurisdiction over a considerable number of Muslims, including many in other lands which Britain did not control. He was in a position to influence Muslim groups towards British interests and could be very useful. In addition to his wealth, which was useful to the British as he would not be seeking financial help, but also as he was of Persian descent he was a lighter colour than most Indians and socially more acceptable. The Aga had already demonstrated that he could adapt to European ways by wearing appropriate dress and displaying, usually, correct demeanour.

*   *   *

The Aga returned to India via Germany where he met the Kaiser to request concessions for his followers in German East Africa. The Kaiser and the Aga enjoyed cordial relations and the concessions were granted. However, the Aga refused to agree that Indian immigrants to East Africa should renounce their allegiance to Britain and become German subjects. Nonetheless, the Kaiser conferred on him the Prussian Order of the Royal Crown, First Class.

*   *   *

And so it was that several months after arriving in Europe he returned to Bombay in the autumn of 1898. He boarded the liner as a short, corpulent individual with a pince-nez and a neat black moustache dressed in a Savile Row suit, cravat with a jewel pin at his neck and a silk hat. He stepped off the liner in Bombay dressed in the robes of a Muslim with a grey astrakhan fez on his head and his feet encased in Oriental slippers. However, there could be no doubt how he would prefer to be dressed from now on.

*   *   *

During his absence in Europe Hashim Shah, a nephew had been shot dead in Poona. The assassin was Jiva Jooma the steward of the Aga's house in Poona. He was tried and sentenced to transportation for life. The reason for the killing was never established but it was rumoured that Hashim Shah was planning to challenge the Aga's leadership. This provided more ammunition for the dissidents to the Aga's leadership.

In response to this the Aga decided upon drastic action. He was convinced that the problem was the world his grandfather had created. The Aga was personally supporting about 2,000 followers with pensions brought to India under his Grandfathers rule. The Aga's solution was to deport many back to the Persian Gulf and to exile others to remote hill stations and prevent them ever returning to Bombay.

To achieve this he was assisted by the Bombay police and supported by Sir William Lee Walker in London and Lord Northcote, then Governor of Bombay. There were even suggestions that the police might be in the pay of the Aga.

*   *   *

Lady Ali Shah was very unhappy that the Aga had spent so much time in Europe and persuaded him to spend more time visiting Khoja communities. He visited Africa and intended to return home via the Riviera which he hoped would coincide with the Queen's annual visit. However, due to the Boer war the Queen stayed at Windsor; he never saw her again.

The death of Queen Victoria in January 1901 affected the Aga considerably. She had always been to him a symbol of majesty and mystery and had wanted to be accepted by her, almost as a child might wish to be favoured by its mother. With her death something had gone forever.

The new King: Edward VII had received a recommendation from Lord Northcote that as recognition of the services the Aga had supplied to the British government the previous year he be upgraded from a KCIE to a GCIE and this was announced in the Coronation Honours List in summer of 1902. The Aga attended the delayed Coronation of The King, who had been taken ill with appendicitis the previous year.

*   *   *

When the Aga returned to India in November 1902 he received a letter from The Viceroy: Lord Curzon, inviting him to become a member of the Legislative Council. With problematic relations between Muslims and Hindus under constant discussion the Aga was scathing about the Indian Congress Party who he considered blind to the needs of Muslims. The Council had no real power but it allowed members to air their views. The Aga was the youngest member and the only serving Indian that had spent much time in Europe. He served two years, but, was not offered a second term, although he suggests in his memoirs that he would not have accepted one had it been offered. The Aga, despite all the honours that he was given, was essentially a religious leader. Despite his efforts he was not a particularly prominent or even very successful political one.

*   *   *

Lord Curzon was concerned that with the death of Queen Victoria India's enthusiasm for the Crown might be wavering. His Lordship once stated that it would take 500 years before the Indians would be capable of governing themselves and considered it vital that they supported the British Monarchy. And so in January 1903 the Aga staged a spectacular Durbar – a ceremonial gathering – and this grand and ostentatious spectacle was deemed a success despite the Aga feeling uncomfortable in his full costume. Clearly the comfort of a Savile Row suit was more to his taste!

*　　*　　*

Not long after the Durbar and, much to his mother's chagrin, the Aga was off again to Europe. She was concerned that there was no heir; being aware that this was unlikely with relations between the Aga and Shahzadi completely fractured. She wanted the Aga to divorce Shahzadi and marry another Ismaili with high connections and get on with the task of producing an heir. However, the Aga had almost certainly made up his mind by this stage that only a European woman would suit him.

The Aga wanted someone he could respect and talk to who shared some of his interests, spoke languages, could travel with him and hold her own in royal society. Indian princesses seldom travelled abroad and usually had a confined education. No; it had to be a European woman. It would transpire that the Aga chose to neglect all but the last of his European wives, giving them little opportunity to display their social skills.

Despite his lifestyle he continued to be in constant contact with his mother and wrote to her almost every day.

*　　*　　*

Sometime during 1903 The Aga met Sir Walter Roper-Lawrence, a man of considerable influence in India; at one time Lord Curzon's private secretary and later a member of the India Council. Although he was only five years older than the Aga, Sir Walter was considerably wiser in the ways of the world. Between 1903 and 1906 The Aga was a complete novice in political circles and almost everything he did in public life was approved by Sir Walter and the Aga became dependent on him in an almost pathetic, childlike way.

However, astonishingly this close friendship was not acknowledged publicly in any way; the Aga makes no mention of Sir Walter in his memoirs, and Sir Walter does not mention the Aga in his: *The India We Served*, published in 1928. That there was such a friendship is clear from the letters between them, although these are almost exclusively from the Aga to Sir Walter. These reveal an amazing assortment of the curious, timid, naïve and, on occasions, unexpected. That the Aga needed help is not surprising as he was living away from home in the European quarter of Calcutta; a city which was, at that time, at the height of its glory. The Aga was, in all probability short of friends as most of the British clubs did not allow Indian members and, in this respect, as a member of the Marlborough Club, he was better off in London than India.

The Aga confessed to Sir Walter that he hankered to return to Persia, although this would be a contradiction in terms as he had never been there! His family were relatively recent migrants to India and he had a romantic notion that the Shah might call him to Persia. This was very unlikely and, with his attitude to India, the Aga was aware that he would not live his life in the manner of his father and grandfather. They had never visited Europe and the Aga was finding life in India suffocating compared to the Riviera and London and, to be blunt, he was bored with orthodox Indian Muslim society.

The Aga made a big error of judgement in December 1903 when on a visit to Bombay he called on the Governor, Lord Lamington, who had been shocked to learn that the Aga had ignored the obligations for Muslims of Ramadan. This had caused offence in the Muslim community and although the Aga's influence had been "useful" to the British he would only continue to be so in future if he was a good Muslim. The Aga thought all this a chore and told His Lordship he could hardly be bothered with Indian society. This attitude could easily have placed in peril the Aga's position with the British government and may even have coloured the views of some government officials in future.

*   *   *

By this time the Cote d'Azur and England were definitely the Aga's preferred domain and not India. He preferred to pursue attractive European women and be in the company of prominent Europeans and he was enjoying a full life. However, his behaviour was giving rise to some critical comments, and, in particular, one serious allegation. The precise nature of these assertions was unknown but the Aga wrote to Sir Walter and said that a "serious charge" had been made against his character.

It would seem that the Aga had upset Lord George Hamilton, the Secretary of State for India by not agreeing with an appointment and earned the epithet from Lord George who called him an "uppity Indian", who, in addition, had too much book learning for his own good! The Aga was rescued from the wrath of the noble Lord by Sir Walter, something the Aga was very grateful for, so much so that he subsequently funded one of Sir Walter's projects.

Notwithstanding all of this the Aga's popularity among the Muslim population was not in obvious decline and this helped to strengthen his relationship with Britain and the Crown. Shortly after the Durbar the Prince and Princess of Wales visited India; the Aga had hoped that they might stay with him at his newly acquired estate in Calcutta. They did not, but did receive him together with Lady Shah. All may not have been totally harmonious however, as the Prince was sensitive to the plight of women in India and not afraid to say so.

*   *   *

By 1906 The Aga Khan was regarded by India's Muslims as their titular leader; Muslims were in total about 25% of India's population at that time of just fewer than 300 million. The Aga was appalled that only seven per cent of his fellow Muslims could read and only one in a hundred women were able to write their names. He was concerned about illiteracy in his followers throughout his life and became determined to improve the standard of education amongst his followers. The Aga was saddened by the illiteracy and brooding fatalism with which his Muslim followers accepted their domination by Hindus who were better educated and more active in trade and public life.

"Educate, educate, educate" the Aga would declaim passionately. "If by education the myriads of India can be taught that they are guardians of the Crown, just as white citizens of the Empire, then the realization that India and the self-governing dominions stand and fall together, bound by a community of interests and a common cause to maintain, will come. It is imperative to give Indians the education to fit them for their future role in the British Empire".

The Aga was asked to petition the Viceroy: Lord Minto, for guarantees for Muslims against the Hindu majority and to have their own representation. Shortly afterwards the All India Muslim League was founded with the Aga as a founding member and first president.

The League was concerned only with Muslim rights and this led to separate constituencies for Muslims and Hindus. Hindus and Muslims had distrusted and disparaged each other for centuries; Hindus regarded Muslims as pariahs; even touching a Muslim hand would cause a Hindu to immediately purify himself with ritual ablutions. Intermarriage was condemned on both sides and virtually unheard of.

The differences between the religions caused many problems: Hindus worshipped God in many forms; animals – the cow is sacred – the sea, the sun, divine incarnations, ancestors and sages. Muslims abhor idols; idolatry, paintings and statues are considered blasphemous; although there are examples of paintings of animals and humans. Hindus were generally more educated and it could be said that the British were probably more comfortable with them than Muslims.

The British in India, far from wanting to unite Hindus and Muslims, were far more concerned that such unity might come about! For example Lord Lamington wrote to John Morley (secretary of state for India): "the real guarantees of our (British) stay in India are as strong as ever over the caste system; the diversity of nationalities, greed and the lack of confidence and trust in one native for another". A wonderful example of divide and rule!

The Aga Khan was perfectly aware that lack of education was an impediment to the advancement of Muslims. He built schools for his young followers and stressed the importance of education at every opportunity. The League did not achieve much in its early years possibly not helped by the Aga spending no more than about two months each year in India. However, it gave the Aga a useful title and a propaganda platform. He remained as president until 1912.

*   *   *

In his memoirs the Aga described the period from 1900 – 1909 as "nine crowded years". Well he was certainly active enough; almost always travelling and visiting Europe as often as he could. However, in nearly fifty pages he says very little of interest. He seemed concerned only to record political and religious events that show him to have been in some way effective and in a favourable light; generally writing platitudes and banalities. Thankfully some of his biographers have been more diligent in their research making it possible to understand more of his life and activities. For example the Aga admitted to a love of the Riviera but was reticent about his pleasures and private life to their almost total exclusion. It could not have been expected that he would disclose details of mistresses but surely he could have said something of his time attending the "playground of Europe"

In addition at this time the Aga was at the height of his, limited, political influence, but was ambitious of not only leading India's Muslims, but all the Muslims of the world. However, his way of life was always going to be against his making any headway as a world leader. He found living in India suffocating and preferred Europe; this meant he was happier speaking on behalf of his Muslim followers from London than actually being amongst them in India.

In truth although his followers in India treated him as a God this was something of a burden to the Aga and he found the duties of an Imam taxing. However he could be light-hearted about them; once in Cairo he was walking with an Englishman when a Khoja follower prostrated himself at the Aga's feet. He blessed the man and turning to his friend said "there, you see, being a God is not all beer and skittles". On the other hand in London being a God to a distant people and being very wealthy brought magic, mystery and fun.

When in Europe, but not London, the Aga established his

headquarters at Aix-les-Bains where he took to the waters. However, Aix-les-Bains had another attraction for him: it was close to the Swiss border and not far from Lausanne University which was a useful listening post for Indian affairs and the Aga was frequently to be seen there.

*   *   *

The Aga was to gradually lose some influence by expressing alarming and indiscreet views and whilst always postulating a position supporting Britain, in reality his only concern was his own position. Sir Harcourt Butler, Commissioner for Lucknow described the Aga as "clever but a weathercock" having expressed the view that Muslims did not have a leader in 1913. Also in November 1909 scorn was poured on the Aga's ideas on reforms advocated by the India Council which seemed to be only to further his own position. "The doubtful advocacy of the Aga Khan is to be dispensed with", said Harvey Adamson, Home member for the Viceroy's Executive Council. In fairness to the Aga being "clever but a weathercock" might have been part of his strategy for survival!

The Aga took some sort of perverse pride from that fact that although he frequently left his followers to visit Europe for long periods; they seemed to be able to manage without him. But upon his return to India he found that the ground had shifted a little more from under his feet and consequently his influence was a little less. The Aga admitted to friends, including British officials, that he was lazy; he liked the ease and comfort of life in England and the South of France. However, he claimed he would give it all up to be able to "bring all that remained of independent Islam under British Influence".

*   *   *

The Aga would continue to be involved with Muslim political affairs for some years, not just in India but everywhere else he had followers, with varying levels of success and considerable anguish as he was frequently thwarted and failed to achieve his objectives. The problem for the Aga was that his political importance counted for nothing with the Rajahs; he was not a prince in their eyes and had no land and was ranked below even the least of the Ruling Chiefs.

At ceremonial occasions he was treated as a Ruling Chief but this did not continue into everyday Indian life, he was just another educated Indian. Even after the Great War and until 1924 he was involved in Muslim affairs to a greater or lesser extent; but it could not be claimed however, apart from one episode during the war possibly, that his successes or influence were in any way significant and on occasions quite the opposite.

*   *   *

Just how effective the Aga had been during these nine years of activity is open to question. However, it was certainly hectic and was to prove damaging, at least in the short term, to his health; his heart was not particularly strong and while visiting the Viceroy in the autumn of 1907 he collapsed and was ordered to rest. However, the Aga had recovered enough and his spell of inactivity was only a short one before he set out on a world tour.

The Aga headed east and visited Malaya, Singapore and China and Japan. He visited Honolulu which he thought a haven of peace and happiness, before he reached the United States. His first stop was San Francisco which had suffered a catastrophic earthquake only the previous year; the place was in almost total ruin and he was glad to arrive in New York. The Aga proved to be a popular figure as he attended parties visited museums the theatre and opera. In addition he was received by President Theodore Roosevelt and attended a lavish ball given by Mrs. Ogden Mills of the famous horse racing family, in the Aga's honour.

The Aga attended the sensational trial of Harry K Thaw, the millionaire husband of the beautiful Evelyn Nesbit, in January 1907. The Aga had met her in London at the home of Baron de Rothschild and was attracted to Evelyn who was known as "Baby face". A friend took him aside and warned him that her husband was violently jealous of anyone paying his wife too much attention. Evelyn confessed to her husband that before their marriage she had been drugged and seduced by the architect Sandford White. Thaw's homicidal rage, induced by this revelation was not improved by his suspicion that White was still pursuing Evelyn. Thaw met White waltzing with a new conquest on the dance floor of the Madison Square Roof Garden. White pulled a revolver and fired six shots into him. Thaw escaped the electric chair on the grounds of insanity. He was released eighteen years later.

The Aga might have thought as he watched proceedings that he might easily have been the victim!

*   *   *

By now fully restored to health The Aga Khan returned to the South of France: Monte Carlo which was at the height of its golden age in 1907. The resort was a magnet for gamblers, conmen and opportunists, both male and female. Rich American heiresses and impoverished titled foreigners used it as a mating ground and many profitable liaisons were sealed there.

As a man with a title and great wealth the Aga never lacked female companionship. In addition to its casinos Monte Carlo also boasted cultural attractions and the Aga had from the time of his introduction to Europe supported the arts; music and ballet in particular but also theatre and art. He was a friend of both Massenet and Puccini and on one occasion when the Aga was visiting the former, he was shown up to his sitting room where Massenet was sitting naked in his bath dictating to his secretary! A flow of inspiration could not apparently be withstood!

The Aga was attending the ballet while his search for a suitable wife was occupying him. This pursuit had not led him to a high ranking European woman; far from it, and in 1908 he fell in love with a ballerina in Monte Carlo. Theresa Magliano, or Ginetta as she was known, had captivated the Aga during a performance with her elegant grace, posture, demeanour and movement. He was so enchanted he returned the following night to see her again. The Aga was determined to get an introduction with probably no other intention than to obtain another demimondaine; after all ballerinas did not enjoy the best of reputations and were considered charming mistresses, but hardly marriage material for someone in the Aga's position.

In his memoirs the Aga claimed that he and Ginetta almost immediately fell in love. She was almost certainly captivated with his exotic status and, as she was an innocent, she probably viewed the attention as like something out of *A Thousand and One Nights!* The Aga wooed her assiduously with fabulous jewels and eventually she agreed to take an apartment, paid by him, in order that they could meet privately.

The Aga was known in Monte Carlo for spending a night with a woman and then sending her an exotic expensive gift then never seeing her again. Ginetta was different; the Aga believed himself truly in love and, even before they became involved sexually, he promised that he would settle a comfortable sum on her, even if she decided against any such involvement. However, if she did bear him a son he would obtain a divorce and marry her.

Whatever her feelings Ginetta was pregnant within a month. The Aga made up his mind that he would marry Ginetta whatever the gender of the child. He returned to Bombay to confront his mother with his decision to divorce Shahzadi, marry a European woman and make his home on the Continent. These were not the only obstacles he needed to overcome: Ginetta was a Roman Catholic whose religion did not recognise marriage to a divorced person. She would need to convert to Islam; something she had not yet agreed to do.

*　　*　　*

The Aga's problems only increased; on his return to Bombay relations between his family and Shahzadi's had deteriorated and her sister was suing the Aga for a share in his property. This was sensational for the times in a Muslim community. The trial was long and bitter with enemies of the Aga spreading anything they could to blacken his name. So outrageous was some of the testimony that the trial judge Mr. Justice Russell was forced to clear the court on more than one occasion. Mr. Russell himself was forced to defend himself against the accusation that he was prejudiced in favour of the Aga because he had dined with him. The Aga's counsel remarked dryly "The same could be said of every judge in Bombay. The judge found in the Aga's favour and his legal triumph was complete.

However, although the Aga had won he felt it inappropriate to proceed with the divorce and he decided to bide his time. But time was not on his side; he returned immediately to Monte Carlo and although he said nothing publicly, he privately declared himself divorced from Shahzadi and wrote a letter to her settling her future financially and giving her an estate in Poona.

He wanted to marry Ginetta as soon as possible; however, his self-decreed divorce was not legal and binding in Europe. Ginetta was trying to cope with pregnancy and the dichotomy of divesting herself of her faith and placing herself in a position where she might never be able to return to her home in Italy. As a Catholic she would be considered a bigamist. However, she also had no wish to continue as a mistress and have her child remain illegitimate. As if this was not enough her mother, Rosa, had always been very ambitious for her daughter and was anxious for Ginetta to marry an exotic prince. Ginetta then miscarried; she was disconsolate; everything seemed to have slipped from her grasp and she was fearful this would lead to the end of her relationship with the Aga.

However, the Aga was besotted with her and far from considering leaving her he was worried she might abandon him! Finally in the spring of 1908 a Muslim ceremony was performed in Egypt and Ginetta agreed to marry him and convert to Islam. This was a *Muta* marriage under Shia Law; this was first practised early in the history of Islam, to allow Muslim warriors, separated from their wives for long periods, to enter temporary associations with one or more other women for a contracted, specific period of time and to legitimize the children of such marriages.

This *Muta* marriage would always be a problem for the Aga and Ginetta. They were never satisfied with this arrangement and in January 1923 in Bombay they were married again. Even this was unsatisfactory; on the 8th December 1926 a week *after* Ginetta's death the Aga finally secured a proper divorce from Shahzadi *who was also dead at that time* in accordance with Shia Law. The exact purpose of this bizarre legal action is unclear. The Aga may have been simply trying to secure freedom for his heir's from any legal action from Shahzadi's litigious family.

*   *   *

The Aga may have "remarried" and his wife pregnant, however, as far as Europe was concerned this was no more than concubinage. Although he undoubtedly loved Ginetta a woman in this condition would never have any physical attraction for him. He was always on the alert for potential mistresses and in1909 Diaghilev, the Russian impresario, brought his ballet to London.

The Aga had met Diaghilev in Monte Carlo and was captivated by the ballet. In his memoirs the Aga would talk about how involvement with the ballet had brought him happiness. He found the dancers enchanting, particularly Tamara Karsavina, a dark lustrous beauty, and he became infatuated with her. Unfortunately for the Aga her list of admirers was a long one and she was not promiscuous.

He made overtures, but Karsavina, while friendly and amusing, would not become his mistress. The Aga, probably keen to find company for himself in his new home in Monte Carlo, had to be content with a blonde dancer called Josefina Kohalevska. Ginetta may not have known about the Aga's dalliances with the Diaghilev's dancers as she was in Nice, but when the Aga occasionally visited her he did not even stay with her at the villa he had built for her. It is anyone's guess why he felt unable to spend time in Ginetta's company, but the Aga stayed in an hotel on the sea front.

*   *   *

In March 1909 Ginetta gave birth to a son Mohammed Mahdi Khan whom she called Giuseppe. The Aga set off on his travels again this time to meet his followers and foreign leaders. The next blow to hit him was the death of the King: Edward VII. The Aga travelled to England for the funeral where he would find himself amongst the grandest ever gathering of the world's great rulers. Among the mourners were nine kings, five heirs apparent, forty imperial or royal highnesses, seven queens (four dowagers and three regnant) plus any number of royal followers. Edward VII had been known as "the uncle of Europe" and as far as the crowned heads were concerned this was a literal description as Queen Victoria's progeny were spread across the continent.

The Aga was worried that the King's death would weaken the Empire. He was also concerned about the growth in Germany's military strength and the increasingly bellicose attitude of the Kaiser. The deteriorating situation in the Near East concerned the Aga as he feared the consequences of German influence in Turkey. He did not want to see a Muslim country become anti-British.

Shortly after the funeral of Edward VII the Aga received a telegram from Ginetta to say that Giuseppe was ill with suspected spinal meningitis. The Aga hurried home but was too late; Mohammed Mahdi, aged one year, was dead.

Ginetta was so distraught the Aga stayed with her for some time until the melancholy eased and her recovery was helped by finding herself pregnant again. She travelled to Turin to be with her family and the Aga, satisfied that she was getting the best medical care, returned to London for the Coronation of George V.

The Aga had always been drawn by the pageantry and magnificence of British ceremonial occasions. London was a feast of colour and he was mesmerised by the spectacle and fully enjoyed all the festivities that accompanied the greatest gathering ever of eminent leaders from all over the world.

While the Aga was in London Ginetta gave birth to a son, Aly Salman Khan on 13th June 1911. It was not an easy birth; Aly was delivered by forceps and Ginetta suffered. Aly was sickly and given considerable attention to help nourish him. It was some weeks before the Aga arrived in Turin to see the child who was born to inherit his status. As there was no legal marriage in force there were no notices in the local paper and the birth certificate stated that his mother was "Theresa Magliano unmarried, twenty-two years old, living on independent means". The Aga Khan was listed as the father. This concerned Ginetta far more than the Aga; giving birth to a child of a Muslim and being in Italy reminded her of the lifelong influence of a Catholic upbringing.

*   *   *

The Aga might have considered the period from 1900 to 1909 to be crowded but even by his standards the year after Aly was born must have been as busy as any. The Coronation of George V in 1911 gave him the chance to meet in London several statesmen. The Aga wished to discuss the worrying situation in the Balkans. He was particularly concerned about any conflict that might develop between Britain and a Muslim country as he wished to spare the Muslims in Turkey an unnecessary war. On a lighter side he helped arrange the first All-India cricket tour of England; they won six matches and lost fifteen. The Aga then undertook a successful and triumphant tour of India's Muslim areas.

Also in 1911 the Aga appeared in *Who's Who* for the first time; he was described as "the acknowledged leader of the Indian Mohammedan"s". He was thirty-four and considered sophisticated and comfortable in the Edwardian world and would always be happier in Europe than Asia. However, he never forgot that he was a Muslim. Wherever he was in the world he carried in his waistcoat pocket a watch with a compass on the reverse side. He always knew the time and direction of Mecca and every Friday he would allow one hour for meditation and prayer and would turn towards the holy city of Islam.

However, the reality was that he had, by self-appointment, changed from an Indian prince to an ambassador without portfolio on matters between East and West. *The Times* said "he was condemned to be the Canute of Muslim India…born to worship Queen Victoria and an Empire upon which the sun never set".

The Aga wrote at that time "My way of life has taken me from the slowly changing east to the west, which is ever swiftly changing. The works I have to do keep me, for most of the time, in Europe, and on the move. I am a pacifist and an internationalist. Yet I belong to no country in the west but only to many people in the east. My skin, my religion, my taste in food, and my way of thinking – all these make me differ profoundly from the people among whom I move". All this is typical of the Aga really; poor syntax, with a touch of pretention, not telling the entire truth and concealing plenty!

* * *

In 1912 the Aga organised a Coronation Durbar for the new king: George V. The ceremonies were as colourful as ever but the Aga in his memoirs is rather sour about the occasion. This could have been because as a result of a problem with the kitchens only enough food emerged to feed the King and a few around him. It is not clear whether or not the Aga was fed; if he went hungry he may well have not been in the best of humour! In addition at his investiture, in which he received his decoration of the GCSI, he was concerned that he might be burned alive! The ceremony was held at night in a brilliantly lit tent, one of the bulbs burst and others behaved erratically and the fear was that the tent might catch fire and incinerate the King and Queen and all inside.

*   *   *

The Aga was soon on his travels again this time to Russia. He made leisurely progress from St Petersburg to Moscow and rather than note the political temperature he commented on the overheated palaces! He did however, observe and note the "truly appalling" gulf between the rich and the poor. On a lighter note in a public steam baths he saw women attendants looking after male visitors passing soap and towels and acting as masseurs. However, he saw that they were old and so ugly that it was impossible to imagine even the slightest impropriety!

*   *   *

The Aga was at this time already beginning to put on too much weight. His principal exercise at this time was probably golf and whenever he was in London he could be seen in the early morning emerging from the Ritz Hotel in his white sports outfit bound for a golf course.

*   *   *

By 1914 the situation in Europe was deteriorating and War was inevitable. The Aga had two main concerns: it was important to him that the British Empire should be secure because much of what he held dear was tied up in it. In addition, in some ways like the Empire, the sun never set on his own religious realm; it was spread around the world in Asia the Middle East and Africa. The Aga had once forecast that in the event of a European War there would be a great uprising with Indian troops mutinying to drive the British out of India. He could not have been more wrong; most Indians rallied to the Empire's cause. The number of fighting Indians eventually reached 800,000 in the various theatres of the Great War.

He was concerned to attend to as much of his affairs as possible and he hurried from Burma to Rangoon and then East Africa; it was whilst he was on the high seas that Austria's Crown Prince Ferdinand was assassinated and events moved towards war. The Aga then made for London.

The Aga was very concerned about Britain's security in the event of war; a conflict in Europe could endanger his considerable financial interests in England. Should Britain become weakened by a protracted war he might become separated from his Ismaili communities and this could block revenues from them to Europe where of course he chose to reside at every opportunity.

The Aga offered his services to the British; he rather dramatically told Lord Kitchener "I will shed my last drop of blood for the British Empire". In addition so there could be no doubt about where his loyalties lay, he returned his German decorations to the Kaiser. Although not uncritical of British policy towards Turkey, which was almost entirely Sunni Muslim, the Aga used his influence to help persuade Muslims everywhere not to follow the Turkish call for a jihad. The Aga considered the Ottoman Empire to be a tool of German imperialism.

* * *

It was vital that the Suez Canal was kept open and when Egypt seemed to be favouring Germany. The Aga claims Lord Kitchener enlisted him to go to Cairo, although neither Kitchener's biographer nor his papers mention any such initiative. In any event it was considered necessary to prop up the pro-British alliance and the Aga went straight to Egypt's most powerful Muslim group: the professors of al-Azhar University. It is hard to say how much influence the Aga

Khan had in keeping Egypt from joining the Central Powers; some documents claim very little. However, Egypt's pro-German leader was deposed and Egypt declared a British protectorate for the duration of the war.

The Aga was rewarded by King George V for his services: the King conferred on him the right to an eleven-gun salute the rank and precedence of a First Class Ruling Prince of the Bombay Presidency. The honour was granted only for the Aga's lifetime; his request that it be in perpetuity was declined. In Imperial Britain no Indian could ask for more; indeed, as the Aga had requested this accolade for himself in a long letter to the Viceroy: Sir Charles Hardinge, in December 1915 there was probably nothing more he could ask for that had any reasonable chance of being granted!

*   *   *

The Aga Khan's reputation fluctuated during the Great War; there was even some speculation as to exactly whose side he was on. That would seem unfair as he always considered himself, with some justification, as a loyal supporter of England. With his financial interests in England he could hardly be in favour of a German victory. He tried to interfere and made suggestions for winning the war, many of which were fantastic to put it kindly and at worst ludicrous.

The Aga offered the British the benefit of his experience and knowledge; did he somehow see himself as taking a prominent part in strategy? Had he lost touch with reality? The Central Powers evidently thought he was dangerous to them; a recommendation that he be killed as a traitor was made to the Indian Independent Committee in Berlin as a warning to other traitors; the Aga received a warning and employed a bodyguard. However, the German-assisted Indian Independence Movement in Europe declared that he was not dangerous, had lost power and was hated, like all Indians who professed loyalty to England.

Nonetheless the Aga definitely seemed to be a thorn, if even a minor one, in the side of the Central Powers. He settled in neutral Switzerland and took a house in Zurich. However, German agents were suspicious, and planned to assassinate him. The Aga had only just recovered from breaking his ankle, which required an operation and took some time to heal, when, despite having his usual appetite, he was ill, losing weight and diagnosed with Graves' disease, which affects the thyroid gland. The Germans threw a bomb at him and poisoned his coffee; the bomb failed to explode and he did not drink the coffee as his medication precluded it.

*   *   *

The Aga was particularly concerned about the fate of Persia during the Great War; he had a natural longing for his lost homeland and he distrusted the Arabs and their revolt against the Ottoman Empire. Although shortly after the War started Persia had declared itself neutral, although this mattered not one jot with any of the warring participants who operated inside the country. German victories had alarmed the Aga who envisaged them marching through Afghanistan and India via Constantinople! For the British, Persia was very much part of its sphere of influence: a wall that secured India. During 1915 and throughout the war the Allies and the Central Powers fought a number of battles in Persia with the Central Powers scoring a number of successes.

The Aga had the ludicrous idea of partitioning Persia with the British taking the South and the Russians the North, but even he could see that this would be highly immoral. Another idea to guarantee Persia's integrity was to supply it with finance and, with America's help, reorganize the country. However, rather cynically he realized that bribes would not work as these would simply be matched by the Germans.

Not surprisingly the Foreign Office was not impressed with either plan despite of the Aga's persistence. The Aga shared the old Persian distrust of Arabs and he had warned Sir Edward Grey about the consequences, as he saw them, in any Arab movement. The British were aware that the Aga and Arabs were antagonistic towards each other; a confidential agent of the political department of the India Office had warned: "one of my informants, who is well in with the Mahommedans, writes and warns me not to allow HH the Aga Khan to associate in any way with Prince Faisul...my informant tells me that the Aga Khan is regarded as "the heretic of heretics" by Mahommedans in general"

* * *

The Aga had been advised to make his base in neutral Switzerland and he had taken a house in Zurich. Neutral or not there were many dark times for the Aga during the war: he lived for eighteen months under the shadow of death, from bombs, poison and natural causes, and the experience lodged deep in his psyche. The original diagnosis of Graves' disease was eventually shown to be wrong but in the meantime an incalculable number of remedies were tried. Eventually a new course of treatment proved more successful and so began the slow return of his health. However, for the rest of his life he never accepted the opinion of any physician, however eminent, without demanding the most detailed explanation. Henceforth every doctor who treated him was subjected to a barrage of questions about his diagnosis and suggested treatment. The Aga's troubled health became well known and subject to all manner of therapies and he became a leading contender for probably the world's most medically knowledgeable patient.

An example of the thoroughness to which he subjected his doctors remedies occurred when he was prescribed sulphadimidine and he promptly asked "Why not sulphadiazine?" The doctor said the prescribed drug was an improvement. "In what way?" he retorted. He was advised it was less toxic. Dr Johnson, his physician, once said "God help me if I could not give him an answer and an adequate explanation". The good Doctor should not have been surprised by the Aga's assiduousness in the matter of medical treatment when it is considered that he had once been immunised against the plague!

* * *

Discovering the truth about the Aga's activities during the Great War is not easy. There are conflicting versions from German agents, his own self-serving memoirs, some of which if taken at face value would rival *Alice in Wonderland*, and the realities of the War. The Germans were irritated by his anti-German and anti-Turkish utterances and might have thought he was the centre of Britain's Muslim ring. The Aga liked to promote the idea that his wide-spread community had acted as British agents; providing information and services that they uniquely could supply. How much is reality is a different matter.

The Germans had monitored and classified the Indian princes into those that were pro and anti-British; the Aga they found difficult to place one way or the other. The Germans must have concluded he was a possible danger as they tried to kill him! British intelligence was convinced the Germans had infiltrated spies into the Aga's camp. The issue of the Aga's contribution to the war will be discussed again when he was proposed for the Noble Peace Prize.

When matters were at their worst the Aga was advised to leave Switzerland and he gave up his house in Zurich but instead of moving the London he saw out the war in Paris.

*   *   *

During the Aga's illness he took time to write a small book: *India in Transition* subtitled "A Study in Political Revolution". It ran to 302 pages and covered many subjects including, bizarrely, a section on domestic animals. However it did provide him with a fleeting reputation as an author and impressed Lady Diana Cooper with his cleverness. She then somewhat spoiled the complement by wondering if he had actually written it himself!

*   *   *

The Aga Khan attended the Paris Peace Conference in January 1919 along with the Indian delegation. The gathering of the victorious allies was the greatest assembled group of such individuals ever, with the purpose of deciding the future of the post-war world. The outcome did not please him as he was concerned that his suggestion that a Commonwealth of Asian States, in association with Britain, was unlikely to be adopted. He also worried about Muslim Turkey and the hostile British attitude towards it.

Incidentally the Aga would have felt at home at the Conference with Lloyd George, who was sleeping with his secretary Frances Stevenson and Lord Beaverbrook who was sharing a suite with

Venetia Montagu, the wife the Secretary of State for India! It is not clear if the Aga had company, if so it would certainly not have been Ginetta!

*   *   *

The end of the war saw the Aga embark on some of the projects that he had cherished for some years. Principally he wanted to enter the world of thoroughbred racing which is covered in separate chapters. Secondly he was determined to restore his health and to this end he began to learn golf; his third ambition.

His tutelage started under the care of the English professional John Henry Taylor. The Aga rarely missed his early morning round before commencing the business of the day. More will be told of the Aga's tribulations on the golf course later on, suffice to say that while his swing progressed it became clear that he would always suffer tribulation with regard to putting.

This problem prompted an onlooker to compose this rather sad quatrain:-

> *He hits the ball from hanging lies,*
> *Or any kind of slant.*
> *Approach and drive the Aga can,*
> *But putt the Aga Khant!*

For a while the Aga attempted to watch his diet but this proved to be somewhat less than successful. Attending so many banquets, dinners or simply eating a normal dinner the Aga did not possess the discipline of restraint. He tried to compensate by throwing himself into exercise with zeal. In addition to golf he sparred at the National Sporting Club and could be seen jog-trotting back to the Ritz across Green Park.

*   *   *

With his movements restricted the Aga and Ginetta probably saw more of one another between 1916 and 1918 than at any other time. There is little doubt that Ginetta was the principal love of the Aga's life; always remembering his fickle regard for all women. However, once peace returned he resumed his old ways: he neglected her with his frequent absences and it was not until she created another life for herself that she was ever really happy. The Aga once said that Ginetta was like a beautiful butterfly; she needed freedom but could not soar very high or fly very far. There is sufficient evidence that the Aga had considerably underestimated her talents.

Ginetta missed her family and found marriage to the Aga, as he envisaged it, hard to accept. She became lonely and depressed and suspected, probably correctly, that the Aga had a mistress. Left alone Ginetta began to suffer bouts of depression. In France she was referred to as Madame Ginetta not "Princess" or Begum". Once when asked if the Aga and Ginetta were legally married his valet replied "nobody knows".

Her life changed when she met some artists on the Riviera and attended a sculpture exhibition following which she decided to take lessons. Ginetta soon became an accomplished sculptor and built a studio in the grounds of her home in Cimiez. It is just as well that Ginetta had an occupation as her suspicions were correct: the Aga now had a mistress. She was an eighteen-year-old French girl called Andree Carron although the Aga always called her Jane despite her friends knowing her as Andree. This was a pattern that he would maintain throughout his life. From now on Ginetta would be happier when the Aga was away and she could fill the house with artists and artisans.

The Aga never took Ginetta on trips or religious tours of Ismaili communities and although he visited India and his mother every year, incredibly, it was not until 1923 that Ginetta saw India for the first time. This was partly due to the Aga's fear that she might not be accepted as the Begum in the same way as she was in England and parts of the continent. The Aga's first wife Shahzadi had recently died so he was free to legally marry Ginetta in the eyes of the western world. The purpose then of the visit was for them to marry in a legally binding ceremony; Aly and Lady Ali Shah were present and Ginetta seemed very happy as she was now addressed as "Highness" and was referred to in the press as Begum Aga Khan.

It was during this visit that Aly, aged twelve, saw for the first time the level of veneration his father's followers had for their leader. He watched in awe as the Aga raised his hands to bless them and how they fell to their knees and kissed the hem of his robes. This had been Aly's first visit to India and as he stood on deck he was perplexed by the Khoja dignitaries on the quayside dressed in impressive *jubas* (crimson gold embroidered gowns) and *paqris* (golden turbans). Aly asked his father "Why have so many magicians come here?" Aly found most of his first experience of being in India pure fairyland.

*   *   *

From about 1921 onwards the Aga became a close friend of Lord Beaverbrook the newspaper magnet. The Aga trusted Lord Beaverbrook almost slavishly and often took his advice with regard to investments. The Aga was a cautious investor who had been well tutored by his mother. When the world financial crisis struck so suddenly in 1929, stock markets began fluctuating, and then, mostly, crashing. The Aga consulted Beaverbrook about possibly liquidating some of his investments. Judging from the list of securities supplied to Beaverbrook in May 1929, the crash occurred in October that year, the Aga's investments in Britain were worth about £2,290,000 (100,760,000). The Aga was not badly affected by the crash and may even have benefitted from it. It is hard to know if he was lucky or not; he had been at Newmarket when he received news of the crash and, just before, had been convinced the market would continue to rise; he was not alone in that opinion of course.

The Aga once advised Harry Wragg to invest into New York Central Railroads; the Aga was sure that the value of railway land in New York was totally undervalued. The shares, however, proved worthless. One wonders if the Aga took his own advice in this instance.

The Aga's income and wealth has been the subject of much speculation. His annual income has been estimated as high as an incredible twelve million pounds (about 432 million). This seems as unlikely as some of the stories of how he accumulates such a sum; his bath water being bottled and sold for example.

However, some of his more devoted wealthy followers would pay huge sums just for the Aga to "name" a child. This is the equivalent of baptising and involves the Aga dipping his fingers in water which is then sipped by the members of the family.

*   *   *

The Indian Legislative Assembly passed a resolution on 5th February 1924 that the Aga Khan was "the fit person for the Nobel Prize for Peace this year". There had been a suggestion in the Indian press that Ghandi be nominated and it is possible that recommending the Aga was a way of derailing Ghandi's nomination. The resolution was dispatched to the India Office in Whitehall to be forwarded to the Nobel Prize committee in Norway. The idea was greeted in London with amazement; Sir Arthur Hirtzel's views are revealing, he observed:-

"To anyone who knows anything about the Aga Khan this recommendation is absolutely ludicrous and I feel strongly that Her Majesty's Government ought not to act even as a post office for forwarding it". Sir Arthur's views were even stronger when the full text and the reports of the debate which resulted in the recommendation were received; in a minute he was scathing about the Aga Khan and his reputation. He wrote;

"I have the lowest possible opinion of the Aga Khan, both as a man, as a religious leader and as a politician. As a politician he is an opportunist pure and simple – always anxious to be in the limelight on the side which he thinks is going to win, seldom anxious to do an honest piece of work for government in obscurity or unpopularity (he has more than once been offered office under the Crown, but always refused). During the war he did nothing of note except issue a proclamation….it was undoubtedly useful, though this loyalty of the Khojas would probably not have been a very great asset if there had been serious trouble in the Muslim world….His doings on the Continent were entirely private – concerned mostly with his pleasures".

"I had him closely watched but the result was only to confirm that he was merely an easy-going voluptuary ready to pay for a quiet life….the Aga had considerable influence on Mr Montagu (Edwin Montagu; secretary of state for India) and used it in the direction of obtaining easier terms for Turkey in the early stages of the negotiations – again pursuing the recovery of his waning prestige in the Indian Muslim world... And if the Nobel Prize is awarded to on these grounds, I consider Mr Montagu has far higher claims".

It would probably have come as a surprise to the Aga that he was watched by the British Government! Neither the Indian or British governments were prepared to support the recommendation with any enthusiasm; in the end the Nobel Peace Prize was not awarded in 1924.

At this stage the Aga's life seemed to be slipping into a pattern: building up his bloodstock empire, travelling to Europe as often as he could, always on the lookout for a new mistress, visiting his followers and trying to look out for their interests around the world. However, there was no doubt he was happiest when able to live the life of a wealthy European and enjoying all the pleasures and delights available to an individual in this fortunate position.

2 The Life of the Aga Khan III; Part II

Dressed in a purple robe, with his decorations and insignia prominently displayed, and sporting a green turban, a distinguished, if rather substantial and heavy man, is looking his military best. A large set of weighing scales with a counterbalancing chair are before him. He eases his huge frame into the seat tilting the scales alarmingly. Gold is then steadily added until the scales are equal. The crowd cheers wildly and for a time it is by no means certain their enthusiasm would be kept under control.

*   *   *

During 1924 there was a picture taken of the Aga showing him wearing horn-rimmed glasses and a trilby; his moustache, still luxuriant, is streaked with white, and he is wearing a three-piece suit which is stretched to the limit in an effort to hold his bulk. At the age of forty-seven the picture captures "Inky" very well; Inky was the nickname some intimates in his gambling circle gave to him. He then weighed 243 pounds (nearly 17 ½ stone, 110 kgs) and ate enormously in the manner of a typical Edwardian gourmandiser.

The Aga had always spoken of the need to keep fit and exercise regularly; clearly he had been neglecting this aspect of his well-being! A few years previously, when approaching forty, he had been diagnosed with goitre; a swelling of the thyroid gland which produces a lump on the neck. In the Aga's case it apparently accounted for his protuberant eyes and he speculated: "Am I going to die a young man or am I going to look after myself properly". He then decided to put himself under the care of the best specialists in Switzerland.

The Aga could certainly talk good sense when it came to diet; "I believe we eat too much, and for this reason I think we should drop one or two meals a week, which is my own practice. That means that on three days a week I take only one solid meal".

However, despite claiming that he took regular vigorous exercise and preaching others to look after their health the Aga had clearly forgotten his own advice. Everyone he came into contact with was usually given advice of some sort. When in London the Aga never shaved himself; the Court Hairdresser: Charles Topper left his shop in Jermyn Street every morning and went to the Ritz to shave him. Whether the Aga was in Ireland or staying at his Deauville villa, Topper would visit to cut the Aga's hair. Once when the Aga was staying in Ireland Topper arrived late in the evening and went to bed. The next morning the Aga and Topper had the following exchange:-

Aga; "Good morning Topper, did you sleep well?"
Topper; "Thank you, Your Highness, very well"
Aga; "Did you have a good breakfast?"
Topper; "Thank you, Your Highness, a very good breakfast".
Aga; "Were your bowels open?"
Topper; "!!!!"
Aga; "You'd better have some green figs"

In that summer of 1924 the Aga's weight was a problem and on the 24th June he suffered a heart attack while attending a meeting in London. It marked the end of that period of the Aga's involvement in politics and from then until 1929 he devoted most of his time to private matters: his pursuit of Andree Carron and building up his racing empire. He still had of course his duties as Imam and remained in contact with his followers. However, he had still had little time for Ginetta and Aly. From 1929, and presumably recovered, he was again rushing energetically about, but these activities mainly involved personal matters. However, even he admitted that from that time until the outbreak of the Second World War he was largely a spectator rather than a participant in politics and world affairs.

*   *   *

Meanwhile Aly was growing up and, although the Aga may not have been in as close contact with his son and heir as most fathers, he ensured that Ginetta and Aly did not lack for comfort and luxury. Aly could ride a horse almost before he could walk and was also introduced to tennis. But he lacked the company of other children; his "playmates" were his uncle Mario and the chauffeur Alfredo. It was not surprising that Aly was moody sometimes high-spirited and on occasions lost in a world of fantasies. However, even at this young age he had an easy charm which endeared him with people.

The Aga began to think about Aly's education; as he was to succeed him as Imam and the Aga would need to be on better terms with his son and that probably meant setting up residence in England. The problem was that the Aga would then be subject to British tax. The Aga had of course made short visits to England in the past and had received enquiries from the Inland Revenue. If he became a resident he would be subject to tax not only on his British investment income but on all of his income; which would be much more serious.

The Aga pleaded that his position was unique, but to no avail: if, as a citizen, he wished to avail himself of the amenities offered by this country, he should share the burden of taxation, he was advised. The Aga decided that Aly's education would continue in England, but he would not take up residence; presumably therefore the Aga realised that his relationship with Aly would probably not improve. A few days at the Ritz would have to suffice and he would continue the pattern of his life: flitting from the South of France to England then after quick visits to India and East Africa back to France. His failure to secure his status as a tax-dodger confirmed his life as a wanderer. He did in time secure suitable tax exemption in France and a permanent home in Switzerland.

*   *   *

Ginetta had returned from India in 1923 with what was described as a "beatific glow" to her handsome Mediterranean features. She thought that matters between herself and the Aga would be different when they returned to Europe. They were now an officially married couple in the eyes of those in Europe and her position as Begum was now official in the eyes of everyone. She was wrong and alone even more than before.

The Aga's neglect of Ginetta and the subsequent solitary times had led her to be drawn to her young chauffeur; probably Alfredo. In 1926 she became pregnant and underwent an abortion from the complications of which she suffered peritonitis. She became desperately ill and was admitted to a Paris hospital.

The Aga was in London where he had just bought a 61 carat diamond known as the Golden Dawn for her; despite the giant flawless gem being labelled unlucky. Weirdly, a short while after he had completed the purchase, he received word that she was worse. Before he arrived at the hospital the following evening she was already dead at the age of thirty-seven. The cause of death was recorded as an embolism. When the Aga learned the full truth he was torn between grief and fury; something that became harsh bitterness. "That woman" he would fume if she was mentioned, "I don't want to hear her name spoken!" That the Aga could work himself up into such a rage over Ginetta's infidelity is probably proof enough that she was indeed the principle love of his life.

Ginetta was buried in the cemetery in Monte Carlo beside the son she had lost in infancy. Aly Khan, just fifteen had not been close to his mother in recent years, but not by his choice, he clearly loved her and could barely control his sobs as the coffin was laid into the ground. Aly was often troubled by his separation from his parents, although by this time he was beginning to thrive in all other respects.

It is impossible not to have considerable sympathy for Ginetta; a talented and beautiful woman who had so much to offer and surely deserved to be treated better.

*   *   *

When the Aga was at his most busy the manner in which he managed the hectic timetable of activities was a constant mystery to all who knew him. He was forever commuting between London and his homes in Deauville, Paris and the Cote d'Azur. He attended conferences in Lausanne and Geneva, ministering to his religious duties as Imam, his mistresses and of course his racing activities in both France and England.

The Aga was concerned to be involved with India's future which was the subject of considerable debate at this time. The Aga was of course principally concerned with regard to the position of Muslims. He was also in the process of building a formidable racing and breeding empire which took up his time as he studied sales catalogues deciding which yearlings he would buy. The Aga's complicated love life alone would surely have been enough to have kept almost any other man occupied most of the time with the beautiful Andree centre of his attentions!

*   *   *

The Aga having divorced his dead first wife and a widower from his second was ready to marry again; a European woman of course but for the moment he marked time. This did not mean inactivity of course and, although the Aga still had little time for Aly, his time was fully occupied. However, when the Aga felt the time was right to re-marry he found it was not easy to persuade the unwilling Andree that she should become his third wife.

*   *   *

As a youngster Aly had been a slender somewhat delicate boy inclined to nightmares and frightened of his father, to whom he was largely a stranger. The War years in particular had been lonely for Aly. He spent hours without company often neglected by Ginetta, and simply watching the chauffeur, Alfredo, polish the sleek automobiles. His Aunt Emmy taught him how to dance and he spoke French and Italian with his mother and her family. Aly spoke English with his father but as he rarely saw the Aga he was not fluent much to the Aga's irritation! On the plus side, and fortunately for him, pictures of Aly in early maturity show clearly and fortunately he had inherited his looks from his mother!

Aly was approaching maturity; he was already strikingly handsome and very exotic, with his mixed Italian and Oriental heritage. His early education had been at the hands of French and Swiss tutors and, although Aly was not confident in himself, he quickly learnt French and Italian. Even so he was not interested in books or learning. An Ismaili scholar acquainted Aly with the rudiments of Islamic history and the basic tenets of his father sect. The Aga was sufficiently kind and considerate enough to recall his own childhood and did not want to subject Aly to high-pressure education.

When the Aga decided not to live in England he asked the India Office to suggest a man to take charge of Aly's education. Charles Waddington was the man chosen, an ex-officer of the Indian Army and former principle of Mayo College at Ajmer where generations of Indian Princes had received their education. Aly went to live with Waddington's family in his fine Sussex country house and was taught style, self-discipline and *savior faire*. It was better the Aga felt that Aly knew how to conduct himself in all situations than have his head crammed with academic knowledge.

The Aga was keen that Aly be presented at court when he was eighteen. It may seem surprising today but this caused some consternation at the India Office in Whitehall: they posed the question: was Aly a legitimate son and the genuine heir? However whatever the difficulties they were overcome and Aly was presented to Queen Mary on the 29th May 1929. It is not clear how the King and Queen felt about Aly but the Prince of Wales loathed him. "David", as he was known, although very popular with the public, was an idle, selfish, inconsiderate, vain individual, a notorious womaniser and a man whose judgement on almost every issue was, at best, peccable, at worst potentially highly damaging and destructible. He had doubtless noted, probably to his consternation that Aly was by some way considerably more handsome and charismatic than he was!

*   *   *

The Aga eventually persuaded Jane-Andree to become his wife. "I shall arrange for you to take the Muslim faith" he informed the "bewitching maid of the Savoy Mountains". Andree shook her head; she was a Catholic and had no intention of changing her faith. The Aga was disappointed as there would be no huge Muslim celebrations. In addition the Aga was forced to agree in writing that he would not pressurise Andree after the wedding to alter her faith and that their children would be brought up as Roman Catholics.

The Aga announced his engagement to Andree on the 24th October 1929 and they married on 7th December in Aix-les-Bains, France in a civil ceremony and on the 13th in a religious one in Bombay. She was twenty-one years his junior, did not, of course, convert to Islam and was known as Princess Andree Aga Khan. She had no interest in horse racing but showed pleasure as a means of keeping the Aga happy; she had been his mistress for ten years. Prior to the marriage the Aga settled $800,000 (£7,410,000) on her plus a house in the South of France, an apartment in Paris and interests in various investments. Only after this did she agree to set a date for the wedding. Aly was not impressed and was at best "cool" towards his new step-mother, although with time this changed and he became very fond of Andree when it was clear she was keen to be an ally and not an enemy.

*   *   *

On 31st October 1929 the Viceroy of India: Lord Irwin made an historic announcement declaring that the goal of British rule in India was to provide the country with dominion status. For this purpose a conference would be held to discuss the issues involved. The Aga Khan's only role was as a channel for Muslim opinion. The conference began badly when Ghandi and the Congress Party refused to attend. Ghandi had been leading campaigns of civil disobedience and such was his power he could wring concessions out of the British. He was imprisoned but released and visited Britain in September 1931 where he made a tremendous impression.

Even his most ardent supporters would have to concede that, physically, Ghandi was excessively unattractive: less than five feet tall, skeletal, frail, puny and by this time bald, toothless and his eyes, magnified by strong lenses, looked disproportionately enormous. He was reputed to eat only dates and drank goat's milk and wore only a simple *dhoti* (loincloth). On one famous occasion when presented formally to King George, and wearing only his *dhoti,* he was asked if he was appropriately dressed for such a regal occasion. He replied

"The King was wearing enough clothes for us both". Despite this he was far from a figure of fun, his appearance merely added to his charm and he was as shrewd an operator as could be imagined, mentally very tough and of course, a committed Marxist.

The full extent of the task facing the Aga in trying to persuade Ghandi to discuss the problems of India is summed up in a short conversation between them. The Aga assured Ghandi that if he showed some feeling towards India's Muslims they would respond in helping Ghandi secure India's independence. Ghandi's ice cold reply destroyed any hope of cooperation: "I cannot in truth say that I have any feelings of paternal love for Muslims…I cannot indulge in any form of sentiment". Later, in 1940, Ghandi told the Aga that these comments had been misunderstood. However, they were largely unhelpful at the time.

Ultimately all three of the conferences failed and no agreement was reached. The squabbling between the factions enabled the British Government to claim that nothing could be done. The Muslims were concerned that Britain might leave India before their rights had been protected and secured. The Aga was caught in the middle and unable to make even the smallest headway. Ghandi had also failed to achieve his goal: independence for India.

*   *   *

In 1932 Lady Ali Shah, the Aga's mother visited Europe for the first time. She was rarely seen in public and stayed mainly in Deauville and London. Her visit was principally to be presented by the King with the Order of the Crown of India which she had been awarded in the Birthday Honours List. She was duly presented to King George and Queen Mary who noted her quick intelligence. She returned in 1935 for the King's Silver Jubilee. On both visits she stayed at Aly's Mayfair flat rather than the Ritz with the Aga; she did not like hotels.

*   *   *

Lady Shah was constantly pleading with the Aga to make a tour of the Khoja communities. Finally in 1932 shortly after Aly had spent a week in hospital recovering from a car crash, the Aga and Aly set off. They both wore Indian dress for the journey, which looked natural for the Aga, but for the twenty one year old Aly, much less used to oriental clothes, the appearance had more the look of stage costume.

The journey was not without its hazards: at that time a sect in India known as the Khoja Reformers Society were very critical of the tone of the Aga's pro-British speeches. Attempts were made to break up meetings at which the Aga spoke and there were threats of assassination. The next tour, undertaken a few months later by Aly alone, was not overshadowed by threats but was not successful in raising funds.

*   *   *

In 1933 the only child of the marriage between the Aga and Andree: Sadruddin Aga Khan was born. Sadruddin, which means Shield of Faith, saw as little of the Aga as Aly had; the Aga claiming he was busy with International commitments. He was certainly working on the plans for constitutional reform the British Government was planning for India. He was worried that these could affect his whole life. Although publicly the Aga was all in favour of the proposed changes he was aware that for all his social status under the law he was merely an ordinary Indian citizen answerable to the law and legislature. If a new elected government stopped him from collecting money from his followers his life in India, and anywhere else come to that, would become impossible.

*   *   *

For seventeen years the position of secretary to the Aga was faithfully occupied by Miss Freda Blain; or possibly Blair. Unfortunately it has not been possible to ascertain for certain which is correct. For the purposes of simplicity she will be referred to as Blain on the understanding that her name might be Blair. An attractive woman and a graduate of a Kensington secretarial college Miss Blain came from a racing family near Newbury and joined the Aga's service in 1922 when she was nineteen. A cultured woman, Miss Blain spoke fluent French, had an excellent knowledge of racing and a first-class memory. The Aga might rattle off a dozen names of people he wished to invite for dinner, it was never necessary for him to repeat anything and she never forgot a name. Her service ended only with the outbreak of war when the Aga moved to Switzerland and Miss Blain wished to remain in England. The Aga told her he could always be reached c/o Lloyds Bank, Geneva. As will be seen later she was able to serve the Aga with considerable distinction again after the war.

*   *   *

A gathering of Indian delegates to the committee on Indian Reform was held at the Dorchester Hotel in July 1933 to honour the Aga. Speaking on behalf of the Indian States Delegation, Sir Akbar Hydari said that the Aga Khan was a most acceptable ambassador of India in Britain. Sir Akbar opined that the Aga's varied interests, which included sport as well as politics, had done great service to India; and never more so than when he won the Derby; a remark which the assembled company loudly cheered.

The Aga Khan might have been a God but unlike the Indian princes he had no territory and in November 1933 he petitioned the British government for some land in India "in order to give my heirs and successor a permanent influential status in India consistent with the prestige and dignity of my ancient lineage and with my family tradition of loyal and devoted service to the British Crown".

The Aga stated that his Grandfather: the Aga Khan I should have been made ruling prince for his services to Sind. Throughout his life the Aga Khan III might have been given many honours, but none were hereditary.

The British had several concerns; the usefulness of the Aga rested on his being a British subject. If he was given land he would be a ruler of state and would cease to be one. Also they were worried whether there might be a considerable migration of Ismailis to any such territory.

The India Office objected to creating states; The Raj had restored states to deposed rulers but there was no precedent for creating a state for someone who had no right to territory. R. A. Butler wrote in a memo: – "He will be of no use to us if he is not a British Subject. The Aga Khan does not seem worthy of special treatment". Another official noted "I believe the Aga Khan's religious and political influence is on the wane….and it is extremely unlikely that his son (Aly) will have any influence at all". The Aga tried all sorts of arguments but the British Government was never going to grant him any territory.

*   *   *

Meanwhile Aly's behaviour was giving cause for concern; the problem of course was his pursuit of, and, attraction to women, plus his hectic lifestyle in which his personal safety seemed, to him, of little or no importance. Aly could be wonderful company and always gave the impression that he was living at twice the pace of anyone else. Paradoxically he always seemed at the same time both restless and relaxed. This ambivalence was expressed in his characteristic gait, combining loose-limbed ease with an underlying sense of urgency. All this was allied to his basic problem that there were only twenty-four hours in a day.

Aly would be in Deauville one minute and then he was off in his private plane to Newmarket. "Inshallah" – as Allah wishes – was his favourite expression, something he used to both welcome and bid goodbye to his guests. Viscountess Astor would remark dryly "I doubt if Allah would often wish it"

Aly plunged uninhibitedly into the hectic life of lively early thirties London; the Embassy Club in Bond Street, the "400" in Leicester Square, the Café de Paris and the Cavendish Hotel, where the original "Duchess of Duke Street" Rosa Lewis presided. This was the London of Noel Coward, Evelyn Waugh and Edgar Wallace and Aly loved it.

The world crisis and Britain's domestic travails and the poverty of the working classes did not darken the skies of those that lived such a life and Aly, often in company with the jockey Michael Beary, melted easily into such an environment. Aly could dance through the night, this was before he regularly spent at least part of the night otherwise occupied, and then set off at the crack of dawn at high speed in his Alfa Romeo to watch the gallops at Newmarket. The following evening he would return to his small house in Mayfair which he shared with his Ismaili valet.

It could hardly have been a surprise that Aly adopted this lifestyle of privilege without responsibility. He was the product of parents from two different religions and cultures: East and West, Muslim and Catholic. His youth had been spent in isolation from other youngsters and then at the age of fifteen his mother died. He was then made to fully realize his father's true stature and that he himself was a direct descendent of Mohammed and in time would be viewed with the same awe as his father when he succeeded.

Aly had not been raised in India but in England and this must have created a dichotomy within himself as he attempted to reconcile the two worlds. Unlike the Aga, Aly did not have the benefit of a strong woman like Lady Shah to guide and advise him. Aly had never had a settled home as a child and, in many ways; he never did although his base could be considered to be the South of France after the war. At this time he was almost twenty-three and developing as a man with all the desires that an extremely handsome man can be expected to feel. He had been involved with several women before he fell deeply in love for the first time.

However, it was two very public affairs that caused the Aga to become concerned about Aly's behaviour: firstly with Margaret Whigham (the future Duchess of Argyle, whose own promiscuity and rapacious sexual appetite would achieve her infamy later in the divorce courts, where her husband cited 88 different men) and with Lady Thelma Furness. She was the twin sister of Gloria Vanderbilt (mother of the future fashion designer), and had been the former mistress of The Prince of Wales for the previous four years, until the egregious Mrs Simpson appeared and began to wreak havoc with the British Monarchy. Mrs Simpson was never really popular with most of the British people and after the Kings abdication in December 1936 the East End urchins produced their own seasonal carol: "Hark the Herald Angels sing; Mrs Simpson's pinched our King".

Aly could be a menace where married women were concerned. The writer and journalist Quintin Gilbey wrote that a friend of his once confided that Aly had slept with the friend's wife and mistress in the same week and that he was going to kill him. However, when the friend tracked Aly down at Epsom he was so utterly charming that he could not bring himself to mention the matter especially when Aly told him to back one of his horses that won. It seems the friend afterwards confronted both women about the matter and they promised it would not happen again. Oh well that's all right then; it had been only a trifling matter which any husband would have happily just shrugged off; especially if one had been tipped a winner!

This story would appear to be far from unique as Aly seemed totally unable to maintain control of his *membrum virile*; one night stands with any wife that took his fancy were followed by irate husbands who often refrained from any reprisals on account of Aly's charm. Many erring women readily confessed to being seduced by him, though they would have strenuously denied any such thing with anyone else. Aly was essentially selfish and self-indulgent and considered rules and regulations only for others; he had hardly been brought up to think much else.

Aly's affairs continued, if it is possible to call a one-night-stand an affair but, unlike his father who generally pursued women of lower rank, Aly was more than happy to seduce women from both the aristocracy and those with husbands prominent in public life; including Joan Guinness. She was the former Hon. Joan Yarde-Buller daughter of Lord Churston and the wife of Loel Guinness, from the brewing family, who had inherited a fortune. Joan had married him at nineteen and when she met Aly in Deauville in 1934 she was twenty-six, tall, elegant, beautiful and, significantly, neglected by her husband.

By this time Aly's relationship with Thelma Furness had run its course and when he met Joan at a dinner party the attraction was almost instant. Loel discovered their inevitable affair, Joan asked Loel for a divorce, but he responded by suing her; citing Aly; Joan did not defend the action and afterwards she and Aly married on 18th May 1936. Seven months later on 13th December 1936 in Geneva Joan gave birth to a son: Karim.

The Aga was not happy with the name and did not think it suitable. Joan thought "It was a beautiful name in any language". Karim means "Generous" and is one of ninety-nine Muslim names for God.

The Aga had hopes that marriage and fatherhood would help Aly settle down; the outcome, however, was someway short of the

Aga's expectations. Aly's eye continued to wander and any beautiful woman he met attracted his attention. It could be argued that Aly, being the Aga's son was only following his father's example: *patris est filius!* The Aga could hardly have been surprised!

In addition Aly seemed addicted to danger; he loved driving cars at maniacal speed and riding horses with almost reckless abandon and ski-ing with such enthusiasm that it comes as no surprise he once broke a leg on the slopes. He had qualified as a pilot and he set off in his plane: Avenger whatever the weather and whenever he felt like it. Lady Ali Shah, looking after Aly's interests, suspected that Andree was plotting to usurp Aly as Imam with her own son Sadruddin and she implored Aly to live a less flamboyant lifestyle. From this time Aly made an effort to improve relations with Andree and eventually they became friends and fond of one another.

None of this should suggest that Aly's life was dominated by the pursuit of women. Although often frivolous his mind was very sharp and his intellect keen. More than one acquaintance was surprised by his ability to immediately grasp any situation, something he demonstrated during his war service. In addition whereas the Aga could not tell one horse from another Aly acquired a good eye for a thoroughbred and was considered to have excellent knowledge of conformation.

Aly's parties were legendary; although he drank very little and did not share his father's appetite for food he could make his guests feel at home and relaxed even though superficially the events appeared formal with guests wearing evening clothes.

Aly could also be an incredibly unreliable host. At one time he owned thirteen homes and, always showing his generosity of spirit, often invited people to stay and then completely forgot about it. Nonetheless no guest was ever turned away and could enjoy the excellent facilities if not the company of their host!

After Aly's death in 1959 the Third Viscount Astor, known as Billy, wrote in Aly's obituary in *The Times* an excellent sketch encapsulating his qualities "If only one knew Aly Khan by repute it was easy to preconceive a dislike towards him. When one met him, it was impossible not to be stimulated and attracted by his charm, his perfect manners, his vitality, his gaiety and sense of fun. But if you were fortunate enough to know him really well, and have him as a friend, you acquired a friendship which was incomparable – generous, imaginative, enduring and almost passionately warm". It is given to few men to have such words written about them.

*   *   *

It is not given to many to be able to claim that they are worth their weight in gold; however, the Aga went through two such ceremonies in 1936. They were fund raising schemes to celebrate the Aga's fifty years as Imam with the money raised used to promote education amongst his followers. The Aga was always concerned that his followers would never progress or improve their circumstances without better education. In addition housing was often poor and health provision almost non-existent. He was particularly keen that Muslim women should be educated; schools for girls were rare in a system that educated boys and girls separately.

The first occasion was a huge ceremony in Bombay; the vast crowd watched as the Aga heaved his considerable bulk onto the seat which caused the scales to tilt alarmingly. Gold was steadily added until the scales were equal; the result was gold to the value of £25,135 (1,281,000). When the amount was broadcast the crowd cheered wildly. A similar ceremony was held in Nairobi and raised £22,773 (1,161,000); had gold gone down in value or had the Aga lost weight between the two ceremonies?

The Jubilee Celebrations came to an abrupt end with the Kings death on 20th January 1936. The Aga's grief was genuine and deep and he ordered that Khoja shops be closed for three days. He was pessimistic about the future the Monarchy might take and he was certain that with the death of George V the India of his dreams was gone.

*   *   *

Sometime during 1936 the Aga took a telephone call from the new King: Edward VIII. The Aga was deeply troubled by the Kings struggle to reconcile the dichotomy of his duty as King and his love of Mrs. Simpson. The details of the call were never disclosed but almost certainly involved the profound sadness and complexity of the drama engulfing the King's life. It seems likely that the King, already preparing for abdication, was looking at possible destinations when he would be required to leave Britain. Switzerland was a possibility and if so the Aga would have been a most suitable host. In the event the King went to the estate of the Austrian Rothschilds at Enzersdorf near Vienna.

*   *   *

The Aga Khan was generally credited with reasonably good judgment of character. However, he was not alone in failing to spot the flaws in Adolf Hitler; Lloyd George was one of many that spoke in his favour including leading members of the British aristocracy and these individuals supported him during the thirties. The Prince of Wales (briefly Edward VIII) was a Nazi sympathiser and friend of Hitler's. The Aga actually lauded Hitler after a meeting in Berchtesgaden in 1937 and came away with a signed photograph of the Fuhrer. He wrote in *The Times*: "Hitler is a firm pillar of peace. Why not take him at his word?"

The Aga expressed support on BBC radio for the Anschluss which united Germany and Austria, failing to understand that this would not be Hitler's only ambition. When Hitler's next territorial demand, which was for the German-speaking Sudetenland, part of Czechoslovakia, the Aga was by then considered one of the appeasers. When Neville Chamberlain returned from Munich with a deal that sealed the destruction of Czechoslovakia, the Aga wrote about "the glorious victory for peace and honour won by the Prime Minister". The Aga was certain that Germany would not attack France and he commended its peaceful policy on Poland. Just a few months later Germany invaded Poland.

To the Aga's credit when war began he sent a strong and unequivocal message to his followers: "Heartfelt, loyal and unstinted service must be given to the cause of the Empire which is the protector of our faith and liberty".

Even someone with as sharp and brilliant a mind as C. B. Fry was taken in, and, at least partially, cast under the Fuhrer's spell. Fry had been asked to visit Germany in 1934 to compare the Hitler Youth

Movement with the Boy Scouts. Fry had a personal interview with Hitler, and, in a long discussion, became convinced that the Fuhrer's intentions by rearming were merely to secure the defence of Germany, and did not involve invading his neighbours.

It is easy to today to condemn those who wanted to keep Hitler happy, after all who wanted another European war just twenty years after the most cataclysmic conflict in World history? However, it soon became obvious that this was the wrong approach with a man already beginning to show signs of megalomania.

Astonishingly Andree when asked who the most attractive man she had ever met was replied "Hitler"! This was in 1938 and presumably she did not maintain this view much longer. The timing of this was unfortunate as the Aga had been elected unanimously as President of The League of Nations earlier in the year.

It should be remembered that in addition to the Aga, the Begum and C. B. Fry plenty of prominent individuals were deceived by the three tyrants of the world stage at this time: Hitler, Mussolini and Stalin. Mussolini, who denied his people a free and fair election for seventeen years but would probably have won one if he had permitted it, was praised by Pope Pius XI. The Pontiff described him as "sent by Providence". Churchill called him "one of the most wonderful men of our time". President Roosevelt regarded Mussolini as his "only potential ally in his effort to safeguard world peace".

Stalin's brand of communism as displayed in the "Russian people's utopia", was hardly that for anyone and definitely not for the estimated twenty million tortured and killed during his reign of terror. However, many figures on the left were almost slavishly devoted to it. Some: George Bernard Shaw visited Russia in 1931 and reported that "her efficient rulers, her atmosphere of such hope and security as has never before been seen in a civilised country on earth". He further opined that the Russian people were "uncommonly well fed" and that as far as Stalin was concerned "he had never met a man more candid fair and honest".

"Barbara Castle (Barbara Betts at that time) visited Moscow in 1937 and reported back in glowing terms about the conditions. "No-one can visit Soviet Union's institutions for mother and child crèches, lying-in hospitals and kindergartens without relishing that these services are an integral part of the lives of Soviet women" she wrote. Staggeringly when reflecting on these views in 1999 she commented "I don't think they were too bad actually". On the credit side Mrs. Castle, when in Government, can be thanked for introducing seat belts in cars!

Hitler, Mussolini and Stalin all had the same thing in common: industrial-strength charisma allied to the potent capacity to enthral those they met and convince them that they had all the solutions to the world's problems and how its people should be ruled. In addition they all had the same method of dealing with the problem of political opposition: simply remove all trace of it. They also had one further idea in common: none of them thought it sensible to allow anyone under their jurisdiction to be completely free.

*   *   *

Towards the end of 1937 the Aga made an emergency flight to Bombay, something that took three and a half days! Lady Shah had suffered stroke shortly after her weekly ritual of a Turkish bath, Turkish and Persian massage, manicure, pedicure and a hair dye. To his great sadness she did not recognize him. The Aga returned early in 1938 but Lady Shah died before he could reach her bedside. The Aga had always promised his mother that she would "Breathe her last with her head on his lap" and he was devastated by her death at the age of 88.

Lady Ali Shah's whole life had been dedicated to her son and although she disapproved strongly of his European lifestyle and decision to reside away from India, she never allowed these differences to come between them. She was highly intelligent, very strong-minded, and active all her life and physically very tough; able to ride well in excess of one hundred miles a day in her efforts to keep the Aga's name constantly before his followers.

*   *   *

Jane-Andree must have been aware of the old adage: "when a man marries his mistress he creates a vacancy". So it was with the Aga;

Andree had always been materialistic and although seemingly putting up with the Aga's mistresses she bitterly opposed him spending money on them. She was aware that the Aga found it difficult to remain a lover to his wives after they had given birth. Andree dealt with the Aga's mistresses better than Ginetta was able to; this was probably because Andree was able to enjoy the trappings of being the Begum.

Although she had considerable status as Begum, Andree could be charmingly unassuming and once greeted the wife of the racing journalist Quintin Gilbey saying simply "I am Andree Khan, I think our husbands know each other". She was rich beyond almost any woman's dreams and a mother in addition to her social status. Andree accepted that she must be above reproach, or at least must not be found out; there were rumours that she was not always alone when the Aga was away. However, the Aga could do as he pleased.

*   *   *

When war again broke out in September 1939 it was not certain the Aga fully realized the position he was in financially. The Great War had not caused the problems in accessing his capital that he would experience now. World War I, as it later became known, had been the most cataclysmic event of the Aga's generation and destroyed so much that he held dear. He had travelled the world totally unrestricted at that time and had not even needed a passport until 1912, when he wanted to visit Russia. For much of the First World War he had moved from the Continent to England relatively freely and the fact that his finances were almost all in England was not a problem. Now he was to discover that using London as a centre for his capital would cause severe problems. Britain imposed export controls and by the winter of 1940 The Aga was experiencing something new and not very pleasant: financial hardship.

The Aga returned to Europe in 1940 and went to his house in Antibes. However, the German offensive in the West was imminent and before he had settled in the Wehrmacht's Blitzkrieg was under way. The Aga set off to neutral Switzerland only just in time as the Nazis closed in.

The Aga, Andree and Sadruddin set up home at the Palace Hotel in St Moritz. The Aga was not alone amongst some of Europe's richest émigrés staying there, who, like the Aga, had been separated from their wealth. Fortunes were made as jewels and property exchanged hands for ready money; mostly at considerably reduced prices. The Aga was in an uncomfortable position: the Germans had taken about one hundred of his horses when they occupied Deauville; although the Aga had managed to transport some to India prior to the occupation and many of the others were recovered after the war. However, the funds for the Indian sales were frozen and the Aga implored the India Office for help. He explained that he needed a minimum of £400 per month (17,600) and asked that this amount be sent to an account in Switzerland; it was the Second World War that led to the creation of numbered Swiss bank accounts.

The Aga decided that whatever happened he would need more money and took the momentous step of selling Bahram and Mahmoud. These sales are discussed more fully in the following chapters; suffice to say that he was still unable to access the proceeds from America. Then a British bank worked out a way of bringing the money from America; the Aga would invest in British companies and the bankers would then be able to advance the funds to him.

The Aga's concern was probably exacerbated because, at least during the first year of the war, he was certain Germany would win. However, by 1942 there were approaching a million Indian troops and volunteers with that number increasing by fifty thousand a month; signifying that there were plenty of loyal Indians prepared to help the rid the world of an evil oppressor.

*   *   *

The Aga Khan was later to refer to the years of the Second World War as the unhappiest of his life and there is little reason to doubt it. He was cut off from the majority of his followers many of whom faced death and injury on the battlefield. He was a spiritual leader separated from his flock and the British had no need of his services. He could not access his wealth, his family was scattered and his son Aly in jeopardy; he had joined the French Foreign Legion and served with distinction chiefly in Syria. Aly was later decorated with Croix de Guerre with palms and the Bronze Star Medal. As if that was not enough the Aga's health was poor, his French stables had been plundered by the Nazis and his Irish studs closed for the duration. He was at one point even forced to use public transport! Imagine; the sheer horror of that experience: travelling with the *profanum vulgus*! Very *infra dig!*

On top of all this his marriage to Andree was in trouble. In truth she was never a suitable wife for him; she lacked spirituality and was materialistic, ambitious and possessive. She was aware that the Aga would always have an eye for beautiful young women and have a mistress, possibly even two, but resented the wealth he lavished on them. The Aga had had one mistress for six years and in1943 Andree could see that her marriage was coming to an end.

The Aga's mistress was French, vivacious, statuesque and very beautiful: Yvonne Blanche Labrousse. She would remain stunningly attractive all her life and photographs taken of her, even when well over seventy, still show her captivating beauty. She was born 15th February 1906, was considerably younger than the Aga, and had been Miss Lyon in 1929 and Miss France in 1930. She was the daughter of a railway porter and a dress maker; the latter being very ambitious for her daughter.

In the late nineteen thirties Yvonne, who was always referred to as Yvette, had intended to marry a young local man she had known for some years. The Aga was aware of this and that she was confused about whether to marry her young man or become the Aga's mistress. The Aga decided to expedite matters; by offering her a large sum which she could keep as an engagement present or if she stayed with him she would have the money and much more to come. She elected to be the Aga's mistress and he bought her a property at Le Cannet overlooking Cannes. The Aga had no plans to divorce Andree and even after the commencement of War and when Yvette went to live in Geneva, he made regular, arduous journeys to be with her.

*   *   *

In September 1943 the Aga divorced Andree on the grounds of

"mutual dislike and diversity of characters". The Aga's behaviour towards his wives may not have been to everyone's taste, but he was never less than generous when the seemingly inevitable parting came. Andree was given a generous settlement and retained the houses in Antibes and Aix-les-Bains as well as an apartment in Paris and a large chalet in Gstaad.

The Aga's attitude to marriage was not entirely at odds with his faith which allowed him to take up to four wives. At any time he had only to state that he no longer loved his wife to secure an Islamic divorce, if he could swear that he had not had sexual relations with her in the preceding three months. Unsurprisingly this does not work in reverse should a Muslim woman wish to divorce her husband. The Aga's religion was very tolerant; it espoused the philosophy that personal serenity and happiness were the main objects of life. The problem was that none of this was legal in the countries in which he chose spend much of his time.

However, the way was cleared and on 9th October 1944 the Aga Khan, now approaching his 67th birthday, married for the fourth time and Yvette became his wife and Begum. The bride was very beautiful, willowy, with wavy chestnut hair and a glowing complexion, had great style but in contrast to the Aga was also almost thirty years younger and six inches taller. There was one significant difference between Yvette and Andree: Yvette converted to Islam. The civil ceremony was followed by a Muslim wedding and the new Begum became Om Habibeh meaning "Mother of the Beloved".

Yvette was highly intelligent and possessed one priceless gift: she was able to make the Aga laugh whatever mood he was in. She had enormous zest and was a keen skier; the Aga, much to everyone's surprise, also tried the slopes but his enthusiasm waned after a fall, which did not cause any great injury. The Aga called Yvette *Yaky*; compounded from their initials and he built a house for her in France at Cannes high upon the hillside overlooking the town called *Yakymour*. The last four letters are taken from the French word for love: *amour*. In public he referred to her as "the Begum"; curiously a title Andree was also allowed to use, and she called him "the Prince". Yvette was called "Highness" by her staff and Yaky by her friends.

Yakymour cost many thousands of pounds to build but in décor and appearance it was not as elaborate or costly as many other luxury villas on the Riviera. The rooms were large and spacious with chintz-covered furniture and many books with one wall covered from end to end in bookshelves and on the opposite side portraits by the Dutch artist Van Dongen. The living room had a wonderful view of the bay over which the Aga would gaze from his vast striped *chaise-longue* which was fitted with rubber tyres to facilitate him being wheeled from room to room. Yakymour was informal and the Aga usually dressed casually when staying there even to receive visitors.

*   *   *

Almost from the beginning Yvette played a more active role in the Aga's life than either Ginetta or Andree who had rarely accompanied him on social occasions. From now on he was almost invariably accompanied by Yvette. The early part of 1945 was much happier for the Aga and the end of the war in Europe in May raised hopes that he could restart his life in particular his racing stables.

Even before the Armistice had been signed but with France in the hands of the western allies, Sir Duff Cooper, the British ambassador in Paris, enabled the Aga to escape to from Geneva to Marseilles. In company with Yvette the U. S. Army offered hospitality and they were housed in comfortable requisitioned property on the coast.

The Aga soon set off on his travels; but not to India but to Africa. He had hardly been mentioned in India during the war when he had been exiled in Switzerland and his influence was possibly less than it was. He need not have worried; he and the Begum were met with an upsurge of affection and emotion.

To celebrate the sixtieth anniversary of his becoming Imam he was weighed again this time against diamonds in Bombay, however, it was Yvette as the new Begum that everyone wanted to see. The Brabourne cricket stadium was packed with 70,000 eager worshipers ready to acclaim their leader. Any doubt about the Aga's importance to his followers would seem to have been removed!

The Aga was due to continue his Diamond Jubilee celebrations and before departing for Dar-es-Salaam he called on the Viceroy: Lord

Wavell to discuss the situation of Indians in South Africa. However, the Aga was not well; looking tired and ill and some way from the smiling avuncular figure so beloved of racecourses. His hair had thinned and was almost white and he was suffering with his dentures. He flew to Nairobi but quickly took to his bed and postponed several receptions. Once he had recovered he was again weighed ceremoniously against diamonds

*   *   *

The post-war world had changed forever; although Churchill boasted that Britain and its Empire were more united and powerful than at any other time, he clearly had not canvased the opinion of many nationals from the "Jewel in Britain's Crown". Although many brave and loyal Indians had fought in the war there were plenty who bitterly resented being dragged into a war without any consultation. Nehru was particularly caustic and when the war in Asia was over in September India was set on its freedom. "As long as we rule India" Lord Curzon had said, "We are the greatest power in the World. However, if we lose it we shall drop straight away to a third-rate power".

His Lordship was about to see if he was right: the tide was now firmly in favour of independence. Although Mountbatten: the last Viceroy of India, put on a typical show which was a combination of arrogance, bluster and splendour in order to display the aura of power, he soon realized that unless he acted without delay he would be faced with civil war.

India was offered absolute independence in 1946, united or divided, within or outside the Commonwealth. The Independence Act was passed in August 1947 and, with Hindus and Muslims still in disagreement, India was partitioned and Pakistan created; in two sections: East and West Pakistan. There followed massacres, arson and violence on a frightening scale.

For the Aga this was all absolutely ghastly. He was devoted to Britain and the Empire and now, despite being on the winning side in a catastrophic war that almost completely bankrupted her, Britain was now only a shadow of the power she had been during Victoria's reign. The Empire was on the wane with its jewel given away with indecent hast; almost as if Britain was in a state of panic about the whole business. The Aga was now in a terminally distraught state; an insoluble dichotomy pervaded his mind: preferring the old world that had by now totally disappeared and unable to adjust to the new one.

*   *   *

Reference was made earlier to Miss Freda Blain the Aga's secretary for seventeen years from 1922 until the outbreak of war from which time she worked in an aeroplane factory. With her characteristic diligence, intelligence and application she was made a foreman. At the end of hostilities the Aga was concerned about his stud in Normandy and cabled Miss Blain and asked if she would investigate. There was no organised transport in Normandy, but the resourceful Miss Blain using a bicycle and obtaining lifts in hay carts reached the stud and organised matters as best she could.

Again in February 1949 when the Aga was quite seriously ill he summoned Miss Blain to help him arrange some of his affairs in case he died. There were no seats available on any scheduled flights from London so Aly chartered a plane in Switzerland to fly to London and collect her. Miss Blain had known all three of the Aga's European wives and had known Aly since he was eleven. She was also on excellent terms with Joan Guinness and Andree and one of the trustees to Aly's two sons. Upon seeing the stricken Aga she felt the best course was a rest period in the mountains which brought about his recovery.

Notwithstanding all that Freda Blain had done for the Aga over many years she does not get even a single mention in the Aga's memoirs; one reason why her true name has been so difficult to establish! This is extraordinary! Her photo and a few recollections would certainly have livened up a most dreary tome!

*   *   *

By the end of 1947 the Aga became a septuagenarian and he was looking his age; his hair had been grey for some time but was now considerably thinner and almost white. There were dark circles under his eyes and the thick magnifying lenses he wore were unable to improve his failing eyesight. He was in steady decline; his health irrevocably damaged and he was becoming increasingly frail. The changing of a world he had known and been part of since Edwardian times changed after the First World War and was now disappearing fast after the Second; and he did not care overmuch for the world that emerged in which he saw no role for himself.

Aly Khan, his son and the man born to be his successor, was approaching forty but showing no inclination to mature and accept his future responsibilities. Aly had divorced and re-married this time to the actress Rita Hayworth and while the Aga had given his tacit blessing the Hollywood-style trappings and the press coverage would have been anathema to him. This does not mean that the Aga was opposed to the marriage; on the contrary he had high hopes that they would be ideally suited to one another. The Aga pointed out that Rita had no social background and had no knowledge of anything apart from motion pictures. "As Aly never reads a book and lives entirely for the present her ignorance will not worry him" he concluded, a shade unfairly most would say.

Rita was never comfortable amongst Aly's racing associates. She did not like taking second place to Aly and did not like being known as "Princess Aly Khan". Aly did not like the name Rita and called her Margarita. However, Aly would deny her nothing; her dress allow-ance was £4,000 (112,000) a year but their clash of lifestyles; some-thing they might have considered at the outset, was a problem.

The Aga had shrewdly noted these differences "I thought Miss Hayworth charming and beautiful but it was not long before I saw, I am afraid, that they were not a well-assorted couple". Aly was warm-hearted, generous and gregarious, was always surrounded by friends and acquaintances while Rita looked on marriage as a haven of peace and rest from her professional work.

Ultimately the marriage failed when Aly began an affair with the beautiful actress Gene Tierney, who he was determined to marry. An exasperated Aga muttered in private "If only Aly could choose his women as he did his horses….!" It is entirely possible that this was the moment when the Aga began to realize that Aly might not be fitted to the role of Imam.

Conversely the Aga was developing a deep relationship with

Karim; or "K" as he was sometimes called. They talked to one another as contemporaries even when Karim was as young as nine and it became a powerful bond. It was probably due to the Aga's influence that Karim was mature beyond his age.

*   *   *

The Aga was subjected to a most unpleasant robbery in 1948. Whilst on his way to Deauville airport with Yvette and two servants their car was forced off the road by a Citroen. They were threatened by firearms and forced to hand over the Begum's jewellery case. The haul was about £70,000 (2,520,000), and was insured by Lloyds of London.

The Aga was depressed in the summer of 1948 by the whole wretched business caused by the partition which was followed by the assassination of Ghandi. Yvette noticed his apathy and organized an African safari, which the Aga greeted with enthusiasm and Sadruddin, on holiday from Harvard, joined them together with some friends of Yvette. This was to be no ordinary safari: it included the Aga's personal physician, a nurse, fourteen trucks of food, four white servants, five white African hunters, sixty native servants including six cooks and six laundrymen. Yvette brought Paris dresses and in the evenings they dined on only the very best food and wine. The party stopped in Nairobi where the previous year Yvette had converted to Islam.

The Aga enjoyed the trip but with his health and spirits much improved he decided to end it prematurely as he was keen to return to his favourite pursuits: breeding and racing, and, despite his age, if rumour is to be believed, chasing women!

*   *   *

The Aga could be remarkably generous when the mood took him. At about this time he was in a car with the Begum and another male relative: Zulfikarali Valiani, on the outskirts of Karachi when they stopped at a junction. A beggar approached the car and the Aga instructed Valiani to give the man 100 rupees (about £7) (240). Valiani had no cash on him and the Aga and Begum certainly didn't have any. Valiani explained to the beggar that they would return with some money. The beggar understandably looked doubtful and implored them tearfully to give him something. So the Aga said "Promise him 200 rupees". The Aga then turned to the beggar and said in Urdu "This man will return in an hour and give you 300 rupees!" Valiani arranged for the sum to be paid to the beggar and as he explained later "His Highness might easily have raised the stakes to 1,000 rupees!"

*   *   *

The Aga returned, to Europe of course not Pakistan, which was now partitioned from India. He returned to the South of France with Yvette and he gradually fell into the habit of spending a few hours each day at the Villa Andree, in Antibes, which was a half an hour drive from Yakimour. Andree was comfortable with the Aga and on very good terms with Aly and, during periods of tension, able to act as an inter-mediary between father and son.

During that winter of 1950–51 the Aga stopped off at Tehran to visit the young Shah of Persia. The Shah conferred the style of a Royal Prince of Persia on the descendants of the previous dynasty. It entitled the Aga to the address of "Royal Highness" which also applied to Aly and, eventually Karim, who is "His Highness" in Europe but "His Royal Highness" east of Suez. The Aga's Persian nationality was confirmed enabling him (and his descendants) to hold a Persian as well as a British passport. None of this has counted for much since 1979 when Persia became an Islamic Republic.

*   *   *

By this time the Aga had no political role, Britain certainly had no use for him in the newly formed Pakistan, and he had looked out of touch with Muslims. During a speech he made to the World Muslim Conference in February 1951 he suggested Pakistan should abandon Urdu as its national language and replace it with Arabic. Urdu he argued was the language of Muslim downfall and was not really a Muslim language but a Hindu one.

Language was an emotive subject on the subcontinent and Pakistani nationalists had clung to Urdu. Iqbal, a poet and inspiration for the idea of Pakistan, had written in Urdu. The Aga's comments were greeted with considerable hostility and this latest *faux pas* only confirmed the view that he was becoming out of kilter with Muslim sentiments. *O Tempora! O Mores!*

* * *

It was about this time that the Aga began, with the help of John Cornell, to write his memoirs. These were eventually published in 1954 and subtitled: *World Enough and Time.* He was unable to use this as a title because there was already a published novel with this title. The Aga then asked for *A Journey through Space and Time*, however, the publishers pointed out that this had science fiction con-notations; to anyone of a generation or so later this title would have brought up an image of *Doctor Who*! Now that really is something the Aga would have loved: a *Tardis,* to move around the world in matter of moments! The kindest thing that can be said about his memoirs is that anyone wishing to study the life of the Aga Khan III would do well not to rely on them too heavily!

In 1952 two biographies of the Aga were published: *Prince, Prophet and Sportsman*, by Stanley Jackson and *His Highness the Aga Khan* by Harry J Greenwall. It may well have been the inac-curacies in these books which convinced the Aga to write his memoirs. Unfortunately he replaced one set of doubtful assertions and anecdotes for some of his own! Astonishingly he had placed a letter in *The Times Literary Supplement* on 14th November 1952 asking for copies of any documents or information that might help him write his memoirs! This would be normal for any writer researching a long dead figure; but hardly an individual's own life. One is irresistibly drawn to the highly entertaining racing journal-ist Jeffrey Bernard; a legendary imbiber of alcohol by any standards, who once placed a request in *The Sporting Life* saying that he was proposing to write his memoirs and asking anyone who knew him between 1960 and 1975 to contact him and tell him what he had been doing!

The Aga had expressed interest in writing an autobiography in 1936 and speculated that such a project would be worth between seven and eight thousand pounds (360,000 – 400,000). Why the Aga's priority should be how much he could make, rather than what he might say, some would consider typical of the man. A London newspaper offered him 2,000 guineas (£109,000) for six articles and said they did not need to be written by him personally! The Aga had wanted Aly to write his biography but this never materialised. When asked why the Aga replied rather brutally "Because my son is a bloody fool"

When the Aga's memoirs were complete and published he made no reference to receiving any help in writing them. However, anyone reading his letters written over fifty years and his memoirs could hardly fail to notice the vast literary gulf; the memoirs, though boring, are organised, grammatically correct and without the Aga's idiosyncratic style. The criticism here is not the Aga's relatively poor command of English; it is that he employed help in writing his memoirs but refused to acknowledge it. Did he think that it was impossible to see what was, in reality, obvious to all? Was he really so naïve? It really did seem that there were times when he assumed that no one could see the truth about him; which is almost beyond belief.

In his memoirs the Aga barely mentions his private life after his childhood; little of him as a person is revealed and, although there had been a number of women in his life, one could be forgiven for thinking each of his first three marriages failed through no fault of his own! The contents are very selective: it would seem from most informed opinion that he was not guilty of outright lies, but many events are almost impossible to equate with accepted historical evidence. For example there are many myths and legends surrounding the Aga Khan many of which have been distorted with time and retelling. In his introduction the Aga laments that such myths and legends exist and then does little or nothing to dispel them. He says nothing about the creation of his wealth which his grandfather struggled so hard to secure from the British.

The Times reviewer lamented of the memoirs "they told us all too little". The Aga omitted any details of women apparently on the advice of Somerset Maugham who wrote a foreword; six pages of not very much! Whoever read the proofs failed to spot that the publishers had omitted a dedication to Yvette, although subsequent editions corrected this.

Reading the memoirs of the Aga Khan III is an exercise in almost relentless, unwavering, stupefying boredom. They are not even enlivened by some interesting or amusing anecdotes or events; even Lord Beaverbrook, a friend of the Aga's, declined to serialise them in the *Daily Express*. Instead the rival *Daily Mail* under Lord Rothermere published extracts; although finding highlights would have taxed even the most imaginative editor.

*   *   *

Possibly because of short-sightedness, playing sport was never a priority for the Aga; unlike many Indians he never took up cricket, however, he did like hockey and introduced the sport to India. He did take daily physical exercise, something he claims to have maintained throughout his life wherever possible. However, as discussed earlier, judging by his frame it can only be assumed it had often not been possible! In youth this comprised, boxing, Sandow's exercises (created by the famous strongman Eugene Sandow), Indian Clubs (swinging exercises using clubs to improve physique), long walks, he once claimed he could walk ten miles in two and a half hours, and cycling tours. Although he had not played sport in his youth he later he took up tennis and, in particular of course, golf.

He played golf for exercise and relaxed by attending the Casino at Monte Carlo. As explained earlier, apart from his putting, he was not a bad golfer and after he had won the Derby for the first time at the age of 52, in 1930, the Aga was supposed to have remarked that he had two great sporting ambitions: "One was to have a Derby winner, and that I have got. My other is to win a great golf championship. I hope to do that before I die. He won the Derby five times but the second ambition, not surprisingly, always eluded him. However, at one time he did play off a handicap of 12 which is decent enough, and once recorded a hole-in-one; something that at least obviated the need to putt out! However, he was some way below the level required to win any tournament open to good players as, even at his best, he would have started any competition at a disadvantage of twelve strokes for each round!

The Aga took lessons from the professional golfer J H (John Henry) Taylor; one day the Aga walked into Taylor's shop and, after waiting until he had served his customers, asked him to teach him how to play golf. The Aga, like many prominent men, took golf very seriously; he and Taylor would play for 25 francs (£13) with Taylor conceding the Aga 16 strokes. Taylor diplomatically allowed the Aga to win on occasions and when Taylor offered the money, although a paltry sum, the Aga would snatch it enthusiastically.

The Aga would go to some lengths to ensure he did not lose money playing golf. Some opponents would let him win and at dinner one night he boasted that he had never been beaten off his handicap, which at that time was 18. Ralph Rafael, who had a handicap of 16 but was capable of playing down to 12, said he would take him on and they arranged to play for £100 (2,800).

The following day Rafael whilst playing a round was driving and produced an outstanding stroke at a dog-leg with just sufficient draw to bring the ball round the corner. He was just picking up his tee when the head of the Aga could just be seen behind a hedge. The Aga had been "touting the gallop" and not surprisingly later that day he approached Rafael and said he had changed his mind and decided friends should not play for money! Someone suggested the Aga should pay a forfeit as he had scratched and so he magnanimously offered to buy Rafael's wife a set of golf clubs. The Aga admired Rafael's wife but when the clubs were produced they amounted to half a dozen clubs from a bygone age that might have been recently discarded. This was typical of the Aga's mind-set: it was not the £100, he would have behaved just the same if it had been £1, it was losing and his churlish gesture was just an extension of this.

Conversely, just after the Great War the Aga invited Taylor to stay with him on the continent; the Aga booked him into a couple of rooms in the Ritz and casually told him that his secretary would pay the bill. Taylor was flabbergasted at such generosity.

*   *   *

The Aga at the age of seventy-five seemed resurgent; possibly as a result of receiving cellular therapy as pioneered by Paul Niehans. The treatment consisted of the injection of cells scraped from unborn lambs and could, apparently, cure cancer, heart disease, and diabetes, cirrhosis of the liver, insomnia, depression and impotence. In addition to the Aga, those sharing his belief in the efficaciousness of Niehans' treatment in halting the ageing process and recreating youth were the following: – W Somerset Maugham, Konrad Adenauer, Pope Pius XII, Thomas Mann and the Duke of Windsor.

The Aga had a new house in Paris in the rue Scheffer, off the Avenue Henri Martin, where he spent about three months each year. He gave and attended some memorable parties and costume balls and was keen to dine out at any restaurant where the food was exceptional. By this time the Aga had given up dancing; "I can't understand you Europeans dancing yourselves. In the East we hire women to do that for us" he would say.

The Aga and food gave rise to some legendary stories. In later years he loved to entertain at his villa in Deauville. Lunch was usually for at least a dozen guests and the food and wine of the highest quality. The Aga had a healthy appetite, often having a second helping, was particularly fond of rich sauces and *soufflés* and was a prodigious consumer of ice cream. The Aga talked continually whilst eating sometimes laying down his knife and fork to relate a story. His guests were often of a cosmopolitan nature which necessitated his telling each story in a different language. On one occasion a story was related in English, French, Italian and Urdu with the Aga laughing more loudly with each telling.

Interestingly his appetite seemed to increase when on a diet! Marcus Marsh records him eating prodigious amounts when in his company, and out of sight of Yvette! At this time he weighed about seventeen stone but was still active; playing golf most days. In addition although he had an attractive wife thirty years his junior rumour suggested he was spending time with a beauty queen! Perhaps the cellular therapy was working…

*　　*　　*

In 1954 the Aga named Yvette Mat Salamat (Spiritual Mother) of the Ismaili. Also at this time the Aga's health was again causing some concern. The seventieth anniversary of his becoming Imam was not due until August 1955. However, it was held in February 1954; when he was weighed against platinum in Karachi. The occasion was not on the same scale and grandeur as his two previous jubilees but he hoped it would raise enough money in order that "by 1960 every Ismaili in Pakistan should have a profession or business of his own". As a result of a diet his doctors had prescribed for him, he weighed only 15 stones exactly (210 pounds; 95 kilos). The ceremony lacked the novelty of the 1936 celebrations or the emotion of the one in 1946.

Following the ceremony the Aga developed a bad cold and a high temperature and returned to *Yakymour* considerably weakened by the journey. The truth of the matter was his health was now in terminal decline: he was nearly blind, his heart impaired, his liver was diseased and, as if that was not enough, he was forced to use a wheelchair. Then a final humiliation; in London billboards advertised a brand of coffee which was "rich and dark like the Aga Khan".

The Aga decided to fight back; while he was at Yakymour recovering from prostate surgery Yvette endured the scorching July heat of the desert and made a pilgrimage to Mecca. Wearing only an *ihram* (a rough cotton robe), her head covered, but her feet bare, she walked over dirt and blistering rock. The only concession to her European sensitivities was a white parasol and dark glasses as some protection from the sun. This was a remarkable and courageous act of dedication by Yvette and her reputation was considerably enhanced by it.

At the same time Karim toured the Ismaili communities in East Africa. Karim was only seventeen but he made a mature and impressive speech to a large gathering in Nairobi propounding the value of education. On the tour Karim had seemed tireless under the harsh conditions, was mature for his age and exuded youth and enthusiasm. Karim's success on this trip was reported to the Aga who was very pleased as he was a firm favourite with him. This is hardly surprising; Karim was much disciplined and showed no signs of inheriting Aly's wild tendencies.

*   *   *

The Aga made a television appearance in June 1954 in which he projected himself as the last great survivor of the Victorian age. He said the most outstanding personality he had ever met was Queen Victoria. He was asked what most fascinated him about horse racing and his reply, not a surprise to anyone involved in racing was "breeding, breeding breeding". At least that is what most assumed he said as it came out sounding more like breathing, breathing breathing!

Just a short while afterwards in August he was ill again with lumbago and sciatica and was virtually a cripple; he spoke mainly now about pain and illness. In September he suffered an attack of bronchitis and a leading heart specialist was called to attend to him.

The Aga recovered sufficiently to attend another weighing ceremony to celebrate his seventy years as Imam, this time in Cairo. He returned to Yakimour but was soon on his travels again this time to London where he attended a ceremony at Buckingham Palace. The Queen invested him with the insignia of a Knight Grand Cross of the Order of St Michael and St George; this had been conferred on him in the New Year Honours' List. He then visited Paris to look over his will…

*   *   *

It is not clear exactly when the Aga Khan decided that his son Aly was not suitable to succeed him. The Aga had admitted as long ago as 1934 to P J Patrick of the India Office that he did not think his son would be able to inherit his mantle. The Aga's will was dated 25th May 1955 when Aly was nearly forty-four; the Aga realised that Aly was too set in his ways to change and the die was cast.

Aly's conduct and behaviour would probably have been sufficient reason in most people's eyes. However, the principal problem was not particularly his behaviour with women, dreadful as that was on occasions: he had conducted his marriages in an even more cavalier fashion than the Aga. However, Aly's status as a religious leader was not at odds with his views on fidelity because of Muslims attitude towards sex; as Evelyn Waugh put it with typically brutal simplicity:

"Muslims are the only people that believe there will be fucking in heaven". As such a playboy religious leader was not to his followers an oxymoron. Another problem, but again not the major one, was Aly's profligate spending. The Aga worried about Aly's attitude to money; his allowance was never enough although he was prevented from touching any capital. The Aga feared this spending would be totally unrestrained after his death and Aly would dissipate the sect's resources. He gambled fearlessly and ferociously and, sometimes foolishly, could lose colossal amounts backing horses, principally chasing losses. For example in that very same year: 1955, Aly's betting showed he was ahead by £26,000 (677,000) after Epsom only to convert this into a deficit of £32,000 (562,000) after Ascot; an astonishing turnaround of £58,000 (1,239,000). Aly made no bones about it: "I am a gambler and I can't help it. Perhaps I will have a monkey or a thousand on someone else's horse I know nothing about just because I have a hunch it might win. However, I might put half as much on a horse of my own that I know all about". Aly was equally unrestrained at the casino and, on most occasions but not all, was usually a good loser.

All of this would have been against Aly but the principal reason the Aga overlooked his son was simply Aly's view on life was from another age. He was unprepared for the world as it was changing and the Aga wanted to pass the succession on to an individual that he considered more suited to the coming, highly technical, age: his grandson Karim, the present Aga Khan.

Aly was of course a man of considerable charm and was liked by almost everyone he met; although because of his tendency towards satyromania there were plenty of husbands who thought him something of a menace! However, his inability to remain faithful to any woman for longer than a week – most one night stands were lucky if he was still with them when they woke up – his wild lifestyle, love of speed and danger, his maniacally fast driving – he was eventually killed in a car crash while driving too fast in Paris in 1959 at the age of 48 – and the hectic pace of his social life probably clinched the matter in the Aga's mind.

In addition the Aga had a premonition that Aly would die

prematurely; a feeling reinforced by Aly's subconscious motto for life: *Carpe diem, quam minimum credula postero*; enjoy today, trust not in tomorrow! Aly could have been killed driving on many occasions; once leaving Newmarket he left the road and ended upside down in a field between Baldock and Stevenage. On this occasion he suffered merely concussion. As if all this was not enough there was his private plane...

The Aga did not want to entrust the welfare of his community to someone who spent his life courting an early death. In seemed that Aly, a man born to be a God and a spiritual leader to millions, would be remembered primarily as a boulevardier with a compulsive zest for life. A man, some thought, who possessed a better judgement of thoroughbreds than women.

Being overlooked by the Aga for the succession was a dreadful blow to Aly softened somewhat by the Pakistan government naming him as its ambassador to the United Nations. Although Aly's staff and the press viewed his arrival at the UN with some doubt and concern he surprised them and was a complete success. In addition to his usual intelligence and charm Aly displayed seriousness, caution and conscientiousness. Lord Astor recorded that the appointment produced the most useful, rewarding and happiest days of Aly's life.

Aly could be a wonderful friend: Lord Astor remembered how he would telephone anyone in trouble or distress wherever he was in the world. To his friends Aly's sympathy, intuition and kindness were rocks that could be relied on. This did not stop at simple words; Aly would provide any practical help to a friend he could; if peace and shelter were needed he would place any of his houses at their disposal for as long as required.

Aly had the endearing and wonderful gift of persuading any interlocutor that at that moment they were the most important person in the world. His natural manner was unaffected whether he was with an eminent person or any ordinary member of the public. "He's a one that Prince Aly. No la-di-da about him," one of Frank Buttes stablemen observed when Aly came to ride work at Fitzroy House one morning.

Aly wasted not a moment of his time; a non-smoker and virtual teetotaller, he was tireless. Returning from a casino at Deauville in the early hours of the morning he would find time to attend to diplomatic or business matters before retiring for the night. However, he would still rise at six thirty and watch horses work or indeed ride them himself. A typical day could be of formidable intensity: a swim, work on business matters with his secretary, tennis, racing, bridge, more work, half an hours work, some exercises and a massage, a dinner party and the casino.

Contrary to appearances which suggest a very confident man Aly had always been a sensitive individual with a curiously defensive attitude to slights both real and imagined. However, once he was assured of an individual's friendship it was returned many times over. Lord Astor recalled the last time he had seen Aly before his death, "An untidy gay figure bustling through London Airport, leaving a trail of laughter by a cheery or courteous word to each person he came into contact with, each of whom he treated as a human being he was glad to see".

Nothing was more typical of Aly was as he lay dying as a result of a car crash his last words were of concern for his female companion: "How is she?" he asked. No man could ever have a more gracious epitaph.

In the final analysis, despite his faults Aly deserves to be remembered in a positive way as a complex, multi-talented, charming, generous, kind, brilliant, restless, brave, fearless and essentially likable man.

*   *   *

The Aga had enjoyed life during the nineteen fifties despite fluctuating health; he was either resting from some ailment or recovered and off on his travels. In July 1956 he suffered a nervous breakdown and his doctors advised complete rest until the spring/summer of 1957. By December 1956 he was well enough to complain about the Suez crisis "this foolish Middle East business". However, by April 1957 he was again ailing and, although he went to Chantilly, he was not well enough to attend the races. He did though complete his set of English

Classics as an owner by winning the One Thousand Guineas with Rose Royale II trained in France by Alec Head.

The Aga was now a sick man and although his mind was sharp he had lost about a hundred pounds in weight (45 kilos) and his enormous appetite was drastically affected. Nonetheless he was adamant that there should be a huge celebration of his eightieth birthday in November.

However, the truth was that there was now no way back and aware that the end could not be far away he was anxious to return home: the Villa Barakat in Switzerland which had become the legal residence of this most nomadic of individuals. He wished to die there in order to leave his affairs in order. In the early hours of July 11th 1957 he was fading and by midday he was asleep and died forty minutes later. His family was at his bedside.

Aly, of course, had no idea that he was not to be the Aga's heir. He said his last goodbye to his father and addressed religious followers and the press that had gathered in the grounds of the villa. He informed them that the Aga was dead and that he had not named his successor on his deathbed. He told them that there would be a press conference and the new Aga Khan; he presumably thought that would be him, would address them.

The following morning the Aga's will was read and Aly learned that he was to be overlooked in favour of his son Karim. Bettina said that the Aga's preference for Karim was a kind of public humiliation and that Aly was never quite the same again.

But Aly behaved impeccably and with considerable stature: he crossed the room to Karim and said "The Imam is dead, long live the Imam". He kissed his son's hand before backing humbly away.

The Aga Khan III was buried at the Mausoleum of Aga Khan on the Nile of Aswan Egypt.

*   *   *

The tributes came: *The Times* headline was "A Citizen of the World"; *The Guardian's* read; "A Monarch without Territory". Both papers carried long life-sketches and editorials seeing his death as a passing of an age.

*   *   *

Yvette Labrousse the fourth Begum was only 51 when the Aga died. They had been married for thirteen years but there seems little doubt that she, of all his wives, made him the most happy, and was without doubt the wife happiest to be married to him. The Aga spent more time with her than any of his previous wives and, while it can only be an assumption, Yvette probably understood him better than the others. As she was from a largely uneducated background Yvette was grateful to the Aga for broadening her horizons, especially in the arts and music. In his turn the Aga was fortunate to have such a devoted wife and carer during his declining years.

After the Aga's death she continued to support his religious mission. For over forty years of widowhood (she never considered remarrying) she remained loyal to this endeavour, keeping in contact with Ismaili communities. Yvette ran a charitable foundation to tackle poverty in Aswan in Egypt where she spent three months each year in a villa at the site of the Aga's mausoleum. For the rest of the time she was usually at *Yakymour*.

As a widow she travelled widely for both charity and pleasure and was a regular visitor to Ascot. He view on fashion was typically astute: "Don't choose what you like but what suits you. To be elegant one must have discretion. The secret is in the detail."

Yvette remained stunningly beautiful to the end of her long life and had only one real regret: she never had children. The Aga once gave her some excellent advice: "Enjoy yourself; it's later than you think".

Yvette died in July 2000 aged 94.

*   *   *

The Aga Khan may have been a God to many millions but as far as Imperial Britain was concerned in India he was still just an Indian, moreover he was without the status of those princes and members of the raj. All Indians were banned from clubs during British rule; when the writer Somerset Maugham visited India the Aga asked him if he had been made an honorary member at the clubs in Bombay and Calcutta. When Maugham replied that he had, the Aga asked him if he knew the difference between the two clubs. Maugham shook his head. "In one they do not allow either dogs or Indians, however, in the other they do allow dogs", was the Aga's baleful reply.

*   *   *

Like many very wealthy men the Aga had no idea of the value of money to those who possessed little of it. For example it was absurd that he should have spent so much time considering whether to tip a caddy or cab driver two shillings or half a crown(about £7). If such individuals had done him a good service, then he should have had the sensitivity to tip generously, in the knowledge that they had been rewarded for a job well done. Did he think a generous tip would corrupt such individuals?

Conversely his blend of Western and Eastern philosophies gave him a unique, at that time, slant on life. He was able to mix with anyone in society; wealthy and titled individuals as well as those who would have been described before the war as "the lower orders". Lady Diana Cooper remembered that between the wars the Aga was much in demand as a lunch or dinner guest with people in high society. Lady Diana herself was at the centre of a clique consisting of such luminaries as Lord Beaverbrook, Mrs Edwin Montagu and of course the Aga. Lady Diana would provide the glamour and select the restaurant together with the guests.

However, he could as easily fit into a heavyweight lunch with such as Lord Astor, Lloyd George, Isaac Foot and various politicians and foreign ambassadors. The Aga may not always say much but would be a dignified presence, a wise leader offering occasional counsel and observations to politicians and statesmen. Equally he could spend an evening at the casino in Deauville or simply play baccarat with a racing or gambling crony. Not considered an impressive public speaker being more effective putting his thoughts in writing than standing on a platform.

The Aga possessed a remarkable memory and read widely. A bibliophile he could converse of a vast number of subjects: once in a Paris bookshop a stranger engaged him in conversation and was astonished that the Aga was so learned about medieval literature.

*   *   *

The Aga had his vicissitudes in public life and politics with his reputation not always surviving the fallout unscathed; but that does not mean that he was not consulted and, on occasions, both useful and taken seriously. Unfortunately the British, while often happy to patronise and regard him with something approaching contempt, as only the British can do with foreigners, they were happy to use him whenever they thought it suited their purposes.

*   *   *

The Aga could be wonderful with children: patient and kind and never making the mistake of talking down to them but able to speak to them in their terms. Sadly he did not find enough time to use this talent often enough for the benefit of his children and grandchildren; particularly Aly who would surely have benefitted from seeing more of his father during his formative years. That he failed Aly as a father can't be given as the reason he lived such a cavalier life; however, it can't have helped that he was a remote, neglectful and frightening figure to his son at a crucial time when Aly should have been undergoing careful grooming as his successor.

*   *   *

What exactly did the life of the Aga Khan III amount to? He lived for over seventy-nine years which saw changes to the World matched by few other periods. Not only did it encompass two cataclysmic world conflicts that changed most parts of the globe for ever, life when he was born bore no relation to that when he died.

In 1877 Britain could still claim to be great; Queen Victoria ruled huge swathes of the world, North America's influence was still in its infancy, Russia was safely controlled by Tsars and many parts of Africa were there for the taking by those adventurous enough to try. When he died in 1957 Britain was barely a shadow of her previous self; almost bankrupted by two wars and divesting herself of her Empire as fast as she could.

North America could claim to be the greatest power in the world but challenged by the mighty bear that was communist Russia. Technology was beginning to transform both how life was lived and the direction the world would take in future. The ideas of just twenty years previously now looked like something from another century.

In the Aga's own memoirs and in various hagiographies written before his death and afterwards, it is claimed that he played a more important role in world affairs than he did. Is it unfair to say that conviction and loyalty were not the Aga's strongest traits? Many believe that almost everything he did was motivated by his own needs and desires. His loyalty to Britain was based on her status and power in the world and in any event was established not by him but by his grandfather the Aga Khan I. The Aga never really believed that Britain would leave India until it became clear in 1946 that they wished to grant independence on almost any terms. The fundamental tenant of the Aga's thinking was always that the British Empire would last forever.

The Aga always wanted a separate Muslim entity as part of a British ruled India with him at the pinnacle. He is considered by some to be one of the founders of Pakistan but in truth the creation of a separate country owed little to the Aga and indeed he was opposed to it. In all probability the Aga Khan's biggest triumph was in simply surviving for over forty years as the leader of India's Muslims who, the Aga convinced, was the only man who could represent their interests to Britain. Conversely British politicians were happier to deal with a man with Western leanings rather than an obviously Indian leader that had no sympathy with British interests.

This view of the Aga from Jawaharlal Nehru is interesting; he was a future prime minister of India and was writing to his daughter Indira, who also became prime minister. "The Aga Khan was the special agent of the English; he lived in England, was chiefly interested in English horseracing and was always hobnobbing with English politicians. He was not even an orthodox Muslim, as he was head of a special sect." Some of this is unfair but the point is that this was how he was perceived by some prominent individuals.

*   *   *

It is sometimes difficult for contemporary Europeans to fully understand the purpose of the Aga Khan III; his fabulous wealth, often
spent in huge amounts purely on selfish gratification, his behaviour
towards women, hard to understand at the time and impossible today.
He was a God to about ten million followers and although he spent
a large proportion of his time pursuing pleasure, he did not neglect
those who believed he should be revered.

In India and East Africa the Aga was instrumental in creating
institutions to enable his communities to regulate their own affairs.
He raised huge sums of money for improving the education of his
followers and building hospitals to care for the sick. He advanced
the welfare, education and expectations of his followers during his
own lifetime. Some may claim he could have done more. This is very
unfair; the Aga was always conscious that his people lacked education and he made strenuous efforts to improve schools for his followers particularly girls who he thought should have the same education
as boys. Considerable amounts of the money raised by donations was
spent on education.

*   *   *

When asked how a man who was a God could spend so much time
racing he replied "And why should God not go racing?" He was once
challenged when drinking wine and asked if it was a sin for a Muslim
to consume alcohol, he replied with a quick wit and gentle humour "I
am so holy that when I touch wine it turns to water!" The Aga would
quote the Ismaili philosophy of happiness when challenged about his
extravagant lifestyle: "One should experience life in order not to be
dominated by it".

The Aga did however leave a legacy which his grandson: Karim
has taken forward. He was always more far-sighted than his grandfather and has used his ability to understand the technological revolution and to carry his community into the modern world by continuing
to help educate and improve themselves. Perhaps then The Aga
Khan's finest legacy was to choose Karim and not Aly or Sadruddin
to succeed him.

In many ways The Aga Khan III was a man of his time and should not be condemned for living his life as he thought fit and taking happiness as he found it. Conversely his reputation does not stand as high as it might have done had he behaved differently on some occasions. The level of respect he ultimately commanded was set as much by the occasions when his judgement was faulty than as the result of his actions.

3 The Aga Khan III; His Life in Racing Part I

A rather scholarly-looking man is sitting atop his hack, his keen eye searching the horizon for four juvenile fillies involved in a gallop. The work is serious and designed to test their progress with races at Ascot in mind. Suddenly an imposing grey filly with a long impressive stride appears cantering some distance in front of her work companions with her rider apparently easing her down when he should have been asking her for an effort. The trainer's first thought is that something was amiss but is staggered when he notices that the other three fillies are being vigorously ridden but are still losing ground on the grey filly.

* * *

In his youth the Aga Khan had horses running in his name throughout Western India; on his father's death he had inherited a sporting establishment of between eighty and ninety horses plus hawks and hounds. However, his mother reduced this respectively to about twenty and thirty, and during his childhood it was these that were raced in his name and under his colours. His interest grew under the influence and friendship of Lord William Beresford, who was military secretary to three Viceroys in succession, and a powerful personality and fearless horseman.

The Aga was a very successful owner in India and wrote "My successes as an owner were not insignificant. I may claim that for a time I – and my cousin Aga Shamsuddin, who was part-owner with me of a number of excellent horses – dominated the turf in Western India. Four times in succession I won the Nizam's Gold Cup – the most important and valuable race in Western India.

The Aga wrote about remembered incidents of English racing from his childhood. "I remember as a child our whole family was almost in mourning and despair at the death of the great jockey Fred Archer. Names such as Ormonde and St. Simon were household names in our family".

During the Aga's first visit to England in 1898 he was delighted that his heredity and interest in horse racing was well known in both turf and Royal circles. He was also surprised and pleased that his colours, red and green, the colours of the Ismaili flag, had been registered. It was only some time later that he discovered that they had been registered as green and chocolate; because green and red had not been available. In England the Aga Khan III always raced in green and chocolate although in France and the rest of Europe his colours were green and red.

The Aga's first experience of racing in England was the Spring Meeting at Epsom; now sadly reduced in all respects. He also attended the Derby and placed a sovereign (£99) on the winner Jeddah at 66–1; his Highness certainly did not get the best of the market as Jeddah started at 100–1! "I shall never forget the thrill of my first Derby", said the Aga some years later. "I stood there gripping the rails as the horses thundered round Tattenham Corner and began to climb the hill. I heard the people shouting "Jeddah! Jeddah!"

The Aga was also granted a Royal Household Badge for Ascot; first by Queen Victoria, who, of course, the Aga would certainly not have met at the course at that time, and subsequently renewed, by successive Monarchs: Edward VII, George V, George VI and Elizabeth II. He also attended race meetings in France where William K Vanderbilt introduced him to his trainer William Duke. Vanderbilt gave instructions that the Aga could have free run of the stables to view trials and training noting; "I think you will get more pleasure out of a free run of my stables than a free run out of my house!

*   *   *

It was however not until the Great War was over that the Aga, by then in better health, returned to his interest in thoroughbred racing. In 1904 on a visit to the Tully stud in Ireland Col. William Hall-Walker, later Lord Wavertree, urged the Aga Khan to take up racing and breeding in England. Significantly The Aga asked Hall-Walker how to best approach the thoroughbred industry from an investment point of view. The Colonel emphasized the need for care in the selection of sound yearlings and suggested that these only come from best female winning lines that money could buy. This was probably the best advice about breeding the Aga ever received.

Col. Hall-Walker was the owner of a successful brewery in Liverpool and a fine horseman who made a profound study of bloodstock breeding and had considerable knowledge. Unfortunately, he was unable to tolerate even the mildest contradiction on the subject and any opposition was liable to make him cantankerous. He had pronounced views on mares: they were, in his opinion, far more important than sires; if one had a good mare then the choice of sire did not matter. Hall-Walker believed that a study of all breeders' methods would bring its own reward and in addition he included, bizarrely, Totemism and most importantly in his view Veidavolani: in-breeding, which he correctly, but probably unnecessarily, pointed out was nothing to do with Astrology!

In 1908 Hall-Walker wrote to the writer and journalist Sydney Galtrey; "There is no royal road to success in breeding, either by the aid of Astrology, Botany or Physiology but these all have their uses if applied in an intelligent manner. Nature cannot be governed by magic, but is ruled by common sense, when by thought study and practical knowledge; men seek its development in the direction they require". He maintained that this was why England maintained her supremacy in breeding animals.

Hall-Walker was never easy to discourse with: he could be astonishingly arrogant and impatient with others, sometimes his demeanour bordered on contempt, and, while it was possible to learn from him, at all times he asserted that only he knew the secret of successful thoroughbred breeding.

This industrial-strength hubris and eccentricity earned him the nickname of "Whimsical Walker" and, probably as a result of his confident certainty that he was always right, was inclined to overestimate the merits of his own horses. Any failings were usually attributed to inadequacies in the trainer and/or jockey and as a result anyone engaged to work for him could, in consequence, only regard themselves as in temporary employment. He once dismissed the very able trainer W T (Jack) Robinson who had trained successfully for him for some years with the words "Goodbye Robinson, you have cost me three Derbys".

The vital decisions in his own life, racing and breeding were based on what the stars forecast. He was born on Christmas Day; family motto *Cura et Industria*, (care and industry) and therefore probably felt he had been born under a favourable star! However, in all probability the horoscope was suffering an off-day when he sold Prince Palatine as a yearling for 2,000 guineas (£184,000); he became one of the best horses Hall-Walker ever bred; winning the Eclipse Stakes, St Leger, Ascot Gold Cup twice, Coronation Cup, Doncaster Cup and Jockey Club Stakes. He later changed hands for £40,000! (3,120,000). When asked why he had sold Prince Palatine instead of racing him, Hall-Walker replied that he had not been satisfied with what the colt's horoscope had told him at the time of foaling!

The employees at the Colonel's stud were certainly aware of his idiosyncrasies; there was an occasion when one of the stud's best mares was enduring a particularly difficult foaling; after the accouchement was over a hot, weary stud hand emerged from the foaling box. When asked what the foal was like he replied "The foal is all right – I just hope the Colonel's bloody horoscope is"!

Some of his employees thought that those foals not considered to have been born under a "lucky star" were not given the best of opportunities as in the case of Prince Palatine. While all of this may make Lord Wavertree appear something of a figure of fun; he did breed some other good horses, apart from Prince Palatine – including the somewhat fortunate Derby winner Minoru, and he also bred the winner of the Gimcrack Stakes four times in five years. He can be thanked, or cursed; contemporaries were by no means unanimous either way, for planting the seed that resulted in the creation of one of horseracing greatest dynasties.

Hall-Walker was ennobled in 1919, becoming Baron Wavertree of Delamere, after presenting his historic Tully Stud to the British

Government along with many valuable mares and foals. Tully was situated near to the Curragh racecourse in Ireland on land now accommodating the Irish National Stud.

In a letter in 1933 to Sidney Galtrey the Aga wrote "It was entirely due to Lord Wavertree and my personal friendship with him that I started to race on the English Turf. I would probably never have been known as an owner west of Suez had he not, during and after my visit to Tully in 1904, urged me to take up racing in England. He undoubtedly gave me much good advice and up to the last I never took an important decision without asking his opinion. Great has have been my successes on the Turf, had I absolutely listened to the advice he gave me; those success would have been infinitely greater. Those who "pooh-pooh" science, knowledge and study in connection with racing do not know what they are talking about".

The Aga really believed in the Colonel's ability to see the future through his faith in the stars; he wrote on 4th February 1933 two days after Lord Wavertree's death…."He – Lord Wavertree – clearly foretold that the King would be very ill and then recover. That winter the King was seriously ill but got over it. Of course Lord Wavertree went by the King's horoscope".

It is a pity His Lordship did not see the Aga's troubles that would beset him during two World Wars; it would have saved British Bloodstock some considerable trouble! The Horoscope failing again!

Ultimately Hall-Walker has three claims to racing immortality: he leased to the King of England Minoru the only Derby winner to carry the Royal colours to victory in the Epsom Classic, he introduced the Aga Khan III to English racing and he gave to the nation the Tully Stud.

* * *

So it was some seventeen years after the seed sown by Col. Hall-Walker – as he was then – bore fruit. Although after visiting the Tully stud the Aga Khan was interested in developing a stud but did not feel the time was right. He noted that "I had neither the means nor time to follow his (Hall-Walker's) advice earlier. Between 1904 and 1921 I was very busy with political work. I wanted to do the thing thoroughly, or not at all. The idea of having a small stud did not appeal to me, so I waited until I could do it as I had planned".

Notwithstanding this the Aga, despite his hectic schedule, was not idle on the subject of breeding during those years: he studied hard and applied his agile and penetrating mind to the study of bloodstock breeding. He eventually decided that he had sufficient funds to set up a breeding operation. The Aga never pretended to have a clue about a thoroughbred's conformation and was only interested in their breeding. He spent at least six of the seventeen years from 1904 in intensive study of breeding in Britain and France; and discussing the theories with acknowledged experts.

The result was that he understood as well as almost anyone which pedigrees offered the best chance of producing good performers. All he needed now was someone to help him acquire yearlings with these pedigrees and a trainer to produce them ready to run on the race-course. The Aga had been about to start a stud in partnership with his cousin Shamsuddin but he died in 1910. Any further plans to start racing were shelved when the world situation deteriorated and his personal, spiritual and political responsibilities took precedence.

$$*   *   *$$

The Aga had resumed going racing in 1919 after four years of war and illness had restricted his opportunities, and he was keen and rarely missed a meeting. "Nothing is more poetic than a man riding a beautiful horse, riding it to perfection, the man and the horse like a centaur, carved as one" was one observation he made at that time.

The result of all the Aga's study of breeding and pedigrees was the belief that the most logical of all the breeding theories was propounded by Lt. Col. John-Joseph Vuillier: the Dosage System; based on Galton's Law of Ancestral Heredity. The Dosage System (also known as the "Lottery" system) was devised in the early part of the century by Vuillier, a retired French military officer, considered a pedigree authority, and an active participant in any pedigree debates at that time.

Vuillier analysed the extended pedigrees of all major European winners, some 650 in total, through twelve generations and considered that Herod had been the most influential sire. Captain Vuillier, as he was then, eventually published this research in *Croisements Rationnels dans la Race Pure* (Rational Crossbreeding in the Thoroughbred) in 1903. A revised edition followed two years later but it was only really brought to prominence when he became associated with the Aga Khan.

And so on the evidence of 650 of the best horses he based a theory, upon which, he would brook no argument. However, what if he had researched the pedigrees of 650 moderate or useless horses? Would he not have found similar conclusions? Was it not simply the case that these ancestors were common to the breed as a whole? This was basically breeding by numbers, taking no account of genetics; preposterous when thoroughbreds are flesh and blood not mathematical formulae.

Vuillier is largely ignored today; his theories fall down in many areas not least that if he was right then all full brothers or sisters would be exactly the same. One's initial reaction to the theory of the Dosage System is of its naivety; just count up a selected number of high-class performers on the racecourse and at stud through twelve generations and if the accumulated score was near enough, using a precise mathematical formula, then *voila!* Nonetheless, the Aga decided to work with Vuillier's system to create his own stud and his apparent reliance on Vuillier's ideas added verisimilitude to this doubtful system. This will be discussed in more detail in the chapter the Aga's breeding methods.

*   *   *

In the spring of 1921 the Aga was dining at Mrs Edwin Montagu's house and sitting next to Mrs Asquith; daughter-in-law of the former Prime Minister and sister of The Hon. George Lambton. They talked horses and she urged him vigorously to take up breeding and racing in England; almost certainly by this time she was pushing at an open door! She then suggested that the Aga ask George Lambton to buy some mares and yearlings.

The Aga decided that he would spend £100,000 (3,600,000) over three years to build his racing stable. He wrote a letter to Lambton and at a resulting meeting asked him to buy some yearlings with the prime objective to setting up a stud. In addition The Aga asked Lambton to train for him. Lambton accepted the offer to buy yearlings; however his position as private trainer to Lord Derby prevented him accepting an offer to train; so Lambton introduced him to Richard C. Dawson who trained at Whatcombe. "I was to concentrate on fillies and only buy a colt if I was really keen on him" said Lambton.

And so the Aga's breeding and racing arrangements in England were settled: Lambton would buy and "Dick" Dawson train. When the Aga returned to Paris he sent for William Duke, whose patron William K. Vanderbilt was now dead, and offered him the job of buying yearlings and training for him in France.

*   *   *

Richard Cecil Dawson had arrived in England from Cloghran in his native Ireland in 1897 accompanied by a five-year-old gelding: Drogheda. The following year as a comparatively unknown he trained Drogheda to win the Grand National. He was an accomplished horse-man but on occasions he had more the appearance of an academic than a horse trainer; dressed in a scholarly fashion and wearing a pince-nez which he pushed to the top of his nose.

Dawson was a man of very positive ideas and was anything but conventional; he could often be observed in various stages of emotion: agitation, annoyance, hurt and indignation. He was rarely if ever seen to be amused as this particular sense was sadly under developed. He and his brother, Samuel, owned a stud in Ireland where he stood Blandford who was to sire four Derby winners in seven years. He had a strange catchphrase: "I can't abide the perfect horse". What he meant by this is hard to say! In any event as anyone involved in buying or breeding horses will confirm; the perfect horse has never and will never exist!

Until the beginning of World War Two it was permissible to give a horse oral medication before a race providing that it was not admin-istrated by a needle: in simple terms dope could be used although in reality these were little more than tonics designed to encourage a healthy appetite and put an effective bloom on their coat. Dawson once sent seven horses to Doncaster races and upon his arrival at the course his travelling head lad was in a panic. His bags had been stolen containing the necessary medication and it was too late to replace it. There was nothing to do but race them without any stimulants; five won and the other two placed!

Incidentally, Dick Dawson was one of the very few trainers who did not saddle his runners. When asked why he replied "Why should I? Surely I can trust an efficient servant to saddle a horse. He can do a thing like that just as well as I can, perhaps better". It is hard to imagine many trainers who would not wish to make sure everything with regard to the saddle and any other equipment, prior to a race, was entirely to his satisfaction. Imagine the effect on Aiden O'Brien if he were to be advised that one of his assistants would in future saddle all his horses in Group 1 races!

*   *   *

The Hon. George Lambton was the fifth son of the 2nd Earl of Durham. His father died while he was at Cambridge, enjoying life but not displaying the obvious traits of a scholar. Lambton was crammed for the Army, something that did not appeal to him any more than study did. What he loved best was riding hoses; particularly in races.

Being a younger son Lambton was often short of money and was reduced to betting to provide the funds he badly needed. However, he was a successful amateur rider until a particularly nasty accident terminated his riding career and he began training.

Lambton was instrumental in the elimination of doping, as practised by North American trainers, at the turn of the century. The Jockey Club did not believe doping to be a problem until Lambton demonstrated exactly how damaging it was by doping six of his own horses that had little ability. Four of them won, one was second and the other was not given a stimulant. Realizing that this was causing chaos to the form, doping was made an offence with warning-off the punishment.

At the time he began his association with the Aga Lambton was aged 62, had been private trainer to Lord Derby for twenty-nine years, had trained seven Classic winners and would train a further six.

A handsome, debonair man who was always immaculately dressed, Lambton possessed considerable charm and was considered an outstanding judge of a thoroughbred.

*   *   *

The Aga began studying the catalogues for the yearlings coming up for sale at the Deauville, Newmarket and Doncaster sales of 1921. He would consider the yearlings on offer in conjunction with Vuillier's, now Colonel he had re-joined the army at the outbreak of war, dosage figures. The Aga was convinced that the figures indicated which he should bid for and which of the "fashionably bred" ones he should avoid. The Aga would indicate to Lambton the yearlings with the correct dosage figures. The Aga was impressed with the amount of statistical research done by Vuillier which, genetics aside, on the face of it, seemed logical using pedigrees of past major race winners.

A combination of the Aga's judge of a pedigree, with Vuillier's dosage theories if they counted for anything, Lambton's eye for a horse and, far more importantly, an enormous budget with which to finance the operation comprised the team to establish the Aga's stud. The Aga would take the catalogue and mark those yearlings he was interested in and Lambton would reject those which he considered untrainable. The Aga was shrewd enough to realize that, important as stamina was, a horse must also have speed to win the best races. He noted that Polemarch; a son of The Tetrarch, had won the St. Leger in 1921 and became convince that speed could produce a horse that could stay but stamina would never produce a horse with speed.

It was the Aga's considerable good fortune that when he began buying yearlings that some wonderfully well-bred fillies came on to the open market. Unlike in recent times, when it has been possible to buy some of the best racehorses at public auction, at that time classically bred racehorses were largely confined to the wealthy owner-breeders; who maintained their position as leading money winners on the turf by supplying their trainers each year with the best bloodstock.

The lists each year of the leading owners varied little, with the same names appearing, and only the order between them changeable. Unless a very special yearling became available a top trainer would have very few horses bought at public auction in his yard.

* * *

So Lambton, armed with the yearling catalogue marked by the Aga, began his assault on the sales. Nearly all available literature, either magazine articles or books, relate the successful purchases made by Lambton in those early days and leave the impression that virtually every yearling was a success with almost no reverses. Certainly Lambton was able to secure some wonderful yearlings which achieved much for the Aga. However, as will be seen Lambton was required to pay vast sums of money to secure the best bloodstock and plenty of them proved subsequently to possess very moderate ability.

* * *

It is instructive to look at some of the purchases made on behalf of the Aga Khan, particularly in those early years. It demonstrates that only with huge resources can any individual enter the world of thoroughbred racing and expect to make any impact at the top level. Armed with as good and knowledgeable man as George Lambton and a cheque book that never cried enough there were, amongst the successes, still plenty of expensive failures along the way.

It all began with the first Newmarket July sales at the end of June 1921; on the second evening Lambton went to 2,400 guineas (£95,000) to secure a filly by the Tetrarch out of Pamfleta by William the Third who was subsequently named Paola. She proved a good racehorse winning the Cheveley Park Stakes and finishing second in the Middle Park Stakes as a juvenile and winning the Coronation Stakes at three. Unfortunately she achieved little at stud.

The following evening Lambton paid 4,000 guineas (£158,000) for a filly by Bridge of Earn out of Addenda by Spearmint; subsequently named Bombay Duck. She won the Richmond Stakes at two but none of her three foals won. To buy two fillies and for both of them to win good races would be considered a success by the majority of owners;

Newmarket sales

© Lionel Edwards Estate by courtesy of Felix Rosenstiel's Widow & Son, London

however, these fillies were bought to found a stud and would not be contributing much towards that.

In addition the Aga spent just over 784,900 francs (just over £6,300) (245,000) on 15 yearlings at the August sales in Deauville to be trained by William Duke. One of these was a filly named Sapience who was a sister to the previous year's French Derby winner Sourbier. She was by Gorgos out of Sapientia and the Aga had to pay 110,000 FF (£4,400) (159,000), a record to secure her. She proved well worth the money but the Aga did not benefit directly. Sapience won only one minor race but her first foal: Samya was later sold by the Aga. Samya produced Samos who won the Prix de l'Arc de Triomphe.

However, Lambton was about to purchase a filly who would become a foundation mare, and miss out on a Classic winner. Listed in the Doncaster sales in September was a yearling filly by Tracery out of Blue Tit by Wildfowler, the Aga urged Lambton to buy this filly and also a colt by Tracery. In his memoirs the Aga records "I wired Lambton and wrote post-haste to Dawson urging the purchase of this colt by Tracery…. Mr Lambton did not like him, finding him too small and on the stocky side. That shows how little we ought to go by the make and shape of a yearling, so long as his legs are sound and he is nearer a giant than a Lilliputian".

The Tracery colt was out of Miss Matty by Marcovil and Lambton decided not to bid for the colt because its make and shape were not to his taste. He was bought on behalf of Mr. Ben Irish for 3,500 guineas (£132,000) who named him Papyrus; he won six races as a two-year-old and the Derby at three.

The loss of this colt because his conformation did not please Lambton, annoyed the Aga and the lesson was not forgotten. He always believed size and conformation to be unimportant; or at best over-valued, no, on reflection as he could not tell one horse from another the Aga would feel it did not matter in the least! He claimed to have had one rule when judging a yearling: is it going to be too tall and heavy or will it always turn out too small and never bigger than a pony. The Aga was then guilty of a *non sequitur* by asking another question: are its legs strong enough to stand hard training? So, that makes two rules then!

Nonetheless, he was making his view clear about conformation. It is possible to sympathise, while not necessarily agreeing with his view; racing history is full of well-bred, wonderful-looking horses that could not run fast enough to keep themselves warm. Even so should not some importance be attached to any inherited, undesirable physical characteristics that run in some families? In addition should not any temperament issues be considered? Sending a temperamental mare to a stallion with an evil disposition is surely asking for trouble; even if their pedigrees are compatible, are outstanding on Vuillier's figures and are well matched physically.

To return to the filly by Tracery, she was a good-looking chestnut filly and the moment George Lambton set eyes on her he was determined to buy her; he and the Aga were in total agreement! "I thought her a beautiful mare; I buy them really on looks, provided they are well-bred. She was very well-bred and a beautiful mare" said Lambton; not sure that was entirely in keeping with the Aga's policy of relying principally on Vuillier's dosage system, but on this occasion their policies coincided!

However, no great knowledge of breeding or conformation was required to make the decision to bid for this filly the eighth foal out of Blue Tit. Her two previous foals: Westward Ho (by Swynford) and Blue Ensign (by The Tetrarch) had been sold at auction for 11,500 (£435,000) and 14,500 (£548,000) guineas respectively. Lord Glanely had been responsible for buying both colts and he was determined to secure their half-sister.

It would not prove easy for Lambton to buy her: the bidding opened at 1,000 guineas (£37,800) and with Lord Glanely in stern opposition the bidding reached 7,600 guineas (£287,000) and only when Lambton signified 7,700 guineas (£291,000) did his Lordship bow out. Mr Somerville Tattersall's hammer came down in favour of Lambton and the filly; to be named Teresina, was led away to join the Aga Khan's racing stable.

Teresina started her career modestly: she was immature as a two-year-old in 1922 and it was not a surprise that she was unplaced in two outings as a juvenile. However, she made great strides as a three-year-old, although she only won one race: the Great Yorkshire Stakes. She was second in the Newmarket, Coronation and Eclipse Stakes plus the Cesarewitch and was third in both the Oaks and St Leger. In the Oaks she participated in a thrilling finish with Brownhylda and Shrove; the distances being a neck and a head; with One Thousand Guineas winner Tranquil very close up in fourth. In the St Leger Teresina was behind Tranquil, who was a convincing winner, and the Derby winner Papyrus. Teresina might have been unlucky in the Cesarewitch; she was beaten only a short-head and suffered a bump inside the final furlong.

At age four Teresina reached her peak with three more wins from seven outings including the Goodwood Cup and Jockey Club Stakes. In the Goodwood Cup she conceded 21 lbs. to a three-year-old colt: Leonardo and in the Jockey Club Stakes she beat Papyrus who was conceding her nine pounds. The pair drew clear inside the final furlong and in one of the seasons most exciting battles Teresina held on grimly by half a length. Both emerged with tremendous credit. Although in total Teresina only won four of her seventeen races she was a most genuine and courageous filly and won £10,944 (470,000) in stakes. She was a high-class stayer but needed a good pace or faster to be seen at her best.

Teresina proved to be a wonderful brood-mare breeding nine winners from fourteen foals; including Theresina, who won three races including the Irish Oaks and Falmouth Stakes, Gino won one race, but it was the valuable Imperial Produce Stakes, and he finished third in the Two Thousand Guineas, Alishah won four races and was fifth in the Derby, and Shahpoor won five races. Theresina also proved to be just as outstanding as her dam breeding ten winners from fifteen foals; the best of whom was Turkhan who won the St Leger. In addition she also produced Shahali and Ujiji, whose stories, in addition to Turkhan, are told later.

It is entirely possible that the best produce of Teresina never reached the racecourse. Alibhai was by Hyperion and clearly had plenty of speed as he was timed covering four furlongs in training in less than 46 seconds. This was impressive because, even allowing for a hand-timed workout, it can probably be assumed, as he had not seen a racecourse, he was not overly pressed at any stage. Unfortunately he split a pastern and never raced; all was not lost as he went to stud where he was a considerable success; particularly as a broodmare sire. Teresina was a wonderful acquisition and was retired in 1944 at the age of twenty four. She died two years later. Her daughter, Theresina was retired in 1949 at the age of twenty two.

Despite missing out on Papyrus Lambton was able to select some other fine prospects at the Doncaster sales of 1921 in addition to Teresina. These included Cos, a filly by Flying Orb out of Renaissance by St Serf, for whom Lambton had to bid 5,000 guineas (£189,000) to secure. Cos was bred by Lord D'Abernon and reared at his Esher Park Stud, then adjoining Sandown Park Racecourse. Possibly because she had sickle hocks (interesting that Lambton was happy that such a horse could be successfully trained) and was by Flying Orb, she was considered by many to have been expensive enough at 5,000 Guineas (£189,000). However, Cos was to prove well worth the money; she was leading juvenile filly in 1922 winning six of her seven races including the Queen Mary Stakes and Imperial Produce Stakes. There are considerable grounds for arguing that she should have been unbeaten. In the most valuable juvenile race of the season: the National Breeders Produce Stakes at Sandown, Cos swerved to the left as the tapes went up compounding the starter's error in giving the winner: Town Guard an "undue advantage" as the stewards found afterwards, following Dawson's complaint.

At three Cos won two of her three races including the Fern Hill Stakes at Ascot, and finished second in the One Thousand Guineas to Tranquil. She had justified her purchase price in win prize money alone; winning £9,602 (403,000). Despite her hocks she was a beautiful mover but tended to run up very light with strong work. She was described as looking like a scarecrow when sent to the Sheshoon Stud. As a brood mare she produced four winners from nine foals; Costaki Pasha, who won the Chesham, Hopeful and Middle Park Stakes as a juvenile, he failed to win at three but won the Cork and Orrery at four. Rustom Pasha, who in 1930 won the Eclipse and Champion Stakes, was second in the St. James's Palace Stakes and third in the St. Leger.

Cos also produced Mrs Rustom who won three races; all as a juvenile: the Gimcrack, Dewhurst and Ham Produce Stakes, she was also second in the Middle Park Stakes. At stud she produced four winners from ten foals; all precocious sorts that failed to train on. The best of which was Masala who won two races as a juvenile. She was small and sparely-made and, like her siblings, did not train on but produced three winners from as many foals before she was exported to North America.

George Lambton spent the Aga's money freely at Doncaster; altogether he bought eight fillies for a total cost of 24,520 guineas (£927,000). In addition to Cos and Teresina he bought five fillies costing 1,000 guineas (£38,000) or more. None proved to be good performers on the racecourse but justified their cost to an extent as brood mares. Tiara cost 4,000 guineas (£151,000) and, although she never won, she bred five winners at stud. Tricky Aunt (Son-in-Law – Rectify by William the Third) cost 3,100 guineas (£117,000) and, although she won only one race; it was the Windsor Castle on her debut, and she bred four winners; the best of whom was Dhoti who won all three of his races as a juvenile including the Chesham Stakes; but that was his final race of the season and, as it turned out, he was the best juvenile owned by the Aga that year.

Eagle Snipe (White Eagle – Snoot by Perigord) cost 2,200 guineas (£83,000) and although a moderate performer she did win one race and bred four winners. Saucer (Chaucer – Tennyson by Wuffy) cost 1,100 guineas (£41,000) and won two races and bred three winners. Bad Joke (Black Jester – Permia by Persimmon) cost 1,000 guineas (£38,000) and, although she did not win, she bred one winner.

However, the best and most shrewd buy was a filly by Volta out of Sun Worship by Sundridge who cost just 420 guineas (£16,000). She was named Voleuse and raced in England as a two-year-old winning three of her five races: a stakes and two plate races, she was also third in the Windsor Castle, but she was finished for the year by the end of July and was sent to France. However it was as a broodmare that she achieved distinction: producing thirteen foals of which nine were winners; then she was covered by Mirza and sent to Hungary. Of her six fillies only two won but they produced five winners, of the four that did not win, three produced ten winners between them. The best of Voleuse's produce was Theft who was close to the very best, La Voleur and Bala Hissar who were both very useful.

In all probability one lot went through totally unnoticed; a filly foal sold at the Newmarket December sales for just 145 guineas (£5,500). She was by Friar Marcus out of Garron Lass by Roseland and was bought by Mrs E Plummer. She must have been very happy with a profit of 105 guineas (£4,300) when Dick Dawson paid her 250 guineas (£10,250) for the filly, as a yearling, on behalf of the Aga Khan. She was named Friar's Daughter and her story will be told later.

At the Doncaster September yearling sales of 1922 George Lambton was able to buy a Classic winner Diophon (Grand Parade – Donnetta by Donovan). This made him a half-brother to Diadem; George Lambton's favourite mare. Diophon cost 4,000 guineas (£164,000) secured after "plenty of bidding" and had attracted much admiration as he was led into the sale ring. Described as "A beauti-fully-balanced, strongly-made chestnut colt" in one quarter, he was not universally acclaimed as his fine physique had to be set against his knees which attracting some adverse comment. Some thought that at the price he was well sold. The Aga would presumably not have been concerned about either of these opinions.

However, Dick Dawson was able to match Lambton by also buying a Classic winner! On a miserable rain-soaked evening Dick Dawson purchased Salmon-Trout (The Tetrarch – Salamandra by St. Frusquin) for 3,000 guineas (£123,000) but again many at the sale did not like him considering him rather straight in front. Both these purchases proved to be a triumph for the judgement of the Aga, Lambton and Dawson. This was almost the peak of success that they enjoyed buying yearling colts; they would not always be so fortunate in future.

Without question the highlight of the sales, and in all probabil-ity many other sales as well, was the auction of a grey filly by The Tetrarch out of Lady Josephine by Sundridge. She was to prove a sensation from her first public appearance and for the rest of her life; being the fastest filly ever to race for the Aga Khan III.

In telling the story of this filly's family it is probably only necessary to start in 1893, with the birth in Ireland of a daughter of Gallinule, named Palotta. She was a winner of two races from 20 starts when, having raced for four seasons, she was purchased by Mr. A. H. Ledlie for 200 guineas (£22,000). It was the first mare he had owned, and all but one of the twelve foals she produced won, including Americus Girl, whose sire, Americus, was imported from America by Mr. R. Croker. Americus Girl raced 6 times at two, winning 5 races includ-ing the Phoenix Plate. Over the next three seasons she won seven more races, earning a total of £8,371(825,000) for Mr. Ledlie, includ-ing the Portland Plate at Doncaster. Americus Girl's speed was such that, at the Derby meeting at Epsom in 1909, she ran five furlongs in 56.8 seconds.

Lady Josephine, a chestnut daughter of Sundridge, and the first of the foals produced by Americus Girl, was offered at the 1913 Doncaster Yearling Sales and purchased by Mr. W. M. Savill for

1,700 guineas (£134,000). She won 4 of her 5 starts as a juvenile, including the Coventry Stakes at Ascot, but foot trouble caused her to be retired prematurely the following year after finishing sixth in her only start, and in July 1915 Mr. Henry Cholmondeley bought her for the Sledmere Stud for 1,200 guineas (£87,000).

She was barren in her first two years at stud and the first of Lady Josephine's foals arrived in 1919. She was named Lady Juror, and being by Son-in-Law, possessed enough stamina to win the Jockey Club Stakes (14f.). Two years later Lady Josephine produced a grey filly by The Tetrarch.

However, this wonderful yearling filly by The Tetrarch was subject to an article that appeared in *The Sporting Chronicle* by "Mankato" (Professor J. B. Robertson) in which he casts doubt on whether she is a fully-fledged thoroughbred and entitled to entry into the *General Stud Book*. However, as the Professor was referring to her TENTH dam, Spitfire, by Beningbrough foaled in 1800, then as far as this writer is concerned it is all totally irrelevant. Purists may bristle at such remarks however; more will be said about these matters in the chapter on the Aga's breeding methods.

Vuillier and Lambton were in agreement that she was the best yearling on offer with an apparently wonderful Vuillier dosage, (a discussion between Hall-Walker, Robertson and Vuillier might be interesting!) and the Aga was adamant that he must have her. However, even at a distance of ninety plus years it is hard not to feel that no great expertise was necessary in the decision to target her. Anyone involved in thoroughbred racing would have bought her; however only one individual had the resources to ensure she was secured whatever the opposition!

She had been consigned to the Doncaster September sales by Lady Sykes's Sledmere Stud and, not surprisingly, attracted plenty of attention; not least because she was a spotted grey yearling. However, she was also a powerful, rangy sort, with size and quality; conformation that could hardly be faulted; rare enough in itself, and, it was amidst almost unparalleled excitement, that she was led into the sales ring. "There was a gasp as she was led into the sale ring" wrote Lord Carnarvon; then Lord Porchester, years later.

Her sire was the original "Spotted Wonder": the blindingly quick The Tetrarch; her dam: Lady Josephine, fast as a juvenile winning four races, was by a sprinter Sundridge; himself out of a sprinter: Sierra. The preponderance of sprinting blood in her pedigree, at a time when stamina was considered more important than speed, gave rise to the concern that she would not stay the distance in any of the Classics; with the possibility that her future value could be compromised. Lady Josephine's first winning foal; Lady Juror, by Son-in-Law, had won over five furlongs, but the previous week had finished second in an eleven furlong race.

However, the risk that she might be a sprinter was, in Lambton's and Vuillier's eyes at least, a risk that was well worth taking to secure such a magnificent creature. After seeing the filly George Lambton was smitten. "As an individual she is wonderful, as near perfection as imagination can conceive. Her conformation is ideal and she has both size and quality." Later he said about her, "I thought her one of the best animals I ever saw in my life".

The bidding began at 2,000 guineas (£82,000) and quickly settled down to a duel between George Lambton and, surprisingly, Captain Percy Bewicke; who was by no means a wealthy man. The bidding reached an astonishing – for the time – 9,000 guineas (£369,000), bid by the Captain. However, Lambton, with the wealth of the Aga Khan behind him and a determination that he must buy the filly, offered 9,100 guineas (£372,000). There was no reply. The hammer came down and she became the most expensive yearling since Sceptre was sold for 10,000 guineas (£1,040,000) to Bob Sievier back in 1900. The Tetrarch filly was named Mumtaz Mahal.

Afterwards Lambton asked Percy Bewicke on whose behalf he had been bidding.

"Myself" was the Captain's reply.

"But you never have that sort of money Percy!" said Lambton.

"I could not have lost with her, she's probably a good animal, but if she isn't, I would have put her in a seller and had ten thousand pounds on her"! (390,000) retorted the bold Captain!

This story, as it stands, whilst undoubtedly true and confirmed from at least two sources, has a rather false ring to it. Was Captain

Bewicke really bidding on his own behalf? If he was considered not to have the sort of money required to buy such a filly why did the auctioneer accept his bids when they went to such a stratospherically high level? Had the Captain an arrangement prior to the sale that his bids were on someone else's behalf? Was the idea to simply find out how much Lambton would go on the Aga's behalf to secure the filly? In other words was Lambton simply being bid up? If so who would have been prepared to pay the huge sum required if Lambton had suddenly shook his head and left the Captain with the filly? Many questions but few answers. However, the feeling persists that most people knew that Lambton would not withdraw however high the bidding went.

So the grey filly named Mumtaz Mahal; she was named after Emperor Shah Jahan's favourite wife who lies buried in the Taj Mahal, was dispatched to the care of Richard Dawson at Whatcombe. It is entirely possible that Mumtaz Mahal was the fastest juvenile filly to race in Britain from the beginning of the Twentieth Century until the present day. In the spring of 1923 she was already towering above the other juveniles in Richard Dawson's large string. Dawson was now too busy to keep a trial book but a record of one gallop at Whatcombe was written down and preserved on a piece of scrap paper. The work was over three furlongs and required M. M.; as she was noted, who carried 9 st. and was ridden by George Hulme, who rode her in her races that year to give plenty of weight away. She conceded Friar's Daughter, who had just been narrowly beaten at Newmarket's Guineas Meeting 22 pounds, ten pounds was conceded to Quakeress, who had also been placed at the same meeting, and close to two stones to a moderate filly who made up the four-runner juvenile fillies gallop.

Mumtaz Mahal "won" the gallop by a very easy three lengths; but that does not tell the full story. Astonishingly, she was clear after a furlong and was being eased down as she passed a stunned Dick Dawson. "I was so astounded that I almost fell off my hack" he reported! From then on until her debut she worked alone in the afternoons to prevent the Whatcombe touts seeing her!

The Aga would like to gaze at her on his visits to Whatcombe.

He would admire her dappled coat, fine shoulders, strong legs with excellent bone and powerful quarters. The Aga watched her as she went out onto the training gallops accompanied by a stable companion without whom she was never happy.

It seems that Mumtaz Mahal was destined to make her debut at Ascot but as she was so precocious, or possibly because Dawson wanted to get a nice winning bet out of her, she made her debut shortly after her trial on16th May at Newmarket. Starting as the even money favourite, the touts must have found something out, she won easily by three lengths in a time of 57.80 seconds; a course record. The time was disputed and was possibly done by hand; nonetheless, it was now clear to everyone that she was well above average. She headed next for Ascot and the Queen Mary where, starting at odds of 4–1 on, she made all the running to win by ten lengths with "astonishing ease". Mumtaz Mahal provided a "remarkable spectacle which will not be readily forgotten". Her time was the fastest over five furlongs throughout the meeting.

Now considered unbeatable she won the most valuable juvenile race of the season: the National Breeders Produce Stakes at Sandown Park, then the Molecomb at Goodwood, both over five furlongs, before winning the Champagne Stakes at Doncaster; over six furlongs. There is archive film of her in the paddock at Doncaster; on her toes and looking very imposing for a juvenile: rangy and unfurnished. The film continues and she is then shown winning the race comfortably.

Unfortunately she was not holding her condition and, easy to say in retrospect, should have been retired for the year. However, she contested the valuable six furlong Imperial Produce Stakes at Kempton on heavy going and, despite showing considerable courage, she was beaten half a length, conceding seven pounds. She had apparently not been herself in the week before the race but Dawson felt she could still win. He would have preferred to withdrawn her on the day when the rain fell in torrents an hour before the race, but he could not contact the Aga Khan; who had left instructions that she was to run. She was placed at the head of the Free Handicap being allotted 9st. 0lbs.

Mumtaz Mahal trained on at three; winning two of her four races. She was trained for the One Thousand Guineas; Dawson was hopeful that she could be persuaded to stay the mile. The 6th Earl of Carnarvon, who had recently inherited the title on the unfortunate death of his father in Egypt that spring, was riding work at Whatcombe and was also enthusiastic about the grey filly's chances. On Guineas day the bold Earl backed his opinion with Ted Heathorn and struck a bet of £1,500 – £1000 (63,000 – 42,000). She was soon 11 to 10 on at which point Dawson rushed up and said not to have a penny on her as she was in season; something that became apparent when he legged up George Hulme in the paddock. "Porchy" went back to the ring only to find that Mumtaz Mahal was now 6 to 4 on and asked if he could hedge his bet which he did by laying Heathorn an even £1,000.

At the bushes Mumtaz Mahal was almost ten lengths clear but her stride shortened and she was comfortably beaten into second place. She had changed her legs and became unbalanced approaching the rising ground and was passed by Plack (Hurry On – Groat by Junior) and only just held off Straitlace (Son-in-Law – Stolen Kiss by Best Man) for second place.

Mumtaz Mahal was then unplaced in the Coronation Stakes at Ascot. She clearly did not stay a mile and, dropping back to sprinting, won the King George at Goodwood and the Nunthorpe at York; by six lengths. She could, and should have remained unbeaten and might have had a reputation as a great sprinter. Heavy ground plus the attempts to make her stay a mile asked too much of a brave and very fast filly. It is impossible to know but Mumtaz Mahal might have been as fast as her sire. She won seven races worth £13,933 (585,000)

At stud Mumtaz Mahal bred seven winners from only nine live foals; but, not surprisingly, nothing as good as herself, although one was close. She was difficult to get into foal; being barren seven times and once she slipped twins. Despite efforts to mate her to stallions with an influence for stamina her blinding speed held dominance with her foals, none of whom was able to show any high-class form beyond a mile. However, when her daughters were retired to stud and mated with staying stallions high-class middle distance performers were produced.

The best of her produce was a very fast colt: Mirza by Blenheim foaled in 1935. Mirza was exceptionally speedy over the first hundred yards; Charlie Smirke was certain he was the fastest he had ever sat on. He raced seven times as a juvenile winning his first five races all over five furlongs; a stakes race at Newmarket, the Coventry Stakes at Ascot, both unchallenged, the July and Chesterfield Stakes at Newmarket; "cantering" in both races at odds of 6/100 and 1/20 respectively and the Lavant Stakes at Goodwood "kept up to his work" at odds of 1/8. The speed he displayed was "amazing" and his opponents were "carried off their feet".

However, when stepped up to six furlongs in both the Champagne and Middle Park Stakes, Mirza faded close home to finish second both times. In the Middle Park he had been at least four lengths clear with a furlong to go. Clearly he did not even stay six furlongs and his chances in the Two Thousand Guineas looked bleak. So it proved; he scraped home in a slowly run Greenham Plate; which was run over a mile at that time, and finished third in the Two Thousand Guineas; he had looked like the winner but failed to stay. He was clearly best at distances of seven furlongs and less. Frank Butters advised the Aga not to have Mirza trained for the Derby but was overruled. He was duly unplaced in the Derby and at Ascot in the five furlong Fern Hill Stakes he was third, beaten under a length. Mirza was then sent to France.

Mumtaz Mahal also produced the useful miler Badruddin by Blandford. He won four races and was third in the Two Thousand Guineas before being exported to Argentina where he was a success as a sire.

One colt produced by Mumtaz Mahal that had plenty of ability but was something of a "head case" was Furrokh Siyar by Colorado. A speedy colt, described as "excitable", he ran once unplaced in England as a three-year-old, was exported to France where his work indicated that he was a more than useful sprinter but was unable to confirm this view on the track. Worse still than Furrokh Siyar was the irresolute Nizami, by Firdaussi, who showed plenty of ability in five races as a juvenile, always placed but was repeatedly described as "not resolute" by *Raceform* and failing to win. As a three and four-year-old he would seem to have completely lost the plot and never looked like winning. However, when exported to New Zealand he did much better as a sire.

Mumtaz Mahal's daughters, although relatively modest on the racecourse did magnificently at stud: Mah Mahal, by Gainsborough, produced seven winners from nine live foals including the Derby winner Mahmoud, by Blenheim, in addition she bred Mah Iran by Bahram, dam of Migoli, by Bois Roussel, and Star of Iran, by Bois Roussel, who was dam of the great Petite Etoile by Petition. Petite Etoile was the best filly ever to race for Aga Khan III, IV or Aly Khan, and that would include Zarkava. As if all this was not enough, Mumtaz Mahal also produced Rustom Mahal, by Rustom Pasha, who was the dam of the great sprinter Abernant. In addition for her crowning achievement she was the dam of Mumtaz Begum, by Blenheim, who was the dam of the magnificent, brilliant, but temperamental and, on occasions, evilly disposed Nasrullah by Nearco; who in turn became one of the great sires of the Twentieth Century in North America.

Rustom Mahal inherited all of her dam's speed but unfortunately she was very quirky. The Aga sent her to the sales in France and she was bought by Lord Woolavington's daughter Mrs. Macdonald Buchanan. Rustom Mahal was a lovely grey filly who was sent to be trained by Fred Darling who adored her and could see immediately that she was very talented. Unfortunately she would swerve sharply left when asked to quicken. Nothing Darling did could cure her and on one occasion, in a gallop, she swerved so violently that she collided with Darling's hack and broke three of the unfortunate animals' ribs! In that same gallop she took Richards' breathe away with her speed at the end of the gallop. Unfortunately Darling would not risk running her in a race as she might easily have taken most of the field out! Richards said that in her work she was the fastest filly he ever rode.

In conclusion, has any filly contributed more to thoroughbred racing both on and off the racecourse than Mumtaz Mahal? There may have been better fillies on the racecourse or mares at stud; but none has combined both roles with such success. It does not come as any surprise to learn that she was "a bit cranky" and would not tolerate a bullock in her paddock; "putting them through the railings in a matter of minutes". She was truly remarkable; a very fast outstanding racehorse and a great foundation mare.

Not all the purchases at this sale turned out to be as successful: a filly by Charles O'Malley out of Enbarr cost 1,450 guineas (£59,000) but died as a juvenile. Teheran (Prince Philip – Vahren by Bona Vista) did better; she cost 1,300 guineas (£53,000) and although she did not win she produced five winners at stud from ten foals. Another of her fillies that did not win: Seistan, produced four foals; all winners. Valhalla (Stedfast – Valkyrie by Eager) cost 1,100 guineas (£45,000); she did not win but produced two winners before dying prematurely. These were the only other purchases above one thousand guineas by Lambton at that sale.

One purchase at the Newmarket's First July sales that proved a success on the racetrack was a filly by Charles O'Malley out of Sunny Ridge by Sunstar. George Lambton paid 2,600 guineas (£107,000) and she was named Charley's Mount. Placed twice in four races as a juvenile she won two of her ten races as a three-year-old: the Park Hill Stakes at Doncaster and the Cesarewitch Handicap.

However, because she was badly beaten in a two mile handicap at Nottingham nine days before the Cesarewitch, apparently looking one paced, her hopes looked forlorn. In addition she went badly in a gallop just before the big race. No jockey had been booked the night before when her odds were 66–1. Probably the only jockey available: T. Pryor, a journeyman sort attached to the Manton stable who rode only nine winners that year, was booked. Charley's Mount, astutely ridden by Pryor, won by a length and a half at the astonishing odds of 100–1. The Aga had only a £10 (390) bet more or less out of habit.

In appearance she was a typical stayer: slightly sparingly made, lengthy and on the leg. Kept in training as a four-year-old she ran well enough without winning until one day in September of that year she "dropped dead" at Whatcombe. She would have made a very useful addition to the Aga's stud and was a considerable loss.

Notwithstanding this at the two consecutive Doncaster yearling sales George Lambton had spent hugely but he had achieved his objective: to provide a sound base for the Aga Khan to build his thoroughbred breeding empire.

In addition in 1922 at the Newmarket July sales Lambton bid 4,000 guineas, (£144,000) for a filly; Hajibibi (Hurry On – Bayuda by Bayardo); she never raced and made a disastrous start to her career at stud; her first three foals, all fillies, failed to win. However, her next six surviving foals all won.

At the Newmarket First October Sales Lambton went to 1,600 Guineas (£65,000) for a daughter of The Tetrarch out of Mariota by St. Victrix. Named Taj Mahal she raced only as a juvenile and won just a maiden from eight starts. At stud she produced four winners from only five foals including her first foal a filly; Taj Mah by Lemberg. She was very small and because of this was sent to the sales at Deauville where she made 250,000 francs (£2,000) (78,000) when bought by M. Simon Guthmann. She won the One Thousand Guineas for him in 1929.

*   *   *

The Aga was a force at the Deauville sales of 1922; again purchasing 15 yearlings at a total cost of 662,300 francs (£5,300) (207,000), the most expensive being a colt; Dandyprat (Sans le Sou – Dame Marie II) who cost 158,000 francs (£1,250) (49,000). However, the best purchase was a colt with, apparently, exceptional dosage figures: Pot-Au-Feu (Bruleur – Polly Peachum by Spearmint). In what amounted to a minor early triumph for Vuillier's figures Pot-Au-Feu rewarded the Aga by winning the French Derby.

1922 saw the Aga's colours: green and chocolate hoops; chocolate cap, on the racecourse. As befitting a wealthy individual who had spent lavishly at the yearling sales the previous year, the Aga had his first winners in England at Ascot! In fact he won with his first runner; Cos in the Queen Mary. She had been working well at Whatcombe; the Trial Book recording that she won a four furlong gallop "easily". She was 7–2 second favourite for the Queen Mary and won by five lengths. What an introduction! On the Friday the Aga won with his second ever runner: Tricky Aunt, who had been third behind Cos in the gallop, winning the Windsor Castle Stakes. Easy this racing game: two runners and two winners at Ascot! All one needs is a huge bank balance!

Principally due to the efforts of Cos and Paola the Aga finished ninth in the table of leading owners. He had five winners of thirteen races and total win prize money of £13,733 (354,000) of which Cos was responsible for six wins and £8,027 (313,000) and Paola for two wins and £1,921 (75,000).

In France he had eleven winners of 23 races value £11,252 (440,000). The principal winners were Niceas (Sundridge – Nika by Ossian), Zoroastra (Sardanapale – Reine III by Ajax) and Saint Illiers (Faucheur – La Pile by J'En Sais Trop).

*   *   *

1923 saw more acquisition by the Aga at the sales through Lambton. At the Newmarket July sales he began his more expensive purchases by spending 2,100 guineas (£90,000) for a filly, by Phalaris out of Velaret by Veles. She was named Velvet and failed to gain even a place in seven races at two and three; including a race called the "Moderate Plate", which probably says it all. At stud she produced three winners but nothing of any note.

Lambton again spent 2,100 guineas (£90,000) this time for a colt by Sunstar out of Airashi by Santoi; unraced at two and named Zambo he justified his cost at three winning six of his nine races and finishing second in two others; he won the St James's Palace Stakes and was second in the Eclipse and St Leger. He failed to win from six starts at four and was exported to France.

The Aga enjoyed mixed fortunes with some colts and fillies bought for less than 2,000 guineas (£86,000). However, La Mauri (Roi Herode – La Maula by Symington) cost a mere 560 guineas (£24,000) and, although she only won a modest race as a juvenile, she produced six winners from eight live foals. One filly: La Boni (Pharos – La Mauri by Roi Herode), that failed to win, produced five winners from seven live foals, one of whom a filly La Li (by Blenheim) won three good races and produced seven winners from nine live foals. Amazing all from a relatively cheaply bought filly foal!

However, a colt by Spearmint out of Judea by Roi Herode and bought for 2,400 guineas (£103,000) and named Zionist, looked potentially as good as anything as a juvenile, and was high-class at three and four.

Of the most expensive purchases of 1923 made by Lambton the highest was bought at the Newmarket "Houghton" sales; Fironze Mahal, (The Tetrarch – Grey Tip by Grey Leg), who cost 5,400 guineas (£232,000). She was to prove only moderate as a racehorse; failing to win at two from nine starts, managing just a second and a third. She made her debut at Ascot in the Queen Mary Stakes and generally kept good company but was eventually tried in nurseries and ended up that year unplaced in a Warwick maiden. At three she did better from five starts; winning once and being placed three times. Although she was third in both the One Thousand Guineas and Coronation Stakes she was beaten 8 lengths and 14 lengths respectively! At stud, she was useful; breeding seven winners, however, there was nothing of particular note, and she left no legacy. The best of her progeny was Shamsuddin, by Solario, who only won one race but usually kept good company. He was twice second to Hyperion, although easily beaten on both occasions and with the great horse conceding plenty of weight.

Brise Bise, (Buchan – Panne by Polymelus) cost 4,200 guineas (£181,000) was unraced at two and made her debut in the Oaks, which seems a shade ambitious, was unplaced and managed just a second and a third before retiring to stud; where she produced three winners. The surprising aspect about this purchase is that Brise Bise was by Buchan a good sire, but rarely ever used by the Aga Khan for his own mares. It has not been possible to locate any winner bred by the Aga sired by Buchan. Ayaz, (Swynford – Eos by Orby) cost 3,400 guineas (£146,000). Unraced at two he was unplaced at three, gelded and exported to India.

Two colts that cost plenty both won good races; Vermillion Pencil, (Gainsborough – Rectify by William the Third) cost 2,700 guineas (£116,000) and won three races value £6,065 (261,000); including the Chester Vase and Queen Alexandra Stakes. He was exported to France. Diacquenod (Diadumenos – Miss Cobalt by Pride), cost 2,000 guineas (£86,000) won three races value £2,412 (104,000) before he was exported to New Zealand.

It could not of course have been known at the time but the Aga's stud had actually made a tremendous start. However, even with limited evidence the Aga was clearly impressed with the contribution of Vuillier; and so much so that, although the Aga had never met him, and after just one year as a consultant, Vuillier and his wife, were offered an exclusive contract to provide the data the Aga felt he needed to select the best yearlings to buy.

*   *   *

The Aga and Lambton were destined to suffer considerable frustration from missing out on two colts that Lambton bid for during 1923 but did not secure. Both would win Classics in 1925. The first was a colt that Fred Darling thought the best yearling in the sale; he was by Phalaris out of Waffles by Buckwheat. The Aga Khan and Lambton also wanted the well-made, medium-sized sort, but as it turned out, not enough. The bidding was between Lambton, Fred Darling, Lady Bullough, Lord Barnby and the representatives of Sir Edward Hulton. Lambton's final bid was 6,000 guineas (£258,000) but the colt was knocked down to Fred Darling for 6,300 guineas (£271,000). He was the most expensive yearling of 1923, was named Manna and he won the Two Thousand Guineas and Derby in 1925. The Aga's Zionist was second to Manna in the Derby.

The second colt was by Gainsborough out of Sun Worship by Sundridge. He was a late foal: 1st May but was sufficiently developed not to look at any disadvantage with his contemporaries. Lambton was the under bidder when the hammer went down to a bid of 3,500 guineas (£151,000) made on behalf of Sir John Rutherford. He was named Solario and he won the St Leger beating the Aga Khan's Zambo.

The Aga later tried to buy Solario as a four-year-old after he had won the Coronation Cup. However, even an offer of £100,000

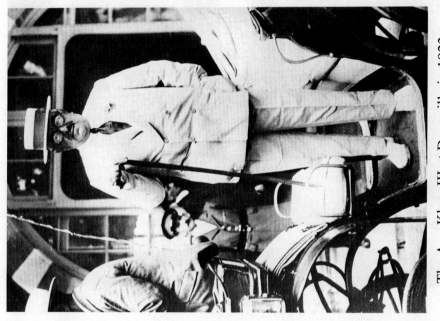

The Aga Khan III at Deauville in 1923

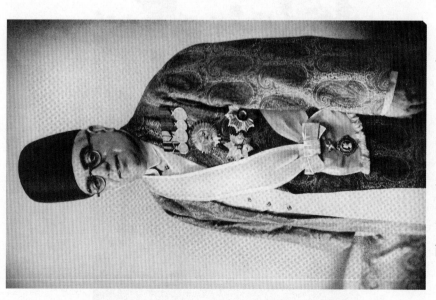

The Aga Khan III in full regalia

Teresa Magliano

The Aga Khan III and Begum Andrea at Epsom 1938

The Aga Khan III playing golf in 1942

The Aga Khan III and Sir Henry Greer at Tully Stud

Miss Freda Blain

The Aga Khan III towards the end of his life.

George Lambton

R. C. (Dick) Dawson

Frank Butters

Freddie Fox

Mumtaz Mahal

Blenheim

Aly Khan and Rita Hayworth

Yvette Labrousse

(4,300,000) could not persuade Sir John to part with his magnificent colt.

At Deauville in 1923 the Aga was the biggest buyer spending 926,500 francs (£7,500) (£289,000) on twenty yearlings.

In 1923 only the second year that the Aga Khan had been active as an owner he finished second in the table of leading owners behind Lord Derby; the Aga was represented by eleven winners of twenty-two races winning £33,409 (1,355,000) in win prize money. Mumtaz Mahal contributed five wins value £11,763 (482,000), Diophon four wins, and £8,140 (334,000) and Paola three wins £5,250 (215,000).

The Aga was responsible for the first two in the Two-year-old Free Handicap with Mumtaz Mahal and Diophon. Diophon won four of his five races starting with the July Stakes at Newmarket. Two weeks later he walked over for the Chesterfield Stakes, despite there being 66 entries and the race worth £1,300 (53,000). Next, despite showing signs of unruliness, he justified favouritism to win the Lavant Stakes. In the autumn he failed to concede a stone to Woodend in the Hopeful Stakes before concluding the year by winning the Middle Park Stakes.

In France the Aga won 33 races value £19,728 (848,000). Niceas won two good races and was second to Le Capucin in the Prix du Jockey Club (French Derby).

*   *   *

George Lambton was in action again in 1924 on a higher scale still; at least as far as paying huge amounts were concerned. For all of the Aga's comprehensive knowledge of pedigrees and Lambton's equally sound judgement of conformation, nothing could protect them from the disasters that lie in wait for purchasers of untried bloodstock. Some have already been mentioned but nothing so far matched the calamity that was Amilcar; a bay or brown colt by Phalaris out of Silver Wand by Lonawand. A portrait of him as a yearling suggests a well-made, good-bodied sort with two white hind legs and any amount of scope.

Amilcar was consigned to the Doncaster sales of 1924 by Lord D'Abernon and in the ring it quickly became a duel between Lambton and Fred Darling; with both seemingly determined to secure the colt. The bidding increased with startling rapidity until Darling probably realizing that, with the Aga's money behind him, Lambton was not going to give way, bowed to the inevitable. When Lambton signalled 9,700 guineas (£438,000) Darling cried enough and the handsome youngster was bound for Dick Dawson. That was the highlight of Amilcar's life: he raced four times as a juvenile, always in the best company, but was unable to manage even a place. At three he was unplaced in the Greenham Plate at Newbury after which he was dispatched, seemingly in disgrace, to North America.

There was more disaster to come; at the Newmarket October sales; usually low key sale with averages of about 300 guineas (£13,500) or so. A colt by Gay Crusader out of Polaire by Sunstar was offered by the Overtown Stud. Described as a "very fine bay colt" Lambton was determined to acquire him but it needed a bid of 6,400 guineas (£282,000) to secure him. The next highest price paid in the 123 lot sale was 2,700 guineas (£122,000) and the average of the other 122 lots was just 315 guineas (£14,200). The Gay Crusader colt was named Nansen and he made his debut as a juvenile in the Coventry Stakes at Ascot where he was unplaced; his only race that year. As a three-year-old he ran three times without winning – a second in a maiden was his best effort – before he was given a one-way ticket to India.

Lambton had more luck with the purchase of Lady Lawless. She was a filly by Son-in-Law out of Entanglement by Spearmint and cost 6,100 guineas (£275,000). She won twice and finished second in the Irish Oaks but did better at stud producing six winners, although nothing of real consequence. A filly: Jan Mahal (The Tetrarch – Palatina by Prince Palatine) cost 5,000 guineas (£226,000) was un-raced at two and failed to win in seven starts at three; although she was second in a minor stakes race. She did though produce two winners at stud; one of whom: Jan Renee, by Grand Parade, produced five winners including Jindani, by Rustom Pasha, who stood as a stallion.

A colt: Phanarite (Phalaris – Osyrua by Desmond) cost 3,200 guineas (£144,000). He won two races: a maiden and the Great

Surrey Foal Stakes at Epsom from four starts at two. However, he was unplaced in the same Greenham as Amilcar and, after another unplaced effort in a valuable handicap; he too was dispatched across the Atlantic Ocean to discover the wonders of the New World.

However, gold was struck in no uncertain terms with the purchase of a filly; Mirawala (Phalaris – Miranda by Gallinule) for 2,900 guineas (131,000). She was the most wonderful acquisition; winning four races. At two she made her debut in the National Breeders Produce Stakes where she was unplaced and then won a plate at Stockton before running unsuccessfully in two valuable nurseries. At three she won three of her eight races; none very important and her winnings were only a respectable £1,955 (84,000).

However it was as a brood mare that she proved outstanding, producing seven winners, including three fillies that in turn produced nineteen individual winners. In addition she produced three other fillies who, although they did not win, produced a further eight winners. In fact every filly produced by Mirawala: a total of six, all produced winners, and she was eventually the proud mother and grand-mother of a total of thirty-four winners! She died the same year she foaled her last filly in 1941 aged eighteen. Despite it being very sentimental and anthropomorphic to think this way; it is hard to avoid the feeling that after all she had contributed she deserved a long and restful retirement.

To digress and move forward a decade for a moment the Aga later sent one of Mirawala's foals: Stafaralla, by Solario, to the sales but Aly, not for the first time displaying better judgement than his father, bought her back! She raced only as a juvenile; was left at the start on her debut but won two other races including the Cheveley Park Stakes. At stud she produced fourteen foals of which ten were winners; including all of the first nine! Of these the best was Tehran, by Bois Roussel, who won the St Leger and whose career is covered in full later on. Interestingly her first five foals were colts and all stood as stallions, she then produced a filly – who won – before producing three more colts; all were winners of course and who in turn then stood as stallions! She only produced one colt that did not win and stand as a stallion. Sadly only one of her fillies produced winners.

A filly; Roshun (Roi Herode – Sabia by Symington) cost 2,500 guineas (£113,000) and although she failed to win she produced two winners at stud. A colt Cimiez (Gainsborough – Sunny Ridge by Sunstar) cost 2,200 guineas (£99,000) and although he kept good company he only won one race value £1,260 (54,000).

The Aga was having good fortune taking everything into consideration. He was paying large amounts by any standards but always buying the best blood, even if he was restricted by his obsession that only those that matched up to Vuillier's figures could be bought. Unfortunately Amilcar was not the only moderate purchase, even worse, if that can be imagined, came in 1926 when the Aga Khan purchased from the National Stud a yearling colt by Hurry On out of Ecurie by Radium which made him a brother to Diligence; a decent sort just below the top level. He was one of two bought at the same time for the huge price of £21,000 (903,000), with the Hurry On colt valued at an astonishing £19,000 (817,000) the largest sum ever paid for a yearling at that time.

The Hurry On colt was named Feridoon and was described as a "very big horse" with a "beautiful action" by Dick Dawson. Unfortunately he was useless as a racehorse at Whatcombe, was sent to France, where he was no better, and sold for about £13 (585); he never raced. He was certainly worth this lesser amount as he did much better when he went to stud in France. He sired a couple of good horses including a filly: Dix Pour Cent who produced Deux Pour Cent who sired Tantieme, an outstanding racehorse and sire.

What about the other colt purchased at the same time as Feridoon and valued at £2,000 (86,000)? He was named Silver Hussar (Silvern – Blanche by White Eagle) which made him a half-brother to Blandford. He did much better as a top-class handicapper winning three races value £4,476 (192,000). Moderate as a juvenile in three races he became a tough and consistent sort and at the age of four won the John Porter Stakes at Newbury; run in the autumn at that time. As evidence of his toughness and durability he raced nine times at three and ten times at four. As a reward for being genuine and trying his best Silver Hussar was gelded at the end of his three-year-old year and sent to India after he had raced at age four.

Feridoon was a disaster but Dick Dawson was not spared the following year either. At the Newmarket second July sales of 1927 a yearling by Papyrus out of Sundart by Sunstar was offered. His portrait suggests an impressive youngster: strong in the body, having plenty of room for the heart and lungs and possessing plenty of scope. The bidding rose swiftly until Mrs Rudd offered 13,500 guineas (£609,000), on behalf, it was understood, of a Texan; Mr. Waggoner, but Dawson, with the unyielding support of the Aga Khan, bid 14,000 guineas (£632,000) and the hammer came down in his favour. The Texan had a lucky escape. Named Aftab the colt was un-raced as a juvenile and only managed one win, a Windsor maiden worth £270 (12,000), from four outings at three and was unplaced in eight outings at four before he was sold at the December sales of 1930 for 125 guineas (£59,000). Incidentally can anyone today imagine a maiden at Windsor worth £12,000? The winner's penalty value for winning a Windsor maiden is today is no more than £3,000.

Interestingly some observers were more impressed by the conformation of a big, lengthy colt by Hurry On out of Carina by Chaucer when Aftab and he were seen together in the pre-sales ring; the Hurry On colt "out looking" Aftab and "surpassing him in movement". The Hurry On colt was bought by Fred Darling for 2,500 guineas (£110,000) and was named Totalisator. He won one race; a match worth £450 (19,500) from ten outings at two and three.

These purchases show again that even with good knowledge, experience and the best possible breeding nothing is guaranteed in the world of thoroughbred racing. Relating the details of these purchases are not designed to show the Aga, Lambton and Dawson in an unfavourable light as there are many examples, right up to the present day, of costly yearlings; bred in the purple and with excellent conformation, but were simply unable to run fast enough, or were not sound enough to stand racing. It is that by relating some of the many yearling purchases made by the Aga it can be seen that an individual was required to invest considerable sums if they were to make any impression in the world of thoroughbred racing.

Paying high prices for untried racehorses that prove to be useless is bad enough; but selling horses that win Classics for other owners is a particularly hard medicine to stomach. After all what is the point of paying many thousands for well-bred stock if not to win the best races? Actually in the Aga's case, where fillies were concerned, finding brood mares were probably more important! When the Aga Khan after six years in which he had spent lavishly for the first time took on the role of vendor it did not prove to be an altogether happy decision.

The Aga's policy would always be to sell in order to buy. Sensibly his idea was to constantly search for new strains in order to increase his chances of success. This policy produced mixed results in the sense that he sold some horses that won Classics and, later on, very nearly sold a Derby winner. In addition, as mentioned earlier, he tried to sell a filly that would later produce a winner of the St. Leger. The Aga, like many before and after, thought that the three most important attributes for a racehorse were speed, speed and speed. However, he realised that quality stamina was also vital if any horse was to stay middle distances and win Classic races. He was particularly impressed by the blindingly fast The Tetrarch who managed to sire St Leger winners.

The Aga sent twenty-one yearlings to the Deauville sales of 1927 and two of them; both fillies, came back to haunt him. Ukrania (Ksar – Uganda by Bridaine) was sold for 970,000 francs, about £7,500 (322,000) to the Comte de Rivaud who won the 1929 French Oaks with her. Taj Mah (Lemberg – Taj Mahal by The Tetrarch) was sold for 250,000 francs, about £2,000 (86,000) to M. Simon Guthmann who won the 1929 One Thousand Guineas with her. It can only be imagined what the Aga thought of this; selling two Classic winners in one year!

However, looking at the breeding of both fillies, based on Vuillier, they would appear to have had unbalanced pedigrees: Ukrania having an excess of St. Simon but a deficiency of Hampton, Galopin, Isonomy and Bend Or. When at stud she would, in Vuillier's view be difficult to place with a suitable stallion as most stallions would add even more St Simon.

Taj Mah was almost the reverse: a deficiency of St Simon and a surplus of Isonomy, Bend Or and Galopin. Finding a stallion to make up the St Simon deficiency would probably increase the surplus in the other three. Interestingly, despite winning Classics neither Ukrania nor Taj Mah were successful at stud; ammunition for advocates of the Vuillier system perhaps? In addition as Taj Mah was a first foal and smallish as a yearling and this, combined with her lack of suitability, as Vuillier saw it, for breeding, probably swung the balance in favour of selling.

*   *   *

Meanwhile on the racecourse the Aga was making his presence felt both in England and France. In 1924 he was leading owner in both England and France. This was also the first time anyone had been leading owner in both England and France in the same year. The amounts were £44,377 (1,900,000) and £46,600 (2,000,000) respectively. Dawson finished as leading trainer with £48,907 (2,100,000)

Diophon won the Two Thousand Guineas without the benefit of a run and may have been fortunate. It was probably not a great renewal; one length covered the first five to finish. Diophon won by a head but so close was the finish that some observers thought the second: Bright Knight might have got up; he would certainly have won in another stride. The Aga was not at Newmarket to see his first Classic winner as he was taking the cure in Aix-les-Bains; the news was conveyed to him in his bath!

The Aga won the St Leger with Salmon-Trout and the Prix du Jockey Club (French Derby) with Pot au Feu. However, the year was not without its disappointments: the Aga failed to win any race at Ascot, Diophon's form declined after his Guineas win and although he ran with credit on occasions some were questioning his resolution. Mumtaz Mahal, of course, failed to stay beyond six furlongs.

Conversely the Aga may have been lucky to win the St Leger with Salmon-Trout in more ways than one. A coughing epidemic caused Alec Taylor to withdraw his four entrants including the compact, smallish St Germans (Swynford – Hamoaze by Torpoint). He had finished an unlucky second in the Derby, third in the Eclipse, had produced an impressive gallop a week before the 'Leger and won five successive races afterwards. Dawson, showing considerable perspicacity, had quarantined Salmon-Trout away from Whatcombe and kept him free from any infection.

Salmon-Trout had won both his races as a juvenile: the Prendergast and the Dewhurst Stakes. As a three-year-old he won three of his ten races; his form had been somewhat inconsistent but by St. Leger time he had won the valuable Princess of Wales's Stakes.

Salmon-Trout was not certain to stay the St Leger trip on pedigree. His work before the race convinced Dawson that he could win if he stayed. The stable commission was £1,500 (63,000) but it was worrying that the more money that was bet on Salmon-Trout he further he drifted and it was clear that the bookmakers were laying him for all they were worth and he drifted from fives to ten to one. As the formbook indicated that he had a good chance of winning, the rumours began to spread that Salmon-Trout could not win; or more likely would not be allowed to win, with his jockey, Brownie Carslake, implicated in the plot; he was supposedly backing Solly Joel's Polyphontes (Polymelus –St. Josephine by St. Denis).

Carslake was thought to be heavily committed to the bookmakers and when this came to the ear of the Stewards they made matters very clear to him. They would be watching Carslake's riding in the race particularly closely. The Aga reacted in a typically shrewd manner: on his authority Dawson told Carslake "I have discussed with the Aga Khan the recent rumours and he has told me to tell you that if you win on Salmon-Trout you will get half the stake minus the percentage due to the trainer".

Salmon-Trout's victory in the St Leger (which meant that Carslake was given nearly £4,000 (168,000) was said to have hit the bookmakers heavily. It also vindicated Dawson's decision to buy him as a yearling against the advice of others. Both Salmon-Trout and St Germans were kept in training but neither was really able to demonstrate that they were any better than the other in 1925.

Meanwhile on the juvenile front the Aga had much to look forward to the following year with Zionist. Dawson had not been able to race him due to the coughing outbreak until September but he impressed in winning his first three races: a plate, a stakes and the Dewhurst Stakes "in a canter". He ran as if something was amiss in his final race the Hurst Park Great Two-year-old Stakes. It seems that the problem had been that Zionist had been suffering some ailment in his knees.

In France the Aga was leading owner with 31 winners of £46,603; over £2,000 in front of Baron Ed. de Rothschild. The Aga wins included the Prix du Jockey Club with Pot-au-Feu; who he later sold to Mr. C. B. Shaffer to stand as a stallion at the Coldstream Stud, Kentucky.

*   *   *

However, the Aga's brief period as a force in France was about to come to an end. In 1925 William Duke made the decision to return to North America and the Aga decided to disperse all his French runners.

*   *   *

The Aga had needed a stud farm for all the fillies he had acquired when the time came to breed from them. Like many before him and since the Aga concluded that the best place to build a stud and rear his stock was Southern Ireland and the man he asked to help him accomplish this was Captain (soon after to be Sir) Henry Greer. Captain Greer was manager of the English National Stud at Tully in Co. Kildare and the Aga asked him to construct an Irish stud farm for him.

Captain Greer, originally a soldier in Co. Tyrone, and who at this time was approaching seventy, was a man of both great charm and an excellent judge of bloodstock. His fortune was based on buying Gallinule (Isonomy – Moorhen by Hermit) for £1,000 (135,000) in the late 1880's even though he had both gone in his wind and was liable to break blood vessels. Although he would not have seemed the most promising of stallion prospects, Gallinule proved to be an outstanding sire, twice champion and sire of four Classic winners, including the immortal Pretty Polly.

Captain Greer found and constructed the Sheshoon stud at Turf

Lodge Curragh in Co. Kildare and the Aga purchased this from him in 1923. Captain Greer later, on behalf of the Aga, brought the Ballymany stud, on the opposite side of the Curragh to Sheshoon, from the Duke of Westminster. Sheshoon was greatly expanded by the purchase of adjoining farms and together with Ballymany became the heart of the Aga's Irish breeding activities. Later Nesbit Waddington brought Gilltown, Ongar and Sallymount studs on behalf of the Aga and Aly to accommodate the increasing number of mares and stallions.

The majority of the Aga's broodmares were based in Ireland because the soil there is rich in natural limestone which is ideal for the development of good bone growth. This has resulted in Ireland being an attractive area and a wonderful environment for young horses and has attracted considerable foreign investment down the years. It can only help that various Irish governments have assisted breeders with moderate taxes on bloodstock. Successive British governments, notoriously blockheaded and unimaginative about most policies with regard to racing, introduced VAT at the full rate and, surprise surprise British bloodstock has suffered. It is a miracle that any breeders stayed in Britain at all when Ireland has better a tax regime, and soil, and France considerably better prize money.

*   *   *

It seems incredible that by 1925 the Aga had never actually met Colonel Vuillier. He was keen to do so and through a mutual friend M. Andre Prevost, he was introduced to the man himself. The Aga was as much impressed by Vuillier in person as by his dosage theory and employed him immediately as his breeding advisor. The Aga made it a condition of the job that Vuillier published no further updates to his dosage formula; the Aga was keen to make sure that only he benefitted from any more research! The Aga would seem to have relented though as Vuillier published an update in 1928! The post of breeding adviser was occupied by Vuillier until his death in 1931.

However, all was not sweetness and light; it can be readily imagined Lambton, who was an authority on conformation and Vuillier, who whilst no expert in the view of many, held strong views on pedigrees, often disagreed. However, one of the Aga's great strengths was as a mediator and he always had the final say and seemed to manage to sooth any professional ruffled feathers.

* * *

In France three smaller studs were purchased: Haras de Marly-la-Ville, near Paris, together with Saint Crespin and La Coquenne in Normandy. The story of how the Saint Crespin stud was acquired is interesting. On the death of M. Edouard Kann in 1927 the Aga Khan purchased his stud; Saint-Crespin in Normandy, and all his blood-stock when they came up for sale in 1927.

Vuillier had advised the Aga to secure two of M Kann's mares: Uganda (Bridaine – Hush by St. Serf) and Pomare (Saint Just – Posada by Gorgos), but the rest of the stock was considered moderate. However, the conditions of sale were that all the stock plus the stud, including two stallions, must be sold as one lot. The Aga was determined to secure these two mares so he purchased everything but then sold all the stock except the two mares, and kept the stud. Pomare proved to be only average at best as a brood mare but Uganda did much better. She was a wonderful mare breeding Udaipur, by Blandford, who won the Oaks and who in turn bred Umiddad by Dastur. Uganda also produced Ukrania but, of course, the Aga sold her.

* * *

In 1925 the Aga finished third in the list of leading owners behind Lord Astor and S B (Solly) Joel. His total of £32,974 was less than £2,000 behind Lord Astor. The Aga was leading owner in Ireland with one winner of one race! Zionist; who won the Irish Derby. The first prize money alone of £4,350 (182,700) was more than any other single owner managed during the entire season. Zionist had been pin-fired the previous winter as a precaution. Firing, also known as thermocautery, divides opinion: some consider it an effective way to cure an injury but the majority view today is that it is barbaric and unnecessarily painful for the horse without any more benefit than could be gained by adequate rest.

In some ways it was a frustrating year: Manna won the Two Thousand Guineas and Derby, a horse the Aga had tried to buy as a yearling. This was compounded as Zionist was second in the Derby. In addition Zambo was second to Solario, another horse the Aga had bid unsuccessfully for, in the St Leger. However, Manna can be considered fortunate that Solario did not come to hand earlier in the year as in the final analysis he was clearly the best three-year-old of the year and would prove to be an outstanding racehorse. Had the Aga secured Solario as a yearling he would have been the second best horse that ever ran in his colours as only Bahram could be considered superior.

Zambo and Zionist had contributed just under half of the Aga's prize money. Dawson had been very patient with Zambo who matured into a most taking individual: almost 16 hands and a substantial and powerful sort. He was unraced as a juvenile and unplaced on his debut as a three-year-old. He then won six races broken only by a second in the Eclipse Stakes: two minor stakes races, Royal Standard, St James's Palace, Richemount and Great Yorkshire Stakes. His final race of the year was a second in the St Leger to Solario.

Zionist at three won the Irish Derby and was second in the Derby, Newmarket and Prince of Wales's Stakes but his season was over by the end of June; the firm ground at the Curragh so jarred him up that he could not run again that year. At four he was second in the Lincoln handicap but failed to win in three races and was exported to France. Incidentally, how many Classic winners since have run the following year in the Lincoln Handicap? Some considered Zionist to have been unlucky not to win the Lincoln. He was set to carry 9st. 1 lb. in recognition of his class and, backed down to 9–2 favourite, failed by a head to concede forty-one pounds to 100–1 chance King of Clubs. The Aga had placed an enormous bet: £50,000 – £1,000 (2,150,000 – 43,000) and Charlie Smirke had been instructed not to talk about his mount's chances as the bookmakers were keen to "hedge" the Aga's bet. Smirke had trouble with Zionist confessing later that he "was a desperately difficult ride".

Diophon had been kept in training as a four-year-old and this was justified as he won three of his seven races, including the valuable Atlantic Cup at Liverpool which was worth £2,595 (109,000). He was second twice and third twice in his other races.

The best juvenile that year was Moti Mahal; a homebred filly by The Tetrarch out of Maglona by Fogleman. She was a smallish sort but genuine enough and won five of her nine starts including the Ham Produce Stakes and was second in the Queen Mary Stakes. At three she won only one of her eight races but it was the Coronation Stakes at Ascot. She was only moderately successful at stud.

*   *   *

1926 was largely disappointing; Zionist and Zambo not really building on their three-year-old form and the juveniles unable to make much impression.

The table below shows that the Aga was still spending large sums at the yearling sales. One colt that all agreed should be brought was a strong-looking colt by Gainsborough out of Lady Burghley by St. Serf. The bidding opened at 2,000 guineas (£88,000) but from 3,000 guineas only George Lambton for the Aga and Mr. R. M. Dale were bidders. It would seem that a value of 7,000 guineas had been placed on the colt and when the bidding went above this figure Lambton signalled enough. However, the Aga then instructed Lord Carnarvon to continue bidding on his behalf! Only when Mr. Dale bid 10,000 guineas (£440,000) did his Lordship retire from the battle. Named Stamford he was exported to North America where he contracted pneumonia. He survived but did not achieve anything of note.

Usually the Aga deputed the bidding at the sales to Dawson, Lambton or Lord Carnarvon. Sometimes he would bid on his own behalf and on one occasion he successfully bid for a yearling only to discover that he had brought the wrong horse! He was under the impression that it was one he was interested in that was to be auctioned later! Sadly it has not been possible to establish the horse concerned.

Before leaving the topic of buying yearlings, as the Aga Khan continued to spend considerable amounts of money at the sales that came nowhere near justifying their cost, a list of the more expensive ones provides a sobering experience. During the winter of 1928 he was quoted as saying "I shall never again buy racehorses. My stud produces about twenty-five yearlings each season. I shall keep twelve and sell the rest". However, he was an active buyer in 1929 but less so afterwards.

Between 1925 and 1929 the following were bought at a cost of 2,000 guineas (£90,300) or more.

Colts:

Feridoon (Hurry On – Ecurie by Radium) – £19,000 (817,000) Unraced; sold (approximately) £13 (585)

Aftab (Papyrus – Sundart by Sunstar) – 14,000 gns. (£632,000) won one race – £270 (12,150) sold 125 gns. (£5,643)

Parwiz (Phalaris – Waffles by Buckwheat) – 10,000 gns. (£451,500) won two races – £3,897 (167,571) exported to Argentina.

Farman Farma (Phalaris – Clear Case by Son-in-Law) – 9,100 gns. (£410,000) maiden; sold 105 gns. (£4,740).

Farhad (Phalaris St. Amour by St. Amant) – 7,000 gns. (£316,000) Won one race £637 (27,391) Gelded and sent to India.

Blanchailles (Swynford – Blanche by White Eagle) – 6,500 gns. (£293,500) Maiden; gelded and sent to India.

Meena (Bachelor's Double – Santa Minna by Santoi) – 6,100 gns. (£275,500) Unraced; gelded and sent to India.

Falko (Phalaris – Cry Help by Irishman) – 6,100 gns. (£275,500) Won one race £935 (40,205), exported to France.

Saleve (Spion Kop –Skein Dhu by Battle-axe) – 6,000 gns. (270,000) Maiden; sold 30 gns. (£1,354). Won one race subsequently value £124 (5,300).

Ganga Singh (Spion Kop – Rackety Coo by Corcyra) – 5,200 gns. (£234,780) Won one race £543 (2,334); gelded sold 380 gns. (£17,157).

Prince Plunkett (Buchan – Plunkette by Prince Palatine) – 5,200 gns. (£234,780) Maiden; sent to France.

Buland Bala (Blandford – Saffian by Stornoway) – 5,000 gns. (£225,750) Won two races £2,710 (94,850) sent to France.

Cobra (Spearmint – White Lie by White Eagle) – 4,600 gns. (£207,000) Unraced; sent to France.

Tetracaun (Tetratema – Deocaun by Buckwheat) – 4,500 gns. (£203,000) Maiden from eight starts as a two-year-old; sold; never won a race.

Nushirawan (Solario – Sword Play by Great Sport) – 4,500 gns. (£203,000) maiden; sold 55 gns. (£2,483)

Halim (Hainault – Three Cheers by Acclaim) – 4,200 gns. (£190,000) Won one race £698 (30,014) gelded sent to India.

Blenheim (Blandford – Malva by Charles O'Malley) – 4,100 gns. (£185,115) Won five races; including Derby £14,533 (624,919) successful stallion; sold £45,000 (2,385,000).

Hakim (Friar Marcus – Honora by Gallinule) – 4,000 gns. (£180,600) Won four races £5,690 (243,000) as juvenile; broke leg and destroyed as a two-year-old.

Sirdar Singh (Swynford – Rectify by William the Third) – 3,600 gns. (£162,540) Maiden from five starts; sold as juvenile for 170 gns. (£7,675)

Prince Firouze (Prince Galahad – Boyne Blue by Lally) – 3,500 gns. (£158,825) Maiden from only start at two; gelded and sent to India.

Hakem (Friar Marcus – Orlass by Orby) – 3,500 gns. (£158,825) Two wins £1780 (76,540) sold 400 gns. (£18,060).

Mario (Buchan – La Tosca by Bayardo) – 3,400 gns. (£153,510) Maiden; gelded and sent to India.

Buland Dar (Diophon – Saffian by Stornoway) – 3,000 gns. (£135,540) Maiden; gelded and sold 105 gns. (£4,740).

Iran (Craig an Eran – Tetrarch's Maid by The Tetrarch) – 2,700 gns. (£121,905) Maiden; gelded.

Faster Still (Hurry On – Belfast by Lemberg) – 2,300 gns. (£103,845) Maiden; gelded and sent to France.

Maharajah (Swynford – Lady Josephine by Sundridge) – 2,100 gns. (£94,815) Maiden; gelded and sent to India.

Ranjit Singh (Gay Crusader – Rackety Coo by Corcyra) – 2,000 gns. (£85,617) Won three races value £2,398 (103,114) sent to France.

Fillies:

Qurrat-al-Ain (Buchan – Harpsichord by Louvois) – 12,500 gns (£564,375) won four races value £11,092 (476,956), including Queen Mary and Coronation Stakes, successful dam: producing six winners from seven foals.

Gay Baby (Gay Crusader – Tete a Tete by The Tetrarch) – 10,500 gns. (£474,075) Won only one race £167 (7,180) but placed in top races; produced three winners from four foals.

Eurydice (Orpheus – Renaissance by St Serf) – 4,800 gns. (£216,720) Won two races £276 (11,868); produced only one foal which died.

Buland Bibi (Blandford – Saffian by Stornoway) – 4,100 gns. (£185,115) Maiden; produced three winners from three foals.

Bartaville (Buchan – Corrie by Roi Herode) – 3,600 gns. (£162,540) Unplaced maiden; two winners from five foals.

Floreat Etona (Blink – Etona by Saint Denis) – 2,400 gns. (£108,360) maiden; one winner from three foals.

Cap d'Ail (My Prince – Capdane by Captivation) – 2,100 gns. (£94,815) unplaced maiden; four winners from nine live foals.

It is noticeable that of the thirty-four expensive yearlings twenty-seven were colts and only seven fillies. At this time the Aga Khan had not won the Derby, in fact he had only won the Two Thousand Guineas with Diophon and the St Leger with Salmon-Trout; both in 1924. He had though sold two Classics winners and failed to buy two colts that won Classics. It suggests that he thought he was on the right path with his fillies and mares: buying the best blood available, and was trying to buy more Classic winners, in particular, a Derby winner.

It is also of interest to note the value of the minor races won by the above. At a conservative estimate ordinary races were worth about three to four times more between the wars than today. In addition the prices paid by the Aga; although hefty enough, are less than would be paid today for the best yearlings. In recent times half a million to a million plus, and on quite a few infamous occasions several millions, has often been paid for yearlings with the best pedigrees.

The Aga did much better with his fillies bought at auction than his colts. Of the twenty-seven colts named above only three showed ability anywhere approaching the quality of their breeding; Blenheim, Hakim and, to a lesser extent, Ranjit Singh. Blenheim of course won the Derby but the Aga suffered desperate bad luck with Hakim; after his debut he was only beaten by Fairway who was a top juvenile and became a great horse. Hakim clearly had the potential to be Classic standard.

The precise Vuillier dosages for all the above expensively acquired yearlings have not been checked, however, it is probably safe to say that all would have met the requirements of the Aga and Vuillier in breeding terms and also Lambton's critical eye with regards to conformation. However, from now on the Aga would achieve most of his success with home breds which was what he had intended from the start.

*   *   *

During these years the Aga was doing well enough on the racecourse without building on the years 1924/25 as well as he might have hoped. During the three years from 1926 to 1928 he finished seventh, third and fourth in the list of leading owners. However, he was well behind the leading owner in these years by huge amounts: £32,000, £18,000 and £45,000. His best horses during this period were well below Classic standard and he must have wondered if any of those expensive horses would ever justify the outlay. He was of course breeding plenty of horses but at this stage nothing of note had emerged.

*   *   *

The best horse to run in his colours during this three year period was probably the French-bred Dark Japan (Dark Legend – Blouzelinda by St. Brendan) who in 1927 won the Chester Cup, Manchester Handicap and Goodwood Cup. Dark Japan had raced in France but was switched to Whatcombe after running unplaced in the Grand Prix de Paris. When Dark Japan arrived at Whatcombe, and for some time afterwards, he was described as "one of the lightest and poorest looking horses that could be seen". He managed just one race that year; a third in a handicap at Manchester in early September. After this he began to improve and Dawson was confident that he could win the Manchester November Handicap but the race was abandoned due to fog.

In 1927 Dark Japan raced six times winning the above three races. He carried 8 st. 11 lbs. to win the Chester Cup and 9 st. 0 lbs. the Manchester Handicap. He won the Goodwood Cup by 12 lengths. He finished third to Foxlaw in the Ascot Gold Cup. In the Doncaster Cup he finished third, finding the huge weight concession beyond him. He failed to win any of his three races in 1928.

The Aga had every reason to be optimistic about his juveniles in 1927. This was despite suffering a most unfortunate blow when Hakim broke a leg on the gallops at Whatcombe towards the end of August and was destroyed. After finishing unplaced on his debut Hakim won a maiden then the New Stakes at Ascot. He finished a head second to Fairway in the July Stakes and then won the Chesterfield and Lavant Stakes. But for his accident Hakim would probably have been placed second in the Free Handicap behind Fairway.

However, the Aga still had Buland, who won Imperial Produce Stakes, Farhad, Criterion Stakes, Ranjit Singh and Parwiz; all yearling purchases, to look forward to.

*   *   *

In 1928 the Aga achieved one of his ambitions; to win the Viceroy Cup in India. Earlier Lord William Beresford had bought Keenan for that purpose but he failed in his mission. The Aga was successful with a French-bred gelding: Astre d'Or (Souviens Toi out of Mon Etoile II by Elf).

In England the Aga appointed Michael Beary as stable jockey. Beary has been described in many ways: the stormy petrel of racing, irrepressible, irresponsible, and volatile of temperament, utterly improvident and useless with his finances; he was declared bankrupt three times. Sidney Galtrey wrote of Beary with wonderful understatement that he was "not the dove of peace and tranquillity when waters are ruffled on the turf... a hard rider with Hitler-like tendencies". However, no one ever doubted that he was, at his best, one of the great jockeys of his time; a superb horseman with style and dash. There can also be little doubt that he did not fully utilise his talent and he had his licence withdrawn three times during his career.

Strange events happened to Beary. On one occasion many years earlier as he entered the paddock at Newmarket Beary was approached by a prominent Irish politician. He told him "I see from the papers that the Prince of Wales is due to visit Punchestown races the day after tomorrow. Don't let him go. We do not control all the guns in Ireland, but we shall be in power next year and then he will be very welcome". Beary cancelled his rides the following day and visited St James's Palace and spoke with the Prince's Private Secretary. The Prince did not go to Punchestown.

*   *   *

1928 was no better than the previous year for the Aga and he had less winners. His three-year-olds did not do as well as hoped with the best of them probably Parwiz who had finished second in the Middle Park Stakes as a juvenile. He won the Gratwicke Stakes but was inconsistent.

However, a juvenile: Costaki Pasha gave the Aga cause to hope that his dream of winning the Derby might be fulfilled. Bred by the Aga out of his mare Cos, Costaki Pasha was an impressive looking sort by Gainsborough. He finished second on his debut at Newbury when "green" and then won his next three races: the Chesham, Hopeful and Middle Park Stakes. Costaki Pasha was very impressive in the last of these and was placed joint second in the Free Handicap a pound behind a filly: Tiffin (Tetratema – Dawn-Wind by Sunstar).

The Aga usually enjoyed better luck buying fillies at the yearling sales than colts. The decision to bid as high as 12,500 guineas (£577,000) for a daughter of Buchan out of Harpsichord by Louvois was, despite some observers considering her "coarse", an inspired one. Named Qurrat-al-Ain she was a decent racehorse but at stud she produced seven winners from eight foals. However, the three winning fillies she produced in turn produced eighteen winners!

At the December foal sales the Aga bid 5,000 guineas (£230,000), a record for a foal. Sir Abe Bailey decided to disperse his mares and foals and a colt by Solario out of Mont d'Or by Orby attracted considerable attention. A photograph shows him as a good sort with plenty of scope and the bidding opened at 800 guineas (£37,000). However, it was Sir Henry Greer bidding on behalf of the Aga that outbid Sir John Rutherford who owned the colt's sire Solario. Named Khorsheed he must have shown something as he made his debut in the Middle Park! However he was unplaced in that race as he was on his only other appearance in the Houghton Stakes.

At three Khorsheed kept the best company and was placed three times from seven starts and was always in the first six. He was placed in the King Edward VII and St. George Stakes and Jockey Club Cup. Although he was just below top-class, Khorsheed was worthy of a *Timeform* rating of 120. He was switched to Frank Butters towards the end of the year and it was under his care that he began his four-year-old career. However, he did not run until the middle of September by which time he had been transferred to the care of Senator J. J. Parkinson in Ireland. Running in Aly's colours Khorsheed finally broke his maiden winning two very moderate contests.

*   *   *

1929 saw the Aga return to the top of the table of leading owners.

Again there were no really outstanding performers among the older horses; his big hope Costaki Pasha largely disappointed.

Parwiz maintained his form and won the City and Suburban Handicap. He was then unplaced at Ascot in the Bessborough Handicap and afterwards sold to Senor Benito Villaneuva for a reported £20,000 (880,000). Parwiz completed his racing career by finishing third in the Eclipse racing in his new colours. The brother to Manna was then taken by Senor Villaneuva to Argentina to stand as a stallion.

However, the Aga had some very promising juveniles to look forward to in 1930: Blenheim (Blandford – Malva by Charles O'Malley), Rustom Pasha (Son-in-Law – Cos by Flying Orb), Qurrat-al-Ain (Buchan – Harpsichord by Louvois) and Teacup (Tetratema – Saucer by Chaucer).

Dawson realised that the Aga had some decent sorts when they worked well during May. Blenheim came to hand first impressing in a gallop during the first week of April by going four lengths clear of his three companions. Ten days later at Newbury, starting as the 2–1 favourite, he beat 31 others to win the Manton Plate by three lengths. He also won a minor plate at Windsor. At the end of April Qurrat-al-Ain won a Newmarket maiden by two lengths at odds of 6–4.

A week before Ascot Dawson worked the Aga's juvenile prospects: Blenheim, Qurrat-al-Ain, Rustom Pasha and Teacup, over the stiff four furlongs on Woolley Down. First Qurrat-al-Ain, conceding four pounds and ridden by Beary, finished ahead of Blenheim ridden by Fox. The time: 50.4 seconds, was good considering the fairly strong headwind. Shortly afterwards a group of four, including the unraced pair Teacup and Rustom Pasha, covered the same ground with Teacup ahead of Rustom Pasha but the time over a second slower.

On the first day the odds-on Qurrat-al-Ain won the Queen Mary. However, she had an extremely hard race; Beary being very tough on an immature, inexperienced filly, she never forgot the experience and it affected the rest of her career. On the second day Rustom Pasha, made favourite on his debut, dead-heated for the Chesham Stakes, on the third day Blenheim won the New Stakes and on the final day Teacup, making her debut won the Windsor Castle Stakes. In addition

Teacup also won the July Stakes at Newmarket and Ann Gudman (Stratford – Flying Home by Barcadaile) the Ham Produce Stakes at Goodwood.

Blenheim raced seven times as a juvenile winning four times including the New and Hopeful Stakes. He was second in both the Champagne and Middle Park Stakes and allotted 9 st. 0lbs. in the Free Handicap.

Possibly to the Aga's chagrin a filly he bred but sold at the Deauville yearling sales won the One Thousand Guineas: Taj Mah. It may have been that because she lacked size, she was a first foal out of Taj Mahal by Lemberg, but nonetheless it was another Classic winner to escape the Aga. When one considers Manna and Solario, not bought, Taj Mah and Ukrania, both sold, that makes four Classics missed. Surely the Aga's luck would turn.

Any disappointment felt by Dick Dawson over the failure of Costaki Pasha to progress as hoped was considerably eased by his training the Derby winner, Trigo (Blandford – Athasi by Farasi), and his finishing leading trainer for the third time.

*   *   *

The Aga had made some impact since his somewhat dramatic entry in 1921 and in eight years from a standing start considerable progress had been made. However, to quote a United States President over fifty years hence "You 'aint seen nothing yet".

4 The Aga Khan III; His Life in Racing Part II

A corpulent owner is ecstatic as his colours are carried over the line and he realizes he has secured an elusive first Derby win. He shouts the horse's name to the world in joy; he has won the Blue Riband of the turf; but not with the horse whose name he has called!

* * *

The Aga was, with considerable help from Lambton and his own unassailable cheque book, creating an enviable brood mare band and was ready to progress to the next stage. Buying yearlings was the only way to begin the Aga's stud, but ultimately it would only be by breeding his own stock that a successful and, importantly to the Aga, a profitable stud would be created. However, he achieved one of his ambitions, not with a home bred, but a colt bought at the sales.

The Aga won the Derby in 1930 with Blenheim and it has to be wondered whether this had any bearing on his decision to cut back at the yearling sales of that year where he bought nothing for more than 2,000 guineas (£94,500). He paid in excess of that sum only once in the next three years; 4,800 guineas (£236,000) for a colt by Sansovino out of Waffles by Buckwheat. Named Shami he failed to win or gain a place in three starts.

Blenheim (Blandford – Malva by Charles O'Malley) was bred by the Earl of Carnarvon who sent him as a yearling to the Newmarket Second July Sales. The Earl was a friend of the Aga's and had often bid on his behalf at the sales. However, at the time of the sale the Earl was accused of bidding up the Aga until the reserve of 4,000 guineas was reached at which point Dawson, on behalf of the Aga, bid 4,100 guineas (£185,000) and secured the colt. Whether true or not this proved to be one high-priced yearling that was well worth the money! One's thoughts are drawn irresistibly back to the time

Lord Carnarvon thought he should have bought Blandford. Was he attempting to recover some of his losses? Or, on the other hand, it is worth remembering that in addition to the Aga, the Earl was also good friends with Dawson…

It should also not be forgotten that, as seen in the examples of Manna and Solario, there were plenty of yearlings that Lambton bid for that he did not buy. It was only where the Aga, Vuillier and Lambton had made up their minds that a certain yearling MUST be purchased that Lambton carried on until all opposition had metaphorically raised the white flag.

The Aga Khan was still selling as well; he looked upon every horse in his stable not as a creature of beauty or something that might provide excitement and entertainment but through its value on the market. Therefore, in some instances the reason for selling could simply have been an effort to balance the books. In 1930 he sent two four-year-old colts to the sales; Le Phare (Phalaris – Eagle Snipe by White Eagle). La Phare was a good, but not outstanding colt, who won four races value £6,151 (289,000) and competed in the top handicaps; winning the Stewards Cup and he made 3,100 guineas (£153,000). Le Voleur (Gainsborough – Voleuse by Volta) and won two races value £4,085 (192,000). He was a high-class handicapper able to compete in, but not win, good Stakes races. He sold for 5,000 guineas (£247,000).

*   *   *

For all of his considerable knowledge of breeding and pedigrees, as stated earlier the Aga had little interest in conformation and it would seem that he could not distinguish one horse from another. For example in the Derby of 1930 he had two runners: Rustom Pasha and Blenheim. The former was second favourite and the latter a relative outsider. Michael Beary, who had become the Aga's jockey after a disagreement between Dawson and Charlie Smirke, chose Rustom Pasha with Harry Wragg on Blenheim. The well-bred Rustom Pasha (Son-in-Law – Cos by Flying Orb) a good-bodied, handsome colt had good form but possibly just short of that required to win an average Derby. However, neither did Blenheim who had finished unplaced in the Greenham and Two Thousand Guineas. As mentioned above, Blenheim had cost 4,100 guineas as a yearling, had shown promise as a juvenile and was ranked fourth in the Free Handicap.

Blenheim, who can be considered a slightly above average Derby winner, was given a fine ride by Harry Wragg (the Aga gave him £5,000 (225,000) as a present) and won well. The Epsom crowd gave "a striking demonstration of enthusiasm when the Aga Khan, hat in hand, and laughing like a happy schoolboy, led the colt through a lane of humanity to the unsaddling enclosure".

However, despite Blenheim being a brown colt with a small blaze and one white sock and Rustom Pasha a light bay with three white socks and a white blaze, the Aga was shouting "Come on Rustom Pasha" as Blenheim swept into the lead! This is understandable of course in the excitement of victory, the Aga's notorious short-sightedness and the fact that he was watching from the stand near the winning post; inside the course. However, he compounded the error by patting Blenheim when leading him in and cooing "Good old Rustom Pasha". Lord Carnarvon, who of course had an interest in the result as the breeder of Blenheim, and was standing near to the Aga, was cheering Blenheim and upon hearing the Aga cheering for Rustom Pasha and declaring "Rustom Pasha wins", His Lordship shouted "No he doesn't, you bloody fool, Blenheim wins".

When teased about this one day by the Earl of Pembroke, one of the few men in a position to rib him, the Aga furiously denied it. This was not the only occasion when the Aga had no idea which of his horses had won; in the 1932 St Leger he had the same problem distinguishing between Dastur and Firdaussi!

After Blenheim had won at the remunerative odds of 18–1 the Aga was summoned to the Royal Box and presented to the King: George V and Queen Mary. The King with a knowing wink asked "How much did you have on?" Not a shilling Your Majesty" the Aga confessed sadly.

Shortly afterwards Lord Carnarvon suggested to the Aga that as the breeder of Blenheim he might have an annual breeding right free. Even in a moment of high excitement and euphoria, and in the company of someone who could be called a friend, the Aga still had his business hat on. He stated unequivocally that the breeder would pay the same price as anyone else!

Rustom Pasha had been second favourite for the Derby at 9–2 but seemed to fail through lack of stamina. However on the evidence of his later races it is clear Michael Beary made too much use of him at Epsom. The ten furlongs of the Eclipse appeared much more to Rustom Pasha's liking when ridden, and held up, by Harry Wragg. These tactics proved most important to Rustom Pasha; when held up for a late run he was able to finish a close up third in the St. Leger and win the Champion Stakes; both times ridden by Wragg. Rustom Pasha's chances in the St Leger may have been compromised as he had begun coughing shortly after the Eclipse and he had not fully recovered until a fortnight before the St. Leger.

Wragg had ridden Blenheim to success in the Derby and Beary of course elected to switch to Blenheim for the Eclipse. When Blenheim was withdrawn from the Eclipse Beary was furious that the Aga kept Wragg on Rustom Pasha, something that did not improve the already strained relations between the two jockeys.

One is drawn to the thought that the Derby result might have been different had Wragg been on Rustom Pasha and Beary on Blenheim. In Michael Seth-Smith's biography of him: *The Head Waiter*, Wragg makes it clear that in his view Rustom Pasha would have won the Derby if held up. Beary was furious when Rustom Pasha won so easily and his resentment of Wragg over the issue, together with Blenheim winning the Derby, festered. Beary of course had the choice on both occasions and got it wrong. Matters continued to simmer and eventually came to a head at Manchester during the final meeting of the season. Beary began arguing with Wragg's younger brother Arthur in the weighing room and Beary challenged Wragg senior to come to his hotel room later to "sort matters out".

Wragg in company with Charlie Smirke and Bobby Jones went to Beary's room where, to their surprise, the bed had been moved and an impromptu "ring" prepared. Beary, who was small even for a jockey, was either very optimistic in "mixing it" with Wragg or may have forgotten that Wragg boxed with some success in his younger days and had maintained his skills. There was not much preamble when the "fight" started and very soon Wragg "belted" Beary. Not lacking courage Beary kept coming back and was trying to wrestle Wragg who then "hit him squarely on the jaw" which knocked him to the ground.

Still Beary got up and so Wragg him again which only made Beary even more angry and coming back for more. By the time the pugilists had finished Beary's cheeks and eyes were a "considerable mess". The following day Frank Butters looked at him and remarked dryly "Did you run into a bus"? Beary replied that he had had a "bit of trouble, but was all right now". Both Wragg, who had badly swollen hands and Beary, rode that day. Happily the feud was now over something Beary was "glad" about.

Rustom Pasha failed to win any of his five races as a four-year-old; Wragg rode him three times and Beary twice. Sadly Blenheim sustained a jarred tendon while being prepared for the Eclipse and never ran again. Dawson was certain he would have made a top-class stayer if kept in training and told the Aga after Blenheim was injured during the Eclipse that he would have recovered enough to race again that year. However, the Aga, always with an eye to a horse's value, did not wish to run the risk that he would be beaten again.

*   *   *

The Aga of course thought he had the Derby in his sights the year before in 1929. He had bred a very promising colt out of Cos by Gainsborough named Costaki Pasha; who won three of his four races as a juvenile, including the Middle Park Stakes, and was placed second in the Free Handicap. However, as a three-year-old he was unplaced in the Greenham Stakes at Newbury having started as the favourite. He was considered a non-stayer and reverted to sprinting where he was unplaced in three runs. Dick Dawson won the Derby that year in any event with Trigo.

1930 saw the Aga as leading owner for the second year in succession and pleasingly it was with the help of some homebred produce that he earned that accolade. Derby winner Blenheim was of course a yearling purchase but Rustom Pasha who won the Eclipse and Champion Stakes, Theresina; Irish Oaks and Falmouth Stakes,

Ut Majeur; Gordon Stakes, Newmarket St Leger and Cesarewitch Handicap and Le Phare; Stewards Cup were all bred by the Aga's studs. Qurrat-al-Ain won the Coronation Stakes at Ascot but she was a yearling purchase.

Qurrat-al-Ain (Buchan – Harpsichord by Louvois) never really recovered from a very hard race in the Queen Mary as a juvenile. Dawson had a very high opinion of her comparing her with Mumtaz Mahal at one stage. Physically she was well-grown with good limbs and a good mover and, after winning on her debut, was backed down to odds on for the Queen Mary. She seemed not to give everything in the race and Beary was extremely forceful on her to prevail. Plenty of observers felt she would not forget the experience in a hurry. As a three-year-old Qurrat-Al-Ain won the Coronation Stakes and although running well enough on occasions, disappointed on others.

In terms of ratings Ut Majeur (Ksar – Uganda by Bridaine) was possibly the best handicapper to run in the Aga's colours, although he was better than such a term implies. However, he was very nearly sold as he had been consigned to the Deauville yearling sales and only with Dawson's insistence that a prohibited reserve of £6,000 (265,000) be placed on him prevented his sale. He did not run as a juvenile but made a winning debut at Newbury in a seven furlong maiden. He ran unplaced in the Craven Stakes before finishing second in the Newmarket Stakes, the most important Derby trial run at that time, apart of course from the Two Thousand Guineas.

Ut Majeur missed the Derby and appeared at Ascot where he finished fifth in the Prince of Wales's Stakes; a completely different race from the one run today with the same name. In 1930 it was a race for three-year-olds only over about one mile and five furlongs; a distance no longer used as it would require the start to be either on a sharp bend or somewhere in No 1 Car Park! Ut Majeur then travelled to France for the Grand Prix de Paris where he was unplaced after suffering interference.

Ut Majeur now started to find his form beginning by dead-heating for the Gordon Stakes at Goodwood. Unfortunately he then suffered a bout of coughing and may not have fully recovered when he ran in the St Leger. It did not help that Ut Majeur also suffered interference and he did well to finish fourth. He then easily won the Newmarket St Leger landing odds of 4–7. After the Newmarket race trainer Dick Dawson was asked if Ut Majeur would run in the Cesarewitch. Dawson indicated that he would be writing to the Aga and recommending that the colt should take his chance. No decision was taken until the Aga arrived in London just two days before the race. The Aga was inclined to miss the Cesarewitch and run Ut Majeur instead in the Lowther Stakes the day after. However, after consulting Dawson the Aga changed his mind and promptly placed a bet of £4,000 to £100 (180,000 to 4,500) on Ut Majeur to win the Cesarewitch and the same bet on Qurrat-al-Ain to win the Cambridgeshire!

Dawson must have known that Ut Majeur was now in prime form and he produced an extraordinary performance to win the Cesarewitch. Ut Majeur's triumph was described as "one of the easiest in the long history of the race". Beary was at his best and, riding with amazing confidence, had Ut Majeur last with ten furlongs to go. He made steady progress through the field and with a quarter of a mile still to travel he had only Friendship for company at the head of the field. Beary had simply to loosen the reins for Ut Majeur to stride away to win by four lengths with five between second and third. Experienced observers compared his win to other notable wins by three-year-olds in the same race: Robert the Devil and St. Gatien. Anticlimactically, Ut Majeur completed the year by being inexplicably beaten in to second place at odds of 2–5 in the Liverpool St. Leger.

In 1931 as a four-year-old Ut Majeur won only one of his six races; the Derby Cup, a mile and six furlong handicap in which he carried top weight of 9 st. 7 lbs. giving away up to 42 pounds to his rivals. He was also second in both the Jockey Club Stakes and Jockey Club Cup. As a five-year-old he failed to win any of his four races but ran with considerable merit; finishing third in the Chester Cup carrying 9 st. 9 lbs. and second in the Manchester Cup carrying top weight of 9 st.6lbs. His other races were in the Ascot Gold Cup and Goodwood Cup where he was third both times. He was then retired to stud.

Although sprint handicaps were not exactly what the Aga had in mind when breeding thoroughbreds he won the Stewards Cup in

1930 with a decent homebred in Le Phare (Phalaris – Eagle Snipe by White Eagle). He was always well thought of at Whatcombe but, although he ran well, he did not win any of his five races as a juvenile. He did better at three winning three races. At four he was largely in the clutches of the handicapper escaping only to win the Stewards Cup.

Teresina's daughter Theresina won two of her four races: the Falmouth Stakes and Irish Oaks. She was then retired to stud where she produced ten winners.

The Aga's juveniles were a shade disappointing with only a filly, Turtle Soup (Tetratema – Eagle Snipe by White Eagle), showing much. Her best run was a second in the Champagne Stakes.

*   *   *

Between 1922, when the Aga Khan began racing in Britain, and the end of September 1931 his horses had been trained by Richard Dawson at Whatcombe. Dawson had done a good job and, although the full benefit had not yet been revealed, his decision to buy Friar's Daughter had been crucial in providing a foundation mare. At a time when George Lambton had been paying stratospheric prices Dawson secured the daughter of Friar Marcus and Garron Lass for just 250 guineas (£10,250). Unfortunately, as mentioned earlier, Dawson was inclined to be humourless, high-handed and autocratic; an attitude which surprisingly did not cause his relationship with the Aga to combust earlier.

There was a suggestion that Michael Beary, himself of course by no means to everyone's taste, was trying to get the Aga's horses sent to be trained by his brother John; behaviour that could only aggravate Beary's less attractive characteristics. In addition Aly was now taking an interest and Dawson a rather stern, humourless and, to twenty-year-old Aly, very ancient trainer, was not someone he could relate to. Beary, who would have been perfectly aware that Aly and Dawson would not be in accord, tried to persuade Aly that his brother would do as well as Dawson. Matters came to a head at the September meeting at Newbury when trainer and the Aga had a fierce disagreement from which there was no way back.

Aly was already friendly with both Michael and John Beary. Michael Beary, in addition to introducing Aly to the delights of London night life, had tutored him in the arts of jockeyship and race riding. Indeed, Aly had ridden in point-to-points until the Aga put a stop to it; however, he was becoming an accomplished rider on the flat. His style of riding in keeping with his somewhat impatient nature, he had a penchant for making the running and, as a good judge of pace, was often successful with this tactic. During the previous month Aly had won an amateur riders event at Gatwick on his own horse, Lights o'London, trained by John Beary, and five days later won on him again at Lewes. Aly was again on board for the United Services Cup on the first day of the Newbury September meeting where he finished unplaced. Despite this latest setback, it can readily be appreciated that Aly would probably have been open to the idea that John should be the Aga's trainer. Michael Beary won the next race, the Newbury Autumn Plate, on Firdaussi, so the Aga would probably have been in good humour.

On the Saturday in the valuable Newbury Autumn Cup the Aga's Isfandiar, ridden by the lightweight Jackie Sirett, ran moderately with the usually competent Sirett riding badly. Worse still, later on the Aga's juvenile Rooz, a well-fancied favourite for the maiden and ridden by Beary, ran badly and this double failure seemed to displease the Aga. A heated argument arose over who should ride Khorsheed in the Jockey Club Stakes the following week. Dawson had engaged Sirett to ride Khorsheed in the Cesarewitch and wanted him to familiarize himself with the horse.

The Aga would not normally interfere with such arrangements but, probably angry by Sirett's poor ride earlier and possibly influenced by Aly, insisted on Freddie Fox riding the horse. An angry exchange took place and that evening Dawson received a telegram that John Beary would collect the Aga's horses on Sunday. Dawson's staff were so angry at the way he had been treated they refused to cooperate in any way. The horses were removed and, while some of the older ones went to John Beary, the majority were sent to be trained by Frank Butters in Newmarket. Freddie Fox rode Khorsheed in the Jockey Club Stakes but Sirett rode him in the Cesarewitch.

Dawson was unlucky with the timing as the Aga had some very promising juveniles in 1931 and these would now be trained elsewhere by a trainer who would benefit from all Dawson's work in preparing them for racing. Dawson was left in his mid-sixties with only a dozen horses and about as many stablemen to lay off. In addition he also had five children to rear and educate. Luckily he had the income from Blandford.

Dawson and the Aga eventually repaired the rift in 1933 and in March of that year a statement was issued as follows:-

"All differences between H. H. Aga Khan and Mr R. C. Dawson have been adjusted to the entire satisfaction of both parties. In those differences no question was involved reflecting on Mr Dawson's character, or ability as a trainer, or on his honesty. Mr Dawson desires to acknowledge that H. H. Aga Khan has dealt with the matter in an entirely fair manner".

This was no more than Dawson was due. The Aga had much to thank him for; in just short of ten years after his first season as an owner the Aga was only once out of the first four in the table of leading owners. This included three years: 1924, 1929 & 1930 when he was leading owner. Dawson also trained two Classic winners and the winner of the Eclipse Stakes.

Returning to the Aga's jockey Michael Beary, according to Charlie Smirke he himself would have been the Aga's jockey but for a misunderstanding. Apparently one day Dawson was critical of Smirke's effort when riding one of his horses. As usual Smirke was unable to remain silent and said "I suppose you don't want me to ride for you anymore". Dawson apparently told the Aga that Smirke did not wish to ride for the Aga any more so the contract went to Beary.

*   *   *

1931 saw the Aga slip to fifth in the list of leading owners and seventh in the list of leading breeders. His best performer was a colt Pomme d'Api (Zionist – Pomare by Saint Just) who won the Ascot Gold Vase.

However, the Aga had plenty to look forward to with his

juveniles. Dastur (Solario – Friar's Daughter by Friar Marcus) won the Woodcote Stakes at Epsom, Firdaussi (Pharos – Brownhylda by Stedfast) the Dewhurst Stakes and Taj Kasra (Gay Crusader – Taj Mahal by The Tetrarch) the Windsor Castle Stakes. All three were products of the Aga's increasingly significant studs.

1931 saw the death of Colonel J-J Vuillier. He was replaced as manager of the Aga's French stud farms in France by Robert Muller; a German who had a good understanding of horses and had been with Vuillier for some time. Madame Vuillier continued to consult with the Aga Khan and his team on breeding matters.

* * *

Good as the first eight years had been there can be no doubt that the great days of the Aga Khan's racing and breeding empire came after his switch to Frank Butters. From 1932 until Butters enforced retirement in 1949 the Aga was leading owner nine times.

The exploits of many his best horses for the next eighteen years are covered in the chapter on Frank Butters. Suffice to say that the Aga never regretted the decision to employ Butters and they enjoyed many successes together. The only downturn in their triumphant progress occurred during the period of the Second World War. The war time also provoked some of the fiercest criticism of the Aga Khan for actions that were considered unpatriotic to the country that had provided the original source of his elevated status as an owner-breeder. The Aga's tribulations during the War have been dealt with in the previous chapter and the implications of selling his best stallions will be discussed more fully in the next chapter.

* * *

Although the Aga makes no mention of him in his memoirs George Criticos Fafoutakis helped the Aga and was, in many ways, very useful to him. It was sometime shortly after the Great War that the Aga entered the Ritz and asked for the Head Hall Porter. He was not available so George stepped forward. George Criticos, as he was known, had come to England as a young man from Crete; he did various jobs before taking employment as a hall porter at the Ritz.

The Aga was doubtful that this man who was volunteering his services could carry out the required tasks. He was wrong and in time Criticos became an unofficial agent and factotum for the Aga in London. The Aga's followers were told that if they wished to contact him to ask for "George at the Ritz". The Aga even gave him a title: the Honourable and caused some confusion at the Ritz switchboard by asking for the Honourable George!

The Aga would pass messages to his stables via George and when the Aga had a runner George would record the result, including details of pedigree, and telephone the Aga in France. Once when the Aga was in Deauville he asked George to lunch; at Lake Geneva. A plane was chartered from Croydon and lunch was taken at a small but very select restaurant where the bill for the whole day was, incredibly, reported to be about £250 (8,750). The cost of the plane would have been considerable but the bill for lunch must have been enough to make most people's eyes water!

It was in the Aga's nature to make an impression when the mood took him; but this seems a shade extreme! George also knew Aly very well, at least as well as he knew the Aga, and would pass on messages and, more often than not, bundles of cash. The Aga invited George to spend his holidays at his Deauville house. George preserved a newspaper cutting from a gossip column: "Mr George Criticos, head porter of the Ritz Hotel in London, is staying as a guest of the Aga Khan in Deauville."

George placed bets for the Aga, not often though on his own horses, his usual stake was £500 (17,500) but double if he was very confident. The Aga named a horse after George but sadly he was of little use.

*   *   *

Despite announcing that he would be buying no more yearlings the Aga could not resist the temptation. At the Doncaster sales, and in buoyant mood after the St Leger, he was keen to secure a colt by Blandford out of Flying-Home by Flying Orb. It came down to a duel between the Aga and Basil Briscoe who was acting for Dorothy Paget. The Aga however practiced some restraint and when Briscoe signalled 4,400 guineas (£240,000) he retired from the fray. Named Blanding he was a very tough sort; but not very good! He won two minor races from twenty-eight starts over three years. The Aga did win one battle with Briscoe: he paid 4,800 guineas for Shami, a brother to Manna and Sandwich, as mentioned earlier.

Earlier in the year the Aga had sold his seven horses in training in France at auction. However, they only made about £1,000 (52,000) in all.

* * *

The Aga continued to trade his horses. In 1933 he sold Zionist, who had finished second in the Derby behind Manna in 1925 and won the Irish Derby. Zionist had been standing in France with some success and then stood in Belgium after he was sold.

However, although on a much reduced scale the Aga was still a force in the yearling market when he was set upon a horse. At the Doncaster September sales of 1933, with Aly bidding on his behalf, he went to 6,400 guineas (£349,000) to secure a half-brother to Royal Minstrel. Royal Minstrel had realized 4,200 guineas (£185,000) as a yearling but had been too backward to run as a juvenile. As a three-year-old he had won the St James's Palace Stakes and Craven Stakes, was beaten a short-head in the Two Thousand Guineas and finished second in the Eclipse Stakes. As a four-year-old he won the Eclipse and July Cup.

The yearling colt half-brother to Royal Minstrel was by Fairway out of Harpsichord (which made him a half-brother to Qurrat-al-Ain) was described as "a very handsome powerful bay". After an initial bid of 2,000 guineas (£110,000) Aly prevailed over Fred Darling and others with a final bid of 6,400 guineas (350,000). The colt was named Hairan and he won five races over three years for a value £6,996 (370,800). He was a contemporary of Bahram and his career is covered later. The Aga sold him as a four-year-old to the Woodhay Stud where he stood for £98 (5,100).

Mrs Rustom won the 1933 Gimcrack Stakes at York and the Aga duly gave the Gimcrack Speech at the annual Gimcrack Dinner in November. He covered several topics, including allocation of prize money for horses finishing second and third. The Aga, quite rightly, pointed out that it is hardly an inducement to run in stakes races if the rewards for being placed were so poor. He covered stipendiary stewards and the practice of relegating disqualified horses to last place instead of, at the discretion of the stewards, merely placing it behind the horse interfered with. He also thought that the bottom weight in handicaps should be less that 6st. 7lbs. in order that apprentices might get more opportunities.

In 1934 with the success of Bahram in the Gimcrack Stakes the Aga was able to present the Gimcrack speech for the second year in succession. He was more robust in his comments than the previous year and spoke of his alarm that the interests of the breeding industry, and the owner-breeder in particular, were being adversely affected by the distribution of prize money. He condemned the growing practice of racecourse executives who reduce prize money for weight-for-age races and transfer the money to handicaps. His point was that there is little point in producing a good performer that is just below the top level, if the better prizes were given to much inferior horses that won handicaps. *Plus ca change, plus c'est la meme chose!*

*   *   *

It was not realised at the time but the Aga had another lucky escape at the Deauville yearling sales of 1934. He consigned a French-bred grey colt by Blandford out of Mah Mahal by Gainsborough. Luckily the colt did not reach his reserve of 5,000 guineas (£ 270,000) and was sent to Frank Butters. Named Mahmoud he won the Derby of course in 1936.

Conversely Aly was adamant that the Aga should buy the four-year-old filly Queen of Scots (Dark Legend – Grand Princess by Grand Parade) privately for a considerable sum. At stud she bred seven winners from eleven foals. This included Queen of Simla by Blenheim, who won the Queen Mary Stakes and at stud produced six winners from fifteen foals. Queen of Scots was then covered three times by Bahram and she produced three non-winning fillies. The first of these: Queen of Baghdad raced only twice as a juvenile but the decision to breed from her was an inspired one. She produced seven winners from nine foals including top performers Noor (by Nasrullah) and Nahar (by Stardust).

*   *   *

The Aga had always wanted Gordon Richards as his jockey and there was a rumour towards the end of the 1934 season about the retainer alleged to have been offered. This was more than Richards was currently receiving as first jockey at Beckhampton from Fred Darling and reputed to be in the region of £7,000 (364,000) a year plus 10% of winning prize money. Darling challenged Richards to declare his intentions and Richards expressed the hope that the Beckhampton patrons would agree to match it; Darling promptly agreed. Richards was thus denied the chance to ride Bahram.

The Aga was leading owner in 1934 with forty-five races won for a value of £64,897 (3,375,000). Second was Lord Glanely with twenty-one wins value £16,160 (840,000); less than a quarter, a quite remarkable difference.

*   *   *

There is an old joke in thoroughbred racing: following yet another unsuccessful attempt to gain election to the Jockey Club a wealthy industrialist declared "to become a member of the Jockey Club you have to be relative of God; and a close one at that!" He was wrong; in the interwar years a God, in the shape of the Aga Khan III, could not obtain the necessary support for an application to succeed. In 1934 he was made an honorary member but was never elected as a full one. Some years later Lord Derby, who considered the Aga his *bête noire,* tried to change the rules and force honorary members to re-apply for election each year. This would have given His Lordship the particular pleasure of blackballing the Aga! Such was Lord Derby's antipathy towards the Aga that he wrote to Lord Rosebery in 1945 asking him to find a way to penalise him!

*   *   *

1935 was of course the year of Bahram which will be covered later, suffice to say he helped the Aga be leading owner with twenty-three wins worth £49,302; twice the amount of Sir Abe Bailey in second place.

The Aga bought two yearling fillies in 1935 for considerable sums that both proved excellent purchases. At the first Newmarket July sales Frank Butters bidding on behalf of the Aga had to go to 5,000 guineas (£278,000) to secure a daughter of Blandford out of Endowment by Silvern. Described as "most attractive" she was named Begum and after failing to earn a place as a juvenile she won two races at three. But as a broodmare she produced six winners from nine live foals. Then at the Doncaster sales Frank Butters bid 4,000 guineas (£147,000) for a daughter of Salamis out of Cinderella by The Tetrarch. She was named Saraikala although she won only one race she produced five winners from as many foals before she was sent to France.

The Aga sold his 1924 Two Thousand Guineas winner Diophon at the second Newmarket July sales. He had not been a conspicuous success at stud and he only fetched 260 guineas (£14,500). His stud fee had been £48 (2,550) and he was later sold again to go to Greece.

*   *   *

1936 saw success for the Aga with Mahmoud in the Derby but he walked headfirst into considerable controversy with his decision to sell the Derby winner Blenheim. The sale was announced on the 7th July and with almost indecent haste the following week he was on board the *Berengaria* leaving Southampton bound for New York. Blenheim's ultimate destination was to be Arthur (Bull) Hancock's Claiborne Stud in Paris, Kentucky. Hancock paid £45,000 (£2,400,000).

When asked why he had sold Blenheim the Aga replied "I have had him in my stud for six years and now have a great deal of his blood, notably his son Mahmoud. Then there are his yearlings and foals, and there will be more foals next year". The Aga had been approached in 1933 to sell Blenheim by Raymond Dale on behalf of a syndicate. While nothing happened at that time negotiations were re-opened in December 1935.

It is not totally clear who was responsible for the misunderstanding during the transactions, but the upshot was that Dale was forced to sue the Aga for commission, which he claimed was due in respect of the work he had performed in arranging the sale. Details of correspondence suggest the Aga was not easy to deal with, but the American syndicate were not without fault as they delayed confirmation that they wished to proceed until after Blenheim's son: Mahmoud, had won the Derby; which of course increased Blenheim's value.

Dale is probably worthy of sympathy and when the case came to court it lasted only a day; the parties reached an agreement including confirmation that Dale's honour had in no way been impinged. Again the Aga's judgment was called into question: Dale was almost certainly in the right so why could the Aga not simply have paid what he owed Dale rather than drag everyone to court? The money of course would have been nothing to him.

Meanwhile British breeders were up in arms as they had booked mares to visit Blenheim in 1937 and 1938 and now had no stallion to cover their mares as any comparable stallion would have been fully booked. One breeder had completed a nomination on the 2nd July, just five days from confirmation of Blenheim's sale! The Aga replied with considerable spirit that all nominations were subject to the stallion concerned being in his ownership at the appropriate time. He pointed out that similar conditions applied to his other stallions with the sole exception of Bahram "whom I decided never to sell". Well that assertion lasted just four years. The Aga compounded the irritation he had caused by selling Blenheim by stating "… no one is a greater or more loyal supporter of British bloodstock and racing, and all that it means". While the Aga may have been within his rights on a strictly legal basis, on any moral level his behaviour can only be described as deplorable.

Why did the Aga sell Blenheim? He liked to balance the books but it was some years later that an explanation came from Marcus Marsh when he was training for the Aga and Aly. Marsh always believed that the sale was motivated by fear. Marsh wrote of the Aga "He was a man who lived very close to the political pulse and, from the mid-thirties onwards, he was convinced that the German armies would one day engulf Europe. He was sure Britain was doomed. And so he came to look upon the United States as a future refuge".

The Aga's judgement about which yearlings to sell, and which to keep, was questioned by Aly that same year. The Aga sent a yearling filly by Solario out of Mirawala by Phalaris amongst a batch twenty-one to the Newmarket Yearling July sales. She was Mirawala's seventh foal and five of the first six had all won!

Named Stafaralla Aly bid 1,850 guineas (£97,000) to retain her. She proved to be well worth the money and as a juvenile won the Cheveley Park and Tattersall Sale Stakes. However it was as a brood mare that her true worth was established; from 13 foals she produced nine winners! The first five were all colts including Tehran. The Aga acknowledged Aly's perspicacity in retaining Stafaralla after Tehran finished second in the Two Thousand Guineas by leasing him to Aly for the rest of his racing career. Better late than never! Aly bought back three more fillies for a total amount of 940 guineas but they could only manage one win in a minor race between them and nothing at stud.

In the same batch two other yearling colts sold for more than a thousand pounds; Faris II (Dastur – Firouze Ranee by Son-in-Law) and Ramtapa (Rustom Pasha – Sultan Ranee by Salmon-Trout). They sold for 3,000 guineas (£160,000) and 1,900 guineas (£102,000) respectively. Ramtapa was trained by Joe Lawson at Manton and more than recovered his purchase price on his debut by winning the New Stakes at Ascot worth £2,970 (149,000). His only other race that year was a third in the Dewhurst Stakes. He did not really train on and won only a plate race in the next two years. As a well-bred colt he still represented a good purchase; however, the Aga probably did not worry much as he had not let a Classic winner slip through his fingers.

*   *   *

1937 saw the Aga as leading owner and breeder; indeed as a breeder the Aga was out on his own. His studs in Ireland and France produced winners of nearly twice as much win prize money as Sir Victor Sassoon who finished second. There were no big stars among the three-year-olds and older, however, the juveniles Mirza and Tahir contributed over half of his winnings.

1937 saw the appointment of Nesbit Waddington as stud manager of the Aga's Irish Studs: Sheshoon and Ballymany. Waddington later undertook the purchase of further studs to accommodate the Aga's ever increasing brood mare band: Gilltown, Ongar and Sallymount.

*   *   *

The Aga's domination was considerable during the 1930's: he was leading owner six times in nine years from 1929, won seven Classics, on four occasions he had the first and second in a Classic. Never had one owner had such a galaxy of stars at any one time and yet what irked the Aga was that unless he won the Derby he could not usually manage to break even. This may go some way to explain why he was keen to be a seller as much as a buyer.

The Aga was again a prominent seller at the Newmarket and Deauville sales consigning sixteen and nineteen yearlings respectively. In addition he sold Rustom Pasha and Badruddin; both were brought to stand as stallions in Argentina.

*   *   *

1938 saw the Aga's dominance reduced: he finished fourth in both the list of leading owners and breeders and again he sold at the Newmarket and Deauville yearling sales. At Newmarket he entered eighteen yearlings to be sold without reserve which realised 10,635 guineas (£536,000). At Deauville the Aga sold seventeen more yearlings for approximately £11,200 (537,600).

He was still a buyer of course and in 1938 paid 1,450 guineas (£73,000) for a colt by Hyperion out of Sister Stella by Friar Marcus. Named Stardust he fully justified his purchase and will be discussed later.

Aly was a good judge of a horse, however, his reputation as a shrewd buyer and seller of bloodstock was not enhanced with a three-year-old colt named Foxglove II (Foxhunter – Staylace by Teddy). Foxglove II was bred in France by Mr. Edward Esmond who sold the colt to Aly as a three-year-old. On his first appearance in Aly's colours, and trained by Frank Butters, he won a very moderate race at Birmingham "in a canter" at odds of 2–7 and followed up at Ayr six days later in an equally poor race also "in a canter" at odds of 1–5.

Aly then sold Foxglove II to Mr. Peter Beatty who sent him to Fred Darling who, spotting his true potential quickly sent him to Ascot. Foxglove won the Gold Vase "easily" but then disappointed at Goodwood. However, if Aly was still thinking he had not done badly out of the deal, to rub it in Foxglove then won the Ebor Handicap.

Following a below par performance in a minor race at Newbury Foxglove won the Jockey Club Cup at Newmarket before finishing the year by running below his best in the Aintree Derby. He was ranked eighth in the Free handicap with 8 st. 10 lbs. There can be no doubt that although Foxglove was not very consistent he won almost £5,000 (240,000) for Mr. Beatty who certainly seems to have got the best of the deal.

Aly's dealings with Mr. Beatty did not end with Foxglove II. He helped Beatty buy Bois Roussel for £8,000 (384,000) and just a few short weeks later he won the Derby! Did Aly not want to buy Bois Roussel? One wonders what the Aga thought of these dealings!

*   *   *

1939 saw the outbreak of World War II and the Aga, who was reported to be "not in the best of health", decided to dispose of his yearling stock at the Newmarket December Sales. The most likely reason was that the Aga was depressed about the outbreak of war and, certain that the Allies would be defeated, had lost his interest in racing.

There was talk of a syndicate being formed to buy the entire consignment *en bloc,* but this proved impractical. Nineteen of his yearlings, including five by Bahram, were offered and fetched a total of 36,710 guineas (£1,773,000), averaging 1,932 guineas (£93,000).

On Tuesday 5th December the following yearlings went under the hammer. It should be remembered that those buying bloodstock with war declared did so in the knowledge that they may not be able to race them. The fillies of course could be bred from but there was still an element of risk:-

Obash c (Ut Majeur – Moti Mahal by The Tetrarch). 330 gns; winner.

Usenge c (Umidwar – Turtle Soup by Tetratema). 160 gns. Failed to win.

Toubo c (Vatout – Boxeuse by Teddy) 3,500 gns; Failed to win.

Khoshbood c (Mahmoud – Farmood by Phalaris) 1,250 gns; Failed to win.

Selim Hassan c (Hyperion – Blanc Mange by Hainault) 4,000 gns; Won 2 races £586.

Firoze Din c (Fairway – La Voulzie by Teddy) 1,200gns; Won 1 race £221.

Mkata f (Dastur – Mumtaz Begum by Blenheim) 730 gns; Won 1 race £75.

Singida f (Solario – Aidetta by Phalaris) 520 gns; did not win.

Samanga f (Solario – Badr-ul-Molk by Blenheim) 2,900 gns; won 1 race £167. Bred 2 winners of 6 races.

Uvira f (Umidwar – Lady Lawless by Son-in-Law) 510 gns; won 5 races £2,009.

Soga f (Solario – Mrs. Rustom by Blandford) 2,200 gns; did not win. Bred 3 winners of 8 races.

Bukumbi f (Bahram – La Douairiere by Spearmint) 1,400 gns; Won 3 races.

Bukhara f (Bahram – Una by Tetratema) 3,500 gns; did not win.

Bura f (Bahram – Becti by Salmon-Trout) 1,200 gns; did not win. Bred 4 winners of 7 races.

Queen of Bombay (Bahram – Queen of Scots by Dark Legend) 3,300 gns; Unraced.

Mambaka f (Mahmoud – Udaipur by Blandford) 3,700 gns; Re-named Clovelly; did not win. Bred 7 winners of 13 races.

Alibhai c (Hyperion – Teresina by Tracery) 3,200 gns; did not win, exported.

Bakhtawar c (Windsor Lad – Friar's Daughter by Friar Marcus) 2,600 gns; won 3 races value £894.

On balance the Aga can consider himself fortunate that none of these became top performers. Of the fillies only Clovelly (ex Mambaka) was a real loss at stud; she would certainly have been a valuable addition to the Aga brood mare band had he not sold her.

The rest of the stock sold at the sale consisted of individuals who were little better than throw-outs from the stud farms, and the 40 others offered that were sold grossed just 2,966 guineas (£143,200), averaging 74 guineas (£3,600) each.

The Aga also decided to dispose of most of his horses in training keeping only a few. He did not sell his stallions, at least not then, or his brood mares or foals.

*   *   *

Those horses that were not sold were raced in the colours of Aly Khan as well as the Aga. By this time Aly had become an authority on the Stud Book and, of course, an excellent judge of a horse.

If the horses owned by the Aga and Aly were added together it would, despite the dispersals, have placed them second in the owners list.

As a breeder though, the Aga was not in the first ten. His travails with his bloodstock are discussed in detail in the following chapter.

*   *   *

When war was declared the Aga, who had no doubt that Germany would win, was for the duration confined to the continent and unable to visit England. Horses still ran in his and Aly's colours of course and he won some big races. However, although he was leading breeder in 1940 he jeopardised his prospects of doing so again by selling Bahram and Mahmoud.

Even with this background and the war going badly for the allies, it was still a shock when the announcement came in July 1940 that the Aga Khan had sold Bahram to a syndicate in the United States for £40,000 (1,760,000), well below the market price. The syndicate comprised of Alfred G Vanderbilt, Sylvester W Labrot, Walter J Chrysler and James Cox Bradley. The latter had a 1/16th interest, while the other three members each contributed $50,000 of the purchase price.

Bahram completed the 1940 stud season at Egerton Stud, and on the 2nd July he was sent to Old Connell, Newbridge, County Kildare, Ireland, before shipment to America. Negotiations, conducted by the British Bloodstock Agency were protracted and difficult, due to complications caused by wartime conditions. Indeed there were even rumours that he was actually on his way to New Zealand. The official announcement that the business had been completed could only be made when Bahram was actually in the ship at Belfast on the 8th August. The most important condition was that the horse must be certified by two veterinary surgeons that he was in good health and condition when he was actually on the ship. This was because war risks could be placed only from "port to port".

Just two months later, on 22nd October, another Aga Khan Derby winner, Mahmoud, also set sail for America, sold to Mr. Alfred

Vanderbilt's cousin Mr. Cornelius Vanderbilt Whitney for £20,000 (880,000), to stand at his stud near Lexington, Kentucky. Incredible, two of the last six Derby winners sold at the same time; a huge body blow to the British Thoroughbred Breeding Industry.

Bahram and Mahmoud became the fifteenth and sixteenth Derby winners to be exported to the United States. This followed Diomed, Saltram, Spread Eagle, Sir Harry, Archduke, Priam, Blue Gown, Kingcraft, St Blaise, St Gatien, Ormonde, Rock Sand, Durban II and Blenheim.

In addition in 1940 the Aga sold all his yearling colts; keeping only the fillies. A special catalogue was to be prepared by Tattersall's and the sale of twenty-six lots was to take place on the evening of July 3rd.

The sale never took place; in the event eleven of the twelve colts bred in Ireland were advertised to be sold privately. The conditions, published in *The Racing Calendar* on 11th July were that these were to be sold privately, as a lot, for 400 guineas (£18,500) each; a total of £4,620 (203,500).

The offer did not remain open for long, and it was announced shortly after that a buyer had been found. Major Alfred E Allnatt had become the proud possessor of eleven of the best bred yearlings, including Bahram's colt named Shah Rookh and Bahram's half-brother Muzloom. It can readily be imagined that these colts would have cost considerably more to buy at any sales conducted outside of wartime. However, buying at such a time was a considerable risk as there was, of course, no guarantee that the buyer would have any opportunity to race them.

Major Allnatt had little knowledge of horses or racing and not much interest. He had made a fortune in property after the Great War and bought the horses purely as a business speculation. Two years later he purchased Lord Glanely's bloodstock – all 134 horses – and resold them all for decent profit except the stallion Colombo which he disposed of separately for a very good one!

Major Allnatt later entered the world of art and in 1959 paid £275,000 (6,100,000) for Ruben's *Adoration of the Magi* which he donated to Kings College Cambridge.

Major Allnatt had secured the following colts out of such wonderful mares as:-

> Ann Gudman: Open Champion; failed to win,
> Farmood: Shah Rookh; won two races value £460 (17,500),
> Fille de Salut: Moemen; won two races value £304 (11,550),
> Friar's Daughter: Muzloom; won three races value £644 (24,470),
> Mir Zadeh: All Joy; failed to win,
> Moti Begum: Joy Boy; failed to win,
> Teresina: Shahpoor; won five races value £2,007 (74,250) (Including Jockey Club Cup).
> Theresina: Ujiji; won eight races value £3,634 (134,450) (Including July Stakes – his only defeat in four races as a juvenile was to Sun Chariot; and substitute Ascot Gold Cup).
> Turtle Soup: Mulji; failed to win,
> Una: Mehrali; won six races value £1,542 (58,600),
> Via Media: Tororo; failed to win.

Major Allnatt had every reason to be pleased with his decision to buy all eleven yearlings; not only was he able to race his horses but on balance he can be said to have got the better of the bargain as he recovered his outlay in win prize money alone! The Aga had only three winners of five races in England in 1940; however, he did have two Classic winners in Ireland.

*   *   *

1941 was not much better for the Aga; not surprising really as he has sold most of his best-bred colts the previous summer. He had only three winners of seven races and possibly because of this he decided to send twelve yearlings from Ireland to Newmarket to be trained by Frank Butters in 1942.

However, the Aga was in the market to buy yearlings! Yes; despite his apparent poverty he began sending telegrams with instructions about those he was interested in. At the Newmarket sales Nesbit Waddington, bidding on the Aga's behalf, went to 8,200 (£325,000) to secure a colt by Hyperion out of Castle Gay by Buchan. Named

Hyderabad he did not race at two and ran only twice as a three-year-old; unplaced both times. At four, when no longer in the Aga's ownership, he managed a win in a modest plate from five outings.

The Aga also splashed out on two mares: Dialia and Éclair. Both were offered at the Newmarket July sales. Dialia (Gainsborough – Dulce by Prince Galahad) was an eight-year-old mare who cost 4,200 guineas (£165,000) and produced two winners of four races for the Aga.

Éclair (Ethnarch – Black Ray by Black Jester) was a twelve-year-old mare that cost 3,500 guineas (140,000) had been a high-class racehorse and had produced five winners from as many foals at the time of her sale. She had been covered by Hyperion and produced four winners from five foals for the Aga including Hyder Ali and Khaled. Éclair was a wonderful racehorse and outstanding brood-mare. She was destroyed in 1951.

With the help of some juveniles in training the Aga finished third in the list of leading owners and second, behind the National Stud, in the list of breeders in 1942. His best two horses were Nasrullah and Umiddad; as they were the following year when the Aga was third in both lists.

The Aga was again in the market to offload good horses in 1943; this time Felicitation who had beaten Hyperion in the Ascot Gold Cup. Felicitation was bought for 4,000 guineas (£152,000) for export to Brazil. He had done reasonably well at stud in England and had sired Morogoro who had finished second in the Two Thousand Guineas and Derby.

At the Newmarket September yearling sales Frank Butters bidding for the Aga went to 7,100 guineas (£280,000) to secure a filly by Hyperion out of Silver Birch by Blandford. Named Hastra she won only a nursery handicap but at stud produced six foals all of whom were winners before she was covered and sent to North America in 1952.

*   *   *

The Aga was still selling at the sales on one hand and buying with the other. In 1944 he sold six lots for 10,920 guineas (£437,700), however, his search for the progeny of Hyperion continued; the Aga could not send any mares to him as Lord Derby had placed a ban on him in retaliation for the Aga selling his stallions. With Frank Butters bidding on the Aga's behalf he bought three yearling colts by Hyperion and one by Blue Peter for a total of 38,400 guineas (£1,530,000), making him the highest buyer at the sales. When asked about the purchases Butters replied "The Aga Khan liked their breeding, he sent me a cable and told me what I could go to". It would have been interesting to know how close to the Aga's limit each colt was!

Details of the Hyperion colts can be found in the chapter on the Aga's breeding methods. The Blue Peter colt: Shere Ali out of Caretta by Phalaris cost 11,000 guineas (£435,000) and managed one win from eight races value £539.

The Aga was leading owner and although only third in the table of leading breeders, if the ones bred by Aly are added then he would have finished top.

*   *   *

Many involved with British racing; breeders for example, may not have voted the Aga Khan as the most popular figure in racing but the public, captivated by his romantic background, the stories of his fabulous wealth and his overtly infectious enjoyment of life itself, regarded him with affection. This was certainly the case up until the Second World War, but perhaps after the Aga decided Germany was odds-on to win the war, the racing public may have had second thoughts! Indeed the survival of Britain from the Second World War was a source of never ending wonder to him. "There is no logic to it, as a racing man I wouldn't have taken any odds on your chances," he once said to Marcus Marsh. Note the "your" instead of "our" chances; loyalty to the Empire seemed to have temporarily evaporated!

The Aga always claimed loyalty to Britain but when it looked as if Britain might be defeated in a war he became detached. From a dispassionate view at the outset of the War Germany would rightly have been an excellent odds-on bet to prevail. Because the Allies won the Second World War it is sometimes forgotten that Britain declared war in circumstances where she was unlikely to win. Ultimately the Aga should not have been surprised by Britain winning the war; Germany's odds would have been extended considerably when Hitler unadvisedly decided to attack Russia. With Japan recklessly deciding to bomb Hawaii and the United States entering the war on the side of the Allies, any self-respecting bookmaker would have bet against a German victory!

*   *   *

When Germany took control of France early in the war the Aga's mares were sequestrated and transferred to Germany. When the Allies were moving to retake Europe from the Nazis in 1945 Aly alerted friends from the armies moving in on Germany to look out for the mares that had been looted from the Aga's French stables.

Aly received a message from General Patton to say the mares had been traced to the German National Stud at Altefelt. Pattern's troops were still some distance away and as the Russians were advancing quickly no time could be lost.

Aly driving a jeep equipped with a horse-trailer and accompanied by a single G. I. headed rapidly across Germany but found that the Nazis were still in control at Altefelt. Not one to be daunted by the situation Aly demanded the return of the horses at the point of a gun. With Robert Muller, who had gone into captivity with the horses, Aly organised their removal transporting the horses over the French border in an expedition which occupied five days and nights.

After the war ended Aly had contemplated making the Army a career but instead even before demobilisation he began to look to the future. Aly became joint-owner with the Aga and shared all the Aga's racing interests. He flew to England to attend the races and travelled on to Ireland to inspect Gilltown of which he was now part owner. Aly was keen to recapture the glory days and had plans for the studs and stables. The new partnership met with immediate success: they were leading breeders in England for the next three years and second in the fourth.

*   *   *

In 1946 Aly, as if revitalised after the war, went to the sales with a vengeance. He was very keen on a magnificent chestnut yearling colt by Nearco out of Eleanor Cross by Hyperion. Aly, bidding on his own behalf, was against Fred Armstrong bidding on behalf of The Gaekwar of Baroda. After some spirited bidding Aly was pushed up to 15,500 guineas but Armstrong came back with a bid of 16,000 (£620,000) and, when Aly caught the eye of the Indian Prince who smiled, he shook his head. The colt, named Star of Gujrath won five races and was rated 118 by *Timeform,* he was sold to Italy as a four-year-old for 3,100 guineas (£112,00).

*   *   *

In 1947 Aly met up with Frank Butters, Robert Muller and Madame Vuillier to discuss the new season. Aly was an instinctive person where horses were concerned and demonstrated this with two horses: a three-year-old colt named Avenger II (Victrix – Minnewaska by Blandford) and, remarkably, a six-year-old mare named Rosa Bonheur (Kerlor – Passiflore by Gaurisankar).

When Aly first heard about Avenger II he asked Muller and Madame Vuillier to look at him. They were not keen and thought him expensive for a maiden. Aly went to see Avenger II and the horse put his head on his shoulder. "Look! He wants me! He's mine!" exclaimed Aly who promptly bought him. Six weeks later Avenger II won the Grand Prix de Paris at Longchamp; in the ensuing excitement Aly was so exuberant he squashed Madame Vuillier's hat! A painting of Avenger II was hung on the wall of Muller's office at Lassy, the stud farm near Chantilly.

It was in 1955 two days before the running of the Grand Prix de Deauville that Aly heard that Rose Bonheur was for sale. She was a good filly but had a moderate pedigree. On that Friday evening Aly forsaking dinner with his friends drove off into the country to inspect the mare. He liked what he saw and bought her for a "modest price". Incredibly she won the Grand Prix de Deauville on the following Sunday; Aly was exuberant! However, Aly did not push his luck with her; she was covered by Nearco and sent to North America!

*   *   *

Just after the end of the war Madame Vuillier was asked to take over the management of the French studs, which she did, assisted by Robert Muller. The studs comprised the Haras de Coquenne, Saint Crespin and Lassy all in Normandy, and Marly-le-Ville, near Paris. It was at Marly that Madame Vuillier set up her headquarters.

*   *   *

In 1946 Aly had formed a syndicate to buy the 1938 Derby winner Bois Roussel. Aly was keen to have access to stamina for his father's mares in France although the purchase was not universally applauded as it seems Bois Roussel did not always match up with Madame Vuillier's dosage formula!

The mating plans for the large number of mares involved a tremendous amount of work. By this time Mme. Vuillier and Robert Muller on one hand and the Irish stud manager Nesbit Waddington would submit suggestions. Mme. Vuillier's would be based on the Dosage system and Waddington would consider conformation, temperament etc. Aly would have his own opinions, including doubts about the Dosage Systems capacity to produce quality stamina. He would also consider conformation while the Aga, of course, would think only in terms of pedigree.

With the Aga getting older and, possibly, not quite as sharp as he was, the quality of horses produced by the studs began to deteriorate. Aly culled some families and, with conformation taking a more prominent role, he sort to produce better physical specimens. He also introduced some North American blood all of which produced an upturn in fortunes.

*   *   *

The Aga had three principle jockeys during his thirty years of ownership in England. When his horses were trained by Dick Dawson they were firstly ridden by Charlie Smirke and then Michael Beary although he only had a retainer from 1928 until 1933 when it was terminated. Smirke was retained jockey to the Aga in 1936, much against Frank Butters wishes. Charlie Smirke rode for the Aga for many years and although he acknowledged that Smirke was a supreme rider on the big occasions, the Aga, despite claims by Smirke to the contrary, was never really happy with him. This may have been due to Smirke's criticism of the training methods used by Dawson and Butters which Smirke considered too severe. The Aga would happily have ditched Smirke if he could have persuaded Gordon Richards to accept a retainer. It was one of the Aga's great disappointments that Richards was never retained as his first jockey. Richards was supremely loyal to his long-standing owners and in particular Fred Darling. Richards did accept a second retainer principally to ride the Aga's lightweights.

*   *   *

The Aga Khan, like many before and plenty since, soon realized that the principal weakness in British racing was prize money. In a letter to *The Times* written before the Tote was introduced in 1928, he supported the introduction of such a mechanism. He wrote "The whole organization of racing seems to be run for the benefit of bookmakers." The Aga, if alive today, would have noticed that nothing much had changed! Twas ever thus and is now and will be for the foreseeable future. Only in the event of today's rather supine leaders being replaced by a strong figurehead who has the best interests of quality racing at heart will there be any change. Some hope; one is inclined to weep with despair whenever it is repeated yet again that big fields and increased turnover should be the aims of racing. Whatever happened to quality?

It has to be wondered what the Aga would say about British racing today with its plethora of Class 5, 6 and even 7 contests for horses hardly worth a rating that in any sensible world would not even be in training. When Bahram won the Gimcrack Stakes at York he made the famous speech at the Gimcrack Club in November. He condemned the growing practice of some racecourse executives of reducing prize money for weight-for-age contests and transferring the money to handicaps. The Aga made a plea on behalf of owner-breeders who he said would be discouraged if the trend continued.

The Aga showed considerable foresight in his observations and he would have been in agreement with the Pattern system that is in operation today. When introduced in 1971 it set out a framework for European Racing and was soon adopted in North America. The Pattern is not perfect and requires constant attention but it has stood the test of time. It can only be speculation; but there is sufficient evidence, based on the historical behaviour of the bookmakers in other areas, to believe that, but for the Pattern system British racing, bad as it is in some areas, would look considerably different today.

The influence of the bookmaking industry, in a lethal partnership with brainless, short-sighted and myopic governments of either colour, and unopposed by supine and unimaginative individuals running racing has in the last fifty years been disastrous for the sport. A toxic combination of a policy of high taxation on betting, together with huge bookmaker profits taken directly from betting have gradually bled racing dry. In addition, with bookmakers demanding, and getting, the racing programme increased in size to its current bloated level, in order to maximize turnover and profits, while returning paltry amounts to racing, has caused a steady remorseless decline in overall quality of the racing programme from which there often seems no way back.

In a world without the Pattern the betting industry would naturally have favoured a programme that, with the exception of the Classics and a few other historical weight-for-age contests, would have consisted almost entirely of handicaps. As it is it has to be wondered what the Aga would think today of the racing programme with many handicaps worth much more than Group 3/Listed races and, incredibly, some are worth more than a few Group 2 races. Who exactly is responsible for this ludicrous situation? The bookmakers are businessmen first and foremost with shareholders to satisfy and can't be blamed if racing's rulers have been spineless in their negotiations.

*　　*　　*

In 1947 to mark the marriage of Princess Elizabeth the Aga presented her with a filly foal by Turkhan out of Hastra by Hyperion. Hastra, who raced only at two winning a five furlong nursery, had been barren to Dastur during her first season at stud and this filly was her first foal. Having dispatched the filly the Aga was distressed to learn that she would probably not stand training. He asked the Princess to choose another filly and she chose one by Stardust out of Bellinzona by Bois Roussel. Named Marsa she was a smallish sort and was unplaced from her only two starts.

However, contrary to earlier fears the Turkhan filly, now named Astrakhan, happily proved sound enough to race. She was second on her debut as a juvenile and then as a three-year-old she was well beaten into third place as the 6–5 favourite on her seasonal debut at Windsor. She then won a mile maiden at Hurst Park before she was tailed off in the Lingfield Oaks Trial. She was rated 98 by *Timeform*. Sadly Astrakhan produced no winners for the Queen at stud and she was exported to North America in 1958.

*   *   *

Aly was convinced that My Love (Vatellor – For My Love by Amfortas) could win the 1948 Derby and made an offer to his owner and breeder M. Volterra. However, the shrewd French owner would only sell 50% and the Aga desperate to win another Derby departed from his normal practice and agreed to a half-share.

The sale was completed on 23rd May with the Aga rumoured to have paid £15,000 (540,000). The Aga was so confident that he defied the Begum's attempts to keep him at home and made an arduous trip to England. The Aga cheerfully tipped My Love to the porters at Waterloo Station after he and the Begum had arrived on the Blue Train. No less confident was My Love's jockey Rae Johnstone who sent a telegram simply saying "My Love to all".

My Love duly won the Derby on 5th June. The colt's trainer was a sixty-four-year-old: Richard Carver who was born in Chantilly but was a British subject although Carver had never visited Epsom before the race. For good measure he also trained the second: Royal Drake; described as "leggy and distinctly plain". My Love also won the Grand Prix de Paris but had trained off by the St Leger where he was unplaced. He was a failure as a sire and exported to North America in 1953 where he did no better.

In addition to My Love the Aga also had the third with Noor (Nasrullah – Queen of Bagdad by Bahram) who, after he was exported to North America, inflicted four defeats on the mighty Citation. In fairness to Citation he was not the force he had been after serious injury had meant a year off the racecourse. At two and three Citation (Bull Lea – Hydroplane II by Hyperion) had won 27 of his 29 starts; not exactly under-raced was he!

Citation should have been unbeaten but before it was realized how exceptional he was, in one race a stable mate was allowed to beat him! On the second occasion Eddie Arcaro rode a bad race; he himself said he had been as "dumb as dumb could be"! When Citation returned to the track after his injury aged five he ran in another 16 races but won only five times. He was brought back to pass a million dollars in prize money; but it was a mistake as he was not the same horse after injury and his reputation suffered.

*   *   *

The Aga was not finished buying expensive yearlings. At the Newmarket October sales a well-related, well-grown good-looking grey son of Nearco out of Infra Red by Ethnarch was offered as part of the late Lord Portal's racing interests. The colt's portrait certainly suggests a most impressive sort. The bidding began at 3,000 guineas (£113,000) and increased rapidly to 14,000 guineas at which point only Aly Khan and Major Holiday were bidding. Aly signalled another 500 and the Major cried enough. At 14,500 guineas (£548,000) he was expensive enough and Dara, as he was named, could not be produced on the racecourse as a juvenile. It might have been better if he had never raced at all. As a three-year-old Dara demonstrated clearly in three outings that his ambitions did not include being a racehorse and was sold at the December sales for 760 guineas £24,000).

The Begum fared no better when, at the behest of the Aga, Harry Wragg was asked to bid for a princely yearling colt by Big Game out of Quick Arrow who was the dam of the Oaks winner Steady Aim. Submitted by Sir Alfred Butt and the Brook Stud Company, the impressive looking youngster attracted considerable interest. The bidding opened at 6,000 (£227,000) guineas and rose quickly to 14,000 (£529,000) when a final bid by Wragg secured the colt. Master Boatman, as he was named, never ran.

*   *   *

Following the accident to Frank Butters which is dealt with in the chapter dedicated to him, the Aga Khan needed a new trainer in 1950 and the choice fell on Marcus Marsh. Marsh met the Aga to discuss the terms and thought, mistakenly, that the Aga looked old and frail. The Aga agreed to Marsh's request regarding numbers and yearlings and then Marsh asked for a five year contract. In a flash the Aga's switched persona from an apparently dying old man to a sharp-minded dealer with a demeanour that brooked no argument. "No" he said "three". Marsh sensibly realized he would not be moved and he accepted.

Marcus Marsh inherited from Butters several promising juveniles; with Palestine (Fair Trial – Una by Tetratema) ranked second in the Free Handicap, the star. Palestine had won six of his seven stars as a juvenile but his breeding did not guarantee his staying a mile as a three-year-old.

Palestine won his trial over seven furlongs at odds of 1–4 but was pushed out to win by ¾ length. The concern over his ability to stay a mile was reflected in him starting as the third favourite for the Two Thousand Guineas at 4–1; the first time he had ever started at odds against. Brilliantly ridden by Smirke, who was at his best, Palestine held on by a short head. Smirke, whose worst enemy, and there were several contenders for the honour, would never accuse him of lacking self-confidence and self-esteem, was again at his best on a big occasion. He had Palestine perfectly balanced at the top of the hill and then drove the grey into the dip for all he was worth and gained more than two lengths on the second, Prince Simon, who failed to negotiate the downhill as well. Prince Simon flew when he met the rising ground but Palestine, now weakening and with Smirke nursing every last ounce of energy, just held on. It had been an outstanding piece of riding and, according to Marsh; Smirke was quite insufferable for days afterwards.

Aly had broken his leg in three places skiing and thought unlikely to attend the Two Thousand Guineas. However, much against his doctors wishes and cheerful as ever, he flew over to Newmarket in his private plane: *The Avenger*, and made his way around the course in a wheelchair. Offers to buy Palestine came in including one from North America of £158,000 (5,400,000), he was syndicated at the end of the season for £3,000 (120,000) a share which valued him at £120,000 (4,080,000).

Palestine dropped back to six furlongs for his next race; The Red Rose Stakes at Manchester and, again with Smirke at his most artistic, landed odds of 1–10 by a short head. He then proved conclusively that he did stay a mile by winning the St James's Palace Stakes by five lengths at odds of 4–7. It is easy to say with hindsight but running in the Eclipse Stakes was surely a distance too far and he was beaten into fourth place; faltering at the distance. Palestine concluded his career by landing odds of 1–2 in the Sussex Stakes. Palestine won eleven of his thirteen races value £38,216 (1,225,000). He did not fully live up to expectations at stud as a sire at Gilltown but was hardly a failure.

Apart from Palestine the Aga's horses were often to prove a shade disappointing during Marsh's time in charge but this was due to a lack of talent not to any deficiencies in Marsh's training. Two of the most promising juveniles failed to progress at three; Diableretta (Dante – Dodoma by Dastur) became sour and badly behaved and was sent to France, but nothing could persuade her to race. Tabriz (Tehran – La-Li by Blenheim) did not appear at all, Dust Devil ran only once unplaced. Tambara did well enough winning the Coronation Stakes; Kisaki was disappointing in two appearances and Éclat, not displaying any sings of temperament, won a race and was placed in the Eclipse while Moondust won only one race; beating Éclat! Khorassan (Big Game – Naishapur by Nearco) who raced only once as a juvenile under Frank Butters, won the Dee Stakes and Kempton's Classic Trial but ran moderately in the Derby and his season was over at Royal Ascot.

1951 was no better and in many ways worse for horses under Marsh's control; Tayeh (Tehran – Rivaz by Nearco) inherited her dam's speed winning the Molecomb but little else distinguished itself. All of this was some way from the glory days of the past and Aly was more inclined to search for a scapegoat rather than take the view that the horses were simply not that good.

Aly, trying to forget Rita Hayworth was seen in the company of the French chanteuse Lise Bourdin; whatever happened to Gene Tierney? He occupied himself by buying Wilfred Harvey's Sandwich Stud of about sixty mares and foals, typically concluding the deal in twenty-four hours. Lawyers had indicated that such a timescale was impossible but Aly would have none of it and signed the documentation as he was leaving the Ritz for Paris. In addition the rather plain-looking but talented Italian three-year-old colt Nuccio (Traghetto – Nuvoletta by Muzio) was bought for £50,000 (1,400,000). Trained by Alec Head he ran moderately until finishing second in the 'Arc. Nuccio did better in 1953 and 1954.

*   *   *

The Aga and Aly as usual sent a draft of horses to the sales from the Sheshoon Stud. They had been doing this for a number of years of course, always without reserve, but rarely achieving very good prices. This is because buyers were suspicious that only cast offs were being offered. However, occasionally one of the "ugly ducklings" turned into a swan. At the Newmarket July sales a colt by Prince Chevalier out of Ann of Austria by Fairway was sold for 1,650 guineas (£52,000). He was named Chivalry and he won nine races value £9640 (290,000).

Other lucky dips into the Aga's bran tub of unwanted thoroughbreds include a colt by Rosewell out of Dasaratha by Dastur offered two years earlier and sold for 500 guineas (£18,000). Named Do Well he won four races, including the Irish St Leger, value £5,724(206,000). A colt by Umiddad out Seed by Solario was sold for 460 guineas (£17,500). He was named Holmbush and won five races value £6,269 (175,000) including the Jockey Club Stakes.

*   *   *

In 1952 Marsh trained the best horse during his short tenure as the Aga's trainer: Tulyar (Tehran – Neocracy by Nearco). Homebred

Tulyar was a small and backward May foal and not much bigger as a yearling and joined Marsh six weeks after the other yearlings from the Aga's studs. He had been useful, but no more than that, as a juvenile: winning two nurseries from six races. However, as he passed the post in a mile nursery at Birmingham it would have taken a huge leap of imagination to predict what would happen the following year. The Aga was clearly not that impressed and Aly tried strenuously to sell him for £7,000 (205,000) over the winter but could not find a buyer.

As a three-year-old the ugly duckling did not turn into a beautiful swan. Tulyar was still no bigger than medium-sized but he was well-proportioned. However, one admirer was John Hislop who described Tulyar thus; "Medium-sized and a dark bay colour, he possess great quality, good length for his height, excellent limbs, a straight hind leg, and a most beautiful, intelligent head. His general outline is symmetrical, and he is only to be faulted in that he might be a little deeper through the girth, and that he has bad feet, these being shallow and rather brittle".

Tulyar began with success in a minor event, then he won the Ormonde Stakes, Lingfield Derby Trial, Derby, Eclipse, King George VI and finally St. Leger Stakes. Before the Derby the gallops at Newmarket were firm and Marsh instructed Smirke to work Tulyar up the peat moss gallop. To Marsh's horror and considerable annoyance Smirke promptly worked him up the parallel grass strip which was like a road. Marsh was furious when Smirke pulled up but the imperturbable "cheerful Charlie" assured Marsh that Tulyar was more effective on top of the ground!

Tulyar won the Derby by three quarters of a length and Aly won £40,000 (1,120,000) in bets but was not happy; he thought Marsh should have ascertained Tulyar's full potential earlier! Smirke really was nerveless; before the Derby he came out of the weighing room and observed to Alec Waugh "you should see that lot in there: as nervous as can be and in and out of the lavatory"!

When Tulyar was aimed at the King George VI Stakes it was obvious Smirke would need to put up overweight. Richard Baerlein wrote in the *Evening Standard* that Gordon Richards should ride as he was the Aga's second jockey and of course able to do the weight. Smirke was furious and chased Baerlein all-round Hurst Park one day saying wasting did not impair his strength! Smirke still put up 2 lbs. overweight which fortunately did not prevent Tulyar from winning. Tulyar won all seven of his races and £76,417 (2,140,000) in win prize money beating the £57,455 (5,840,000) record established by the great Triple-Crown winner Isinglass between 1892 and 1895. In real terms of course Isinglass's record was considerably greater than Tulyar's.

Despite this outstanding record Tulyar was not a great horse; he was too one dimensional to be considered as such, although he was very tough. It is hard not to conclude that Bahram would have comfortably out-speeded him in any race over any distance both as a juvenile and a three-year-old. On the credit side Tulyar won on any going, was indolent by nature and blessed with a placid and easy-going temperament.

Despite this success the Aga, like Aly, only reflected that Marsh should have run him in the Two Thousand Guineas! He convinced himself that Tulyar would have won of course, and was annoyed that, in his view, he had been deprived of a second Triple-Crown. Nonetheless to general surprise Marsh was able to announce that Tulyar would remain in training as a four-year-old. However, by now the racing world knew the Aga far too well; and it was no surprise when in February 1953 it was announced that he had sold Tulyar to the Irish National Stud for £250,000 (7,000,000). Marsh first discovered this when he was listening to the radio! Tulyar was sold again in 1955 to North America and departed after the 1956 covering season. Sadly he was in poor health and was a failure.

Marsh trained one of the best juvenile fillies the Aga ever bred or owned in Neemah (Migoli – Naishapur by Nearco). From Migoli's first crop Neemah a rangy sort in the image of her grandsire Nearco, won three of her five races. However, the performance that stamped her as potentially high-class was the manner in which she quickened past the 2–5 favourite, and future Derby winner Pinza, in the Royal Lodge Stakes. Pinza franked the form by easily making all and winning the Dewhurst Stakes by five lengths.

Masai King (Big Game – Nikellora by Vatellor) was a tall leggy colt with scope but unfortunately he was rather straight in front and slightly back at the knee. He won two races easily but was well beaten on firm ground in the National Breeders Produce stakes at odds-on.

At the end of the 1952 season the Aga was leading owner for the thirteenth time and Marcus Marsh leading trainer. Notwithstanding this he removed all his horses from Marsh's yard at the end of 1953 and sent them to Noel Murless who had been sent some horses earlier in the year. By this time Aly Khan had been taking increasing responsibility for the management of the ageing Aga's racing affairs and it was Aly who decided that Marsh's contract would not be renewed.

Aly had often been guilty of overrating some of the horses in Marsh's care and surprisingly did not really seem to understand that much of the produce of the studs were in steady decline. When horses were beaten Aly, who lost money betting on them, blamed Marsh. Murless, great trainer that he was could, not surprisingly, do no better.

Aly behaved shamefully over his treatment of Marcus Marsh; Aly had taken the decision to transfer most of the horses to Noel Murless at the end of 1953. Murless had moved from Beckhampton to Newmarket. However, Aly did not have the grace to inform Marsh who discovered his fate by accident when Nesbit Waddington told him at Goodwood that he was sorry the horses were to be removed. Waddington naturally had assumed Marsh would have been told.

Noel Murless took over the horses that Marsh had trained and also some yearlings. The best horse was a filly Bara Bibi (Bois Roussel – Masaka by Nearco). She was a small, only 15.1 hands, but an attractive sort, full of quality and as a juvenile she showed some promise winning a six furlongs plate at Brighton before producing a decent performance to win the Histon Stakes over seven furlongs at Newmarket. As she was bred for middle distances better could be expected as a three-year-old.

Bara Bibi proved to be the only really decent performer trained by Murless during 1954. She won two races; the Princess Elizabeth Stakes at Epsom and the Park Hill at Doncaster and, as long as the ground was not soft, usually ran with credit. Probably because of her size she was sold when the season was over.

*   *   *

At the end of 1954 Aly and the Aga Khan removed most of their horses from England and made France their racing centre. He cited the cheaper costs of having horses trained in France coupled with the higher prize money. Alec Head was appointed trainer of the horses bred by the Aga and Aly at Chantilly. The Aga Khan after over thirty years had effectively turned his back on British racing. He had won every major race in Britain apart from the One Thousand Guineas and he corrected that omission just before he died. As it transpired The Aga and Aly continued to have some horses trained in England by Murless and Harry Wragg but the majority would be trained in France.

In that same year Nesbit Waddington retired and it was necessary to appoint a successor as manager of the Irish Studs. Major Cyril Hall, manager of the Irish National Stud was approached. The Aga and Aly knew Major Hall and he was summoned to the South of France and made a most generous offer. Major Hall accepted the position and took control of the Aga's seven stud farms: Gilltown, Sheshoon, Ballymanny, Sallymount, Ongar, Williamstown and Eyrefield.

The Aga never really established with Marsh the sort of relationship he enjoyed with Dawson and Butters. Although happy to have Smirke riding for him in the big races, the Aga knew full well that Smirke often rode for himself on other occasions. The Aga was also suspicious of Smirke always in the background trying to influence Marsh. Whatever Smirke said or did had little effect on Dawson and Butters but Marsh was a different matter altogether. Smirke rode out for Marsh and on occasions simply ignored his instructions about how to ride work and ride in races. Although Aly was largely in charge of the horses the Aga never entirely relinquished the reins of power.

*   *   *

The Aga can hardly be blamed for wishing to switch the training of most of his horses to France; Tulyar won seven races in 1952 including the Derby, Eclipse, King George VI and St Leger winning a record £75,103; the most by any horse in one year in Britain. However, with Nuccio, trained in France by Alec Head, he won £29,704 for the Prix de l'Arc de Triomphe alone. Nuccio also won the Coronation Cup at Epsom the day after Tulyar had won the Derby; the prize money was just £2,270 (63,500) for a race that should have been the highlight for older horses at that meeting. That year the Champion Stakes was worth just £2,253 (63,100); many big handicaps were worth well over £3,000 (84,000)! In England it was clearly better to own a horse rated 90 that could run to 100 than have one rated two stones better and capable of winning the best weight-for-age races. What a mess: in what other sport are second division performers often better rewarded that best ones? Racing was being run moderately with the Jockey Club apparently clueless about improving matters.

It did not help that Governments of either colour had little sympathy with racing's plight; the entertainment tax on racecourse admissions was almost 50%. In 1950 racing paid £1,780,000 (56,960,000) in duty. Imagine what racing could have done with just a quarter of that! Racing was being bled dry by uncaring governments and then from 1961 with the opening of betting shops and a "licence to print money" bookmakers together with governments completed the misery! The Aga predicted that racing in England would continue to decline and it is hard to argue that he would not have been proved right. Prize money has continued to decline in real terms and only the welcome life-saving intervention of the Maktoum family and Khaled Abdulla have propped up the prestige of British racing since they arrived in the late 1970's.

It is tiresome to be continually told by smug, uncritical, malleable observers, usually those whose income is not dependent on levels of prize money, also representatives of racings governing bodies, racecourses and bookmakers, in that unrelentingly upbeat manner that Britain has the best, most prestigious racing with more variety than is available in any other country in the world. There may be some truth in this; but who pays for it? Some claim that it is punters that keep the racing show on the road. They make their contribution of course but without owners there would be no racing for punters to bet on.

In recent years one particular bellicose observer in the media has repeated *ad nauseam* that nobody is forced to own a racehorse. What a stupid statement! Does this individual not realize that without the investment of those that buy thoroughbreds or breed their own, then there would be no racing? That would mean of course, no blood-stock industry, no employment for thousands of hard-working stud and stable staff, not to mention thousands more employed in ancillary industries, no careers for trainers and finally no betting. Is it too much to ask that such individuals who provide the investment might, not necessarily to make a profit, but to get a better return on their often considerable outlay than an average of 21%?

Owners in Britain suffer the worst return on investment of any principal racing nation; it is as near a certainty as possible that anyone thinking of entering racehorse ownership in Britain today, at any level, will lose money; quite possibly everything they invest. All owners in Britain love the chance to race their horses at the major meetings, particularly Royal Ascot, even though the prize money, except for sprinting of course, is gradually falling behind similar races around the World. There will surely come a time when prestige alone is unable to bridge the gap between the rewards in Britain and those in other parts of the world.

*   *   *

Most of the Aga's horses in France were trained by Alec Head. One horse he trained: Hafiz was, in terms of *Timeform* ratings, the second best horse ever to race in the Aga's colours. Hafiz (Nearco – Double Rose by Macaron) first appeared in 1954. However, he was not owned by the Aga when he reached his peak! A big, heavy-topped colt that carried plenty of condition Hafiz first raced in Britain in 1955 when he won two of his three races. He was unplaced in the Derby after which he won the Queen Elizabeth II and Champion Stakes.

At the end of the year the Aga tried to syndicate Hafiz. Each of the forty shares would cost £2,000 (48,000) with the proviso that he could race Hafiz until the end of the 1956 season. Extraordinary! The Aga seeking to keep a horse in training rather than dispatch him off

Swynford

Blandford

Friar's Daughter

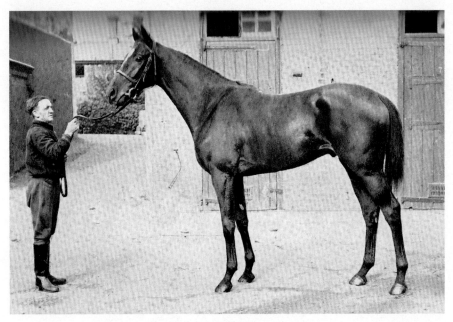

Bahram as a Two-year-old

Bahram on his way to post on his debut

The finish of the National Breeders Produce Stakes

Bahram – nearest the camera – canters over his work companion.

Frank Butters watches work with Michael Beary.

Bahram going to post in the Two Thousand Guineas

Bahram wins very easily

Frank Butters after the race

Bahram after his easy win.

FOURTH RACE. **Bretby Stakes Course.**

3 15—THE MIDDLE PARK STAKES of 20 sov. each, and 10 sov. extra if not declared by October 9th, with 1000 sov. added, *for two yrs old;* colts and geldings 9st, fillies 8st 11lb; the second to receive 10 per cent. and the third 5 per cent. of the whole stakes; Bretby Stakes Course, six furlongs. (122 entries, forfeit declared for 104). Closed October 31st, 1933.

No.		st	lb	
1	Mr A. F. Basset's b g **GODOLPHIN** *by Baytown—Phalanstery*	9	0	**LIGHT BLUE & YELLOW HOOPS,** (Persse) *scarlet sls & cap*
2	Ld Derby b c .... **PLASSY** *by Bosworth—Pladda*	9	0	**BLACK, WHITE CAP** (C. Leader)
3	Ld Derby's ...... **FAIRHAVEN** *ch c by Fairway—Drift*	9	0	**BLACK, WHITE CAP** (C. Leader)
4	H.H. Aga Khan's b c **HAIRAN** *by Fairway—Harpsichord*	9	0	**GREEN & CHOCOLATE HOOPS,** (Frank Butters) *chocolate cap*
5	H.H. Aga Khan's ...... **BAHRAM** (late Bahman) *b c by Blandford— Friar's Daughter*	9	0	**GREEN & CHOCOLATE HOOPS,** (Frank Butters) *chocolate cap*
6	Sir Charles McLeod's gr c **CONSEQUENTIAL** *by Son and Heir—Quento*	9	0	**WHITE, TARTAN SASH,** *black cap* (Higgs)
7	Miss Dorothy Paget's b c by *Diomedes*—**RACLA**	9	0	} **BLUE, YELLOW HOOP** on body & sls, (Briscoe) *yellow cap with blue hoop*
8	Mrs C. B. Robinson's gr c **MARMADUKE JINKS** *by Mr Jinks—Mill Belle*	9	0	**DELPHINIUM BLUE,** *black star on* (M. D. Peacock) *back, qtd cap*
9	Mr William Woodward's b c **FRESH FOX** *by Gallant Fox—Filante* (bred in U.S.A.)	9	0	**WHITE, RED SPOTS,** *black cap* (Boyd-Rochfort)
10	Ld Woolavington's b c **BEN MARSHALL** *by Gainsborough—Fair Diana*	9	0	**WHITE,** one **BLACK HOOP,** *red cap,* (F Darling) *gold tassel*

The weights have been added for the convenience of the public but are not guaranteed as correct.

1st 5   2nd 1   3rd 6

Two lengths & 3 lengths

3 - 4 - 7 - 10   did not run

to stud! In any event the offer was not sufficiently attractive so the Aga sold him outright for a reputed £80,000 (1,920,000).

In 1956 and racing in the colours of Mr. L. S. McPhail, Hafiz won only one of his six races: a small race in France. He was beaten in all of his four races in Britain. His form was disappointing and it was not until his final race: the Cambridgeshire that he recovered his form and indeed produced the performance of his life in carrying 9st. 7 lbs. into second place, beaten only half a length, and he was overhauling the winner, to whom he was conceding 27 pounds, at the line. Hafiz was rated 136 by *Timeform* on the strength of this one effort.

Before this, in both 1953 and 1954, Head had sent Nahar (Stardust – Queen of Bagdad by Bahram) to England to run in the Lincolnshire Handicap, staged at that time on the now defunct Carholme course at Lincoln. It probably says much about British racing that Nahar rated 109 by *Timeform*, only raced once in England, in a valuable handicap, in each of those two years. The Lincolnshire Handicap was worth more in both 1953 and 1954 than the Princess of Wales's Stakes and Champion Stakes. In 1953 the almost black Nahar, ridden by Gordon Richards, stopped inside the final furlong having hit the front. The following year ridden by the French jockey Jean Massard, who was having his first ride on the course, Nahar was produced by his jockey to perfection and won comfortably.

One filly trained by Alec Head in France was raced principally in England! Foaled in 1953 Palariva (Palestine – Rivaz by Nearco) was a half-sister to four winners and her dam of had been a blistering fast filly. Palariva's grand-dam was Mumtaz Begum and her great grand-dam Mumtaz Mahal! A neat, strong filly Palariva was, not surprisingly, a fast sort who tried to burn off her rivals from the off. As a juvenile she was raced only at five furlongs and won a minor race at Maisons-Laffitte and the Great Surrey Foal Stakes at Epsom, despite her saddle slipping. She was then beaten into second place in the National Breeders Produce Stakes before winning the Chesham Stakes at Royal Ascot, run that year in July because of the national rail strike. She was beaten a short-head in the Molecomb Stakes but was bumped and awarded the race. It was probably a mistake to hold her up in the Lowther Stakes where she finished second, before running a very disappointing race in the Prix d'Arenberg at Longchamp. Palariva's principal asset was her ability to break quickly and reach top pace in matter of strides; she was rated 126 by *Timeform*.

As a three-year-old Palariva won six of her seven races demonstrating that she possessed tremendous courage to accompany her speed. She won all four of her races in France and the King's Stand and King George Stakes in England. She was rated 131 by *Timeform* which means that only Petite Etoile and Mumtaz Mahal can be considered superior to her of all the fillies that raced in the colours of the Aga Khan III and his family during his time.

At stud she produced three winners from nine foals before her death in 1972. However, one of her foals, a filly Khairunissa by Prince Bio, produced seven winners from nine foals before being retired in 1980. Her best produce was Kalamoun by Zeddaan who won three Group 1 races: Poule d'Essai des Poulains, Prix Lupin and Prix Jacques le Marois, and was an outstanding sire producing Group 1 winners: Kenmare, Bikala, Kalaglow, Persepolis and Shakapour.

*   *   *

The Aga had added Harry Wragg to his ranks when he began training in 1947and Wragg looked after the horses that ran in the name of the Begum. Wragg had ridden for the Aga and won many big races so it was no surprise that he decided to support him when he began training. Wragg trained some well-bred sorts for the Aga but taking everything into consideration he did not enjoy the best of fortune.

When the Aga decided to switch the majority of his horses to France some horses stayed with Wragg and he was to receive more patronage for some years to come. Noel Murless also trained for the family and after the Aga's death would train the best filly ever produced by the Aga Khan studs: Petite Etoile (Petition – Star of Iran by Bois Roussel). It was a shame that the Aga never saw her race, although whether he would have allowed her to race over four seasons is extremely doubtful!

The best horses trained at Abington Place for The Begum by Harry Wragg were Fraise du Bois, Neron, Military Court, Golovine and Noble Venture.

The most talented of these was Fraise du Bois (Bois Roussel – Sugar Hills by Coroado); a handsome good-bodied colt that was bred to stay. However, he had enough speed to win over five furlongs on his debut in the Errol Stakes at Ascot and added the Royal Lodge Stakes later in the year. However, he was always going to be better over middle distances and, although he only won one race at three, it was the Irish Derby. He was second in the St Leger and placed on two other occasions. Fraise du Bois began the season by finishing a disappointing third in the Dee Stakes when as the short-price favourite he was not given the best of rides by Smirke. Fitted with a hood he refused to jump off in the Derby until the field had covered a hundred yards, but for which he might easily have been placed.

The Aga had been very bullish about his chances; during the Annual Derby Lunch at the London Press Club he said that Fraise du Bois "stood a good chance and thought he would win". However, he told the cloakroom attendant as he left "I am *certain* he will win". The Aga liked to attend these lunches especially if he had a fancied runner. There was an amusing incident when one year he was greeted on arrival by Horace Sanders who was the chairman. Sanders, like the Aga, was built on generous lines; "Please proceed me", requested the Aga. Worrying about protocol Sanders replied "I don't know how far I should precede Your Highness". "Well" said the Aga glancing at Sanders "it is evident that we cannot proceed side by side"!

Fraise du Bois was placed in the Eclipse Stakes at four but broke a leg and was destroyed the same year. He was in some ways an unlucky horse and had the ability to have done better.

Neron (Nearco – Love's Legend by Dark Legend) won four races including the Queen Anne Stakes and Military Court (Court Martial – Solanum by Solario) won the Lincoln Handicap in 1955. Military Court in all won seven races but was somewhat difficult to train.

Golovine (Precipitation – Coppelia by Son-in-Law) was not the best horse trained by Wragg; a highest *Timeform* rating of only 102, he was not very consistent and may not have been completely genuine. However, he was a durable; he raced for four seasons, and was a decent handicapper on his day. He won the Chester Cup in

1956 when benefitting from a shrewd ride by Peter Robinson who got up close home on the 9–2 favourite.

In addition to the prize money the winning owner: in this instance the Begum was presented with an enormous Cheshire Cheese weighing 50 pounds (23 kilos). It was so big that it was only with the greatest difficulty that it was transported back to the horsebox and then on the Abington Place. As it could not be kept fresh for too long it was decided that it would be cut up and Harry's Wragg's wife Marjorie was assigned the not inconsiderable task of dividing it up into manageable pieces. It was then given away to the staff and friends. Unfortunately The Begum remembered it about a month or so later and, seemingly not thinking how or where it had been stored in the meantime, asked for it to be delivered to her in order that it might be of use during Ascot week!

Marjorie Wragg had little option but to organize a replacement, brought by Harry, and despatch it forthwith to the owner who was blissfully unaware of the consternation she had caused!

*   *   *

The Aga had a major clear-out of fillies and mares in July 1956 selling 41 in a package deal to the American Rex Ellsworth. Amongst them were some excellent mares that had produced plenty of winners.

The family had only two horses that ran in the Classics that year: Buisson Ardent (Relic – Rose O'Lynn by Pherozshah) who finished third in the Two Thousand Guineas and was unplaced in the Derby and Yasmin (Migoli – Plume II by Vatellor) who finished third in the Oaks. Both were trained in France by Alec Head and Charles Semblat respectively.

The Aga had to wait until the last race at Royal Ascot; the Kings Stand Stakes for his only winner: Palariva as discussed earlier.

*   *   *

1957 was the year that saw the final runners to race under the name of the Aga Khan III. He did not have a runner in the Two Thousand Guineas but he completed his set of Classic wins when Rose Royale II (Prince Bio – Rose of Yeroda by Nearco) won the One Thousand

Guineas. It was a family one-two as Aly owned the second: Sensualita (Polynesian – Peace of Mind by Beau-Pere). Rose Royale won two other races that year including the Champion Stakes and was a possibly unlucky third in the Oaks. Her story does not have a happy end; she was due to be covered by Ribot but died of a tumour in the large intestine in December of that same year.

In the Derby the Aga's final runner was Prince Taj (Prince Bio – Malindi by Nearco) who finished ninth. Malindi was a sister to Nasrullah. Prince Taj, who was trained by Alec Head, had been second favourite but lost all chance when he was sideways on to the gate when it went up. In any event he was better with some give in the ground.

The Aga died on the 11th July 1957 and did not attend what would have been his final Royal Ascot meeting. He only had one winner but it was the impressive Toro (Tudor Minstrel – L'Horizon by Bois Roussel) who triumphed by an emphatic four lengths in the Coronation Stakes. Toro, whose dam was a full sister to Tehran, won the French One Thousand Guineas as a maiden and also the Prix du Casino. At stud Toro was virtually a complete failure: just one living foal; a winner, before her retirement at the age of twelve.

From the time of the switch to France Aly would be mainly responsible for the Aga's racing empire, although the Aga would still have some measure of control. After the Aga's death Aly had to dig deeply to buy out the Begum and his brother: Prince Sadruddin. Aly was only to survive the Aga by just under three years. The future of the Aga's breeding empire was in peril for some time as; again, there were three heirs to what had become Aly's racing and breeding empire. Karim was left 40% as was his brother Amyn and Yasmin, Aly's daughter by Rita Hayworth inherited 20%.

However, if it is assumed that Aly had more input into the breeding and buying side from about 1955, when the Aga's health entered its final gradual decline, then matters began to improve from that time on. During the period 1956 until 1962 the following outstanding horses were bred and raced by the Aga, Aly and, after his death, the Aga Khan IV: – Charlottesville, Petite Etoile, St. Crespin II, Sheshoon, Opaline, Venture VII, Taboun and Empire. Aly would have had an input into all of the matings for these horses and it is not in the least fanciful to suggest that had Aly lived the studs would have prospered under his leadership to a level at least as great as under the Aga during his heyday.

*   *   *

The Aga Khan IV: Karim, just twenty-three when his father Aly was killed, decided to buy out his partners and rebuild the studs. When the Aga had died, in order to meet death duties, Aly had been forced to sell some of the best mares. Now Karim was faced with a similar dilemma and more stock were sold. With debilitating death duties paid twice in three years there was a contraction of numbers and loss of quality. This would need to be rebuilt if the glory days were to return.

It would have been a tragedy if the Aga Khan III's racing empire, continued by Aly Khan had simply been dissipated. It can't be under-estimated just what was required to re-establish and re-build those wonderful bloodlines. It is to His Highness's immense credit that, despite an admitted lack of both knowledge and, initially, interest, he decided to continue the tradition begun many years before by his grand-father.

To do this it was necessary for him to acquire knowledge of all aspects of breeding. With the help of excellent staff, slowly the studs began to recover. Karim became very knowledgeable about breeding and despite other claims on his time, was able to oversee much of the recovery. However, it would not be until 1981 that the colours of the Aga Khan IV would be carried to victory in a major race in England. How appropriate that the mighty Shergar should be the one to hail the return to Britain of this great racing dynasty.

Today the empire begun by the Aga Khan III is in safe hands and it is unlikely that it will decline again and has every prospect of pro-ducing more outstanding thoroughbreds. The only sadness is that Karim has turned his back on British racing; none of his horses are trained in Britain and, although he has many suitable horses, he has very few runners, a quite unjustified slight on racing in this country. Admittedly prize money is derisory in Britain compared with France, but not that far behind Ireland where, in addition to France, he has his horses trained. The best races in Britain compare favourably with all but the Arc de Triomphe in Europe and the British Classic races are rightly considered preeminent. It is significant that when Karim won his fifth Derby in 2016 with Harzand, to equal his grandfather, he was very proud. Hopefully the family will relent and horses will again be trained on British soil and the colours of the Aga Khan can again be seen regularly on British racecourses.

*   *   *

In conclusion it is clear that the Aga Khan III was the most remarkable owner and breeder. He may not always have been the most popular but even his most fervent doubters cannot argue about his achievements. Starting from scratch in 1921 until 1961 when one of the last of the horses he bred: Petite Etoile ran her final race, he was leading owner thirteen times and leading breeder eleven. In addition he was either second or third ten times in the list of leading owners and seven times second or third in the lists of leading breeders. Despite never having large numbers of horses in training in Ireland the Aga was leading owner five times between 1925 and 1956. In 1948 he had nine winners of thirteen races.

The achievements of the Aga Khan III in partnership with Frank Butters, Dick Dawson, George Lambton, Aly Khan *et al* and continued by the Aga Khan VI and in recent years assisted by his daughter: Princess Zahra, both on the racecourse and breeding shed are unlikely to be surpassed.

5 The Aga Khan III; His and other Breeding Methods

"All the breeding theories I've read about – great or otherwise – are equivalent to palmistry, phrenology, scientology, and astrology etc. –all pseudo-intellectual excreta".

Phil Bull.

* * *

The Aga Khan III was a successful breeder by any standards; although it is probably true to say he set his own. When it is considered that, from a standing start, within fifteen years he was outperforming such well-established owner-breeders as Lord Derby, Lord Rosebery, Lord Astor, Sir Abe Bailey, the Duke of Westminster, Lord Dewar and Lord Woolavington the speed of his progress can be readily appreciated.

However, how he achieved this level of success is a matter that provokes some disagreement. Beginning with his friendship with Lord Wavertree (then Col. Hall-Walker) the Aga was, from his earliest days, impressed by his Lordship's reliance on the dosage system as propounded by Col. Jean-Joseph Vuillier. The famous polymath and founder of *Timeform* Phil Bull, almost certainly the finest mind ever to devote time to thoroughbred racing and a successful breeder, described the dosage system as "a load of nonsense". He was not alone in his views.

Bull on various occasions expressed strong views about "breeding experts" some of whom propounded theories and ideas that were in Bull's view preposterous and the perpetrators little better than snake oil salesmen. This was his opinion written about the effect of a stallion with each generation, firstly Tehran in *The Best Horses of 1945*:-

"The popular talking point about him (Tehran) as a stallion is, of course, the possibility that he may re-establish the St. Simon tail-male line. When the more bone-headed of our breeding commentators are tired of extolling the mystical virtues of a tail-female descendent from one of Bruce Lowe's renowned "tap roots" they transfer their attentions to the tail-male descent and bleat about revivals of the tail-male lines of Matchem and St. Simon etc. Apparently, they have eyes only for the top and bottom lines of a pedigree, as though these two "lines" were more important than any other "lines".

Tehran inherited his sex and secondary sex characters direct in the tail-male from St. Simon but so far as his character as a racehorse goes, or his potentialities as a stallion, the Bois Rousel – Vatout – Prince Chimay – Chaucer – St. Simon "line" is of no more moment in Tehran's pedigree than the Bois Rousel – Plucky Liege – Spearmint – Carbine – Musket "line", or any other line. Owing to random gene selection inherent in the mechanism of heredity, these so-called "blood-lines" are not continuities in reality in the same sense that they are continuities on paper. For all we know to the contrary Musket may have contributed more to the heredity make up of Tehran than St. Simon. So where is the sense in prating about Tehran's being a representative of the St. Simon line? It is a fact but what of it?"

Similarly:-

"To suggest that that magnificent stayer of my youth: Brown Jack, bought as a yearling for 110 guineas (£5,200), was bred well enough for the long distance races because he was in-bred to St Simon in the fourth generation with a fifth cross of St Simon's sire Galopin close up in his pedigree, is just a joke".

The top amateur rider, authoritative bloodstock writer and breeder John Hislop, who bred the great Brigadier Gerard, always liked to believe that part of the Brigadier's ability stemmed from his being bred from a mare who was a tail-female descendent of Pretty Polly. Bull noted, or more likely snorted in response, "So far as I am concerned Pretty Polly is merely one of 32 individuals in the fifth generation of Brigadier Gerard's pedigree".

Bull had earlier eviscerated another breeding method: that which used Bruce Lowe's figure system. Lowe's work in tracing back through the female families of the winners of the Derby, Oaks and St Leger to the original mares in the Stud book is of some interest; or as Bull states "He (Lowe) accomplished an unobjectionable though not particularly useful piece of work". Lowe produced a list of 43 original mares: families, which he then placed in order of "merit": number one being the family that had produced the most Classic winners and 43 the least. However, as a guide to breeding durable, faster, sounder and better horses it was, and still is, useless! This did not stop plenty propounding this absurd system including the well-respected journalist William Allison who published Lowe's work after the latter's death. Lowe did not suffer false modesty describing his work as able "to a great extent revolutionise the present methods of mating thoroughbreds".

Despite this work not undergoing detailed critical scrutiny Bruce Lowe's figures were regularly used by breeders for some years. About 1944 Mr. John Loder wrote in *The Field* "Since 1894, the last year Bruce Lowe included in his analysis, there have been 149 more races for the Derby, Oaks and St Leger and the winners of 62 of them (41.6%) have come from families 1 – 5. I think the record of the first five families takes a bit of explaining away", concluded Mr. Loder with extravagant hubris.

In response Bull wrote in *Best Horses 1945* "The trouble with Mr. Loder is that, like nine out of every ten commentators upon thorough-bred breeding, he thinks only in terms of the best horses. Therefore I deem it desirable that just for once his attention should be drawn to the *worst* horses".

To demonstrate this Bull asked Dick Whitford to produce a list of the worst horses to run in selling races during the seasons 1938 and 1939; the last two years for selling races at that time as they ceased to be staged during the Second World War. Whitford produced a list of 430 horses that had each finished last at least once in selling races during the years concerned. Mr. H. Mansfield of *The Sporting Life* then traced the Bruce Lowe family numbers of 379 of them; 46 could not be traced and five were half-bred. Bull was amused and not at all surprised that the families that produced most of these extremely moderate horses were represented in almost exactly to same proportions as Classic winning horses since 1894. Families 1 – 5 produced 154 of the 379 useless selling palters (40.6% as against 41.6%). Quite simply families 1 – 5 produce more Classic winners than any other family and more useless platers for the simple reason that there are more of them!

Any reader interested in more detail should consult pages 470 and 471 of *The Best Horses of 1945* by Phil Bull. It contains a full explanation of Lowe's Figure System and also the full list of "Bruce Lowe Families of Worthless Platers" for the years 1938 and 1939. Extremely entertaining reading and Phil Bull at his best!

In a letter to *The Sporting Life* in 1976 Bull was also in fine form:-

> "This business of tracing back tail-female lines to the nth generation, as though it told you something material about the horse itself is a typical example of the "blood-line buggaboo" (what a great word!). "It is the traditional mystique that I condemn. No geneticist could think in this way".

Bull had little time for those who sought to theorise about the elements of breeding. After Hard Ridden; sired by a sprinter Hard Sauce, had won the Derby in 1958 pedigree analysts were in shock. Bull pointed out that the Derby winner is usually most unlikely to be sired by a sprinter partly because so few such horses ever run in the race. In the previous ten years only three horses sired by a sprinter had even run in the Derby. If a sprinter-bred horse stays middle distances Bull insisted there was no point in searching for the source of the stamina: "He just inherited it and there is no mystery about it whatever, except in the minds of those who think about heredity in terms of "blood". Among the various breeding systems to be found in current literature on the thoroughbred are the family system, the sanguinary system and the fisherman system. The first deals in "tap roots", the second in "blood" and the third in "lines" and their adherents all think in the same dam fool way".

In a letter to Abe Hewitt, the American racing historian in 1984:-

"All the breeding theories I've read about – great or otherwise – are equivalent to palmistry, phrenology, scientology, and astrology etc. –all pseudo-intellectual excreta".

This was his view on books about breeding in 1978:-

"There is practically nothing on breeding in print that is worth reading. The few books on the subject have as much relation to the realities of the matter as astrology has to astronomy – tap roots, inbreeding, out-crossing, sire lines, pre-potency etc. overlaid with the dressing of genetics, mostly misunderstood – it is a world of fantasy".

In saying this Bull was being a little hard on written matter dealing with breeding; he was justified only if an author claimed that his research showed some kind of golden highway to future success. Lowe exposed himself to ridicule, not because of his work which is admirable and interesting in some ways, but because of his preposterous claims for it.

This author has always enjoyed reading books and articles about the theory of breeding thoroughbred racehorses, and is fascinated by the lineage of the best performers. However, no matter how learned the writer, nothing he has ever read convinces him that he is reading anything that offers better prospects of future success, or, even better than average chances of producing a top performer. Better that is than simply breeding well-bred, as opposed to "fashionably-bred", good class racing mares to well-bred top-class racehorses that are proven stallions; if a moderately-bred, non-winning mare is put to a middle or lower ranking sire, the most likely outcome is a below average, poor or useless racehorse; and there are plenty bred along these lines at present.

Conversely if a well-bred mare is sent to a top stallion then there is a better chance, no more, of producing a good or better performer. Obvious isn't it? Yet matings of, at best, ordinary bloodstock still take place on a large scale; resulting in a plethora of very ordinary thoroughbreds. Can anyone justify racing horses that can't run to a minimum rating of 60? Oh, of course, how could anyone forget; the British Horseracing Authority would seem to think the purpose of breeding so many horses is to fill the surfeit of Class 5, 6 and 7 races staged for the benefit of bookmakers! Must get those field sizes up! Never mind the quality just look at all those runners! Whatever happened to those noble ideas of improving the thoroughbred?

Earnest individuals write passionately about certain types of mating, crosses, nicks etc. yet with the benefit of over two hundred years of data and experience, producing a high percentage of good horses, with any regularity, remains tantalisingly elusive. There is far too much "fashionable breeding": sending mares to sprinter-miler stallions that are considered "safe" in that if the produce has good, correct conformation then it will sell at the sales. Few commercial breeders ever seem to consider sending their best mares to be covered by stallions whose pedigrees are not considered by the industry cognoscenti to be acceptable. The result of this is that some perfectly good stallions, usually those that were effective over 10–12 furlongs plus, are being badly underused or worse, if such a stallion does produce a good performer, even from a good mare, and it is a colt, it will be shunned by commercial breeders when it is sent to stud; because, as a stayer, he is unfashionable!.

It is fair to say that simply because Bull had a wonderfully incisive mind, and the capacity to scythe through any fallacious argument, that does not mean that he was always right. However, those who wished to dispute any of his statements would have needed to marshal their case with considerable acuity if they were to prevail in any debate. However, Bull, if he was still alive, could have taken solace (not that he would have done as he rarely, if ever, suffered from self-doubt) in a book: *Pedigree Theories and the Science of Genetics* by Dr Matthew Binns and Tony Morris which exposes many theories and other ideas on thoroughbred breeding which do not stand up to close, sustained examination.

Notwithstanding John Hislop's sentimental thoughts about the breeding of Brigadier Gerard when asked by Richard Baerlein about the Vuillier system he replied "It is interesting to know how many times St Simon, Hyperion, Nearco etc. appear in a pedigree but impossible to tell the scale of their genetic representation. The Vuillier system is genetically nonsense because genes do not conform to a mathematical pattern. If they did all full brothers and sisters would be exactly the same".

On the other hand Nesbit Waddington, who for twenty years until his retirement in 1954 was the under-manager and then manager of the Aga Khan's studs, said "The Aga spent more than twenty years studying and reading every book and theory of breeding racehorses and discussing them with acknowledged experts before finally settling on Colonel Vuillier's ideas. Whatever Bull says, it is a wonderful guide to tell you exactly what proportions of the great horses in the pedigrees of successful racehorses would appear in any intended mating, not guesswork as is usually done by looking at the pedigree of sire and dam". He seems to be saying that the Dosage System does not offer any guarantees with regard to producing a better than average number of top-class racehorses. But it does ensure that there is not too much inbreeding, unless, of course, that is what the objective is.

Notwithstanding this Waddington does not explain how Vuillier helps breed better, faster, sounder and more durable horses with greater regularity. The Aga Khan III may have spent years studying in detail which pedigrees were most likely to produce a good racehorse. However, a more likely reason for his success was simply that he had the resources to out-bid all-comers for the best female blood, and then breed them to the best stallions. It is certainly hard to claim that Dosage was responsible for the good horses bred or, indeed was at fault for the many moderate ones.

H. E. (Harry Edward) Keylock studied the dosage system to assess if it had any merit. He examined the stud records of eight of the best mares: Scapa Flow, Jennie Deans, Selene, Mumtaz Mahal,

Plymstock, Friar's Daughter, Lady Wembley and Resplendent. His verdict was: "Nothing can be found in the results which supports Vuillier's dosage figures".

Vuillier, speaking with industrial-strength hubris, believed completely in his own infallibility: "I can say to those who may be tempted to deny the law of dosage: It is so – and your denial will not alter it, for it is in nobody's power to prove that truth is error".

Even after the dosage system was proved largely ineffective there were still those who sought to provide credibility. Franco Varola during the 1970's revised Vuillier's work in his *New Dosages of the Thoroughbred.* He acknowledged the criticism of Vuillier's theories but was unable to understand the force of the argument. An excellent and concise explanation and faults of the dosage system can be found in Peter Willett's *An Introduction to the Thoroughbred* on pages 56–61.

*   *   *

The result of the Aga's breeding and buying operation in Europe over thirty years, bearing in mind that he was using plenty of the best blood available, was about what might have been expected: one genuinely great horse by any standards, some excellent ones, some very good horses, some good ones, some moderate ones, plenty that were very ordinary and more than enough that were either useless or totally useless. When he used his chequebook the proportion of good horses to others was, again, about what could have been expected when purchasing the very best stock. He bought plenty of colts that were disappointing and a few that never reached the racecourse. However, he did well with the fillies buying enough that became foundation mares for his studs.

On balance he can be considered to have done a shade better than could have been expected; because he employed the best individuals in Lambton, Dawson and Butters and was well organized. Notwithstanding this, it could easily be argued that the Aga's record of breeding Classic fillies was moderate. He bred only two winners of the One Thousand Guineas, one he sold, and two winners of the Oaks.

Earlier it was stated that the Aga was outperforming many leading owner-breeders. However, it is interesting to compare the Aga with the most prominent of them: the Seventeenth Earl of Derby. The Aga had a considerable rivalry with Lord Derby for many years; both were prominent for almost forty years over more or less the same period. Both bred many good horses, however, Lord Derby spent only a fraction at the sales compared to the Aga. It is true to say that Lord Derby inherited a stud and the Aga started from scratch, but he soon made up any lost ground by buying many well-bred fillies in the early years.

The Aga certainly bred and raced many more good horses than Lord Derby. So he should, he had considerably more mares at stud and spent much more at the sales. However, when winning the very best races then Lord Derby fared almost as well as the Aga. Lord Derby owned twenty British Classic winners against twenty-one by the Aga; including My Love which the Aga bought into just before he won the Derby and four that won Classics after his death. Of the other principal races Lord Derby owned five winners of the Eclipse against two by the Aga and if Alycidon is included both owned two winners of the Ascot Gold Cup. Not surprisingly the Aga owned and bred many more juvenile winners then did Lord Derby.

One area interestingly where Lord Derby performed better was the breeding of Classic fillies. Although both bred two winners of the Oaks, Lord Derby bred seven winners of the One Thousand Guineas against the Aga who owned and bred one and bred but sold another. Petite Etoile – winner of the One Thousand Guineas and Oaks – could be added to the Aga's score, because although she raced after his death, she was bred when he was still alive.

Therefore although the Aga probably had a greater knowledge of pedigrees, certainly possessed a much more robust check book and had the services of Col. Vuillier, Lord Derby was still able to match and beat the Aga when it came to producing the best horses. Indeed of those horses generally considered great the Aga bred and raced only Bahram. Lord Derby bred and raced Hyperion and Fairway; in addition although he did not live to see him race, he also bred Alycidon.

In fairness if Alycidon is mentioned then Petite Etoile should be included also.

It seems almost unfair to point out that Lord Derby bred more Champion Sires than the Aga as the Aga did not give most of his best horses the chance to be champion sires before he sold them! Lord Derby bred Phalaris, champion sire twice, Pharos, Fairway, four times, Hyperion six times and Alycidon. The Aga bred Nasrullah who was champion sire once in England and five times in North America. The Aga can also be given credit for Tehran; Champion Sire once and a horse that was strictly speaking bred by Aly Khan. Just imagine; Lord Derby achieved all this without the help of Col. Vuillier and his fancy theories!

It was not as if the Aga started with limited resources, and by using Vuillier's theories, built up a great stud. Waddington together with Madame Vuillier, Robert Muller and the Aga Khan worked out each of the matings. Without detailed analysis of each mating it can only be conjecture, but it is a reasonable assumption that, however much a stallion matched up in terms of Vuillier's theories, he was only used because he had high-class racecourse form and was, by any criteria, well-bred. Notwithstanding this, the success of the Aga Khan's breeding programme was credited to Vuillier's system, and brought it a measure of credibility. Vuillier died in 1931 but his wife continued and the Aga consulted her afterwards. However, it is worth noting that other leading breeders of the period such as Federico Tesio, Marcel Boussac and, of course, Lord Derby did not adopt Vuillier's theories. Despite the Aga giving credit to Vuillier and his dosage theory for helping to build up his thoroughbred empire it is strange that the Aga makes no mention of Vuillier in his memoirs.

Vuillier settled on fifteen stallions and one mare calculated to have appeared with approximately the same frequency in the twelve generation pedigrees of 650 of the most successful racehorses. However, there were five successful stallions: Beresford, Friar Marcus, Foxlaw, Bosworth and Buchan, that, as far as it is possible to tell, were never used by the Aga; presumably because they did not match up to Vuillier's system:-

The table below shows the fifteen stallions and one mare as selected by Vuillier with the standard dosage and the five stallions not used by the Aga Khan with their dosages compared.

	Standard	Beresford	Difference	Friar Marcus	Difference
Pantaloon	140	114	−26	140	0
Voltaire	186	226	+40	224	+38
Touchstone	351	404	+53	412	+61
Birdcatcher	288	296	+8	192	−96
Gladiator	95	96	+1	128	+33
Bay Middleton	127	140	+13	128	+1
Melbourne	184	198	+14	232	+48
Pocahontas +	313	296	−17	368	+55
Newminster	295	416	+121	384	+89
Stockwell	340	304	−36	384	+44
Hermit	235	128	−107	128	−107
Hampton	260	512	+252	512	+252
Galopin	405	512	+107	384	−21
Isonomy	280	256	−24	256	−24
Bend Or	210	128	−82	256	+46
St Simon	420	256	−164	512	+92

Stallion	Standard	Foxlaw	Difference	Bosworth	Difference	Buchan	Difference
Pantaloon	140	44	−96	64	−76	118	−22
Voltaire	186	180	+6	124	62	184	−2
Touchstone	351	464	+113	462	+111	410	+59
Birdcatcher	288	308	+20	232	−56	236	−52
Gladiator	95	112	+17	260	+165	60	−35
Bay Middleton	127	184	+57	168	+41	68	−59
Melbourne	184	248	+64	276	+92	248	+64
Pocahontas+	313	264	−49	256	−77	312	−1
Newminster	295	304	+9	336	+41	384	+89
Stockwell	340	416	+76	416	+76	376	+36
Hermit	235	256	+21	192	−43	192	−43
Hampton	260	256	−4	256	−4	192	−68
Galopin	405	448	+43	320	−85	64	−341
Isonomy	280	512	+232	128	−152	128	−152
Bend Or	210	0	−210	128	−82	256	+46
St Simon	420	0	−420	0	−420	128	−292

+ Pocahontas was the only mare

Incidentally it is worth asking why Vuillier thought only one mare was worthy of inclusion. Were mares really so unimportant in his view? If this author is ever going to be convinced that a breeding method had any chance of consistently breeding high-class performers, it would need to address, at least to some extent, inbreeding to certain mares.

*   *   *

Breeding thoroughbred racehorses has always been, and will remain, a fascinating study; not least researching pedigrees and tracing various lines and crosses and discovering the nuances of how they were bred. But the evidence suggests that, as with finance and investment, past performance is no guarantee to future results! Nothing, it seems, is certain; however, it would appear that after more than two hundred years of selective breeding; those in possession of mares with the best pedigrees have more chance of producing a good horse than any breeder whose mares are moderately bred; even if the latter have access to better stallions. Stating the obvious isn't it!

On a least one occasion, however nature probably knew best: Quintin Gilbey wrote that one knowledgeable and successful breeder, sadly not named, endured several lean years broken only when one of his stallions escaped into a paddock where some of his mares were grazing. One of the mares to whom the stallion gave his attention subsequently produced a foal which, much to his astonishment, was a top performer! If only Gilbey had revealed the horse concerned! Perhaps the breeder was too embarrassed to admit how the horse had been bred: that it was purely a chance occurrence and not an example of his perspicacity!

Conversely consider any breeder who, in addition to a detailed knowledge of his brood mares' blood lines, also understands their physical and mental strengths and weaknesses. Suppose he breeds with the latter elements foremost in mind and only uses a stallion which will marry in well with these characteristics and in addition had proved his soundness and durability on the racecourse over a minimum of three seasons; irrespective of whether the mating would meet with a pedigree expert's approval. Might not such a breeder fare as well on some occasions as those who spend hours studying pedigrees; searching for an elusive as yet undiscovered pattern or, like some modern breeders, simply want to use the latest "fashionable" sire; but do not consider conformation and temperament?

Cavaliere Ginistrelli was convinced his mare Signorina had fallen in love with a stallion that was regularly walked past her paddock. They neighed at each other when they met, something the "Chevalier", as he was known, took to indicate at least a strong affection and, as an Italian romantic, he was convinced it was a love match! He decided that the stallion, the Cesarewitch winner Chaleureux, was worth his nine guineas (£600) covering fee and sent Signorina to him. The result was a filly, Signorinetta, who remarkably won the Derby and Oaks of 1908! *Amor vincit omnia et nos cedamus amori!* There are those today that would smirk and sneer at this story; however, having had a good laugh, they might like to reflect on their own record of breeding Derby and Oaks winners!

In any event, it would seem safe to say, that if anyone, from any side of the bloodstock breeding industry, thinks that they have discovered the secret of how to consistently breed good, correct, sound and durable horses that possess, in proportion, stamina and speed, they should, perhaps, consider spending some time in what the American's euphemistically refer to as a "clinical facility".

The evidence is inarguable: the percentage of horses produced, even by the best stallions out of the finest brood mares, where the mating was the result of considerable knowledge and expertise, that can't run very fast or are not sound enough to stand training, does not appear to be decreasing. Tattersall's "horses in training" autumn sale; where dreams often go to die, there are plenty of well-bred horses that go through the ring for a fraction of their cost the previous year as yearlings.

In no other walk of life is it possible to move so quickly, to use an automobile metaphor, from the slick showroom of the pristine Ferrari and Porsche to the Arthur Daley second-hand car lot. Some are reasonably well-bred fillies that are ether unsound or just simply too slow, these are picked up cheaply and then some optimistic individual will send her to a middling stallion or sometimes worse, a very cheap failing one. The resultant foal will in all probability be another dream which has only a very remote chance of being realized. Therein lies the genesis of over production.

This failure to improve the percentage of good runners to foals suggests that either stallion owners are happy for their horse to cover any old mare; possible with some moderate, underused stallions but most unlikely with the best ones. It is more probably that no one has yet discovered a fool-proof, or even a sound and plausible method, of mating that regularly produces good, sound and durable horses that have stamina and speed to a high degree. In most cases they are simply playing percentages.

It is not so long ago that a top stallion would be restricted to covering forty mares a year. However, that might mean no more than about four possibly five good performers each year and sometimes only one or two. The number of mares gradually increased when modern veterinarian knowledge improved and it was possible for a mare to be accurately assessed when she was ready to be covered. Stallion owners began thinking that if their stallions covered twice, three times or even five times as many mares would this not increase the chances of producing more top performers?

Take for example the top stallion in Europe: Galileo. In 2014 he was represented by as many as 35 horses that could be classed as "good" performers or better: winners as two-year-olds and up at Listed and Pattern level in Europe. However, to achieve this he was covering over 150 mares each year and in the four years from 2011 to 2014 he had covered 214/196/193/179 mares respectively in those years! It works then! Cover four to five times as many mares and produce proportionately more good performers. So that's all right then. No it is not! It not only fails to produce proportionately more good horses but what about the contracting gene pool? It is already difficult to find a stallion or mare "free of Northern Dancer". In addition was it certain that Galileo, wonderful stallion though he is, was the best one suited to every mare he covered? The great Frankel when he took up stud duties could not cover some good mares because they were by Sadler's Wells or Danehill; he will need to make his way with some non-Northern Dancer line mares. Comparing stallions of the past that covered just forty mares with any leading stallion today is impossible due to the number of mares covered at present by many of the most popular stallions.

These excessive numbers also result in plenty of the progeny by leading sires that are moderate or worse. The percentage of mares bred too has increased from 23% about forty years ago to 52% today. Are they all really worth breeding from? What percentage were sound enough to stand training? How many were maiden racehorses and had not produced a winner at stud? Even with the best mares nothing is remotely certain; how many yearlings in the last thirty years have sold at public auction for in excess of one million dollars/ pounds? What percentage of these was able to win at Pattern level? Remarkably few, yet all of them would have had at least a reasonable, in some cases a good and, in many, outstanding conformation. In addition, most yearlings in this group would have had a flawless pedigree, or if not, at least, a "fashionable one". Those responsible for buying at the sales might also like to reflect that as well as paying plenty for some moderate sorts in recent years outstanding performers Golden Horn, Treve and American Pharoah were all led out unsold when presented at the sales. However, this may have been because the respective sires for these three champions were Cape Cross, Motivator and Pioneerof the Nile; none of whom are top of the lists of most bloodstock agents.

For all the claims of various well-qualified, experienced breeders: those whose job it is to decide which stallion a mare should be covered by, often using so called "nicks" and what one "respected" observer wrote recently "cutting edgy genetics and statistics", whatever that might mean; the feeling persists that the old rule, however simplistic it is, might still produce comparable results: based on racecourse performance; mate the best to the best and hope for the best. Just one proviso: make sure that the sire has been thoroughly tested on the racecourse and the dam is well-bred, has good racecourse experience is sound and matches up with him physically and temperamentally!

The outstanding dual Derby and International Stakes winner Australia is a good example: by Galileo; Derby, Irish Derby, King

George winner out of Ouija Board; Oaks, Irish Oaks, Nassau Stakes, Breeders Cup Filly & Mare Turf etc, a tough mare raced and fully tested over four seasons. That was a mating which hardly required the services of any breeding consultant! Ouija Board helped to explode another myth that is constantly trotted out: over-raced mares often fail at stud.

Joe Estes, legendary editor of *The Bloodhorse*, who spent years compiling statistics on breeding and who treated all theories with considerable suspicion, concluded that "there is no more sense in laying down rules for breeding racehorses than laying down rules for throwing dice". He believed that any theory claiming that by breeding along certain lines a disproportionately high number of good horses will be produced, should also publish figures showing the percentage of moderate horses produced by the same methods.

This is not intended as a diatribe against those involved with breeding, buying and owning racehorses. The contempory blood-stock market is a difficult area in which to make money and is cursed with "fashionable" ideas and an obsession with sprinter/miler stallions. In addition the ill-considered stated aim of the BHA to increase the number of horses in training will not improve the quality or the standard, something that should surely be one of the objectives of breeding thoroughbreds. On the contrary it is likely to result in more moderate, unsound and largely useless horses; many not even good enough for those dreadful class 5, 6 and 7 races.

To conclude, although there are many who may dispute this, as far as breeding thoroughbred racehorses is concerned, it is probably fair to say: *"vitam regit fortuna non sapientia!"* it is mostly a matter of luck!

*   *   *

The Aga Khan's mares were mated studiously according to Vuillier's principles. This resulted in him banking heavily on the alliance of the high-class stamina of Gainsborough and Blandford with the speedier elements derived from Phalaris and The Tetrarch. The great majority of his brood-mares eventually carried the blood of Blandford, whilst of his five Derby winners; Blenheim and Bahram were sons of Blandford and Mahmoud was a grandson. Udaipur and Umidwar were also by Blandford.

*   *   *

It is interesting that in his autobiography the Aga discusses the great horses he has seen. The best two in his opinion were The Tetrarch and Spearmint. He also notes Ard Patrick, Sunstar and Sardanapale and suggests that Sceptre and Pretty Polly are the only fillies that can be compared with these. However, his most interesting observation concerns a colt named Prestige about whom he says "I am not at all sure that Prestige was not the most impressive racehorse I ever saw".

A contemporary of Prestige (Florizel II – Orgueilleuse by Le Pompom), was Maintenon (Le Sagittaire – Marcia by Marden) who won the French Derby in 1906 but was beaten by Spearmint in the Grand Prix de Paris. However, according to the Aga, when tried together, even after a hard gallop Maintenon could not get "within twenty lengths" of Prestige. Their trainer William Duke claimed that no weight – even three stones – could bring them together. Unfortunately Prestige was never entered for the Classics and was unbeaten and largely untested in 16 races – usually making the running. Prestige was said to be on the smallish side with a charming disposition and his lasting legacy was that he was the sire of Sardanapale. Bearing in mind that the Aga considered conformation to be overrated it is perhaps the comments of Duke that should carry more weight!

*   *   *

Even his strongest defenders would find it impossible to convince anyone that the Aga Khan considered racing a sport. He saw it as a business that had the immense attraction of testing his considerable mental powers to their maximum. The problems and challenges involved in attempting to breed champion racehorses fascinated him. However, whenever success was achieved the satisfaction thus gained was never tempered by sentiment. It is for this reason that praise for the considerable achievement of building probably the greatest bloodstock empire ever seen at that time, and probably since, is tempered by a feeling that he badly let down both the British race-goer and bloodstock breeders.

The Aga rather disingenuously claimed that he kept horses because they bought pleasure to millions. If that was true he would have tested them more thoroughly on the racecourse which in turn would have provided tremendous entertainment. Aly would have none of it; "after all, father and I are just a couple of horse traders. Some people are in this business for fun, we are in it for profit" he said rather more candidly.

This writer contests that in Bahram the Aga Khan bred possibly the greatest racehorse since the beginning of the Twentieth Century. But the truth of this will never be known; because the Aga showed no interest in thoroughly testing Bahram on the racecourse. He was never fully extended in either a race or a gallop and retired sound. The Aga was quoted as saying "To breed another Bahram is beyond my wildest dreams". Notice he said "to breed" not "to breed and race".

To the Aga producing a thoroughbred as good as Bahram was the end in itself; the feeling persists that racing to him was sometimes an incidental: a rather tiresome adjunct that had to be gone through to prove the point. Having said that he did enjoy leading in a big-race winner! Had someone like Lord Derby bred such a horse he would have stayed in training and contested weight-for-age races as a four-year-old. This will be discussed in more detail in the chapters dealing with Bahram.

The Aga Khan also retired Mahmoud, although he had plenty to prove after an unfortunate Classic year, even though he did win the Derby. Retiring fillies is possibly a different matter, although it was not until Aly Khan had Petite Etoile that an outstanding filly from the Aga's empire was fully tested beyond the age of three. She was without doubt a great racehorse and a popular filly who gave immense pleasure, excitement, and, on occasions, some nerve-racking moments, to race-goers.

"I'm a great believer in my own young stallions because they have not been over-raced. If mares are better for not being over-raced, then it should apply to horses as well. My horses are not submitted to long periods of training and racing". These words spoken by the Aga Khan III in the late thirties show how little he considered the racecourse to be all important. But was he right? Some outstanding stallions had many hard races without it causing any harm. Certainly it would be unwise to over-race a horse with a light frame or weak constitution; but who would breed from such a horse anyway?

The Aga states that it is better not to over-race fillies as if this is some rule that must not be disobeyed. He had clearly never heard of Beeswing (Doctor Syntax out of an un-named mare by Ardrossan). Foaled in 1833, Beeswing stood just 15.2 hands, with a "sweet head" and "although rather light of bone" she had "capital hips and ribs". She raced for eight seasons and won over 50 races including the Champagne Stakes, Ascot Gold Cup, Doncaster Cup, on four occasions and Newcastle Cup six times. She was retired after her final victory in the Doncaster Cup. In those times the training for cup races was particularly arduous, even brutal, and Beeswing was exceptionally tough. After a year where she was used as a hack she was covered by Touchstone and produced in 1846 Nunnykirk who won the Two Thousand Guineas and was second in the St Leger. She also produced in 1848 Newminster (also by Touchstone) who won the St Leger and was Champion Sire twice. In addition she produced the fillies Honeysuckle and Honeydew; both by Touchstone. Newminster is thought to have founded a great male line and Honeysuckle was the ancestress of many famous winners. Beeswing was considered a most influential tap-root mare.

The Aga might also have liked to reflect that his own Teresina was raced seventeen times over three seasons. Although she won only four races she was placed in six races; four of which are today ranked as Group 1 races, plus the Cesarewitch. At stud she produced nine winners from fourteen foals; racing obviously did her no harm!

Considering Champion Sires who raced from the beginning of the Twentieth Century several were thoroughly tested on the racecourse. The following table shows horses that were all raced over at least three seasons and raced more than any of the Aga's best horses:-

	Number of times Champion	wins/starts	ages raced
Polymelus	5	11/31	2–5
Bayardo	2	22/25	2–4
Lemberg	1	17/22	2–4
Phalaris	2	16/24	2–5
Buchan	1	11/17	2–4
Tetratema	1	13/16	2–4
Pharos	1	14/30	2–5
Fairway	4	12/15	2–4
Hyperion	6	9/13	2–4
Alycidon	1	11/17	2–4
Ribot	3	16/16	2–4
Mill Reef	2	12/14	2–4
Kris	1	14/16	2–4

In North America the figures are even more startling:-

Bold Ruler	8	23/33	2–4
Bull Lea	5	10/27	2–4
Sir Gallahad	4	12/25	2–4
Broomstick	3	14/39	2–4
Fair Play	3	10/32	2–4
Heliopolis +	2	5/15	2–5
Princequillo	2	12/33	2–4
Halo	2	9/31	2–5
Deputy Minister	2	12/22	2–4
Round Table	1	43/66	2–5
Dr Fager	1	18/22	2–4
Alydar	1	14/26	2–4
Broad Brush	1	14/27	2–4

+ Raced principally in Britain
All of the above raced over at least three seasons.

Missing from the above is Nearctic who was never leading sire but produced Northern Dancer. Nearctic was an exceptionally tough, brave, front-running, fast horse that won 21 of his 47 races over four years. However, until retirement from racing, the only fortune Nearctic enjoyed was to be trained initially by Pete McCann; in all other respects the only luck he had during his racing career was bad. His owner, other trainers, particularly Horatio Luro, a racing manager who refused to listen to McCann and some of the ten different jockeys that rode him, badly let him down. On one occasion he was raced with bucked shins (inflammation of the cannon bone) and when he put his head to one side in pain his jockey: George Walker, struck him in the eye with his whip. He was frequently raced with quarter cracks in his near fore hoof; and blinkers were fitted when he tried to run out due to the pain.

Despite all of this Nearctic always tried his best; such courage is humbling, how could he possibly have still trusted those in charge of him? Nearctic was criminally used and over-raced and that he survived such appalling abuse is no thanks to anyone involved in his care – McCann apart, who was always given the job of nursing him back to health when the others had seemingly done their worst – and to sire Northern Dancer, is close to a miracle.

It is significant that few high-class, well-bred or "fashionably-bred", North American colts that showed classic form as a three-year-old and offered the potential to be a commercial stallion, has been fully tested on the racecourse in recent years. The golden age of North American racing, which began in the thirties, probably ended with the retirements of Sunday Silence and Easy Goer in 1990. Since then the vast majority of top performing colts have been retired to stud at age three. This is partly due to increasing unsoundness, caused by a combination of a policy which is obsessed with speed which has breed out stamina and, in many cases soundness and durability. Breeders have overused some fast but unsound sires and combined with the use of race-day medication soundness and durability has definitely suffered. Breakdowns of the leading colts in North America are commonplace every year and there can be no doubt that the typical North American thoroughbred is significantly less tough and sound than their predecessors of 30 or more years ago. Keeping California Chrome in training as a four-year-old was a welcome change, although it is not imagined that breeders were desperate for his services. What is encouraging is that he has improved again as a five-year-old and as this is written has raced twenty-one times. When he does retire to stud he can be marketed as a stallion that was fully tested on the racecourse!

Unfortunately, even more enlightened owners-breeders such as

Juddmonte Farms and Sheikh Mohammed have retired horses that should have been raced as four-year-olds in order to demonstrate their soundness and ability. Empire Maker was obviously considered to have done enough by winning three Grade 1 races at age three. So after just four wins from eight starts at age 2 & 3 he was dispatched to stud by Juddmonte Farms. He was described as retiring sound and "an extraordinary physical specimen with the genetic prowess and raw racehorse ability of a modern day Man'o War". This author saw him in the paddock and on the racecourse as a three-year-old and would concur with most of that statement with the exception of the Man'o War claim, which is preposterous. Empire Maker was seriously under-raced.

Bernardini raced only as a three-year-old winning six of his eight races, including three at Grade 1 level, before he too was sent to stud. He was described as "A brilliant, beautiful Champion"; this is true: this author also saw him in the paddock and racecourse and has seldom seen a more imposing, attractive sort. There was no excuse not to race him as a four-year-old.

It is possible to have some sympathy with the Aga where fillies are concerned; such was the ignorance prevailing that during the thirties when physical exercise was popular among the masses it was the intelligent view that women should not be too energetic. Medical men earnestly entreated them not to take vigorous exercise as it might impair their prospects of conceiving! However, there is sufficient evidence to suggest that his views on not over-racing colts were, to put it kindly, misguided and possibly dangerous to the future prospects of the thoroughbred. Plenty of colts have raced strenuously and still been outstanding sires. It has not been possible to find any other leading figure at that time who concurred that colts should not be subjected to a thorough examination on the racecourse. On the balance of evidence the Aga's view on restricting the number of races his top horses run in has little substance: *cadit quaestio!*

*   *   *

The Aga Khan III was probably the first owner-breeder to routinely retire his best horses prematurely whilst still sound. Until his time horses were bred to race and then after a colt had achieved all that he could on the racecourse the most successful were used as stallions. Commercial breeders were in the minority and racing was essentially about racehorses with stamina and soundness considered most important. Today of course it is principally about breeding; establish a colt's reputation as quickly as possible and then retire him to stud. One owner of a top three-year-old was quoted as saying that there was no question of the colt racing next year as breeders could not wait to use him! Those who continue to race their horses after they have won at the top level are to be thanked and congratulated.

This practice of retiring thoroughbreds prematurely is also the *modus operandi* of the present Aga Khan: Karim. When asked in an interview about retiring three-year-olds to stud he replied "Each sport has its own dynamic. A golfer or tennis player will have a professional career which will be longer than a skier or skater. I personally don't think one can change the dynamic of horse racing. What we have to recognise is that it is an issue and try to work around it". Apart from being a masterpiece of diplomacy that would do credit to any high-ranking diplomat, this is no answer at all.

The Aga Khan IV continued when asked if prematurely retiring colts was a matter of losing a year's income or the chance the colt's value may decrease; "It's a two-fold question. The first is; what's the probability that a four-year-old career will add credibility or value to the horse? Secondly, you lose a breeding year. Statistically, the younger stallions are the most successful. As the ageing process goes on they tend to slip off the radar. Very few stay up there throughout their lives. So it becomes a question of good sense and logic more than anything else".

This was an answer his grand-father would have been proud of: the competition on the racecourse is of far less importance than that between breeders! Since when did breeding become a spectator sport! In another, earlier interview he was more succinct: "Stallions are the economic driver for the rest of the operation". This is definitely so; but can't it wait just one year while the colt concerned proves that he really is tough, sound, durable and top-class by beating the next generation?

To be fair to His Highness it should be made clear that he stated at the beginning in 1960, following his father Aly's death, that racing would not be a pastime: "I made up my mind to run the studs and the racing not as a hobby but as a business". He would therefore be following the practice of his grand-father.

Without putting words into his mouth is Karim saying that older-horse racing is only for those below Group/Grade1 standard? Sheikh Mohammed, despite Bernardini, has demonstrated that the best horses can be raced at four and it is to the benefit of both breeders and race-goers. Khalid Abdulla, despite Empire Maker, kept Workforce and Frankel in training at four when he could easily have retired them after their three-year-old careers. It did not prove a successful decision in Workforce's case but with Frankel the racing world was able to marvel at the sight of a mature thoroughbred, in his case the best there has ever been in Europe, at the peak of his powers.

Coolmore, despite sadly dispatching Australia to stud prematurely, have kept more good horses in training at four and helped to provide some exhilarating older horse racing in recent years. One can only have the most enormous sympathy that Camelot; a very talented horse with outstanding conformation; this author's idea of an outstanding thoroughbred physically, not only failed to win the Triple Crown, but, after a severe attack of colic, failed to reproduce his best form as a four-year-old. Despite the best of efforts of Aiden O'Brien and those at Ballydoyle it is quite probable that Camelot's true potential was not fully realised on the racecourse. Camelot has everything a breeder could wish for in a stallion: exceptional conformation, high-class speed and stamina in equal proportion and, for a Montjeu, an excellent temperament. It is hoped he will be highly successful and replace his much lamented sire at Coolmore.

Whilst trying to be fair the feeling persists that the response of the present Aga Khan to keeping his best three-year-old colts in training indicates a cold and detached view of thoroughbred racing. It suggests that nothing is owed to the sport that helped establish a horse's reputation and confirms the view that the purpose of racing at the top level is simply to establish what a colt is worth as a breeding tool. It also shows an incredible lack of curiosity about how a top three-year-old might perform as an older horse. Instead of worrying about loss of value consider the possible increase if he beats the best of the next generation!

There is only one example of a three-year-old horse, colt or filly, bred and raced by the Aga Khan IV, that was rated 130 or better by *Timeform,* being raced at aged four and older.+ This was Vayrann; who was rated 133 by Timeform at three and 123 at four. Sadly Vayrann broke down at four and could not in the event justify the decision. However, at least his soundness was tested; as it should be in an ideal world. Conversely the decision to keep Azamour in training proved to be a great success. He was rated 128 at three but 130 at four when he won the Prince of Wales's Stakes and King George. Curiously neither race was staged at their normal venue: Ascot, which was undergoing rebuilding at that time.

In addition Sendawar, rated 129, was kept in training and, although he was only rated 125 at aged four, he did win a race and provided vital opposition for Dubai Millennium in the Prince of Wales's Stakes at Ascot; thus essential racecourse evidence for breeders was combined with high quality entertainment for the race-goer!

There are only two other examples to consider: Lashkari; who was rated 128 at three and 127 at four and was thoroughly tested on the racecourse. Behkabad was rated 125 at aged three but broke down in his only race at four. There are, however, another twenty-three Group 1 winners from 1960 to the present day all of which were retired after their three-year-old seasons.

At a risk of stating the obvious, the great advantage of keeping horses in training is that a new generation can be tested against the best of a previous one. Is that not the purpose of breeding thoroughbreds: to test them against each other? Surely thoroughbred breeding is about producing racehorses based on pedigree, soundness, durability and performance and testing the best ones to the limit on the racecourse. Then using the best and most sound to produce the next

+ Daylami was rated 124 by Timeform after his three-year-old season. He was subsequently rated 138 but was by then owned and raced at ages 4 & 5 by Godolphin.

generation. No of course it isn't! It should be but that has not happened for many, many years and the sport at the top level is considerably the poorer for it.

None of the foregoing is in any way intended to detract from the wonderful breeding operation run today by the Aga Khan Studs. It should also be remembered that when His Highness inherited the studs in 1960 they were in decline and run by mature individuals somewhat stuck in their ways. It required considerable time, patience and expertise to rebuild. They have since achieved pre-eminent status, not least because of their willingness to use stallions that commercial breeders would consider "unfashionable". In addition while conscious of the need for high-class speed, Karim's studs aim to produce horses that can race over a variety of distances, including twelve furlongs plus, something most commercial breeders seem terrified of doing. This is simply a plea to His Highness to race all his best produce, particularly the colts, and thoroughly test them on the racecourse against different generations. It can only be to the benefit of the sport and the breed.

In addition Karim has sensibly reduced any reliance on Vuillier's dosage method as he rightly points out that with stallions now covering such large books of mares it would produce an imbalance. It is also significant that Karim is different from his grandfather in one particularly important respect: conformation. In an interview he gave in the late 1990's he said "Conformation is also a major issue. There are families that are "long in the back", "light of frame" or "temperamental". Others have their own particular traits and idiosyncrasies that in my experience are consistently hereditary. These are the reasons why the Dosage System, though still an important consideration, is for me less dominant than it was".

Returning to the Aga Khan III, an even greater disservice was done to British bloodstock by the selling of his best stallions to North America. Shortly after Mahmoud won the Derby in 1936 he sold his sire: the Derby winner Blenheim for £45,000 (2,160,000). This was bad but nothing compared to his selling Bahram for £40,000 (1,760,000) and Mahmoud for £20,000 (880,000).

This decision drew universal condemnation, particularly from Lord

Derby, and he responded by banning the Aga from sending any of his mares to his stallions, which of course included Hyperion. The only way the Aga could get into Hyperion was by buying at the sales. His endeavours in this respect were not entirely successful, although the Aga's purchase of Stardust out of Sister Stella by Friar Marcus for 1,450 guineas (£62,400), from the National Stud, was a definite plus as Stardust won £7,582 (310,900) in winning prize money and was a successful sire.

The Aga also bought a 12 year-old mare with a relatively moderate record of production: Éclair (Ethnarch – Black Ray by Black Jester) for 3,500 guineas (£150,700), who was tested in foal to Hyperion. The resultant progeny was a colt called Khaled; who was unbeaten as a juvenile but went in his wind as a three-year-old. He was sold abroad to North America; but this was more because he had a wind problem but nonetheless was a success at stud. Incidentally the buyer of Khaled: Rex Ellsworth was considered a good judge of thoroughbred and spent a considerable amount of time studying a horse before he brought it. Harry Wragg went with Ellsworth to view Khaled and exclaimed "You can't buy him, he makes a noise". Nonetheless Ellsworth went ahead and purchased Khaled for $160,000 (£40,000) (1,360,000). So successful was Khaled that Ellsworth founded his stud upon him. Probably the best horse he sired was Swaps (out of Iron Reward – Beau Pere) who won the Kentucky Derby.

However, the Aga was less successful with some of his other purchases of Hyperion progeny:-

Hyderabad (out of Castle Gay by Buchan) – 8,200 guineas (£353,000); he looked very immature in his portrait but otherwise nice enough.
Hyder Ali (out of Éclair by Ethnarch) – 8,200 guineas (£353,000).
Al Dakhil (out of Queen Christina by Buchan) – 12,500 guineas (£538,000)).
Al Wassat (out of La Cerenentola by Miracle) – 8,200 guineas (£353,000).
Al Nasser (out of Olein by Colombo) – 6,700 guineas (£288,400).
El Hawa (out of Silver Birch by Blandford) – 7,600 guineas (£327,200).

In total his spending on the above progeny of Hyperion amounted to 53,970 guineas (£2,323,400).

They won between them £5,988 (245,508) and made a total of 10,290 guineas (£442,990) when re-sold. The reader can probably guess that Al Dakhil, the most expensive, raced four times as a three-year-old without winning; including the Eclipse Stakes, and recouped only 2,100 guineas (£90,400) at the sales. His picture shows a colt very much in his sire's image and looked very taking. So desperate was the Aga to use Hyperion he bought the Sandwich Stud; in all probability because it had a nomination to Hyperion. According to Marcus Marsh the Aga was very excited about the purchase!

To return to The Aga selling his best horses, although it was not fully realized at the time, possibly his worst and most damaging decision was the one to sell Nasrullah. Although the Aga did not sell Nasrullah to North America he spent only one year in England before transferring to Ireland and then to North America six years later. It is easier to understand this sale as Nasrullah had possessed temperament problems when racing and was, if anything, worse in retirement and he had been savage and almost unmanageable at the Barton Stud. Even so he was beautifully bred and should, perhaps, have been given a better chance in Europe. He was more tractable when transferred to Ireland, although few who had been in close contact with the horse at the Barton Stud, regretted his departure.

Nasrullah was sold after standing for that one season in Newmarket to the "Nasrullah Syndicate". This consisted of only two men who passed him on to Joe McGrath for 19,000 guineas (£718,200). In late 1950 he was sold to "Bull" Hancock; acting on behalf of a syndicate of American breeders for $370,000 (£128,000), (£4,590,000).

When in North America Nasrullah was much better behaved, particularly after "Bull" Hancock had hit him over the nose, and he would prove to be a colossal influence in North America; siring many fine horses including Bold Ruler who sired the mighty Secretariat, probably the greatest racehorse ever foaled.

These were not the only horses disposed of; as discussed in the previous chapter, it seemed that almost any colt with potential as a stallion was sold. However, in some of these cases, as with, for instance Palestine, the horses were transferred to syndicates in which he retained a large number of shares. In this way he was able to still send mares to these stallions.

Had he done this with Blenheim, Bahram, Mahmoud and Nasrullah there would have been no ill-feeling and of course British breeders would not have missed out and the Aga would have realised some of his asset. Something that in today's rather vulgar parlance would have been called a win/win situation.

Cashing in on his best bloodstock was painful enough for a British breeder but, astonishingly, in his later years in discussion with Quintin Gilbey he lamented the dearth of good stallions. It is impossible to believe that he did not understand that this was in part caused by his own practice of selling his best horses to North America! As late as December 1956 he started a controversial correspondence in the Times under the heading "Saving British Racing".

In view of his decision to remove almost all of his horses from Britain this on its own shows a certain lack of sensitivity but when he commented on the "steady flow of our best horses to North America" he was fortunate the opprobrium he attracted was not more venomous. Lord Rosebery, ostensibly an old friend of the Aga's, but who in reality had very little affection or regard for him, was content to chide him as being "by far the worst offender...though by no stretch of the imagination could he be called a poor man". In his letter *The Sporting Life* editor, Mr A. B. Clements, included in the statement "The Aga Khan's interest in bloodstock is primarily that of a dealer."

Lord Derby, who was of course very hostile to the Aga Khan, and expressed himself forcibly on several occasions; writing to Lord Rosebery in 1942 he clearly had no time for the Aga; "What a rotten fellow he is, I was always against electing him an Honorary Member of the (Jockey) Club and should like even now to get rid of him, but do not know if we can...I cannot stand the man myself". On another occasion he wrote to Lord Rosebery "I like you hate the idea of the Aga Khan winning any big race. He is very mean. He is not prepared to do anything to help racing. All he wants is to get his money".

With regard to selling his best stallions, in fairness to the Aga it is only right to put his side of the argument. He admitted that he sold

Blenheim when well off and not in need of any money. But he says nothing on the decision to change his mind about keeping Tulyar in training, simply stating that he could have sold him for $1,000,000 (£340,000), (9,520,000) to North America but instead sold him to the Irish National Stud for £275,000 (7,700,000), claiming that it was the prospect of him remaining in Europe that attracted him to the sale, which was without any restrictions on the contract. Lord Rosebery made reference to the sale of Tulyar in his 1952 Gimcrack speech and stated "A leopard does not change his spots". Tulyar stood for three years in Ireland before being sold to North America. He was seriously ill on arrival and largely a failure.

However, his defence for selling Bahram and Mahmoud are more interesting. Both were considered to be worth huge sums before the war: between £175,000 (8,400,000) and £200,000 (9,600,000) each. However, they were sold for £40,000 (1,760,000) – Bahram and £20,000 (880,000) – Mahmoud. Why? The Aga claims he was forced to decide between selling his best two stallions or breaking up his stud and parting with his best mares and thus parting with blood lines built up between 1921 and 1940.

Between 1940 and 1945 he claims his position was misunderstood. This was discussed in the previous chapter and he was definitely short of money. At this time the Battle of Britain was beginning and the majority of France was occupied. In addition he was being treated for a serious glandular problem amongst other things. During those years he claims his family lived on the sale of those two horses.

Despite this it still does not explain the sales of Blenheim before the War and Nasrullah and Tulyar afterwards, although in the latter's case at least the horse stayed in Europe, if only for a limited period. The feeling persists that all that would have changed was the amount paid: if there had been no war, offers would have been made from North America and in all probability the Aga would have sold. In any event at least he was honest and he never claimed that he would not have sold in different circumstances.

In his autobiography the Aga discloses that he offered his stallions and mares to the National Stud at the outbreak of the War for about one tenth of their value. Lord Rosebery wrote to Lord Derby in 1942 to say the Aga had offered his entire stud to a friend of his in September 1939. Assuming the former offer to the National Stud was true then it seems astonishing that the Ministry of Agriculture should decline this offer. Was Lord Derby or the Jockey Club consulted? If Lord Rosebery informed Lord Derby about an offer then he, Lord Derby, probably was not.

The Aga says that he then travelled to Florence in order to offer the Italian government the chance to buy all of his horses for about half their value. He states that in 1939 the Italian's were non belligerent and he hoped to use the money to buy British War Loans. An agreement was reached at the highest level with two conditions: the money was to be paid immediately and the horses were not to be delivered until hostilities had ceased. However this was forbidden by Mussolini personally.

In the event he sold all his yearling colts in 1940 and retained the fillies. As there were no sales at Doncaster and Newmarket the Aga offered eleven of the twelve colts he had bred for sale as a lot for 400 guineas (£18,500) each. Had they been sold at an auction individually in normal times they would have realized ten times as much. This generous offer was quickly accepted by Mr A E Allnatt and he became the proud possessor of eleven of the finest bred colts possible. There was a downside: buying colts in war time was risky with the possibility that there might not be any chance of racing them.

*   *   *

In the final analysis it must be conceded that the Aga Khan's decision to enter thoroughbred horse racing and breeding was to the benefit of the sport. However, if a question was asked "Did the Aga Khan III's decision to enter the world of thoroughbred racing and breeding enrich and benefit BRITISH racing and breeding"? The answer then would probably be "on balance partially yes, but more so, no."

The Aga bred and raced some wonderful horses; but retired many without testing them thoroughly, which deprived the British race going public of the chance of seeing them doing, what after all should be the purpose of their existence: racing. At that time the best horses were usually raced as four-year-olds and therefore, by the Aga retiring them early, breeders were denied the chance to check on their durability and soundness.

The Aga did not benefit British racing because he sold his best horses abroad which deprived breeders of the chance to use them. Under different circumstances, it is entirely possible that the horses he bred could have been bred by others if they had owned the mares the Aga brought and bred. It is also possible that had the same horses been bred and owned by more sporting owners, they might have raced more. The colts could then have stood in Britain and benefitted British breeders. Even those who disagree with this analysis would have to concede there is, at least, a case to answer.

Conversely a leading journalist of the Aga's time: Sydney Galtrey, who knew him well, believed that if the Aga had been able to influence matters he would have removed the severe restrictions placed on the tote by Act of Parliament. The Aga would have seen the problems which beset the tote at the time and have done so right up to the ill-advised sale just a few years ago to a bookmaker which has effectively killed it. He would have expanded it and reduced the influence of bookmakers and thus bringing prosperity to the sport.

By further restricting the Tote deductions to six per cent racing could have been transformed with the wealth created; better prize money, new racecourse facilities built and a thriving breeding industry to compare with anywhere in the world. How many individuals in racing today, whose employment does not depend on bookmakers, would say he was wrong? The current desperate state of racing in Britain might have been prevented...

*   *   *

The Aga's breeding empire had been showing signs of a steady, gradual decline but enjoyed a slight renaissance under Aly. The Aga was essentially a theoretician somewhat inflexible, obsessed with bloodlines, utterly committed to Vuillier's doubtful theories, ignorant about racehorses as living creatures and uninterested in conformation. Aly was much less theoretical and more practical and broad-minded; he thoroughly understood horses, was a competent amateur rider and a good judge of conformation.

Under Aly's guidance between 1955 and 1961 horses bred during that time and running in the family name again won the best races in Europe. This was despite him having to buy out his siblings and Yvette on the death of the Aga. Aly had inherited only two fifths of his father's breeding and racing empire and after heavy death duties the number of mares had been reduced from 174 to about half this. By the time of Aly's death just three years later he had ninety mares and seventy horses in training, sixty-four with Alec Head. This required some retrenchment and the studs were further reduced after Aly's death when Karim took over. It was many years before the studs under Karim regained their prestige. Carefully and gradually he rebuilt the studs and returned them to their place of prominence that they have enjoyed for forty years.

6 Frank Butters; Part one

It is a perfect summer's afternoon on Eclipse Stakes Day at Sandown Park. In the paddock before the big race a trainer looks particularly tense as he studies his runner carefully. The colt seems relaxed but on his previous appearance on Derby Day at Epsom, when a warm favourite, he had become very upset and fractious and lost all chance of securing the Blue Riband. If the horse again becomes overwrought, he, as the trainer, would be subject to considerable criticism. The trainer can only watch and hope that his charge will stay calm and produce his best.

*   *   *

Joseph Arthur Frank Butters was born near Vienna in December 1878. He was the eldest son of Joseph (Joe) Butters, and his wife Janet, daughter of James (Jimmy) Waugh and sister of Willie, Charles, Dawson and Tom Waugh, all of whom were trainers. Joseph and Janet had four sons: Frank, Fred (who trained Mid-day Sun to win the Derby in 1937, Jim and Oliver (who trained Reichenau winner of the Austrian Derby in 1918) and a daughter: Isobel who married the trainer William Rose Jarvis.

Isobel and William had a son: Ryan Jarvis who trained at firstly, Clarehaven Stables and then Phantom House Stables where his son: William Jarvis trains today. William Rose and Isobel also had a daughter: Bridget who married the famous jockey William (Bill) Rickaby.

Frank's father Joseph Butters was born on the estate of the fourteenth Earl of Derby (who was Prime Minister on three occasions) at Knowsley in Lancashire in 1847 where his father, also Joseph was kennel man. At the age of thirteen Joseph Butters junior was apprenticed to John Scott at Whitewall near Malton, although his indentures were later transferred to the above mentioned James Waugh.

However, due to a lack of opportunities in England he accepted an offer in 1873 to ride for the Emperor Franz Josef in Austria-Hungary.

Frank's father had married in February 1878 and returned to Austria with his bride. In December of that same year Frank was born. Joseph was a greatly respected figure who rode the winners of many important races in Austria, Hungary and Germany and, although afterwards a successful trainer for Baron Nathan de Rothschild. Joseph returned to Newmarket in 1903 with an excellent reputation as a developer of horses.

Joseph's first employer in England was Prince Soltykoff, a prominent member of the Jockey Club. However, this was soon terminated by the Prince's death and, as Joseph had been abroad for thirty years, he experienced some difficulty in stablishing himself. Slowly he built up his stable until by 1911 he had fifty horses in training at Kremlin House.

The best horse he ever trained was Nassovian (William the Third – Veneration by Laveno). Owned by an American John Sanford Nassovian was foaled in 1913. Physically he was unfurnished as a juvenile, kept good company, but could manage only a second in five starts. As a three-year-old he improved considerably; having furnished to his frame and began with a third in the Two Thousand Guineas behind Clarissimus and Kwang-Su; a half-brother to Bayardo and Lemberg.

Nassovian then headed for the New Derby. Unfortunately Mr. Sanford decided to replace regular jockey Nathan Spear with a more fashionable American Frank O'Neill. O'Neill was Champion jockey in France but lacked experience of riding at Newmarket. This may well have been a factor in a driving finish with Nassovian beaten a neck and a head into third place behind the filly Fifinella and Kwang-Su. Spear was back on board for Nassovian's final race of the year which was the Princess of Wales's Stakes which he won comfortably with odds of 5–2 laid on him. A cracked heel kept him from racing again that year.

That proved to be his only win. At four he could only manage a third; well-beaten behind the great Gay Crusader in the Champion Stakes, and two unplaced efforts before he was retired to stud.

Joe Butters trained until 1926 and died in 1933 at the age of eighty-six leaving behind him memories of a cheery, kind-hearted man who liked to do a good turn to everyone. He was a picturesque character; short of stature, with sharply-chiselled features, always in a hurry but never failing to respond to a chorus of "Good morning Mr Butters". He was until his dying day, a spruce, spare figure who believed the maxim: "Up with the lark and breathe the pure morning air".

It can be seen that on both sides of his family, Frank Butters was closely related to Newmarket trainers, and no family has done more to contribute to the town's fame as a training centre, with Butters the most famous representative. However, Frank Butters was neither born in Newmarket nor was he established there until he was nearly fifty.

*   *   *

Frank Butters had spent his youth among the horses in his father's stable near the Imperial City. He returned to England to be educated at Framlingham College in Suffolk spending his school holidays with his Waugh relatives in Newmarket. Among his contemporaries was Alfred (later Sir Alfred) Munnings. On leaving Framlingham Butters re-joined his father as his assistant. Some years later Frank was engaged by Herr Von Mautner-Markhof, a very rich brewer, a member of the Austrian Jockey Club and a leading owner-breeder. Butters was employed as a private trainer in charge of Von Mautner-Markhof's strong stable of between eighty and one hundred.

Probably the best horse Butters trained in Austria was San Gennaro a bay colt by Gomba out of Celestine by Cyllene. Despite the problems presented by the Great War he won the Austrian Two Thousand Guineas and Derby plus the Hungarian St. Leger in 1917 amongst other important races. He won sixteen of his twenty starts. Butters had earlier won the Austrian Two Thousand Guineas in 1912 and 1913 with Mokan (Tokio – Moneta by Kisber Ocscse) and Blondel (Blocksberg – Blindes Gluck by Ladas) respectively.

*   *   *

Frank had three brothers who all became trainers: Fred who joined

Frank in Austria before returning in 1919. He trained at Beverley House Stables, where John Berry trains today, and then at Heath House, where Sir Mark Prescott is in majestic control. Fred took over at Kingsclere, where in the 1880's John Porter had trained the mighty Ormonde, in 1934 and won the Derby with Mid-day Sun in 1937 but when Kingsclere was closed down in 1939 Fred returned to Newmarket. He retired in 1950 and died in 1967.

Jim Butters always wanted to be a vet but his father insisted he work at the stables as a secretary and liaison with the owners. He served in the Great War and stayed on in the Army afterwards.

Oliver was a trainer in Austria but a riding accident at an early age affected him mentally and his career ended.

*   *   *

During the Great War Frank Butters and his brother Fred were held captive, along with other members of the British racing community in Austria-Hungary. However, as the American Embassy stood surety for their good behaviour their detention was only nominal. It is fair to say they enjoyed a degree of freedom; certainly greater than was granted to internees in other counties. Frank was able to carry on training in much the same way as he had before war was declared but on a reduced basis. After the Armistice Fred returned to England but Frank, with most of his savings now gone, remained in Austria in the hope that the stable would recover to its pre-war eminence. This proved impossible under the Bolsheviks and on the advice of Prince Kinsky he left and took up an appointment in Italy.

Butters' time in Italy was very successful winning over a thousand races in just six years, including all the Classics, for the Razza Bellata stable. Butters "would always be remembered not only as an able trainer but also a thorough gentleman who made many friends while sojourning in Italy".

*   *   *

In 1926, and approaching fifty, Frank Butters returned to Newmarket as private trainer to Lord Derby at Stanley House, having being offered a four-year contract. Although he had been a successful trainer until this point, from this time onwards the great years of Frank Butters' career were about to begin.

*   *   *

George Lambton had suffered a nasty fall at Stanley House stables during October 1925 and was not in the best of health. Lord Derby discussed retirement with Lambton with the end of 1926 considered the most suitable time. Butters had already been approached about the possibility of taking over at Stanley House when Lambton retired.

From Lord Derby's point of view Butters was a most suitable choice with his family association and history. Even so Lord Derby was a sensitive man and probably realised that taking over from Lambton would be no easy task for Butters despite his experience.

Butters was initially paid an annual salary of £1,500 (63,000) plus 10% of winnings, and for 1926 only, he was to assist George Lambton whose salary was £2,000 (84,000). This was hardly a satisfactory arrangement as, although Lambton was someway short of being in the best of health, he was certainly well enough to be constantly looking over Butters' shoulder and ever ready to criticise his methods. It might have been worse as the original idea had been that Butters would not take over until 1928, an option he would probably have declined. This idea was that Butters would spend 1926 travelling about to familiarise himself with English racing, spend 1927 as Lambton's assistant and take over in January 1928. It seems it was George Lambton's decision that Butters should assist him in 1926 and take over in 1927.

So it was that Butters was responsible for the training Lord Derby's horses from 1927 and Lambton for entering and running them; a recipe for discontent one might think! So it was to prove. It could not have helped that Lambton considered Butters to be "not much of a horseman!"

*   *   *

In 1927, his first season in sole charge, Butters was leading trainer narrowly beating Alec Taylor; who retired as trainer at Manton at the end of the season. The principle money winner for Butters was the four-year-old Colorado (Phalaris – Canyon by Chaucer), the Two Thousand Guineas winner of the previous year, who in 1927 won five races including the Eclipse and Princess of Wales's Stakes. Had the medium-sized, good-looking and powerful Colorado been able to maintain his best form throughout his three seasons racing, he would have been rated with the greats. Unfortunately, after a most promising juvenile season, where he won the Coventry Stakes before losing form, fortune did not favour him at three.

After his Guineas win Colorado's chances in the Derby were compromised by Lambton's instructions to Tommy Weston to hold him up; the pace was moderate and he could not make up the ground. Coronach was a well above average Derby winner and it was not at all certain that Colorado would have beaten him in any circumstances on Derby day. Colorado was below form at Ascot; he was suffering from some sort of equine rheumatism and did not run again that year.

As a four-year-old Colorado was slow to come to hand but by the time of the Eclipse Stakes in July he was back to his best. However, George Lambton refused to consider running him in the race as he thought Colorado had no chance of beating last years Derby winner Coronach! It has not been possible to discover what the trainer's view was! Butters was in charge of training and advised Lord Derby of their health and form. Lambton as manager decided where the horses would run and advised Lord Derby accordingly. Colorado's jockey Tommy Weston was unable to persuade Lambton to change his mind; so he took the bold decision to approach Lord Derby directly.

His Lordship was persuaded by Weston's pleas and allowed Colorado to run against Coronach in the Eclipse. There were only three runners but Colorado vindicated Weston; who was very confident and said as much to anyone within earshot. Colorado beat Coronach, winning easily by six lengths. Sadly though, Coronach had gone in his wind; he failed to hang on for second place, and the victory lost some of its lustre.

In 1927 Butters trained his first Classic winner in the Oaks with Lord Durham's homebred Beam (Galloper Light – Mistrella by Cyllene). Beam, the best horse ever bred by His Lordship, was a big rangy filly with a tremendous stride and was not the sort of horse thought to be suited by Epsom. Her size meant that she was not trained too hard as a juvenile and her only win came on her fourth appearance in the Houghton Stakes at Newmarket run over a mile. Displaying excellent stamina she won by 8 lengths.

As a three-year-old she won a mile handicap and was then fourth in the One Thousand Guineas; running on after losing ground at the start. Her next start was the Oaks a tremendous race with Beam prevailing by a head from Lord Astor's Book Law (Buchan – Popingaol by Dark Ronald). They were six lengths clear of the third: Sir George Bullough's Grande Vitesse (Hurry On – Lanessa by Corcyra). The time; 2 mins 34.60 secs, was the fastest in the history of the Oaks at that time.

Unfortunately Beam's next race was her last; the Gold Vase at Ascot. Weston was not considered to have given the filly the best of rides and she had a very hard race in defeat and was never really sound afterwards. It was unfortunate that she was not entered for the St Leger, because in those circumstances she would probably not have run at Ascot and Doncaster would have suited her admirably.

Stanley House could also boast the champion juvenile: Fairway (Phalaris – Scapa Flow by Chaucer), who looked to be an outstanding prospect for the classics; winning the Coventry, July and Champagne Stakes. In addition Butters trained the winners of the Middle Park; with Pharamond (Phalaris – Selene by Chaucer) and Dewhurst Stakes with a filly, Toboggan (Hurry On – Glacier by St. Simon). Although by Hurry On Toboggan looked nothing like him and had more the look of St. Simon. Lord Derby headed the lists for both leading owner and breeder.

*   *   *

Butters followed up by retaining his title in 1928 beating Fred Darling by over £25,000 (1,100,000). He may have been the leading trainer in terms of money won but this level of success brought its own pressure; an example of which occurred in 1928 after Fairway had proved a huge disappointment in the first two classics. He missed the Two Thousand Guineas with a mouth abscess; but he soon recovered and won the principal Derby trial, after the Two Thousand Guineas, the Newmarket Stakes, easily.

It can only be conjecture but it may be that if Lambton was ever correct about Butters it could have been with regard to his training of Fairway in the early part of his three-year-old season. Lambton had noted how light he was as a two-year-old and had written in an article in early April 1928 that "he is a light-framed colt that in the early part of the season may be difficult to train. I can foresee some anxious moments for Frank Butters". Fairway's sire and grand-sire had both taken time to come to hand as three-year-olds and Lambton feared that Fairway would be the same.

In suffering from an abscess luck had not favoured Fairway causing him to miss the Two Thousand Guineas, but he threw away his chances in the Derby by getting very over wrought. As if this was not enough he then suffered from the attentions of his admirers; who mobbed him and pulled hairs out of his tail in the parade which caused him further considerable distress.

Theodore Felstead asked Butters what had gone wrong with Fairway in the Derby. Butters replied "He had been difficult to train; he had gone too light, as I watched him parading for the race and then going to the post, I gave up all hope". As Lambton had noticed that Fairway was light-framed then one can only assume Butters was aware of it too. In addition it was known that Fairway was a nervous, highly-strung colt. By Butters own admission Fairway was light in condition, something Lambton noticed as well, and it is not unreasonable to conclude that his training schedule may have been too arduous for a lightly-made sort who had not come to hand. The result was that he was in no state to contest the Derby. Tommy Weston always believed that Fairway was "overstrained and stale" before the race.

Whatever, the truth there can be no denying that Butters care of Fairway was exemplary between the Derby and the Eclipse Stakes where he confirmed his quality; winning by eight lengths. In addition to supervising Fairway's recovery from his unpleasant Derby experience, Butters had to contend with Fairway developing a cough and slight temperature which placed his participation in doubt. Even so, according to his memoirs, Tommy Weston felt compelled to lie to Butters one morning between the Derby and the Eclipse. Weston felt Fairway was getting overly stressed and was not in any state to gallop six furlongs; his work scheduled for that day. Butters, taking Weston's word, agreed that the work should be abandoned; something that in Weston's view prevented any harm to Fairway.

After the Eclipse Butters betrayed the pressure he had been under by confessing to Eric Rickman "I shall sleep tonight for the first time for weeks". Whatever the truth behind Butters handling of Fairway's training up to the time of the Eclipse, it was faultless from then on as he also won the St Leger and Champion Stakes as a three-year-old; and five of his six races as a four-year-old. Fairway was rather leggy, light-framed sort but according to George Lambton possessed "beautiful shoulders and the best set of legs and feet I have ever seen on a racehorse; hard ground or soft came alike to him". Fairway was due to stay in training as a five-year-old with the Ascot Gold Cup as his objective; unfortunately he sustained an injury, for which Lord Derby held Butters responsible, and he was retired.

Close behind Fairway in winning stakes for 1928 was the filly Toboggan who also won four races including the Oaks, Coronation and Jockey Club Stakes. She was slow to come to hand and it was not possible to get a preparatory race into her before the One Thousand Guineas where she ran on to take third place. The race brought her on considerably by the time the Oaks was run and she had the race in safe keeping some way out and prevailed by four lengths and six. She then won the Coronation Stakes at Ascot before walking over at Chepstow in the Welsh Oaks.

However, starting at odds of 7–2 on Toboggan was beaten at Liverpool in the £2,779 (117,000) St. George Stakes. No reason emerged for this disappointing effort and it may have been the ground which was in a "bad state". She concluded her career by winning the £5, 687 (240,000) Jockey Club Stakes. Unfortunately she broke down afterwards and was retired.

Toboggan suffered from a bad mouth but was intelligently ridden by Weston who never restrained her and felt she was always a better filly when allowed to run her races in her own way.

*   *   *

Butters continued to enjoy success finishing third in the trainers table in both 1929 and 1930, winning the One Thousand Guineas in the latter year with Fair Isle (Phalaris – Scapa Flow by Chaucer) which made her a sister to Pharos and Fairway.

Fair Isle stood at only 15.2 hands. However, she was of considerable quality, and, like her brother Fairway, a wonderful mover and preferred firm going. Unfortunately she was not a good "doer" and could not stand much hard work. She was also a bad traveller and would kick and sweat and this, on occasions, compromised her chances.

As a juvenile she won three of her five races; including a walk-over. As a three-year-old she won two of her five races: the One Thousand Guineas and Midsummer Stakes. The Guineas was a tremendous battle with Fair Isle, the 7–4 favourite, prevailing by a short head from Anthony de Rothschild's Torchere (Pomme de terre – Torchlight by John o' Gaunt) with Sister Clover (Friar Marcus – Miss Sainfoin by Sainfoin) a further neck away.

Hopes were high that Fair Isle would win the Oaks. However, she became very upset on the journey to Epsom and did not eat up. She seemed more herself on the day of the race and went into the paddock looking restored. She was made the 11–10 favourite but failed to show any sparkle behind Rose of England (Teddy – Perce Neige by Neil Gow). Incidentally she was bred by Lady James Douglas the first woman to officially own a Classic winner. Lady James saw her colours carried to victory by Gainsborough in 1918 when he won the Triple-Crown.

Fair Isle was at her best on the Bunbury Mile winning the Midsummer Stakes. She conceded 11 pounds to each of five colts in opposition and won "comfortably" by three lengths. Unfortunately dropped back to six furlongs at Goodwood in the King George Stakes she had run up light, sweated, was slowly away and never able to threaten. She concluded her career with a creditable third in the Champion Stakes behind The Aga Khan's Rustom Pasha (Son-in-Law – Cos by Flying Orb).

One horse that promised much was Hunter's Moon (Hurry On – Selene by Chaucer). As a juvenile in 1928 he had shown promise in two outings: the Prince of Wales's and Gimcrack Stakes. Although by Hurry On Hunter's Moon was only medium-sized but well-made and possessing a long stride. Unfortunately he did not like firm ground and at three in six outings he was favoured by heavy ground only once. After finishing second in the one mile Union Jack Stakes at Liverpool, Hunter's Moon won a ten furlong stakes race at Newmarket then finished fourth in the Two Thousand Guineas. He re-opposed the Guineas winner: Mr. Jinks (Tetratema – False Piety by Lemberg) in the Newmarket Stakes and, benefiting from an excellent front running ride by Weston, beat him a short head in a pulsating three way finish with Midlothian (Son-in-Law – Lammermuir by Sunstar) a further short head away in third.

Hunter's Moon again made the running at Epsom and ran a fine race to finish fourth unfortunately the effort left him with sore shins. He was rested to recover from this and produced another decent performance to win the valuable: £2,388 (105,000) Gratwicke Stakes at Goodwood. However, shortly afterwards Lambton warned that the ground was causing Hunter's Moon problems and he was retired and sold to a breeder in the Argentine. It is not hard to imagine that in a wet summer Hunter's Moon could have achieved much more.

Considered equally good as Hunter's Moon and sharing a similar going preference was Bosworth (Son-in-Law – Serenissima by Minoru), who had been beaten a short-head in the 1929 St Leger. Bosworth was a well-made sort and a natural stayer; Butters noted "The offspring of Son-in-Law are considered better on hard going, but Bosworth prefers it a little on the soft side, which he did not enjoy as a three-year-old".

Bosworth had been backward as a juvenile and had raced only once; finishing third. As a three-year-old he won two of his eight races: the valuable: £2,612 (115,000) St. George Stakes at Liverpool and a moderate plate race. However, that does not tell the whole story; his overall form was only just below the very top as he finished placed in four good races: Royal Standard Stakes where he was second, King Edward VII – third, St. Leger – second, Jockey Club Stakes – second.

Butters had done well to keep Bosworth going for as many as eight races as he disliked fast going and preferred some give in the ground. However, the ground for all his races varied from good to hard and Bosworth did not race on any ground with give in it all season.

In 1930 Bosworth won two of his four races: the Burwell Stakes and Ascot Gold Cup. The latter one of the slowest renewals of all time: over five minutes due to a crawl until halfway. The Gold Cup was run on soft going which must have been very agreeable to Bosworth. His other races were a second in the Princess of Wales's Stakes on hard ground, and his last race where he sadly broke down, a third in the Atlantic Cup, ironically run on soft ground.

However, all was not well. At the York August meeting Lord Derby informed Butters by letter that, due to the acute world-wide economic crisis, he would be compelled to reduce his racing commitments. The result was that Butters' contract would not be renewed in December despite Lord Derby finishing as leading breeder and third in the list of leading owners. Butters himself finished third in the list of leading trainers, and had been in charge of the winners of the One Thousand Guineas, Ascot Gold Cup and Jockey Club Stakes!

Lord Derby may well have been feeling the cold economic drought that was prevailing following the disasters of the previous year, when many prominent individuals had found themselves bankrupt. However, it would seem that he had always harboured some misgivings about Butters training methods and, at Lambton's instigation, considered this a good opportunity to be rid of him.

Lord Derby had shown concern in 1929, a relatively moderate year for his horses, and considered terminating Butters contract at that time. Furthermore in a letter to Lambton he expressed himself quite forcibly:-

"Everything tends to prove that Butters is quite incapable of training a big stable. I do not know what we are to do. I feel that one will probably have to give him a chance again next year, but if he does not do better next year I shall certainly make a change. We cannot go on like this. He is doing just what you say, not giving the horses enough slow work when the ground is hard, and then rushing at them as soon as it begins to get soft, and breaking them down".

Despite this Butters still finished third in the trainers table with sixty winners! Lord Derby continued to have doubts during the winter and became convinced that Lambton should have more day-to-day management of the stables something he confided to him in June 1930. Finally both agreed that Lambton should take over the training of the Stanley House horses which necessitated dismissing Butters and this decision was communicated to him at York. His Lordship, on his own admission, took a cowardly course by not speaking to Butters directly but instead giving him a letter.

In addition to the world-wide financial crisis the letter also blamed higher taxation, plus the unfortunate loss of three top-class stallions and, while this was certainly true, a feeling persists that a face-to-face meeting, honestly telling Butters that he was also unhappy with him as a trainer, would have been better. It must be remembered that, although the Great War changed many aspects of life in Britain, there was still considerable class distinction. Lord Derby had been accustomed to dealing with George Lambton, who was his social equal. Possibly because Butters' father, and indeed grandfather, had been born on his estate, Lord Derby would have dealt with him as an employee. This would not have been as comfortable when compared with the more relaxed relationship he enjoyed with Lambton.

Essentially a kind man it is to Lord Derby's credit that he offered to help Butters in any way he could and confided to Lambton that he did not want it made public the real reason for Butters dismissal. He then states that he "has not the slightest doubt that Fairway, Caerleon and Bosworth would still be in training if it had not been for this absolute lack of knowledge on Butters part" He is then guilty of a *non sequitur* by saying that if Butters were to set up a stable he would be inclined to send him two or three horses! Strange if he felt Butters had broken down three of the best of them!

George Lambton, who had never agreed with Lord Derby that he was too unwell to train, certainly had no remorse for his part in Butters removal. A vet in Liverpool expressed the view that Bosworth had not been suffering from a chill; but was simply too tired when beaten at the July meeting; he never ran again. Lambton wrote that after speaking to Lord Derby's jockey Tommy Weston, he had even less pity for Butters' plight and that Weston was delighted that Lambton was to take over again. Lambton is guilty of hypocrisy for he wrote shortly after that he was "most genuinely sorry for Butters"! In addition he wrote "at times I hated myself for having brought it about"! Weston has nothing further to say to Butters detriment in his autobiography *My Racing Life* so he can add nothing on this point.

With regard to Bosworth this seems rather harsh; Butters had kept him going when the ground was firm and hard so he could hardly be as incompetent as that otherwise Bosworth would not have seen out his three-year-old season. It is hardly surprising that Bosworth was tired; simply being trained for the Ascot Gold Cup is arduous enough but presumably Bosworth had been working well enough otherwise he would not have run so well in both his races afterwards.

With regard to Caerleon (Phalaris – Canyon by Chaucer); a full-brother to Colorado, Butters could not have done all that much damage as he won the Eclipse Stakes the following year! Fairway developed tendon problems in the spring of his five-year-old season although how much of this can be attributed to Butters training or just one of those things is hard to say. Certainly in the case of Fair Isle he did little wrong in safely getting her to the races ten times in two years despite her somewhat delicate nature.

Lambton's biggest worry was that he might blurt out the real reason for Butters' dismissal, which was not economy, but that "he was quite incapable of managing a big English stable". Lambton remained convinced that Butters started giving the horses' fast work too soon. He clearly had a moderate view of Frank Butters; he even told Lord Derby, when Butters first arrived, that he was not much of a horseman when discussing the subject of hacks!

*   *   *

Frank Butters four year tenure at Stanley House can nonetheless be considered successful. He trained four classic winners plus the winner of the Ascot Gold Cup and the Eclipse Stakes twice. It is impossible to say whether the results would have been better if Lambton had been in sole charge or, indeed, not as good. It is to an extent speculation but the available evidence seems to suggest that once George Lambton had returned to full health, he longed to be in full control again. He felt that, as Butters did not train horses in the same manner as he did, they would be better off under his care. Lord Derby would have taken Lambton's advice and in the circumstances it is not surprising that the outcome was the eventual dismissal of Butters and Lambton's return as trainer at Stanley House.

The conviction that it was George Lambton, and not Lord Derby, who was the instigator of the idea that Frank Butters was an incompetent trainer, stem from His Lordship's apparently genuine praise for him at moments of success, and just as importantly, when enduring narrow defeat. After Butters first year of training: 1927, Lord Derby wrote to him with congratulations on being leading trainer. In addition he thanked him for "all the care and attention you have given to the stable and to which I attribute our very great success". When Fairway won the St. Leger Lord Derby wrote to Butters praising his "training and patience with the horse". After Bosworth's brave defeat in the St Leger, Lord Derby wrote sympathetically to him, noting that he had "never seen a horse look fitter or better" he then congratulated him on his training.

Much of the foregoing does not seem to show George Lambton, in particular, and, to a lesser extent, Lord Derby in a very favourable light. This should not be taken as a slight on either of these two distinguished men of the turf. However, this chapter is primarily about the life of Frank Butters and how Lambton and Lord Derby featured in his professional life. Most of the available evidence suggests that they should probably never have employed Butters; as the circumstances placed him in a situation where he found it almost impossible to do his job to the satisfaction of both. The chapters on the Aga Khan's life in racing and breeding are a better reflection on George Lambton's judgement and Lord Derby, it should not be forgotten, was a giant of the turf and highly distinguished in many other walks of life as well.

*   *   *

All this meant that as 1930 drew to a close Frank Butters found himself unemployed aged 52 and with his reputation potentially at risk whenever George Lambton discussed him! Butters displaying considerable courage and faith in his ability and, without the promise of a single horse, took a lease on Fitzroy House stables; owned at that time by Victor Sassoon, and subsequently bought by Butters. The previous trainer was J. H. Crawford who had moved to Fitzroy House in 1926 to be the private trainer to Sir Victor. After Crawford's death Sir Victor moved his horses from his own yard to Carlburg Stables to be trained by Charlie Waugh.

Butters first two patrons were A W Gordon, who sent two horses inside a fortnight, and Sir Alfred Butt who included in his draft a rebellious sort: Lord Bill, a four-year-old maiden who was reputed to hate racing. Butters however, thoroughly reformed Lord Bill and persuaded him to win eight races from fifteen outings, including the Chesterfield Cup; not something that a trainer who was too hard on his horses would have managed it might be thought! Butters ended the year with 49 winners and finished ninth in the trainers table. Considering that he started from scratch this was a remarkable achievement; it was also 19 more than George Lambton trained at Stanley House with a full yard of better bred horses than Butters had!

*   *   *

Frank Butters had survived his first year and would have had every reason to be satisfied with it and could justifiably have been looking forward to 1932. However, his prospects were suddenly enhanced by an event that was of seismic proportions in the world of racing. Butters training career was about to be transformed.

7   Frank Butters; Part two

It is a few minutes after 7 a. m. on a morning of gentle breezes and pleasant sunshine on Newmarket gallops. A rather stern looking figure sits atop his hack as the charges under his care gallop past him in groups of two's and three's. He tenses slightly, sits up straighter and looks with extra vigilance as a trio of particular interest come towards him. As they pass, he notices that two of the riders are hard at work in an effort to persuade their mounts to keep pace with the third horse, which is moving effortlessly alongside displaying an easy, long stride. The rider on this horse is virtually motionless glancing over his shoulder in wry amusement at the futile efforts of his work companions. As he views this most satisfactory spectacle the stern-faced man allows the merest trace of a smile to pass over his face.

*   *   *

The Aga Khan's horses were trained by Richard Dawson at Whatcombe and the association had enjoyed considerable success. However, as was explained in the chapters on the Aga Khan, their relationship was under strain as a result of disagreements over policy. Such lack of harmony could only eventually end one way and the Aga's horses were removed and, although some went to Michael Beary's brother John, the majority: seventeen were sent to Fitzroy House. This decision is dealt in more detail in the chapter on the Aga Khan's life in racing. Surmise to say that Butters reputation plus his handling of the horses under his control during 1931 had obviously produced a favourable impression. "I had gone racing a lot on the continent" said the Aga, "and I knew Butters' reputation well in Germany, Austria and Italy. I knew the pre-eminence and honesty of Butters".

The Aga's altercation with Dawson at Newbury was on 26th

September and just four days later, after the Aga's horses arrived at Fitzroy House Butters sent out Bahram's half-brother Dastur (by Solario) to finish a close-up third in the Hopeful Stakes at Newmarket. When he first arrived Butters formed the view that Dastur had a nervous temperament. However, this proved not to be the case it was simply that Dastur took some time to settle in at Fitzroy House.

At the end of October Butters saddled Firdaussi (Pharos – Brownhylda by Stedfast) to win the Dewhurst Stakes which today would almost certainly be a juvenile's last race of the season. However the Dewhurst was worth £1,505 (70,700) and, although an important race, was not the most important juvenile race in those days; that was the Middle Park Stakes worth £3,180 (149,400) and a month later there was a race at Hurst Park worth more than the Dewhurst! The Hurst Park Great Two-Year-old Stakes was worth £1,550 (72,850). Imagine a course today of a similar standing to Hurst Park, (which closed in 1962 taken by rapacious property developers) putting on a race of any description worth that amount! Firdaussi finished second.

In April Butters had been able to welcome a decent sort in the form of the four-year-old Orpen (Solario – Harpy by Swynford). As a three-year-old in the care of Joe Lawson he had finished second in the Two Thousand Guineas and third in both the Derby and St Leger. Entered at the dispersal sale of the late Sir John Rutherford at Newmarket in April Sir Alfred Butt went to 6,600 guineas (£332,600) to secure him. With the depression and the bloodstock market in a somewhat volatile state Orpen could be considered well bought at the price. Unfortunately he proved disappointing winning only the two mile Churchill Stakes at Ascot from three runs; in both the other two he was unplaced. He did not race again that year after Ascot but did much better in 1933 winning the Yorkshire Cup (handicap) and finishing second in the Ascot Gold Cup which was his last race.

*   *   *

Butters first full year in charge of the Aga Khan's horses: 1932 saw success in the Oaks and Coronation Stakes with Udaipur (Blandford – Uganda by Bridaine). In the St Leger he saddled four horses for the Aga Khan, who could not make up his mind which ones to run, so ran all four of them, and they finished first, second, fourth and fifth. This remarkable monopoly caused King George V to remark "I hear they call it the Indian Circus". Firdaussi, who won the St Leger, also won the Jockey Club Stakes and Dastur, who finished second in all three Classics and the Champion Stakes, was successful in the Irish Derby. In the St Leger Firdaussi had been the third of the four Aga Khan's runners in the betting at 20–1. However, Frank Butters bet Geoffrey Gilbey ten shillings (50 pence) (£26) that he would finish in front of the other three. Butters had been certain that Firdaussi would run a big race as he had only recently managed to get strong work into him as the going eased.

The Aga had no idea which horse had won between Dastur and Firdaussi; "Firdaussi" someone shouted to him! "Splendid" the Aga retorted; "That comes of managing my own horses. I insisted on running him because I thought he had a great chance". Before the race the Aga had been heard to say his best chance of winning lay with Dastur or Udaipur. Indeed, Dastur carried the first colours and Udaipur the second! Almost everyone else thought Dastur; second in the Two Thousand Guineas and Derby, would win, although Frank Butters of course gave Firdaussi a chance.

The Derby winner, April the Fifth (Craig an Eran – Sold Again by Call o' the Wild), was well beaten in 13th place. However, he had suffered a bad knock to a knee and was sore only a week before the race and had been a doubtful starter right up to the last moment. He could not possibly have been ready for a race like the St Leger.

Winning two Classics in his first season training for the Aga removed any pressure Butters may have been feeling. Udaipur raced only as a three-year-old as she was too backward to be trained as a juvenile. She won four of her eight races: the Oaks – as a maiden – Coronation Stakes at Ascot, a minor stakes race at Hurst Park and Newmarket Oaks. She was unplaced in the One Thousand Guineas and fourth in the St. Leger. She was a good if not outstanding filly but physically she was "a lengthy filly of great quality, deep through the heart, with exceptional length from hip to hook". Her Oaks was not a great race and even Butters remarked that she "was the best of a moderate lot". He also said she was "possessed of a splendid disposition and was very game". At stud Udaipur produced six winners from nine foals the best of which was Umiddad by Dastur whose career will be covered later.

The handsome Dastur was a good horse but below the level where he could be considered equal with the very best. Butters described him as "just about a model of a horse", Dastur was "exquisitely moulded, stood about 16.00 hands and combines great strength with exquisite quality. He is perfectly balanced on the best of limbs". Dastur finished second in all three Classics. However, had these performances been sufficient to have won the Triple Crown he would undoubtedly been the worst horse to have achieved that accolade; and that includes Common. Dastur was comfortably out-speeded by Orwell (Gainsborough – Golden Hair by Golden Sun) in the Two Thousand Guineas, and although beaten less than a length by April the Fifth in the Derby, few would claim Dastur was a better horse.

In the St. Leger Dastur was beaten a neck by his stable companion Firdaussi with the third four lengths further back. Finally in the Champion Stakes he was easily beaten by the previous year's Derby winner: Cameronian (Pharos – Una Cameron by Gainsborough).

To his credit, Dastur was a tough, consistent and genuine sort; as a juvenile he won two of his five races, as a three-year-old he won three of his eight races. Apart from his seconds in the Classics and Champion Stakes Dastur won the King Edward VII Stakes at Ascot, The Irish Derby and Sussex Stakes. In addition he was second in the Free Handicap. He was therefore not out of the first two all year and ran from April to October. At four he won two of his six races; the Coronation Cup and Champion Stakes (dead-heated). Sadly he was not great success at stud.

Firdaussi had more the look of his dam than his sire and was not as good-looking as Dastur; more leggy and weak as a juvenile and still looking a shade unfurnished as a three-year-old. As a two-year-old he won three of his five races. As a three-year-old he was beaten in his first five races, but won his last four. In addition to the St Leger he also won the Jockey Club Stakes beating Cameronian. However, during the early part of the year he had been coughing and was a sick horse and endured an interrupted training schedule and it was only in the second half of the season he was able to demonstrate just how good he was. After returning to form in the Eclipse Stakes, where he finished third, Firdaussi won the Gordon, Duke of York, St. Leger and Jockey Club Stakes.

Kept in training as a four-year-old Firdaussi won only one of his seven races; and that was a match with odds of 25–1 laid on him. He was first past the post in the John Porter Stakes – run in September at that time – but was disqualified. He did finish second in the Eclipse but the final judgement was that he could have done better, although it must be said he did not have much good luck. In addition Frank Butters said Firdaussi suffered leg trouble from the time he came over from Ireland. He spent a year at stud in England and was then exported France and subsequently to Rumania.

Bulandshar (Blandford – La Douairiere by Spearmint) had run unplaced on his only start as a juvenile in a Newmarket back-end maiden. He began the year with a second in the Union Jack Stakes at Liverpool before breaking his maiden by winning the Chester Vase by four lengths. He failed to win again but ran with credit finishing third in both the Newmarket Stakes and Hurst Park St Leger trial. He was sold and achieved little as a four-year-old.

Amongst the juveniles three showed the most promise: a colt Gino (Tetratema – Teresina by Tracery), a filly Moti Begum (Gainsborough – Moti Mahal by The Tetrarch) and a colt Felicitation (Colorado – Felicita by Cantilever). The beautifully bred Gino dead-heated for first place in Buckenham (Post Produce) Stakes, a valuable stakes race at Newmarket but was disqualified for boring. Strangely it was discovered months later that Gino was not qualified for the race as the Aga was no longer the sole owner having transferred a share to Aly. Gino won the second most valuable race for juveniles; Imperial Produce Stakes at Kempton. His portrait shows a colt needing to grow in to his frame and plenty of improvement could be expected.

Moti Begum won only the Ham (Produce) Stakes but was placed in several big races. Felicitation won only one of his six races, had that number doubled when awarded the Middle Park Stakes. Disconcertingly he had swished his tail and looked possibly un-genuine.

Young Lover (Son-in-Law – Tryst by Rochester) a colt owned by Sir Alfred Butt won the Gimcrack Stakes but did not impress as a top-class prospect.

*   *   *

1933 saw Butters narrowly headed in the list of leading trainers by Fred Darling. Butters did not win any of the Classics or many other big races but he had plenty of talent.

The performances of Orpen, Dastur and Firdaussi have been covered. Of the three-year-olds Gino failed to win any of his ten races. However, he was placed four times, including Two Thousand Guineas and Sussex Stakes and was also fifth in the Cambridgeshire. He was used as a pacemaker in the Eclipse Stakes and finished the year in a handicap at Birmingham. Moti Begum achieved little from four starts.

An example of Frank Butters' ability to get the very best out of a horse came with the stayer Felicitation. He had been a good juvenile awarded the Middle Park Stakes and was considered by Butters his most likely Derby horse. However, as a three-year-old he had suffered from sore shins, common among two-year-olds but rarer in older horses, the result was that although he raced eight times he failed to win; although he was second in the St Leger.

As a four-year-old Felicitation won five of his eight races, including two in consecutive days at Ascot; on Wednesday he won the Churchill Stakes over two miles and on Thursday he won the Gold Cup over two miles and a half beating Hyperion.

In the Ascot Gold Cup of 1934 Butters had heard that Hyperion had not trained satisfactorily prior to the race, and determined that Felicitation would set a fast pace. The day before, Wednesday, by way of warming up for his task Felicitation had beaten a moderate field in the two-mile Churchill Stakes. Starting at 1–2 Felicitation made all the running to win with facile ease. He was a relatively fresh horse on Gold Cup day and with Gordon Richards setting a cracking pace he made the running. Headed for a while, Felicitation, having regained his second wind, retook the lead and stayed on strongly. To the surprise and chagrin of the huge Ascot crowd, already wet

THIRD RACE   Armlet—YELLOW

About One Mile and a Half

3.0.—THE 152ND RENEWAL OF THE DERBY STAKES

of 100 sov. each, 50 sov. ft. if declared by the Tuesday in the week before running, 25 sov. ft. if declared by the last Tuesday in March, 1935, or 5 sov. only if declared by the first Tuesday in July, 1934, with 3000 sov. added, for entire colts and fillies, foaled in 1932; colts, 9st, and fillies 8st 9lb; the owner of the second to receive 10 per cent. and the owner of the third 5 per cent. of the whole stakes; the breeder of the winner to receive 500 sov. out of the stakes; about one mile and a half (292 entries, 50 sov. forfeit declared for 62, 25 sov. for 100, and 5 sov. for 112).—Closed October 31st, 1935.

		Trainer.	Jockey.
1—Ld Astor	FIELD TRIAL	Lawson	R. Dick
	b or br c by Felstead—Popingaol		
	light blue, pink sash & cap		
2—Ld Astor	PLYMOUTH SOUND	Lawson	J. Brennan
	b c by Coronach—Plymstock		
	light blue, pink sash & cap		
3—Sir Abe Bailey	JAPETUS	Day	F. Lane
	b c by Son-in-Law—Oceana		
	black & gold hoops, gold cap		
4—Sir Abe Bailey ROBIN GOODFELLOW		Cottrill	T. Weston
	bl c by Son and Heir—Epple Adair		
	black & gold hoops, gold cap		
5—Mr A. E. Berry PEACEFUL WALTER		Sneyd	D. Smith
	b c by Walter Gay—Turtledove		
	black, pink hooped sleeves, pink cap		
6—Mr F. W. Dennis	ST. BOTOLPH	Digby	H. Beasley
	b c by Son-in-Law—Dame Caution		
	blue & white (halved), red sleeves & peak		
7—Ld Derby	FAIRHAVEN	C. Leader	R. Perryman
	ch c by Fairway—Drift		
	black, white cap		
8—Mrs C. Evans	FIRST SON	Allden	R. A. Jones
	ch c by Son and Heir—Widow Twankey		
	mauve, cerise hoop on body & sleeves, cerise cap		
9—Ld Glanely	SCREAMER	Hogg	A. Wragg
	b c by Beresford—Saxham Cat		
	black, red, white & blue belt & cap		
10—Mrs Corlette Glorney ASSIGNATION		Cundell	S. Donoghue
	br c by Son-in-Law—Tryst		
	old gold, green sash, quartered cap		

For continuation of this race see next page

THE 152nd RENEWAL OF THE DERBY STAKES—cond.

11—Mr C. W. Gordon	SEA BEQUEST	J. Jarvis	B. Smith
	b by Legatee—Ocean Light		
	cherry, cornflower blue sash & cap		
12—H.H. Aga Khan	THEFT	Fk. Butters	H. Wragg
	b c by Tetratema—Voleuse		
	green & chocolate hoops, chocolate cap		
13—H.H. Aga Khan	BAHRAM (late Bahran)	Fk. Butters	F. Fox
	b c by Blandford—Friar's Daughter		
	green & chocolate hoops, chocolate cap		
14—H.H. Aga Khan	HAIRAN	Fk. Butters	Gordon Richards
	b c by Fairway—Harpsichord		
	green & chocolate hoops, chocolate cap		
15—Lt.-Col. Giles Loder	FAIRBAIRN	Gilpin	C. Smirke
	ch c by Fairway—Baby Polly		
	yellow, dark blue sleeves, black cap		
16—Mr H. W. W. Simms	PRY II.	Digby	M. Beary
	b c by Priori—Edwina (bred in France)		
	pink, black sleeve, hooped cap		
17—Mr E. T. Thornton-Smith BARBERRY		Templeman	S. Smith
	b c by Beresford—Toybridge		
	blue, scarlet belt, gold cap		

GENTLEMEN PREFER **Zoppot**
Free State of Danzig

for a real change

Internat. Casino ★ Roulette ★ Baccara

TO STAY IN ZOPPOT COSTS SO VERY LITTLE

[Information from Thomas Cook & Son, Ltd. and all leading Travel Agencies]

Racecard for the 1935 Derby Stakes

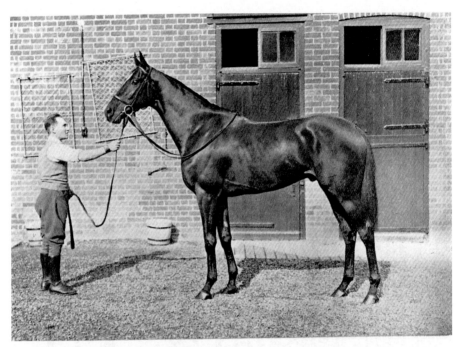

Bahram as a three-year-old.

Bahram being led along Epsom High Street prior to the Derby

The Derby Field after half a mile.

Rounding Tattenham Corner; Bahram is beginning his challenge;
marked with an x

Two views of the finish as Bahram wins easily

Bahram is led in by a delighted Aga!

Charlie Smirke

Freddie Fox with Joe Childs

Frank Butters with Theft, Hairan and Bahram

Frank Butters ready for the races

SEVENTH RACE.   Old Mile.   Armlet—PINK.

5.0.—THE ST. JAMES'S PALACE STAKES

of 100 sov., each, h. ft., or 10 ft. if declared by March 26th, 1935, with 1000 sov. added for the winner, 400 sov. for the second, and 200 sov. for the third, for three yrs old; colts, 9st, fillies and geldings, 8st 11lb; maidens allowed 7lb.; Old Mile (96 entries, 10 sov. forfeit declared for 68).—Closed October 17th, 1935.

Declaration of forfeit to Messrs Weatherby & Sons only.

		st	lb	
1 Lord Derby's........FAIRHAVEN	ch c by Fairway—Drift.	9	0	BLACK, WHITE CAP
2 Mr Edward Esmond's.....ROSECRAG	br c by Craig an Eran—Necklace II. J. Jarvis	9	0	WHITE, BLUE SLEEVES, yellow cap
3 H.H. Aga Khan's.........BAHRAM	b c by Blandford—Friar's Daughter. (into Bahram) Frank Butters	9	0	GREEN and CHOCOLATE HOOPS, chocolate cap
4 H.H. Aga Khan's...........HAIRAN	b c by Fairway—Hurrahford. Frank Butters	9	0	GREEN and CHOCOLATE HOOPS, chocolate cap
5 H.H. Aga Khan's............THEFT	b c by Tetratema—Voleuse. Frank Butters	9	0	GREEN and CHOCOLATE HOOPS, chocolate cap
6 Lord Astor's.........PORTFOLIO	b c by Swinford—Short Story. Lawson	8	7	LIGHT BLUE, PINK SASH and cap
7 Sir Abe Bailey's.........ZINGARO	br c by Solario—Graecila. Lawson	8	7	BLACK and GOLD HOOPS, gold cap
8 Miss J. B. Courtauld's.......SPANNER	b c by Manna—Spinney. B. Jarvis	8	7	PRIMROSE, LIGHT BLUE HOOPED SLEEVES, primrose cap with blue hoop
9 Sir Frederick Eley's....MERIDIAN BOY	b c by Tetralemon—Decoran. Templeman	8	7	SCARLET and WHITE CHECK, black cap
10 Lt.-Col. Giles Loder's.....FAIRBAIRN	ch c by Fairway—Baby Polly. V. Gilpin	8	7	YELLOW, DARK BLUE SLEEVES, black cap
11 Lt.-Col. Giles Loder's.......APENNINE	ch c by Apelle—Bridgemount. V. Gilpin	8	7	YELLOW, DARK BLUE SLEEVES, black cap
12 Miss Dorothy Paget's.....DESERT CLOUD	gr c by Blandford—Donatella. Brunce	8	7	BLUE, YELLOW HOOP on body and sleeves, yellow cap with blue hoop
13 Sir Victor Sassoon's........JOSHUA	b c by Solario—Persuasion. B. Jarvis	8	7	PEACOCK BLUE and OLD GOLD HOOPS, OLD GOLD SLEEVES, peacock blue cap
14 Mr William Woodward's.....FRESH FOX	b c by Cathurst Fox—Flaunt (bred in U.S.A.). Boyd-Rochfort	8	7	WHITE, RED SPOTS, black cap

1st..........3   2nd..........6   3rd....2.........

One length & 4 Lengths.

1·4·5·8·9·10·11·12·13 Ald not run.

Racecard for the St James's Palace Stakes and Bahram afterwards. This was the only race he did not win easily.

from the rain, their hero, that great and wonderfully popular horse Hyperion, backed down to 8–11, was galloped into the ground and beaten almost ten lengths.

Felicitation later that year won the John Porter Stakes and Jockey Club Cup and also finished third in the Prix de l'Arc Triomphe. At the age of five in 1935 he won the Yorkshire Cup, a handicap in those days, carrying top weight. It was fortunate that Felicitation won as he was conceding between 12 and 28 pounds to his seven rivals. It would have been a travesty if he had been denied the £1,580 (84,000) first prize by a horse in receipt of considerable weight beating him in those circumstances. Thankfully no horse today capable of running to a *Timeform* rating of 135 would be expected to run in a handicap.

A good example of the frustrations and perversities of thoroughbreds which make trainers want to tear their hair out was a grey filly called Una (Tetratema – Uganda by Bridaine). As a juvenile she split a pastern, which might go some way to explaining her performances, and raced only once, unplaced in the Acorn Plate at Epsom's summer meeting. At three she started by producing an excellent performance to beat the Lincoln Winner: Dorigen (Franklin – Trilogy by Son-in-Law) at Lingfield in April. She then ran disappointingly as the 4–1 second favourite when unplaced in the One Thousand Guineas.

A week or so later Una was working with Young Lover, a decent enough three-year-old colt and the above mentioned Felicitation. It was a misty morning and only the last furlong of the gallop was visible to trainer Frank Butters who was astonished to see the grey filly emerge from the mist several lengths clear of the two colts. Thinking that the work had been messed up in some way a somewhat irate trainer demanded to know what had happened. Butters astonishment only increased when the riders informed him that the work was carried out exactly to his instructions and that Una "won" on merit. Shortly afterwards Una ran disappointingly in the Haverhill Stakes and Young Lover won the Newmarket Stakes. Una was never anywhere near her best again. However, she more than made up for her failings at stud producing seven winners from eight foals including the Two Thousand Guineas winner Palestine by Fair Trial.

It should not be forgotten that while the Aga Khan provided the majority of the horses at Fitzroy House Frank Butters also trained for 5th Earl of Durham, George Lambton's elder brother, Sir Alfred Butt and Thomas Lant. It was for Lord Durham that Butters trained a filly Light Brocade (Galloper Light – Trilogy by Son-in-Law) who had been a top-class juvenile in 1933 winning four races, including the Molecomb and Cheveley Park Stakes. She was ranked third in the Free Handicap. In her Classic year she won only one of her four races but it was the Oaks and she was second in the One Thousand Guineas.

The best juvenile at Fitzroy House in 1933 was Mrs Rustom (Blandford – Cos by Flying Orb) which made her a half-sister to Costaki Pasha and Rustom Pasha. Physically she was rather spare and on the leg but she won three of her five races: the Ham, Gimcrack and Dewhurst Stakes. In addition she was second in the Middle Park Stakes.

Alishah; a full-brother to Gino but a bay instead of a grey was probably the best juvenile colt. Described as a "better-made colt that his half-brother Alishah won the July and Buckenham Stakes and was second in the Champagne Stakes.

One very promising juvenile of 1933 was a bay colt Umidwar (Blandford – Uganda by Bridaine). He was the last foal of Uganda and a typically fine son of his sire. He ran only once but won the Hurst Park Two-year-old Stakes. So impressed by Umidwar was Lord Woolavington that he offered the Aga £2,000 (106,000) during the following winter. However, Butters held Umidwar in very high regard and the offer was refused.

Another juvenile colt Badruddin (Blandford – Mumtaz Mahal by The Tetrarch) a grey, was badly gored in the quarters by a bullock as a yearling at a stud farm in France and only raced once as a two-year-old. He showed promise finishing second in the Clearwell Stakes at Newmarket. He was a useful three-year-old winning four of his nine starts, including the Waterford and Sussex Stakes, and finishing third in the Two Thousand Guineas. As a four-year-old he was campaigned in the top handicaps but a fourth was the best he could manage. He became a useful sire in the Argentine.

* * *

When Butters took over the training of the Aga Khan's horses Michael Beary came as first jockey and his retainer continued in 1932 and 1933. He and Frank Butters were the antithesis of each other; one a carefree and voluble Irishman and the other a dour and conscientious individual, for whom attention to detail was paramount and who enjoyed a quiet life. It was no surprise when after two years their association ended and Beary's contract was not renewed for 1934. It was a wonder that it lasted as long as it did.

From Beary's point of view he left at just the wrong time because 1934 saw astonishing dominance by horses owned by the Aga and trained by Frank Butters. The Aga easily headed the list of leading breeders with twice as many winners and four times the amount of prize money. Butters was leading trainer with over three times as much prize money as Marcus Marsh in second place. At one stage Butters looked certain to beat Joe Lawson's record of £93,899 set three years previously but in the end fell just short with £88,844(4,620,000).

As if this was not enough Butters saddled nine winners at Ascot; seven owned by the Aga, from twenty eight races. An astonishing achievement at the most competitive four days racing each year anywhere in Britain. For good measure he also saddled six winners at Goodwood.

Apart from Felicitation and Light Brocade who have both been covered the best three-year-old was Umidwar. He had surprised Butters by winning his only race as a juvenile when thought too backward. He did not enjoy much good fortune in the early part of his three-year-old career; he was due to appear in the Greenham Stakes but was cast in his box. This is usually a relatively minor problem but it hampered Umidwar for several months.

Consequently when he ran in the Two Thousand Guineas he was not ready and although he showed speed and was prominent for six furlongs he managed only fifth. He would not have beaten the winner, Colombo (Manna – Lady Nairne by Chaucer), under any circumstances as he was one of the best winners of the race for many a year. Unfortunately Umidwar sprained a hock in the race and, although Butters was able to be prepare him for the Derby, the inter-ruption did not help. Neither did the very firm conditions as the dry weather, which was becoming a drought, persisted. Not surprisingly he finished a moderate seventh in the Derby, although he travelled well until the straight. Again he would not have beaten the winner Windsor Lad (Blandford – Resplendent by By George!) who was one of the great horses of the era.

By the time the Eclipse Stakes was run Butters had Umidwar in better shape and he was second to King Salmon (Salmon-Trout – Malva by Charles O'Malley). However, both Umidwar and King Salmon should have been beaten by Windsor Lad, who finished third, but was given a ludicrously over confident ride by Charlie Smirke who got himself boxed in. He was in front just after the line and going away. In fairness to Smirke he even admitted himself that he was at fault and suffered considerable disapprobation from punters who had confidently backed Windsor Lad down to favouritism. Umidwar then won the Gratwicke Stakes and, after finishing fifth in the St Leger, won the Jockey Club and Champion Stakes.

Alishah continued to progress winning four of his nine races including the Rous Memorial and Atlantic Cup. Mrs Rustom failed to win any of her six races but ran well enough on occasions.

*   *   *

Frank Butters trained for owners that wanted to win the Classics and weight-for-age races. That is not to say that he could not prepare a horse to win big handicaps when he had a suitable candidate.

Butters' most notable handicap success was in the 1935 Cesarewitch with Sir Alfred Butt's Near Relation (Son-in-Law – Youyou by Simon Square). Sir Alfred was not an easy man to train for; a theatre magnet, a big-time gambler and a man who lost his temper easily when matters did not go well. He was also inclined to hold his trainer personally responsible for the success or otherwise of his betting. Not the sort of individual that Frank Butters would be able to act in harmony with one would have thought. However, they seemed to have rubbed along well enough.

Sir Alfred made two entries in the Cesarewitch: Near Relation and

Lucky Patch (Spion Kop – Enrichment by Tracery) who was proven in staying handicaps, although not as far as the severe two miles and a quarter of the Cesarewitch. Sir Alfred began backing Lucky Patch and gained in confidence after he had won at Ayr over the Cesarewitch distance.

In the meantime Near Relation won the twelve furlongs Edinburgh Cup under Harry Wragg. One observer: James H. (Jimmy) Park, one of the few men whose judgement Phil Bull completely trusted, told Wragg that Near Relation would win the Cesarewitch. Wragg was certain he had won comfortably and that there was more to come and confided to Sir Alfred that he would win the Cesarewitch with Near Relation and not Lucky Patch. Neither Butters nor Sir Alfred had considered Near Relation for the race and so decided to start both horses.

Near Relation worked better than Lucky Patch in the build-up to the race and Sir Alfred backed both horses to win the same amount. In the event Near Relation won comfortably at 25–1 and Lucky Patch twelfth at 9–1. As a postscript Near Relation came close to winning the following year as well; he was beaten a neck into second place having swerved in the last half-furlong.

While Bahram was winning the Triple Crown in 1935 Fitzroy House had a juvenile of considerable promise who won three of his six races including the Champagne Stakes at Doncaster: Mahmoud (Blenheim – Mah Mahal by Gainsborough), who was placed third in the Free Handicap. Mahmoud developed acute lameness which could not be located as a juvenile. Butters decided that rest was the answer and after about three months the problem corrected itself.

When Mahmoud was entered for his debut in the Spring Maiden Stakes at Newmarket in May it was a fiasco. There was a false start and thirteen of the sixteen jockeys thought the race was off and ran the full five furlongs. These included Mahmoud who was withdrawn when the race was re-run. Ironically Butters won the four-runner race (one of the runners completed the course twice) with Sir Alfred Butt's filly Windsail (Winalot – Himera by Phalaris).

The reader will recall the Aga had tried to sell Mahmoud at the Deauville yearling sales but he did not reach his reserve of 5,000 guineas (£270,000). On the day that Mahmoud was sent to Butters the Aga telephoned him and asked:

"What do you think of the grey colt I sent you from France?"
"I think he is all right" Butters replied.
"What do you think he would fetch at auction in England?"
"About 8,000 guineas" (£437,000).
"Do you really? In that case I think I will keep him!"

As a three-year-old Mahmoud won only one of his five races, but that one race was the Derby, in impressive style and a record time. However, there is some evidence to support the claim that he was unfortunate and with better luck may have also won the Triple Crown. At the end of the 1936 season Frank Butters wrote to Eric Rickman as follows:-

"I think that it will be generally admitted, on reflection that with ordinary luck Mahmoud would this year have repeated Bahram's great achievement of the previous season, by winning the Classic 'Triple Crown'. We saw how much ground he lost at the start of the Two Thousand Guineas, and wider evidence of this was given by photographs and the cinema. He failed to win only by a short head. He won the Derby very easily by three lengths, with the Two Thousand Guineas winner Pay Up (Fairway – Book Debt by Buchan) only fourth this time. Before the St Leger every horse above the age of two in my stable had the heel bug, with one exception, and he was too slow to catch anything.

I believe that my horses had the infection in its most virulent form, and Mahmoud was one of the worst cases. He had it in all four heels. His preparation for the St Leger was, of course, interrupted to a very serious extent, and his heels had so recently healed when he went to Doncaster that they broke open during the race. Considering the circumstances he put up a fine performance, and finished third to Boswell and Fearless Fox, both of whom had been a long way behind him in the Derby. I think that the effects of the heel bug and my consequent inability to give him a normal preparation robbed him of the race".

*   *   *

By this time the Aga's studs were producing so many horses that Frank Butters did not have enough room at Fitzroy House to stable then all. It became necessary to find boxes for the overspill and these were rented at Stockbridge House and Queensbury Lodge. Both these yards were round the corner from Fitzroy House in the High Street opposite The Terrace where today the BBA have their offices.

*   *   *

This period was just as susceptible to hyperbole as today with regard to horses that were considered much better than they eventually proved. Such a colt was foaled in the same year as Mahmoud and was named Bala Hissar (Blandford – Voleuse by Volta) which made him a half-brother to Le Voleur and Theft. He was among the yearlings which the Aga Khan sent into training in the autumn of 1934 and according to Eric Rickman he was strikingly handsome and he certainly looked very impressive in his portrait as a four-year-old. Blandford was the most successful sire of the time; his sons Windsor Lad, Brantome and Bahram had been outstandingly brilliant during that season. Voleuse in addition to Le Voleur and Theft was also the damn of four other winners. Rickman on a visit to Fitzroy House that winter was struck by his good looks the moment he entered Bala Hissar's box; and thought that, although he had already seen many equine aristocrats in the stable, this was the Adonis among them. When he was introduced to the young colt he had 'magically assumed an aureole'.

Long before he raced he was the subject of much gossip and favourable report. He ran twice as a two year old and due to his reputation odds were laid on him for his debut. However, he was beaten easily by his only opponent: Concordat (Coronach – Short Story by Buchan), but of course a lack of racing experience was a ready excuse. Bala Hissar had, in fact, shown nothing at home in any gallop which had really satisfied Butters. However, a fortnight after his debut he was made favourite and won the Dewhurst Stakes on the strength of which he was placed top of the juvenile Free Handicap;

something the Jockey Club handicapper was widely criticized for. He was not the first or the last handicapper to wrongly assess a horse on its reputation rather than its actual form. As a three year old in 1936 Bala Hissar managed to win just one of his six races: a plate worth £181 (9,412) at Haydock Park, beating three very moderate performers, a couple of weeks before the Derby. Butters already knew how limited Bala Hissar really was after he had performed moderately in the Two Thousand Guineas.

Frank Butters

© Lionel Edwards Estate by courtesy of Felix Rosenstiel's Widow & Son, London

Following the first Classic Butters was asked 'How is your Derby horse?' He replied 'I should like you to tell me first which my Derby horse is!' He had concluded that there was not any hope for Bala Hissar. Charlie Smirke, who had been retained by the Aga Khan as first jockey that year, had been one of his strongest admirers, a rare misjudgement, and had been confident of another Derby triumph. Smirke complained that he was not allowed to ride Bala Hissar before his seasonal debut in the Craven Stakes at Newmarket. He finished fifth and Smirke jumped off to unsaddle and said to Butters "He's no good", "I can't help that" replied Butters, "after all this is the horse that you yourself picked to ride in the Classics". Smirke was very disappointed by Bala Hissar's poor showing in both the Craven and the Two Thousand Guineas and blamed Butters for not allowing him to "grow or develop", and was keen to get off him for the Derby.

Smirke was a good judge but even he had been taken in by this "paragon". He was relieved when given Mahmoud to ride although he would have preferred Taj Akbar (Fairway – Taj Shirin by Gainsborough). He had shown promise as a juvenile in three runs without winning and this year had won the Nonesuch Plate at Epsom and the Chester Vase under Gordon Richards. Richards, who had been retained as second jockey by the Aga, would ride Taj Akbar in the Derby. Smirke was furious as he was first jockey and felt he should have been allowed first option to ride Taj Akbar. He was though allowed to switch to Mahmoud, still a sparely made sort, under 16 hands, out of a moderate sprinter and considered a probable non-stayer. Smirke was allowed a couple of gallops before the Derby during which he let Mahmoud run "idly" as he thought such a lightly-made colt would not be favoured by strong gallops. Butters was convinced that over twelve furlongs Taj Akbar was superior to Mahmoud and was keen to keep Smirke off Taj Akbar.

However, in exceptionally dry conditions that year at Epsom the course was "like a road" and this suited Mahmoud admirably. Smirke was reduced to tears after his convincing win, probably because Mahmoud would have been third choice at best if he had been asked about his Derby mount at the start of the year.

Smirke was an outstanding jockey with what was once memorably described as "terrifying confidence" but was an arrogant and often disagreeable individual. In his autobiography he admits that he can be considered boastful and significantly does not offer any rebuttal to this aspect of his reputation. This sometimes unreliable memoir tells of other events which are at variance with the views of other contemporary observers.

In the paddock before the Derby in company with The Aga Khan, Frank Butters and the other three jockeys riding the horses trained by Butters: Richards (Taj Akbar), Bobby Jones (Bala Hissar) and Perryman (Noble King owned by Sir Alfred Butt) Smirke was at his least likeable. "Never mind the others your Highness; I will win the Derby for you". Then pointing at Gordon Richards he continued "and one horse I'm sure to beat is Taj Akbar". Richards looked anxious, Butters embarrassed and the Aga simply chuckled. The Aga was perfectly well aware that Smirke's riding could, on occasions, to put it euphemistically, not be entirely trusted. However, the Aga's principal objective was to win the major races and on the big occasion no jockey had a better temperament, judgement or determination to win than Charlie Smirke.

Smirke was fond of quoting stories when matters worked out in his favour or he thought another jockey, usually Gordon Richards, had not ridden well. In his autobiography Smirke was more reticent about the occasions when he was wrong! Taj Akbar finished second and Bala Hissar, wearing a hood, was well beaten.

The going was probably as hard as it has ever been at Epsom; a stone was thrown up and might easily have blinded Tommy Burns. Smirke was at his best: his timing was perfect as he kicked on in the straight and was never in danger. He records that he looked back at Richards "with glee". The other jockeys reported Smirke as saying to Richards in the weighing room afterwards "Hey there Moppy! I'm tired – come and pull my boots off". Smirke denies saying this; so the other jockeys just made it up then!

Frank Butters had a strong dislike of Charlie Smirke; whose hubris and tendency to rodomontading he would not have found endearing. In addition Butters would have been aware, as stated earlier, that Smirke sometimes rode horses for his own benefit rather than the owner and trainer. Butters was certainly not alone in this view of course the Aga knew and Harry Wragg also discovered this tendency when Smirke rode for him in the 1950's. Butters would never have been in favour of putting Smirke up on anything if he had had his way. In turn Smirke felt that Butters was too hard on his horses; Smirke wrote that Butters was "tough and ruthless in training horses". In Smirke's view it was "only the number of horses that the Aga had that withstood the many mishaps that afflicted the horses in Butters care". It should be mentioned that Smirke also failed to work harmoniously with both Dick Dawson, in the nineteen twenties and Alec Head in the nineteen fifties. It should also be made clear that all of the trainers Smirke rode for agreed that on a big day there was no better jockey.

There also seems little doubt that given the choice the Aga would always rather have Gordon Richards riding rather than Charlie Smirke. In 1946 when the Aga had a second retainer on Richards, Smirke was engaged to ride Anwar (Umidwar – Stafaralla by Solario) in the St Leger. Richards being booked to ride Edward Tudor for his first retainer with Fred Darling. When Edward Tudor (Hyperion – Mary Tudor II by Pharos) was withdrawn Smirke was replaced by Richards, the assumption being that the second retainer would take precedence over Smirke's engagement. Smirke, as anyone could have predicted, was smarting with indignation and threatened to inform the Stewards. He could only be placated when Aly offered to pay Smirke the same present as Richards in the event that Anwar won. He was unplaced behind Airborne (Precipitation – Bouquet by Buchan).

Conversely Smirke was not only a brilliant horseman but one who genuinely cared about horses. During the 1947 Prix Royal Oak (French St. Leger) his mount Imphal (Airway – Nymph II by Sansovino) snapped a leg turning into the straight. Smirke's efficiency and tender ministrations to the stricken animal went way beyond his duty until the dilatory French authorities finally put Imphal out of his misery.

Smirke wrote in his autobiography that he offered on many occasions to ride the Aga's horses at exercise; but after driving from London would have to watch the stable lads riding the Aga's horses across Newmarket heath. Smirke resented this but does not make clear whether there was any arrangement for him to ride. Smirke must have known that Butters preferred work riders to jockeys for training and also that he disliked him in any circumstances. Some of Butters' work riders had been with him for some time and he could trust them to do as he asked. In the circumstances there was little chance that Butters would allow Smirke, a man he disliked to ride work for him when he had his own riders.

Smirke rode Mirza as a two-year-old and of course claims that he told Butters that he would not stay six furlongs. It is unlikely that Butters would have needed Smirke to tell him this as he himself was of the opinion that Mirza was the fastest juvenile he had ever trained. Mirza was a very fast colt and indeed did not stay six furlongs as a juvenile but did manage to win over a mile as a three-year-old; under Harry Wragg in a slowly run moderate renewal of the Greenham Plate. In the world according the Charlie Smirke he was always right and never wrong. He was a brilliant jockey and must have been right on many occasions but it is sometimes hard to sort out for certain when this was the case.

There is a lovely story which unfortunately is apocryphal. The story goes that during the war someone spoke to Butters on the Limekilns: "Have you heard the news Mr Butters?": "Charlie Smirke has been awarded the VC".

Really! What for? Asked Butters. "For stopping a German tank" came the reply.

"I am not in the least surprised. When he was riding for me he would stop anything" came the riposte from Butters.

*   *   *

This business of training horses too hard should not be allowed to affect Frank Butters reputation. Training for the Aga Khan was a great honour and anyone in this position would never be short of well-bred stock. However, it can be readily imagined that the Aga, who was without a shred of sentimentality about horses, would want to know as soon as possible which of his horses was up to classic standard. A thoroughbred racehorse has a short career at the top level; sometimes not much more than a year to eighteen months if they achieve enough to become a stallion.

A trainer working for the Aga would see his job as establishing a pecking order by the end of their juvenile year. It was therefore incumbent on him to press on whenever possible to establish the merit of each horse. That some broke down or failed to progress was inevitable, but the Aga would not have been concerned with this if Butters was able to say there were a few good ones among them. It should be remembered that William Duke, who trained for the Aga in France, had a reputation for not sparing horses in his care. This is not to say he was cavalier in his approach or did not look after them; it is simply that thoroughbreds are born to race and the sooner the trainer finds out how fast they can run the better. A trainer only deserves criticism if he works a horse when too immature or if it is carrying an injury. Once a horse is fit and well then there is every reason for pressing on.

Horses were trained differently in Butters' time than today. Although there was a tan gallop there were no all-weather gallops for Butters to resort to when the turf gallops became to firm. George Colling would say "Get them fit in the spring, because you can't work them hard enough in the summer when the gallops are too firm".

Throughout history no two great trainers prepared their horses in an identical manner. In recent times Newmarket saw two great practitioners of the trainer's art in Sir Michael Stoute and Sir Henry Cecil; both without doubt as good as any trainer in the history of racing. However they adopted different approaches to training horses. However, as both were immensely successful it is impossible to say one or the other adopted the better method.

Frank Butters' record in the most important two-year-old races suggests that he was able to successfully identify and prepare juveniles for the best races. During the 'thirties he farmed many of the best races with horses bred to win Classics. While some inevitably did not train on, or found a Classic preparation too much and failed to show form as three-year-olds, his record shows that not only did plenty progress as three-year-olds, but in most cases, improved or reproduced their best form when kept in training as four-year-olds.

Frank Butters trained nineteen horses – Palestine is excluded as he did not train him as a three-year-old – for the Aga Khan capable of running to a *Timeform* rating of 124 or better as three-year-olds. Of these thirteen raced as four-year-olds: Felicitation, Tehran, Migoli, Theft, Umiddad, Dastur, Umidwar, Alishah, Ut Majeur, Hairan, Taj Akbar, Badruddin, and Firdaussi. All were given a Classic preparation, but with the exception of Alishah, Hairan, Taj Akbar and Badruddin, all showed form at least as good at aged four as aged three. This would not have been possible if Butters' methods, although searching, had not conducive to his charges welfare and progression.

That Butters could when required, train horses with delicate constitutions or lacking soundness has been demonstrated on many occasions. There is little doubt that with different owners with moderately-bred sorts he would not always have trained then as rigorously during the early part of their careers.

*   *   *

This was the zenith of Frank Butters training career and this was probably the time he was at his happiest. A typical day would start about 6–00 am with "first lot" out by seven. The first lot are usually those due to run in the near future and horses that are fit enough to accompany them in their work.

After first lot has worked which would be about 9–00 am Butters would have time for breakfast after which "second lot" would be ready for the exercise grounds. These are horses that are either backward or not in full training for some reason.

Butters would then return to Fitzroy House to change and depart for racing, assuming the stable had a runner. Butters would usually be driven to the races and would return home that evening if at all possible. On his return to Fitzroy House Butters must find time to eat dinner, answer any correspondence and prepare the work schedule for the following morning.

In addition to the above mentioned duties Butters would need to consult vets and, as the Aga was not usually in Newmarket, Butters would need to speak to him over the telephone. This took place most evenings and could result in some long calls to the continent. In addition to all this Butters also managed Sir Alfred Butt's stud at Newmarket.

At this time Butters was ably assisted by his efficient son Victor, who had by now enough experience to take some of the load. This domestic scene was completed by Frank's wife, Cossie. This provided a staunch and happy family circle.

*   *   *

The story has drifted away somewhat from 1936. Taj Akbar continued to run well and won the Princess of Wales's Stakes, beating the previous year's North American Triple Crown winner Omaha (Gallant Fox – Flambino by Wrack) by a neck Taj Akbar was in receipt of seven pounds more than weight-for-age and although this win does him great credit Omaha was not the horse that he had been the previous year. He had suffered lameness after winning the Triple Crown and although he showed decent form afterwards he was capable of better. Taj Akbar was then second in the Sussex Stakes before winning the Great Midlands Breeders Plate at Nottingham. He stayed in training but only raced twice in 1937, early in the season when he won a handicap at Chester before he was sent to France.

The juveniles of 1936, like all the horses at Fitzroy House, were affected by heel bug including the best of them: Le Grand Duc (Blenheim – La Douairiere by Spearmint). He had won the New Stakes at Ascot in fine style but was then off the course until September when he ran dismally in the Champagne Stakes having not recovered sufficiently from the malady.

A colt; Sultan Mahomed (Massine – Rollybuchy by Filibert de Savoie) won only one of his five races but it was the Dewhurst Stakes at 20–1. He was below the top level and at ages three and four he kept good company and won three more races including the Lowther Stakes.

*   *   *

1937 saw the Aga back on top as leading owner and Butters, although only third in the list of trainers, had some very promising juveniles in his care. Mirza's career has been dealt with earlier with his dam Mumtaz Mahal, and in addition Butters had Tahir (Tetratema – Qurrat al Ain by Buchan), who won three of his six races, including the Chesham and Ham Stakes. Tahir was also second in the National Breeders Produce and Gimcrack Stakes. Queen of Simla (Blenheim – Queen of Scots by Dark Legend) won the Queen Mary Stakes; Ann of Austria (Fairway – Ann Gudman by Stratford) won three of her four races including the Molecomb Stakes. Finally Stafaralla (Solario – Mirawala by Phalaris) would have been unbeaten but she whipped round at the start of the Molecomb Stakes on her debut. She then won a sales race before winning the Cheveley Park Stakes "on the bit most of the way".

Le Grand Duc ran well enough; he only won a modest match race at odds of 1–25 but was third in the Derby which was enough for him to be sold to stand as a stallion in Belgium.

*   *   *

1938 proved that even with the resources of the Aga Khan a moderate batch of juveniles can appear. The 1938 vintage was, according to Charlie Smirke the worst ever. On this occasion he was almost certainly right! However, there were some promising sorts: a colt Dhoti (Dastur – Tricky Aunt by Son-in-Law) a filly Yakimour (Blenheim – Una by Tetratema). Dhoti must have been showing plenty at home as he was backed down to 8–11 on his debut in early April. The race was the Granby Stakes which he won by five lengths and then at odds of 4–11, he followed up when a three length winner of a minor race next. His final race of the year was at Ascot where he won the Chesham Stakes comfortably as the 4–5 favourite. Yakimour raced eight times, won twice and was placed three times. Neither Dhoti nor Yakimour trained on at three and failed to win a race between them.

One filly trained by Butters but not owned by the Aga was Belle Travers (Mr. Jinks – Futurity by Blandford). She was bought as a yearling at the Doncaster September sales for 2,600 guineas (£142,000) by Mr. T Lant. Mr. Lant had owned Maltravers who was a full-brother to Belle Travers, also trained by Butters. She won the Queen Mary and although unable to add to this victory in a six starts she kept good company and ran well except on her final race of the year.

This year saw the Aga finish fourth in the owners lists with only 19 winners compared with 50 for Lord Derby. In 1939 he was eighth with only ten winners. Butters did however, have horses for other owners that did well enough during those two years but nothing of any significance.

The juveniles of 1939 were much better and included Stardust (Hyperion – Sister Stella by Friar Marcus) and Turkhan (Bahram – Theresina by Diophon). Stardust cost 1,450 guineas (£73,000) as a yearling and justified his purchase price by winning three races as a two-year-old, including the National Breeders Produce Stakes at Sandown the most valuable race for juveniles. This was not without controversy as he was awarded the race on the disqualification of an unnamed colt by Colombo out of Rose of England by Teddy; a fine strong-looking individual, a quality colt who moved effortlessly through his races. Turkhan won the Coventry Stakes.

As three-year-olds both progressed Stardust finished second in the Two Thousand Guineas and New St Leger and was first past the post in the Champion Stakes but was disqualified. Turkhan won the Irish Derby and New St Leger. The Rose of England colt was named British Empire, he made only one appearance; finishing last in the Craven Stakes, before being exported to Argentina.

*   *   *

Butters' son Victor, a happy and charming young man who was his assistant died tragically died whilst on holiday in Switzerland in February 1939. Victor did not survive emergency surgery for a mastoid. He was Butters' only son and just thirty at the time of his death. Not surprisingly this was the great sadness of Frank Butters' life and afterwards he was seldom seen not wearing a black tie.

*   *   *

War was declared on 3rd September, just a few days before the St. Leger and Doncaster yearling sales. The sales were cancelled, and all racing was abandoned until further notice. Racing eventually resumed at Newmarket on 18th October, when a two day meeting was held on the July course, featuring a substitute Cambridgeshire Handicap run over a mile in two divisions. Yearling sales were held at Park Paddocks on 17th October, when prices, although low, were better than they might have been in the circumstances.

*   *   *

After war broke out Butters continued to train for The Aga Khan and others, but of course, things were not the same. Even the most prestigious stables had to surrender their staff to the requirements of defending the realm. As a trainer Butters might have had all the resources of the Aga Khan at his command but in wartime he was in no better position than any other trainer in Newmarket. Everything was scarce: oats, beans, straw and saddlery and most important of all: labour. Also horse-boxes were scarce and the railways out of the question. Drastic economies were demanded of civilians and Butters in a typical gesture gave up his car and used a bicycle to watch the horses work.

Ironically their counterparts in occupied France were better off! The Germans allowed racing to continue in and around Paris; probably to amuse themselves as much as the locals but also to convince the French people that life could still go on normally under their occupation. While the Aga still had horses trained by Butters, he sent many of his fillies to Hubert Hartigan and Gerald Wellesley at the Curragh. Butters trained only 23 horses in 1940; about a third as many as normal.

Newmarket felt the wrath of Hitler when it was bombed in 1940. Racings Headquarters was surrounded by airfields with Lakenheath not far away, something the Germans were aware of. There was even a warning that enemy parachutists might be sent to the area. During the air raids The White Hart hotel, the Post Office and Marlborough Club were all destroyed.

There was a reduced program of racing in Britain during 1940. The season commenced on 25th March at Hurst Park and Birmingham and concluded on 23rd November at Thirsk. However, following the fall of France on 14th June racing was cancelled from 18th June and did not restart until the 14th September. The first four Classics were all run on the July course at Newmarket. The St. Leger was not run until the final day of the season at Thirsk and run as the Yorkshire St. Leger. There was no Ascot and it was not possible to rearrange any of the races, including the Gold Cup.

There were six runners in the 'Leger and the Aga had two of them: Stardust and Turkhan. Gordon Richards did not have a mount so accepted Butters' offer to ride the second string: Turkhan, Harry Wragg was on Stardust. The distance was one mile and seven furlongs; slightly more than the normal one at Doncaster. Richards was convinced that Stardust, who had won the Champion Stakes on merit but was disqualified, was not a true stayer. He was confident that Turkhan had plenty of stamina and set out to make all the running at "a pretty hot pace throughout". Turkhan stayed on bravely to resist Stardust who, despite the assistance of the "head waiter" Harry Wragg, was held by three-quarters of a length.

Although Butters won the St Leger with Turkhan, he had good reason to believe that he would have won the Two Thousand Guineas and Derby as well if the Classics had not been re-opened. Butters trained the second in both races: Stardust in the Guineas and Turkhan in the Derby. Both races were won with French horses not originally entered: Djebel (Tourbillion – Loika by Gay Crusader) and Pont l'Eveque (Barneveldt – Ponteba by Belfonds). It is possible to sympathise with Butters as for many years the top French races, except the Grand Prix de Paris, were not open to British Horses.

*   *   *

In 1941 racing in England began at Lincoln on 26th March and concluded at Newmarket on 6th November. There were 86 meetings scheduled to be run over 13 courses; in peacetime the number would be 330. Of the 86 days racing Newmarket staged 27. The first four Classics were run at Newmarket and the St Leger at Manchester as Doncaster was out of commission. Newmarket staged the principal Ascot races, including the Gold Cup.

The first meeting of the year was scheduled to be staged at Salisbury but was cancelled in mysterious circumstances. It later emerged that the King was attending troop exercises on Salisbury Plain that day in conditions of great secrecy.

Frank Butters trained just eleven horses and won no major races, although he did train the promising juvenile filly, Mah Iran (Bahram – Mah Mahal by Gainsborough) which made her a three quarters sister to Mahmoud. She was originally sent to Gerald Wellesley at the Curragh as a yearling where she was prepared for her juvenile career. She made her debut on 7th May at Phoenix Park where she was second in a Plate. She was then transferred to Newmarket and under Butters care she won a stakes race on Oaks day: 19th June.

Mah Iran ran modestly in the Queen Mary Stakes and then finished second three times in as many weeks in the Chesterfield and Molecomb Stakes and a nursery. Her final race was also in a nursery which she won. She was ranked fourth in the Free Handicap behind Sun Chariot, Big Game and Watling Street.

As a three-year-old it was always possible that Mah Iran would have too much speed to stay beyond six furlongs. The influence of Bahram's stamina did not prove sufficient against the speed of Mumtaz Mahal and she failed to stay in the One Thousand Guineas. She reverted to sprinting where she won three minor races.

*   *   *

The racing programme in 1942 was further reduced from 86 to 80 meetings. Racing became regional and was staged at just five courses. About 40% of the 540 races run were for two-year-olds and 22.5% for three-year-olds. Fixtures were originally arranged until the end of July with racing at Newmarket confined to horses trained at Newmarket; racing at Salisbury and Windsor to horses trained south of the River Trent; and racing at Pontefract and Stockton confined to horses trained north of the Trent. However, the following races at Newmarket were open to all horses; One Thousand Guineas; Two Thousand Guineas; Derby; Oaks; St. Leger; Gold Cup; Jockey Club Cup; Champion Stakes; Nunthorpe Stakes. The following juvenile races were also open; Coventry, Rous, Queen Mary, Cheveley Park and Dewhurst Stakes.

The second set of fixtures to the end of the season still confined Newmarket horses to Headquarters, but allowed Epsom trained horses to race there until 15th September, when rail transport facilities for racehorses were officially withdrawn. Epsom trained horses were also excluded from running at Salisbury.

The future of Newmarket racecourse itself was in jeopardy with the call-up of all able bodied men under age forty-five. Of eighteen men employed in maintaining the track twelve were eligible for the service. In addition the Royal Air Force was thinking of extending the area for landing aeroplanes and heavy bombers to include the section between the Rowley Mile grandstand and the Ditch. This requisition would last ten years which might place the whole viability of racing at Newmarket into question.

Frank Butters trained just 23 horses in 1942; better than 1941 but still well down on his peacetime numbers. However, included in the horses housed at Fitzroy House was the only horse owned and bred by the Aga and trained by Frank Butters that had enough talent to be compared with Bahram: Nasrullah. Foaled in 1940 by Nearco out of Mumtaz Begum by Blenheim he was about as well-bred a colt as was possible; Mumtaz Begum was a daughter of Mumtaz Mahal. Nasrullah was destined to have a greater influence on the turf than any other horse bred by the Aga Khan; he was to prove a better sire than all of his five Derby winners put together.

Nasrullah was a big, handsome, bay colt, standing a shade over 16.1 hands, with huge nostrils and talent to equal his looks and breeding, and, as if that was not enough, he was also the most wonderful mover; the best Gordon Richards ever rode. Unfortunately, he was not the perfect package he seemed; due to the war and regional racing he could only race at Newmarket and Nasrullah hated the place. According to Gordon Richards he did not like him much either! Richards felt that if Nasrullah could have raced away from Newmarket he would have proved himself one of the greatest horses ever. He worked alongside the July course and had to race on it and the monotony must have driven Nasrullah to distraction. There were some fraught mornings while they tried to persuade Nasrullah to gallop; he would hold the whole string up and on occasions only by dodging between the banks of the Devils Dyke could he be persuaded to work at all.

As a juvenile he won two of his four races: the Coventry and Great Bradley Stakes and, although he sweated up, he was beaten only a neck in the Middle Park. These performances plus his performances against the clock convinced Phil Bull that he was a horse apart, although Bull's sharp eye had spotted signs of temperament.

In his classic season he won three of his six races but threw away his chances in the others by simply refusing to try his best. He should definitely have won the Two Thousand Guineas; he would not go on, then he would, then changed his mind and would not cooperate. Nasrullah finished fourth; beaten a short-head, head and half a length. How exasperating was that! For Phil Bull very; he noted "No doubt it had come to his (Nasrullah's) knowledge that I had obtained £500 – £400 (18,500 – 14,800) a place only about him"! Gordon Richards felt he should also have won the Derby but blamed himself for making his effort too soon. He was almost certainly being too hard on himself; if he could not unlock Nasrullah's talent to the full it is unlikely anyone else would have done better, with the possible exception of Harry Wragg, or maybe Charlie Smirke.

There can be little doubt that his temperament deprived the Aga Khan and Frank Butters of a possible second Triple Crown Champion and Gordon Richards of what would be his only one. Having said this Gordon Richards said that Nasrullah did not stay in the St Leger. However, how he could know this on a horse that habitually kept the level of both his ability and stamina to himself it is hard to say. In addition to Richards Nasrullah must have tried the patience of Butters to the limit and he must have despaired of getting the best out of him. On more than one occasion he could be seen behind Nasrullah as the truculent animal stood motionless at the paddock gate, Butters armed with his umbrella opening and shutting it in an effort to persuade the unwilling horse to canter off to the start. Eventually in the Champion Stakes Richards held him up until the last possible moment and although he timed his run to perfection Nasrullah's head went up and he was stopping at the line.

In *Best Horses of 1943* Bull wrote; "If conformation and innate ability count for anything he may make the name for himself as a stallion which his unfortunate temperament prevented his making for himself as a racehorse". These words were to prove prophetic; but it would not be until he stood in North America that his true greatness was revealed.

Aly Khan never forgave Nasrullah for his display in the Derby; Aly lost several large bets on Nasrullah which would not have endeared him to the colt, and this may even have influenced the decision to sell him later. Nasrullah was just as obstreperous out of training and a blank was once fired over his head shortly after arriving at Claiborne Farm following his purchase. "Bull" Hancock went into his box and Nasrullah advanced towards him with his mouth open. Hancock was not known as "Bull" for nothing: he was a very big, strong man and wacked Nasrullah over the head as hard as he could with the stable broom he was carrying. Nasrullah never gave him any trouble thereafter.

Butters later trained another horse by Nearco: Masaka (Nearco – Majideh by Mahmoud), who also had temperament issues, and he once confessed to Nesbit Waddington; "I have had some brilliant Nearco's but I sometimes never want to see another one in the yard". Nasrullah was a great sire in North America; with probably only Northern Dancer better. He sired many outstanding horses including Nashua, Bold Ruler and Never Bend who themselves became out-standing sires.

Interestingly Nasrullah's full sister: Rivaz, was the antithesis of all that he was and stood for. Foaled in 1943 she was a leading juvenile winning three of her five races, including the Queen Mary and July Stakes, and finishing second in the other two. Whereas Nasrullah as a juvenile was always going to be a better three-year-old, having any amount of scope, Rivaz was an early sort, neat, racy, strong but slightly below average size. She would show speed from the gate and continue from start to finish on the bridle. Nasrullah for the whole of his career needing plenty of attention from the saddle, none of it welcome of course! Rivaz did not race as a three-year-old but pro-duced six winners from her first seven foals.

A juvenile of 1942 that was not as talented but a great deal more genuine was Umiddad (Dastur – Udaipur by Blandford) who won both his races including the Dewhurst Stakes. A good-bodied colt, in the mould of his sire, he looked almost mature, unlikely to grow much and carried condition. Umiddad beat eighteen others on his debut at odds of 33–1 at the end of July and his only other race was the Dewhurst stakes in September. Starting as the 6–4 favourite he won "cleverly".

Nasrullah and Umiddad were second and third respectively behind Lady Sybil (Nearco – Sister Sarah by Abbots Trace) in the Free Handicap.

*   *   *

1943, a fourth year of wartime restricted racing in England saw the number of meetings reduced again. Racing took place on just 67 days at six courses. Ascot was added to the five in 1942 which meant racing was staged for the first time ever at Ascot outside the formal meeting; now known as the Royal Meeting in June. Nine individual days were staged but none of the races normally staged there in June during peacetime.

Frank Butters trained 35 horses but apart from Nasrullah and Umiddad – who was placed in the New Derby and Champion Stakes – nothing else out of the ordinary.

Umiddad won two of his six races; both minor stakes events but he was second in the Derby and third in the Champion Stakes. He was unlucky to be badly bumped in the St Leger where he could have been expected to run well given the amount of stamina in his pedigree. Umiddad was something to look forward to in next year's staying races.

Notwithstanding this Butters might have reflected that, but for the Aga selling the majority of his juveniles in 1940, he would have trained the winner of the substitute Ascot Gold Cup. Ujiji (Umidwar – Theresina by Diophon), bred by the Aga, but now owned of course by Mr. Allnatt and ridden by Gordon Richards, won by eight lengths.

*   *   *

With the tide of war gradually turning in the allies favour, there was a slight increase in the racing programme in England for 1944. Although there was only one extra days racing (68 against 67 in 1943), there were 556 races (an increase of 85 over the previous year), mainly due to numerous entries and many divided races, with some meetings staging marathon 12 race cards. Racing began at Windsor on 10th April, and ended at the same course on 4th November. The same six courses were again used: Newmarket staged 21 days, the Southern Area 26 and Northern Area 21.

In 1944 Butters trained 40 horses including the winner of the New St Leger with Tehran (Bois Roussel – Stafaralla by Solario), who had been too backward to be seriously trained as a juvenile when he was unplaced in two races. However, Gordon Richards was aware of his latent talent and spoke well of him over the winter. After breaking his maiden in the Culford Stakes (traditionally a conditions race for promising sorts sadly no longer run) he was third in the Two Thousand Guineas, then second in the Derby, beaten a neck by Ocean Swell (Blue Peter – Jiffy by Hurry On). After winning a minor race at long odds-on he won the St Leger; with Ocean Swell behind him. The Aga Khan effectively imprisoned in Switzerland heard of these triumphs by telegram. Tehran's win in the St Leger benefited the Indian Army Comforts Fund as the Aga had decided at the outset of the War to donate all his winnings in England to this charity.

On St Leger day there was "open war" in Newmarket between taxi and lorry drivers. Car restrictions made it impossible for racegoers to reach Newmarket in one journey from Cambridge on one side and Bury St Edmunds on the other. Relays and changeover points were arranged although this did nothing to save valuable fuel. Taxi drivers were charging an astonishing £2 (75) for a seven mile journey. However, they did not profit as much as they might have hoped as lorry drivers were offering to drive twenty to thirty spectators a time for ten shillings (50 pence) (£19) each!

Frank Butters was champion trainer for the sixth time in 1944 helped by the improving four-year-old Umiddad who won three of his four races. He began with two wins in minor races at Newmarket. First, in a handicap over 14 furlongs, he was required to concede between 16 and 35 pounds to his five rivals. He was brought with a well-timed run by Gordon Richards to win by a head and the same with the Champion Jockey at his strongest in the finish and Umiddad at his bravest. Next over the same trip he beat two rivals including Persian Gulf in the Thorney Stakes at odds of 8–13. Umiddad, who was receiving four pounds, showed great courage to hold off Persian Gulf (Bahram – Double Life by Bachelor's Double) by a neck but the race had been run at a farcically slow pace and the form could be safely ignored. At level weights Persian Gulf got his revenge in the Coronation Cup, run at Newmarket of course, when Umiddad, who started favourite, was beaten into third place by over three lengths.

All was set for the substitute Gold Cup run in early July at Newmarket over two miles and a quarter in what transpired to be a thrilling contest. Unfortunately Persian Gulf was injured and missed the race. Although there were five runners the race was always a match between Umiddad and Bright Lady (April the Fifth – Bright Spot by Solario), a six-year-old mare. Bright Lady had won the Cesarewitch and finished second in the Jockey Club Cup the previous year. Gordon Richards was at his best on the very brave Umiddad, who tracked the pace making Bright Lady and, taking the lead running into the dip, won driven out. Umiddad was rolling about with exhaustion inside the final furlong, but refusing to surrender, managed to just hold on from the equally brave Bright Lady. Umiddad was reduced to a walk immediately after the line and it proved to be his last race.

In the final analysis Umiddad, although high-class was below the very best. He was an out and out stayer although not one in appearance and after his juvenile days he needed a minimum eleven furlongs to be seen at his best. No horse ever had more courage and Frank Butters and Gordon Richards must have speculated that had Nasrullah possessed even half of Umiddad's commitment and bravery, he would surely have been the best horse the Aga, Butters and Richards had ever been associated with; possibly better even than Bahram.

*   *   *

With the war in Europe ending on 8th May 1945, a day before the Two Thousand Guineas, racing started to slowly return to normal.

The 1945 season began on 2nd April at Ascot and Pontefract, and closed at Newmarket on 1st November. Racing returned to the Rowley Mile for the first time since 1939.

The war years produced some strange racing at times but, as far as Newmarket was concerned at least, it was very competitive. Due to the shortage of races the field sizes were above average and races difficult to win. Frank Butters once told Nesbit Waddington that it was sometimes as hard to get a place in races during the war years as win them in peacetime.

*   *   *

Tehran was kept in training as a four-year-old in 1945 – the Aga being unable to make the decision to retire him – with the Ascot Gold Cup as his objective. He won his three preparation races easily; in the second he again beat Ocean Swell, and all seemed set for Ascot. However, Tehran was a heavy-topped, long striding colt who hit the ground very hard and, although he acted on any going, unfortunately for him, the ground at Ascot was almost hard. Although odds-on he was most uncomfortable on it; every serious observer noting his inability to stride out, and he could finish only second to Ocean Swell. He pulled up feelingly and appeared lame.

Tehran was a lazy sort who took some getting fit and in the view of his jockey Gordon Richards a most "gallant" horse a "really tremendous battler with the heart of a lion" who would simply not accept defeat. On one occasion when he was in a desperate finish with Ocean Swell he kept finding more when it seemed certain Ocean Swell would pass him. Many congratulated Richards on an outstanding ride to keep Tehran in front. However, in his autobiography Richards modestly makes it clear that the credit must all go to the horse.

Even Frank Butters, who rarely spoke effusively about any horse, said "He is the right sort; the beggar does nothing but eat and sleep"! Butters thought the placid, intelligent and kind Tehran could be considered unlucky not to have won the Triple Crown. It had not been possible to get him fully fit for the Two Thousand Guineas and he had been badly drawn. Tehran suffered a slight setback in his preparation for the Derby, serious for a horse that needed as much work as he could get. Incidentally, Ocean Swell was the last Derby winner to win the Ascot Gold Cup; sadly, there is no prospect of him losing this distinction.

When asked to name the six best horses he had trained Butters did not include Tehran. However, apart from his last race, he was unfortunate in that he ran only at Newmarket. Although he needed at least twelve furlongs to be at his best, there would seem to be sufficient evidence that he was worthy for inclusion with the very best: not far behind Bahram and Fairway.

The three-year-olds did not amount to much the best of which was a filly: Naishapur (Nearco – Udaipur by Blandford) which made her a half-sister to Umiddad. Naishapur raced only once as a juvenile when as a "well-grown" sort she was outpaced. She began 1945 with a win in a minor stakes race at Newmarket over seven furlongs as the odds-on favourite. She next ran in the Oaks, still run on the July course at Newmarket, where, looking in "grand trim" she was beaten a short-head into second place by Sun Stream (Hyperion – Drift by Swynford). Some observers felt Naishapur may have been unlucky; however, as Sun Stream was owned by Lord Derby it must have given his Lordship considerable pleasure to have beaten the Aga!

Naishapur was disappointing next time when beaten comfortably at odds of 2–7 in the Falmouth Stakes. She recovered herself to land odds of 1–7 in the Rutland Stakes; which turned out to be her last win. She was unplaced in the St Leger before concluding her career by failing to land odds of 5–6 when second in the Great Foal Stakes. Her best form was good but she was not consistent. At stud she produced four winners from seven foals before being sent to North America.

The two best juveniles in Butters yard were Nasrullah's sister Rivaz who has been discussed and a colt, Khaled (Hyperion – Éclair by Ethnarch) who was unbeaten in three races including the Coventry and Middle Park Stakes. The Aga, who of course was barred by Lord Derby from sending any mares to Hyperion, bought Éclair in foal to Hyperion for 3,500 guineas (£140,000) in 1942.

It can only be imagined what his Lordship thought when Khaled beat his horse, Sky High (Hyperion – Pyramid by Papyrus), in the

Coventry Stakes! What made it worse was that Sky High was the odds-on favourite at 2–7! It is stretching matters too far to imagine that Lord Derby strolled across the Ascot unsaddling enclose and, grasping the Aga warmly by the hand, congratulated him on his win!

*   *   *

1946 saw racing return to something like normality; in more ways than one. Frank Butters headed the list of leading trainers, with almost twice the win prize money as Fred Darling in second. Butters trained the winner of the Oaks for Sir Alfred Butt. Steady Aim (Felstead – Quick Arrow by Casterari) won a small race as a juvenile and the Oaks was her only win at three from two starts. She was injured whilst being trained for the St Leger and never raced again. Steady Aim was described as a "plain-looking" filly with "weak-looking bent hocks" and "not much behind the saddle". However, she was better in front with an "honest head and eye".

Khaled trained on winning the Column Produce and St James's Palace Stakes. He was second in the Two Thousand Guineas albeit a respectful four lengths behind comfortable winner Happy Knight (Colombo – Happy Morn by D'Orsay). However, Khaled did not really stay beyond a mile; there was little stamina on his dam's side, and he failed to stay in both the Derby and Eclipse Stakes. He retired to stud in Ireland but stood for only one season before he was sold and exported to Argentina.

Early in July a colt: Claro (Colombo – Clovelly by Mahmoud) was transferred to Butters from Ireland where he had been trained by Hubert Hartigan. Claro, described as "a grand stamp of bay colt", raced nine times as a juvenile in Ireland winning twice and finishing second four times. As a three-year-old he won the Irish Two Thousand Guineas and finished second in the Irish Derby before he was transferred to Fitzroy House. Within a week he won the Dullingham Stakes but then ran moderately in his next three races before recovering his form in the Great Foal Stakes at Newmarket. He concluded the season with seconds in the Champion Stakes and Cambridgeshire. He looked set to win good races in 1947 but failed to win any of his eleven races although he was placed six times. He might have won on one occasion if he had not been attacked and savaged in the last 100 yards and was only beaten a neck.

Claro was a tough sort but there is a suggestion that Butters may not have handled him as well as he might. Claro raced eleven times over the course of the year, without a break, in the best company in stakes and handicap races. It may have been that Claro's work suggested that he was taking his races well. However, the evidence of some moderate performances suggested that the hard races he endured, during which he did not flinch, eventually took their toll. Claro raced 27 times in three years and, although he won only four races, he was second or third fifteen times. At his best he could run to a *Timeform* rating of 125.

Sir Alfred Butt had a very smart juvenile in Petition (Fair Trial – Art Paper by Artist's Proof) who won The New, Richmond, Gimcrack and Champagne Stakes and in most years would have topped the Free Handicap. However, Petition who was a beautifully made colt with a pleasant disposition and a "glorious" action was unfortunate to be foaled in the same year as Tudor Minstrel (Owen Tudor – Sansonnet by Sansovino).

In the Dewhurst Stakes the Aga and Frank Butters were represented by a maiden from four starts that had seemed to lack speed for the top level. However, Migoli (Bois Roussel – Mah Iran by Bahram) was just waiting for the opportunity to race over seven furlongs and gave every impression of quickening out of the dip as he ran on strongly to prevail. He looked a promising stayer for next year.

The best filly was Neocracy (Nearco – Harina by Blandford). She was unplaced on her debut but then won the Lonsdale Stakes at Epsom and the Princess Elizabeth Stakes at Ascot. She had a hard race at Ascot and it probably left its mark as she was below her best when third in the July Stakes at Newmarket. This was her final race of the year and she ran only once as a three-year-old; unplaced in the One Thousand Guineas. Physically she was an unprepossessing sort; leggy and light-framed, however, this did not stop her from being very successful at stud. She produced nine winners from eleven surviving foals in fifteen years including Tulyar (by Tehran), Cobetto (by Migoli) and Saint Crespin III (by Aureole). She had earned her retirement when it came in 1966 when she was twenty-two.

*   *   *

Tudor Minstrel proved to be an outstanding winner of the 1947 Two Thousand Guineas; possibly the best ever until the arrival of Frankel. However, even if Tudor Minstrel had run below his best Petition would still not have won. After winning a minor stakes race by ten lengths Petition ran very moderately in the first colts Classic. He was beaten at halfway and was then sick and off his feed. He returned short of full fitness and was beaten in the Sussex Stakes at odds on. His only other race was moderate third in a minor stakes race. That was his final race of a disappointing year and it could only be hoped he would do better next year as a four-year-old.

Migoli did much better winning six of his eight races: Craven, Royal Standard, King Edward VII, Eclipse and Champion Stakes. He was second in the Derby and third in the St Leger. Strangely for a horse that lacked speed he did not seem stay in either the Derby or St Leger and was at his best over ten furlongs. He would be kept in training as a four-year-old.

If Frank Butters thought that Nasrullah had stretched his patience and emotions to the limit he was about to discover another of Nearco's progeny possessing exasperating tendencies. This time it was the female of the species in the form of Masaka who was out of Majideh by Mahmoud. As a juvenile she did not give much cause for concern; she won a minor stakes race at 2–5 on her debut, the Queen Mary convincingly and the July Stakes, beating colts. Then she began coughing and when she returned she was third in a valuable stakes race and her final race resulted in a fourth in the Gimcrack Stakes. She had looked the winner but, perhaps displaying an early sign of temperament, did not run on…

The best juveniles apart from Masaka were two colts by Nasrullah: Noor out of Queen of Bagdad by Bahram and Nathoo out of Taj Shirin by Gainsborough. Noor, a leggy, narrow sort raced seven times over five and six furlongs winning twice; nurseries at Doncaster and Newmarket. He was bred to stay ten furlongs. Nathoo was unplaced in his first four outings but a second in a Manchester Nursery indicated that he would do better as a three-year-old.

*   *   *

Both Migoli and Petition justified the decision to keep them in training in 1948. Petition won the Victoria Cup carrying second top weight, was surprisingly beaten in the Rous Memorial at Royal Ascot in a match, before concluding his career by winning the Eclipse Stakes. Petition was a very brave and courageous horse. He did reasonably well at stud but his crowning achievement was to sire the great Petite Etoile out of Star of Iran.

Migoli won four of his eight races, but he might easily have done better; he won three relatively minor stakes races, was beaten only a neck in the Coronation Cup and, although he was only fourth, he was beaten only a length in the Eclipse Stakes behind Petition. However, both his and Frank Butters big triumph was to win the Prix de l'Arc de Triomphe. Although it must be conceded that the race lacked Goyama (Goya – Deveriness by Finglas) and both Pearl Diver (Vatellor – Pearl Cap by Le Capucin) and Rigolo (Puits d'Amour – Riberac by Kircubbin) failed to show their form. Nonetheless for Migoli to win "easily" was no mean achievement, he was a very brave, genuine and consistent horse that never gave up.

Handling Migoli and Petition was something Frank Butters took in his stride but training Masaka had him tearing out what little hair he retained. All began well enough when she won the One Thousand Guineas Trial at Kempton after which she was made favourite for the One Thousand Guineas itself. Her supporters never entertained hopes of victory at any stage; she resolutely refused to start with the rest of the field, swerved left and only then, and with great reluctance, did she consent to run but was unable to challenge.

Masaka did not race again before the Oaks where following her mulish display in the 'Guineas she was 7–1 third favourite under a new jockey: Billy Nevett. This time she was far more accommodating and after making rapid headway six furlongs out she forged clear to win by six lengths. If Butters thought he had found the answer to her he was sadly wrong. At Royal Ascot she was a warm favourite for the Coronation Stakes but was at her recalcitrant worst; very unruly at the start and refusing to race.

Masaka was transferred to Ireland to the care of Hubert Hartigan probably with the Irish Oaks in mind. With Aubrey Brabazon aboard she was backed down to even money favourite and never gave her supporters any cause for concern, winning comfortably. On returning to unsaddle Brabazon might have expected Aly to have a congratulatory word for him. Unfortunately Aly, probably with Masaka's temperament in mind, had backed his other runner in the race Amina. She was an 8–1 chance, and finished second carrying Aly's £500 (18,000) bet. "You bastard" was all Aly said looking in the direction of Brabazon and Masaka. It summed matters up really, was he talking to the jockey or the filly! It had to be Masaka of course but Brabazon must have wondered what Aly was so annoyed about! Frank Butters lost out on a Classic winner but was probably very relieved to see the back of the highly talented but mercurial Masaka.

Noor progressed without being quite top-class. Nonetheless he won two minor races and was third in both the Derby and Eclipse Stakes. However, he improved again when sent to North America to race as a four-year-old; which has been covered in an earlier chapter. Nathoo won the Irish Derby before he was sold to race in North America.

* * *

Frank Butters was by now seventy but there were no signs that he was losing his touch; in 1949 he was champion trainer for the eighth time. He had a host of juvenile talent and prospects for the 1950 classics looked bright. In Palestine (Fair Trial – Una by Tetratema) and Diableretta (Dante – Dodoma by Dastur) the Aga and Butters had the year's best two-year-old colt and filly. However, it had been an exceptionally dry summer and many juveniles could not be adequately trained and failed to see the racecourse.

For most of the year Palestine had looked as good as anything the Aga had ever bred and Butters trained. He reeled off six wins: the Sandown Park Stud Produce Stakes at odds of 2–5, Coventry 1–2, National Breeders Produce 4–6, Richmond 6–100, Gimcrack 1–25 and Champagne Stakes 1–9. He had never started at odds against, was never shown the whip and won these six races by a combined distance of twenty-six lengths. Significantly the going was good, firm or hard in all his races and Palestine clearly relished the conditions. The going for the Middle Park Stakes had some give and this combined with Palestine being a shade stale resulted in his first defeat. He went off at 2–7 but although Richards tried to restrain him to conserve as much energy as possible Palestine was comfortably beaten by Masked Light (Signal Light – Mashaq by Massine). This defeat meant that Masked Light and not Palestine topped the Free Handicap despite the relative wins and prize money being three and £4,777 and six and £16,931 in favour of Palestine.

Diableretta was beaten on her debut but then won seven consecutive races: a minor stakes, Acorn Plate, Queen Mary, July, Cherry Hinton, Molecomb and Hopeful Stakes. Diableretta fought a tremendous battle with Corejada (Pharis – Tourzima by Tourbillion) in the Cheveley Park Stakes where she was beaten a head. However, there are grounds for believing that Diableretta should never have contested the race. She endured a very hard time which unfortunately left its mark and she was never the same again.

Diableretta was odds-on for all her races except her debut and the Queen Mary. Her seven wins had earned £12,088 (410,000) in win prize money. At three she won a minor stakes race at Hurst Park, where she was wilful and un-cooperative before the start, then ran badly in the One Thousand Guineas and was retired. At stud she produced seven winners from eight foals before she was sent to North America.

Neither Palestine nor Diableretta would have run in their final races of the year if the decision had been left with Butters. After Palestine had won six races and Diableretta seven, Butters decided that both had done enough for the year. He made it clear to all that both would be put away and trained for their respective Guineas in 1950.

On the Sunday before Newmarket's Second October Meeting Press Association reporter Norman Fairchild made his routine call to Frank Butters to ascertain the Fitzroy House runners for the coming week. To his amazement he was told by Butters that Palestine would run in the Middle Park and Diableretta the Cheveley Park. Aly had been mesmerised by the idea that the Aga could become the first owner ever to win £100,000 (3,400,000) in England in one season. Aly persuaded the Aga to run the pair against Butters better advice.

Butters was horrified at the prospect of both horses running in big races when every instinct and a lifetimes experience told him they were not in a suitable condition for the task. His worst fears were realized: both had "gone over the top" and were beaten. It is not clear whether the Aga knew that Butters was very displeased about the decision to Palestine and Diableretta but he did stay at Fitzroy House for the meeting. The Aga and the Begum instead stayed with Harry Wragg and his wife at Abington Place. Wragg, of course, trained horses that ran in the name of the Begum.

Ironically Aly became the first owner to achieve the feat of winning over £100,000 in 1959 with the mighty Petite Etoile supplying over half of his winnings. Interestingly like Diableretta, Petite Etoile traced back to Mumtaz Mahal in the tail female line and in the tail male line she was a grand-daughter of Palestine's sire: Fair Trial.

A grey colt Tabriz (Tehran – La Li by Blenheim) won the Windsor Castle and Royal Lodge Stakes but was beaten five lengths in the Houghton Stakes at odds of 2–5. His portrait shows an immature sort that would do better with time.

Kisaki (Blue Peter – Clovelly by Mahmoud) was a good-bodied filly who made her debut in the Rous Stakes at Doncaster, finishing third, before making all the running to win by four lengths in the Imperial Produce Stakes at Kempton. The Aga and Butters had a one-two as Éclat (Stardust – Éclair by Ethnarch) finished second. Kisaki was then well beaten in the Dewhurst Stakes. Éclat was then disappointingly beaten at odds-on in the Prendergast Stakes and rather worryingly had displayed signs of temperament.

Tambara (Nasrullah – Theresina by Diophon), a lightly-framed filly, was third on her debut in the Princess Margaret Stakes and then won the Rous Memorial and Clearwell Stakes.

The best three-year-olds that year were Moondust (Stardust – Mah Iran by Bahram) which meant he was a half-brother to Migoli, and Dust Devil (Stardust – Udaipur by Blandford) which made him a half-brother to Umiddad. Moondust raced only once as a juvenile finishing third in the Chesterfield Stakes. As a three-year-old he raced nine times and proved himself a tough performer just below the top level. He won the Craven and Diomed Stakes before finishing first in the Irish St Leger but was disqualified. Dust Devil raced twice as a juvenile winning the Dalham Stakes. He was troubled by a splint and did not reappear in 1949 until the St Leger when he finished second. He won the Jockey Club Stakes from three further races.

Butters had every reason to look forward to the 1950 season. Unfortunately fate intervened in as cruel a manner as could be imagined.

*   *   *

Towards the end of 1949 Butters left home on his bicycle, a legacy of his wartime economy, to attend a committee meeting at the Rous Memorial Hospital. Returning home he stopped in the middle of the High Street to turn into Blackbear Lane and was knocked over by a lorry resulting in Butters sustaining serious head injuries. The Aga Khan arranged for him to be sent to the greatest neurosurgeons in the world; but the damage to his brain was considered irreparable and he was forced to retire. He was reduced to the status of a man that was still alive but with his principal mental faculties destroyed.

For the last 18 years Frank Butters had enjoyed almost unbroken success training mainly the blue-bloods of the Aga Khan's racing and breeding empire. He trained the winners of eleven Classics and had a further fifteen placed. He trained the winners of all the Classics for the Aga Khan with the exception of the One Thousand Guineas. The Derby was won in consecutive years and the Oaks and St Leger both four times each. He trained Felicitation to win a second Ascot Gold Cup and Migoli and Petition to win the Eclipse Stakes. In addition Migoli won the Prix de l'Arc de Triomphe.

Frank and his wife Cossie left Fitzroy House and settled at Paddocks Lodge in the Avenue next to Tattersalls to live out what remained of their lives as best they could. Butters was attended by a male nurse who would walk with him during his daily constitutional. Each afternoon when he had had tea Butters would look at his watch and remark "Time for stables now". Frank Butters spent eight years in retirement in Newmarket before eventually he was forced to move into a nursing home in Northampton where he died on 31st December 1957.

*   *   *

Frank Butters was a truly great trainer ranked third by *A Century of Champions* behind only Vincent O'Brien and Fred Darling. The Aga Khan described him as "the greatest trainer of all" within his experience of racing. Notwithstanding the view of George Lambton, which was shared by Lord Derby, Butters was generally regarded as a great trainer by almost all other observers. However, there is no doubt he belonged to the old school of trainers who believed in giving his horses plenty of strong work to make them hard and fit; the inevitable result was that some broke down. However, he was fortunate in that his principal patron, the Aga Khan, could well afford to regard himself as better off without any horse that could not stand up to his trainers searching preparations.

Notwithstanding this Eric Rickman wrote of Butters that he would "very rarely have them ridden out at the end of a strong gallop to make it a thorough trial". Unlike many trainers Butters did not keep a "trial book" preferring to use his eyes and experience to judge when a horse was ready. This method would seem to have worked well enough except, of course, when handling a horse like Bahram; who kept the true level of his talent and fitness strictly to himself!

The Aga Khan made his views on training horses clear in his 1954 memoirs; "There is too much coddling at present, far too much cotton wool. Since nearly all trainers subscribe to the current fashionable views it does not matter greatly, but I think if any of them came up against one of the hard men of the past…they would show up badly". He continued "The reason given is doubtless that in the old days, many horses were broken down in the process of training". He cites the example of Peter Gilpin – who trained Pretty Polly – and worked his horses hard and who once broke down a filly that was favourite for the Derby; just a few days before the race. Gilpin was not at all ruffled and did not even apologise to the owner! He stated that if he had spared her in the gallop she would not have won the Derby. From this it can be construed that the Aga would prefer his horses made fit for their races and not asked to race when "short of a gallop".

It should be remembered that winning top races has rarely been possible with a horse that was not completely fit and well. No trainer could have won as many of the most important races if he simply worked his horses hard and sent them to the races. Horses trained in such a manner can win one race, possibly two, but will not be able to maintain their form. The secret of successful training is to be able to map out each horses path for the season and prepare them so that they can meet each challenge in the appropriate condition. A horse with classic pretentions, for example, will not last long if he is presented for his trial in absolute peak condition. A good trainer will have him about 80/85% fit and able to progress from the race. Once the horse is fit he will not maintain his health and strength for long if the trainer continues to give them hard work instead of keeping them ticking over and mentally happy.

Butters was dedicated to ensuring that his charges were fit to run for their lives on a big race day. His only concern was winning Classics and major races and had little interest in handicaps.

*   *   *

Butters once said that he would have liked to train a champion sprinter but he never had a suitable horse in his yard. That is not to say that plenty of the best horses in his care could not have won good sprint races but the emphasis in his time was to breed horses that could win over the Classic distance of twelve furlongs. Any horses that were below the top level that could not win at 8–12 furlongs would not have the speed to win sprints.

In the same way Butters was never really a force in big handicaps. His stable and his owner's policy was to concentrate on weight-for-age races and in addition there was little or no consideration given to betting. Horses that are aimed at the best non-handicap races soon have the true level of their ability exposed to the handicapper and are therefore vulnerable to underexposed sorts.

*   *   *

That Frank Butters managed year after year to train horses at the top level; and to keep their form through the year, amply demonstrates that he knew how much work each needed at any time. Put quite simply Lord Derby and George Lambton, although fine men, were wrong about Frank Butters and the proof of that statement is confirmed by eighteen years at the top of his profession, training for a demanding owner, and the results he obtained.

Butters, like Dick Dawson, preferred to use work riders rather than jockeys for gallops. Charlie Smirke could not understand why this was so and said neither explained to him why. In all probability both felt that a stable lad would carry out the trainers instructions for fear of the consequences; a jockey, particularly Smirke might just be tempted to find out what the horse could do if asked for more. In any event Butters only had time for Gordon Richards, Harry Wragg and Doug Smith and of course he had a strong dislike of Charlie Smirke!

*   *   *

Frank Butters was completely loyal to the interests of his patrons and was only concerned with getting his horses fit and well for the engagements made for them. He had very little interest in betting and his limit would seem to have been £5 (240) each way on a horse with a chance at long odds. In 1938 he sent a cheque for £10 (480) to Eric Rickman in payment for a losing bet. Enclosed was a note which concluded "I am pleased I do not bet much, or I would be very much on the wrong side".

This might surprise some who assume the trainer always knows when his horses will win. The truth in most cases, with even the best trainers, is that they only know when the horse is ready to perform at their best. The only occasion Butters had a sizable bet was on Fairway for the Derby; and on the day both he and George Lambton knew Fairway had little chance, before the race was run, due to the state he had got himself into. Those of his owners who enjoyed a bet knew he hated to give an assessment of any horse's chances; and others who sort such information received very short shift.

*   *   *

Bahram was the best horse Butters ever trained, however, there have been occasions when he named Fairway as the best and there was probably not much between them. In any event when asked about the six best horses he had trained by journalist Eric Rickman he said he had no difficulty with the first four: Bahram, Fairway, Colorado and Toboggan. He concluded that he could complete the list with Felicitation and Mahmoud. He said "Bahram was certainly the best… and he was very lazy at all times and never beaten, not even I knew how good he was".

*   *   *

Despite his workload he found time to help Sir Alfred Butt manage the Brook Stud in Newmarket owned by Sir Alfred. The journalist Quintin Gilbey wrote "Frank Butters was introspective, and behind that open countenance and those steadfast blue eyes there was a deep suspicion of his fellow man".

Richard Baerlein had early experience of Butters' suspicion with the fourth estate. In those days there was no two-day or even overnight declarations, the latter were not introduced until 1960. The editor of the *Evening Standard,* for whom Baerlein was writing, asked him to try and organise their own list of runners; instead of relying on the Press Association which sent a list of probable runners to all newspapers. These could only be supplied with the goodwill and cooperation of trainers who were under no obligation to supply anything. Baerlein realised that this would be impossible without the help of Frank Butters so he was the first trainer he contacted for support. "I give my runners to Norman Fairchild of the Press Association on Sunday morning at 10 am and that's how it will remain" was the firm retort.

*   *   *

Theodore Felstead once asked Butters if he knew all of the horses in his stable by sight, and their pedigrees, "Why not" he retorted. Felstead thought this remarkable; but anyone who has visited a stable will be impressed by the ability of the trainer to recognize each of the horses under his control and how they were bred. In addition many trainers who train for large owner-breeders will receive the progeny of horses they have trained in the past and will be well aware of any aspects of family temperament and any physical characteristics. Felstead noted that Butters had no time for bad horses; they cost the same to keep as good ones. It is a question of economics and time: once a horse is established as moderate it is better out of a top stable without delay.

*   *   *

Strangely the Aga Khan was of the opinion that neither William Duke, who trained for him in Paris, or Butters, attached much importance to a horse's appearance. Both apparently believed that one yearling was as good as another as long as it had good health, nervous energy and the capacity to rest and sleep. He said Duke hardly ever looked at a horse before he brought it. This seems incredible: no matter how well-bred a horse is, if it has poor conformation, it can hardly represent a promising racing and breeding prospect.

*   *   *

Frank Butters was a man of the utmost integrity in both his professional and personal life; being essentially kind, considerate and dedicated to his job. He was said to have far more patience with thoroughbreds than humans and did not suffer fools and could be terse with anyone wasting his time. He did once display some public displeasure when a young gentleman, (sadly not named) who later became a Senior Steward at the Jockey Club, was bolted with on the Heath and unable to prevent his mount from galloping through the Aga Khan's Ascot two-year-olds!

Frank Butters was an old-fashioned trainer: he watched both lots each day from his hack and checked each horse in the yard twice each day; after morning work and at 6–00 p m promptly each evening.

He would work the yearlings before Christmas by galloping them on Saturdays along a three furlong strip of ground adjacent to the Cambridge Road. The yearlings would work four times along this same strip, Butters thought that not only would they find this educational but the exercise and experience would ensure they would be tired the following day: Sunday when everyone had a day off!

When he had spare time his hobbies were keeping budgerigars and gardening. In addition he enjoyed some shooting in the winter and an hour occasionally watching a cricket match. He also attended the reunions of the Twelve Club (despite its name it was restricted to 100 members, the name coming from the number of selections each member made: a sort of early, but restricted ten to follow) and the Old Framlinghamians.

Frank and his wife Cossie were looked after by a German house-keeper named Marie from their time in Austria. Marie moved with them to Italy back to England and Stanley House Stables where she ruled their home: Fairway House with considerable efficiency running the abode "like clockwork" and then carrying on the good work at Fitzroy House and finally at Paddocks Lodge. Marie was particularly punctilious about meal times and the gong would sound at 1–00 p m promptly to summon everyone to lunch!

*   *   *

The Aga was an infrequent visitor to Fitzroy Stables but when he did he would stay usually with Frank and Cossie. Just outside the house near to Blackbear Lane a small three-sided building; a sort of summer house, with a mosaic floor was constructed. This faced Mecca and enabled the Aga to pray at the same time each day.

*   *   *

During the autumn of each year and, accompanied by his wife Cossie, Butters would visit the Aga Khan in the South of France. Sadly after his accident he was no longer able to accept the invitation; although the Aga continued to extended one each year and was greatly disappointed that Butters' health precluded travel. Apart from the war years the Aga spoke to Butters each evening on the telephone to discuss stable plans. The Aga Khan described Mrs Butters as "delightful, courageous".

*   *   *

In his memoirs the Aga Khan wrote "From 1931 onwards I had the great good fortune of having my very dear friend Mr Frank Butters to train for me, for whom we all in my family have the greatest affection. Mr Butters, one of the most delightful human beings one could ever wish to meet, with a nature as clear and clean as a diamond but without its harshness…for me he trained a succession of magnificent horses…even more wonderful than his success with the great horses was his way with quite moderate ones. He had a knack of getting out of any horse the very best that the horse could do. In some ways Butters and Duke were alike, particularly in that neither attached the importance that most other trainers attach to the detailed appearance of the yearlings which came to them".

Whilst this eulogy may seem a shade grandiloquent it confirms beyond doubt that after eighteen years as his trainer the Aga Khan, not an individual easily impressed, held Frank Butters in the highest esteem. The Aga was not alone and this calm, honest, decent and dedicated man will be remembered as one of the great practitioners of his trade.

*   *   *

8   Freddie Fox

It is Manchester November Handicap day; the last of the season. The Champion Jockey for the last three seasons is facing a serious opponent for his title. The challenger: an experienced, reliable light-weight, a well-liked and honest, if journeyman rider, has the mount on the favourite in a nursery; if he can win he will achieve a lifetime's ambition.

*   *   *

Frederick Sydney Fox was born in 18th February 1888 at Condover, Durrington in Wiltshire. At 18 he was apprenticed to trainer Fred Pratt in Lambourn. Pratt was a nephew of Fred Archer and established a long relationship with James de Rothschild for whom he trained from 1903 until his retirement in 1945. Mr. de Rothschild was famous in many ways not least because he enjoyed a heavy tilt at the betting ring and brought off a substantial coup in the 1919 Cambridgeshire with Brigand (Lemberg – Plyte by Earwig), trained by Pratt.

Fox rode his first winner on Mr. W Nichols' Purdysburn (Fortunio – Helen's Bay by Hollywood) at Warwick on 8th April 1907 in a maiden apprentice selling plate. He followed up with his second winner the following day on Mr. A W Wood's Purslet (Aperse – Periscope by Hagioscope) in another selling handicap.

Fox's first experience of the hazards of race riding came six weeks later at Hurst Park during the Whitsuntide Meeting. He was riding Bessborough for James De Rothschild in the three-runner Open Plate when he collided with a mounted police horse and fell off! It has not been possible to establish if Fox faced any potential charges for dangerous riding! The King: Edward VII was present and expressed concern about the condition of Fox and the mounted policeman both of whom were taken to hospital. They survived unscathed and Fox would always claim that this was the only occasion he ever had any trouble with the law!

At the beginning of Fox's riding career Fred Darling was training for Lady de Bathe (Lillie Langtry) and in 1908 Darling put Fox up on Yentoi (Santoi – Rot by Sainfoin), owned by Lady de Bathe, in the Cesarewitch. Benefitting form an excellent ride by Fox, Yentoi won and this began a long association for him with the Beckhampton stable. Further success came in 1909 when he won the Ascot Gold Cup on Bomba (Carbine – St Neophyte by St Simon), trained by Pratt and owned by de Rothschild. This was quite a notable triumph for a young jockey of just twenty-one and Fox confirmed his promise when he won the valuable Liverpool Autumn Cup (handicap) worth £1,375 (130,000) in successive years in 1908/09 on Mr. George Edwardes' Santeve (Santoi – Wedding Eve by Rhidorroch).

However, Fox surpassed this in 1911 when he rode his first Classic winner on Atmah (Galeazzo – Mrs. Kenny by Tenny) in the One Thousand Guineas. It was a desperate finish with Fox managing to get the filly up virtually on the line to beat Mr. Jack Joel's Radiancy (Sundridge – Queen Elizabeth by Ladas) by a short head. This was the only race Atmah, owned by de Rothschild and trained by Pratt, ever won although she raced another seven times that year. She was also Fox's first ride in the Derby where she was a 33–1 outsider and did not finish in the first nine. Fox might have won his first Classic in 1910 when beaten a short head in the St. Leger. Fox was aboard Mr. Rothschild's Bronzino (Marco – Flitters by Galopin) and Frank Wootton on Lord Derby's colt magnificent Swynford (John O'Gaunt – Canterbury Pilgrim by Tristan): the grand sire of Bahram. It might have been thought that this excellent start would launch Fox's career but as will be seen matters are not always that simple.

Like many jockeys Fox was more successful as an apprentice than when he lost his allowance. During the three years he was an apprentice to Fred Pratt he rode 124 winners from 1,094 rides. In the seasons 1910/11 although he was hardly a failure the winners declined and he was offered fewer rides. Pratt and Fred Darling both advised Fox to ride in Germany; Darling had spent two years training for the powerful von Weinberg stable, and Fox rode for them during 1912 and 1913. The Australian jockey Frank Bullock rode in Germany from 1908 until 1913 and became Fox's chief rival. Fox learned the hard way from Bullock about how to ride the turning German courses; Bullock would slow the pace until the straight then gain lengths by quickening away.

*   *   *

Fox returned to Britain full-time in 1914 where he was only moderately successful. During the years of The Great War Fox, like all jockeys had far less rides and in truth he looked booked for a career as a journeyman jockey at best, the sort that makes only a moderate living.

Notwithstanding this in 1918 his 30 winners placed him third behind Steve Donoghue (65 winners) and Brownie Carslake (42) and it seemed possible his career might be progressing. The best horse Fox rode during this period was undoubtedly Mr. James White's Irish Elegance (Sir Archibald – Sweet Clorane by Clorane). A big strong colt Irish Elegance was foaled in 1915 and, as he was a half-breed, was not eligible for the stud book. Described as "a magnificent chestnut of great range, scope and quality", his photograph shows a horse of tremendous substance. Irish Elegance was the greatest handicapper in the history of racing and the second best sprinter of all-time. As a juvenile he won one of his three races, coming second in the other two.

As a three-year-old in 1918 he won three of his seven races. He began over seven furlongs in a handicap at Newmarket where he finished fourth and followed this with a third in a six furlong handicap at Manchester. Shortly afterwards, and with Fox in the plate on both occasions, Irish Elegance won two seven furlong handicaps at Newmarket.

Irish Elegance's next race was the July Cup which today would be considered a considerable step up in class. But in 1918 the two handicaps that he had won were worth £715 (24,000) and £585 (19,500) respectively and the July Cup £265 (8,900)! The value of the July Cup today might be preposterously high when compared with the One Thousand and Two Thousand Guineas but few would argue that its value should be higher than handicaps! In any event Irish Elegance won by five lengths and six at odds of 6–4 on.

That sadly was the last time Fox rode Irish Elegance. After the July Cup he was slightly disappointing when unplaced in a mile handicap over the Rowley mile but his final race of the season was a fine effort in the Cambridgeshire. Carrying the highest weight for a three-year-old of 8st. 12 lbs. he was beaten a head and the same.

Although Fox did not ride Irish Elegance again it is interesting to consider this great handicappers career as a four-year-old in 1919 when he reached his magnificent peak. He won four of his six races, however, these figures tell only a fraction of the story. He began the season winning a valuable £930 (30,750) six furlong handicap at Manchester. Starting at 8–13 and carrying top weight of 9 st. 9 lbs. he gave up to 38 lbs. to his rivals and won by six lengths. Next he was off to Ascot for the Royal Hunt Cup where he carried top weight of 9st. 11 lbs. giving away up to 49 lbs. to his rivals and, after racing prominently all the way, he won "brilliantly" by a length and a half and four lengths. He conceded 26 lbs. to Lord Jersey's Arion (Valens – Post Horn by Galloping Lad), a decent four-year-old handicapper, who finished second.

Shortly afterwards he ran in a valuable handicap £830 (27,500) at Newbury over six furlongs. This time carrying top weight of 10 st. 3 lbs. and conceding at least 27 lbs. to all his rivals, he could manage only third. Nothing daunted Irish Elegance then tackled the Stewards Cup at Goodwood where he carried 10 st. 2 lbs. and, conceding between 20 and 53 lbs. to his rivals, he finished second beaten under a length. He conceded the winner 44 lbs. Despite this huge weight concession, in the view on many observers he would have won but was slowly away.

Weight can stop a train so the old saying goes, and the handicapper, merciless it would seem on occasions, had Irish Elegance firmly in his grip. However, no handicapper, no matter how unfeeling could prevent this brave and magnificent horse from prevailing. After a short rest he went to Doncaster where he successfully carried 10 st. 2 lbs. in the Portland Handicap, conceding between 20 and 58 lbs. The winning margin was three lengths. Despite the incredible weight concession, Irish Elegance started favourite at 9–4 and was given a "tremendous" reception on Town Moor when he secured an "easy victory" That was effectively his career over, Irish Elegance's swan-song was something of an anti-climax when he walked over for the Select Stakes at Newmarket in October. Rating a horse capable of conceding such huge amounts of weight is difficult, *A Century of Champions* rated him 137 and it is hard to argue with that. Sadly he was a failure at stud.

*   *   *

With the War over Fox moved from Wantage to Newmarket where he rode for the next three years. He was retained by Sir Abe Bailey for the 1919 season. With the racing programme largely restored Fox had almost twice as many rides as the previous year and won 56 races. Probably the best horse Fox rode for Sir Abe that year was Southern (Sunstar – Pretty Dark by Dark Ronald) who won the Gimcrack Stakes and Lancashire Breeders' Produce Stakes. A tough sort Southern won three of his eight races as a juvenile but was comfortably held in the Champagne, Middle Park and Dewhurst Stakes. He was given 8 st. 3 lbs. in the Free Handicap; 18 pounds behind Major Dermot McCalmont's Tetratema (The Tetrarch – Scotch Gift by Symington).

*   *   *

In 1920 Fox was retained by Reg Day and in 1921 by both Day and Colledge Leader. He still rode for Sir Abe Bailey and, although relatively successful, Fox would not have been considered as one of the leading half a dozen jockeys of the period. He was not particularly in demand; for example he had no rides at Chester in 1920 and at the York Spring meeting he had only one for Sir Abe Bailey. At Ascot he rode in ten of the 28 races and at Goodwood eight of 28. Fox's mounts at the big meetings would decline over the following couple of years.

One good horse that Fox rode during this period was Major Harold Cayzer's Poisoned Arrow (Spearmint – White Lie by White Eagle) trained by Captain Gooch. Unraced as a juvenile Poisoned Arrow; foaled in 1919, was a consistent and genuine handicapper. He raced twenty-four times between the ages of three and five, winning seven times. He was very consistent and placed many times, usually conceding plenty of weight. Sadly Fox was not aboard for Poisoned Arrow's biggest win in the valuable £1,680 (72,500) Duke of York Stakes at Kempton. In addition Fox was replaced by Joe Childs for all of Poisoned Arrows races as a five-year-old.

Racing was at the mercy of industrial action on occasions and during 1920 the Houghton Meeting at Newmarket was abandoned due to a miners strike. This meant no Dewhurst Stakes or Cambridgeshire Handicap that year. Racing ceased on Monday 18th October and did not recommence until Friday 5th November. The miners were on strike again the following spring and racing was suspended from Monday 4th April until Friday 29th. This meant that the trials for the Two Thousand and One Thousand Guineas were not run and indeed it looked at one time as if the Classics themselves would be lost.

However, strong representations were made to the government and it was agreed that Newmarket could stage a one day meeting in order that both Classics could be run. This was on the understanding that the railways could not be used for either horses or spectators. The roads to the Rowley Mile were jammed with an endless stream of vehicles of all descriptions and the fields for the seven races were large including 26 for the colts' race and 24 for the fillies. The strike continued until the end of June and racing lost more fixtures.

*   *   *

At this stage of Fox's career it is surprising that after his early successes and his ability to ride at 7 st. 6lbs. that he was so relatively unsuccessful during the period from 1913 to 1925. But for the support of Captain Richard Gooch, who trained at Hodcott House, West Ilsley, and who used Fox to ride his handicappers with light weights, he might have fallen into obscurity. Fox had returned to Berkshire in 1922 and was to be based in East Ilsley, Beckhampton and Wantage for the remainder of his riding career.

Fox's best ride during this time was probably Major Cayzer's four-year-old Bhuidhaonach (Royal Realm – Countess Zia by Gallinule) in the Manchester Cup of 1923. His win by two lengths convinced Captain Gooch that he should ride the stables light-weights in handicaps. Nonetheless the next three years saw Fox's fortunes decline steadily with both the number of mounts and winners much lower. 1924 was to prove the nadir of Fox's career; his mounts dropped to just 283 and the number of winners to 20. 1925 saw some improvement to 35 winners from 372 mounts.

The best horse Fox rode in 1925 was the filly Tatra (Lemberg – Whitetor by Torpoint), trained by Gooch and owned by Mrs. Harold Cayzer. Tatra was only medium-sized but "was not lacking in depth, range and scope, and was particularly good behind the saddle". She was bought by Major Cayzer for 2,300 guineas (£94,000) as a year-ling. Although lacking in size she was not an early sort and was slow to come to hand and raced only once as a yearling.

Tatra was also backward as a three-year-old was unplaced in four races, and, in addition, disliked firm ground. It was not until the autumn that Captain Gooch persuaded Tatra to produce her best form. She then won three races in succession: two handicaps and then she beat Lord Astor's St. Germans (Swynford – Hamoaze by Torpoint) and Mr. Somerville Tattersall's Hurstwood (Gay Crusader – Bleasdale by Martagon) in the £6,334 (266,000) Jockey Club Stakes. There were only four runners and it was considered a match between the two colts and considerable surprise was generated when Tatra beat them both comfortably by three lengths with four lengths between second and third. It was decided to run her in the Cesarewitch but she developed leg problems and could not race again. Fox won his third Liverpool Autumn Cup (handicap) on Sir Hedworth Meux's Donzelon (Chaucer – Tortor by Volodyovski).

*   *   *

1926 marked a sharp upward turn in Fox's fortunes. This year he was riding principally for Captain Gooch, T. A. Foster and Dick Dawson, and his mounts increased by 200 and he more than doubled his number of winners from 35 to 74. Fox would have had more rides and ridden more winners but the National Strike again affected racing with the third day of Chester being abandoned. There was no racing from 6th until 20th May.

The best horse that Fox rode in 1926 was the filly Bongrace (Spion

Kop – Vaucluse by Dark Ronald); a somewhat leggy filly owned and bred by Lord Rosebery and trained by Jack Jarvis. Raced only once; unplaced, as a juvenile Bongrace won 8 of her 12 races as a three-year-old. Fox was aboard her only twice when she was required to carry a light weight and he did not actually win on either occasion. First in the Gold Vase at Ascot she finished third and in the Doncaster Cup where he finished second. At Doncaster Bongrace had won the Scarborough Stakes over a mile on the Thursday and was then declared for the Doncaster Cup on the Friday over two and a quarter miles. Fox was booked to ride as she was to carry only 7 st. 5 lbs.; the lightest weight that Fox ever rode at.

Starting as favourite at 9–4 Bongrace was in command halfway up the long Doncaster straight when Solly Joel's Glommen (Pommern – Lady Gladys by Sundridge) ridden by Harry Wragg challenged but in doing so rolled onto the filly hampering her to such an extent that Fox had to stop riding. Glommen went on to win by four lengths but nobody was surprised when the stewards altered the placings and awarded Bongrace the race. Bongrace and Glommen met again in the Jockey Club Cup but on different terms. At Doncaster she was receiving 35 lbs. but at Newmarket she was getting only sixteen but showing tremendous battling qualities she held on the win by a neck.

Bongrace suffered from setfast, an alarming if harmless condition where a horse is unable to walk because it can't bring its hind legs towards the front ones. Bongrace usually suffered an attack when she was not in strong work. For that reason Jack Jarvis kept her on the go throughout the season. Fortunately she possessed an excellent disposition and racing took very little out of her. Her trainer Jack Jarvis thought Bongrace was so lazy she would make a race of it with a donkey. She was unplaced in her only race in 1927. At stud she produced four winners including Ribbon (by Fairway), who won five races including the Middle Park Stakes beating Nasrullah.

In retrospect it can be seen that 1927 saw the turning point in Fox's career at a time when he seemed a journeyman rider at best. He was now 39 and although the previous year was better than recent seasons from now on it would a story of continual progress. The difference was that Fox was now riding more horses for the Aga Khan. Usually retained jockey Charlie Smirke would be on the most fancied runner and Fox on the "second string". At that time an owner had to state which horse was better fancied if he had two or more runners in any one race: the Aga Khan declared to win with …" Sometimes it was difficult to be sure which of the Aga's runners was the most likely winner. When a horse won that had not been declared to win with it was often greeted with hostility by the punters who considered that some sort of stroke had been pulled on them. Fox therefore would often ride one of the Aga's outsiders. He would usually be first choice for any light weight rides as Smirke could not ride at less than 8 st. 3 lbs.

Fox rode 72 winners as opposed to 74 the previous year but had many more rides: 714 compared with 571 the previous year suggesting that he was more in demand. He achieved the biggest win of the year when he steered Solly Joel's Trelawny (Son-in-Law – Polkerris by Polymelus) to victory in the valuable £2,847 (122,000) Royal Standard Stakes over a mile at Manchester's Whitsuntide meeting. As a three-year-old Trelawny was required to carry only 7 st. 5 lbs. it was an ideal mount for Fox.

Fox had begun 1927 by winning the Lincoln Handicap on Priory Park (Rocksavage – Chatham II by Darley Vale) for Jack Joel. However, he was in trouble at the Epsom Spring Meeting for his riding of Birth Control (Bachelor's Craft – Baby's Fate by Roi Herode) owned by W. A. Read and trained T. A. Foster. Incidentally, what wonderful naming! Clearly Mr. Read possessed a lively imagination! The Stewards: His Lordships Lonsdale, Durham, and Dalmeny, were not happy that Fox had ridden the horse to win. Lord Lonsdale was "in such a blazing temper that he would not listen to anything anyone said". The result was that Fox was suspended for the rest of the meeting. At the inquiry held by the Stewards at Newmarket on 26th April Fox's explanation was accepted.

That same year Fox rode Baytown (Achtoi – Princess Herodias by Poor Boy) who was no more than a useful handicapper but very kind, brave and consistent, and he simply thrived on racing. Physically he was workmanlike but very powerful and strong. Baytown was foaled in Ireland and ran his first three races there, winning the first two after which he was bought by Sir Charles Hyde for 5,500 guineas (£250,000). Fox rode Baytown for the first time on his third appearance at Phoenix Park; his first for Sir Charles. Baytown was then switched to the care of Norman Scobie at Whitsbury and ran three further times that year without success, but running with credit.

In 1928 Baytown won five of his twelve races, was second four times third twice and his winning stakes amounted to £7,861 (340,000). Fox rode him in ten of these races, winning three times. Baytown's wins came in the Irish Two Thousand Guineas and Derby, Fox being aboard both times, the Free Handicap and two minor races; Fox was the jockey in one of these races. Baytown was also an unlucky second in the Wood Ditton Stakes at Newmarket, which was not a contest for unraced three-year-olds at that time. He was also second in the Cesarewitch and third in the Champion Stakes. As a four-year-old Baytown was cast in his box in the spring and unable to race before Ascot. He raced only five times, winning once. By this time Fox had been replaced as jockey and did not ride him in any of his races. As a five-year-old he won two of his nine races. Fox was aboard for only one race, a second in the Jockey Club Cup. Baytown won ten of his thirty-two races and seldom ran a bad race.

In 1928 Fox rode 89 winners, more than he had done previously in any one year. However, he suffered a bad fall at Catterick and was fortunate to escape unscathed when the field galloped over his prostrate body. Bad as this was, it was nothing compared to the horrific accident that befell Captain Gooch a short while afterwards. Whilst hunting with the Quorn he fractured his spine in three places crippling him for the last ten years of his life.

*   *   *

Fred Fox was now forty years of age and although since the Great War he had been a reliable light weight, had done well and been successful winning many important handicaps he was now to enjoy the best years as a jockey. In 1929 Fox had looked at one stage as if he would win the jockey's title. Fox and Gordon Richards were closely matched for a time partly due to Richards suffering a fall which kept him out of Goodwood. The betting had Richards at 4–5 and Fox 6–4;

20–1 bar. Yes that is correct: those prices represented an under round of 5% in favour of the backer! The press coverage centered on the battle between "youth" and "a veteran" something that annoyed Fox who did not want to be reminded that he was forty-one years old and had ridden his first winner when Richards was just a boy of three! In the end Richards ran out a comfortably victor by 139 winners to 120.

At Sandown in June Fox rode five winners from six rides, and shortly afterwards after he rode Lord Ellesmere's filly Tiffin (Tetratema – Dawn-wind by Sunstar) to win the July Cup in a most thrilling race. Tiffin won all three of her races in 1929: the Fern Hill Stakes at Ascot, The July Cup and the King George Stakes at Goodwood, with Fox in the plate for all three races. At Ascot a heath fire was raging within a furlong of the finishing post but the dense clouds of smoke did not interfere with the race. Those really were different times; can you imagine the carnage those obsessed with health and safety "issues" would have caused if such an event occurred today! The course would have been cleared and race abandoned.

In the July Cup there were only three runners but it provided a memorable spectacle. The Aga Khan's Le Phare was slowly away and never in the race; Tiffin made the running and quickly established a two length lead. The race looked all over when "Jock" Whitney's Royal Minstrel (Tetratema – Harpsichord by Louvois) started to close the gap but with both jockeys asking their mounts for a maximum effort it was only when Royal Minstrel finally cracked that the filly was able to regain the lead close home to win by a short head.

In some quarters Fox was criticized for his ride in the 1929 Derby on Lord Woolavington's Walter Gay (Captain Cuttle – William's Pride by William the Third). However, Fox said that he was the most unsuitable mount he had ever ridden in the race. He could not act on a downhill course or firm ground. In addition he lacked the early speed necessary to find a good position. Not surprisingly Fred Darling had been dubious about running him. As if all this was not enough Walter Gay suffered interference when Solly Joel's Kopi (Spion Kop – Suncroft by Sunstar) fell but ran on well to take second.

Fox also rode the promising juveniles Press Gang (Hurry On – Fifinella by Polymelus) and Fair Diana (Hurry On – Daughter-in-Law by Son-in-Law); both owned by Lord Woolavington and trained by Fred Darling. Press Gang won the Rous Memorial, Middle Park and Hurst Park Great Two-year-old Stakes ridden by Fox and was ranked second in the Free Handicap with 9 st. 2 lbs. Fair Diana won the Champagne Stakes at Doncaster and was given 8 st. 9 lbs.

*   *   *

Fox was retained as stable jockey by Fred Darling at Beckhampton for 1930 and this helped considerably in his battle with Gordon Richards for the Jockey's Championship. With two days to go Fox led Richards by two, even though Fox had not ridden a winner for a week. Richards was being offered mounts even from stables he would not normally ride for and his brother: Clifford had willingly given up a mount at Warwick earlier in the week to enable Richards to ride another winner. Fox would not normally be happy to accept rides from outside stables that provided him with retainers. However, he was equally determined to win the title which was a life's ambition.

On the last day of the season; 22nd November, there was racing at Manchester and Lingfield Park. Both Fox and Richards were at Manchester where the big race was the Manchester November handicap. Although called Manchester the racecourse had several homes the final one being Castle Irwell situated two and half miles outside the city. Manchester closed for the final time in November 1963.

Richards won the first on Mr. R Clifford's Rivalry (Chivalrous – Renira by Renown) to draw level. Fox was runner-up in the second on Baron F de Tuyll's Canfield (Phalaris – Candescent by White Eagle). Richards went ahead by winning the November Handicap on Lord Glanely's Glorious Devon (Pommern – Skyglory by Sky-rocket) at which point with only three races to go most would have backed Richards to prevail even though Fox had two rides to come and Richards only one.

However, Fox was aboard two favourites, the first of which was Mr. D Goold's Landsong (Orpheus – Land Girl by Spearmint), a 5–1 chance in a highly competitive six furlong selling handicap. Fox won by a head with a short head between second and third, and Richards was down the field on his last mount of the season, Lord Glanely's

Good Sport (Westward Ho – Damask by Lemberg). They were now level and with Richards surprisingly having no rides in the last two races Fox's task was a simple one: win on his final mount in the next race and he was Champion Jockey.

Fox's final ride was the odds on favourite; Mr. H F Clayton's Isthmus (Belsize – Lady Lucy by Wargrave or Sir Edgar), in a mile nursery. He duly obliged by six lengths and Fox was Champion Jockey by one winner 129 to 128. Gordon Richards was drinking tea during Isthmus's race as he did not have a mount. The roar of the crowd told him that he was no longer Champion Jockey.

Three weeks later Fox entertained his fellow jockeys in the traditional Champions Dinner at the Piccadilly Hotel where his speech quite possibly set a record for brevity. "I thank you" he said and promptly sat down! Those present who had at any time been subjected to one of Fox's interminable yarns must have breathed a sigh of relief!

1930 had begun well for Fox when he won his second Classic in the Two Thousand Guineas aboard Diolite (Diophon – Needle Rock by Rock Sand). Fox had ridden Diolite as a juvenile to win his maiden but not when he had won the Coventry and Molecomb Stakes. Brought by his trainer F. G. Templeman on behalf of Sir Hugo Hirst; the Chairman and Managing Director of the General Electric Company, as a yearling, for just 480 guineas (£21,500) Diolite had proved a bargain by the end of his juvenile year. However, the Two Thousand Guineas was his only win of the season and the only time Fox rode him. Diolite was subjected to some rather eccentric placement after finishing third in the Derby: he ran in the Fern Hill Stakes at Ascot over five furlongs.

At Ascot Fox rode Mr. J. A. Dewar's The MacNab (Abbot's Trace – Sunny Moya by Sunstar) to win the Royal Hunt Cup trained by Fred Darling. However, that would not be the story of the day. There had been a heavy storm overnight and the Royal Stand sustained damage through a lightning strike. Shortly after noon rain began again and by the time the runners for the Hunt Cup had reached the paddock there was a heavy downpour. The MacNab made most of the running but little of the race could be distinguished in the mist and rain.

However, shortly after the finish of the race a tremendous thunderstorm hit the course and raged for almost an hour causing devastation. A bookmaker was killed in the Tattersall's enclosure and there were various other casualties. The numbers for the next race were being put into the frame, which caused mild amusement, as it was clear to anyone that further racing would be impossible. The deluge quickly converted the paddock into a lake and parts of the course were under water; just beyond the winning post a considerable area was submerged. The Stewards had no option but to abandon the remainder of the card. The five races not run were added to the Thursday and Friday cards which meant ten races and nine respectively were staged. The MacNab also won the Chesterfield Cup at Goodwood month later. Fox's success on the MacNab was one of the first since he had accepted a retainer from Fred Darling. Darling had wanted Gordon Richards to replace Joe Childs but Richards was retained by Lord Glanely.

Another big win for Fox in 1930 came in the Princess of Wales's Stakes at Newmarket on Press Gang. He also rode him to dead-heat for the Gordon Stakes with the Aga Khan's Ut Majeur. The other promising juvenile from the previous year Fair Diana showed little in two races.

*   *   *

Fox probably thought the zenith of his riding career had been reached in 1931 when Cameronian (Pharos – Una Cameron by Gainsborough) gave him his third Classic win. The year had begun well as Fox again won the Lincoln Handicap, in gloriously sunny spring weather, this time on Captain A. Stanley Wilson's five-year-old Knight Error (Prince Galahad – V.A.D. by The White Knight). Capt. Wilson had acquired Knight Error only three months previously from Sir George Noble for £500 (23,500). As the Lincoln was worth £1,730 (82,000) Capt. Wilson had got back his "monkey" with considerable interest!

Cameronian was a typical grandson of Phalaris being of beautiful quality and standing 15.3. Cameronian made history as the first horse to be able to run in a Classic after his owner had died. Prior to 1929 when an owner died all the entries made on behalf of their horses became void. This was unsatisfactory in many ways as it meant that a good horse could be prevented from running in any important races. The Jockey Club instigated a "friendly" action against the writer Edgar Wallace which resulted in a change in Rule 86 which was amended to read "Entries and Subscriptions made after 9th May 1929 shall not become void on the death of the person in whose name they were made or taken". Thus when Cameronian's owner and breeder the 1st Baron Dewar died on 11th April 1930, his nephew John Arthur Dewar, who had inherited his racing interests, was able to continue with Cameronian's Classic engagements.

Cameronian had been brought along with typical patience by Fred Darling and won his only race at two, a minor race at Salisbury, and was fancied to win the Craven Stakes at Newmarket on his three-year-old debut. However, he disappointed and finished only third. Subsequently

Cameronian was beaten in a gallop by Lord Ellesmere's Lemnarchus (Friar Marcus – Lemnos by Lemberg), who had won the Nonesuch Stakes at Epsom's spring meeting. Consequently Fox rode Lemnarchus, who was by this time Beckhampton's more fancied runner, in the Two Thousand Guineas.

Fox had been confident that Lemnarchus would win the first Classic but suffered the galling experience of watching Joe Childs ride Cameronian to a "smooth" victory. As if that was not bad enough Fox suffered more agony in the One Thousand Guineas, when unable to make up his mind about his mount. The choice was between Lord Ellesmere's Four Course (Tetratema – Dinner by Dinneford) and Lord Woolavington's Windybrae (Manna – Windyridge by Swynford) with Charlie Elliot to ride whichever mount Fox rejected. As Fox's indecision seemed never ending Lord Ellesmere suggested that Fox and Elliot tossed a coin to decide who would ride which filly. Elliot won and chose Four Course who beat Martin Benson's Lady Marjorie (Sansovino – Florena by Orby), ridden by Richards, a head. Windybrae finished eighth. Richards should have won on Lady Marjorie; as she was challenging inside the final furlong Richards applied his whip causing his mount to swerve and become unbalanced. She then produced a terrific turn of foot to be narrowly denied.

The view of most observers was that she would have won if Richards had simply ridden her to the line.

Cameronian did not race between the Classics but gave every satisfaction in a searching trial over twelve furlongs at Beckhampton when ridden by Childs. However, Fox was to ride him in the Derby. Epsom on Derby Day was at its glorious best with a mammoth crowd, the sun blazing down, it was also the King's birthday, and Cameronian was well backed. Fox was understandably nervous and Joe Childs gave him some kind advice: "Just ride as though you are in a seller, you have nothing to fear". Cameronian stormed home to beat Sir John Rutherford's Orpen (Solario – Harpy by Swynford) by three quarters of a length. "I brought out my whip and gave Cameronian a tap. He pulled out a bit extra, like the good horse he is, and for the last quarter of a mile I was always holding Orpen", reported Fox.

Cameronian easily won the St. James's Palace Stakes at Ascot and was odds on for the St. Leger where, ridden by Fox, he ran deplorably. Restless at the start where he kicked Orpen, he refused to settle in the race and finished tailed off. Fox told reporters "It was obvious when I got Cameronian to the post that there was something wrong with him. He was very upset and kicked Orpen. He then literally went mad, ran himself right out, and was completely done with once the straight was reached".

Although Cameronian had a temperature of 103 Darling refused to concede that he may have been "got at". When it was suggested to Darling that Cameronian had been subject to attentions of some miscreant he retorted "There are various causes for horses going suddenly wrong in this way, and I put no sinister construction whatever upon the occurrence. There is no question of the horse being "got at" or anything of that kind",

The Stewards incredibly took no action! Darling's stubborn stance seems to indicate a possible fear that anyone should question the security at Beckhampton or that Darling's staff were unable to protect one of his horses at the racecourse. In addition if Cameronian had been found to have been doped, then Darling, as the trainer, would have been responsible and his license withdrawn. Better to simply deny that any such thing was possible. Kept in training as a four-year-old

Cameronian continued to suffer from a high temperature until the autumn, a year after the St. Leger. He recovered his form enough to defeat Dastur in the Champion Stakes. Fox's successful year continued to the end and he won the Cesarewitch on Mr. F H W Cundell's Noble Star (Hapsburg – Hesper by Herodote), a horse Fox was also successful on in the Ascot and Goodwood Stakes.

Notwithstanding being the Champion Jockey of 1930 Fox was surprisingly removed as principal jockey to Fred Darling in 1931. After he had become champion there were rumours that Fox would retire. Bearing in mind that he was only 42 it was no surprise when he scotched any such thoughts "Why should I retire? Luckily, I enjoy very good health, and I have little or no trouble keeping my weight normal" he said.

Fred Darling had always wanted to appoint Gordon Richards as his stable jockey but Richards had a retainer to ride for Lord Glanely. Despite Fox being both the stable and Champion jockey the previous year Darling asked Fox if Richards could ride for the stable when available at which times Fox would have to ride the lesser stable lights. Fox was as genial a man as one could wish to meet but this was a most humiliating request and he declined to have any part of it.

Nonetheless Darling approached Gordon Richards about the position of stable jockey. However, Gordon Richards, who despite not being entirely happy with Lord Glanely was very loyal and he would not consider moving. However, Darling's offer persuaded Richards to ask Lord Glanely if he was prepared to match it. His Lordship was unable to do so and Richards felt able to accept Darling's offer.

This of course meant that Fox would no longer be first choice at Beckhampton. He was stunned and shocked to learn he had been replaced as first jockey. Darling had been determined for years to secure the services of Gordon Richards and it was hardly Richards's fault that Fox lost out. However, the manner in which Darling conducted the matter did his reputation no good whatsoever. Instead of telling Fox privately that he had been replaced the first he knew about the matter was when told by the press.

The result of this was that during the winter of 1931–32 Fox decided that he would ride free-lance which he did in 1932 and 1933.

Both years saw no decline in the number of mounts offered to Fox but his winners were reduced. However, he was riding for the Aga Khan and this would have a profound influence on the remaining five years of his career. By this time Michael Beary had replaced Charlie Smirke as principle jockey to Dick Dawson after Smirke had been warned off in 1928.

Fox had ridden the winner of the Victoria Cup; then run at Hurst Park, on Knight Error, the horse's only win of the season. But more importantly Fox's first big win of the year for the Aga Khan came in the Chester Vase, which at that time was for three and four-year-olds. Although the younger horses received considerable weight from their elders, the amount varied with various penalties, and they were still at a disadvantage. With Fox putting up a pound overweight at 7 st. 5 lbs. it was a good performance for Bulandshar to win by four lengths. This was Bulandshar's only win of the year but he ran with credit on other occasions, although Fox did not ride him again. He was, of course, trained by Frank Butters. Fox also rode Firdaussi for the Aga Khan and Frank Butters to win the St. Leger. The story of this race has already been related.

Fox again rode for the Aga Khan in the 1933 Chester Vase on the three-year-old Shamsuddin (Solario – Firouze Mahal by The Tetrarch) who was to carry 7st. 4 lbs. Fox put up two pounds over-weight on the useful, but some way below top-class, Shamsuddin who finished second. The overweight did not cost him the race as the winner was Hyperion! At this stage Fox was usually only asked to ride for the Aga when the horse concerned was due to carry a low weight or was a second string.

Fox won the valuable, £2,040 (108,000) Manchester Cup (handi-cap), on Robber Chief (Sherwood Starr – Rockmills by Mushroom) for Sir Alfred Butt. It was to be Robber Chief's only win of the year and Fox, perhaps surprisingly, rode him only twice from the thirteen times the tough gelding raced that year.

Fox won the Stewards Cup on Pharacre (Pharos – Sweet Acre by Orby) owned by Capt. Arnold Wills, a member of the tobacco firm, and trained by Frank Butters. It was an ideal ride for Fox as Pharacre had been given just 7st. 4 lbs. Fox put up a pound overweight and may have been a shade fortunate to win. The top weight: Mrs. C L Mackean's Solenoid (Soldennis – Shannon Jug by Athlone) who had won the previous year carrying 7st. 10lbs., was now burdened with 9st. 7lbs. Despite this Solenoid might still have won but for meeting interference a furlong from the finish. He was third, beaten a head and three quarters of a length. Fox enjoyed a decent Goodwood as he was also successful in the Lavant Stakes on Sir Richard Garton's juvenile Propaganda (Bachelor' Double – Betsy Trotwood by Flying Orb) and in the Trundle Stakes (Handicap) on Mr. J E Widener's Seminole (Diligence – Blanche by White Eagle) who carried 7st. 7lbs.

Doncaster's St. Leger meeting brought Fox more success in the Aga's colours when he rode the filly Pomme au Four (Spion Kop – Pomare by Saint Just); 7st. 6lbs. to victory in the Prince of Wales's Nursery.

Fox enjoyed his best win of the year at the Newmarket Second October Meeting when he rode Seminole to victory in the Cesarewitch. A four-year-old gelding, Seminole was bred at the National Stud and was a half-brother to Blandford. Diligence was by Hurry On and Seminole looked every inch a descendent of him, having plenty of size and strength, whilst not exactly the most handsome horse in training.

Seminole was unraced as a juvenile and only really came to himself when four. In the build up to the Cesarewitch Seminole had been pricked whilst being shod and was lame causing his trainer Capt. Cecil Boyd-Rochfort to regard his prospects as hopeless. It was announced that Fox would ride another horse in the stable, Lady Zia Wernher's Sandals (Manna – Simon's Shoes by Simon Square). However, Seminole made a quick recovery and then began to work so well that Fox was switched back to ride him. What is normally a most competitive race was won decisively by Seminole; the distances were two lengths and four.

* * *

In 1934 Fox rode not only for Capt. Gooch but also the King: George V. However, it would be his riding of Bahram that would ultimately define his career which is covered in the chapters on Bahram. Michael

Beary was no longer retained by the Aga Khan and this would lead to Fox getting more rides. An early example was Fox riding Gino in the Lincoln Handicap; Gino carried 8st. 7lbs. and was second favourite so could not be considered merely an outsider with a light weight. Notwithstanding this it should not be forgotten that the Aga would always prefer Gordon Richards whenever he was available.

Fox rode a treble at the Liverpool Spring Meeting for three different owners. At that time the flat season opened on a Monday at Lincoln for a three-day meeting with the Lincolnshire Handicap run on the Wednesday. Then racing moved to Liverpool for a three-day mixed meeting with the Grand National staged on Friday. As the "Lincoln" and Grand National were staged in the same week each year this was the origin of the "spring double".

The Aga had Umidwar and Badruddin in the Two Thousand Guineas with Harry Wragg on the former and Fox the latter. Neither stood any real chance against the 2–7 favourite; Lord Glanely's mighty Colombo (Manna – Lady Nairne by Chaucer) who won very easily. Fox managed to finish third with Wragg unplaced. Fox had an equally impossible task when given the leg up on Felicitation in the March Stakes. Standing in his way this time was the great Hyperion who obliged at odds of 40–105. Nonetheless it was clear that the Aga was willing to use Fox more and more on the big occasions. In the One Thousand Guineas Fox rode Mrs. Rustom for the Aga but she was unplaced.

Fox was engaged by Marcus Marsh to ride H. H. Maharaja of Rajpipla's Windsor Lad at Chester in the Vase. The course would not have been suitable for a big long-striding horse like Windsor Lad but Marsh felt the experience would teach him to be handy and learn how to negotiate a sharp left-handed track. Normally Windsor Lad would have been ridden by Charlie Smirke but he was set to carry only 7st. 12 lbs. about five pounds below his minimum.

Smirke predictably was livid; "Damn it Marky, even putting up five pounds overweight you know we'd still be a certainty".

"You probably would" replied Marsh, "but overweight might mean giving him a harder race than I or Windsor Lad wants at this stage. Remember, there's only a month to go before the Derby"

Bahram at stud.

© Lionel Edwards Estate by courtesy of Felix Rosenstiel's Widow & Son, London

Bahram shortly after he retired to stud.

The artist Alfred Haigh at work on the painting.

3rd RACE. 1 Mile, 6 Fur., & 132 Yds.

(Paddock Badge Armlet—Yellow).

THE ST LEGER STAKES of 5 sov. each, 20 sov. extra if not struck out to Messrs Weatherby and Sons by the first Tuesday in July, 1934, 25 sov. more if not struck out by the Tuesday after the Newmarket Craven Meeting, 1935, and 50 sov. in addition if not struck out by the Tuesday in the week before running, with 4000 sov. added, *for entire colts and fillies, foaled in 1932*; colts, 9st, fillies, 8st 11lb; the owner of the second to receive 10 per cent. and the owner of the third 5 per cent. of the whole stakes; the breeder of the winner to receive 500 sov. out of the stakes; St Leger Course (about one mile, six furlongs, and 132 yards)—277 entries, 50 sov. forfeit declared for 67, 25 sov. for 95, and 5 sov. for 104—Closed October 31st, 1933.

There will be a Parade for this race.

1—Lord Astor's.............................**FLASH BYE,** ch c by Hurry On—Picture.......R. A. JONES
    Light blue, pink sash, gold cap *(Lawson)*

2—Lord Astor's.............................**FIELD TRIAL,** b or br c by Felstead—Popingaol...R. DICK
    Light blue, pink sash and cap *(Lawson)*

3—Lord Derby's.............................**PLASSY,** b c by Bosworth—Pladda ....R. PERRYMAN
    Black, white cap *(C. Leader)*

4—Lord Glanely's ....**BUCKLEIGH,** b c by Sansovino—Surbine.........H. WRAGG
    Black, red, white and blue belt and cap *(Hogg)*

5—H.H. Aga Khan's....................**BAHRAM** (late Bahman), b c by Blandford—
    Green and chocolate hoops, chocolate cap *(Frank Butters)*   Friar's Daughter... ——

6—H.H. Aga Khan's ....**HAIRAN,** b c by Fairway—Harpsichord...............C. SMIRKE
    Green and chocolate hoops, green cap *(Frank Butters)*

7—Lt.-Col. Giles Loder's.............**FAIRBAIRN,** ch c by Fairway—Baby Polly......G. RICHARDS
    Yellow, dark blue sleeves, black cap *(Gilpin)*

8—Sir Malcolm McAlpine's..........**SOLAR RAY,** b c by Solario—Trincomalee...........J. SIRETT
    McAlpine tartan, gold cap *(V. Smyth)*

9—Mr H. W. W. Simms'...............**PRY II.,** b c by Priori—Edwina.............................M. BEARY
    Pink, black sleeves, hooped cap *(Digby)*   (bred in France

Racecard for the 1935 St Leger Stakes.

Two views of Bahram as he wins the St Leger very easily. The judge's verdict was only five lengths!

Bahram immediately after the race.

Bahram led in by Aly.

Bahram at stud

Turkhan.

Big Game

Persian Gulf

Bahram in later years

Nasrullah.

Smirke had to endure the ordeal of watching Windsor Lad win "cleverly", handling the turns with aplomb and pricking his ears as he passed the post. Strangely Fox was not totally convinced "He is a nice horse all right" said Fox "but at Epsom he'll have no chance with Colombo. He'll never match his speed. Still, he might be a Leger horse". Windsor Lad won the Derby, but supporters of Colombo never had a chance as the Australian Rae Johnstone had a wretched experience and gave him a very moderate ride.

At Chester the day after the Vase Fox landed the big race of the week: The Chester Cup, on a wonderful mare Mr. Montague Evans' seven-year-old Blue Vision (Etheric – Perimeter by Perigord). However, what should have been a splendid day in agreeable weather was horribly marred by an awful incident resulting in the death of a horse and injury to jockeys. As the field of twenty runners was approaching the short straight, Lord Carnarvon's filly Sibell (Achtoi – Star in the East by Roi Herode), was knocked over by a horse thought to be forcing its way through. She in turn brought down the favourite Roi de Paris (Cerfeuil – La Panade by Negofol) ridden by Gordon Richards, in addition Barrage (Somme Kiss – Cornice by Hounam) also fell. Richards escaped unhurt but the other two jockeys were taken to hospital. Sibell broke a shoulder and was destroyed.

This ghastly incident rather took away some of the credit due to Blue Vision who carried 7st. 11lbs. and was trained by Ivor Antony at Wroughton. Sir Harold A. Wernher's mighty Brown Jack (Jackdaw – Querquidella by Kroonstad) finished third carrying 9st. 6lbs. Blue Vision had won the Northumberland Plate in 1931 as a four-year-old but broke down during the running of the Cesarewitch the following year. She would have been retired to the paddocks but her trainer persisted with her and although she missed all of 1933 she returned during the winter of 1933/34 to race five times over hurdles winning twice. She appeared just once more after Chester; unplaced in the Yorkshire Cup.

In the Derby Fox rode Badruddin for the Aga. However, although the Aga had three runners, Umidwar, Alishah and Badruddin, he had little chance of winning with Windsor Lad and the unfortunate Colombo against them. The following day Fox was aboard

Mr. A C Bostwick's six-year-old entire handicapper Mate (Prince Pal – Killashandra by Ambassador) in a substandard renewal of the Coronation Cup. Mate started favourite against just two opponents but could only finish second.

Fox had rides in most of the races at Ascot and enjoyed three wins. The best of these was on the Aga's Felicitation in the Churchill Stake which was a curious race in that it was for four-year-olds only. He started at odds of 1–2 and won by ten lengths. It is not clear why Richards, who finished second, was not on board.

However, it can be seen that Fox was now getting rides on fancied horses in big races. He was aboard the 7–4 favourite Bright Bird (Biribi – Pretty Swift by Swynford), owned by Lord Astor and trained by Joe Lawson, in the Princess of Wales's Stakes at Newmarket when they won easily by five lengths. This famous race was already in steady decline but at this time it was still worth £2,570 (136,000) to the winner. Compare that to 2014 when the winner collected a mere £56,000! Yet another middle distance race fallen prey to the contemporary voracious craze that racecourses have for sprinting! Interestingly in the following race which was the July Cup was worth £855 (45,000) to the winner. In 2014 the winning owner of the July Cup took home a staggering £289,000! For a sprinter; good grief!

Some readers may feel that this author rather hammers on about the decline in middle distance races in Britain in favour of sprinting. Does it matter? Well yes it does if British racing wishes to stage good middle distance racing in twenty or thirty years' time. Almost all races at twelve furlongs and above for four-year-olds and up have declined in value over the last twenty to thirty years and, in some cases even longer. At the same time races at 5/6 furlongs have had money poured into them. The result is that any owner in possession of a decent middle distance horse just below the top level is better of selling it abroad, usually to Australia or the Far East, than racing it in Britain. Today the majority of commercial breeders are not interested in breeding horses that are going to need twelve furlongs plus to be effective. Why? It is because at all levels below Group One the money is gravitating towards races at 6–8 furlongs. The sales catalogues increasingly feature the progeny of mares, with stamina in their pedigree, that have been mated with a sprinters rather than a 10–12 furlong stallion.

Fox had a double at the Second Newmarket July Meeting with Badruddin in the Midsummer Stakes and then, with Mr. T Lant's Maltravers, who was a work companion of Bahram, in the Chesterfield Stakes. Maltravers had the Aga's Alykhan, who was odds on, back in third place.

The Eclipse Stakes should probably have been a relatively straight-forward affair for the Derby winner Windsor Lad. Fox was riding Umidwar for the Aga who also had Alishah in the race. At this time penalties applied in many races and Windsor Lad carried a ten pound penalty for winning the Derby. This, combined with Charlie Smirke giving Windsor Lad a ride he would prefer to forget, resulted in Sir Richard Brookes' King Salmon winning with Umidwar second and the frustrated Windsor Lad third. The distances were half a length and the same. Had Smirke not managed to get Windsor Lad trapped on the rails he would have won comfortably. In his autobiography Smirke confesses that it was the worst ride he had ever given any horse.

Wins in the better races continued and Fox was aboard Lord Astor's Adept (Gainsborough – Pennycomequick by Hurry On) trained by Joe Lawson when winning the valuable St. George Stakes; £1,791 (95,000) at Liverpool's Summer Meeting. Adept started at odds of 1–2 and won by four lengths. The party continued the following week at Goodwood where on the Tuesday Fox won the Gratwicke (Produce) Stakes; £2,342 (125,000) for the Aga aboard Umidwar who beat his sole opponent comfortably by four lengths. The Wednesday produced a treble in the first three races: the Sussex Stakes, Lavant Stakes and Goodwood handicap Stakes. The icing on Fox's metaphorical Goodwood cake was Bahram easily winning the Rous Memorial Stakes on Thursday.

At York Fox rode a double but not of course Bahram who was ridden by Dick Perryman. This was not a case of Fox being "jocked-off" as Perryman had been aboard Bahram when he won at Sandown. Fox drew a blank at Doncaster and rode Umidwar who was unplaced in the St Leger.

Newmarket's First October Meeting brought yet more success for Fox as not only did he ride Bahram to an easy win in the Boscawen (Post) Stakes but he partnered Umidwar to success in the Jockey Club Stakes worth £4,025 (213,000) to the winner. The Jockey Club Stakes was instituted in 1894 and run over one mile and six furlongs. Mr. Harry McCalmont's mighty Isinglass (Isonomy – Deadlock by Wenlock) was the first winner and his owner collected a colossal £11,302 (1,220,000). However, the Jockey Club decided they could not afford this after 1916 and the value was halved when run again in 1918. In 1922 it became a sweepstakes with £2,200 (86,000) added to the stakes. The race began its steady decline after the Second World War and during the 1950's it declined in both actual and real terms. The race was effectively destroyed in 1963 when it was switched to the Spring Meeting, the distance reduced to twelve furlongs and the value reduced to just £1,600 (34,000) to the winner. Today it is staged as a Group 2 but worth just £56,000 to the winner.

At Newmarket's Second October Meeting Fox was again in terrific form. On the Wednesday he was aboard the Aga's Umidwar when he won the Champion Stakes as the 5–4 favourite, the Newmarket Oaks on Lord Astor's Miss Erene (Buchan – Gay Bird by Gay Crusader) and then he completed a treble in the following race in a nursery. The following day Fox won the Challenge Stakes on 10–1 chance Mate and later that afternoon cruised home on Bahram in the Middle Park Stakes.

There was an interesting incident later in October at Wolverhampton's Autumn Meeting. The first race was the Shrewsbury Selling Plate which was a match between Double Event (Prestissimo – Pride of Priestown by Invincible), ridden by Fox and Up Rivers (Upsalquitch – Reine d'ete by Roi Herode); the 2–7 favourite, with Gordon Richards in the plate. Richards displaying all his characteristic determination got up to win by a neck. Fox lodged an objection on the grounds of bumping and boring. The Stewards after hearing evidence from both jockeys and the Judge sustained the objection. Richards was known for staying on the right side of officials but in this instance his charm failed to carry the day!

Fox won only two races at Newmarket's Houghton Meeting but one of them was on the Aga's Hairan in the Dewhurst Stakes. It had been an excellent year for Fox who finished second in the jockey's table with 132 winners; the most he would ever achieve in one year. Good as this was Fox had only a distant view of Gordon Richards who was Champion jockey with 212 winners.

*   *   *

1934 was to prove the zenith of Fox's career in terms of winners. His rides and winners declined considerably in 1935. It is hard to say why he was riding for the same connections and of course his profile could hardly have been higher after he had ridden Bahram to success in the Two Thousand Guineas and Derby. He failed to ride a winner at the Newmarket Craven or the Epsom Spring Meetings. He won the Two Thousand Guineas on Bahram of course but was beaten at odds on aboard Felicitation in the Chippenham Stakes. He drew a blank at Chester where he had few rides and also at Newmarket's Second Spring Meeting. At York's Spring Meeting his luck changed when Felicitation won the Yorkshire Stakes; a handicap at that time.

Fox rode only one winner at the Epsom Derby meeting but that was Bahram! He was denied a Classic double when second in the Oaks; beaten a short head on Mrs. G B Miller's Ankaret (Blandford – Sister Stella by Friar Marcus) trained by Frank Butters. However, the winner Quashed would have been a very unlucky loser; the pace was so slow the fillies' were getting in each other's way and Quashed was last and looked without any hope. Eventually she made her way to the front only to find that Ankaret had gone clear. It was amidst considerable excitement that, galvanized by the veteran Henri Jelliss, Quashed showing tremendous determination, closed the gap and was only in front with the final stride.

At Ascot Fox gained compensation by winning the Coronation Stakes on Ankaret; his only other win coming on Bahram in the St. James's Palace Stakes. Fox may not have been winning many big races but he was still riding plenty of horses for the Aga. At Goodwood he won the Gratwicke (Produce) Stakes on Mrs. Arthur James's Louise (Finglas – Devonshire House by Swynford). However, Fox's season came to a juddering halt at Doncaster. He did not ride again in 1935 following his fall from Sheldrake (Old Rowley – Sarcelle by Lomond) at Doncaster. It is entirely possible that this fall not only cost Fox the chance to ride Bahram in the St. Leger but also deprived him of another Derby.

Fox had ridden Mahmoud in all his races as a juvenile. Mahmoud began with an unplaced effort in a stakes race at Newmarket and was then third in the New Stakes at Ascot. He broke his maiden by winning the Exeter Stakes at Newmarket, and then won the Richmond Stakes at Goodwood. At Doncaster on the Tuesday Fox rode Mahmoud to victory in the Champagne Stakes, the race before Sheldrake's selling handicap in which Fox was so badly injured. As Mahmoud would not have been Smirke's first choice to ride the following year, it is not unreasonable to assume Fox might easily have ridden Mahmoud as a three-year-old.

While Fox lay injured on the track at Doncaster, someone relieved him of his whip. He appealed for its return believing that it was lucky; well not perhaps when he was riding Sheldrake! Fox went to South Africa for the winter to help his recuperation and on his return from Cape Town was delighted to discover that the whip had been sent to his home in Wantage.

*   *   *

Returning to the saddle for the 1936 season his first winner was at Kempton on Easter Monday when he rode Feola (Friar Marcus – Aloe by Son-in-Law) to victory. She carried Lord Derby's colours as King George V had died. But Fox enjoyed little success that summer and he decided to retire and announced the decision in October. At forty-eight he probably had another couple of years left in him. However, he had had enough of race riding and made plans to begin training firstly by assisting Captain Gooch in 1937 before training on his own account.

*   *   *

Having left the stresses of riding, Fox found that home life, and enjoying his leisure in a part of the country with which he had been so long associated, was a more attractive proposition than training. So he decided devoted himself to the life of a country gentleman at Letcombe Regis near Wantage. He was appointed as a Justice of the Peace, rode to hounds regularly and became known to the racing world as "unofficial Mayor of Wantage"! Fox enjoyed the winter months when he could hunt, usually with Old Berkshire, and he also played golf and tennis.

Many people who love horses will talk to them and Fox would often stop in the street and "chat" to a horse between the shafts of a van and each morning he would visit his favourite hunter Tim, in his paddock. Tim was over twenty years old and Fox would enjoy some companionable time and share an apple with him and probably tell the unfortunate Tim one of his interminable stories!

Fox did not desert racing entirely and he was persuaded to write a few articles for *The News of the World*; these were considered well enough but the feeling persisted that he was not as entertaining as a writer as when he was talking! Good gracious! What were his articles like? Nonetheless he contributed an excellent chapter on jockeyship in the *Flat Racing* volume of the *Lonsdale Library* series. He stayed in touch with those he had enjoyed working with and when, in 1938 two weeks before the Derby, there was a strike by 300 stable lads in Lambourn, Fox came out of retirement to help Fred Templeman.

Fox had a sensitive side and feeling for his fellow jockeys. In 1931 Gordon Richards and Joe Childs had a temporary disagreement over a couple of incidents and relations were cool to say the least. When Fox gave a celebration dinner to mark his Derby win on Cameronian he deliberately placed Richards and Childs together. For most of the evening sparks flew between the protagonists but as the fine food and wine percolated through reconciliation was achieved.

Fox also worked for the protection of old horses. In 1933 at a dinner held at the Eccentric Club he said "I am organizing and supporting a movement for the protection of old horses. It is not known to the people of England that old horses are sent abroad and exported to Spain, where they are used in bullfights. What happens to those horses I hardly dare mention. They are doomed to a terrible death, often a lingering death, and nothing is done to prevent such a thing happening". Shortly afterwards he wrote a letter on this subject which was published in *The Morning Post*. He wrote that he hoped to get a bill framed in Parliament limiting the export of horses valued at less than £25 (1,300) so as to eliminate the traffic in animals too old or unfit for any kind of active service. Months later he spoke at a meeting held at Central Hall, Westminster, called by the International League against the export of horses for butchery and Our Dumb Friends League.

Freddie Fox vulpine by name and, curiously also in looks, was able to ride at 7st. 6 lbs. throughout his career. Short, dapper and always well-groomed Fox was usually business like and unostentatious. He had a thin high-pitched voice which would often trail into incomprehensibility if he became agitated or excited. He was only ever tiresome when reciting for the umpteenth time a, usually long, story he considered amusing and expected all around him to share that opinion. It was possible to know when one of these apparently interminable yarns was drawing to its close when Fox began to chuckle contentedly; before embarking on another! It is a small fault in a man anyone would be proud to call a friend. He once said that he never regretted his career as a jockey and would do the same again, except, possibly, he might like to have been a huntsman with a good pack of hounds!

During the early days of Fox's career his contemporaries were Steve Donoghue, Danny Maher, "Skeets" Martin, Frank Wootton, Bernard Dillon and Walter Earl. When he retired in 1936 they were now Gordon Richards, Charlie Smirke, Eph. Smith, Harry Wragg, Joe Childs and Tommy Weston. It is to his credit that while he may not have been considered superior to those named Fox was more than able to hold his own in their company. He deserves his place amongst the best jockeys of the twentieth century, a good rider and an intelligent, thinking jockey.

Of his fellow jockeys Fox had the highest opinion of the skills of Danny Maher. However, he was not impressed with the manner that Maher handled Bayardo! Well he was not alone in that; just ask Alec Taylor! Fox rode in the notorious three-runner Goodwood Cup in 1910 when Bayardo was sensationally beaten at odds of 1–20. He noted that Maher made up ground on the uphill sections which must have tired Bayardo and helped run the finish out of him. The lesson of this race was not lost on Fox when in the 1928 running of the Goodwood Cup, aboard Kinchinjunga (Juggernaut – Maid of the Mountains by Amadis), he made all the running. Fox was careful to ensure that his mount freewheeled down the declines but he managed to get a "breather" into him when he reached the inclines. Consequently Kinchinjunga, although almost out on his legs, was just able to hold on by half a length at the line from the fast finishing Bois Josselyn (Ayala – Puntarenas by Maintenon).

In addition Fox felt that Maher cost him the 1910 St. Leger on Bronzino (Marco – Flitters by Galopin) although he does not explain how. The race was won by the magnificent Swynford on whom Frank Wootton rode an exemplary race whereas Maher was accused of riding an over confident one on the Derby winner Lemberg (Cyllene – Galicia by Galopin). However, nothing Maher could have done would have changed matters: Lemberg was simply outstayed by a better horse over the extended one mile six furlongs. As it turned out Swynford was probably a better horse than Lemberg but either way Bronzino, decent horse that he was, would have been below the level of both of them.

Fox felt that Epsom was a difficult course to ride, took some knowing and was the most severe test a racecourse could set. He thought that had Rae Johnstone been better acquainted with its unique terrain he might have won the Derby in 1934 on Colombo. As the winner was the great Windsor Lad Fox must have thought that Johnstone was culpable indeed! Johnstone managed to get himself boxed in coming down to Tattenham Corner and by the time he was clear the principals had gone. That Colombo was only beaten just over a length at the finish gives some indication just what a brave and magnificent horse he was. It is worth remembering that Charlie Smirke, who rode Windsor Lad, also said that he would have won the race had he been riding Colombo.

Someone once suggested to Fox that game and honest horses were fools and that rogues that refuse to exert themselves show greater intelligence. Fox would not agree "That is altogether too sweeping, some horses have intelligence which we admire. Others are just cunning which we hate. The best horses I have ridden have been intelligent without being cunning. A really stupid horse is seldom good for anything. I will certainly admit that all jockeys ride some horses which, if they were humans, would be "certified" as mentally deficient".

Fox's enjoyment of retirement sadly did not last long; within five years his only son Michael was killed during the war while serving with the Royal Air Force. This blighted the final years of both Fox and his wife and in Fox's case these years were to be cut short by further tragedy. On the 12th December 1945, aged just 57, he was killed in a car accident. He was travelling with his wife, with Fox at the wheel, between Wantage and Oxford when near Frilford his car was involved in a head-on collision with a lorry. At the subsequent inquest the lorry driver claimed he had been waived on by another lorry. The impact caused Fox to be thrown on to the steering wheel and he was killed instantly. His wife, though injured, survived. An inquest held in Abingdon recorded a verdict of "Death from misadventure".

Fred Fox was buried at the church in Letcombe Regis and left an estate valued at £23,285 (86,000).

His Classic wins were as follows:-

1,000 Guineas:	1911 Atmah
2,000 Guineas:	1930 Diolite
	1935 Bahram
Derby:	1935 Bahram
St. Leger:	1932 Firdaussi

His annual summary of rides is as follows

	Winners	Mounts	Percentage
1907 *	19	214	8.87
1908 *	39	313	12.46
1909 *	66	567	11.64
1910	42	509	8.25
1911	31	419	7.39
1912 +			
1913 +	10	116	8.62
1914	32	291	10.99
1915	17	183	9.28
1916	10	164	6.09
1917	16	163	9.81
1918	30	252	11.90
1919	56	440	12.72
1920	38	434	8.75
1921	43	456	9.42
1922	47	453	10.37
1923	23	353	6.51
1924	20	283	7.06
1925	35	375	9.33
1926	74	571	12.95
1927	72	714	10.08
1928	89	672	13.24
1929	116	754	15.38
1930 ++	129	802	16.08
1931	89	783	11.36
1932	71	789	8.99
1933	71	669	10.61
1934	132	716	18.43
1935	40	423	9.45
1936	30	403	7.44
	1,487	13,281	11.19

* Apprentice + Riding abroad ++ Champion Jockey

Pedigree of Bahram

			Isinglass
		John o' Gaunt	
		B. 1901	La Fleche
	Swynford		
	Br. 1907		Tristan
		Canterbury Pilgrim	
		Ch. 1893	Pilgrimage
Blandford			
Br. 1919			Gallinule
		White Eagle	
		Ch.1905	Merry Gal
	Blanche		
	B. 1912		Bendigo
		Black Cherry	
		Br. 1892	Black Duchess

Bahram
B c 13 April 1932

			Cyllene
		Cicero	
		Ch. 1902	Gas
	Friar Marcus		
	B. 1912		Persimmon
		Prim Nun	
		Br. 1906	Nonesuch
Friar's Daughter			
Br. 1921			William the Third
		Roseland	
		Br. 1912	Electric Rose
	Garron Lass		
	Br. 1917		St. Simon
		Concertina	
		B. 1896	Comic Song

9   Blandford

A yearling colt is resting in his paddock and does not see any danger as a group of carthorses approach. Had he noticed the unusual hostility they exuded he could have run away but he felt no need as he had always felt safe in his environment. He was unaware that these were not companions placed to keep him company but intruders that had broken in. The carthorses attacked and buffeted the unfortunate youngster so severely he was left in a very sorry state. His injuries were so severe it was necessary to hand feed him and even his very survival was in the balance.

*   *   *

Bred at the National Stud at Tully in Ireland, Blandford was a brown colt by Swynford out of Blanche by White Eagle. He was a late foal: 26th May 1919, and his early years were plagued with problems. Noble Johnson manager of the Stud recalled that as a foal and a yearling Blandford was very backward. "He was always getting into trouble in the paddock. As a result he was usually covered in scars".

The paddocks at Tully were divided by high boarded fences: stallion barriers, designed so that the stock should not look over into the adjoining enclosure. However, Blandford used to put his forelegs on the top and see what was on the other side and one day injured himself badly doing this. Then, followed the attack by carthorses, he contracted rheumatic fever.

The vet who attended him following the attack Mr. Thomas Griffin, was able to save his life but thought he had no future as a racehorse and, that it would not be possible to even train him much less win any races with him. The Director of the National Stud, Sir Henry Greer was so unimpressed by Blandford's prospects that he offered the colt as a gift to Mr. Griffin; who declined him! As a consequence of his various misfortunes Blandford missed joining the Tully draft at the July sales and instead was entered for the Newmarket December yearling sales.

The Earl of Carnarvon always claimed that he should have owned the colt that was to be named Blandford. As Lord Porchester in 1920, and a British Army Officer, Dick Dawson told him about the colt by Swynford that the National Stud had submitted to the sales. Dawson expressed the view that it would not fetch much of a price so "Porchy", as he was known, told Dawson to go up to 2,000 guineas (£70,000). Dawson said he thought he could be obtained for far less than that.

During the bidding Dawson assumed he was buying for Lord Porchester, however, his brother Sam persuaded him that he was buying on behalf of themselves and when the hammer came down at just 730 guineas (£25,300) the Swynford colt was now owned by Dick and Sam Dawson! This is the story as told by Porchy and he claimed that "My whole life would have taken on a completely different hue had this tragedy not occurred".

Tragedy is rather a strong word to describe missing buying a yearling colt. However, Lord Porchester could certainly have used the money that Blandford might have earned him. The sudden death of his father in 1923 left him at the mercy of death duties and it was not always certain he could save Highclere Castle which it may have been necessary to sell.

Dick of course was a trainer in England, and Sam owned the Cloghran Stud in Ireland. Blandford made a good recovery and, against the odds, made up into a reasonable specimen; that is if one is prepared to overlook his somewhat heavy-topped physique and moderate forelegs, very short straight pasterns and, in addition, he was over at the knee.

The Dawson brothers had officially brought the colt on their own behalf and as time would show; what a bargain they had secured! There was only one drawback: entries for the 1922 Classics had closed several weeks before Blandford had been sold. If he was top-class he would not be able to prove it in any of the Classic races.

Blandford's sire Swynford was bred by Lord Derby out of his mare Canterbury Pilgrim. Foaled on 30th January 1907 he was one of the first foals sired by the Two Thousand Guineas and Derby runner-up John O'Gaunt. John O'Gaunt was a temperamental character with bad feet, round joints and upright pasterns; it can only have been his impeccable pedigree, he was by Isinglass out of La Fleche by St. Simon, which made him in any way acceptable as a sire one would have thought! John O'Gaunt's sire: the mighty and all-time great Isinglass, won the Triple Crown and was beaten only once in twelve starts. However, physically Isinglass was plain to put it politely.

Even with this lineage to recommend him, his physique would have been enough to persuade many breeders to happily give John O' Gaunt a miss. Fortunately many of the worst of these traits were not passed on to Swynford, who although a big, rather plain individual; a "very ugly customer" according to George Lambton, had "a good head, legs and feet. He was also was a fine mover when he chose to extend himself". Despite this foreleg problems did resurface in some of his descendants. Incidentally, John O' Gaunt never sired another horse of comparable ability to Swynford. Kennymore (out of Croceum by Martacon), who won the Two Thousand Guineas came closest.

Swynford was unplaced on his sole juvenile start in the Exeter Stakes at Newmarket and afterwards he threw a large thoroughpin – a swelling in the area between the hock and the gaskin. However, he was thought good enough to make his three-year-old debut in the Derby, but was struck into and finished unplaced. None the worse for this he reappeared at Ascot where he finished third in the St James's Palace Stakes and then the following day won the Hardwicke Stakes which was at that time open to three-year-olds. He carried only 7st. 7lbs. and won "cleverly".

Swynford then found his form; winning the Liverpool Summer Cup by five lengths. Next came the St. Leger where from the off Swynford charged to the front and, either making the running or always prominent, held on gamely under strong driving. Bronzino was second and the Derby winner and odds-on favourite Lemberg third. Swynford concluded the season by walking over for the Liverpool St Leger. His three-year-old form would entitle him to a *Timeform* rating of about 133.

Kept in training at four, Swynford was even better and won four races from five starts: The Chippenham, Hardwicke, Princess of Wales's and Eclipse Stakes. In the latter he carried 10st. 1lb and, storming clear, again beat Lemberg by four lengths. His only defeat came when he was second to Lemberg in the Coronation Cup. Swynford was a long-striding colt that excelled when allowed to stride out along in front; significantly he suffered his only defeat as a four-year-old when held up.

In September 1911, when he was being prepared for the Jockey Club Stakes and another clash with Lemberg, Swynford broke a fetlock which would normally be fatal; however, Lord Derby spared no expense in trying to save him for stud. Through the skilled efforts of the eminent Newmarket veterinarian Mr Livock, together with Swynford's placid temperament, his life was saved and after eighteen months devoted skill and care Swynford's recovery was complete and he was pronounced recovered sufficiently to take up stud duties at his owners Woodland Stud in Newmarket in 1913. *A Century of Champions* rated him 137 as a four-year-old.

His trainer the George Lambton had a very high opinion of Swynford: "far and away the best horse I have ever trained" he said. Lambton claimed that when he had him right "he had no bottom". It has to be said that this was not the most attractive turn of phrase in which to describe a horse with limitless courage and ability! Swynford won eight of his twelve races; after being unplaced on his first two outings, and third in his third race. He therefore won all but one of his remaining nine races; second when held up in the Coronation Cup. Whether Swynford can be described as a great horse is arguable: he was certainly capable of producing great performances at distances of ten furlongs and up as a four-year-old but he showed nothing at two and although he won the Liverpool Cup over ten furlongs as a three-year-old, he was receiving twenty-six pounds from the older Dean Swift. In conclusion Swynford was a brave front-running horse with a tremendously long and impressive stride. It would have been interesting to see if that would have been enough to take the sting out of the finish of a great stayer with a turn of foot like Bayardo.

Such was Swynford's reputation that he was immediately booked for the covering seasons of 1913, 1914 and 1915 at a fee of 300 guineas (£28,500). Swynford began well when one considers that his first crop to race was in 1916 at a time when the Great War was at its ghastly zenith. His second crop, including the One Thousand Guineas winner Ferry (out of Gondolette by Loved One), enabled Swynford to finish sixth in the list of stallions for 1918. Over the next few years he rarely dropped below this level, securing the title in 1923 and finishing runner-up in 1924 and 1925, by which time his stud fee had risen to 400 guineas (£17,200).

Generally his fillies were better than his colts, for in addition to Ferry he sired three more One Thousand Guineas winners in Bettina (out of Bobbina by Desmond), Tranquil (Serenissima by Minoru) and Saucy Sue (Good and Gay by Bayardo), while another daughter Keysoe (Keystone by Persimmon) won the St Leger. Saucy Sue and Tranquil also won the Oaks and St Leger respectively. Swynford's sole male European Classic winner was Lord Derby's 1924 Derby winner Sansovino who was a full-brother to Ferry. At stud Sansovino was not a great success although he did sire 208 winners.

Swynford's other high-class colt was the Coronation Cup winner and Derby runner-up St. Germans (Hamoaze by Torpoint). From the same crop as Sansovino, the smallish St Germans was exported to the Greentree Stud in America, where he proved a shy-breeder, and, in the circumstances, rather surprisingly, became champion sire in 1931. In that year he was represented by the Kentucky Derby and Belmont Stakes winner Twenty Grand (Bonus by All Gold), a horse that proved completely sterile. St. Germans sired another Kentucky Derby winner in Bold Venture (Possible by Ultimas). A further son of Swynford to make his mark on the race was the Hardwicke Stakes winner Lancegaye (Flying Spear by Spearmint), when his son Cavalcade (Hastily by Hurry On) won the Kentucky Derby in 1934.

To return briefly to Hamoaze she was foaled in 1911 and first covered in 1915. She foaled Buchan by Sunstar in 1916 was barren in 1916 and 1917 then in successive years produced three more colts: Tamar by Tracey, Saltash by Sunstar and St. Germans. Despite attempts to get her in foal she was barren in 1922, 23, 24, and 25.

She died in 1929. Incredibly all her foals became Champion sires; Buchan in England, Tamar in Austria, Saltash in Australia and St. Germans in North America.

Another of Swynford's sons to cross the Atlantic and become champion sire was Challenger II (Sword Play by Great Sport). An unbeaten juvenile in England, Challenger II's racing career was compromised by injury, and although standing in Maryland where opportunities were limited, he sired two champions out of mares by Sir Gallahad III: Challedon and Gallorette, the former helping him to secure the stallion crown in 1939. However, it was Blandford who carried forward the Swynford line in England and this proved to be the only surviving line of his illustrious grandsire: Isinglass.

As a broodmare sire Swynford was champion in 1932. The two Classic winners out of Swynford mares: Sun Stream (One Thousand Guineas and Oaks) and Tide-Way (One Thousand Guineas) were daughters of Hyperion and Fairway respectively.

Swynford died suddenly on 18th May 1928; his influence had been considerable and his offspring won a total of 351 races worth £233,125 (9,791,250). His stamina index was 9.45 furlongs.

Blandford's grandam: Black Cherry, by Bendigo out of Black Duchess by Galliard, won only once from nine races. However when retired to the paddocks she did much better. In all Black Cherry had 13 foals, and produced 9 winners of 41 races worth £30,543 (2,750,000). Her most notable produce were in order of foaling: – Full Ripe; colt by Fullerton, won 6 races, Half Caste; colt by Fullerton, won 5 races and Jean's Folly; filly by Ayrshire, won 6 races.

However, it was her next foal: Cherry Lass, a filly by Isinglass that secured her reputation. Cherry Lass won ten races, including the Anglesey Stakes, Free Handicap, One Thousand Guineas and Oaks, St. James's Palace and Nassau Stakes, Duchess of York Plate and Newmarket Oaks. She was also third in the St Leger.

Subsequently Black Cherry produced two colts both by Count Schomberg: Black Arrow, who won six races, and John Amendall; who won five. A third colt: Kingston Black, by Royal Realm won one race.

Conspicuous by her absence in the list of winners out of Black

Cherry is Blandford's dam: Blanche a bay filly by White Eagle and foaled in 1912. White Eagle, who won the Sussex Stakes, sired nothing of note, but earned a deserved reputation for producing some good broodmares, including Dolabella and Lady Peregrine.

Although Blanche failed to win she was thought good enough to run in important juvenile races such as the Coventry Stakes at Ascot and Newmarket's Cheveley Park Stakes. At three she started in the Oaks, but in five starts at two, and five more at three, she failed to be placed. When retired to the paddocks Blanche produced 6 winners, from only 10 surviving foals, that won between them 20 races worth £16,384 (740,000). In 1919 she produced her third foal and the first of these six winners: Blandford. Blanche died while foaling a colt which also died in 1933, aged twenty-one.

Blandford entered training at Whatcombe with Dick Dawson who admitted he tried the colt very hard as a two-year-old. During June 1921 Blandford, as yet unnamed, was asked to concede 23 lbs. to a filly Malva (Charles O'Malley – Wild Arum by Robert le Diable), who was owned by Lord Carnarvon. At that time she was unnamed but had won a race at Salisbury beating Lord Glanely's Drake's Drum (Corcyra – Seadune by Ayrshire) who then finished second in the Coventry Stakes at Ascot. Blandford was to meet Malva again in the future this time in the breeding shed; a union that produced Blenheim.

Blandford, still unnamed, made his debut at Newbury on 8th June in the five furlong Kennet Stakes as Blanche colt and ridden by a stable lad P Mason. Sent off second favourite at 5–2 in a field of nineteen he took up the lead about two furlongs from the finish and won by ¾ length from Lord Jersey's Scamp (Son-in-Law – Campanula by Chaucer) with the favourite: Col. A W B Spencer's Innes of Court (Son-in-Law – Flora Temple by Chaucer) a further two lengths back in third. Nine days later he lined up, still as Blanche colt, as the even money favourite in the Windsor Castle Stakes also over five furlongs. Unfortunately he was suffering from sore shins and he stumbled just short of the line and was beaten a neck by Mr. W T de Pledge's Alaric (Captivation – Zenith by Lesterlin); who he had beaten at Newbury and to whom he was conceding ten pounds. Sore shins then kept Blandford off the racecourse for the rest of 1921.

However, the form of Blandford's races held up well; Scamp won the New and Gimcrack Stakes. At the end of the year, and by now named Blandford, he was given 8 st. 9 lbs. in the Free Handicap; five pounds below a filly, Mr. M Fields' Golden Corn (Golden Sun – Corn Cockle by St. Frusquin), who won the Champagne and Middle Park Stakes. Blandford's form as a juvenile would entitle him to a *Timeform* rating of about 119.

In 1922 he reappeared on the 29th April in the ten furlong Paradise Stakes at Hurst Park. Sent off the 11–8 favourite in a field of eleven he won easily from Lord Howard de Walden's Captain Fracasse (Tracery – Sauce Hollandaise by William the Third) and Major Giles Loder's Spike Island (Spearmint – Molly Desmond by Desmond); who later won the Irish Derby. Dawson noted; "Although he won this race in such good style, Blandford was not ready; he was coming on every day".

Blandford, of course, had no engagements for any of the Classics but Dawson claimed he would have beaten Lord Woolavington's Captain Cuttle (Hurry On – Bellavista by Cyllene) if they had met in the Derby. Such claims are frequently made on behalf of horses that miss big races for various reasons. Dawson based his claim on some work at Whatcombe before the Derby which demonstrated that Blandford was of equal merit with the Earl of Carnarvon's four-year-old colt Franklin (Volta – Cambric by Sainfoin) who won an above average renewal of the Coronation Cup at the Derby meeting.

Captain Cuttle won three of his four races; Wood Ditton, Derby and St James's Palace Stakes and was only beaten in Two Thousand Guineas when finishing third. Unfortunately there are no reliable form lines to tie the form of both horses together. The simple truth was that Captain Cuttle had been entered, was well prepared, fit and won the Derby by four lengths and three in a then record time for the race. Blandford of course had not even been entered.

Blandford's next, and as it turned out final race, was the once highly prestigious twelve furlong Princess of Wales's Stakes at Newmarket on the 29th June. However, it had by then been reduced in value to about a quarter of that of the Derby and St Leger and a third of the value of the Eclipse. Blandford was sent off the 11–10 favourite in a field of nine and won handsomely by two lengths and the same. He took up the running before the field had covered a mile to win comfortably.

Unfortunately afterwards he injured a tendon and it was not possible to train him afterwards. He had never had the best of forelegs, something he could probably thank his maternal grandam Black Cherry, for she had a similar problem. Nonetheless in four races he amply demonstrated his merit; he had immense latent ability, and earned his place at stud. His two wins as a three-year-old would entitle him to a *Timeform* rating of about 126.

*   *   *

Blandford did not of course race at four, but neither did he retire to stud. Dawson may have kept him in training but had been unable to ready him for the racecourse. In any event he retired to Cloghran Stud in 1924 at a fee of 148 guineas (£6,700); his first yearlings were not enthusiastically received in the sales ring. However his progeny soon proved they could run and from that first crop came two of the best juveniles in England and Ireland: Buland – out of Saffian by Stornoway and bought by the Aga Khan as a yearling for 900 Guineas (£39,700) and Athford – out of Athasi by Farasi. At the end of the year Blandford had five winners of ten races value £8,361 (359,500).

He did not do as well in 1928 although he did have a promising juvenile in Ireland: Trigo – out of Athasi by Farasi; a brother to Athford. 1929 was Blandford's breakthrough year; he was second in the list of leading sires with Derby and St Leger winner Trigo leading the way. A decent juvenile: Blenheim out of Malva by Charles O'Malley and the four-year-old Athford also contributed. His fee as a result was raised to 300 guineas (£14,000).

Siring a Derby and St Leger winner helped raise Blandford's profile but, apart from Blenheim's Derby, 1930 was disappointing producing only six winners of ten races. Blenheim accounted for £10,086 of Blandford's progeny winnings of £12,335. 1931 was worse; although he had fourteen winners of twenty races there were no stars and he finished 26th in the list of leading sires. Despite these slightly poor results his fee for 1931 was raised again to 400 guineas (£19,750). However, with two Derby winners he was assured more and better patronage.

1932 was not much better and only with the considerable help of Oaks and Coronation Stakes winner Udaipur, owned and bred by the Aga Khan, was Blandford able to finish in seventh place by contributing over 60% of his winning prize money.

Due to the tax on foals in Ireland; the Irish government levied 40% tax on foals leaving for Great Britain, Dawson decided to transfer Blandford from Cloghran to stand at Whatcombe in 1933 in time for the 1934 covering season. His fee remained at 400 guineas.

Blandford's best years as a stallion, in terms of results, were about to begin: led by Mrs. Rustom, the only outstanding performer that year, he rose to fourth place in the sires list in 1933. However, the following year he was leading sire for the first time; his total of £75,707 being more than three times the amount of the sire in second place: Tetratema.

Windsor Lad, winner of five races; the Derby, St Leger, Chester Vase, Newmarket and Great Yorkshire Stakes, accounted for almost a third of Blandford's total. Bahram contributed nearly twelve thousand, Umidwar; winner of the Jockey Club and Champion Stakes and Campanula; winner of the One Thousand guineas, over seven thousand each.

There is a strong case to argue that possibly the best of all Blandford's progeny, Bahram and Windsor Lad included, was the French trained Brantome bred by Baron Edouard de Rothschild out of Vitamine by Clarissimus and foaled on 27th March 1931. Physically unimpressive Brantome stood just 15.1 hands and was rather light of bone and delicate looking. However, on the credit side he possessed a "wonderful" shoulder and straight hind legs. In addition, like many high-class horses he had a lovely fluid action. His somewhat fiery temperament only became a problem when he was a four-year-old.

Brantome was the "brilliant" winner of all four of his races as a juvenile including the Prix Robert Papin and Prix Morny both over six furlongs and he completed the year by winning the Grand Criterium over a mile. He had demonstrated both speed and stamina and was clearly the outstanding French juvenile of 1933. He headed the juvenile French Free Handicap with 63 Kilos (9st. 13lbs.); eight pounds ahead of the second horse. A *Timeform* rating of about 132 would not be flattering him.

As a three-year-old in 1934 Brantome progressed and can be rated one of the best French-trained horses between the wars. Indeed contemporaries described him as a "crack" and the "horse of the century". He began the year by winning a minor event over a mile by six lengths before easily winning the French Two Thousand Guineas by three lengths "pulling up" at odds of 1–10 on the pari-mutuel. Next he annexed the Prix Lupin over ten and a half furlongs easily by two and half lengths at odds of 2–5 with his jockey waiting in typical French style before taking the lead towards the finish.

The French Derby looked a formality but Brantome contracted a cough and was withdrawn. Unfortunately he also missed the Grand Prix de Paris as he had not fully recovered. He returned to win the Prix Royal Oak over fifteen furlongs in September but was not at his best prevailing by only a neck. The stage was now set for the Prix de l'Arc de Triomphe on 7th October. The Aga Khan's Felicitation, trained by Frank Butters was in opposition with Brantome the even money favourite and Felicitation at 3–1.

The race, run in heavy ground, was dramatic: Felicitation took the lead and looked the winner but Brantome challenged and with "electric speed" won easily by two and half lengths from Assuerus with Felicitation a length further away in third. Brantome was given a hero's reception from the enthusiastic Longchamp faithful. He was indeed a "crack"! He was rated 139 by a *Century of Champions*.

Brantome was kept in training in 1935 as a four-year-old but did not enjoy much good fortune. His principal target was the Ascot Gold Cup and all was proceeding according to plan when he opened the year by winning a minor event from moderate opposition over nineteen furlongs. Eleven days later he won the Prix du Cadran over twenty furlongs by fifteen lengths in record time. He had now won all eleven of his races and his warm-up race for the Ascot Gold Cup looked a formality. This was to be the Prix de Dangu at Chantilly, a minor race over twenty furlongs. However, he broke loose on the way to the course and injured himself on the concrete surface as he galloped around the town, dodging cars and in the process sustain some cuts. He was given anti-tetanus and, easy to say in retrospect, he should never have run at Ascot when, clearly below his best, he finished fifth. In the autumn he won the Prix du Prince d'Orange over twelve furlongs as preparation for the 'arc. However, he failed to produce his best and was retired to stud. Brantome had won twelve of his fourteen races. He was trained by Lucien Robert in Chantilly and ridden in all his races by Christophe Bouillon. His best form as a four-year-old would give him a *Timeform* rating of about 134.

Brantome has sound claims to being considered the equal of Bahram; he was arguably better as a juvenile and but for misfortune would have won the French Derby. He stayed in training at four and demonstrated high-class stamina. However, luck does play its part in all walks of life and on the evidence of the racecourse Bahram must be rated the better horse.

However, just as Blandford was establishing himself as the pre-eminent sire of the day he died of pneumonia on 26th April 1935 aged 16. He had seemed well on Easter Sunday but on the Monday appeared to be suffering from either a chill or infection caught from a visiting mare. The following day one of Newmarket's leading vets: Brayley Reynolds travelled post-haste to Whatcombe and diagnosed pneumonia. There were no antibiotics at that time and Blandford succumbed the following day.

Blandford's loss to thoroughbred breeding was all the more poignant when he retained his title that year. His progeny won £57,538; being over twice that of the runner-up; Fairway. Bahram provided over £31,000 and he was helped by Windsor Lad who won four races, including the Coronation Cup and Eclipse Stakes, and contributed over ten thousand. As if to reinforce his loss Blandford was also leading sire in France in 1935; he had been second in 1934. This was largely due to the exploits of Mistress Ford, out of Polly Flanders by Teddy. She won all of her six races including Prix Robert Papin,

Prix Morny and, in facile manner, the Grand Criterium. She won only one race as a three-year-old but it was the French Oaks: the Prix de Diane.

However, the following year in 1936 not only did Blandford did not have a star performer but his progeny won only eight thousand pounds and he dropped to twenty-first in the list of stallions.

With the quality of mare sent to Blandford in the two years prior to his death it was inevitable that he would do better and in 1937 he finished third behind Solario and Fairway. However, Blandford lacked an outstanding performer amongst the fourteen winners of twenty-four races.

Blandford was leading sire for the third and last time in 1938; beating Felstead by just over two thousand pounds. Pasch (Pasca by Manna), a consistent rather than outstanding sort and winner of three races including the Two Thousand Guineas and Eclipse Stakes contributed two thirds of Blandford's total. Pasch was the last of the high-class progeny of Blandford.

The last winner to be sired by Blandford was in 1940 when, with pleasing symmetry, the four-year-old filly Avena was the final winner. She was out of Athasi who was the dam of Athford, one of Blandford's first winners from his first crop in 1925. Incidentally Avena was the seventh winner produced by Athasi and sired by Blandford. Between 1924 and 1936 Athasi was covered by Blandford twelve times in thirteen years. She was barren in 1928 and 1934 and covered by Cygnus in 1927; which resulted in Athnus; a winner! After Blandford's death Athasi was covered by two sons of Blandford: Umidwar and Windsor Lad. She foaled two winners by Umidwar: Chico and Soldado.

Athasi (Farasi – Athgreany by His Majesty or Galloping Simon) was a moderately bred staying mare who had even run over hurdles. From her nine foals by Blandford she produced, in addition to Athford and Trigo, the Irish Derby and St Leger winners Harinero and Primero, plus Harina, winner of the Imperial Produce Stakes. Harina became ancestress of Tulyar, Saint Crespin III and Time Charter, plus the mares Centeno and Choclo whose descendants numbered Aintree Grand National heroes Grittar and Maori Venture. Athasi was retired in 1941 and died in 1944 aged 27.

Blandford's pedigree possessed just one strain of St. Simon, a stallion who at that time saturated many pedigrees. He achieved a high level of success despite not being the most fertile of stallions, and being very slow to cover his mares; this trait has been inherited by some of his descendants. In addition Blandford covered many ordinary mares in his early years.

Blenheim and Bahram apart, Blandford was a disappointing sire of sires; not helped by their being sold off before the Second World War at an indecent rate. The following sons or grandsons of Blandford were sold abroad: – Bahram, Blenheim, Badruddin, together with his grandson Mahmoud. In addition Windsor Lad died aged just 12.

Champion North American sire in 1941 Blenheim kept up the classic connection via sons Donatello II and Mahmoud in Europe and Jet Pilot and Whirlaway in America, but his most enduring legacy to the breed was to sire Mumtaz Begum, the dam of Nasrullah and granddam of Royal Charger.

Blandford maintained his worldwide influence via his sons Badruddin, Blue Skies and Brantome (France), Bulandshar and Solicitor General (New Zealand), Midstream (Australia), Pigling Brand (South Africa) and Primero (Japan).

As a sire of broodmares Blandford never ranked higher than third place in 1944, but his daughters produced Umiddad (Ascot Gold Cup), Lambert Simnel (Two Thousand Guineas) and Why Hurry (Epsom Oaks), while in Ireland the mare Morning Dew produced the Irish Classic winners' Good Morning, Grand Weather, Morning Madam and Morning Wings.

Other important broodmares sired by Blandford were La Furka (grandam of Tantieme), Reine Isaure (dam of Cranach) and Wild Violet (dam of Wild Risk), but perhaps Blandford's most influential daughter was Dalmary. Winner of the Yorkshire Oaks, her descendants included El Condor Pasa, Lorenzaccio, Nureyev, Sadler's Wells, Thatch, Thatching and Topsider.

But it will principally be as one of the greatest classic sires of the 20th Century that Blandford will always be remembered, most of his best progeny were good tempered and lazy. Physically they were usually rather light-framed, had good actions and acted on good ground. In addition his sons were usually sound and did not inherit the bad forelegs, particularly joints, of their male ancestors.

Blandford had been a quiet placid animal for a stallion whilst at Whatcombe and there were often birds in his box with him. Dick Dawson's two daughters: Kitty and Eleanor would even ride him as little girls round his boarded paddock.

Blandford's Classic winners:-

One Thousand Guineas
1934 – Campanula

Two Thousand Guineas
1935 – Bahram
1938 – Pasch

Derby
1929 – Trigo
1930 – Blenheim
1934 – Windsor Lad
1935 – Bahram

Oaks
1932 – Udaipur

St. Leger
1929 – Trigo
1934 – Windsor Lad
1935 – Bahram

His year-by-year record as a sire

Year	Winning horses	Races won	value	position in sires list
1927	5	10	8,631	18th
1928	8	15	6,453	27th
1929	15	30	40,247	2nd
1930	6	10	12,336	13th
1931	14	20	7,380	26th
1932	13	21	23,080	7th
1933	22	38	28,206	4th
1934	26	58	75,707	1st

1935	13	23	57,538	1st
1936	19	26	8,487	21st
1937	14	23	21,390	3rd
1938	16	27	31,840	1st
1939	6	8	6,545	19th
1940	2	3	332	–

Blandford sired 179 winners of 312 races value £328,172. His average stamina index was 9.70 furlongs.

10 Friar's Daughter

It is a chilly day at the Newmarket Tattersalls December sales and a smallish brown filly-foal is walking round the sales ring. She is not particularly impressive to look at, and her pedigree, although reasonable has produced no winners on her dam side for some generations. However, the woman who has just bid 145 guineas to secure her seems happy enough.

*   *   *

Friar's Daughter was foaled in 1921 and was a brown filly by Friar Marcus (Cicero – Prim Nun by Persimmon by St. Simon) out of Garron Lass (Roseland – Concertina by St. Simon). Roseland was by William the Third by St. Simon therefore Garron Lass was inbred to St. Simon 3 x 2 and Friar Marcus introduced a third cross of St. Simon within four generations of Friar's Daughters pedigree. For what it is worth in terms of Vuillier's figures Friar's Daughter carried 1,024 points of St. Simon compared to the standard dosage of 420.

Friar Marcus was bred at the Sandringham Stud of King George V. Foaled in 1912 Friar Marcus was a "very good-looking bay colt very strong in the quarters" by Cicero out of Prim Nun by Persimmon. Friar Marcus was trained by Richard Marsh, who described him as "a mottled brown colt….very kind and good-tempered" and as such always a favourite with the King. He was a perfect model of what a sprinter should look like: "he was short-coupled and very strong in the back quarters and arms" wrote Marsh. "He had a beautiful head and neck, the best of shoulders while his hocks were all that they should be" he continued. Although bred to stay middle distances it was no surprise when he turned out to be a sprinter.

Friar Marcus was "well tried" by Marsh as a two-year-old before his debut on 28th April at Newmarket. As such Marsh knew that he should run well but, as word of his potential had not spread and the newspapers had not mentioned him, the assumption was that he would start at generous price. However, someone in the stable had evidently been talking and the colt opened up at 2–1 in a field of twenty-four! Friar Marcus made all the running to win by a length and a half.

Friar Marcus won all his five races as a juvenile: debut maiden, Great Surrey Foal Stakes at Epsom, both over five furlongs, Prince of Wales's Stakes at Goodwood, over six, Rous Memorial Stakes at Newmarket, back at five and finally the Middle Park Plate at Newmarket over six furlongs. He had not been able to run at Ascot as he was coughing and very ill with an "alarming temperature".

However, with his "robust" constitution Friar Marcus pulled round. Marsh found that Friar Marcus was not back to his best prior to Goodwood and feared that the six furlongs might find him out. In the event he just lasted home by a neck. After winning the Middle Park Marsh had doubts about how far such a "herculean and tremendously muscular and compact type" would stay as a three-year-old. Marsh noted that Friar Marcus's type did not win staying races; in addition he lacked scope as a juvenile.

Over the winter Friar Marcus grew just "a quarter of an inch" but was still under sixteen hands. In his favour was his wonderful temperament. Marsh had no trouble preparing him for the Two Thousand Guineas; unfortunately Friar Marcus made the running and ran too fast for six and a half furlongs. In the circumstances it was decided not to train him for the Derby. However, some damage was done and he failed to show any form in his next three races; a sweepstakes and a handicap over six furlongs and another handicap over five. However, he rallied to win his final two races; both handicaps one over five furlongs and one over six.

Kept in training as a four-year-old Friar Marcus won two of his three races, all at Newmarket of course, carrying top weight in all three and all before the end of May: he won the Crawfurd Plate (handicap) over six furlongs, was second in the Bretby Handicap over six furlongs, and won the Chesterfield Handicap over five furlongs.

At stud Friar Marcus would eventually prove reasonably successful; producing good-looking stock but most were unable to stay middle distances. His best progeny were Brown Betty; winner of the One Thousand Guineas amongst a total of six wins value £11,637. The very fast Lemnarchus; who won nine races value £11,249 plus Hakim, Beresford, Morals of Marcus, Nun's Veil and Waterval. In all he sired the winners of 368 races value £143,072 with an ASI of 7.56 furlongs. With the help of Bahram he was leading brood mare sire in 1935.

Friar's Daughter's dam: Garron Lass was unraced and the final foal of an unraced mare Concertina who was also out of an unraced mare: Comic Song, who cut little ice as a brood mare and was exported to Russia in 1898. This was hardly promising even if Concertina was by St Simon. In the circumstances it would have been no surprise if Garron Lass had never been covered. It was necessary to go back before Comic Song to find any decent breeding but her dam; Frivolity was from one of the very best families.

Concertina produced 9 winners from her 14 foals, including Aurium (Prince Edward Handicap, Manchester), Orchestration (Middlesex Plate, Hurst Park), Research (International Two-year-old Plate, Hurst Park) and Plucky Liege (Great Sapling Plate and Suffolk Nursery); although none were anything other than average.

Plucky Liege, by Spearmint, however, proved an outstanding broodmare producing eleven winners including the Lincoln winner Sir Gallahad III (by Teddy), Grand Prix de Paris winner Admiral Drake by (Craig an Eran) and the top North American sire Bull Dog (by Teddy). Finally at the advanced age of twenty-three she produced the Derby winner Bois Roussel (by Vatout).

Concertina's final foal: Garron Lass arrived in 1917. She was by the moderate miler Roseland who won the July Stakes as a juvenile. Roseland was equally anonymous as a stallion with his only important winner being Bower of Roses who won the 1930 Irish Cesarewitch Handicap, although he was also maternal grandsire of 1938 Irish Derby winner Rosewell. However, as mentioned earlier, Roseland's pedigree did provide some interest, as he was by St. Simon's son William the Third, which meant that Garron Lass was inbred 3x2 to St. Simon. However, once again this failed to ignite the family, and after Garron Lass failed to see the racecourse, she died when only six after producing just one foal; the diminutive Friar's Daughter in 1921.

Although Friar Marcus would prove to be a useful stallion, at the time he covered Garron Lass his first crop had yet to race and he stood at just 98 guineas (£7,100). However, once again Friar Marcus had a pedigree of interest for his maternal grandsire Persimmon was by St. Simon, making Friar's Daughter inbred 4x4x3 to the champion sire.

This was Friar's Daughter's modest background when she was sold as a foal by her breeder, Colonel F. Lort Phillips from Pembrokeshire, to Mrs Plummer for 145 guineas (£5,200) at the 1921 Newmarket December Sales. Even that modest price looked to be less than a bargain when Friar's Daughter soon became seriously ill, and was only nursed back to health by the care and attention of her owner. The full story of this wonderful care by her devoted owner can be found in the chapter dealing with Bahram's Derby win.

Friar's Daughter returned to the sales ring on 14th September 1922 at the Doncaster Sales, and was purchased for 250 guineas (£10,250) for the Aga Khan by Dick Dawson. George Lambton had asked Dawson to purchase some yearlings of his own choosing and, although Friar's Daughter's dam was a non-winner, she matched up to Vuillier's dosage requirements. This was probably for two reasons: the high St. Simon dosage: inbred 4x4x3, and because her female line was held in high esteem.

Friar's Daughter went into training with Dick Dawson. She did not present the most promising proposition; not particularly attractive, smallish and from a family where the previous three dams were all non-winners. Notwithstanding this she was to prove a tough filly racing nine times as a juvenile. She began promisingly winning on her debut 7th April at Alexandra Park in the Enfield Plate beating thirteen opponents as the second favourite at 3–1. Behind her was the even money favourite: Mrs. T H Ratliffe's Golden Knight (Greenback – Pretty Bess by Saxham), who was already a winner. The distance was two lengths.

A month later she contested Division 1 of Newmarket's May Stakes (5f.), but despite being made a 1–2 favourite she could only finish a length and a half second. She returned to Newmarket later in the month, but this time could only manage third place, just over a length and a half behind the winner. After she was unplaced in the Speedy Plate (5f.) at Windsor, Friar's Daughter failed by just a neck to win Sandown Park's Great Kingston Plate (5f.), and she occupied the same position three weeks later in the Astley Stakes (5f.) at Leicester, a length behind the winner. In her final three starts Friar's Daughter raced twice over six furlongs in Nursery Handicaps at Doncaster and Windsor, finishing unplaced both times, either side of a head second in the Reading Nursery Handicap (5f.) at Newbury.

Although she did not win again she finished second four times and third once, admittedly never in the best company. However, she was sound and had kept going from April until November. Nesbit Waddington was convinced Friar's Daughter would have made a useful sprinter if she had been slightly bigger. She was simply not big enough to carry any penalties. She was though very game and considering her unfortunate start in life she had done well enough.

This was her only season to race and she was covered as a three-year-old. Although only a moderate racehorse and the only winner in three generations, the only one to race in fact, on her dam's side

FRIAR'S DAUGHTER—FOAL BY BLENHEIM.

© Lionel Edwards Estate by courtesy of Felix Rosenstiel's Widow & Son, London

she was considered to have an attractive enough pedigree; largely through the inbreeding to St. Simon. However, breeding from such a small filly was a risk as her produce might also be lacking in size.

However she became not only a successful brood mare, producing 11 winners from 13 foals, but a tremendous character. Whenever she was let out into her paddock she would immediately set off to complete three or four circuits of her paddock at full pace. As she usually had a foal with her the youngster would take a lead from its mother and do the same. As might have been expected Friar's Daughter soon lapped her foal but, in most cases, they would struggle on until exhausted. This would happen every day and sometimes more frequently and could be alarming to watch. However, none of her foals came to any harm, and who knows, perhaps she knew best what her foal should be doing to prepare itself for a life in racing! Lord Derby's fine mare Scapa Flow did the same thing apparently.

The history of Friar's Daughter illustrates how events in turf history can hang by a slender thread. Friar's Daughter was the only foal produced by her dam, and she herself nearly died as a yearling. In addition nobody could be blamed for thinking the family line was totally dormant. Few mares produce a Triple Crown winner, but Friar's Daughter nearly did it twice, with her son Dastur finishing runner-up in the Two Thousand Guineas, Derby and St. Leger.

The total prize money won by Friar's Daughter's offspring amounts to £66,702. At the time of her death this placed her third behind Scapa Flow (£86,084), dam of Fairway, Pharos and Fair Isle; and Galicia (£83,776), dam of Bayardo and Lemberg.

Friar's Daughter died at the Aga Khan's Sheshoon Stud in County Kildare, in early November 1950. She was 29 years old and it is comforting that it was reported she was "quite happy and contented up to the end".

The following are details of Friar's Daughter's stud career:-

Foal	Subsequent Career
1925 Fille D'Espoir (b or br f by Hurry On)	Placed twice over 5 furlongs in England at two, then transferred to France

Foal	Subsequent Career
1926	Fille D'Amour (b f by Hurry On)	Won 1 race at two worth, £890, namely the Prince of Wales's Nursery (8f.). 4th in Oaks & 4th in Yorkshire Oaks at three. At stud produced Fille de Poete, the dam of Irish 2000 Guineas and Derby winner The Phoenix.
1927	Myron (b c Diophon)	Won 2 races over 5 furlongs at two, worth £337 in England and sent to India where he won 6 races worth £2,470 between 1931 & 1936.
1928	Fille de Salut (b f by Sansovino)	Won 4 races at three in France over 2150m. 2000m. (twice) and 2300m. worth 91,370 francs. At stud produced 1945 Cambridgeshire Handicap winner Esquire
1929	Dastur (b c by Solario)	Won 7 races, including one dead-heat, worth £11,625.50, including Woodcote S, King Edward VII S, Irish Derby, Sussex S, Coronation Cup & Champion S (dead-heat). Runner-up in 2000 Guineas, Derby & St. Leger. At stud sired Ascot Gold Cup winner Umiddad.
1930	Parsan (b f by Solario)	Won final 2 races, both dead-heats, at three over 8 furlongs worth £125 in England. Sent to France in 1936 where she had two foals, and then to Germany 1940.
1931	Not Covered	
1932	Bahram (b c by Blandford)	Unbeaten in 9 races worth £45,308.50
1933	Niloufer (b f by Sansovino)	Unplaced in all 4 starts at two. Sent to France in 1936
1934	Barren to Solario	
1935	Sadruddin (b c by Solario)	Won one race in France, Prix de Saint-Gratien (10.5f.) worth 15,870 francs in 1940. Stallion in France.
1936	Sadri (br c by Solario)	Foaled in France, while visiting Blenheim. Unraced at two, raced three times in England at three, finishing third to Heliopolis on final start in Gratwicke Stakes. Later exported to South Africa and won 4 races worth £5,680, including 1941 July Handicap (10.5f.) and 1943 Peninsula Handicap (8f.) (dead-heat). At stud sired South African Derby winner Dancing Flame & July Handicap winners Gay Jane and C'est Si Bon.

	Foal	Subsequent Career
1937	Alrabia (b f by Blenheim)	Won 1 race at three over 9 furlongs worth £42 in England.
1938	Bakhtawar (b c by Windsor Lad)	Won 1 race at three over 14 furlongs and 2 races at four over 12 and 14 furlongs worth £894 in England. At stud sired the dam of 1978 Aintree Grand National winner Lucius.
1939	Muzloom (gr c by Mahmoud)	Won 1 race at two over 5 furlongs and 2 races at three over 8 furlongs worth £644 in England. Exported to Argentina in 1943 and stood as a stallion there.
1940	Barren to Umidwar	

Friar's Daughter was also barren in 1941, 1942 and 1943. She was not covered again and retired.

Friar's Daughter bred 11 winners from 13 foals.
England & Ireland – 28 races (including 3 dead-heats) worth £57,645
France – 5 races worth 107,240 francs (£906)
India – 6 races worth £2,471
South Africa – 4 races (including 1 dead-heat) worth £5,680.

At the time of her death Friar's Daughter's descendants had already secured her a place as an important broodmare. The Phoenix, a grandson of Fille D'Amour, started by winning the 1943 Irish Two Thousand Guineas and Irish Derby, while two years later Fille de Salut's son Esquire won the Cambridgeshire Handicap. Esquire's older full sister Fille de Soleil, produced Sunny Boy, a useful race-horse and champion sire in France in 1954, when his winners included Oaks winner Sun Cap, and Prix de L'Arc de Triomphe winner Sica Boy.

Group1/Grade 1 winners descended from Friar's Daughter:-

Horse	G1 races won
African Boy	1979 Gran Premio Cruzeiro do Sul
Alondite	2006 Japan Dirt Derby

Horse	G1 races won
Bannaby	2008 Prix du Cadran
Daily Busy	1985 Ramona Handicap
Eastern Joy	1985 Easter Handicap
Esprit du Nord	1983 Preis von Europa, 1984 Gran Premio di Milano
Etiqueta Negra	2004 Clasico Independencia
Grison	1985 Gran Premio Cruzeiro do Sul, 1985 Gran Premio Brasil
Guadanini	1978 Grand Prix de Saint-Cloud
Kyoei Promise	1983 Tenno Sho Autumn
Literato	2007 Champion S
Livernon	1989 Gran Premio Estado do Rio de Janeiro
Manacor	1975 Gran Premio Piratininga
Orban	1987 Premio Roma
Passing Shot	2003 Personal Ensign Handicap
Pernod	2002 Invitation S
Piachay	2003 Brisbane Cup
Rajput Princess	1964 French 1000 Guineas
Regal Exception	1972 Irish Oaks
Right Win	1983 Gran Premio D'Italia
Russian Pearl	2003 Levin Turf Classic, 2006 Hong Kong Stewards Cup
Sakura Chiyono-O	1987 Asahi Hai Sanai S, 1988 Tokyo Yushun (Japanese Derby)
Sakura Hokuto-O	1988 Asahi Hai Sanai S
Shadai Kagura	1989 Oka Sho (Japanese 1000 Guineas)
The Phoenix	1942 Phoenix S, 1943 Irish 2000 Guineas, 1943 Irish Derby
Zug	1971 French 2000 Guineas

Winners of Principal Races with a duplication of Friar's Daughter within their first four generations

Horse	Inbreeding via	Principal races won
Baba Au Rhum	3x3 Bahram/Alrabia	1958 Prix Quincey (8f.)
Burnt Brown	4x3 Fille D'Amour/Dastur	1948 Cornwallis Stakes (5f.) 1950 City & Suburban Handicap (10f.)
Crawley Beauty	3x3 Bahram/Dastur	1950 Molecomb Stakes (5f.)
Darranour	4x4 Fille de Salut/Bahram	1962 Prix Morny (6f.)
Great Bear	4x4 Dastur/Dastur	1967 Diadem Stakes (6f.) 1969 Duke of York Stakes (6f.)
Khalif	4x4 Bahram/Dastur	1966 Victoria Derby (12.5f.)

Horse	Inbreeding via	Principal races won
Proud Chieftain	3x4 Bahram/Bahram	1960 Column Produce Stakes (8f.) 1961 Rosebery Handicap (10f.) 1961 John Smith's Cup (10f.)
Regal Light	4x4 Bahram/Dastur	1967 Royal Hunt Cup (8f.)
Samson	4x4 Dastur/Bahram	1962 Doomben Cup (10f.) 1964 All Aged Stakes (8f.)
Sir Dane	4x4 Bahram/Bahram	1964 Turnbull Stakes (12f.) 1964 W S Cox Plate (10f.)
Tahiri	3x4 Bahram/Dastur	1963 City & Suburban Handicap (10f.)

11 Sandown Surprise

The horses have just passed the post in the big race of the day and the most valuable two-year-old race of the year. The winner is a 20–1 outsider that has beaten the favourite. Both horses are owned by the same man and the crowd is not happy...

*   *   *

Bahram was a bay colt foaled at the Aga Khan's Sheshoon stud on 13th April 1932. He was by Blandford out of Friar's Daughter who was by Friar Marcus. The details of his ancestry have already been dealt with; he was bred to be no more than a good horse and the Aga Khan had produced more regally-bred foals from better mares at his studs.

Friar's Daughter had been delicate as a foal and Bahram as a youngster was not very robust either; "Bahram's lungs were affected by pneumonia" said Colonel Peacocke the stud manager, "and as a result he was a delicate foal. But he was a plucky little animal, and never left his feed. As a yearling he was very handsome. We thought he was a prince".

However, pneumonia is very serious for a foal but thanks to the skillful care of Colonel Peacocke, who in addition to being stud manager was also an experienced veterinary surgeon, Bahram began to improve. He was an excellent patient with a good appetite and this, allied to his equable temperament, gave him every chance and he made a full recovery. He grew to become, in the opinion of those at Sheshoon, a handsome youngster and was able to join the other yearlings at Fitzroy House in Newmarket under the care of trainer Frank Butters.

Bahram had hardly got comfortable in his stable when another problem emerged: his name, it had been the intention to name him Bahman and it was this that was submitted to Weatherbys. However, this name had been previously registered by the late J B Hornung for one of his colts so the name Bahman was refused to avoid any possible confusion. So Bahram was substituted; a name with romantic associations of "that great hunter" of Edward FitzGerald's *Rubaiyat of Omar Khayyam*. This was an infinitely more suitable name for a colt that would become the greatest racehorse the Aga Khan III ever bred and raced and would become one of the giants of the Twentieth Century.

However, it is by no means certain that this was the Aga's intention when he named his son of Blandford and Friars Daughter Bahram, pronounced Bahr-arm with the second syllable being stressed. The Aga had a cousin: Prince Bahram of Persia who was drowned during the Great War when the ship *Sussex* was sunk. On reflection this was probably what the Aga had in mind. However, in view of Bahram's subsequent achievements, preference is definitely for his being named after "the great hunter".

Good-looking as Bahram was he was not considered quite as handsome as his half-brother Dastur; who had the frustrating distinction of finishing second in all three Classics of 1932, Bahram though was bigger. The stud may have thought he was a prince but as a juvenile he was not a horse which immediately attracted the eye: there was nothing magnificent or particularly distinguished about him, but he was difficult to fault.

As a two-year-old he was tall and well-formed enough to be easily mistaken for a three-year-old. He had the stamp of quality all over him, except perhaps his head which was rather plain and his tail which was "short and scanty".

These minor quibbles apart he was tall: sixteen hands, but beautifully proportioned, with perfect symmetry: a good long neck, deep in both shoulder and from withers to the lower chest and also below the elbow in front and the stifle joint behind. He was perhaps a little light in bone and overall gave the impression of somewhat lacking in substance, however, he possessed very good shape and quality: short in the back and well ribbed up. He had good hocks: no sign of sickle hocks, good short canon bones, short pasterns, at the correct angle and feet that looked as if they would suit a horse with a far heavier build.

However, it was his action that was his most distinctive trait. Archive film shows him to have been the most wonderful walker and mover; when walking he displayed an easy, relaxed, athletic, loose-limbed gait. When cantering he was nothing out of the ordinary, however when galloping he was a tremendous mover, with a long stride showing an action that never seemed to hurry. Bahram, although a lightly-made sort, was essentially an athlete. Photographs taken at ages three and four suggest that he did not change much; but he had grown and had reached 16.2 on Derby day, however, he did look lighter as a three-year-old; something that will be discussed later.

* * *

As would be expected Bahram was entered for all the top juvenile races: a total of eleven. He was to run in five of them. He was listed as Bahram (late Bahman) in recognition of his name change. The first entries were for the Coventry and New Stakes at Ascot; then the British Dominion Plate at Sandown and the July Stakes at Newmarket. Not surprisingly he also had an entry for the most valuable race run all year for juveniles: the National Breeders Produce Stakes at Sandown. Entering this race required some foresight as will be explained later.

In addition he held entries for the Ham Produce stakes at Goodwood; the Aga actually won this race but with another horse, and also the Rous Memorial Stakes. Bahram was also entered for the valuable juvenile races towards the end of the season: the Gimcrack Stakes at York, Champagne stakes at Doncaster and finally the Middle Park and Dewhurst Stakes at Newmarket.

* * *

Bahram was not the most forward of the Fitzroy House juveniles and the early two-year-old races went by, in addition to the big races at Ascot, without any prospect of him making his debut. The most valuable race in the early part of the year was the Sandown Park Stud Produce Stakes and this was won by a filly: Major Dermot McCalmont's Vallema (Tetratema – Valla by Poisoned Arrow), it was her only win of the year from five starts; she did not really progress and finished the season running unsuccessfully in nurseries. However, the second: Mrs. Arthur James's colt Gynerium (Phalaris – Figliastra by Son-in-Law), won three of his seven races and earned 8 st. 7lb. in the Free Handicap.

The next race of importance was the Woodcote Stakes at the Derby meeting over six furlongs. This was won by Vicomte de Fontarce's Bagman (Foxlaw – Grand Pet by Grand Parade); his only win from seven races, he made little impression thereafter although he was given 8 st. 1lb. in the Free Handicap.

Juvenile racing stepped up considerably when Ascot arrived. It should be remembered that the meeting in June, now known as Royal Ascot but in Bahram's time simply as Ascot Heath, was the only meeting of the year held at the course. Consequently each race over the four days carried considerable prestige and many two-year-olds made their debut during the week. On the first day: Tuesday, then, as now the principal two-year-old race was the Coventry Stakes run, at that time, over five furlongs. It was probably a good, if not a vintage, renewal and the Aga Khan's Hairan (Fairway – Harpsichord by Louvois)), trained by Frank Butters, won comfortably from Col. W F Story's Pampas Grass (Papyrus – Silver Grass by Phalaris), Mrs. Derek FitzGerald's The Jesuit (Mr Jinks – Lay Sister by Abbots Trace) and seven others at odds of 9–4 on. Hairan started slowly but finished impressively and was a comfortable winner at the line. He had earlier won on his debut at Manchester.

On Wednesday it was the Chesham Stakes run, at that time, over five furlongs and won by the Aga Khan's colt Shahali (Sansovino – Theresina by Diophon) who beat Mrs. Corlette Glorney's Winandermere (Beresford – Grasmere by Chaucer) and Gynerium. Shahali won three of his five races and was given 8st. 13 lb. in the Free Handicap. Mr. C Jarvis' Knighted (Sir Cosmo – Bellona by Happy Warrior); a two-year-old gelding, won the Fern Hill Stakes, this was for two and three-year-olds over five furlongs. Although it was only the 20th June this was incredibly Knighted's seventh race and he had won them all. He ran only once more at the end of the season and finished third.

On Thursday the most valuable juvenile race of the week, and the most important at that time, was the New Stakes run over five furlongs; known today as the Norfolk Stakes. The winner was Sir Abe Bailey's unnamed colt by Son and Heir out of Eppie Adair by Duncan Grey who beat another unnamed colt: Miss Dorothy Paget's colt by Diomedes out of Racla by Clarissimus who will feature later in races against Bahram. The Eppie Adair colt, who remained unnamed at the end of the season, won two of his four races and was given 8st. 8lb. in the Free Handicap. The following year he was named Robin Goodfellow. The Racla colt was later named Radamedes.

The final juvenile race was staged on Friday: the Windsor Castle Stakes, and was run over five furlongs, as it is today. By the end of the season it was to prove the best of the four Ascot two-year-old races; something extremely unlikely to happen today! The Aga and Frank Butters had first and third. It was won by Theft (Tetratema – Voleuse by Volta) who beat Lord Derby's Bobsleigh (Gainsborough –Toboggan by Hurry On) and the Aga's Alykhan (Diophin – Teresina by Tracery).

Named after the Aga's son Aly, Alykhan was a most promising sort; this was only his second race and he then won the Exeter Stakes and was third in the Chesterfield Stakes, both at Newmarket. Unfortunately he did not progress and by the end of the year he had been gelded! One or two husbands might have thought this operation could usefully have been performed on Aly! The horse Alykhan was sold at the Newmarket December sales in 1935 for 300 guineas (£16,700) and purchased by the trainer W Carr on behalf of Mr. A. J. Redman. Alykhan was renamed Tereson and raced with moderate success until he was a seven-year-old. It can only be speculation but did the Aga have any part in the changing of the horse's name?

Theft and Bobsleigh were to be ranked third and fourth respectively in the Free Handicap.

*   *   *

The July Stakes at Newmarket's three day meeting was reduced to match and won by Hilla (Son-in-Law – Cos by Flying Orb); a filly owned and bred by the Aga Khan and trained by Frank Butters. The other principal race at that meeting was the Exeter Stakes and was annexed by the same owner and trainer combination; this time with Alykhan who beat Godolphin, a gelding (Baytown – Phalanstery by Phalaris) and two others. It was his only win from seven races.

*   *   *

Bahram had been noted doing "canters" over four and five furlongs, usually in company with other juveniles, but it was not until 11th July that anything specific was recorded. He was noted as working 5 furlongs "half speed" with Theft; an indication that he was considered above average. As Theft had won the Windsor Castle Stakes Bahram must have been thought potentially at least useful to be able to keep company with him in a gallop. However, Theft "won" the gallop ridden by Gordon Richards with Dick Perryman on Bahram and afterwards Butters asked Richards what he thought of Theft; "He'll do for me" he replied.

On the 15th July Bahram worked five furlongs "fast" in company, on the 18th he cantered on the tan gallop, on the 19th he worked 5 furlongs "sharp" with the Aga's Hindoo Holiday (Blandford – Pagan Sacrifice by Cicero); who had finished seventh in the New Stakes at Ascot.

*   *   *

Bahram might have been considered to be potentially above average by Frank Butters but it still seems surprising that it was decided that he would make his debut in the most valuable juvenile race of the year. His work might have suggested he was ready to make his debut, but in a maiden or minor stakes perhaps. In addition it is known that Butters thought Bahram needed more time and this, together with a lack of experience, meant he could not be expected to beat his stable companion Theft, even in receipt of 9 lbs. Bahram was therefore set to carry the Aga's second colours with Theft, ridden of course by a confident Gordon Richards, carrying the principle ones.

The National Breeders Produce Stakes was the most valuable race of the year for juveniles and its conditions seem strange now. It was for the produce of mares covered in 1931: foals of 1932 and juveniles of 1934. However, the race closed on 26th July 1931 BEFORE any of the eventual runners had even been foaled. Entries were made on behalf of 267 potential foals.

There were seven various forfeit stages costing a total of £122 (6,350) until the runners were eventually reduced to 24; of these ten were declared to run. The course added only One Thousand pounds (52,000) therefore the owners, including those that did not declare at all seven stages, contributed approximately 84% of the prize money! This was undoubtedly very mean of the racecourse, but not to be compared with today's ghastly "sales" races where the owners put up well over 90% of the prize fund and the sponsors what little remains!

Today even the best races are often largely paid for by owners. For example the 2015 Two Thousand Guineas was advertised as £450,000 guaranteed. However, by declaration time £419,000 had been paid by owners in forfeits! Not much left for the racecourse and sponsors: Qipco to find. Why can't the racecourses return to the days when races were advertised as say, £200,000 added to the stakes. If Newmarket had done this in 2015 then the race would have been worth £619,000 and the winner would have received about £354,000 instead of £282,841.

Racecourses might argue that by guaranteeing the amount owners always know the minimum prize money on offer. However, taking the example of the 2015 Two Thousand Guineas, for the course to be seriously out of pocket the number of entrants, which amounted to 83, would need to have been below fifty!

It could have been expected that Theft with the best form would start favourite; he had won the Windsor Castle Stakes on his debut. However, as sometimes happens, logic and the form book were ignored as the "work watchers" thought they had seen something out of the ordinary. Dick Dawson's Duke John (Blandford – Orcelone by Orby) had impressed in his work at Whatcombe with Lord Carnarvon's Satyr (Tetratema – Nigella by Galloper Light) and Sir Albert Stern's Dictator (Stefan the Great – My Dame by Littleton); both good but by no means top-class three-year-olds. On the strength of this he was made favourite. Nothing in Bahram's work encouraged such confidence and he was allowed to start at 20–1.

Meyrick Good thought the field was "a good-looking lot" with Lady Zia Wernher's Nymph Errant (Hurry On – Double Life by Bachelor's Double) and Jock Whitney's Baba au Rhum (Tetratema – Phyllis Dare by Sunder) the most backward. Bahram and Duke John, both of whom were by Blandford, he noted "there is a great similarity about them in make, shape and colour. Bahram may be a trifle shorter backed". Good also noted Bahram's short tail; in his view it detracted from his appearance and made him looked shorter.

Duke John displayed traces of greenness and appeared too docile in the paddock; Good expected him to improve and be all the better for the race. Interestingly he observed "It could be seen why he has not run before. He has a big splint just under his off-knee, and will probably be seen to most advantage, when, if ever, we get really soft ground again". This was during a severe dry spell; was there a hose-pipe ban one wonders! At least at that time the ground was consistent: no over eager, water-happy clerks of courses, eager to keep the bookmakers happy creating false going!

A splint is a bony growth found anywhere on the cannon bone. They are more common in young horses and can be caused by working on firm ground. Splints can vary in size from barely discernible to the size of an egg, and can often be troublesome when found high under the knee, as in this instance. It may well be the reason Duke John was unable to race again as a juvenile.

Lt.-Col. Giles Loder's Fairbairn (Fairway – Baby Polly by Spearmint) was a "racing-like colt; a little on his toes leaving the paddock and again at the post.

The National Breeders Produce Stakes has declined considerably since Bahram's time; it is now run at the end of May, with entirely different race conditions, and has only Listed status.

Sandown Park Saturday 21st July Going; Firm
National Breeders Produce Stakes of £50 each £43 if dec. by July 10 1934
£22 if dec. by March 27 1934 £6 if dec. Oct 10 1933 or £1 if dec. Mar 28
1933, with £1,000 added of which breeder of the winner recd £300, breeder
and owner of second each £200 and owner and breeder of third each £100
two-year-olds; colts 8st 10lbs fillies and geldings 8st 7lbs; winner of any race
400 sov. 5lb, of two races 400 sov. each or one 800 sov., 9lb ex. 5 furlongs

(267 ents., viz., 24 at £50 55 at £43 56 at £22 56 at £6 and 76 at £1 – £5,559)
(294,600) – Closed July 28 1931

1	Bahram	8st 10 lb	R. Perryman	112 ++
2	Theft	9st 5 lb	G Richards	119
3	Highland Lament	8st 7lb	H Wragg	99
4	Red Biddy	8st 12lb	H Beasley	
5	Fairbairn	8st 10lb	C Smirke	
6	Duke John	8st 10lb	C Ray	
7	Nymph Errant	8st 7lb	P Beasley	
0	Sequalo	8st 7lb	M Beary	
0	Golden Araby f	8st 7lb	B Carslake	
0	Baba au Rhum	8st 7lb	J Childs	

Betting; 13/8 Duke John, 5/2 Theft 6/1 Fairbairn 10/1 Red Biddy & Golden Araby f 100/8 Sequalo 20/1 Bahram 25/1 bar

Won by a neck; 2 lengths between second and third.
Time 1 min. 0.20 sec. (fast by 1.40)

Sporting Life race analysis;
Babu au Rhum began slowly, losing several lengths. The pace was a good one, those most prominent when the barrier rose being Theft (on the far side) Sequalo, Bahram, Highland Lament (on the stand side), Golden Araby filly and Red Biddy. Theft and Bahram were leading the field below the distance, pursued by Highland Lament, Duke John, Sequalo and Red Biddy. Bahram mastered Theft in the last half-furlong and got up to win by a neck.

There were five races over five furlongs during the two days of the meeting; both of which were staged on firm ground. It might have been expected that Bahram's time would be the fastest of the four juvenile races but it was also quicker than the handicap for three-year-olds and up; by 0. 80 of a second! Meyrick Good noted in *The Sporting Life* that it was the fastest juvenile time he had recorded over the Esher straight course that year.

Bahram carried more weight than all of the runners in the handicap with the exception of the winner, a four-year-old, who carried 9st 6lb. A juvenile should receive 20 pounds from a four-year-old over five furlongs in July; Bahram carried ten pounds less so could have been said to have produced a performance in which he could have given ten pounds-weight-for-age to an older horse and beaten him four lengths! It should not be forgotten that Theft, beaten only a neck, conceded Bahram nine pounds; clearly the first two were well above average.

Bahram won comfortably; Capt. Long (Augur of *The Sporting Life*) thought that not only did Bahram win "cleverly" but also gave the impression he would have won even more comfortably over a furlong further. Despite being beaten easily Theft could also be considered to have run well: his performance was equal to giving a four-year-old nineteen pounds and beating him about three and a half lengths. It is not hard to imagine a twenty-four year old Phil Bull; the great polymath and founder of *Timeform* and an early advocate of time, seeing these times and salivating about the prospects of both Bahram and Theft.

Theft's performance, without Bahram in the field, would have been considered a good one in its own right and it was his only defeat from five outings as a juvenile. It also demonstrates just how good this debut performance by Bahram was. Both ran on their merits as the Aga Khan cared only about winning and would only have wanted Bahram to beat his stable companions once his reputation had been established. On this occasion he would have expected and been quite happy if Theft had beaten Bahram.

Theft had won the Windsor Castle at Ascot on his debut beating a fellow debutant: Bobsleigh. After the National Breeders Produce Stakes Theft won the Ham Stakes at Goodwood, the Nottinghamshire Breeders Foal Plate and finished the year by beating his sole opponent in the Buckenham Stakes at Newmarket. He was given 9st. 6lbs. in the Free Handicap a pound below Bahram. Bobsleigh ran only once more after; winning the Richmond Stakes at Goodwood.

Of the others only Major Dermot McCalmont's filly Red Biddy (Tetratema – Hesperia by Diadumenos) won a race that year; winning three times and had also finished second in the Queen Mary at Ascot. She was given 8 st. 0 lbs. in the Free Handicap. Duke John was unfortunate enough to sprain a hock at the start and did not race again that season. This in addition to his splint was very unfortunate. Fairbairn simply lacked the pace to challenge. Sir George Bullough's filly Highland Lament (Coronach – Vesper Bell by Pommern) did not race again that year. She had been thought good enough to make her debut in the Queen Mary at Ascot and then ran well against winners in a conditions stakes at Newmarket.

The result was not popular with all race-goers; there was a demonstration by a small ill-behaved section of the crowd due to the Aga Khan winning with what they considered to be the "wrong" horse. As Bahram was wearing the second colours and was a much bigger price some punters felt cheated when Bahram won. This provoked some discussion about whether in such circumstances it should be possible to back the owner in a race and include all his runners. Over the years there had been several instances of the Aga Khan winning with an outsider and beating one of his own horses that had been a much shorter price. Nothing ever came of it of course and, while bookmakers have the final say, nothing ever will!

Bahram had made an impressive debut; albeit surprising everyone it seems! Nonetheless he had beaten horses with good early-season juvenile form and the decision to run him in such a high profile race on his debut was justified.

Frank Butters stable of high class juveniles had just been strengthened by one more; this one though might just be a bit special.

12 Glorious Goodwood and York

The Knavesmire is packed for the Ebor meeting. The principal race for three-year-olds has been won by the Derby winner. The following race was the major juvenile contest of the meeting and has been won by a most promising sort. One observer speculates that he might have seen two Derby winners on one afternoon...

*   *   *

Following his promising debut at Sandown Bahram's work was restricted to canters on most days, but he did work 5 furlongs "sharp" on 26th. He left Newmarket for Goodwood on Monday 30th with the Ham Produce Stakes on the following day his intended race. However after rain fell it was decided to run Theft; who beat Lord Woolavington's Ben Marshall (Gainsborough – Fair Diana by Hurry On) and Lord Derby's Trade Wind (Fairway – Serenissima by Minoru). Bahram had not been entered for the Richmond, Lavant or Molecomb Stakes and the only other nomination he held at Goodwood was for the Rous Memorial Stakes on Thursday.

The Richmond Stakes was won in commanding style by Lord Derby's Bobsleigh who beat his nine opponents in a fashion that convinced many they had seen a future Classic winner. Bobsleigh was by Gainsborough out of Toboggan by Hurry On, however, he looked nothing like a son of Gainsborough, which was unusual as most progeny of Gainsborough resemble their sire. Bobsleigh resembled his dam side and was a typical Hurry On. Unfortunately this was to be his last race that year; Lord Derby was worried about the prevailing firm ground and persuaded his trainer: Colledge Leader, not to run Bobsleigh again. Lord Derby was certain Bobsleigh would have won the Windsor Castle Stakes at Ascot but for Tommy Weston's incompetent riding. His Lordship is entitled to his opinion; however, as Bobsleigh was beaten two lengths by Theft; both were making their debuts, and the subsequent form of Theft suggests that nothing Weston could have done would have ensured victory. In addition Bobsleigh showed greenness at Ascot by displaying a high head carriage; something he did not show at Goodwood.

The Lavant Stakes was won by Maltravers (Mr. Jinks – Futurity by Blandford), trained by Frank Butters. He won five of his eight races as a juvenile and was given 9 st. 0 lbs. in the free handicap; fifth behind the "big four": Bahram, Hairan, Theft, and Bobsleigh. His form suggested a decent colt; not quite good enough to beat the first four. The Molecomb was won by a filly: La Gaiete (Gainsborough – Lady Lawless by Son-in-Law) owned by the Aga Khan and trained by Frank Butters.

The principal juvenile race at Goodwood today is the Champagne Stakes but it was not inaugurated until 1975. At that time it did not have pattern status and had a penalty value to the winner of £3,315 as compared with £13,561 for the Richmond Stakes. It was not until 1998 that the two races were of comparable value. Today they attract different horses as the Richmond Stakes is still over six furlongs and the Champagne, as it always has been, is over seven.

The Rous Memorial Stakes was discontinued in 1982 when a three-runner renewal was so uncompetitive that no starting prices were returned. It had enjoyed listed status the year before. Unfortunately the executive at Goodwood at that time were over-quick to drop any non-handicap race, regardless of its history, if there was an uncompetitive renewal. "Only four runners next year it will be run as a handicap" was the mantra from the management during the eighties and several races were affected.

This obsession, often at the behest of the bookmakers and the ever greater drive for yet more betting "turnover", resulted in many non-handicap races that did not attract eight runners, being dropped and replaced by handicaps. It did not take into account that inexperienced horses need racecourse experience in order to help them progress. It can ruin a juvenile who wins first time out and then must run in Pattern /Listed Company or nurseries against more experienced sorts. It also ignores the view of race-goers who are often happy to see a good horse run and often don't mind that the race is uncompetitive.

Anyone who doubts this has only to witness any good horse when it wins a race as the overwhelming odds-on favourite, being clapped by the appreciative race-goers in acknowledgement. In the event of any race-goer not being interested they could always retire to the tea room or bar and refresh themselves with a suitable beverage!

It was stated earlier in the day, exactly by who is not clear, that Bahram would not run in the Rous Memorial Stakes. However, when the numbers were hoisted on to the board to general surprise Bahram's number was amongst them.

Goodwood Thursday 2 August Going; Good
Rous Memorial Stakes £20 each £10 if dec by July 3 1934 or £3 if dec by Oct.
17 1933 (the forfeits on this date being added to the Rous Memorial Fund),
with £400 added for owner, and £100 for breeder of winner, second rec. £100
and the third £50 out of stakes, for two-year-olds; colts 8st 7lb fillies and geld-
ings 8st 4lb, winner of a race 300 sov. 5lb., of two races 300 sov. each or one
of 500 sov. 9lb, of two races 500 sov or one 800 sov 14 lb ex., 6 furlongs (83
ent. Viz. 23 at £20 35 at £10 and 25 at £3-----£1,140) (60,400))

1	Bahram	9st 7lb	F. Fox	122++
2	Racla colt	8st 7lb	H. Beasley	107
3	Fifine colt	8st 10lb	B. Carslake	104
4	Battle Note	8st 4lb	R. Perryman	
5	True Tilda	8st 4lb	G. Richards	
6	Polette	8st 4lbs	H Packman	

Betting; 4/5 Bahram 4/1 True Tilda 11/2 Racla c 6/1 Battle Note 100/7 Polette
100/6 Fifine c

Won by a neck; two lengths between second and third
Time; 1 min 15.00 sec. (Slow by 2.80)

Race analysis; Racla colt led from True Tilda, Battle Note, Bahram and Polette. Bahram made his effort in the final furlong, and, travelling better than Racla colt, he won cleverly.

There were seven races over six furlongs during the four days of the Goodwood meeting and Bahram's was the slowest. This was, however, not by any means a moderate race; Racla colt had good form but was comfortably beaten by Bahram who was conceding a stone. Even so Racla colt probably ran slightly below his Ascot form.

The Racla colt, by Diomedes, was unnamed as a juvenile and it was not until the following year that he was named Radamedes. He raced ten times as a two-year-old, winning twice. Making his debut as early as 18th April he was slow to understand what was required of him, but finished second on his fourth start in the New Stakes at Ascot; the Rous Memorial was his sixth race. On his next start he won the valuable Manchester Autumn Breeders Plate and followed up the next start by winning the Hopeful Stakes at Newmarket before finishing the year with two unplaced efforts. He was a useful if not very consistent colt and was given 8st. 6 lbs. in the Free Handicap; fifteen pounds behind Bahram. As a three-year-old he raced eight times winning once; a five furlong handicap at Newmarket. After failing to see out a mile at Epsom he was dropped to five furlongs for the remainder of the year. As his sire: Diomedes was a very fast horse whose average stamina index as a sire was 5.67, this was hardly a surprise.

The Fifine colt was by Sansovino and eventually named Sansofine; all year to think of a name and that was the best Lord Glanely could come with; good grief! He raced five times as a juvenile, winning once: a Newmarket maiden on his debut. The Rous Memorial represented his best form. He failed to win as a three-year-old and was sent to Australia.

The other three runners won just a nursery from twenty outings.

*   *   *

Bahram continued his education; merely cantering most days but he did do a solo piece of work over five furlongs at "good pace" on the 8th August. His work was mainly canters over 5 and 6 furlongs until 26th when in preparation for his next race he worked over six furlongs at "good pace" with Maltravers and Hilla.

*   *   *

The only race Bahram had a nomination for in August was the Gimcrack Stakes at York's August Meeting which, although a good race today, and has Group 2 status, it was usually a much better race in Bahram's time. It was inaugurated in 1846 and is one of the oldest juvenile races. The winning owner earns the right to make the annual Gimcrack speech at the dinner in December. During its history there have been some splendid occasions with very entertaining orations.

York Thursday August 30 Going; Hard
Gimcrack Stakes of 1,000 sov. added to a sweepstake of 10 sov. each half forfeit
if dec by Aug 21 or 2 sov. if dec by Tues after the Newmarket Craven meeting;
of which the second recd £150 and the third £50 two-year-olds ; colts 8st 7lb.
fillies and geldings 8st 4lb ; winner of a race 750 sov. 5 lb ext. six furlongs
straight (134 entries viz 9 at £10 94 at £5 and 31 at £2 – £1,142) (60,500)

1	Bahram	8st 12 lb	R. Perryman	120+
2	Consequential	8st 7lb	C. Smirke	112
3	Phalange colt	8st 12 lb	C. Ray	105
4	Eton Blue	8st 7lb	H. Wragg	
5	Happi	8st 7lb	E. Smith	

Betting; 2/7 Bahram 5/1 Consequential 100/6 Phalange c 33/1 Eton Blue 50/1 Happi

Won by a length; four lengths between second and third
Time; 1min 12.60 sec (slow by .70)

Race analysis; Happi took a slight lead over Bahram and Eton Blue with Phalange colt and Consequential in rear. At half-way Bahram was moving well in front of Phalange colt and Consequential. At the distance Consequential challenged, but failed to catch Bahram who won easily.

Rapier writing in *The Illustrated Sporting and Dramatic News* felt that Bahram was finding Sir Charles McLeod's Consequential (Son and Heir – Quento by Friar Marcus) hard to "polish off" just under a furlong from the finish. However, Perryman was well aware of this and pulled his whip with no intention of using it other than to "threaten" Bahram who was running lazily; the move sufficed and he exerted himself sufficiently to comfortably hold the second. *Rapier* also noted that Bahram winning meant that The Aga Khan would be making the Gimcrack speech at the annual dinner for the second year in succession.

Over the three days of the August Ebor meeting there were only two races over six furlongs. Bahram's time was faster than a welter handicap. The times for the six races over five furlongs suggest the ground was very fast.

Consequential raced six times as a juvenile winning twice: the Beckhampton Plate at Newbury on his debut in April and a stakes race at Newmarket in early May. Incidentally there were 36 runners in the Newbury race; thirty-three of them debutants! Charlie Smirke and his brother were both cautioned for taking each other's position at the start. It is surprising anyone noticed! Consequential was then off the track for almost four months until the Gimcrack. Afterwards he raced three more times; finishing second in the Champagne Stakes at Doncaster behind Kingsem and third behind Bahram in the Middle Park. He was a big colt with every expectation that he would be better at three and was given 8 st. 11 lbs. in the Free Handicap.

Sir Frederick Eley's Phalange colt, by Tetratema was later named Quadrille Boy, ran ten times winning three. He won a stakes race at Manchester and the Champagne Stakes at Salisbury. The Gimcrack was his sixth race and he finished the year running in three nurseries; winning one. Lord Rosebery's Eton Blue (Felstead – All's Blue by Buchan) and Sir Laurence Philipps's Happi (Horus – Catharis by Son-in-Law) both failed to win as juveniles.

The race before the Gimcrack; the Great Yorkshire Stakes – sadly discontinued after the 1955 meeting having being run for 130 years – was won by the Derby winner: Windsor Lad. One enthusiast remarked after the Gimcrack that in one afternoon he had seen this year's Derby winner and also next years! It has to be hoped that he backed his opinion at the same time!

13   Middle Park Stakes

The most important juvenile race of the season has just been won in commanding fashion. Many are talking enthusiastically of his chances in next year's Classics. Others are less impressed...

*   *   *

Now unbeaten in three races Bahram was ready to step up and challenge for the big autumn races which establish the pecking order for juveniles. These were the Champagne Stakes at Doncaster, The Imperial Produce Stakes at Kempton and the Middle Park Stakes at Newmarket, all over six furlongs.

The St Leger meeting at Doncaster in early September featured only two juvenile races of any note: the Champagne Stakes and the Tattersall Sales Stakes. The latter race was restricted, as are similar ones today, to horses bought at the sales and as such the results are often meaningless as home-bred produce are excluded. The Champagne Stakes was, and is today, one of the most important two-year-old races. In Bahram's time it was over six furlongs and was first run in 1823.

The renewal of 1934 looked well up to standard and Hairan was the warm favourite at 7–4 on. However, the ground was very firm and Hairan either could not or would not exert himself in such conditions. He was beaten into third place behind Sir Charles Hyde's Kingsem (Tetrameter – Pomona by Stornoway) and Consequential. Kingsem won four of his nine races as a juvenile and was given 8 st. 11 lbs. in the Free Handicap. He had previously won the very valuable Lancashire Produce Stakes run at the Liverpool Summer Meeting at the end of July.

The sales race was won by Lord Derby's colt Bunker (Fairway – Wandering Maid by Diadumenos), who beat Lord Glanely's

Screamer (Beresford – Saxham Cat by Saxham) and Lord Rosebery's Veldschoen (Felstead – Fallen Star by Flying Orb). Bunker was a good winner and he was given 8st 10 lbs. in the Free Handicap. The other two however, won only two of their twelve races that year. Veldschoen's efforts earned him a one-way ticket to North America.

Bahram was considered for the Champagne stakes at Doncaster but in the end Hairan was preferred. Bahram was not noted doing any strong work between the Gimcrack and the Champagne Stakes – run on 11th September – and, although it can only be speculation, in all probability Butters was giving Bahram an easy time in preparation for the Middle Park.

Notwithstanding this on 16th he went six furlongs "half-speed" with Maltravers; on the 23rd on Racecourse side he went five furlongs at "good pace" also with Maltravers. On the 26th he cantered six furlongs on racecourse side; on the 30th September he went five furlongs "sharp" on Bury Side in company with the Aga's Crème Caramel ((Coronach – Blane Mange by Hainault). On the 2nd he cantered six furlongs again with Crème Caramel which put him in good shape for his next race which was effectively a "trial" for the Middle Park; the Boscawen Stakes at Newmarket.

The Boscawen Stakes was last run in 1958 and is one of many races abandoned in the rush to move racing into a modern era.

Newmarket; Wednesday 3 October Going; Hard
Boscawen (Post) Stakes of £100 each of which the second rec. £100, for two-year-olds; Rous course five furlongs (8 subs. – £600) (31,800)

1	Bahram	9st	F. Fox	105++
2	Trade Wind	9st	T. Weston	93
3	Flash Bye	9st	R. Dick	82

Betting; 1/10 Bahram 10/1 Trade Wind 25/1 Flash Bye

Won by three lengths; the same second and third.
Time; 1 min 4.40 secs. (Slow by 5.30 secs.)

Race analysis; Flash Bye and Bahram were in close company until half-way. Bahram then made his effort and quickly drawing clear won in a canter.

There were eleven races over five furlongs during the four days of the meeting; and Bahram's was the slowest! Proof if any were needed that he did not exert himself to any great extent! This was little more than a public workout; neither Trade Wind nor Lord Astor's Flash Bye (Hurry On – Pictura by Holiday House) was able to win that year.

Three days later at Kempton the valuable Imperial Produce Stakes £3,931 (204,000) was run: in terms of prize money the most valuable after the National Breeders Produce Stakes at Sandown. This was yet another race won by the apparently unstoppable force that was the Aga Khan and Frank Butters; this time with Shahali (Sansovino – Theresina by Diophon), who beat Ben Marshall and Mr. D Sullivan's Lady Gabriel ((Tetratema – Resplendent by By George); who was making her debut. Shahali won three of his five races as a juvenile and was given 8 st. 13 lbs. in the Free Handicap.

Bahram was now prepared for his most important test as a juvenile: the Middle Park Stakes. On 8th October he went five furlongs at "half speed" solo on Racecourse Side; on the 10th he worked six furlongs at "good pace" in company with Hairan also on Racecourse Side; at least one observer thought Hairan worked best. This is evidence of Butters observations that Bahram often failed to exert himself on the gallops. On the 13th Bahram cantered five furlongs in company; on the 16th he did his final piece of serious work: going six furlongs at "good pace" with Hairan on Racecourse Side. He completed his preparation by cantering five furlongs on Racecourse Side on the 16th.

It was decided that Bahram would run in the Middle Park Stakes; Frank Butters was, however, far from sanguine. So indolent was Bahram and his work so sluggish that his trainer was by no means certain he had him fit enough. Butters was always convinced Bahram was an exceptional colt; it was simply that so unimpressive was his work that he was worried he had been deceived about his level of fitness.

It should be noted that the Dewhurst Stakes, considered the principal juvenile race today, was not as important in Bahram's time as the Middle Park. This remained the situation until the 1960's when

RETURN FROM EXERCISE, TOP OF WARREN HILL.

© Lionel Edwards Estate by courtesy of Felix Rosenstiel's Widow & Son, London

the races were of roughly equal value. It was not until the mid to late 1980's that the Dewhurst began to forge clear in terms of both value and status. The Dewhurst is currently worth approximately twice as much as the Middle Park, although both have Group 1 status. The Middle Park generally attracts more sprint-bred types as against potential miler colts that run in the Dewhurst. Middle distance sorts are aimed at the Royal Lodge and Racing Post Trophy over a mile; there were no races for juveniles of a mile or over in Bahram's time.

It was a fine day and Bahram was noted as looking "as well in the paddock as he had at York" by *The Times* correspondent; probably R. C. Lyle.

Newmarket; Thursday 18 October Going; Good
Middle Park Stakes of 30 sov. each or 20 sov. if dec. £1,000 added; second to receive 10% and third 5% of the whole stakes, for two-year-olds Bretby Stakes course, 6 furlongs; colts and geldings 9 st. fillies 8st 11lb., (122 ents. Viz. 18 £30 104 at £20 – £3,047) ( )

1	Bahram	9st.	F. Fox	127++
2	Godolphin	9st.	S. Donoghue	120
3	Consequential	9st.	C. Smirke	111
4	Plassy	9st.	T. Weston	
5	Fresh Fox	9st.	J. Childs	
6	Marmaduke Jinks	9st.	H. Graves	

Betting; 2/7 Bahram, 11/2 Consequential, 100/7 Fresh Fox 20/1 Godolphin 50/1 Plassy & Marmaduke Jinks

Won by 2 lengths; 3 lengths between second and third.
Time; 1 min 11.40 secs (Fast by .80 sec.)

Race analysis; Godolphin was quickly away with Bahram, Consequential and Plassy. Marmaduke Jinks was tailed off. Consequential was under pressure coming out of the dip where Bahram was asked for his effort. Bahram had no difficulty holding Godolphin to win cleverly.

"Bahram won very easily; there were no fireworks, his performance was not brilliant, there will never be anything sparkling about such a lazy colt. The half-brother to Dastur pulls out no more than is required of him". These were the views of Meyrick Good writing in *The Sporting Life*. However, as far as he was concerned these were assets and not liabilities; it meant that Bahram was more likely than not to be able to stay the following year.

Good further opined that Mr. A F Basset's blinkered Godolphin (Baytown – Phalanstery by Phalaris) led Bahram "a nice gallop" to the Bushes where Consequential – highly-regarded he noted – was being hard driven to keep his place; Mr. William Woodward's Fresh Fox (Gallant Fox – Filante by Sardanapale) was finding the pace all too much it seemed. After the bushes and as they met the rising ground Bahram reached Godolphin's girths and after a "sharp rally" Bahram took the lead. Good noticed that Fox was required to "hand ride" Bahram to the line in order that he would not ease up.

Freddie Fox spoke to the Aga Khan afterwards and told him that Bahram does little from the moment he hits the front and that he has "seldom thrown a leg over a more lazy youngster".

Capt. Long writing as Augur in The Sporting Life wrote:-

"The Aga Khan's brilliant colt Bahram added to his fame by winning the Middle Park Stakes at headquarters yesterday in a style only associated with a high-class colt. Any doubts we may have harboured as to his being the best of his age are certainly dispelled more especially as Consequential was strongly fancied to lower his colours.

Faith in Sir Charles McLeod's grey came as a surprise since Bahram conceded him 5 lbs. and a clever beating in the Gimcrack Stakes at York. The belief that the improved going would assist Consequential appreciably lacked confirmation. He failed to get in a blow at the leaders Godolphin and Bahram.

As I pointed out overnight Bahram is notoriously lazy, a characteristic often noted of a good horse. It came as no surprise to find Fox shaking him up a furlong from home, but once reminded Bahram tackled Godolphin to go on and win by two lengths – a pleasing and satisfactory performance".

There were six races over five furlongs and seven races over six furlongs during the four days of the second October meeting. Only two were faster than the standards used for this exercise; the Challenge Stakes won by a six-year-old carrying 8st 12 lb and the Middle Park where Bahram carried two pounds more and recorded a time 0.40 seconds faster. A juvenile should be receiving sixteen pounds from an older horse during October over six furlongs. Bahram could be said to have given eighteen pounds and beaten the older horse two lengths; a beating of about 24 pounds!

This was a remarkable performance; Bahram beat the standard and recorded the fastest time at the meeting over the distance, but did it winning easily! It is possible to crab the opposition in any race but the clock is an unforgiving element. A good horse may, on occasion's record a modest time; a bad horse can't record a fast time in comparison with good horses.

That Bahram recorded a fast time on its own means nothing. But he recorded a fast time in comparison with others and did it unextended. That is only possible with the very best horses.

Godolphin ran in four stakes races winning one. The Middle Park was his final race of the year and he was given 8 st. 11 lbs. in the Free Handicap.

Consequential ran close to his Gimcrack form, Lord Derby's Plassy (Bosworth – Pladda by Phalaris) and Mrs. C B Robinson's Marmaduke Jinks (Mr. Jinks – Mill Belle by Tredennis) were both, remarkably making their career debuts. Plassy had impressed Good in the paddock as a "well-grown but backward sort"; he thought he might make a "nice" three-year-old. Fresh Fox failed to win in four starts but was placed in two Stakes races and ran below expectation here.

Bahram concluded his juvenile season with his fifth straight win. He was probably the best juvenile but his preeminence was not universally acknowledged. There were plenty of observers confident he could be beaten the following year.

14 Champion Juvenile

Damn with faint praise, assent with civil leer,
And, without sneering, teach the rest to sneer,
Willing to wound, and yet afraid to strike,
Just hint a fault, and hesitate to strike.

Alexander Pope

*   *   *

Bahram was champion juvenile, and given top weight of 9 st. 7 lbs. in the Free Handicap, although it was by no means clear cut. However, he finished the season unbeaten in five races. At the time the Middle Park was the most prestigious race and the National Breeders Produce Stakes the most valuable, Bahram won them both.

Listed below were the principal races for juvenile colts and geldings in 1934 that were worth £1,000 (53,000) or more, they are given in order of value, races for fillies only have been omitted:-

Race	Value (£)	Winner
National Breeders Produce Stakes	5,559	Bahram
Imperial Produce Stakes	3,931	Shahali
Middle Park Stakes	3,047	Bahram
Ham (Produce) Stakes	2,861	Theft
New Stakes	2,840	Eppie Adair c
Lancashire Breeders Produce Stakes	2,760	Kingsem
Champagne Stakes	2,485	Kingsem
Windsor Castle Stakes	2,230	Theft
Coventry Stakes	2,110	Hairan
Chesham Stakes	1,780	Shahali
Molecomb Stakes	1,763	La Gaiete
Sandown Park Produce Stakes	1,507	Vallema
Lavant Stakes	1,500	Maltravers
Dewhurst Stakes	1,500	Hairan
Gimcrack Stakes	1,412	Bahram
Fern Hill Stakes +	1,380	Knighted
Richmond Stakes	1,358	Bobsleigh
Rous Memorial Stakes	1,140	Bahram
Hurst two-year-old Stakes	1,135	Flying Orders
July Stakes	1,130	Hilla

Coworth Stakes	*1,087*	*Gynerium*
Tattersall Sale Stakes ++	*1,060*	*Bunker*
Exeter Stakes	*1,050*	*Alykhan*
Champion Breeders Foal Plate	*1,038*	*Annabel*
Prendergast	*1,035*	*Mythical Monk*
Woodcote Stakes	*1,026*	*Bagman*

+ For two and three-year-olds only.
++ Restricted to juveniles sold as yearlings at Tattersall's Doncaster sales.

However, *The Bloodstock Breeders Review* was by no means alone when it stated in the 1934 annual published in December: "The situation with which we are confronted when we turn to the two-year-olds is a remarkable one. Four of the first six youngsters in the Free Handicap published at the end of November are owned by the Aga Khan, while those four and another, Maltravers, are trained by Frank Butters, who must feel embarrassed by the plethora of talent in his stable. That Bahram, Hairan and Theft were, according to public form, the best of their age was the general opinion, but there was not, and probably is not now, unanimity concerning the respective merits of the three colts. As will be seen Mr. Fawcett, the compiler of the handicap, rates Hairan and Theft equal, and gives Bahram 1lb. more. If he had allotted them all the same weight, few people could have blamed him. Lord Derby's Bobsleigh is placed fourth. It will not, however, be surprising if, when the Free Handicap for three-year-olds is published next October, we find him at the top".

The general view was that Mr. Fawcett, strictly on the formbook, was unable to place Bobsleigh any higher. Well that has not stopped handicappers from such folly in the past and won't restrain them in the future. It could be argued that as the only principal race Bobsleigh won: the Richmond Stakes was the seventeenth in the list of valuable races for juveniles, he was placed high enough. That he won impressively from three debutants at odds of 1–3 suggest he did no more than he was entitled to do. He did not contest any races later in the year and it can only be speculation that he would have been good enough to have troubled Bahram, Hairan or Theft.

The top ten in the two-year-old Free Handicap for 1934 are as follows:-

	St	lbs.
Bahram	9	7
Hairan	9	6
Theft	9	6
Bobsleigh	9	3
Maltravers	9	0
Shahali	8	13
Godolphin	8	11
Flying Orders	8	11
Consequential	8	11
Kingsem	8	11

There follows an order of merit based on the *Timeform* scale and calculated on the same principles as used by that organization since 1948 and *A Century of Champions* from 1900 until 1947. The second figure is the number of times each horse ran together with the number of wins. These are the top ten colts and geldings together with the highest rated filly, five of the top seven were trained by Frank Butters:-

* Trained by Frank Butters.

Bahram c *	127+	5/5
Theft c *	124+	5/4
Hairan c *	122+	4/3
Godolphin g	118	4/1
Bobsleigh c	117+	2/1
Maltravers c *	117	8/5
Shahali c *	115	5/3
Flying Orders g	113	8/4
Caretta f	113	6/3
Consequential c	110	6/2
Kingsem c	110	9/4

The ratings calculated by these two publications can be used to compare different generations; a horse rated 125 in 2016 can be considered the equal of one with a similar rating from 1934 and anytime since the beginning of the Twentieth Century. Bahram's rating is based on the one given in *A Century of Champions* and used as a base for calculating the other ratings all of which are this author's.

It should be remembered that *Timeform* do not calculate their annual ratings in the same manner as a handicapper handicaps horses. *Timeform* ratings are based on what a horse has achieved on the racecourse based on time and form. The handicapper is attempting to rate horses in order that each would have a similar chance in a race; this means that the rating given to any one horse may reflect what in *the handicapper's opinion* that horse is capable of; not necessarily what it has actually achieved. This can result in connections sometimes complaining that a horse has been "harshly treated" by a handicapper; meaning his weight is higher than his form strictly warrants.

It is readily understood that there are plenty who will claim that different generations can't be compared. However, enough horses stay in training each year for different generations to be compared. *Timeform* when publishing their annual ratings for the *Racehorses* annual have by scrupulously returning each year's ratings to a recognized "mean" has ensured that ratings have neither risen more than they should nor suffered the fate of official ratings: slippage. This is where international handicappers have allowed ratings to decline year by year until a situation is reached where horses of the present time are rated, sometimes ludicrously, much lower than horses that raced twenty or so years ago; the International Classifications only began in their current form in 1986, they had been even worse, if that is possible, before that date when they used a scale of 0–100. For example, Grundy in 1975 was officially rated 101, Troy in 1979 was given 96. Timeform rated both at 137: official slippage of about five pounds in four years!

Since 1986 the International ratings have gradually "slipped"; here are a few examples the first figure is *Timeform* the second the official international one: – Dancing Brave 140, 141, Reference Point, 139, 135, Generous 139, 137, Zafonic (French trained) 130, 130, Lammtarra 134, 130, Mark of Esteem 137, 133, Dubai Millennium

140, 134, Montjeu 137, 130, Sea The Stars 140, 136, Frankel (2011) 143, 136, Frankel (2012) 147, 140.

As if this was not bad enough in 2012 it was decided to retrospectively re-handicap the top horses of the previous 25 years! This was because due to slippage it was not possible apparently to rate Frankel properly. His generally accepted superiority over horses like Dancing Brave, Dubai Millennium and Sea The Stars created an insoluble problem.

What threw the official rankings out of kilter was the above average number of outstanding horses that raced in a relatively short period: 2008–2012. History shows that a great horse will appear about every 8–10 years but there have been much longer periods without any racehorse appearing that could be sensibly described as great. The following all raced within a span of six short years which is unusual: Frankel, Sea The Stars, Black Caviar, Zarkava, Goldikova and Zenyatta. Something similar happened in North America when in just seven years: 1973 – 1979 the following horses competed: Secretariat, Spectacular Bid, Seattle Slew, Affirmed and Alydar. These are five of the best ten horses ever to race in North America. Three won the Triple Crown and Alydar would have done but he was foaled in the same year as Affirmed! Imagine: two of the best horses ever to race running over three seasons against each other.

In Europe similarly between 1965 and 1974 the following raced; Sea Bird, Brigadier Gerard, Mill Reef, Nijinsky, Vaguely Noble and Allez France. Brigadier Gerard and Mill Reef were also foaled in the same year but only ever met once.

Whatever the problem it is hard to imagine a more stupid solution than rewriting history! This totally barmpot idea attracted deserved ridicule and disapprobation. The operation was called "Recalibration" and was accompanied by an astonishing document setting the whole dreadful mess out; an exercise in futile obfuscation which would be difficult to better. It stated that "handicapping methods and practices have evolved over 35 years" Rubbish! The International Classifications and the World Thoroughbred Rankings simply failed to assess continuity with any accuracy as the each year went by. Did no one ever look at their handiwork and think: don't some of these look a little on the low side compared with a few years ago? Did they think the thoroughbred was getter slower and in decline? What a cock-up!

It could be clearly seen that the official ratings were slowly reducing. Does it matter? Well yes it does! What is the point of "official" ratings if – as has been admitted – today's ratings can't be compared with those of years gone by? If *Timeform* does not exist in fifty years' time how will students compare horses from today with contemporary ones?

One of the most important aspects of *Timeform* and its 60 odd years of consistently using the same method is to be able to instantly assess the approximate ability of any good horse since 1948. Generally *Timeform* rate good handicappers and Listed level and some Group 3 performers between 100–115, good horses 116–123, very good horses 124 – 131 and outstanding horses 132–139. However, any rating of 140 and above is usually reserved only for the true greats: those horses capable of rare and remarkable feats which place them significantly apart from their contemporaries. Fillies and mares ratings would be about three to six pounds less than colts and geldings; thus the great fillies and mares are generally rated 134 and above.

Notwithstanding this reference has been made to the Free Handicap of 1934 in calculating the ratings. Bahram's rating of 127 is not particularly high for a top juvenile. Plenty have been rated higher. However, all contemporary observers agree he won races easily or comfortably. As he was never ridden clear of his fields it is not possible rate him any higher. However, what is surprising is that so many did not consider Bahram that much better than other two-year-olds of his year and that so many were confident that Bobsleigh would prove a better three-year-old. Bahram won the most valuable juvenile race and the most prestigious.

The most striking aspect of the juveniles of 1934 is the number of times each of the top horses ran. With the exception of Bobsleigh all the leading contenders raced at least four times. The more evidence there is the easier assessing any group of horses will be; the juveniles of 1934 were at least average and in the view of some slightly above. The evidence for this is simple; Bahram was unbeaten as a juvenile, however, there were a number of good judges who thought he would not be able to confirm his superiority as a three-year-old. Therefore the view must have been that it was an above average year and that there were some exceptional sorts with considerable improvement in them. Unbeaten juveniles that win five races, including two of the most prestigious, like Bahram are rare.

The above were the leading ten colts and geldings of Bahram's juvenile year. It was unlikely that he would meet any fillies in his Classic year but the best juvenile filly was Caretta (Phalaris or Solario – Daumont by Diligence). She won three of her six races including the Queen Mary and she raced against colts which proved her quality. Unfortunately she was beaten half a length into second place in the Cheveley Park conceding the winner fourteen pounds.

Theft ran five times winning four. His only defeat came when opposing Bahram in the National Breeders Produce Stakes at Sandown. Theft won the Windsor Castle, beating Bobsleigh, before winning the Ham Stakes at Goodwood, the Nottinghamshire Breeders Foal Plate and then Buckenham Stakes at Newmarket. Theft, who was not as big as Bahram as a juvenile, was well-made and thickened out as the year progressed.

Hairan ran four times being beaten only once. Hairan won a plate race at Manchester and the Coventry Stakes before running well below expectations in the Champagne Stakes at Doncaster where he started at odds of 30–100. In this race Hairan gave every indication that he hated the very firm ground. The going was also firm in the Dewhurst where he liked neither the dip nor the surface, but when he hit the rising ground he was able to assert himself and forge two lengths clear of Ben Marshall who was receiving ten pounds. Hairan, who was given 9 st. 6 lbs. in the Free Handicap, was a big horse at 16 hands and his picture suggests he needed to fill out. He had cost the Aga 6,400 guineas (£349,000) at the sales and was giving every indication of being worth the money.

Godolphin had been gelded which would have ruled him out of the classics. He won one of his four races: a stakes race at Newmarket and was placed in the other three, including behind Bahram in the Middle Park. His position compared to other juveniles is as a result of his surprising second to Bahram and it remains to be seen if he could justify this next year.

Bobsleigh ran only twice; finishing second on his debut to Theft in the Windsor Castle and then winning the Richmond Stakes at Goodwood easily at odds of 1–3. After the Windsor Castle several judges declared he would win the Derby next year. This view was only strengthened when he left a deep impression when disposing of ten moderate opponents at Goodwood. Soon afterwards he damaged a hind fetlock and was put away for the year. Bobsleigh had shown greenness at Ascot by holding his head too high. However, there was no sign of this at Goodwood where he was shown to best advantage; displaying a long stride and graceful action. There seemed much to look forward to.

Maltravers, (surely a name for a butler or valet not a racehorse!), ran eight times, winning five. He began with an unplaced effort in a Newmarket stakes race and then won a similar contest. Stepping up in class he finished sixth behind Theft and Bobsleigh in the Windsor Castle before winning the Chesterfield Stakes at Newmarket and the Lavant Stakes at Goodwood. He ran below expectations in the Prince of Wales's Stakes at York, failing to justify odds on favouritism, before concluding the year with two more wins. These were in the Rous Memorial Stakes at Newmarket and the Malton Plate at York. Maltravers was a medium-sized, strong-quartered colt, consistent, but just below the top level.

Shahali raced five times winning three. After a third in a stakes race at Newmarket he won the Chesham Stakes, but was then off the track for over three months, before returning the win the Imperial Produce Stakes at Kempton; the second most valuable race for juveniles after the National Breeders Produce stakes won by Bahram. He finished the year winning the Criterion Stakes at Newmarket and finishing second to Flying Orders in a stakes race at Hurst Park. Considered a handsome colt there was every chance he would do better at three.

Flying Orders was also a gelding that raced eight times winning three. He was another reliable yardstick to assessing the value of juvenile racing that year. He was a cheap yearling; he cost only 40 guineas (£2,200) and it could not be expected that he would have much influence the following year. He was not to be given the chance as he was sold to race in India.

Consequential met Bahram twice in his six races of which he won two. He was a big colt and there was the possibility that he might do better next year.

Kingsem ran nine times winning four. Taking three races to find his form he then won four in succession including the Champagne Stakes at Doncaster where he beat Consequential and Hairan. He then lost form somewhat. Incidentally the tradition of the Champagne Stakes, which was instituted in 1823, was that the winner presented six dozen bottles of Champagne to the Doncaster Race Club. Kingsem's owner: Sir Charles Hyde, elated by his colt's victory, remembered the tradition and decided to revive it. He acted accordingly and it can only be imagined that the Committee and their friends greatly was appreciated the donor's gesture!

That the first three were all owned by the Aga Khan and trained by Frank Butters should not affect how each is assessed; they ran on their merits on each occasion. In addition Butters trained Maltravers and also Shahali, who was of course, owned by the Aga Khan. Five of the top seven juvenile colts were trained at Fitzroy House. The prospects for the Butters yard in 1935 looked good indeed!

Looking at the portraits of the leading juveniles the one that stands out as possessing the most physical potential is undoubtedly Bobsleigh. It is not difficult to see why he was regarded with such enthusiasm by many.

Bahram contributed £11,758 in prize money, more than any other horse, in making the Aga Khan the top owner and breeder and Frank Butters the leading trainer.

15 Two Thousand Guineas

A stable lad looks into the box of one of his charges and checks that all is well; to his surprise he sees that the feed tub is still half-full. The horse is clearly not himself and is due to run in a few days' time. He immediately alerts the trainer who understands only too well that, not only will the horse miss his intended race, but probably the first Classic of the season as well.

*   *   *

In 1935 before the event of the Pattern, which was not inaugurated until 1971, the Classics were the most important races for three-year-olds. Many of the best races below Classic level carry the same name today and, although similar, or greater, in monetary value, were of lesser importance to a horse's reputation. The best races were referred to as "Principal" or "important" races and nominations were required well in advance: the previous year.

The following is a list of the principal races of 1935, excluding handicaps, apart from the Free Handicap, open to three-year-old colts; fillies' only races are excluded. The figure following is the value to the winner and then the equivalent race and its value today. It should be noted that the values shown for races today include any additional stakes that are added in respect of horses being supplemented. For example the value of the Two Thousand Guineas to the winner in 2015 was £282,000. However, that included money added from two horses being supplemented which added £60,000 to the prize money. Some races from the past using the original name are run as different races today and some distances have also been altered:-

Union Jack St.8f	*£1,008 (53,424)*	*No longer run*
Greenham Plate 8f	*£840 (44,520)*	*Greenham Stakes £31,000*

Column Produce St. 8f	£746 ((39,538)	No longer run
Craven St.8f	£1,005 (53,265)	Craven St. £31,000.
Free Handicap 7f	£1,155 (61,215)	Free Handicap £18,000.
2000 Gns. 8f	£9,339 (494,967)	2000 Gns. £282,000.
Chester Vase 12f	£1,605 (56,175)	Chester Vase £31,000.
Dee St. 12f	£854 (45,262)	Dee St. £31,000
Newmarket St.10f	£1,875 (99,375)	Newmarket St. £22,000.
Payne St.12f	£670 (35,510)	No longer run.
Derby St.12f	£9,216 (488,448)	Derby St. £751,000.
Royal Standard St.8f *	£2,882 (152,746)	No longer run.
Red Rose St.5f	£1,468 (77,804)	No longer run.
St James's Palace St. 8f	£3,230 (171,190)	St James's Palace St. £167,000
Prince of Wales's St.13f	£2,430 (128,790)	No longer run.
King Edward VII St.12f	£2,345 (124,285)	King Edward VII St. £85,000.
Waterford St. 8f	£2,310 (122,430)	No longer run.
Rous Memorial St. 7f*	£1,040 (55,120)	No longer run.
Granville St. 5f+	£8,210 (441,013).	No longer run
Jersey St.7f	£1,660 (88,033)	Jersey St. £39,000.
Gold Vase 16f*	£2,170 (115,010)	Queen's Vase £34,000*
Hardwicke St.12f*	£3,180 (168,540)	No longer open to three-year-olds.
Beeswing Plate11f	£865 (45,845)	No longer run
Royal Plate 10f*	£1,260 (66,780)	No longer run
Sandringham Foal Plate 10f	£890 (47,170)	No longer run
Princess of Wales's St. 12f *	£2,720 (144,160)	Princess of Wales's St £61,000.
Welsh Derby 12f	£593 (31,429)	No longer run
Dullingham St. 12f*	£730 (38,690)	No longer run
Eclipse St. 10f *	£7,569 (401,157)	Eclipse St. £241,000.
St George St. 13f	£1,561 (82,733)	No longer run
Atlantic Cup 10f*	£1,630 (86,390)	No longer run
Gratwicke (Produce) St.12f	£2,084 (110,452)	No longer run
Sussex St. 8f	£1,098 (58,194)	Sussex St £179,000
King George St 6f*	£1,219 (64,607)	King George St. £56,000.
Goodwood Cup 21f *	£1,230 (65,190)	Goodwood Cup £56,000)
Gordon St. 12f	£815 (43,195)	Gordon St. £34,000.

Londonderry St.13f	*£657 (34,821)*	*No longer run*
Durham County Produce Pl. 10f	*£642 (34,026)*	*No longer run*
Duke of York Plate 10f	*£865 (45,845)*	*No longer run*
Great Yorkshire St. 12f	*£1,474 (78,122)*	*Great Voltigeur St. £90,000*
St. Leger St. 14f	*£9,543 (505,779)*	*St. Leger St. £312,000)*
Doncaster Cup 18f*	*£890 (47,170)*	*Doncaster Cup £57,000*
Welsh St. Leger St. 14f	*£519 (27,507)*	*No longer run*
John Porter St.13f*	*£1,830 (96,990)*	*Geoffrey Freer St. £32,000.*
Great Foal St.10f	*£1,373 (72,769)*	*No longer run*
Jockey Club St.14f*	*£4,287 (227,211)*	*No equivalent race*
Champion St.10f*	*£1,310 (69,430)*	*Champion St. £738,000.*
Liverpool St Leger St.14f	*£798 (42,135)*	*No longer run.*

* Open to four-year-olds and up. + Open to two-year-olds as well.

With very few exceptions most races are worth far less today in real terms that in Bahram's time. There were also more non-handicap races for a three-year-old to run in. It is impossible today to imagine a course like Chepstow putting on two non-handicap races: the Welsh Derby and Welsh St Leger, with a value to the winner of £31,429 and £27,000 respectively. They would only attract about four runners each which would not please either the BHB or the bookmakers! The Welsh racegoers interests would not be considered! It should be remembered also that most of these stakes and plate races required winners to carry penalties. These could on occasions amount to anything up to 28 lbs.

The biggest fall from grace is unquestionably the Princess of Wales's Stakes run at Newmarket in July for three-year-olds and up over twelve furlongs. This race was inaugurated in 1894 and run over ten furlongs with the mighty Isinglass the first winner. It was one of the three great "ten thousand pounders" run during the year. The other two were the Eclipse Stakes and the Jockey Club Stakes. In 1894 the value to the winner of each race was respectively: – £9,285 (649,950), £10,911 (763,770) and £11,362 (795,340). By 1935 all three had been significantly downgraded and today only the Eclipse can still, just about, hold its head up. Isinglass had won the Triple Crown as a three-year-old and as a four-year-old was aimed at these three races only and, brilliantly handled by Capt. Machell, he won them all.

*   *   *

To return to 1935, Bahram's preparation for the year began in early January with canters over five and six furlongs, usually in company and, when weather permitted, on the Southfields gallop, or confined to the paddocks when conditions were cold and there was frost. These canters, or what was described as "steady work", increased to seven furlongs from the middle of the month. It was not until the 12th February that he moved across town for a five furlong canter on Warren Hill, which was followed the day after by a ten furlong "steady" piece of work on the Southfields gallop, that the pace increased. Two days later the work was stepped up slightly to "half speed" over seven furlongs.

His first piece of work that took place with only one companion was on 21st February when he went seven furlongs "half speed" with Alykhan. On the 27th again in company with Alykhan, he went a mile "half speed". The following day he had his first piece of stronger work when he went a mile at a "nice pace" in company with Tramaway (Tetrameter – Hark Forrard by King William) and Maltravers. Tramaway was a five-year-old handicap stayer; he was tough and probably able to run to a *Timeform* rating of about 90, Maltravers was a three-year-old sprinter probably about ten pounds below Bahram as a juvenile but he did not really train on as a sprinter. Neither, however, would have been within three stones of Bahram by this time. On the 8th March he went five furlongs "sharply" in company on Warren Hill and did the same on 15th. Otherwise he did canters, steady work and half speed work often in company with Tramaway, Alykhan or Hairan.

Frank Butters was gradually building up Bahram's fitness in preparation for his seasonal debut, due in the Craven Stakes on Thursday 11th April. On the 25th March he went a mile on Bury Side, exactly where was not specified, at "useful pace" in company with Theft and Sir Alfred Butt's Lucky Patch (Spion Kop – Enrichment by Tracery). This was his probably Bahram's first piece of serious work as he was joined by Theft for the first time that year. Lucky Patch was a five-year-old gelding good enough to be given 8st. 7lbs. in the Cesarewitch and probably worth a *Timeform* rating of about 110.

Bahram's work now consisted of gallops over five and six furlongs "sharply" or, on one occasion, a mile "half speed" with Tramaway and Maltravers and once, just with Maltravers. On the 3rd April he went a mile at "good pace" with Tramaway and Maltravers and the following day a six furlong solo canter, in rain and sleet, on the tan. Then, again solo, but this time in fine weather, five furlongs "sharp" on Bury side on 5th. All looked set for his seasonal debut.

Unfortunately that night: Friday, he left half his feed and had a temperature. He was not able to work on Saturday and would not now be able to run in the Craven on the following Thursday. He had trotting exercise on Monday 8th and it was now a question of getting him ready for the Two Thousand Guineas on 1st May without a prep race.

* * *

For many years Rapier of *The Illustrated Sporting and Dramatic News* had an annual contest with Robin Goodfellow of the *Daily Mail*, whereby each chose twelve horses, and the winner was decided by money won assuming each horse was backed on each run to a pound level stakes. For 1935 Robin Goodfellow chose Bahram but Rapier did not. Was this because he did not have faith in Bahram, or that he would start at such short odds each time he ran he would not prove worthy of inclusion!

* * *

Following Bahram's minor indisposition he did only canters and half speed work until 12th April when in fine weather he worked solo over five furlongs "sharp"; on 13th he went seven furlongs "half speed" in company with Tramaway, Alykhan and Theft. Again on his own he went a mile at "useful pace" on the 15th and on the following morning, a wet one, five furlongs "sharp".

Between then and 20th, amongst some canters and half speed work, in fine weather, he went a mile at "good pace" in company with Hindoo Holiday, Maltravers and Sir Alfred Butt's Powerful Prince (Rose Prince – Puisne by Junior); the latter a three-year-old maiden good enough to keep excellent company over a variety of distances and he could probably run to a *Timeform* rating of about 100. On 24th Bahram went a mile at "good pace" with Hindoo Holiday, Badruddin; a four-year-old handicapper good enough to be allocated 8 st. 10 lbs. in the Royal Hunt Cup, and Tramaway. The choice of work partners was interesting: enough to lead Bahram but not good enough to really stretch him and, of course, the work watchers were not overly impressed!

* * *

Newmarket's Craven Meeting was over and the principal Guineas trials had now been run. The Union Jack Stakes at Liverpool had been won by Mrs. Esmond Harmsworth's Cyrus (Abbots Trace – Roshun Ara by Abbots Trace); who had been unplaced in his only race as a juvenile. Trade Wind and Godolphin were both unplaced. Theft, although not pleasing much in his work, won the Greenham Plate as he should have done at odds of 5–2 on. He also did not impress all observers at Newbury with his performance. The Column Produce Stakes was won by Major J S Courtauld's Tiderace (Fairway – Panic by Hurry On) whose three previous runs had not suggested he was good enough to win an average Two Thousand Guineas; Lord Astor's Portfolio (Sansovino – Short Story by Buchan) was second and Trade Wind third.

In Bahram's absence the Craven Stakes was won by Lord Glanely's unraced colt Buckleigh (Sansovino – Surbine by Bachelor's Double) beating the Aga's Hindoo Holiday (Blandford – Pagan Sacrifice by Cicero) and Sir Abe Bailey's Zingaro (Solario – Gracella by Phalaris). That Buckleigh was considered good enough to make his debut in what was considered a leading Two Thousand Guineas trial gives some indication of the high regard he was held. That he was able to beat a reasonable field by three lengths at odds of 20–1 indicated that he could be threat in the first classic. In addition he did an impressive time: 1min.-38 2/5 secs. However, it transpired that he ran simply because his owner: Lord Glanely wanted Gordon Richards's opinion about him! Nonetheless, this performance by Buckleigh in winning the Craven Stakes on his first ever appearance would qualify him for a *Timeform* rating of about 110 – 115. Most horses able to run to this level on their debut's today would be considered Group 1 material.

Of the other leading pretenders Mr. C W Gordon's Sea Bequest (Legatee – Ocean Light by Sunstar) had failed to win in six outings as a juvenile and ended the year running in nurseries. However, he had progressed over the winter and had raced twice; winning a Plate Race at Liverpool before finishing second, beaten a neck with the third was six lengths further back, by Lord Woolavington's four-year-old Easton (Dark Legend – Phaona by Phalaris) in a minor Stakes race at Lingfield. Sea Bequest was receiving 12 lbs. more than weight-for-age but this was a good performance as Easton was a top-class sort; second in the previous year's Derby and capable at his best of running to *Timeform* rating of 130.

It seemed clear to many that the Aga had the best prospects in Bahram and Theft; but apparently not to everyone; Bobsleigh was attracting considerable interest as a result of his work, mainly on the opposite side of Newmarket to his two main rivals. Bahram would never be praised for his homework; indeed it has not been possible to find any reference to his work ever being described in any other fashion that good or ordinary. Only by watching closely could it be seen that although rarely – if ever – was Bahram more than an neck or half a length in front he was usually only cantering against workmates that were under much greater pressure. In addition Bahram, although a fine athlete with a long stride, was physically never the sort of colt that connoisseurs of conformation speak of in an exalted manner. However, Bobsleigh was just such a colt; big strong and handsome, and a good worker as well. He was by Gainsborough but he looked nothing like his sire and closely resembled his dam's side and had all the characteristics of Hurry On. Curiously although Bahram was 16.2 hands some thought that Bobsleigh was bigger such was the impression he gave.

*   *   *

On Friday 26th April *The Sporting Life* considered the Two Thousand Guineas to be "fraught with considerable uncertainty". Mrs. Henry Hawkins' Guest of Honour (Son and Heir – Dionysia by Diadumenos), whose juvenile form placed him at least a stone behind Bahram, won a handicap at Birmingham after finishing second to Theft at Newbury. Whilst this did not do the Greenham form any harm it can hardly be said to have enhanced it by very much. Theft was not still not impressive on the gallops, however, Butters thought this only laziness.

The thinking was that Bahram would not run unless his trainer was happy that "he was sufficiently straight in condition". *The Sporting Life* noted that although Bahram was not "exactly showing marked superiority over companions of late, he was at least giving satisfaction, which is really more than this lazy colt ever did as a two-year-old". It further opined "Bahram is of the kind who will race with a donkey in private or in public until fully roused, when he responds in no uncertain fashion – a characteristic associated with high-class racehorses in the past".

On 27th on a dull and cold day he went a mile at "good pace" with Tramaway on racecourse side, his last piece of strong work before the Two Thousand Guineas. *The Sporting Life's* Newmarket observer considered that Bahram was seen to "great advantage" in the gallop; so he should, he was about three stones superior! Theft and Powerful Prince worked well, also over a mile, but Bahram's work was considered better. However, it was the mile gallop by Bobsleigh that caught the attention of the work watchers. This was just the latest impressive piece of work noted by Lord Derby's colt.

Frank Butters had done all he could to prepare Bahram for the Two Thousand Guineas but must have been worried. A horse that works lazily always benefits from a race and his inability to contest the Craven Stakes was a disadvantage. Whether the work that Butters had managed to get into his charge would make him fit enough to win a Classic would soon be known.

Of the 253 original entries only 18 were left in at the final forfeit stage. There were no runners from Beckhampton and only one from Manton: Lord Astor's Plymouth Sound (Coronach – Plymstock by Polymelus), who seemed to have little chance at that stage, although he did win the valuable £2,882 (152,000) Royal Standard Stakes at Manchester a month later. As Fred Darling had no candidate Gordon Richards was free to accept the ride on Theft for the Aga and Frank Butters.

The betting market had Theft favourite, but at the Victoria Club call over which took place at noon on Monday 29th April the following odds were quoted:-

100–30	Bahram
100–30	Bobsleigh
5–1	Theft
9–1	Buckleigh
100–8	Robin Goodfellow
100–7	Sea Bequest
20–1	Desert Cloud
25–1	Screamer
28–1	Consequential
33–1	Bar.

There was only light betting with the front two both backed to win about £1,500 (80,000). Bahram was quoted at 4–1 for the Derby with Bobsleigh at 9–2.

The final Victoria Club call over took place the evening before the race and quoted Bahram at 5–2 and Bobsleigh at 7–2.

* * *

The value of the Two Thousand Guineas to the winner in 1935 was almost twice as much as today when inflation is taken into account. A sad indictment of how a Classic race has been devalued by the Newmarket executive. This is all the more curious when it is considered that some in the breeding world today think the race is more important that the Derby. These are the sort of individuals who only consider what is fashionable but have little consideration for the future of the thoroughbred. If left to them racing in Europe will follow the disastrous example of North America where speed is an obsession and over 99% of all races are run at nine furlongs and below. Breeders who think only racing up to a mile is important are a menace to the sport.

This is bad enough one might think but extraordinary when one considers that that the July Cup is currently worth more to the winner than the Two Thousand Guineas and an unbelievable FIVE times more in real terms than the July Cup was worth in 1935; £256,000 to £1,085 (57,505). What can this all be about? What IS this obsession with sprinting? Times change the Newmarket executive might assert: every racecourse executive is seemingly obsessed with attracting the best sprinters from around the world. But has Newmarket forgotten which race is supposed to be a Classic? They might also like to consider the respective average end of year *Timeform* ratings of the winners of the Two Thousand Guineas and July Cup. Since the ill-advised decision to make the July Cup worth more than the Two Thousand guineas nine years ago, these have been133 and 127 respectively. The Newmarket executive should face the facts: better horses win the Two Thousand Guineas than the July Cup!

*   *   *

On 'Guineas day *The Sporting Life's* "Warren Hill" (Willie Standring) discussing Bahram wrote "Whether Bahram will be able to hold Buckleigh, whose race has obviously done him good, or the long striding Bobsleigh, is a matter of greater interest as I look at it". "I feel sure that if training luck is equal all round, there will come a day, and not that far ahead, when Bobsleigh will show marked superiority to all of his age trained here". He tipped Bobsleigh to win and Buckleigh to finish second.

"Augur" of the same paper wrote; "It would appear Lord Derby's colt (Bobsleigh) has given such great satisfaction in his latest gallops that his connections believe will require all the beating the best can give him in the first of the Classics". "Home gallops can prove misleading the racecourse alone proving the acid test. Working on these lines I consider Bahram entitled to preference in the face of the confidence reposed in Bobsleigh. Excepting for the possibility of being proved wrong in discarding Theft, Buckleigh alone would appear to threaten serious danger to Bahram and Bobsleigh".

The papers "Man on the spot" noted that Newmarket was divided equally between those who would not hear of defeat for either Bahram or Bobsleigh. As Theft had not been impressing watchers in his work no other colt was considered. The most likely danger seemed to be from Buckleigh who had won the Craven Stakes so well and had worked impressively since. In the end "Man on the spot" gave Bahram slight preference over Bobsleigh with Buckleigh the most likely to finish third.

*   *   *

In the event two horses were not declared this left 16 runners to stand their ground. Newmarket had seen a good deal of rain in the week preceding the race and the day began "dull and dismal in town" and fine but cool at the course and in any event too chilly for May. Most of the rain missed the heath and the going on the Rowley mile was considered perfect. Although 16 runners were declared it was possible to completely rule out ten of them as having no chance whatsoever based on racecourse form. Of the other six Sea Bequest and Robin Goodfellow (raced as Eppie Adair colt as a juvenile) had outside place prospects only. The winner was almost certain to come from the first four in the betting.

The Aga Khan was in the South of France but a commentary on the race was given to him over the telephone. In his absence he was represented by Aly.

In the paddock Bobsleigh made a very favourable impression; he had a commanding presence and when both walking and cantering showed a free and smooth action; "nothing moved with better regulated stride". Bahram was fit and well but more finely made and although not impressing in his slower movements when stretching out it could not be bettered. Clearly some disagreement here: both

Bahram and Bobsleigh could not have been the best mover! Bahram was reported as noticeably taller than the previous year. However, it was unlikely he had grown much. Theft was "all wire and whip-cord". Sea Bequest was noted to be "very fit". Bahram had the worst of the draw: on the extreme outside. However, Mr. F W Horlock's Apollo (Son and Heir – Blue Mermaid by Milesius) behaved very badly at the start and, like some errant schoolboy, was ordered by the starter to surrender his place and go to the outside. It can only be assumed that Bahram and Freddie Fox were none too pleased to see him!

Newmarket; Wednesday 1 May, Going; Good
2,000 Guineas Stakes of 100 sov. each £50 if dec. by 23 April 1935 or £5 if dec. 3 July 1934, with 2,000 Gns added; second to receive 10% and the third 5% of the whole stakes; for three-year-olds entire colts and fillies ; colts 9 st fillies 8st 11lb; Rowley Mile (253 ent. viz. 18 at £100 134 at £50 101 at £5 – – £9,339) (494,967)

1	Bahram	9st	F. Fox	131+
2	Theft	9st	G. Richards	127
3	Sea Bequest	9st	E. Smith	122
4	Bobsleigh	9st	R. Perryman	117+
5	Apollo	9st	H. Beasley	111
6	Buckleigh	9st	A. Wragg	
7	Screamer	9st	G. Nicoll	
8	Fairbairn	9st	C. Smirke	
9	Consequential	9st	R. Jones	
10	Robin Goodfellow	9st	T. Weston	
11	Bouldnor	9st	H. Jelliss	
0	Plymouth Sound	9st	R. Dick	
0	Powerful Prince	9st	W. Nevett	
0	Desert Cloud	9st	H. Wragg	
0	Marmaduke Jinks	9st	B. Rook	
0	Auf Wiedersehen	9st	F. Lane	

Betting; 7/4 Bobsleigh 7/2 Bahram 11/2 Theft 8/1 Buckleigh 100/7 Sea Bequest & Robin Goodfellow 20/1 Desert Cloud 33/1 Consequential & Screamer 50/1 others

Won by a length and a half; two lengths between second and third; unofficially there was two and a half lengths between third and fourth; two and a half lengths between fourth and fifth.
Time; 1 min 41.40 secs (Slow by 2.80 sec.)

Race analysis: –
Apollo was unruly at the post and was ordered by the starter to the extreme
outside of the field from which position he ran.

From a level breakaway the first to show in front were Screamer (stands
side), Apollo (racing wide on the far side), Consequential (far side) and Robin
Goodfellow.

These were followed by Sea Bequest, Bahram and Theft. Screamer kept
up a good gallop for fully five furlongs and then gave way to Apollo and
Consequential.

Consequential was the first to weaken and Screamer also began to drop
back. Theft was prominent at this point with Bahram beginning to make a pro-
gressive move in front of Bobsleigh.

Buckleigh also took up a flattering position. In the dip Theft was at the
head of the field, pressed by Bahram and then came Sea Bequest, Apollo,
Bobsleigh and Buckleigh

Bahram had the measure of Theft from the time the rising ground was
reached and won comfortably.

The betting was all about Bobsleigh with substantial support forcing his
price down from 100–30 to 7–4 favourite. In the face of this Bahram drifted
out from 5–2 to 7–2 at the off.

As expected the first four in the betting filled the first four places
but not in the order anticipated. Bobsleigh failing to live up to the
huge level of expectation.

The ground for the three days of the meeting was given as good
for the first two days and firm for the third. However, no race in the
meeting dipped below the standard times used for this exercise; and
several were well above. The heavy rain had probably been sufficient
to take any semblance of firm out of the ground by the off. The time
in itself was moderate for a Two Thousand Guineas; there had been
several instances of sub 1 min. 40 sec. renewals with the record at
that time being 1 min. 37.60 sec by Sunstar in 1911.

Bahram was observed to "make a spurt" as the ground slopes down
to the dip which brought him alongside Theft. They matched strides
for a short while before Bahram's long stride began to assert and he
had the race at his mercy half a furlong from the finish. "The advantage of one and a half lengths could have been increased had Fox so
desired" noted the *Bloodstock Breeders Review*.

Meyrick Good wrote glowingly about the race "Bahram has
only to keep well to justify the faith of those who made him winter

favourite for the Derby. In keeping his unbeaten record intact in the Two Thousand Guineas, the Aga Khan's colt gave a thoroughly pleasing display. I cannot visualise any of his rivals turning the tables at Epsom five weeks hence". Good continued "Never has there been better going for the Two Thousand Guineas. Quintin Gilbey wrote "I shall always think that in winning the Guineas as he did Bahram accomplished one of the best performances I have seen". Gilbey continued "Theft was a nailing good miler and furthermore he had had a race which was another 5 to 6 pounds in his favour yet Bahram went and beat him as he wanted to". There was no excuse for any of the vanquished on that score".

Bobsleigh was going with a "well balanced and nicely measured stride, and he got almost in line with the leaders going up Bushes Hill". However, immediately after making this forward move Perryman became uneasy and began to "urge the favourite forward with his hands". Then he was described as "green" and "all at sea" as he raced into the dip. However, he was seen "to greater advantage after meeting the rising ground than he did when descending into it".

However, while Bobsleigh lost ground going down the hill, Bahram raced up to his stable companion: Theft, who did not go down without a struggle. However, as they came out of the dip he was no match for Bahram who won "in game and decisive fashion".

However, *Warren Hill* (Willie Standring) was having none of it; having tipped Bobsleigh to win, his Newmarket letter the following Saturday was headed "Bobsleigh at his best will beat Bahram". He asked two questions: Will Bahram stay the Derby distance? Will time and circumstance permit of the more backward Bobsleigh being presented fit at Epsom? To the first question he concluded that yes Bahram will stay. To the second he was concerned that if the ground were to dry out then this would affect the chances of Bobsleigh turning up at Epson in a sufficient state of fitness to defeat Bahram who he averred would not be inconvenienced by a spell of dry weather.

In conclusion he wrote "All continuing well with Bobsleigh I think he will beat the Two Thousand Guineas winner sooner or later, but

Bahram will be less affected if we get a rainless month". Warren Hill's opinion of Bahram was lukewarm; he even gave his view that Hairan may prove to be the beat of the Aga's three-year-olds. He observed Hairan working much better than Near Relation and noted "I shall not be surprised if, in the course of time, he is able to do the same to the natty Bahram". Oh dear: how patronizing!

It was announced that Bobsleigh would run in the Newmarket Stakes over ten furlongs before the Derby. There was no Dante Stakes in those days and the Newmarket Stakes was the principal Derby trial at that time; apart from the Two Thousand Guineas of course. Bahram was unlikely to race again before the Derby, and Warren Hill expected Bobsleigh and Hairan to be the main protagonists for the Epsom Classic after the Newmarket Stakes.

However, Meyrick Good further opined "The colt (Bobsleigh) has had very little racing and it was not altogether surprising that he should have run a little green. There is no disguising the fact however, that he has a deal of improvement to report before he can be put on the same plane as Bahram, who has the battling qualities of most of Blandford's progeny".

Bahram had won the Two Thousand Guineas convincingly. However, he would continue to attract adverse comment from those who could not or would not see the true extent of his merit.

16 Derby & Ascot

The Derby field is approaching Tattenham Hill and the jockey
on the favourite is sitting comfortably. However, he is trapped
on the inside behind horses. He was starting to get anxious but
was then able to take a position behind his stable companion.
He shouts to the jockey in front of him to let him through; if he
does the jockey knows he will win, if he refuses matters might
well become very difficult…

*   *   *

Bahram was now the firm favourite for the Derby at 7–4 with
Bobsleigh 11–2. Just imagine today what price a horse would be for
the Derby if he was unbeaten in six races and had just easily won
Two Thousand Guineas! Getting even money would not be easy but
7–4; impossible!

*   *   *

Following his easy Two Thousand Guineas win Bahram was given
only "healthy exercise", canters and "half speed" work with only a
mile at "nice pace" in company with Alykhan to break things up on
8th. On the 14th on a cold wet morning he went 6 furlongs at a "nice
pace" with Hairan, Powerful Prince and the Aga's Ben Sultan presumably just to keep him warm! On a couple of occasions he worked
over ten furlongs but only at "half speed".

*   *   *

On the 15th May, the day of the Newmarket Stakes, "Augur" wrote
in *The Sporting Life* "From the date when races commenced to be run
through from end to end, it has become increasingly difficult to keep
a horse fit for any length of time, and since the Derby is by far the
most important race of the year a prospective candidate's preparation
is timed accordingly".

"Thus, it has been found, especially of late years, that while an animal may fail in the Two Thousand Guineas for want of complete condition, his progress is such as to enable him to win the Epsom Classic".

"Herein lies the strong point favourable to Bahram if I am correct in thinking that he has been trained with the Derby mainly in view".

"That his stable companion Theft, was fully wound up for the Guineas leaves no room for doubt and yet Bahram, in spite of having to be eased in his work for a day or two, accounted for Theft and other opponents in really good style".

"As a set-off to this argument it should be observed that Bahram, as a lightly-fleshed individual, probably does not require as much work as most, and certainly the son of Blandford – Friar's Daughter did not, on Guineas day, look capable of making exceptional improvement".

"Appearances, however, can prove deceptive in this respect and, so far Frank Butters has got Bahram through his racing career unbeaten".

"Despite the obvious claims of Bahram I remain convinced that Bobsleigh held the greater scope for improvement but whether he can make up the best part of six lengths on his rival in the Derby is a debatable point".

This was a most interesting commentary not least the first point concerning keeping horses at peak condition. It is not always readily understood nowadays that before the so called "American invasion" from 1898 thoroughbred racing in Britain changed beyond recognition within five years. Before North American jockeys appeared, races were often run at a crawl until the furlong pole and then a sprint ensued with the capacity of a jockey to win by a short head considered an act of artistry. However, when races were run at a fast pace from the flag more strain was placed on horses and they were not able to run as often or remain as fit and sound as before.

*   *   *

Bobsleigh, who had finished fourth behind Bahram in the Two Thousand Guineas, won the Newmarket Stakes easily from Hairan. In the paddock Hairan, who was making his seasonal debut, looked leggy and did not compare favourably with Bobsleigh who drew universal admiration and was considered to have progressed and thrived since the Guineas and possessed a "lordly demeanour". Bobsleigh's performance delighted his admirers, particularly his finishing effort up the hill which demonstrated that stamina would not be a problem at Epsom. He had also negotiated the run down into the dip well which banished fears that he would not cope with run down to Tattenham Corner. Bobsleigh had atoned for his disappointing display in the Guineas and everyone began to speculate about a battle royal between Bahram and Bobsleigh at Epsom.

On the Friday two days after the Newmarket Stakes, under the heading "Anticipating the defeat of Bahram at Epsom" *The Sporting Life's* "Warren Hill" was trumpeting the virtues of Bobsleigh:-

"In winning so easily on Wednesday Bobsleigh was once more demonstrating how valuable is public practice to horses at his time of life. I have no doubt that it will be argued that the major points go to Bahram on this early-season showing. Bahram had the greater experience of the two last year, but the winter months are long, even though this latest time round they have passed agreeably for man and beast, and Bahram and Bobsleigh could be rated as having met on even terms in the Two Thousand.

I can well imagine anyone, blindly partisan on the side of Bobsleigh, saying after the Two Thousand that the form so far as it concerned Lord Derby's colt was too bad to be true. An impartial observer would probably have said that if Bobsleigh had then finished, say, a good second, it was a case of farewell to his Epsom chance. He was many lengths behind Bahram at the judge's box and Bahram had not needed pressing to beat the stable-companion, Theft.

As against that, it could be argued that Theft was a non-stayer, so that Bahram was flattered by the result, while I fancy that, amongst those who closely watched the race, there would be some who formed the opinion that Bobsleigh did not fail for want of stamina, and that, he was, after a long absence from the racecourse, just a gawky baby. It would, I think, have been noted that day that although Perryman had accepted the situation and dropped his hands, the big colt was going up the hill with fine stride. Had the distance of the Two Thousand been a mile and a quarter, Bobsleigh would have taken closer order with Bahram.

Great credit, however, went to the latter. He won in unimpeachable style justifying all the good words one had written of him in his juvenile days.

The nattier Bahram will be the stable's main hope for some time, and I am led to believe, with all my admiration for that dapper colt that he will meet with his first defeat when he next meets Bobsleigh".

It seems strange that Bahram, who stood 16.2 hands, should have been described as "nattier" or "dapper" but never mind!

The Newmarket Stakes had the effect of bringing Bobsleigh right back into the Derby reckoning; the following day the Derby betting was:-

Bahram	13–8
Bobsleigh	5–2
Hairan	100–7
Theft	8–1
Sea Bequest	22–1
Duke John	28–1
50–1	bar

*   *   *

However, whilst cantering the following Monday, over seven furlongs on Long Hill, Bobsleigh sustained an injury. He returned to his box apparently sound but was found to be "walking peculiarly" as he moved around his box an hour later. A vet was called and although he seemed to be sound trotting outside his box he was found not to be using his near hind properly. A belladonna plaster was applied and his trainer: Colledge Leader hoped that Bobsleigh would be able to canter the following day. Before this injury became known the betting had changed slightly with Bahram quoted as favourite for the Derby at 15–8 with Bobsleigh 9–4.

*   *   *

On the 18th Bahram went ten furlongs at "good pace" in company with Tramaway, Umidwar and Shahali. The use of Umidwar; a four-year-old and winner of the previous year's Jockey Club Stakes and Champion Stakes and also second in the Eclipse, suggests the work was probably important and designed to take his Derby preparation a stage further.

* * *

Meanwhile the Aga was still undecided who would join Bahram in the Derby lineup. His other entries were Hairan, Theft, Vermeil II and Hindoo Holiday. "Fred Fox will ride Bahram for certain" said Frank Butters, "Should the Aga Khan have another runner then Gordon Richards will take that mount".

* * *

Duke John, who had made such a good impression on the gallops as a juvenile prior to his debut, was having plenty of luck; all of it bad. He was scratched as Dick Dawson could not ready the colt in time.

* * *

On Tuesday 21st all betting on the Derby was suspended following reports that Bobsleigh might not run. A "leading firm of bookmakers" opined that if Bobsleigh did not run then Bahram would be a two to one on shot. With regard to Bobsleigh, Leader said" I am still very worried about him".

Bobsleigh was not recovering from his slight setback as well as might be hoped. The problem had been identified and was located in the near hind fetlock. He was unable to work on Wednesday 22nd and was restricted to walking and trotting in the paddocks. He was walking soundly but was not right when he trotted. Leader remained hopeful that Bobsleigh could be worked the following Saturday.

Meanwhile Bahram was reaching his peak and worked over the full Derby distance of a mile and a half on Wednesday 22nd in company with Umidwar, Shahali and Aly's Antar II (Odol – Roseal by Fairy King). However, he still did not impress everyone.

* * *

Bobsleigh began to drift and Bahram harden for the Derby. At Thursday's call-over Bobsleigh could be backed at 11–2 (from 9–4 the previous Monday) and although some 11–10 was obtained about Bahram evens was soon the best price available. Of the others 10–1 was available about Sea Bequest, 100–8 Theft and Hairan and 50–1 Fairbairn. Of these others only Fairbairn was a certain runner.

On Thursday following Leader's comments that Bobsleigh was now sound his odds contracted to 9–2 (from 11–2) and was taken so that 4–1 was the best on offer. The next call-over for the Derby would be the following Monday the 27th at 12.30 pm.

*   *   *

On Friday 24th Bahram was dispatched to Lingfield in company with Shahali. Both were entered in the Derby Trial Sweepstakes (the equivalent of today's Lingfield Derby Trial but run much closer to the race itself) the following day. Shahali was declared and finished unplaced as the 6–4 on favourite behind Lord Astor's Field Trial (Felstead – Popingaol by Dark Ronald). *The Sporting Life* reported "He (Bahram) walked as soberly as could be in the paddock, and pleased every critic by his action round the left-hand bend and down the hill when he was galloped with Tramaway".

Meyrick Good reported "Bahram has greatly improved in appearance since Guineas day. He has put on muscle, and Frank Butters will have him "timed" to the hour for the great test. Now that he has a more trained appearance, he seems a taller and more lengthy colt. Although his mile and a half gallop was only a half-pace affair, and Fox could have left Tramaway when and where he liked, it served to confirm the opinion that the Aga Khan's colt could not be in better heart".

This trip to Lingfield was a good move for such a lazy colt, as it took Bahram away from Newmarket for the first time since his victory in the Gimcrack Stakes at York the previous August. Apart from the benefit that a change of environment usually brings, it was an opportunity to gallop left-handed round the bend at Lingfield and into the straight, something that has similarities with Epsom's Tattenham Corner.

*   *   *

Between then and the Derby, Bahram would do only canters, except when he went twelve furlongs at "nice pace" with Tramaway on 29th, and on Saturday 1st June he went ten furlongs at "good pace" with Mr. T H Lant's four-year-old colt Achtenan (Achtoi – Nantenan by Hainault) and the Aga's five-year-old gelding Conversion (Legatee – Thamar by Golden Myth) on the peat moss gallop. This piece of work in particular was reported in *The Sporting Life;* "Bahram, who is usually a sluggish horse in training work, went particularly well". It also reported that Hairan, working with Umidwar and Shahali, and Theft accompanied by Lucky Patch and Tramaway, both over ten furlongs, also "pleased".

That was it Frank Butters had done all he could it was now up to Bahram. If he were to fall short then it was hoped that Hairan or Theft would oblige.

*   *   *

Meanwhile everything possible it seemed was conspiring against the unfortunate Bobsleigh; he pulled up "very lame" after trotting exercise in the Stanley House paddock on Monday 27th. *The Sporting Chronicle* reported on Tuesday 28th that his prospects of running in the Derby were now "hopeless". Colledge Leader had initially been quoted as saying he was satisfied with his charge; however, later reports cancelled that view. With the final forfeit for the Classic due on Tuesday 28th at 10.00 p. m. it looked more and more certain Bobsleigh would be scratched.

However, on Wednesday 29th May "Warren Hill" writing under his name of Willie Standring in *The Sporting Life* was very optimistic: "Backers of Bobsleigh, who were pardonably despondent on Monday night, are likely to have a run for their money next Wednesday. Lord Derby's colt pleased his trainer in a half-speed gallop yesterday morning, and although there were signs of the leg trouble again last evening, the outlook is regarded more hopefully".

"Newmarket opinion is sharply divided regarding the Derby prospects of Bobsleigh. "Warren Hill" (meaning himself of course!) is among those who have not lost faith in the Stanley House champion, as is indicated by the following wire received last night:-

"This evening Bobsleigh again betrayed a halt in his gait when given bouts of trotting, and to diagnose his ailment might require some Heaven-sent genius. I suppose the stiffness, or whatever it is, will recur while the colt is engaged in this light business after warmer blooded work such as he had this morning. His case continues to remain, from the training point of view, more interesting than alarming. Bobsleigh wore a bandage again last tonight, He did not carry a rag this morning. The stable programme is to give the colt light exercise tomorrow morning and a gallop on Thursday".

Writing under his *non de plume* of "Warren Hill" he wrote the same day "The report which I have to present of Bobsleigh this morning (Tuesday) is the brightest since his training programme was broken into more than a week ago. With Robber Chief for companion he went six furlongs at half-speed, trotted out sound after the spin and walked off home showing not a vestige of halt. It would seem that the fault is simply intermittent and yields to treatment".

Later in the same article he commented that the Aga would declare all three of his Derby hopes: Bahram, Hairan and Theft. He noted that Bahram had impressed at Lingfield the previous Saturday but could not resist a jibe by suggesting that Bahram will need to travel faster next Wednesday. So it was fine when Bobsleigh works half-speed but not when Bahram did!

Standring drew some comfort from speculating that as Bahram had never raced on a soft surface and May had been more unsettled than usual it may be a Derby run with give in the ground.

*   *   *

Any optimism with regard to Bobsleigh proved unfounded: on Friday 31st May "Augur" wrote in *The Sporting Life* "As the mishap to Bobsleigh has proved of a more serious nature than anticipated at the time, I much fear we must be prepared for the worst, and so have to eliminate Lord Derby's colt as a really live factor for the Blue Riband".

"Although Bobsleigh was nicely forward in condition when

winning the Newmarket Stakes, he could scarcely afford a day's idleness during the comparatively short time at the trainer's disposal to
fit him for the fray at Epsom. The general belief that Bobsleigh might
reverse the Guineas placing's with Bahram was based mainly on
the assumption that the son of Gainsborough held the greater scope
for improvement which would, it was thought, be manifested in the
searching preparation which every Derby aspirant has to undergo".

"In the circumstances, it would be difficult to over-estimate what
the loss of several days' work means to Bobsleigh. His enforced
idleness is in striking contrast to the gallops which Bahram is being
subjected day by day. I should not have greatly fancied Bobsleigh to
defeat Bahram at Epsom even had all gone well, and now misfortune
has overtaken Lord Derby's colt I dismiss him from further serious
consideration".

*   *   *

On the Monday at the Victoria Club call-over about £7,000 (371,000)
was wagered on Bahram at odds varying from 11–8 on to 6–5 on.
The full betting was as follows:-

Bahram	5–6
Hairan	100–8
Theft	100–8
Sea Bequest	15–1
Bobsleigh	18–1
Field Trial	22–1
Fairhaven	25–1
First Son	33–1
Fairbairn	35–1
Pry II	40–1
Screamer	50–1
Assignation	66–1

The Aga Khan and Frank Butters were responsible for the first
three in the betting. It seemed almost certain the Bahram would
start at odds-on. The last odds-on favourite to oblige had been Mr.

J Gubbins' Galtee More (Kendal – Morganette by Springfield) who won at odds of 4–1 on in 1897. Capt. Greer's Slieve Gallion (Gallinule – Reclusion by St. Florian) had started at 13–8 on when finishing third to Mr. R Croker's Orby (Orme – Rhoda B by Hanover) and Col. E W Baird's Wool Winder (Martagon – St. Windeline by St. Simon) in 1907.

Bobsleigh was left in the Derby at the final forfeit and Colledge Leader was quoted as saying that his charge was never more than "slightly lame". On the Tuesday the colt was again brought out at 5.00 p. m. and given trotting exercise with a view to galloping him the following morning if all was well. However, despite all his best efforts Leader had to concede that, following a canter on the Wednesday morning with Lord Derby's Robber Chief (Sherwood Star – Rockmills by Mushroom), Bobsleigh was again showing signs of lameness. He contacted Lord Derby immediately and on his instructions the colt was scratched at 12–47 p. m. Such was the severity of the injury that Bobsleigh did not return to the track until 29th October when with odds of 13–8 laid on him he finished second to his only opponent: William Woodward's Alcazar (Achtoi – Priscilla Carter by Omar Khayyam), in the Limekiln Stakes at Newmarket.

As a four-year-old Bobsleigh raced six times but never really fulfilled his potential. He won only once: the Chippenham Stakes at Newmarket. He did finish second to both Fair Trial and Omaha in moderate plate races at Newmarket and Kempton respectively; but his career ended with a disappointing fifth at 6–5 on in the Dullingham Stakes. Bobsleigh's career and misfortune have been covered in some detail because he was considered for a time by many to be at least as good as Bahram.

Bobsleigh must have been a tremendous sort physically; Sir Walter Gilbey, considered to be "one of the best judges in the Kingdom" had seen almost every Derby runner in the paddock for fifty-seven years and he could not recall ever seeing a more beautiful colt. Bobsleigh must have impressed the Aga at some stage as he placed a bet on him to win the Derby; possibly to cover his bets on Bahram and Hairan.

It is impossible to say how good Bobsleigh might have been as a three-year-old had he stayed sound for more of the year. It is however unlikely that he would ever have beaten Bahram and in retrospect there are few who would contend that Bobsleigh was in the same class as Bahram as a racehorse, even if Bobsleigh was the superior colt in physique.

*　　*　　*

Frank Butters did not take any special precautions to protect Bahram from possible interference from those who might prefer matters better if he were unable to start in the Derby. However, no unauthorized persons were allowed near him in the stables.

*　　*　　*

The Aga Khan was expected to arrive in England the following Monday or Tuesday before the race. He would not decide how many of his entries would run in the race until then. It seemed certain, however, that Bahram, Hairan and Theft would all be declared.

In an article in the *Sporting Chronicle* on 29th May, headed "Aga Khan's Happy Family" and subtitled "Bahram called the perfect racehorse", it was reported that, whereas Leader had endured problems with Bobsleigh, Frank Butters had not had a moment's concern training the three colts of the Aga's: Bahram, Hairan and Theft. Sounds like it was written by someone who has never spoken to a trainer about preparing a horse for a big race!

*　　*　　*

In the days just prior to the Derby the journalist Eric Rickman received the following letter:-

Bridge House
Staverley
Harrogate
Yorkshire

Dear Sir
As I see you think that Bahram will win the Derby, I am writing to tell you I hope he does as I bought his dam, Friars Daughter, as a

foal at the Newmarket December Sales for 120 guineas, and sold her as a yearling to Mr. R C Dawson (on behalf of the Aga Kahn) for 250 guineas. When I got her home from the December Sales, she developed a cold and was very ill and would not eat for a week, but I nursed her night and day and she pulled round. I was very afraid that she would die.

I only wish that Bahram was not favourite, as something always seems to happen in these days to prevent the favourite winning the Derby, so don't praise him too much in print. I cannot afford it or I would so much like to see the race run. If Bahram wins I would like his photograph, and I wonder if you would ask the Aga Khan to send me one with his autograph.

My father, W Sanderson, was a trainer and my brother George a jockey. I used to sell the yearlings I bred at Doncaster.

I do not want you to mention anything in this letter in the paper, until after Bahram has won the Derby and if he does that I shall feel very proud of the bonny little foal whose life I saved. She was a most beautiful mover and a good disposition.

Yours faithfully,

E M Plummer (Mrs.)

Rickman showed the letter to a delighted Aga before the Derby and, after receiving congratulations from Rickman after the race, he said Mrs. Plummer would have her photograph.

*   *   *

Meanwhile Freddie Fox was apparently doing his best to injure himself! The previous week, at York, he had suffered cuts about the head when his mount, Tewkesbury, struck into the heels of another horse and came down. Then at Birmingham on Tuesday 28th he was kicked at the start while waiting to line up on Solomon's Crown.

*   *   *

The Monday evening of Derby week saw the final call-over; apart from some betting on Theft there was little or no betting. The combined odds of the Aga's three runners were 2–5.

Bahram	10–11
Hairan	100–12
Theft	100–9
Field Trial	100–8
Sea Bequest	13–1
First Son	25–1
Fairhaven	28–1
Fairbairn	28–1
50–1	bar

*   *   *

In Tuesday's *Sporting Life* "Warren Hill" (Willie Standring) wrote in his "Newmarket Letter";

"The annual all-round test which the Derby sets to early-summer three-year-olds, will, I think, reveal Bahram to be the best of our Newmarket-trained horses. A little later in the season and the trial might be a fairer one all-round, even after such a mild, and therefore favourable, winter such as we have gone through.

There are people who say, as did a Franco-American owner who declined to run his horse some years ago, that this mile and a half course at Epson is a travesty. They argue that it is suited only to horses of a particular type – handy horses able to come down a long section of it as goats come down a mountain track. But something more than adaptability to the long down gradient is needed to win the Derby if the race is truly run.

Long before the "dive" to Tattenham Corner has to be made there is that half-mile climb from the starting post. A turn, akin to Chester's, opens on to more level ground, then comes the falling gradient, which takes in a still sharper turn into the straight. More downhill until a furlong from the finish; and then a rise which beats all but the stoutest heart. The Derby puts all-round ability into the melting-pot. It must bring every muscle into action. Whatever a particular candidate may not have done before, and no matter what the subsequent failure, I always think that the winner must be a good horse on the day.

Now that Bobsleigh has gone, I make out that Bahram is the one horse which most nearly meets the requirements of the race. Anyhow, I find less to say against him than against any other of ours. If he does not fulfill expectations, he cannot be excused on the ground concerning his training. I like him for being a lazy worker, Laziness was characteristic of my earliest favourite amongst racehorse – Isinglass. It generally denotes an ability to keep on pulling out a little more when it is wanted amidst the inspiring influence of a race.

The Two Thousand running showed that Bahram is capable of smart quickening effort, and when he had beaten Theft at seven furlongs he continued up the hill after the manner of one which would not be troubled by another half-mile. As that was probably the impression created in the trainer's mind, Bahram has not been formerly tried as other owners and trainers of the past would have tried him.

His improvement from the day he was first seen on a course and when, taking 9lb from Theft, who had already been in public, he squeezed home by a neck, was to be noted in his Two Thousand effort. Again Theft had enjoyed public experience, whereas the other colt (Bahram) was coming out for the first time since Cesarewitch week.

There is no proof that Bahram can get a truly-run mile and a half, but his Two Thousand finish impressed me most favourably with regard to his stamina potentialities… Bahram does not seem to mind firm going and I fancy he can place himself on any kind of course".

So Bahram to win; but it was hardly a ringing endorsement!

*   *   *

Also on Tuesday, before the Derby at the Press Club luncheon, Lord Derby showed that he had clearly read plenty of the praise heaped upon Bobsleigh; he alluded to 1935 being a disastrous year as far as racing was concerned, and then said "If Bobsleigh was running, even with Mr. Frank Butters in the room, I should have told you he was going to win". His Lordship continued after a reference to Fairhaven; "May I make a suggestion? If, about the middle of next year the Aga

Khan finds that he has two or three horses outside those he intends to run, would he think of leasing them to other people? Then we might get a very interesting race, and, who knows the outsider might turn up!"

His Lordship concluded irrelevantly: "If I were to express a preference for either of the Aga Khan's horses, it is not because I think Hairan is the best, but because I would like him to win for the sake of his sire."

Hairan was by Lord Derby's stallion Fairway. In addition, in may also have been in His Lordship's mind, that a win for Hairan would not do Bobsleigh's claim to be the best three-year-old colt any harm, as he had convincingly beaten Hairan in the Newmarket Stakes! From this it can clearly be seen that Lord Derby was harbouring some resentment towards the Aga, and may not have been exactly overjoyed that his ex-trainer Frank Butters was in charge of the horses of his nemesis!

The Aga was unable to be present at the luncheon and was represented by Frank Butters who confirmed that all his three runners had done half-speed canters that day on the Limekilns. Considering that he had an unbeaten Two Thousand Guineas winner to represent him, the Aga was not confident and requested a constant supply of stable information and weather reports. He was concerned about soft ground for Bahram an in such circumstances preferred the claims of Hairan.

To take his mind off the Derby the Aga went off to play golf at St. Cloud. His playing partner was waiting for him in the club house when a girl caddy, who had seen the Aga doing his Swedish exercises on the tee and misinterpreted what he was doing, said to his partner "His Highness is praying on the first tee"!

The Aga and the Begum, in company with two-year-old Sadruddin, caught the Blue Train from Nice to Paris and from there they flew on to Croydon airport.

* * *

Some final thoughts by Meyrick Good on Derby day appeared in *The Sporting Life* these are those concerning Bahram:-

"Courage and a disposition that is not easily ruffled count for as much if not more than good looks and make and shape in a race-horse...Bahram has good looks and disposition to recommend him.

Nothing appears to upset the Aga Khan's favourite, and he does not appear to really show his mettle until half-way through his races. He then finds plenty of dash, and does all that is necessary. Bahram, because of his docility, reminds me of April the Fifth. Nothing used to upset Tom Walls Derby winner.

Few horses have kept their strength and at the same time grown and lengthened as Bahram has done since his two-year-old days. His trainer told me last year that he thought his charge stood sixteen hands. Certainly Bahram did not as a youngster look so big, which shows how truly he has turned.

When I saw Bahram at Lingfield recently, when he was given a gallop on the course with his stable companion Tramaway, I was impressed by the improvement that had been effected in his looks. Now that he is a thoroughly trained individual he appears to stand over a lot more ground. This may be due to the fact that work has muscled him up, and hard tissue has taken the place of softer substance.

Another thing about the favourite that impressed me at Lingfield was the handy way he took the turn into the straight. It was in marked contrast with the running of April the Fifth when he won the Derby trial at Lingfield. The Epsom-trained horse took Lane almost to the centre of the track. Bahram had his stable companion on his inside. Except for this, he would have "taken a coat of paint" off the rails.

This confirms Fox's opinion, which is that Bahram would turn on a sixpence and is the most sensible and handiest horse he has ever ridden – a tribute indeed from a jockey of such vast experience.

Unlike his stable companion Hairan, who is appreciably straighter in front of the saddle, Bahram does not ride so high off the ground when galloping or bend his knees so extravagantly, which points to his preferring firmer going than does Frank Butters second string".

*   *   *

On the Wednesday: Derby day both principal writers in *The Sporting Life* tipped Bahram to win. Meyrick Good had always been amongst Bahram staunchest supporters and "Warren Hill" (Willie Standring), with his beloved Bobsleigh out of the race, presumably had little choice!

The Aga was up early to be greeted by a day that had begun wet, damp and depressing and continued in this fashion for five hours with the prospects not improved until well after midday. The King: George V arrived in the rain with all the dignitaries to be greeted by the dismal sight of sodden downs and damp spectators. However, the clouds then began to disperse and by the off time of three o'clock the sun was shining. The Aga said that the rain would help Hairan but not enough had fallen to really change the going it merely perfected the condition of the course.

Although King George V and Queen Mary, who were celebrating twenty-five years on the Throne together, with the Prince of Wales, Princess Royal, Duke of Gloucester, Duke and Duchess of Kent and Princess Nicolas of Greece had arrived at 1–00 o'clock with the rain still falling. When they made their way to the paddock a much more cheerful sight greeted them.

In the paddock Field Trial impressed the most as "a handsome and beautifully turned out colt". Fairhaven and Fairbairn were sweating slightly; Bahram was much admired but was edgy, on his toes and sweating slightly and did so also in the parade. Fox later described how he felt when he saw Bahram "My heart sank into my boots and I thought for the first and only time he *may* (his italics) get beaten. He was pulling the boy round the parade ring and sweating so much that it (the boy) is running off his feet". *The Times* correspondent noted that Bahram was "sweating and excitable".

However, by the time he started to canter to the start his coat had dried and he was relaxed. Bahram moved "magnificently" to post, Robin Goodfellow was also noted moving well; Hairan it was noted did not possess Bahram's easy rhythm.

The Aga had three runners; Bahram carried the first colours: green and chocolate hoops with chocolate cap, his other runners were distinguished by a yellow cap for Theft and red one for Hairan.

As the horses were leaving the paddock Aly Khan appeared and placed his hand on the shoulder of Quintin Gilbey and said "I can't stand the strain, I need a drink". Over a bottle of Bollinger Aly confided that he had placed the biggest bet of his life on Bahram. Aly did not say how much his bet was but Gilbey had £80 (4,200) on Bahram and thought that relatively speaking this would be larger than Aly's for the simple reason it was £80 he did not have! However much Aly had bet at least he would be able to pay – eventually – if Bahram lost!

On Derby day Bahram was 16.2 hands tall, 69 inch girth (175 cm), 7 ½ inches (19cm) of bone beneath his knee and had 47 inch (119cm) reign.

Epsom Downs Wednesday 5th June. Going; Good/firm
The 156th renewal of the Derby Stakes with £3,000 added. There were 292
entries, viz. 18 at £100 62 at £50 100 at £25 and 112 at £5. Breeder of winner
to receive £500, second 10% of the whole stakes viz £1,096 and the third 5%
namely £548. For three-year-old colts and fillies; colts 9 st., fillies 8st 9lbs.
Run over the Derby course of about one and a half miles. (£9,216) (448,448).

1	Bahram	9st	F. Fox	132+
2	Robin Goodfellow	9st	T. Weston	127
3	Field Trial	9st	R. Dick	126
4	Theft	9st	H. Wragg	119+
5	Fairhaven	9st	R. Perryman	109
6	Sea Bequest	9st	E. Smith	108
7	Hairan	9st	G. Richards	104
8	Assignation	9st	S. Donoghue	99
9	Fairbairn	9st	C. Smirke	
10	First Son	9st	R. Jones	
11	Peaceful Walter	9st	D. Smith	
12	Screamer	9st	A. Wragg	
13	Japetus	9st	F. Lane	
14	Pry II	9st	M. Beary	
15	Barberry	9st	S. Smith	
16	St. Botolph	9st	H. Beasley	

Starting prices; 5/4 Bahram, 5/1 Hairan, 9/1 Field Trial, 100/8 Sea Bequest
and Theft, 100/6 Assignation, 25/1 Japetus, Fairhaven and First Sun, 40/1
Fairbairn, 50/1 Robin Goodfellow, screamer and Pry II, 100/1 Peaceful Walter
and 200/1 others.

Distances; won by two lengths, half a length between second and third. Unofficially the distances thereafter were three and a half, six, half a length, two lengths and three lengths.

Time; 2 min 36.00 secs. (fast by 0.40)

Race analysis:-
The first to break the line was First Son who was followed by Pry II, Theft, Bahram, Sea Bequest, Screamer and Field Trial. These were in front of Peaceful Walter, Barberry and Robin Goodfellow, Japetus being the back marker. Going to the top of the hill after about half a mile had been covered First Son was leading from Pry II, Sea Bequest and Field Trial. Sea Bequest did not appear to act well down the hill approaching the straight, and began to lose ground. Before reaching Tattenham Corner, Field Trial had raced to the front pressed by First Son and Pry II. At this point Bahram was in a prominent position and shortly afterwards took closer order with the leaders. Field Trial swept round the bend in front of First Son, Pry II, Bahram and Hairan. Robin Goodfellow then began to make headway; First Son and Pry II were beaten two furlongs from the post. Bahram was then in touch with the leader. He was given his head below the distance, where Robin Goodfellow deprived Field Trial of second place. Robin Goodfellow stayed on well, but failed to overhaul Bahram who went on to win decisively.

Archive film shows Bahram as a convincing and comfortable winner and Fox was never required to be particularly animated. Interestingly although there were sixteen runners and, although Bahram's name began with a B, he carried the number 13 on his weight cloth. This was because horses were listed under their owner on the racecard so the Aga's runners were grouped together under K for Khan. If any horses listed on the racecard were not declared to run then each horse that ran kept its original number. This was almost certainly as a result of a request from the tote that horses be numbered on the racecard in order that they could set up their machines in advance. Declarations for all races at that time were made less than an hour before it was due to take place.

There were eight races over the four days of the meeting run over distances of ten furlongs and above. Three were run at faster than the standard times used for this exercise: the Derby, a handicap over ten furlongs and the Coronation Cup. This was won by Windsor Lad in a time of 2 min. 33.20 sec. fast by 3.20 sec. Windsor Lad was a four-year-old carrying 3 pounds more than Bahram.

Weight-for-age in early June would have a three-year-old receiving 13 pounds from older horses. So Bahram could have been said to have been beaten by 2.80 seconds (about 14 lengths) giving ten pounds more than weight-for-age! This despite a pace described as "muddling" by jockeys and "wretched" by an observer and about which several jockeys complained as it caused considerable interference.

Bahram's time was still faster than the average for the race since race times had improved from the turn of the century. That Bahram never raced against Windsor Lad was a sad indictment of the attitude of the Aga to competition. That two giants of the Twentieth Century had been foaled just a year apart and yet never raced against each other is a travesty for the sport.

The overall opinion was that Bahram won very easily; Meyrick Good observed that he had the race won two furlongs from home. "Bahram raced up to Field Trial and in half a dozen strides was alongside, Fox sitting perfectly still". Freddie Fox said "It was not a particularly fast gallop, but I was nicely placed throughout lying just behind Gordon on Hairan. I knew the race was mine, bar accident, half-way down the straight".

Steve Donoghue paid tribute to Fox's riding "Fox has to thank Harry Wragg who quickly saw what was happening and pulled Theft away to let the favourite go through. I have never ridden in a Derby in which there was so much trouble and the winning horse and jockey came out of it with flying colours. Bahram must be a smashing good and plucky horse". High praise indeed from the rider of six Derby winners and a jockey considered to be the master of riding Epsom. Tommy Weston said that Robin Goodfellow was "pocketed" when making the turn into the straight, and, although he did not think he would have won, felt he might have "stretched" Bahram with a clear run. Weston said that Bahram was "A good colt, make no mistake about that".

After the field had covered about a furlong First Son had been making the pace followed two lengths behind by St. Botolph and Theft. They were followed by Screamer, Field Trial, Sea Bequest, Bahram, Peaceful Walter, Pry II and Hairan. The incident which attracted so much attention happened soon after. "Ajax" of the *Evening Standard* described what happened

"They had not reached the top of the hill. First Son was then setting the pace to Pry II, Field Trial and Hairan. Just behind the trio was Theft, racing on the bit and Bahram in anything but a happy position on the inside. (Theft was drawn fifth and Bahram third; nearer the rails). The next thing I saw was that Theft had dropped back and Bahram had got his position. Harry Wragg (on Theft) told me how it happened and how at that point Bahram had been able to win the Derby. "I had a lovely position going up the hill. I had intended to go along just behind the leaders and not wait as so many people thought I would do. Before we reached the top of the hill I heard somebody shout. I had a glance over my shoulder and found that it was Freddie Fox trying to squeeze through. There was not room for him to do so, but when I realized it was Bahram, and I was also riding for the Aga Khan, I gave way and he was able to take a position which might have been mine".

It was Wragg's view that but for that incident Theft, who was running on late, would have finished second. While this is entirely possible it is equally likely that Theft ran on through beaten horses after he himself had been taken out of the firing line. He had been so far behind at Tattenham Corner that Wragg must have entirely given up hope of winning and would only have asked Theft to run on. Horses running on late are usually thought to be unlucky, it is only when they are asked to race in the heat of a race that their true merit is known. Theft had proved that he was top class over a mile in the Two Thousand Guineas but would need to prove that he was equally effective over 10–12 furlongs.

When the Stewards heard about this Wragg was interviewed as they were not satisfied with his riding. The point of contention was of course Wragg's decision to pull out Theft to allow Bahram a clear run; the stewards drew Wragg's attention to Rule 139 which stated: "Every horse that runs in a race shall be run on its merit, whether his owner runs another horse in the race or not". Wragg sensibly admitted he had contravened the Rule, was cautioned, and warned that if he or any other jockey disregarded the Rule in future they would be severely dealt with. The Stewards had addressed the jockeys before the race and warned them about keeping their places and avoiding interference.

In the past if an owner had more than one runner he could make a declaration to win with one particular horse and any others could be pulled aside to let it through. The rule was altered partly because the Aga and a few other owners were keen on having more than one representative. They disliked a declaration whether or not this was optional. Finally it was stressed that every owner's horse had to race on their own merits: a horse put in the race solely as a pacemaker was against the rules of racing.

A fortnight before the Derby Theft had been heavily backed for a place. Had Theft managed to come second or third the bookmakers would have had some serious losses to bear.

Too much should not be made of this incident. After all it took place with still ten furlongs to race and it is unlikely that Fox would not have had any opportunity to extract Bahram. As Bahram had plenty of speed he would have needed to be boxed in almost to the line to fail to have won. In the event Bahram came with a "space devouring stride" and drew alongside Field Trial and, although for a few strides they were level, Bahram then forged ahead. Subsequently "Augur" (Capt. Long) of the *Sporting Life* wrote, without offering any detail, "I have reason to believe that Bahram got into more trouble in running than is generally believed".

The win was describe as "immensely popular" and gave rise to a "veritable tornado of cheering". "The demonstration began when Bahram got the better of Field Trial and gained in volume until the race was over". This was hardly a surprise as Bahram was the favourite!

Freddie Fox talking after the Derby said:-

"I was never out of the first seven. After I got through going up the hill I was able to follow Gordon Richards on Hairan. My colt was always giving me a good feel, and he goes just as well uphill as downhill. He came down the descent to Tattenham Corner much smoother than Hairan, and I was able to go into 4th place without asking him to increase his pace to any extent. As we turned into the straight I was in a position to challenge the leaders. I was going so well that I knew I would win. First Son dropped away a furlong in the straight and that left me in 2nd place, just behind Field Trial. Without having to press the colt I had no difficulty in passing Field Trial as we came to the path which crosses the course. Bahram continued to gallop strongly and we were never in danger of defeat."

Bahram became the first horse since the great Isinglass in 1893 to win the Derby as an undefeated horse. Before that the mighty Ormonde had achieved the same distinction in 1886. According to Meyrick Good Bahram had only to maintain his superiority over Bobsleigh, Hairan and Field Trial to take his place with the greats. However, not everyone shared that view. Already there were those quick to claim that the three-year-olds were a moderate lot which have not taken much beating. In addition there were plenty who thought that if Bobsleigh could be produced fit and well on St Leger day there would be no Triple Crown for Bahram.

Immediately after the Derby the Aga was not basking in the euphoria of Bahram's success but more typically reflecting on what he had cost to produce! He observed "All told Bahram cost me about £600 (32,000) to breed. I gave £200 (9,000) for his dam and there was the stud fee for Blandford (which was 400 guineas – £20,000). I think that was cheap". Although the facts were – largely – true one would still need to be wealthy to be able to do it! And of course he had spent prodigiously on many yearlings that proved to be moderate or worse!

The evening of Bahram's Derby triumph the Aga was guest of honour at a celebration dinner for Jockey Club members at Buckingham Palace, for which the tables were decorated in the winning owner's colours of green and chocolate. This had been Queen Mary's own idea. His Majesty King George V proposed the Aga's health and the following day he and the Begum were guests for lunch at 10 Downing Street.

*   *   *

With only thirteen days between the Derby and Ascot Bahram needed only to be kept ticking over. Bahram had been nominated for six races over the four days: St James's Palace Stakes, King Edward VII Stakes, Waterford Stakes; a mile race for three-year-olds: a sort of poor man's St James's Palace Stakes no longer run, Rous Memorial Stakes; an all-aged race over seven and a half furlongs, Jersey Stakes; the same as today but over half a furlong further and Hardwicke Stakes, same as now but then open to three-year-olds. In terms of importance then, as now, the St James's Palace Stakes was the most valuable and prestigious.

Bahram did light exercise on the 7th and the following day seven furlongs at "half speed" with Theft, who it was felt had not fully stayed the Derby trip and was being prepared for the Jersey Stakes, which he won. Bahram went six furlongs at "useful pace" on the tenth.

The Times on the 14th June carried the news that Bahram would be retired to stud at the end of the year. The news was described as "surprising" but would be welcomed by breeders following the death of Blandford earlier in the year. It was stated that Bahram would be limited to 16 mares including those of the Aga Khan.

On that same day, a fine morning, Bahram, blissfully unaware of the delights that awaited him the following February, went six furlongs "nice pace" with Shahali on the Limekilns. On 15th he went "good pace" with Theft, Hairan and Powerful Prince to complete the preparations for all of those who were to run at Ascot. However, only Bahram and Theft were successful. Bahram departed for Ascot on Monday 17th.

The significant falls in the value of races at the Royal meeting are an indication of the complacent attitude of the executive. They rely on the meetings status to make up for the relatively modest prize-money. The absurd elevation in the value of the sprint races provides another illustration of how British racing is obsessed with 6–8 furlong events to the detriment of middle distance racing. The values of all races at what is today known as Royal Ascot were increased for 2016. However, they are still well behind what is available in other parts of the racing world for prestigious races.

Ascot Heath Tuesday 18th June. Going; Soft
St. James's Palace Stakes of £100 each half forfeit or £10 if declared with
£1,000 added for winner £400 for the second and £200 for the third for
three-year-olds; colts 9st fillies and geldings 8st 11lb maidens allowed 7 lb
; Old mile; (96 entrants viz. 5 at £100, 23 at £50 and 68 at £10----£3,230)
(172,000)

1	Bahram	9st	F. Fox	112+
2	Portfolio	8st 7lb	R. Dick	102
3	Rosecrag	9st	E. Smith	100
4	Zingaro	9st	T. Weston	
5	Fresh Fox	8st 7lb	M. Beary	

Starting Prices; 1/8 Bahram, 100/7 Portfolio, 100/6 Rosecrag and Zingaro,
33/1 Fresh Fox

Won by one length; 4 lengths between second and third.
Time; 1 min 48.20 sec (slow by 7.50)

Race analysis:-
Fresh Fox set the pace to Zingaro, Portfolio and Bahram; but after going four
furlongs Portfolio headed Fresh Fox, Bahram being next.
Bahram was asked for his effort soon after turning into the straight and
mastering Portfolio won by a length.

There were only three races over the old mile during the four days and all were slowly run. Ascot was reconfigured in 1955 and 2006 and comparing times in any meaningful way in different eras is very difficult.

Nonetheless it could hardly be claimed that Bahram had impressed, Fox had found it necessary to draw the whip to remind him that a race was still to be won. Although he then won comfortably enough he was clearly not himself. The form was not in any way franked by Lord Astor's Portfolio ((Sansovino – Short Story by Buchan) in any of the three races he ran in afterwards. In his final race that year he was beaten half a length by Robin Goodfellow who was conceding Portfolio nineteen pounds; seven more than Bahram had done at Ascot. There is no escaping the fact that Bahram ran at least a stone below the form he had shown in both the Two Thousand Guineas and Derby.

Almost certainly the Derby had taken the edge off him; no matter how easily a Derby is won the race always takes its toll. The day is full of new experiences for all the runners, and coping with these pressures is all part of demonstrating that a horse has, not only the ability to win a Derby, but also the temperament as well. Fox said he thought Bahram found the Derby experience "nerve-racking".

Bahram was now unbeaten in eight races during which he had hardly been pushed to beat his opponents. It only remained now for him to prove just how great he was by beating all-comers and all ages...

17 Triple Crown Champion

It is St Leger day and the long odds-on favourite is being led out of the saddling boxes. His trainer is alarmed to see that his coat is standing up almost reminiscent of a hedgehog. He is concerned that something may be seriously amiss with his charge...

*   *   *

The News Chronicle reported on 25th June that Bobsleigh was still lame and may not be able to run in the St Leger. In the course of its report the *Chronicle* stated that "Bobsleigh was confidently expected to beat Bahram in the Derby"! The report did not make it clear exactly who was of this opinion; certainly there were those who confidently thought Bobsleigh could beat Bahram before the Derby, and there were those who felt that he might have beaten him had Bobsleigh managed to line up for the race. However, there is little hard evidence that Bobsleigh could ever have been confidently backed to beat Bahram over any distance. Quintin Gilbey wrote that Bobsleigh had been heralded as "a horse and a half" but his view was that he would not have beaten Bahram if "he'd had five legs"!

The doubters would not, however, be silenced. Early in July "Warren Hill" (Willie Standring) who, of course, had always had his reservations about the extent of Bahram's ability, and had championed Bobsleigh at every opportunity as being the superior horse, wrote an article in the *Sporting Life* which began as follows:-

"A valued correspondent: "Isonomy" from Norwich, in running the rule over the leading three-year-olds pleasantly criticizes those writers on the racing press who have shown a tendency to look rather disparagingly upon the Derby winner. I suppose that without being directly charged, I am one of the number for, while I realized more than thirty years back, that it was foolish to harbour prejudices in matters affecting racing, I have had to say of Bahram that good, honest, fighting colt that he be, I do not regard him to be in the same rank as other Epsom winners I have known. Let my correspondent have his say on this and other things":-

"The chief inference I draw from these writings is that the running of Hairan (in the Derby) and his position – as I expected it to be – with regard to Theft shows what a completely misleading reading has been made of Bobsleigh's two lengths beating of Hairan, after a good fight in the Newmarket Stakes.

The Derby running shows that this fuss made of Bobsleigh's performance was all nonsense; it took no great horse to win the Newmarket Stakes. I take it that as Theft beat Bobsleigh so far (in the Two Thousand guineas) and in the Derby beat Hairan much farther it is hardly fair to keep harping on Theft's lack of stamina and Bobsleigh's and Hairan's (problematic) possession of it".

"Warren Hill" respects "Isonomy's" view but infers that his form reading is simplistic as the Epsom course is so different from Newmarket's Rowley Mile. "Warren Hill" refers to Isinglass as a wonder horse; true Isinglass was a great horse but any comparison between horses that ran before 1900 and those that ran afterwards are largely irrelevant. This is because races were so much more slowly run before the "American invasion" when "Tod" Sloan *et al* began the fashion for riding shorter and ensuring that races were run at a faster pace. From 1900 race times were reduced significantly, and it is therefore impossible to have any idea how Isinglass would have performed in either the Derbys of 1934 or 1935 run, as they were, nine and seven seconds faster respectively.

The view of "Warren Hill" is that Windsor Lad was a superior Derby winner to Bahram and further opines that the former more resembles a Triple Crown winner! Good grief! So, because Bobsleigh can't beat Bahram it is necessary to write something as asinine as that! It may have escaped Standring's notice but Windsor Lad did not even contest the Two Thousand Guineas of 1934 where, if he had, he would have been soundly beaten by Colombo, one of the best winners of that race for many years. Indeed, Colombo, who started at odds of 2–7, would also have beaten Bahram in the Two Thousand Guineas had they been able to meet. Had Bahram and Windsor Lad been able to meet as juveniles then it is hard not to conclude that Bahram, unbeaten in five races and awarded top weight in the Free handicap would have easily beaten Windsor Lad, fifth and fourth in his first two races and the winner of a minor stakes race on his only other appearance!

The evidence of the form book suggests that Bahram had more speed than Windsor Lad both as a juvenile and as a three-year-old, certainly in the early part of the season. Therefore as Bahram easily stayed twelve furlongs, what evidence is there that Windsor Lad would not have been out-speeded by Bahram in a Derby had they been able to meet? Or to put it another way; what evidence is there that Windsor Lad would have been able to beat Bahram in either the Derby or St Leger?

In conclusion "Warren Hill" asserts that Hairan will prove a stouter stayer than Bahram in the St Leger but feels that, if Bobsleigh can't be produced fit and well at Doncaster, neither will cope with Field Trial. The inference is that a fit and well Bobsleigh would, of course, win the St Leger!

*　　*　　*

Bahram had been nominated for the Eclipse Stakes at Sandown on 19th July. However, it seems clear that there was never any intention of running him. The problem may well have been quite simply that he would not have been in any fit state to run in such a race at that time. The Derby had clearly taken quite a lot out of him as his rather lacklustre performance at Ascot confirmed. For Butters to ready him for the Eclipse would have meant getting him back to peak fitness, for what would have been his third race in 44 days. For Bahram, a rather lightly-made colt, this could well have meant no attempt on the Triple Crown as Butters would have had just 54 days to get him ready for the final Classic after what would have been, win or lose, a tough race against Windsor Lad and Theft.

The plan therefore seemed to be the St. Leger in an effort to complete the Triple Crown which had not been achieved since Pommern,

Gay Crusader and Gainsborough had won all three Classics during the Great War and not since Rock Sand in peacetime in 1903. Bahram had a nomination for both the Sussex and Gordon Stakes at Goodwood at the end of July which would have been ideal in terms of timing. However, his work which consisted almost entirely of canters and half-speed work suggested that Butters was giving him an "easy" time. Bahram might even go to the St. Leger without a race since Ascot. Then it was muted that he would run at Derby just a week before the 'Leger in the Breeders St Leger, over twelve furlongs.

*   *   *

However, a more sinister element was about to be introduced: Newmarket had been ravaged by a virulent outbreak of coughing and many stables were virtually closed down. Fitzroy House had its fair share but Bahram had not been reported as one of the sufferers. The spell of exceptionally dry weather was providing perfect conditions for the infection to spread.

Bahram's work was stepped up and he worked at "useful pace" on the Limekilns in company on the 8th August, and then on 10th ten furlongs at "nice pace" on the peat moss gallop. This was followed on the 12th by a mile at "nice pace" on the Limekilns.

Then on the 13th August Bahram was diagnosed as suffering from a cough; it was a relatively mild attack and he did not have a temperature. Unfortunately the timing was not good: his work was just being stepped up and the St Leger was only a month away. There was little option but to ease off with his training and wait for the attack to subside. He was confined to walking and trotting and on the 20th was reported to be still coughing.

"Mankato" a veterinary surgeon wrote in the *Sporting Chronicle* about the coughing epidemic "The infection is as old as the domesticated horse…. There is no vaccine or serum which can give immunity to this coughing enzootic, but there are many which can do no little harm to the horse's system. The affection is air-borne, and both arises and spreads most rapidly after a period of drought. Pure air from dust is the best cure. Immunity after an attack is not permanent, and two and three-year-olds are more susceptible than older horses to the visitation of the microbe, which varies in strains in different outbreaks".

During this period Butters had to leave Bahram and go to Deauville to see the French-bred yearlings which the Aga Khan was sending to the sales there, and to suggest the appropriate reserves to be placed on the most promising. There was frequent telephoning between Deauville and Newmarket and the report from Fitzroy House was always the same: "Bahram's temperature is normal" Had it risen, as it has a tendency to do with coughing, his chances of running in the St Leger would probably have been considerably reduced. As a result his odds drifted out to 6–4.

He was able to resume work on 24th August and on a dull morning he went a mile with Tramaway and Hairan at "useful pace" on the Limekilns. That Bahram was able to work with these two suggested he was largely over his malaise. Clearly he would not be able to run at Derby so Butters would need all his skill to have him fit and ready to run and win a Classic in just 18 days.

On the 26th he went ten furlongs "steady" on the Limekilns with Tramaway and Hairan but also now with Theft. On the 28th on a fine morning he went twelve furlongs at a "good gallop" with Hairan and Tramaway. On 31st on a wet morning on racecourse side he went fourteen furlongs at "good pace" in company with Hairan, Conversion and Ben Sultan. This was likely to have been serious work; Conversion was a miler and set a good pace with Ben Sultan joining in as pacemaker after seven furlongs. Hairan accompanied Bahram on this gallop. However, as Bahram never did more than he was asked it would not have been easy for Butters to decide how much work to give him.

On Wednesday 4th September at Derby in the Breeders St Leger, Robin Goodfellow, who had finished second to Bahram in the Derby, warmed up for Doncaster the following week by conceding weight to his four opponents. This would have put him spot on following his second to Fairbairn in the Great Yorkshire Stakes six days earlier.

On the same day as the Breeders St Leger Bahram – who was ridden by Fox instead of his normal work rider – did his final piece of strong work in preparation. This was over fourteen furlongs at "good pace" in company with Hairan, Ben Sultan and Conversion. This gallop was a repetition of the previous Saturdays on racecourse side: Conversion led for seven furlongs with Ben Sultan joining in to lead for the second seven furlongs: just at the turn near the Cambridge Road at the top of a sharp rise. Hairan kept Bahram company for twelve furlongs before Bahram went steadily away from Hairan. Fox could not conceal his pleasure on dismounting. On 7th Bahram went thirteen furlongs at "good pace" with Tramaway.

On the same day the final acceptors for the St Leger were declared. Eleven had been left in but it transpired that two French entries had been left in by mistake! This error cost the owner: Comte de Rivaud £100 (5,300) in respect of each horse. So there were only really nine left in then! These were; Bahram, Buckleigh, Fairbairn, Field Trial, Flash Bye, Hairan, Plassy, Pry II and Solar Ray. Robin Goodfellow had been withdrawn.

On the 10th the day before the St Leger Bahram departed for Doncaster with Frank Butters endorsement: "Bahram has pleased me in his work since he left off coughing. I think he should win the St Leger if he keeps well". Butters observed dryly that most of his horses were affected by the cough and those that had not were so slow they could not catch anything!

On the night before the race little business took place at the final call-over; Bahram was backed at 400–700 (twice) and 80–150 (several times).

Bahram	4–7
Field Trial	17–2
Fairbairn	10–1
Solar Ray	100–6
Plassy	20–1
Buckleigh	25–1

The Aga Khan was not able to be at Doncaster as he was in Geneva attending the League of Nations Assembly as the principal delegate for India. He was no more than optimistic about his horses' chances in the St Leger; "If my horses are none the worse for coughing I hope they will run well. I am optimistic of Bahram winning the Triple Crown but fearing the worst".

The principal opposition would seem to be from Field Trial, whose trainer Joe Lawson would also saddle outsider Flash Bye, and who said "Both suffered during the coughing epidemic. Since then they have done well and are improving. If Bahram is at his best I fail to see how we can beat him".

Field Trial, like Bahram, had not run since Ascot when he won the King Edward VII Stakes beating Sir Malcolm McAlpine's Solar Ray (Solario – Trincomalee by Tetratema) who would also be in the St Leger field. Field Trial had of course already been beaten by Bahram in the Derby. Unfortunately Field Trial had been a major sufferer from the coughing outbreak and it must be conceded that he could not possibly have been fit enough for the St Leger.

Solar Ray was progressing well; after the Edward VII Stakes he had won the Sandringham Foal Plate at Sandown and the Hyperion Stakes at Hurst Park. Both Field Trial and Solar Ray could be expected to stay the St Leger trip.

Fairbairn had been very busy since easily eclipsed by Bahram in the Two Thousand Guineas and Derby; he had run in six races winning three times. After the Derby he had finished second in the Prince of Wales's Stakes at Ascot to Assignation – also behind Bahram in the Derby – then two days later he was second again behind Sea Bequest in the Waterford Stakes.

Sea Bequest had also finished behind Bahram in both the Two Thousand Guineas and Derby. Fairbairn's best performance came in winning the prestigious Princess of Wales's Stakes at Newmarket but he was subsequently beaten by Hairan in the Sussex Stakes, the mile over Goodwood's tight terrain almost certainly too short a trip for him. He then won the Great National Breeders Foal Plate at Redcar and the Great Yorkshire Stakes at the main York meeting; both over twelve furlongs. He looked certain to stay the Leger trip.

Plassy had made his seasonal debut at Ascot in the Edward VII Stakes finishing third. He then won his only other two races before the St Leger: the St George Stakes at Liverpool over thirteen furlongs and the Duke of York Plate over ten. He would stay the trip and was relatively fresh.

Buckleigh was very interesting; he had not raced since finishing sixth in the Two Thousand Guineas after which he was lame. He had been weak in his forelegs as a juvenile and a recurrence of this problem meant a period of rest. If he could be produced fit and well on 'Leger day he would be a threat as he was certain to stay the trip. One possible problem for Buckleigh was the going. Like many of Sansovino's progeny he was thought better with some give and his trainer, Captain Hogg, was anxious that the prolonged dry spell would mean firm conditions. Rain had begun to fall around the country but not in sufficient quantities to help Buckleigh's cause to any great extent.

The previously mentioned Flash Bye had finished third on his seasonal debut in the Newmarket Stakes behind Bobsleigh before winning the Gold Vase at Ascot over two miles. He was unplaced in the Princess of Wales's Stakes then finished second in the Gratwicke (Produce) Stakes at Goodwood. Only Pry II can be said to have no chance whatsoever; he had been well beaten in the Derby and won just one of his fourteen races that year and nothing he ever did suggested he should be in the race.

"Warren Hill" of *The Sporting Life* (Willie Standring) seemed to be accepting that Bahram would win the St Leger; his letter the day before the big race was headed "Bahram, fit and well, will remain unbeaten". After noting that the coughing epidemic is "gradually losing its grip" helped by rain the previous night settling the dust.

Of Bahram he wrote "In the case of a light-actioned horse like Bahram, the matter of surface conditions, firm or easy, is of less consequence than was the break in his training time-table which occurred over a fortnight ago, for he has quite an easy gait when extended. It is his indolence which inspires a thought that he keeps something up his sleeve and that he could have won the Derby and again at Ascot more easily but for indulging this lazy humour. He has been just the same on the gallops and I must say that I like his type".

Even before the race there was drama; Bahram's jockey Freddie Fox suffered a heavy fall from his mount Sheldrake, who slipped and fell at the entrance to the straight in the Strand Selling Stakes. Fox had ridden Mahmoud to victory in the Champagne Stakes just half an hour before. He was taken to hospital with suspected broken ribs, some neck damage and concussion. It transpired that he had fractured his skull. Charlie Smirke, who would have ridden the Aka Khan's second string Hairan, was confirmed as Bahram's replacement jockey after Aly Khan had contacted the Aga.

On the eve of the race Hairan was withdrawn; it is not clear why this decision was taken; was it because no satisfactory jockey could be found or was it that the evidence of his gallops with Bahram seemed to confirm that he would not stay the extended fourteen furlongs. On balance it was most likely that as Smirke, who was to ride Hairan, and had been switched to Bahram, meant that no suitable jockey was available.

The Sporting Life on St Leger day spoke of a "general optimism" that Bahram would prevail and become the first horse to complete the Triple Crown for thirty-two years. It continued "...but I find a few good judges inclined to oppose him on the grounds that the time since he fell a victim to coughing has been all too short for his trainer to deliver him to post fully wound up".

This view was understandable; Frank Butters had had only three weeks to complete Bahram's preparation. However, Bahram would have been close to full fitness before he began coughing and he was only held up for a short while. Bahram had also been held up prior to the Two Thousand Guineas and Butters had presented him on the day trained to perfection. Also it should not be forgotten that Bahram was a lightly-made sort and would not take all that much work to regain any fitness he may have lost.

Losing Fox was unfortunate enough but there was a further alarm less than an hour before the race. When Bahram came out of his box in the stable-yard near the racecourse to walk to the paddock there seemed to be something seriously amiss with him. "His coat was standing up and he looked like a hedgehog" said Frank Butters, "I was very worried for a moment but by the time Bahram had reached the paddock he was all right again. He always felt the cold very much, and his staring coat must have been caused by coming out of a stuffy box into the cool air".

The weather was fine, the course described as "in splendid condition" and the "crowd assembled on the Town Moor as huge as usual" by starting time.

Meyrick Good noted as Bahram cantered to post that "Although his ribs were visible as he cantered to post no one could suggest that he was light or too finely drawn. I should say that the colt was appreciably heavier than on Derby day."

The St Leger in 1935 was worth about 40% more than today. However, the executive at Doncaster can be praised for maintaining, as far as possible, the value of this wonderful race in the face of some asinine views that races further than ten furlongs are an anachronism and that the St Leger should be run at that distance.

The field of eight was the smallest since 1909 when seven lined up and Bayardo won very easily; there were eight in 1911 when Prince Palatine was successful.

Doncaster; Wednesday 11th September, Going; good.
St Leger Stakes of £100 each £50 if declared by Sept 3 £25 if dec Apr 16 1935 or £5 if dec by July 3 1934 with £4,000 added; breeder of winner recd £500 out of the stakes owner of second recd 10% and of the third 5% of the whole stakes; for three-year-olds entire colts and fillies colts 9st fillies 8st 11lbSt Leger course of 1mile six furlongs and 132 yards(277 entrants viz. 11 at £100 67 at £50 95 at £25 104 at £5--- – £9,543) (505,779)

1	Bahram	9st	C. Smirke	138+
2	Solar Ray	9st	J. Sirett	124
3	Buckleigh	9st	H. Wragg	118
4	Plassy	9st	R. Perryman	112
5	Fairbairn	9st	G. Richards	
6	Field Trial	9st	R.Dick	
7	Pry II	9st	T. Weston	
8	Flash Bye	9st	R. Jones	

Starting prices; 4/11 Bahram, 9/1 Field Trial, 10/1 Fairbairn, 100/6 Plassy and Solar Ray, 25/1 Buckleigh, 33/1 Flash Bye, 100/1 Pry II

Won by 5 lengths; 3 lengths between second and third, unofficially the distance between third and fourth was 3 lengths.

Time; 3 min 1.80 sec (fast by 4.20)

Race analysis: – Flash Bye quickly led from a good start, followed by Pry II, Fairbairn, Bahram, Solar Ray and Buckleigh with Plassy the whipper-in. After about half a mile had been covered Flash Bye was attended by Field Trial with Bahram next. Flash Bye still led from Field Trial into the straight where Bahram was third in front of Fairbairn, Solar Ray and Buckleigh. Bahram was given his head about a quarter of a mile from the post and immediately went to the front with Field Trial Fairbairn and Solar Ray the most prominent of the others. Field Trial gradually weakened from the distance where Solar Ray came up on the outside and Buckleigh also improved but neither had any chance with Bahram who forged ahead and won in great style.

The official distances were five lengths and three lengths; however, by viewing archive film and a still photograph of the finish it can be clearly seen that the distance between first and second was at least two and almost three times the distance between second and third. Bahram could therefore be given a winning distance of about seven or eight lengths. The photograph of the finish shows clearly that the distance was at least eight lengths. His rating in the race reflects this and also the time of the race. Also in calculating Bahram's rating the ability of Solar Ray is taken into account; if Bahram had not run Solar Ray would have been considered a moderate or below average St Leger winner for that period, although very close to the average in recent years. This view is based on the time he would have recorded in relation to other times over the meeting. Solar Ray's rating is about 3–5 pounds below what an average St Leger winner would have recorded in the race at that time.

If all seven races of ten furlongs and up over the four days of the meeting are used as a guide Bahram's time for the St Leger is the only one faster than the standard times used for this exercise. One time; for the Doncaster Cup is unfortunately probably wrong, as it is given as 3 min. 46.60 sec. which would be almost two seconds faster than the record today!

Bahram had become only the second undefeated Triple Crown winner equaling the feat of the great Ormonde. *The Sporting Chronicle* noted "there were remarkable scenes of enthusiasm when it was seen that Bahram had won. A dense throng of people rushed to the paddock to welcome him". He was led by Aly Khan in the absence of the Aga.

There was "a long delay" to the start but the eight starters got away together. Bahram was well placed throughout the early stages of the race and after a brief struggle with Field Trial he was ahead over two furlongs from the finish. Ridden only with "hands and heels" until Smirke, looking behind, noticed Solar Ray making ground. Smirke had only to shake the reins for Bahram to draw away and win by "the longest five lengths I ever saw. It would not have surprised me in the least if the judge had given the distance as ten lengths, so easily did he win" according to R. C. Lyle. Buckleigh who at one stage looked to be tailing off ran on the take third. Field Trial, doubtless exhausted by his efforts to keep pace with Bahram, faded in the straight.

The Aga was of course detained at Geneva as the representative of India at the meeting of the League of Nations dealing with the Italo-Abyssinia dispute. He was deeply involved in proceedings when he was called to the telephone and told about Bahram's win; "It is the horse of the century!" he exclaimed jubilantly. Frank Butters send him a telegram saying simply "Won easily by five lengths Butters".

In the absence of his father Aly led Bahram in but did not look happy and carefree. Any joy he may have felt was overshadowed by gloom that his escapades with Joan Guinness were about to cause a scandal and that news of this would shortly reach the Aga. When knowledge of the Guinness's divorce, in which Aly had been named and against whom costs had been awarded, the Aga was angry. He was only slightly mollified when Aly told him he and Joan Guinness would marry as soon as possible.

Meyrick Good wrote the following in *The Sporting Life* the following day: "Hard held as he passed the post five lengths ahead of his nearest rival Bahram's St Leger victory was the easiest of his distinguished career…there were scenes of great enthusiasm as Prince Aly Khan led Bahram to the unsaddling enclosure, and congratulations were showered upon Frank Butters and Charlie Smirke".

The first person to grasp Frank Butters by the hand was Dick Dawson.

Butters speaking about Bahram said "The point about him is that we have never got to the bottom of him. Whenever he has run he has always "kept a little bit up his sleeve". Look at him today; he stayed with the others long enough to make a race of it then came away as he liked.

Charlie Smirke, who rode Bahram "with supreme confidence throughout" said "He could have won with 12 st. on his back and two men on his back". Freddie Fox listened to the race in a Doncaster nursing home; it would be a few days before he could be sent by air back to his home in Berkshire. The Aga gave £1,000 (53,000) to both Smirke and Fox which was some compensation for the latter deprived of a "once-in-a-lifetime" opportunity.

Jackie Sirett, who finished second on Solar Ray, said "When Bahram went to the front in the straight I followed him, but my mount simply could not make any impression on him".

The disappointment was Field Trial who seemed not to stay and performed well below his Ascot form.

Not every observer was exactly overwhelmed by Bahram's success. "Hotspur" in *The Daily Telegraph* wrote about the race (there was) "never a thrill, never a moment of suspense. Everything worked like a piece of machinery". "Bouverie" in the *Daily Mirror* was equally underwhelmed "Well, Bahram is the first triple-crowned hero since Rock Sand. The Aga Khan's colt retires from racing to join the few great horses that went through their racing careers unbeaten. All that and yet it was one of the tamest St Leger days I can remember.... Never have I seen Tattersalls so sedate before a big race, and the preliminaries in the paddock and the parade left the feeling that it was all merely a preliminary to a Bahram canter. And that is all that it proved to be".

These are splendid examples of two racing hacks unimpressed, not by Bahram, but by the day not providing enough for them to write about! Generally speaking sports journalists and commentators like something of a sensationalist nature to occur rather than a predictable event, even if perfection is taking place in front of them. Bahram was far and away the best three-year-old and barring accidents would win in a canter; when it happened they had little to fill their column inches, if praising one of the greatest thoroughbreds ever to race, did not appeal to them.

The Aga Khan announced towards the end of September that Bahram would run in the Champion Stakes in order that he could see his champion race one more time before retirement. Although Bahram was reported as working as if in preparation for another race, probably to no one's surprise nothing came of this.

With that the career of a great racehorse came to its conclusion. In total it lasted just fourteen months from start to finish and consisted of nine races all won either comfortably or easily with Bahram never needing to call upon his reserves to prevail. How much would he have found if asked? Is it possible he was simply a "bridle" horse, albeit a high class one? Freddie Fox wrote later that it had been his intention to ask Bahram for his effort coming into the straight. Fox was certain that Bahram was a stayer and thought he might win by a distance! He kept this plan to himself of course as Butters would almost certainly have forbidden Fox from doing any such thing.

That Fox was denied the opportunity to set him alight four furlongs from the finish at Doncaster almost certainly deprived racing of spectacular sight. Could it have rivalled the immortal Secretariat's performance in the Belmont? These questions can of course never be answered.

Despite his total lack of sentimentality if he had known he would never breed another horse nearly as good as Bahram would the Aga have let him race as a four-year-old? The question is asked because in modern times owners of outstanding horses have raced them after their second season. Khalid Abdulla raced Frankel as a four-year-old possibly because he knew that as he approached his eightieth birthday it was unlikely he would ever breed another as good and wanted to appreciate him. Coolmore; not exactly noted for sentimentality, have made it known that history is important and by running Camelot in the St Leger endeavoured to be part of it. In addition they kept him in training as a four-year-old when as a Two Thousand Guineas and Derby winner they could easily have retired him to stud. Sadly Camelot, a handsome, most imposing, correct and impressive looking colt, failed to show his form as a four-year-old.

Had Bahram raced as a four-year-old there would have been the prospect of one of the all-time great races: the meeting of two Triple Crown winners from either side of the Atlantic meeting in the Ascot Gold Cup of 1936. Omaha winner of the North American Triple Crown: Derby, Preakness and Belmont of 1935 travelled to England where he was beaten in the Gold Cup in a pulsating finish by the filly Quashed. How much better would the race have been if Bahram had been there too!

Was the form of the St Leger upheld afterwards? Solar Ray was beaten at odds of 1–2 in the Great Foal Stakes at Newmarket; he was not even in the first three. Buckleigh won the Newmarket St Leger and was then second in the Champion Stakes to the decent four-year-old Wychwood Abbot. Plassy paid the best complement to Bahram by winning the Jockey Club Stakes over two miles. The race was worth £4,287 (225,000) to the winner.

Interestingly Robin Goodfellow second in the Derby ran a total of ten times in 1935. He never met Bahram again after the Derby and his form was somewhat inconsistent. However, he won three races and was second also three times. His best form, apart from his second in the Derby of course, was a second in the Liverpool St Leger when he conceded nineteen pounds to the winner Santorin and the third Portfolio. He also conceded seven pounds to the fourth Fairhaven. A *Timeform* rating of 127 does not flatter Robin Goodfellow at his best; however, it would not be wise to assume he could always run to it!

The following ratings are calculated in the same manner as those for 1934. They are on the *Timeform* scale with reference to the three-year-old handicap published on the 10th October 1935.

Deciding where to place the level of ratings for the three-year-olds of 1935 was no easy matter. There were several very useful horses all capable of form of a decent standard. The problem was their lack of consistency, together with the effects of the cough which affected many horses during the summer.

However, there are just enough lines of form; some against older horses, to settle on some meaningful ratings. There can be little doubt that, Bahram and Theft apart, they were no better than average. There have of course been worse years and, while this can only ever be a matter of opinion, from 1900 until 1935 the following year's three-year-olds were probably worse than those in 1935: – 1913, 1919, 1924, 1931 and 1932. In some other years they were no better or worse. The simple truth is that there are very few vintage years and this was a time of great horses; apart from Bahram, Hyperion, Windsor Lad and Blue Peter were also foaled during the 1930's.

Bahram	c	140+
Theft	c	131
Field Trial	c	128
Robin Goodfellow	c	127
Fair Trial	c	126
Plassy	c	125
Bobsleigh	c	124
Solar Ray	c	124
Buckleigh	c	123
Sea Bequest	c	123
Mesa	f	123
Hairan	c	122
Fairbairn	c	122
Quashed	f	122
Ankaret	f	120
Assignation	c	120
Coppelia	f	120
Fairhaven	c	117
Pampas Grass	c	117

Bahram retired to Egerton House Stud, Newmarket at a fee of 500 guineas (£28,000), making him the most expensive stallion in the British Isles, alongside Solario and Tetratema, and 100 guineas (£5,400) more than successful sires such as Fairway, Gainsborough and Hyperion. This attracted some opprobrium from Lord Derby who asserted that no stallion should stand for more than 400 guineas.

Egerton House Stud was leased to the Aga Khan, and the following year Bahram was joined by Mahmoud. Originally built in the early 1890's by Lord Ellesmere as a training establishment for Richard Marsh, Egerton House had been home for the racing careers of Derby winners Persimmon, Diamond Jubilee and Minoru.

18 Bahram the Great

Veni, vidi, vici.

Julius Caesar.

*   *   *

Bahram won the Triple Crown; something achieved fourteen times from 1853 until 1935 but only once since. This is not because only one horse has been capable. No, far from it, plenty have had the opportunity but breeding fashion is against potential stallions running in the final Classic.

Winning the Triple Crown is astonishingly difficult; to achieve this feat a horse must come to hand early in the season, be fit and possess enough high-class pace to win at the beginning of May over the Rowley mile. Have the adaptability, athleticism and stamina to add to his speed and win at Epsom, probably the most difficult terrain anywhere in the world that a thoroughbred is required to perform on. Finally, after a long season early in September, on one of the fairest course in Britain, he must then demonstrate the capacity to retain his form and gallop the relentless one mile six furlongs and 132 yards of the St Leger, often needing to beat fresher horses, whose principal attribute is stamina, and may have been reserved specifically for the final Classic. Surely it is true to say of any horse able to win all three of these races; *"sic itur ad astra!"* This is the path to immortality!

A Triple Crown winner! What breeder would not want to send his best mares to such an animal? Surely a colt able to perform such a feat would be the most valuable of stallions! Certainly such a horse should be valued well above horses whose principal asset is stampeding for five or six furlongs. Sadly in this modern world of commercial speed-obsessed breeding there are plenty. Quality stamina in the modern thoroughbred is becoming rarer as commercial breeders gravitate, like so many sheep crowding into the corner of a field, to breeding from sprinter/milers. For an example look no further than the current must breed-to stallion: Dark Angel; a horse that was a pure sprinter and did not even race at three being retired sound after his two-year-old career!

It is not that horses that can show their best form over middle distances are not being bred; they are, except in much smaller numbers. Increasingly the best mares, Coolmore, Juddmonte Farms, Ballymacoll, Aga Khan Studs and one or two others excepted, are being bred to sprinter/miler stallions because that is where it is believed the "commercial" advantage lies. Has no such breeder noticed the decline in North American racing?

It is no surprise that in recent years the Derby has been dominated by horses bred, and sometimes also owned, by those breeders that arrange matings with the aim of producing quality stayers. The pattern was broken in 2015 when Golden Horn triumphed for owner-breeder Anthony Oppenheimer. However, by this own admission Oppenheimer was trying to breed a miler and Golden Horn was not even entered for the Derby! When it was clear that he stayed ten and a half furlongs well enough he was supplemented against a considerable weight of opinion that he would not stay twelve furlongs.

However, contrary to his breeding Golden Horn easily stayed the distance and can be rated an above-average Derby winner. Golden Horn had been led out unsold when offered at the yearling sales; not exactly a triumph for those charged with buying untried bloodstock! Or could it be that, despite siring Sea The Stars, Golden Horn's sire: Cape Cross is no longer considered fashionable! Certainly the number of mares he covered last year; 114, is way down on his peak of 173 in 2010. Depressingly it is almost certain that breeders sending mares to Golden Horn at stud will be trying to breed horses that do not stay beyond 8–10 furlongs.

The obsession with speed in North America means that over 50% of races are sprints: over five, six and seven furlongs, and less than 1% of races at ten furlongs and over. The Belmont Stakes; the third leg of the American Triple Crown, is these days usually a somewhat pathetic spectacle with most of the runners unable to stay twelve furlongs and virtually at a standstill two furlongs from the finish. The winner usually takes up to thirty seconds to cover the last two furlongs.

In 2015 American Pharoah won the Triple Crown, however, in the Belmont he was able to set easy fractions and was unchallenged! Hardly a test of stamina! North America hailed their first Triple Crown winner for 37 years and in the hysteria the uncompetitive nature of the final leg was almost unnoticed.

Do we really want racing in Britain to be an unremitting diet of sprinting and mile races in future, with only one paced plodders running at twelve furlongs and up? Only drastic action now will stop the inevitable slide towards this.

The situation is in steady and remorseless decline: in 2012 a leading bloodstock advisor actually stated that the most important race in Britain now, from a breeder's point of view, was the Two Thousand Guineas! Extraordinary; it can only be hoped that his influence is not very extensive! It could have been worse: he might have nominated the July Cup for that exalted position. It is bordering on criminal behaviour that "respected" figures in thoroughbred breeding are allowed to continue this drift away from quality stamina. Modern commercial breeders may well be guilty of contributing to reducing future racing to an orgy consisting mainly of mediocre 6–8 furlong racing that could be in danger of killing high class stamina. History will not be kind to such thinking.

Encouragement must be given to breeders to produce quality stayers. Currently middle-distance horses rated by *Timeform* at 115–125 are often sold to Australia for the Melbourne Cup or Hong Kong because owners of such horses can sell them for far more than could ever expect to win in prize money in Britain. These horses have the ability to run in some European Group 1 races, but would normally be aimed at Group 2 & 3 races which are worth between £60,000 and £125,000 to the winner, so a horse would need to win at least six of these to come anywhere near the amount they could be sold for. As a consequence middle-distance races in Britain and Europe outside Group 1 are weakened. This leads to a spiral of decline: the level of the ratings for the first four to finish gradually reduces and the races concerned become in danger of being downgraded. This drain of Britain's Pattern quality stayers must be arrested.

What can be done? Well recently a welcome move to encourage the breeding of stayers has been made. However, more must be done: racecourses should, as far as is possible under modern legislation, be compelled to stage races at twelve furlongs and up as part of the levy payment. It is already noticeable that if a course stages a valuable handicap over twelve furlongs for three-year-olds officially rated 90 to 100, particularly during the first half of the turf season, they are rewarded with fields of 4 or 5 whereas a race over six, seven or eight furlongs would guarantee a field of a dozen at least. The Derby trials are always seemingly under pressure because of small fields; even when the winner of such a race then wins at Group/Grade 1 level! In addition prize money for Group 2 & 3 races over twelve furlongs and up must be increased.

Since Bahram won the Triple Crown in 1935 eight horses have won the Two Thousand Guineas and Derby; only one: Nijinsky completed the Triple Crown. Of the other seven Blue Peter would probably have done so in 1939 had the War not caused the cancellation of the St Leger. Nimbus only just stayed twelve furlongs and had not been entered for the St Leger. Crepello and Royal Palace would also most likely have prevailed, but injury prevented both from running in the St Leger. Sir Ivor, although entered for the St. Leger, did not make the attempt and almost certainly lacked the stamina to succeed.

The Coolmore team made a brave attempt in 2012 when the Aidan O'Brien trained Camelot failed to win the Triple Crown, probably because he had trained off after a brutally hard race in bottomless ground when winning the Irish Derby. The disappointment was intense and it can only be hoped that it will not deter those with more sense of history than "commercial interests" from attempting the feat in future.

Coolmore stud have done more than most to preserve quality stamina in the modern thoroughbred. Firstly with Sadler's Wells, then the late lamented Montjeu, and currently with the great Galileo. Coolmore have bred horses capable of winning big races over twelve furlongs but were not devoid of the necessary speed which is essential to win at the top level over any distance.

An eventual replacement for Galileo is becoming a matter of urgency and it is hoped that Camelot and Australia will eventually fill the inevitable void at Coolmore. Galileo's best son: Frankel, standing under the Juddmonte banner, will need to be given the opportunity to cover mares with quality middle distance blood if he is to sire a Derby winner. It can only be hoped that Coolmore will produce many more horses capable of attempting to win the Triple Crown and that they will revive a great tradition by succeeding soon. It is also encouraging that the 2009 Derby winner: Sea The Stars is producing stock that possesses quality stamina and he was responsible for the 2016 winner: Harzand. It can only be hoped that he continues to receive good support. The sport will be all the better for it.

To return to horses that won both the Two Thousand Guineas and Derby and should have run in the St Leger both Nashwan and See The Stars could and should have done so. Winning the St Leger would have been a tremendous boost for racing; and the reputation of neither horse would have suffered not one jot as both had already displayed high-class speed by winning the Two Thousand Guineas. It is inconceivable that any breeder, even those whose obsession is sprinter/miler speed, would have decided that they would not send their mare to either horse just because it had run in the St Leger.

A rather stupid legend has built up that running in the St Leger somehow cost Nijinsky victory in the Arc de Triomphe. What is seemingly overlooked is that Nijinsky was fortunate to be racing at all after the King George at Ascot in July; he suffered an attack of ringworm which would have kept a lesser horse out of the St Leger and racing for that year. He had seemed in good health before the St Leger but returned 29 pounds (just over 13 kilos) lighter after the race. This was not the St Leger's fault; it was the after effects of ringworm; Nijinsky should have been retired for the season after the 'Leger, and kept in training as a four-year-old with the 'Arc as his principle target. However, as the decision to retire him had already been taken it was the 'Arc that year or not at all. The breeders got their hands on Nijinsky a year too soon and racing suffered as did Nijinsky's reputation as a racehorse.

Even after Nijinsky's debilitating illness and St Leger all might still have been well if Lester Piggott had done as Vincent O'Brien told him and not held him up as far back as he did. Nijinsky's heroic effort to extract Piggott from a hole of his own making should not be considered as a failure but on a par with many winning performances. Those who would defend Piggott's ride should ask themselves if it was sensible to have Nijinsky in the last four half a mile from the finish. When he began his run he was ten lengths behind the winner and initially denied a clear run. Had he been mid division Nijinsky, even well below par as he was, would surely have won.

In addition it is also seemingly forgotten that Alleged won the first of his two 'Arcs after a hard race in the St Leger, where he was outstayed by the Queen's Dunfermline. Piggott was not at his best and made the mistake of tracking/setting a brisk pace and then pressing on only to be passed inside the final furlong as Alleged's stamina drained away. Alleged was a great horse by any standards and a much better horse than Dunfermline but not with a fast pace over Doncaster's stiff fourteen furlongs. However, despite Piggott asking for everything from Alleged, the race did not seem to do him any harm and he was able to win the 'Arc convincingly; beating Dunfermline, on whom Carson did not shine; he held her up in a moderately run race. Alleged has the distinction of being probably the best horse to finish runner-up in the St Leger since the beginning of the twentieth century; according to *Timeform* he ran to a mark of 133, which would have won the vast majority of renewals since that time. The third horse was a further ten lengths behind.

It is reasonable to assume that with average luck, since Bahram, there could have been not one Triple Crown winner, but five. The sport would have benefitted enormously from the anticipation that would have built up as the St Leger approached. That a silly and short sighted view should dictate the course of history is galling enough; but that a horse's stud value should be at risk through such views is preposterous.

*   *   *

Winning the Triple Crown, although considered a major achievement and, as such, qualifies a horse for a place alongside the greats in the sports history, it did not endear Bahram to everyone. Unfortunately there were plenty of observers who found it difficult to get excited over Bahram; his wins were efficient rather than impressive or spectacular. By the time of the St Leger most thought he had only to turn up and consent to run round the track to win. Unfortunately, due to the injury to Freddie Fox, Bahram, although ridden out, won easily enough and confirmed those expectations.

In addition the horses he beat in the Derby and St Leger were considered undistinguished by Classic standards; in short Bahram's Triple Crown lacked glamour. He never looked in danger of defeat so he engendered very little excitement and, in the absence of Bobsleigh, most observers thought there was nothing for him to beat. However, it should not be forgotten that Frank Butters who trained Fairway and Mahmoud, considered Bahram the best horse he ever trained. Bahram was his own worst enemy: he was said to be indolent, an indolence which sprang from "complete self-confidence". Whatever he had been asked to do both in training and on the racecourse Bahram accomplished with the minimum of fuss. In these circumstances he was bound to feel that he would always be able to prevail over any other horse that tried to run faster than him.

Bahram's demeanour could be extraordinary: though easy-going and disinclined to exert himself unduly, he was clearly happy to be in the public gaze. He formed the habit, when under scrutiny, of leaning against the wall of a stable in what seemed a self-satisfied manner with his front legs crossed and looking around him in a supercilious manner. A cravat and smoking jacket, glass of champagne and a cigar would have completed the picture!

Freddie Fox, who had ridden him in most of his races, considered him the laziest horse he ever rode. Fox wrote that Bahram was a "perfect gentleman, a great racehorse; the best he had ever seen, without a doubt, but with the manners of a ladies hack". Fox continued "In his two-year-old days he was a little inclined to be over-anxious at the gallops end, or at the starting gate, yet as soon as he jumped off was as placid as any old hunter, and any kid could have ridden him in his races".

*   *   *

Were the horses beaten by Bahram in 1935 really so moderate? The feeling persists that, because Bobsleigh was unable to run in the Derby and St Leger, and, as so many believed fervently that he was Bahram's superior, these individuals were never going to be impressed with Bahram beating "second raters" and winning races they were convinced Bobsleigh would have won if only he could have been prepared for them. However, even when he was able to run after a break in a match against Alcazar in the Limekiln Stakes at Newmarket at the end of October, he was beaten at odds on.

Alcazar was a four-year-old who raced nine times that year winning three times – including the match with Bobsleigh. He had some good form: second to Ascot Gold Cup winner Quashed in the eighteen furlongs Jockey Club Cup at Newmarket the day after he beat Bobsleigh. Alcazar was third in the Champion Stakes behind the four-year-old Wychwood Abbot (The Black Abbott – Sweet Hainault by Hainault) and the three-year-old Buckleigh who had been behind Bahram in both the Two Thousand Guineas and St Leger. However, on form Alcazar should not have beaten Bobsleigh and certainly not so easily that he could race the following day and win again!

It is not difficult to imagine the excitement that would have prevailed in 1935 had Bobsleigh been as good as his admirers thought and he and Bahram had engaged in three epic battles for the Triple Crown races. In North America in 1978 this was exactly the scenario for their Triple Crown: Kentucky Derby, Preakness and Belmont. The two protagonists were Affirmed (Exclusive Native – Won't Tell by Crafty Admiral), a fairly moderately bred sort by Classic standards, and the regally-bred Alydar (Raise a Native – Sweet Tooth by On-and-On). They had met as juveniles and there was not much between them. In the Kentucky Derby Affirmed won by 1½ lengths. There followed two titanic struggles for the Preakness and Belmont where the distances were a neck and a head. In both races they were locked together in pulsating stretch runs that sent the ecstatic racegoers into raptures. Both races were won by Affirmed and it was he that was a Triple Crown winner, had there been no Affirmed then Alydar would have been lauded as one. Incredibly fate had thrown up two great horses in one year; an unprecedented event that has so far never been repeated, although Sunday Silence (Halo – Wishing Well by Understanding) and Easy Goer (Alydar – Relaxing by Buckpasser) came close in 1989.

However, Bobsleigh, despite his magnificent conformation was unable to stay sound for his supporters and Bahram was left on his own to dominate all that could be mustered against him. Bahram's stable companion Theft, who was easily beaten three times by Bahram, and was never able to get him off the bit, had excellent form. In the Two Thousand Guineas Theft produced a performance that would have won plenty of other renewals. Although his jockey: Harry Wragg, felt he had plenty of stamina, he seemed not to fully stay in the Derby, but won the Greenham Stakes and was second to the great Windsor Lad in the Eclipse beaten under a length.

Although Windsor Lad finished the race lame, he was still able to run on. In addition Theft won the Jersey Stakes at Ascot. His form was close to many three-year-olds that were champion of their year. As a four-year-old Theft ran only at ten and – once – at twelve furlongs; he won the Rosebery Handicap giving at least a stone or more to all his rivals but in the Coronation Cup he "found nil" when asked for his effort according to *Raceform*. The evidence suggests that he was high-class at distances from 7–10 furlongs but did not really stay twelve.

Field Trial's form was not far below that of Theft but it has to be conceded that after that most of the Classic generation were no better than average. But is it not often the case that each Classic generation is condemned as mediocre? The inescapable truth is that no horse was able to trouble Bahram and his dominance was total.

In 1962 after a series of average or moderate Classic winners Nesbit Waddington wrote an article claiming high virtue for the thoroughbred in 1962 "The speed of the average racehorse today is much superior to that of the average racehorse of fifty years ago and it is much more difficult to produce a racehorse which towers over its contemporaries".

This of course was rubbish; there is no evidence which suggests that the thoroughbred has progressed much, if at all, since the beginning of the Twentieth Century. No less a figure than Peter Burrell, director of the National Stud asserted that the thoroughbred had reached the highest level attainable before the Great War, and that further significant improvement was unlikely.

Waddington, who seemed to have forgotten Ribot and Crepello, was to be proved wrong in dramatic fashion as within ten years Sea Bird, Vaguely Noble, Nijinsky, Brigadier General and Mill Reef all emerged to dominate their contemporaries. There followed a period of over thirty years with only three great horses emerging: Shergar, Dancing Brave and Dubai Millennium. Then after a short while within the space of five years Zarkava, Sea The Stars and Frankel appeared. Apart from Sea The Stars's debut these three horses ran a total of thirty-five times unbeaten and totally dominated their contemporaries. There will always be periods when no horse is able to dominate but that does not indicate that the average thoroughbred has improved.

*   *   *

Bahram would seem to have been very intelligent; again according to Fox who wrote; "His intelligence was way above the average, and he soon got over his anxiety to be off, and he was helped a good deal in this by his trainer, Mr. Frank Butters, having me out to ride him cantering as well as in his fast work". Fox went on to explain "A jockey usually rides a horse in his fast work only, and he (the horse) soon learns to associate the two and become more liable to get "on his toes" on that account when his usual jockey gets up. Horses have a very retentive memory, especially one with a high degree of intelligence, and they never forget a road or a place with which they have become acquainted".

Fox said Bahram only ran one race which defied understanding. At Ascot as a three-year-old he ran in the St. James's Palace Stakes.

Bahram was the 1–8 favourite and expected to canter in. However, much to his surprise, Fox found it necessary, for the only time in his career, to give Bahram a smack with the whip. Bahram responded and won easily; however, Fox felt through the race that Bahram was disinclined to exert himself. He was sure the horse had not recovered from his nerve-racking Derby experience, where he sweated and was on edge in the parade ring.

It was particularly unfortunate that Fox was unable to ride Bahram in the St Leger. In his final gallop before the race Bahram showed Fox something that the jockey had always believed: that he was a true out-and-out natural stayer. Bahram had always been ridden for speed: waited with until inside the final furlong before out-speeding the opposition. Fox made up his mind to show the world exactly what sort of horse Bahram was by asking him for his effort some way from home and see how far he finished in front of the field. He did not even tell Frank Butters as he feared Butters would forbid him to do any such thing! Fox believed that if he could have let Bahram go about five furlongs from home he would have finished a furlong in front by the line! Charlie Smirke could not have been expected to ride Bahram in such a manner and, of course, he was ridden for speed. Again the fates denied an opportunity to find out more about just how good Bahram really was. To allow one's mind to wander and imagination to take flight again for a moment, with Fox in the plate is it possible that Bahram could have raced down Doncaster's long straight alone in a manner similar to Secretariat in the Belmont Stakes 38 years later?

Smirke, whose judgment on various matters was not always reliable; he had a lifelong "chip on his shoulder", and was not overly impressed with Bahram. In his autobiography he stated that Bahram did not give him the same feel as Windsor Lad when the former was winning the St Leger. The famous hands must have been suffering an off day as Bahram returned an almost identical time to Windsor Lad in their respective 'Legers and was being eased before the finish and could hardly have won more easily.

*   *   *

In a previous book on *Bayardo* some criteria were established for a horse to be considered great. These are shown below:-

1. Undoubted superiority at age two, three and preferably four.
2. Ability to show dominance at a variety of distances.
3. Able to beat older horses as a three-year-old and three-year-olds as a four-year-old.
4. Able to overcome difficulties and still prevail.
5. Able to act on any going.
6. Able to act on a variety of courses.
7. Have the necessary temperament to show their best form in big races.
8. Able to reproduce a top-level of form regularly over a period of time.
9. To lose very few races.

Of the nine Bahram can only satisfy 2, 5, 6, 7, 8, 9; He was not given the opportunity to achieve number 3 and with regard to number 4, apart from the Derby, he never really got into any difficulties.

1. He was undoubtedly superior to his contemporaries at age two and three. However, he did not race at age four.
2. He won nine races; five of which are Group 1 today and one that is Group 2 over distances from five to fourteen furlongs.
3. He never met an older horse.
4. Apart from the Derby, when Harry Wragg let him through, he almost never faced any difficulties.
5. As a juvenile he raced only on good, firm or hard going. As a three-year-old he raced three times on good and once on soft going.
6. He raced on seven different courses.
7. He won all his races and never displayed signs of temperament. He did sweat up and became edgy but this was only anticipation.
8. At two he won five races from July until October and at three he won from May until September.

9. He was never beaten.

How does Bahram compare with other great horses since the beginning of the Twentieth Century? In *Bayardo* a list of the best horses since the beginning of the Twentieth Century was produced with ratings based on the *Timeform* scale. The list is reproduced here with the addition of Frankel and Treve, and the record of Goldikova brought up to date.

The following colts were capable of running to a *Timeform* rating of 138 or better. Horses marked * are generally considered to be great horses. Ratings marked + indicate that there is evidence to suggest the horse may have been capable of running to a higher rating than indicated.

Frankel*	133	143	147	7–10	14/14
Sea Bird*	129	145		7–12	7/8
Brigadier Gerard*	132	141	144	5–12	17/18
Ribot*	?	133	143	5–15	16/16
Bayardo*	131	140	142	5–20	22/25
Hyperion*	120	142	134	5–14	9/13
Tudor Minstrel*	133	142		5–8	8/10
Abernant*	133	136	142	5–7	14/17
Mill Reef*	133	141	141	5–12	12/14
Pharis	–	–	141+	12–15	3/3
Hurry On*	–	–	140+	8–20	6/6
Bahram*	127	140+		5–14	9/9
Vaguely Noble*	132	140		7–12	6/9
Nijinsky*	131	140+		6–14	11/13
Shergar*	122	140		8–12	6/8
Dancing Brave*	110	140		8–12	8/10
Dubai Millennium*	108	132	140	8–10	9/10
Sea The Stars*	109	140		7–12	8/9
Windsor Lad*	110	136	139	6–14	10–13
Brantome*	119+	139	134	5–20	12/14
Epinard	?	139	?	5–8	12/20
Pappa Fourway	114	139		5–6	12/15

Reference Point	132	139			8–14	7–10
Generous	115	139			6–20	8–10
Fairway*	124	134	138		5–18	12/15
Sardanapale	?	138			6–15	11/16
Coronach	126	138	138		5–14	10/14
Colorado	119	136	138		5–12	9/16
Nearco*	?	138+			5–15	14/14
Blue Peter*	122	138+			8–12	4/6
Dante*	130	138+			5–12	8/9
Pinza*	129	138			7–12	5/7
Alleged*	112	137	138		7–12	9/10
Roberto	127	138	131		6–12	7/14
Troy	122	138			7–12	8/11
Nashwan	106	138			7–12	6/7
Daylami	112	124	126	138	8–12	11/21

The following are the best fillies rated 133 and better. Note that seven of these raced at aged five.

Pretty Polly*	130	137	137	129	5–18	22/24
Sun Chariot*	114	137+			5–14	8/9
Allez France*	126	132	136	132	8–12	13/21
Sceptre*	110	136	136	130	6–13	13/24
Dahlia	?	132	135	128	5–13	15/47
Coronation	118	135	132		5–12	6/13
Pebbles	114	124	135		6–12	8/15
All Along	?	129	134	125	8–13	9/21
Godiva	118	134			5–12	6/8
Treve*	?	134	129	129	8–12	9/13
Zarkava*	117	133+			8–12	7/7
Goldikova	101+	129	133	133	7–9	17/27

The arguments for and against comparing horses of different generations are thoroughly covered in *Bayardo,* and it is not proposed to repeat them again. Suffice to say that it should always be remembered that any of those listed above could have beaten any of the others;

all that is required is for one horse to be inconvenienced by going, distance, pace and fitness and for another to find in such conditions they were able to produce their optimum form. For a full and detailed explanation of the merits of the horses rated please refer to *Bayardo* and the chapter on greatness.

Only two other horses that raced at least nine times were unbeaten: Nearco and Ribot. Both were great horses who won many easy races that were little more than public work outs. In theory at least six of Bahram's races should have been competitive: the National, Gimcrack and Middle Park stakes as a juvenile and all of his races as a three-year-old. In fairness The St. James's Palace Stakes should not have been competitive but Bahram's lethargy induced some interest. However, only the National Stakes and the Two Thousand Guineas could be described as in any way exciting and even in those races he eventually won comfortably as he did in all his other races.

What claims Bahram may possibly have to being considered *primus inter pares* with the greatest racehorses since the beginning of the Twentieth Century, lie in his tremendous versatility. Of those listed the following either did or could have won the National Stakes on their debut in a similar manner to Bahram; Brigadier Gerard; who did not, Bayardo, Tudor Minstrel, Abernant – all three of whom did; Dante and Mill Reef did not but could have done. All had displayed tremendous speed as juveniles by the end of July over five furlongs. However, only Bayardo, who won the St Leger, Dante, who suffered setbacks and could not be readied for it, and possibly Mill Reef, who won the 'Arc and was a much better horse than that year's Leger winner Athens Wood, could also have won the St Leger.

Some observers from the time always insist that Windsor Lad was better than Bahram. It is entirely possible that Windsor Lad was superior to Bahram as a Derby and St Leger winner as the evidence is not conclusive either way. However, based on their performances on the racecourse, what is beyond all argument is that Windsor Lad would have stood no chance against Bahram as a juvenile and at any distance up to and including a mile.

In terms of versatility Bahram was inferior to Bayardo as the latter also stayed in training at four and won the Ascot Gold Cup. Unfortunately Bayardo was beaten in both the Two Thousand Guineas and Derby when well below form.

Does the time of Bahram's races give an indication of his ability? The clock never lies is the mantra of those who swear by its evidence. Certainly one thing is beyond dispute: no bad horse can both run a fast time and produce a good speed figure. Evidence of such is confirmation that the horse concerned is, at the very least, useful. The clock does supply some evidence of Bahram's greatness as all of his races were run on good ground or faster, except the St James's Palace Stakes which was run on soft ground. However, as Bahram was the 1–8 favourite not much was ever going to be learned either way from the time of the race unless, possibly, he had been beaten.

By taking the times of all races at each course during Bahram's career run on ground that was good or faster it has been possible to produce some approximate "standard times". *Raceform* standard times have also been used in conjunction to produce a time that an average horse of 1934 and 1935 should have been able run to over each distance on good ground or faster carrying 9 st.

Bahram won all five of his juvenile races; the clock indicates above average performances in two races, a good performance in one and merely average performances in the remaining two.

On his debut Bahram ran the stiff five furlongs at Sandown in a time of 1 minute 0.20 seconds; very fast but at the weights Theft comes out better as he was giving nine pounds and was beaten a neck. However, this simply confirms that both performances were exceptional; in all probability Theft produced the best performance in the history of the National Breeders Produce Stakes that did not win the race.

Bahram's performance in the Rous Memorial Stakes at Goodwood was an easy win in a slow time and nothing was learned. Next in the Gimcrack Stakes Bahram again won easily in a reasonable but not particularly quick time. The Boscawen Stakes was won very easily in a slow time. Finally in the Middle Park Stakes he won impressively in a very good time: 1 minute 11.40 seconds.

The two races to focus on are the National Breeders Produce Stakes and Middle Park Stakes. Both were won comfortably in good times. However, what is particularly impressive is that both in the past and right up to the present the only horses that were able to better Bahram's times were sprinter/milers and not horses bred to win middle distance races the following year.

The period from 1900 until 1961, when the one mile *Timeform* Gold Cup was first run, races over five and six furlong were the most important, even for potential Derby and St Leger candidates. During this period the most valuable and important races for the best colts were the National Breeders Produce Stakes, the Imperial Produce Stakes and the Middle Park Stakes; the latter was rather misleading known as "the two-year-old Derby". No horse won all three races and only Pretty Polly, Bayardo and Bahram were able to win two of the three and then win a Classic the following year over middle distances. Pretty Polly won the fillies' Triple Crown and Bahram of course won the colts. Bayardo won the St Leger and the following year the Ascot Gold Cup; a unique achievement in the Twentieth Century for a horse that had also won the National Breeders Produce and Middle Park Stakes. With regard to the Middle Park Stakes, and its misnomer of two-year-old Derby, only four horses had won both races in the previous sixty years: Lemberg, Call Boy, Bahram and Dante; it was hardly fulfilling its purpose of identifying potential Derby winners.

Targets for juveniles that are potential stayers have changed dramatically since the *Timeform* Gold Cup was inaugurated; for one thing it was worth a staggering £21,893 (482,000) to the winner. This was more than three times as much as the next most valuable juvenile contest: the six furlong Gimcrack Stakes; £5,917 (131,000). It was worth more than the One Thousand Guineas, Oaks, Ascot Gold Cup, Eclipse and Champion Stakes. It was worth only slightly less than the Two Thousand Guineas and King George VI & Queen Elizabeth Stakes.

The *Timeform* Gold Cup was the brainchild of Phil Bull who made the perfectly valid point that Britain was the only leading European country that did not stage a major race for juveniles over a mile; France had staged one: the Grand Criterium for the previous 97 years! As the Jockey Club was displaying its usual ineptitude and lack of foresight and was clearly not going to introduce such a race, then Bull, despite some objections from the usual and predictable short-sighted sections of racing, did so himself. Bull clearly wanted a strong race hence the remarkable prize money.

Now run as the Racing Post Trophy, Phil Bull would be proud that his race is of such importance today. Although it no longer towers over its rivals in terms of prize money, and is worth only a third of its original value in real terms, it has a long and distinguished history, and has been won by some of the best staying horses in the past forty years. One great horse: Shergar was even beaten in it! A juvenile today bred to be a Derby winner is more likely to run in the Racing Post Trophy than the Dewhurst Stakes which, quite rightly, is more likely to attract potential Two Thousand Guineas prospects. The Middle Park Stakes is now the principally the province of sprinters.

As a three-year-old Bahram won all four of his races but in terms of the clock only the time of his St Leger really stands out. Bahram's time in winning the St Leger has been bettered only four times in the history of the race. Coronach in 1926, a better than average Derby winner, returned a time of 3 minutes 1.60 seconds. In 1934 Windsor Lad returned an identical time to Coronach; just 0.20 seconds faster than Bahram.

Although from archive footage it would appear that Bahram was being eased and winning a shade more easily, it is, as already stated, almost impossible to split these two magnificent horses over distances of twelve furlongs and up. However, Bahram was much faster as a juvenile than Windsor Lad who was unplaced twice before winning the Criterion Stakes at Newmarket. In addition Bahram won the Two Thousand Guineas; a race neither Coronach nor Windsor Lad would have had the speed to win. It is appreciated that Coronach was second in the Two Thousand Guineas but he was beaten very easily by five lengths.

Without wishing to digress too much it is worth considering

Coronach for a moment. As a juvenile, after winning his first three races very easily, he was beaten in a three-runner renewal of the Middle Park Stakes at odds of 15–100. Despite Fred Darling's protestations that nothing was wrong with him Coronach refused to eat for the next two days. When Coronach was beaten in the Two Thousand Guineas he had apparently been upset prior to the race. As a four-year-old he won two races but had clearly "gone in his wind" when beaten twice afterwards. The magnificently powerful Coronach, by all accounts and looking at his portrait, a most imposing sort, had every attribute to be a great horse by any standards. Circumstances simply conspired against him demonstrating this beyond all doubt.

*   *   *

Bahram's time has been bettered twice since; in 2007 and 2011 but this was after the track had been altered: it had been levelled, re-seeded and some of the drains realigned. This produced a slight change in the course's characteristics, with the emphasis in staying races subsequently very slightly more biased towards speed than previously.

Frank Butters wrote the following to Eric Rickman; "Bahram was certainly the best horse I ever trained and I shall be extremely fortunate if I ever have another like him. He was very lazy, which is a common characteristic among the good ones. He would do just sufficient to win his races and was even less inclined to exert his real merit in his work at home. If it had been my custom to keep a trial book, nothing I could have noted in it would have shown the true Bahram, because no gallop ever tested him entirely".

A gross or heavy-topped horse that is also lazy is difficult to get fully fit and maintain in that condition. However, Bahram though perfectly proportioned and of considerable quality, could be described as light whilst in training and did not put on superfluous weight. The art of training lies largely in the preparation of each individual horse according to their needs and giving them the correct amount of work to build them up physically and mentally. In this respect Bahram was probably not a difficult horse to train despite his laziness.

He was fit enough to win on his two-year-old debut and, although Butters had wanted to give him a preliminary race, he was able to win the Two Thousand Guineas first time out as a three-year-old. He had two races; the Derby and St James's Palace Stakes, close together and then he was off the course for three months before the St Leger. These are long absences and would not have suited many horses and it is to both Butters and Bahram's credit that he was turned out tuned to the minute for each race.

Plenty of the Newmarket "touts" did not think Bahram had done enough work to win the Two Thousand Guineas. Before a horse is given a canter or gallop he is trotted. It was Bahram's habit to cough once or twice each morning before starting to trot. This initially caused concern but when it became clear that this was simply an idiosyncrasy, and not a symptom of any ailment, it was ignored. He did however, fall a victim to the epidemic of coughing just before the St Leger.

Although Bahram was quite a light-framed sort when in full training, Quintin Gilbey said he had two magnificent "ends" and was one of the most beautiful movers he had ever seen. He wrote …. "Although a horse of magnificent constitution and of equable temperament, Bahram required careful training in that a race would lighten him up terribly. When he appeared for the St. James's Palace Stakes at Ascot thirteen days after the Derby, he must have weighed many stones lighter than he did on Derby Day; after a race he always required building up again".

Gilbey considered Bahram's win in the Two Thousand Guineas to be amongst the best performances her ever saw. This is not surprising as Theft produced a performance that would have won many other renewals. Of Bahram's other three-year-old performances he wrote "Bahram's task in the Derby was, I think, considerably easier. Theft at a mile and a half was but a shadow of what Theft is at a mile, and the rest of the opposition was not of any great account judged by Classic standards. No horse however, could have won the race more fluently than he did. By Ascot he had run up very light and his victory in the St. James's Palace Stakes was not particularly impressive, but he ran on with great gameness when Fox got at him, though just for a stride or two I had a vision that something frightful was going to happen".

Gilbey continued, "In the St. Leger he put up a glorious display. When a horse wins that easily there are always a number of detractors who declare he beat nothing. Maybe the horses opposed to Bahram at Doncaster were not the most brilliant we have seen, but they were the best we had. Bahram, during his glorious career could do no more than win and keep on winning. As a true son of Blandford there was nothing flash or spectacular about his victories, they were simply the outcome of a great and sensible horse who always gave of his best at the moment his jockey called upon him".

It seems that with hindsight some observers felt Bahram may have been underestimated. Writing in 1968 Franco Varola observed "We find that commentators have now been regretting for many years that there has not been another Bahram after 1935 in England. Not only because no other colt has been capable of winning the Triple Crown, but also because there has not been another horse which could convey the same impression of absolute physical excellence, of a perfectly balanced specimen, which is at the same time towering above its contemporaries".

Along similar lines in 1970 John Hislop wrote "As with men, posterity can be unduly eulogistic or harsh. Thus, to take a couple of the late Aga Khan's famous horses as an example, Tulyar was over-rated and Bahram's merit never fully recognized. Often a horse's true merit is not immediately evident. He may run up an impressive succession of victories against moderate horses and himself be really good, or only a little better than those defeated by him.

Neither Bahram nor Tulyar beat truly outstanding horses; Theft was probably the best horse either ran against, but Bahram, who was unbeaten, was the best two-year-old of his year and won the St Leger in near-record time, despite being eased a long way from home. Tulyar, on the other hand, won only a couple of nurseries as a juvenile and none of his performances at three match the intrinsic merit of Bahram's St Leger.

*   *   *

In conclusion it is clear that Bahram was a truly great racehorse one that can be truthfully described among Twentieth Century Thoroughbreds as *sui generis*; just how great will never be known. Neither his trainer Frank Butters, his regular jockey Freddie Fox nor any of his work riders ever knew the limit of his ability. In this respect Bahram can be bracketed with the great St Simon; when his trainer Matt Dawson was asked if he was a truly great stayer he replied "I really don't know; no horse ever went fast enough to find out!"

There is an old equestrian saying that "there is no secret so close as that between a rider and his horse"; well there is: it is the secret of the true extent of his ability that Bahram kept from all that were privileged to be connected with him and, ultimately, it was a secret known only by the horse himself and his maker.

*   *   *

Bahram was retired in 1936 to stand at the Egerton Stud in Newmarket at a fee of 500 guineas (£27,500); more than Solario, Tetratema and Blenheim. Bahram was full for the first three years.

Sir Charles Leicester noted about Bahram at stud; "I remember seeing him at Egerton Stud, Newmarket, when he looked the lord of all he surveyed and with the most charming and equable temperament".

Bahram was controversially sold to stand in North America in 1940. He was bought by a syndicate comprising Alfred G. Vanderbilt, Sylvester W. Labrot, Walter J. Chrysler and James Cox Brady. The price paid was £40,000 (1,760,000), a considerable sum of money, however, it seriously under-valued Bahram.

Bahram was shipped from Belfast in late 1940 during a time when German U-boats were attacking allied shipping, usually when vessels were eastward bound. The Aga and the buyers were represented by veterinary surgeons Joe Cosgrave and Jim Parkinson. Unfortunately the winch to lift Bahram into the hold was being operated by an inexperienced hand and by the time he was lifted aboard Bahram was in an awful lather. As the stall was being lifted aboard it was let down so rapidly and that it hit the hold with a sickening bang. Bahram collapsed and only after Cosgrave had swiftly administered digitalis did the stricken champion recover. Not the best way to start his journey to the New World!

*   *   *

Bahram stood for five years in North America: firstly at Mr. Vanderbilt's Sagamore Stud in Maryland and later at Mr. Chrysler's North Wales Stud in Virginia.

Bahram was sold again in 1945 this time he was bought by an Argentinian syndicate to stand at the Haras Chapadmalal Stud owned by Sociedad Jose A. y Miguel Martinez de Hoz. The agent was Mr. Charles Lund and the reputed sum of $130,000 (£32,260) (1,194,000).

*   *   *

Bahram had a long stud career in three different continents. His career can therefore be divided into three parts: 1936 to 1940 when he stood in England, 1941 to 1945 in North America and 1946 to 1955 in Argentina.

Bahram was only a qualified success in any of the three locations he stood in. He had made a very promising start in England and it has to be wondered whether moving him large distances to different countries, environments and climates was detrimental to him. In any event it was hardly conducive to producing the best from him. However, it would be unfair to say that he was a failure as a stallion.

Bahram died in Argentina on 24th January 1956 in his twenty-fourth year.

Details of his stud career can be found in the appendix.

*   *   *

Notwithstanding what has been written before somehow it is a comfort to know that Bahram's "line" is still alive with three sons currently standing at stud in Europe. However, as he is only one of 32 influences in Monsun's pedigree and one of 64 in the pedigrees of Manduro, Shirocco and Novellist it is not imagined or claimed that Bahram contributed in any greater proportion than that to the success of any of them or their progeny:-

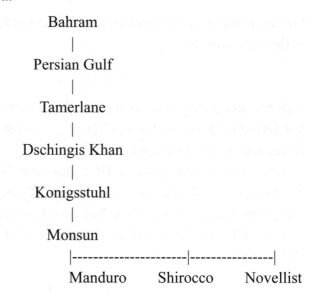

Bahram
|
Persian Gulf
|
Tamerlane
|
Dschingis Khan
|
Konigsstuhl
|
Monsun
|----------------------|----------------|
Manduro   Shirocco   Novellist

Here is a summary of Bahram's racing record:-

Year	Distance	Race	Course	Placing	Race Rating	Winnings
1934	5f	National Breeders Produce Stakes	Sandown	1st	112++	5,559
	6f	Rous Memorial Stakes	Goodwood	1st	122++	1,140
	6f	Gimcrack Stakes	York	1st	120+	1,412
	5f	Boscawen Stakes	Newmarket	1st	105++	600
	6f	Middle Park Stakes	Newmarket	1st	127++	3,047
1935	1m	Two Thousand Guineas	Newmarket	1st	131+	9,339
	1m 4f	Derby	Epsom	1st	132+	9,216

Year	Distance	Race	Course	Placing	Race Rating	Winnings
1935	1m	St James's Palace Stakes	Ascot	1st	112+	3,230
	1m 6f	St Leger Stakes	Doncaster	1st	138+	9,543

Total earnings   £43,086
(2,284,000)

19 Turkhan, Big Game & Persian Gulf

A full review of Bahram's stud record can be found in the appendices. However, it is felt that these three, the best of his produce, deserve detailed attention.

Turkhan

Turkhan was a strongly built, good-looking bay colt, foaled in Ireland on 9th April 1937 by Bahram out of Theresina by Diophon. Theresina was a daughter of Teresina who produced nine winners from fourteen foals. Theresina was good racehorse but even better as a brood mare. She won a valuable five furlong race at Newmarket as a juvenile on her second and final appearance of the year. As a three-year-old she won two of her four races: the Irish Oaks and the Falmouth Stakes. However, it was as a broodmare that she left her lasting legacy. Of her fifteen foals ten were winners including Turkhan and Ujiji.

Turkhan, who stood 16 hands, ran in the colours of Aly Khan and was sent into training with Frank Butters. As a juvenile Turkhan made his debut at Newmarket on 11th May in the Norfolk Two-year-old Stakes over five furlongs where he finished sixth in a field thirty eight at odds of 100–6. The race was won by Tant Mieux (Asterus – Tantine by Solario) who was later assessed as the leading juvenile in the Free Handicap.

Turkhan then ran in the Coventry Stakes at Ascot, where he attracted much favourable comment in the paddock, and was sent off at odds of 100–8. He had benefitted considerably for his debut run and beat a field of sixteen, initially outpaced, he ran on strongly, to win easily by three lengths. However, time was to show that the Coventry Stakes form was moderate; the second The Aga's Jindani (Rustom Pasha – Jan Ranee by Grand Parade) did not win a race.

Turkhan's next race was at Goodwood in the Ham (Produce) Stakes over six furlongs. He carried top weight of 9st. 5lbs. was the 11–8 favourite and took up the running a furlong out only to be caught on the line by Hippius (Hyperion – Edgelaw by Ellangowen) to whom he was conceding three pounds. Hippius had been behind Turkhan in the Coventry Stakes. This form was better as Hippius was a progressive sort and won the Champion Stakes the following year.

Turkhan's last race of the season was an unplaced effort behind Djebel (Tourbillion – Loika by Gay Crusader) in the six furlong Middle Park Stakes which attracted a field of twenty; the largest number of runners for the race at that stage in the twentieth century. Djebel was trained in France and although it was now 1st November and war had been declared two months previously his trainer had organized an efficient raid to steal this valuable race before heading home with the spoils. He won comfortably by two lengths form Tant Mieux and a filly, Godiva (Hyperion – Carpet Slipper by Phalaris).

Turkhan was allocated 9 st. 2 lbs. in the Free Handicap; five pounds and seven places below Tant Mieux. Djebel would have topped the rankings but as he was trained in France was not given a weight. Turkhan's assessment rather flatters him; in all probability the handicapper, Mr. Fawcett, had overrated the Coventry Stakes form.

At three with war declared Turkhan began his sophomore year in April at Newmarket finishing seventh of fourteen when an unfancied outsider in the Craven Stakes. He was also unplaced when equally unfancied behind Djebel, on yet another successful raid, in the New Two Thousand Guineas. Turkhan was finding a mile too sharp and he was stepped up in trip for his next race the Newmarket Stakes over ten furlongs. He finished fifth running on but beaten over eight lengths. It was beginning to look as if he was not really top-class and had been overrated. His form improved on his next start when he was third in the Derby Trial Plate at Hurst Park to Tant Mieux; beaten five lengths.

This form may have been better but it looked optimistic to let him take his chance in the New Derby run at Newmarket 12th June. His improved form meant that he was joint fifth favourite at 100–7.

However, Frank Butters must have felt he would perform well otherwise he simply would not have let him run. Butters was right: now able to demonstrate his stamina Turkhan ran on strongly inside the final furlong to take second place on the line. He had no chance with the comfortable three lengths winner Pont L'Eveque (Barneveldt – Pontebra by Belfonds). Turkhan had looked fit and well in the paddock but "sweating slightly".

The sight on the day the New Derby was staged with special trains and long streams of cars and coaches aroused the suspicion amongst those always on the lookout to condemn racing and claim that plenty of people were not taking the war seriously. Questions had already been asked in House of Commons particularly one "whether the Home Secretary would take steps to avoid squandering war resources by prohibiting motor-coach tours, horse racing and hunting". However, the Jockey Club took the decision themselves on 19th June to cancel all racing until further notice.

Racing in Britain ceased after the meeting at Wolverhampton on 17th June. The meeting scheduled for Brighton on the 19th and 20th was the first casualty. Also cancelled was a two-day meeting at Newmarket scheduled for Friday and Saturday 21st and 22nd June where some races transferred from Ascot were due to be run.

With no opportunity to race in Britain Turkhan was dispatched across the Irish Sea for his next race the Irish Derby at the Curragh on the 26th June. It may surprise some but this was not a level weight contest despite being considered a Classic. There were seven runners and Turkhan and Teasel (Pharian – Chardon by Aldford) were required to carry 9st. 5lbs. and the other five 8st. 12lbs. In all probability it would have taken stones not pounds to bring the runners together and Turkhan went off at odds of 4–11, which looked very generous by the finishing post.

Turkhan won with Smirke not needing to let him out of a canter to beat two British trained horses Golden Tiger and Claudius by two lengths and the same. However, unless Golden Tiger ran well below form this was as good a performance as Turkhan ever produced. Golden Tiger did not win any of his five races in 1941, however, he had some reasonable form and although it would have been a surprise if Turkhan had been beaten, winning so easily was impressive. The locals had the consolation of knowing that the winner although trained in England had been bred at the Sheshoon Stud close to the Curragh. If they had needed further solace Turkhan's sire and dam were also bred locally too!

Opposition to racing continued with *The Times* publishing many letters condemning racing and a leading article claimed there would be "widespread resentment" if racing was resumed. Unfortunately it was an element of class resentment about some of these comments that emerged with "class warriors" seeing nothing wrong with huge crowds at football matches and greyhound racing but having the strongest objection to horse racing; perceived as a pastime of the rich and privileged. A statistic emerged which just about summed up the lunacy of these idiotic, hypocritical types who saw the war as a chance to berate the wealthy: if all the oats provided to race horses were instead given to poultry, one more egg could have been provided per head of population every FOUR years!

Racing in Britain did not resume until 14th September at Ripon where there were 97 runners for the six races. The St Leger had been scheduled for the 11th September but was abandoned.

Turkhan's next race was the New Jockey Club Cup run at Nottingham on 2nd November over two and a half miles. The trip was a long way for a three-year-old but nonetheless he ran disappointingly. Starting as the fourth favourite at 5–1 he finished fifth of seven weakening and beaten 19 lengths. He was either short of fitness after an 18 week layoff or he did not stay.

In any event the race would have sharpened Turkhan up for the Yorkshire St Leger. Having been abandoned the race was subjected to considerable debate and had been "tossed, as it were from pillar to post". The race was eventually saved and run at Thirsk on the last day of the season; 23rd November. This was the latest date the final Classic had ever been run.

Turkhan started joint second favourite in a field of six and won by ¾ lengths, with the same between the second and third. Gordon

Richards took Turkhan to the front almost immediately and resisted all challenges until the finishing post was reached. He was described as running his race out with "fine courage and persistence" and that both horse and rider were warmly applauded as the post was passed. The Aga and Aly were responsible for both first and second with Stardust following Turkhan home.

Shortly afterwards it was announced that both Turkhan and Stardust would go to stud. This was a pity as Turkhan would have made an excellent Cup horse. However, keeping him in training with racing constantly under threat would have been risky.

Turkhan won only three of his twelve races. However, he is better than that suggests; he won the Yorkshire St Leger and was second in the New Derby. He was placed in two others and he had enough speed to win over five furlongs as a juvenile and enough stamina to win over 15 furlongs as a three-year-old. He was sound and would almost certainly have made a better four-year-old. His final *Timeform* rating of 126 places him as just about Group 1 level by today's standards and his three wins are today classified as Group 2 – Coventry Stakes – and both his Classic wins are of course Group 1. It would however, be hard to claim that his Irish Derby and Yorkshire St Leger were high-class renewals, although in the Yorkshire St Leger both Turkhan and the second Stardust, were well up to the standard of the race.

Here is a summary of his racing career:-

Two-year-old
1939

Distance	Race	Course	Placing	Race Rating	Amount won £
5f	Norfolk 2 y o Plate	Newmarket	6th	76+	–
5f	Coventry Stakes	Ascot	1st	112+	2,500
6f	Ham (Produce) Stakes	Goodwood	2nd	115	–
6f	Middle Park Stakes	Newmarket	–	–	–

Three-year-old
1940

1m	Craven Stakes	Newmarket	6th	97+	–
1m	New 2000 Guineas	Newmarket	–	–	–

1m 2f	Newmarket Stakes	Newmarket	5th	104	–
1m 2f	Derby Trial Plate	Hurst Park	3rd	109	–
1m 4f	New Derby Stakes	Newmarket	2nd	123	–
1m 4f	Irish St Leger	Curragh	1st	126	2,500
2m 4f	New Jockey Club Gold Cup	Nottingham	5th	–	–
1m 7f	Yorkshire St Leger	Thirsk	1st	126	980

*   *   *

Big Game

Big Game was a rich bay colt bred by the National Stud and foaled on 24th January 1939. He was by Bahram out of Myrobella by The Tetrarch; which made him about as well-bred as it is possible to be. His sire: Bahram was an unbeaten Triple Crown winner, and his dam: Myrobella was a well-bred, very fast, high-class racehorse. Both Big Game's sire and dam headed the Free Handicap as juveniles.

Myrobella, who was foaled in 1930 when her dam: Dolabella was nineteen years old, was leased from the National Stud by Lord Lonsdale and trained by Fred Darling at Beckhampton. Dolabella bred six other winners but Myrobella was by some way the best. A grey filly Myrobella was "big and extremely good-looking" and "powerfully made, especially behind the saddle, while her chest was broad and deep and her limbs clean and hard." Her portrait taken as a juvenile certainly suggests a handsome sort with plenty of scope. In addition she had an action that was "light and graceful".

Myrobella suffered her only defeat as a juvenile on her debut in the five furlong Salisbury Stakes on 26th May 1932 when, as the 11–8 favourite, she was beaten under a length into second place. She returned to Salisbury on 5th July and broke her maiden as the 8–15 favourite in the five furlongs Salisbury Maiden Plate. Next was the most valuable juvenile race of the year: the National breeders Produce Stakes over the straight five furlongs at Sandown. Despite some of her opponents having shown good form at Ascot Myrobella started as the 21–10 favourite. She was fast away, looked the winner before halfway and was able to cruise home by five lengths.

The St Leger meeting at Doncaster was her next stop for the six furlong Champagne Stakes. The extra distance plus the soft going produced some doubt about her winning in the minds of some and 2–1 was available against her chances. Those who backed her down to 11–8 never had a nervous moment as she "cantered home" by six lengths. Myrobella completed the year with two facile wins at odds of 2–13 and 8–100, both were races over five furlongs at Newmarket; the Hopeful and Prendergast Stakes respectively. She was placed top of the Free Handicap with 9 st. 7 lbs. where unusually the first three horses: Myrobella, Betty (Teddy – Miss Cavendish by Chaucer) and Brown Betty (Friar Marcus – Garpal by Phalaris), were all fillies. Her performances would have earned her a *Timeform* rating of 127, a figure allotted by *A Century of Champions*, well-deserved for one of the fastest juvenile fillies of the Twentieth Century. The future Derby winner Hyperion was allotted 9 st. 0.lbs.

As a three-year-old Myrobella began with a slightly unconvincing win over five furlongs at Newmarket in the Severals Stakes. She was conceding at least 16 pounds to each of her four rivals and started at odds of 1–5. With so much speed in her pedigree, together with the pace she had displayed as a juvenile, there was always some doubt about Myrobella staying a mile. So it proved when she started in the One Thousand Guineas; fast away, and racing on the unfavoured far side of the course, she was soon clear and had built up a "substantial lead" by halfway. However, her stamina ebbed away and she was beaten just under two lengths into third place.

While Myrobella stayed a mile it was obvious that she would be better back at sprinting distances. So with this in mind Fred Darling plotted her year around five and six furlong races. For her next race she was sent to Ascot for the Fern Hill Stakes over five furlongs where she easily disposed of four opponents by five lengths at odds of 2–5. Tougher assignments now awaited her starting with the July Cup at Newmarket over six furlongs. She was now to lock horns for the first time with Concerto (Orpheus – Constellation by Sunstar), an extremely tough five-year-old entire. He was fresh from winning the Wokingham Stakes for the second year running, this time conceding between 9 and 38 pounds to his rivals. Despite this Myrobella was backed down to favouritism at 4–6 with Concerto at 3–1 in a four-horse field.

The weights were interesting: Concerto carried 10 st. 8 lbs. and Myrobella 9 st. 7 lbs. The weight-for-age scale at that time would have a three-year-old receiving 13 pounds from an older horse. Today for example the *Timeform* scale would allow a three-year-old just five pounds. Being a filly Myrobella would be allowed three pounds so she can be said to have received seven pounds more than she would be today. As Myrobella won by only a head this probably made a difference.

A month later the protagonists met again at Goodwood in the King George Stakes run, at that time, over six furlongs. There were again four runners and the weights similar: Concerto 9 st. 11 lbs. and Myrobella 8 st. 11 lbs. This time Myrobella won "easily" by two lengths and, as she was receiving seven pounds more than she should, Concerto and Myrobella can be assessed as almost equal.

The third "leg" took place at York's August meeting in the five furlong Nunthorpe Stakes. There were three runners and the weights Concerto 8 st. 12lbs. and Myrobella 8 st. 4 lbs. This meant that Myrobella was only three pounds better off than she should have been. It was a titanic struggle with Concerto prevailing by a short head from Myrobella and the third horse: Gold Bridge (Swynford or Golden Boss – Flying Diadem by Diadumenos), just a neck away. Myrobella completed the year by winning the Challenge Stakes at Newmarket over six furlongs. It was a match but Myrobella was set to concede ten pounds (she should have been receiving eight pounds including the fillies' allowance) to a decent six-year-old horse: Heronslea (Bachelor's Double – Dinah Desmond by Marcovil) who had the Wokingham as a four-year-old. Despite being eighteen pounds "wrong" Myrobella prevailed by a head. Myrobella's *Timeform* rating based on her three-year-old efforts was slightly below her juvenile one at 125.

Myrobella was kept in training as a four-year-old but won failed to show her previous level of form winning only a handicap from two races. A high-class sprinter in all she won eleven of her fifteen races and won £16,143 (840,000).

At stud she bred six winners from ten live foals, but Big Game was the best of them.

Big Game grew into a handsome colt that would eventually stand just over 16.1 hands. Physically he was a massively built, most impressive individual with considerable power in his quarters, and an unusually large girth with plenty of heart room. He was described as "covering the ground smoothly" when moving. On the debit side he was rather too heavy in the shoulder. His portrait as a juvenile shows a particularly imposing sort. He probably inherited his size and physique from Myrobella and her influence for speed would have an effect on Big Game's career as a three-year-old.

Big Game was undoubtedly the best of Bahram's progeny; he was leased to His Majesty King George VI for his racing career by the National Stud and trained at Beckhampton by Fred Darling. Perhaps surprisingly for a big colt he made his debut as early as 19th April at Salisbury. It was wartime of course and the normal racing programme had been cancelled and racing restricted to twelve courses. The race chosen was the Hurstbourne Plate over five furlongs; Big Game had not been named at this stage and ran as Myrobella colt.

Big Game's work at Beckhampton could hardly have been a secret as he started at odds of 4–9 to beat his nineteen moderate opponents. Ridden by stable jockey Gordon Richards this he duly did despite running "very green" and wandering about at one stage and he had three-quarters of a length to spare at the line over the second. The form was moderate and the second failed to win in eight outings that year.

Big Game was back at Salisbury on 9th May for the five furlong, twelve runner Cranbourne Stakes; and he had clearly learnt much from his debut. Starting at odds of 2–9 he made all and won by five lengths, in a "canter" according to *Raceform,* under Harry Wragg. He was to have been again ridden by Richards but an hour before Big Game's race Richards was kicked at the post by another horse. His injuries were serious enough for him to be taken to hospital and to prevent him riding again in 1941.

Big Game's third race was again at Salisbury on 2nd June in the five furlongs Salisbury Plate. Only five turned out against him and again, running as Myrobella colt and under Wragg he landed odds of 2–9. The distance was only a length but *Raceform's* comment was "tight rein; smoothly".

Ascot was not staged during the war but racing was run at the course from 1943; the first time ever outside the meeting in June, and substitute contests were staged for some of the more important races. The Coventry Stakes, over five furlongs at that time, was run at Newmarket's July course on 2nd July. There were five runners lining up against Big Game, by now named, including a colt that he would oppose several times over the next year or so. Watling Street was bred by the 17th Earl of Derby, by Fairway out of Ranai by Rabelais. He was a tall, rather leggy colt, somewhat narrow and possessing a look in his eye that was not altogether kindly. He was trained at Stanley House by Walter Earl.

Prior to the Coventry Stakes Watling Street had won a Plate Race and then finished second as the even money favourite in a Stakes race, both at Newmarket. The betting for the Coventry Stakes indicated what was expected: Big Game was 2–9 and Watling Street 8–1. At no stage did Big Game's supporters have any reason for concern. He went to the front after two furlongs "hardly seemed to be out of a canter….he swept impressively and with extreme ease to the winning post". "There was something lazy and yet magnificent about his action; he simply drew away from his opponents as if they did not exist".

Watling Street, who was not in the best of moods, finished four lengths behind in second place. The distances thereafter were a further four lengths and five lengths. The fourth horse was beaten thirteen lengths: just over forty pounds! Yet Big Game was hardly out of a canter. It is no surprise that observers reached for the full lexicon in an effort to convey his full majesty and total domination. The time for the race was one minute exactly. During the period that the Coventry Stakes was run over five furlongs; it was first run over six furlongs in 1955, it is hard to imagine a more impressive winner.

Big Game's final start of the year was at Newbury on 6th September in the substitute running of the Champagne Stakes over six furlongs.

This step up in trip was not thought to be in any way a problem for Big Game. Although his dam was a sprinter Bahram would surely impart enough stamina. There were six runners including Watling Street who, since they had last met, had redeemed himself with an impressive win in the five furlong Chesterfield Stakes at Newmarket.

The betting suggested that a closer race was expected than in the Coventry Stakes; 1–2 Big Game, 7–2 Watling Street, 9–1 bar. It proved to be a thrilling race; Big Game jumped off well and seemed to be going comfortably with Watling Street and the outsider Birikan (Bahram – Carola by Tetratema) disputing the lead for four furlongs. One and a half furlongs from the finish Watling Street established a lead of about a length and a half. With a furlong to go to the line Big Game had only cut the deficit by half a length and Wragg drew the whip. Big Game produced a huge effort and took the lead only strides from the post but Watling Street fought back gamely and the two flashed past the post together. The crowd waited in silence until the judge gave the verdict to Big Game by a short head. The was a suggestion that many observers were convinced that Watling Street had won and as a result a Royal victory was not greeted with the normal enthusiasm.

The race at least demonstrated that Big Game lacked nothing in courage and he had responded generously to the whip. However, either Watling Street had improved considerably or Big Game was not as effective over six furlongs as five. The form was not sustained when Watling Street ran below form in his final race of the season; the Middle Park Stakes.

Big Game and Watling Street were the two best juvenile colts of 1941. However, neither of them topped the Free Handicap. This honour went to a filly that was destined to take her place among the very best of her gender: Sun Chariot.

Bred by the National Stud and leased to King George VI she was by Hyperion out of Clarence by Diligence. Sun Chariot was so backward that trainer Fred Darling arranged for her to be sent to Ireland. Fortunately there was a delay in issuing the export license and a week before it was received at Beckhampton Sun Chariot produced a gallop that amply demonstrated what she was capable of. Plans were changed and she was trained for her debut race. She progressed rapidly and was unbeaten in four races including the substitute Queen Mary and Middle Park Stakes; in the latter she beat colts "very easily" having made progress "on the bit". She was selected above Big Game for the Middle Park; an indication of the high regard she was held in by that time. She was ridden by Harry Wragg in all her races. Sun Chariot was allocated 9 st. 7 lbs. in the Free Handicap a pound more than Big Game and two more than Watling Street. *A Century of Champions* rated Sun Chariot 128, Big Game 127 and Watling Street 126. Few years at any time were blessed with three such juveniles in one season.

Despite the War being at its most fearsome, there was much to look forward to in 1942 for those who enjoyed thoroughbred racing. Racing was restricted to five racecourses: Newmarket, Salisbury, Windsor, Pontefract and Stockton. With the exception of the substitute Classics, horses trained at Newmarket were restricted to racing at headquarters, those in the south Salisbury and Windsor, those in the north, Pontefract and Stockton.

As a three-year-old Big Game's first objective was the New Two Thousand Guineas and in preparation his first race was at Salisbury on 2nd May in the Salisbury Stakes over seven furlongs. None of his six moderate opponents had the form to trouble him and he won very easily by two lengths at odds of 2–5. In the circumstances it is a surprise that the time was a; 1 min. 29.6 secs. was a course record. At least he seemed to thoroughly stay seven furlongs!

On Two Thousand Guineas day 12th May Big Game totally dominated the paddock and odds of 8–11 were confidently bet on. Watling Street had begun the year with a win in a minor stakes race where he had to be shown the whip to get home. He was fourth favourite at 13–2. Big Game was always going easily, if a shade too keenly, took up the running about four furlongs from the finish and, striding out impressively, won by four lengths with Watling Street second. Assuming Watling Street had improved, or at least not regressed, this was a most impressive performance and on at least the same level as Bahram's performance in the same race and probably better. He was given a "splendid reception" by the crowd not least because he was both the favourite and owned by the King! Unfortunately he could not be present to witness Big Game's triumph.

His next objective was the New Derby and a challenge that could no longer be avoided: a thorough test of his stamina. Bahram would certainly have supplied more than enough stamina for twelve furlongs. However, Myrobella was a different proposition. She had been outstayed in the One Thousand Guineas and had reverted to sprinting and her pedigree offered very little encouragement that Big Game would have the stamina for middle distances. None of this was lost on the connections of Watling Street; his jockey was the highly intelligent Harry Wragg. Both he and Watling Street's trainer Walter Earl would know that a strong gallop would favour their colt. The owner of the second favourite: Hyperides (Hyperion – Priscilla by Phalaris), Lord Rosebery and his trainer Jack Jarvis shared this opinion and they took the precaution of employing a pacemaker to ensure a strong gallop.

The press and most pundits however refused to consider the possibility of defeat for Big Game. He was unbeaten and considered to be the "Horse of the Century". At this stage of his career almost all observers rated Big Game as potentially better than his sire. He had a record that was comparable, was better bred and was, by some way, a much more imposing and impressive sort physically.

Sadly it was not to be; on Saturday 13th June in the presence of the King and Queen Big Game came into the paddock and again towered over his opponents. He "stripped magnificently, he was a mass of muscle and yet was big and round". Meyrick Good wrote "I have seen every Derby candidate for 44 years and never have I beheld a three-year-old of such strength and maturity". One observer certainly felt he could have passed as a four-year-old. Watling Street was described as "harder trained and not nearly so impressive"

It all proved too much for Big Game who did not settle for Gordon Richards and although he took the lead about three furlongs out his stamina ebbed away. He was a well-beaten sixth about seven lengths behind Watling Street who had tracked and then produced a good turn of foot to beat Hyperides a neck. Gordon Richards expressed disappointment that Big Game did not settle but it is hard to argue that the result would have been in any way changed whatever Big Game had done. He was simply not a stayer.

There was of course little point in taking up his nomination for the New St. Leger and so with little else to aim for Big Game's final race was the Champion Stakes. He faced four opponents including Hyperides, Ujiji and Afterthought (Obliterate – Plack by Hurry On), all of whom were keen to test Big Game's stamina over ten furlongs. Confidence was not high and Big Game started at the rather generous odds of 11–10. There was no need for any real concern; Richards had him well settled in last place until half-way, then challenged, took the lead in the dip and strode away. There was a minor alarm as his stride shortened close home but he had one and half lengths to spare over Afterthought at the line. This represented top form as Afterthought had been second in the New Oaks and replacement Gold Cup. Big Game had restored his reputation and the memory of his wins would hopefully outlast the disappointment of his performance in the New Derby.

At the end of the year Big Game was placed equal top of the free handicap alongside Sun Chariot on 9 st. 7 lbs. with Watling Street five pounds behind. *A Century of Champions* rated both 136 which is about right. With the fillies allowance Sun Chariot would have beaten Big Game over ten furlongs plus. However, his Two Thousand Guineas performance was probably superior to hers in the One Thousand. Sun Chariot won the filly's Triple Crown; her Oaks performance almost defying belief. She was left almost half a furlong at the start but was still back on the bit by the line. Her performance in the St Leger was equally impressive: she took the lead "on the bit" and won "easily" from Watling Street. One respected observer said she made a "hack" of the New Derby winner. Watling Street was not rated by *A Century of Champions* but this author calculates that, on the *Timeform* scale, a rating of 129 would be fair which would make him a marginally above average Derby winner.

In the final analysis Big Game fell short of the required level to be described as "great". However, his performance in winning the Two Thousand Guineas was arguably better than Bahram's in winning the same race. However, whereas Bahram then progressed to winning both the Derby and St. Leger Big Game failed through lack of stamina in the New Derby. Nonetheless his performance in the Two Thousand Guineas could be rated with any in the Twentieth Century up to that date with the possible exception of Colombo. Phil Bull thought him the most brilliant miler he had ever seen at that time. However, he also stated that Big Game would only stay ten furlongs when ridden with caution and that he would be ineffective beyond that distance. Bull was proved correct. In addition Big Game's performances to win the Coventry and Champion Stakes rank high up with any performances in the history of both races.

Big Game was a sedate, well-mannered horse and inclined to be lazy. However, he was absolutely game and genuine. He was retired to the Aislabie Stud in Newmarket in 1943 at a fee of £250 (9,250). Details of his career at stud can be found in the appendix.

Big Game was destroyed on 3rd July 1963 at the age of 24.

Here is a summary of his racing record:-

Two-year-old
1941

Distance	Race	Course	Placing	Race rating	Amount won
5f	Hurstbourne Plate	Salisbury	1st	88++	166
5f	Cranbourne Stakes	Salisbury	1st	104++	206
5f	Salisbury Plate	Salisbury	1st	97++	252
5f	Coventry Stakes	Newmarket	1st	127+	1,217
6f	Champagne Stakes	Newbury	1st	124	806

Three-year-old
1942

7f	Salisbury Stakes	Salisbury	1st	119++	316
8f	New 2000 Gns.	Newmarket	1st	136	2,083
12f	New Derby Stakes	Newmarket	6th	116	–
10f	Champion Stakes	Newmarket	1st	132+	782

*   *   *

Persian Gulf

Persian Gulf was foaled on 26th March 1940 by Bahram out of Double Life by Bachelors Double and owned and bred by Lady Zia Wernher. Double Life was a rather lightly-made, unimpressive individual with a plain head standing just 15.1 hands. Persian Gulf was a slow developer who nonetheless eventually made up into a decent sort.

Despite her unprepossessing aspect Double Life was bought for 600 guineas (£28,000) as a yearling and sent into training with Cecil Boyd-Rochfort. She won two minor races as a juvenile but suffered misfortune at the start of her three-year-old career: she was disqualified after winning a handicap at Kempton and then badly interfered with at Ascot. She was progressing however and won a Plate at Newcastle and the Chesterfield Cup at Goodwood. Stepping up further she won the Duke of York Handicap at Kempton which earned her a ten pound penalty for the Cambridgeshire. Showing excellent determination she hit the front close home and prevailed by a neck after which she was retired to stud.

Double Life was probably worth a *Timeform* rating of about 109. Her trainer said of her "She was a filly of charming disposition with a heart of gold, and I never trained a gamer filly". At stud she produced four winners from eight foals the best of which were Precipitation and Persian Gulf. She became very lame and it was necessary to destroy her in December 1943, aged seventeen.

Persian Gulf was a slow maturing sort and it was not possible to race him as a juvenile. He did not appear on a racecourse until 1st June 1943when he showed some promise in finishing sixth, beaten four and a half lengths, in a moderate twelve furlong maiden on Newmarket's July course where he ran all his races.

Persian Gulf must have been showing Boyd-Rochfort more than just promise as his next race was in the New Derby. Not surprisingly he started as a 50–1 outsider in a field of twenty-three; however, Persian Gulf ran well above expectations by finishing fourth, beaten just under a length behind Straight Deal (Solario – Good Deal by Apelle), Umiddad and Nasrullah.

This performance represented an improvement of over three stones from his debut! Moreover he did something very surprising for a horse of so slight experience in a big race: he made the running. He galloped with total honesty and determination up the long Newmarket straight and only faltered close home. It has to be wondered whether he would have won had it been possible to get more experience into him. However, with the first five to finish being covered by just over a length, it did not look a particularly strong renewal of Britain's principal three-year-old race. This impression would be shown to be wrong.

A maiden looked at his mercy but in his next race, an eleven runner maiden over twelve furlongs, he was beaten a short head at odds of 1–2. On the formbook those odds look generous but that would have been no consolation to those who took advantage! Despite this defeat Persian Gulf ran his next and final race of the season in the New St Leger Stakes. He was again prominent and took the lead briefly two furlongs out, before finishing fourth beaten just under two lengths behind a filly: Herringbone (King Salmon – Schiaparelli by Schiavoni), Ribbon (Fairway – Bongrace by Spion Kop) and Straight Deal. Again not much separated the first four to finish. However, both the New Derby and New St Leger were truly run races and returned high value speed figures demonstrating that, unusually, although both races produced blanket finishes the horses concerned are worth their relatively high *Timeform* ratings. Straight Deal 132, Herringbone 131, Ribbon 130, Persian Gulf 129, Umiddad 129, and Nasrullah 128.

At the end of the year Persian Gulf was given 9st. 1lb. in the Free Handicap; six pounds behind Straight Deal. Many observers might feel that as Persian Gulf had been beaten twice by Straight Deal in two Classics by no more than a length on each occasion, he might have been placed within three pounds of the Derby winner.

Phil Bull writing in *Best Horses of 1943* put it neatly when he said "Persian Gulf was only a racehorse in the making last season". It was Bull's view that the firm ground prevailing that year retarded Persian Gulf's progress as he possessed a high pounding action unsuited to fast going. In addition Bull averred that Persian Gulf lacked speed and was a dyed-in-the-wool stayer and would need at least two miles to shine together with a strong pace. Despite Bull's observations about his lack of pace it is worth remembering that Persian Gulf produced two fast speed figures in both the Derby and St Leger thus demonstrating that, although he was a dyed-in-the-wool-stayer, he was no long distance plodder.

As a four-year-old Persian Gulf improved considerably. He was of course still a maiden and began in a match for the twelve furlong April Stakes where he impressed Phil Bull immensely in the paddock. Persian Gulf had made tremendous physical progress over the winter and had shed some surplus bulk and replaced it with muscle and now looked sleek, fit and his coat shone. In addition his body language was that of a positive horse keen to start his work for the year. In short he was now a "commanding specimen". Gordon Richards set a sound but not fast gallop and Persian Gulf strode home by six lengths. Interestingly Bull noted that his knee action was absent when he stretched out.

Surprisingly for his next race he was dropped in trip for the eleven furlongs Linton Stakes. Bobby Jones, riding Persian Gulf for the first time, set a searching gallop and he held on bravely to win by a neck from High Chancellor (Fair Trial – Chincona by Buchan); an enormously big, strong colt who stood over 17 hands. Back up in trip next for the fourteen and a half furlongs Thorney Stakes Jones's judgment was faulty and he rode a poor race. There were only three runners and Jones set such a moderate gallop that the 66–1 outsider was able to lie up with the two principals for twelve furlongs. Jones compounded his error by allowing Gordon Richards on Umiddad, who was receiving four pounds, to take the lead from him and go a length up before asking Persian Gulf to fight back. He did so courageously but found Richards in strong form and Umiddad just as brave and there was a neck between them at the line. As Umiddad was the 8–13 favourite he was probably the better horse but the only way Persian Gulf could win was with a searching gallop. The race was so slowly run that it did not merit Phil Bull recording any speed figures.

Next came the Coronation Cup, which due to the War, was switched from Epsom. This time Persian Gulf and Umiddad met at level weights. Jones had clearly learnt the lesson from the last race and this time set a "decent gallop" and, although he was only three quarters of a length up at the line, was in no danger of defeat from High Chancellor, who was receiving ten pounds, with Umiddad third. Persian Gulf's time for the race was very fast, a course record, due mainly to a strong tail wind; the actual time value of the performance although good, was relatively modest.

Persian Gulf's next, and as it transpired his last, race was in the two mile Fen Ditton Stakes where he landed odds of 8–100 easily by ten lengths. He was now on target for the substitute Ascot Gold Cup but sustained an injury during his preparation. He cracked the lower end of his cannon bone in his near foreleg and that was the end of his season. The injury responded to treatment and Persian Gulf was back exercising on the Heath by the end of October, without bandages, and the hope must have been that he would recover enough to be fully trained the following year. Despite Capt. Boyd-Rochfort's efforts it was not possible to ready Persian Gulf to race again and he was retired to the Heath Lodge Stud at Newmarket. His fee was 300 guineas (£11,700).

How good was Persian Gulf? Probably a shade better than he was able to show in most of his races. Phil Bull was certain he would have won the Gold Cup in 1944 but for his injury. He would have met his old foe Umiddad who showed tremendous courage to win and Persian Gulf would have needed to have been able to produce his best over two and a half miles; a trip he never raced over. Nonetheless if as good a judge as Bull thought he would win this suggests Persian Gulf was a stayer close to the best. As a three-year-old his *Timeform* rating would have been 129 and as a four-year-old 135; which would place him towards the top of those horses that could be considered high-class but below the very best.

His record at stud can be found in the appendix. Persian Gulf died of heart failure 22nd July 1964.

His race record is as follows:-

All races staged at Newmarket's July course.

Year	Distance	Race	Placing	Race Rating	Amount won £
1943	12f	Harston Plate	6th	88+	–
	12f	New Derby Stakes	4th	129	–
	12f	Spring Hall Plate	2nd	100	–
	14f	New St Leger Stakes	4th	125	–
1944	12f	April Stakes	1st	117+	410
	11f	Linton Stakes	1st	128+	418
	14f	Thorney Stakes	2nd	128	–
	12f	Coronation Cup	1st	135	876
	16f	Fen Ditton Stakes	1st	112++	419

Statistics for the Aga Khan III
& Frank Butters

Statistics

The Aga Khan III

The following are the best horses to run in the colours of the Aga Khan III, Aly Khan and other members of the family, mostly in Britain and Ireland, between 1922 and 1962 together with their ratings as two and three-year-olds, and, where applicable, as four and five-year-olds, and in one case a six-year-old. These are based on the *Timeform* scale. Some ratings for the period 1948 to 1962 are taken directly from the *Racehorses* annual; others have been adjusted slightly. Prior to 1948 some ratings are taken form *A Century of Champions* and the rest are the authors.

Horses bred by the Aga Khan and his family that did not race in their colours are not included. Horses owned in partnership with individuals outside the family are included. Ratings for horses sold in training are also omitted from the time they no longer ran in the families colours. 1962 effectively marks the end of the breeding empire of the Aga Khan III. After 1962 there weren't any significant horses racing in the colours of the family bred by the Aga Khan III.

As a rough indication it is generally considered that horses rated 140 and above by *Timeform's Racehorses* annual are great horses capable of performances well above the normal and a horse of this standard appears, on average, about once every ten years. Those rated 132 to 139 are outstanding horses, usually but not definitely, below the standard required to be considered great, but capable of winning multiple Group/Grade 1 races. Those rated 124 to 131 are very good horses capable of winning at Group/Grade 1 level but often falling just short of the very top level in that they lose at Group/Grade 1 level at least as often as they win. Those rated 116 to 123 are good horses, capable of winning some Group/Grade 2 races and most Group/Grade 3 and Listed races. Generally these ratings can be reduced by about three to five pounds for fillies and mares.

What is impressive is the huge number of horses that raced in the colours of the Aga Khan III and his family that can be considered good and above. Although he only ever owned or bred one truly great horse: Bahram and ten outstanding horses, his studs produced an extraordinary number of good and very good horses over a period of 35 years.

The year following the name of each horse is that of foaling. Almost all the horses listed won or were placed in races that are, or have been, part of the "pattern", or high-value handicaps; those that are today considered Heritage Handicaps. Some won races that were valuable but are no longer run.

* Indicates homebred. # indicates trained by Frank Butters.

Bahram (1932) * #	127+	140+		
Felicitation (1930) * #	116	128	135	
Charlottesville (1957) *	114	135		
Tulyar (1949) *	119	134		
Tehran (1941) * #		134	132	
Petite Etoile (1956) f *	120	134	134	131
My Love (1945)	?	133+		
Palestine (1947) * #	126+	133		
Nuccio (1948)		132	133	127
Mumtaz Mahal (1921) f	129+	132		
Migoli (1944) * #	121	131	132	
Mahmoud (1933) * #	121	132		
Saint Crespin III (1956) *	128+	132		
Sheshoon (1956) *		120	132	
Theft (1932) * #	124+	131	123	
Palariva (1953) f *	126	131		
Blenheim (1927)	118	130		
Al Mabsoot (1954)	123	130	126	124
Magic North (1954)		130	122	113
Chief III (1953) *		122	130	? 124
Zambo (1922)		130	120	
Opaline (1958) f *	130	120		
Umiddad (1940) * #	124	129	130	
Venture VII (1957) *	129+	129		
Rose Royale III (1954) f *	?	129		
Buisson Ardent (1953)	125	129		
Toro (1954) f *	+	129		
Neemah (1950) f *	129	–		
Nasrullah (1940) * #	125+	128+		
Dastur (1929) * #	113+	127	128	
Rustom Pasha (1927)*	115	128	119	
Umidwar (1931) * #	90+	128	125	
Taboun (1956) *	124	128		
Hafiz II (1952) *		128		
Empire (1957) *		118	119	128
Alishah (1931) * #	112	127	112	
Ut Majeur (1927) * #		127	125	125
Hairan (1932) #	123+	126	117	
Diophon (1921)	125+	125	126	
Sind (1933) * #	+	126		
Stardust (1937) #	119+	126		
Turkhan (1937) * #	115	126		
Taj Akbar (1933) * #	92+	126	122	
Badruddin (1931) * #	100+	126	115	
Salmon Trout (1921)	120+	126	124	

Fraise Du Bois (1948)	126	124	122	
Pot-Au-Feu (1921)		126		
Avenger (1944)		126		
Princillon (1956) *	126	120	117	
Zionist (1922)	119	125	122	
Ann of Austria (1935) f * #	114+	125		
Masaka (1945) * #	119+	125+		
Firdaussi (1929) * #	122+	124	125	
Claro (1943) *	105	125	125	
Shikampur (1949)	125	124		
Esprit de France (1944)	85+	125		
Let's Fly (1951)	125	120		
Pampa (1949) f	?	?	125	
Sallymount (1956) *	?	125	124	
Cos (1920) f	122	124		
Mirza (1935) * #	124	119		
Khaled (1943) * #	119	124		
Naishapur (1942) * #	+	124		
Buland (1925)	124	121	95	
Mah Iran (1939) * #	124	117		
Éclat (1947) * #	105	124	120	
Empereur (1949)	+	124		
Rosa Bonheur (1949)	?	?	?	? 124
Tahir (1935) * #	123+	107		
Costaki Pasha (1926) *	123+	105	110	
Tant Mieux (1937)	123+			
Saravan (1944) #	122	123		
Parwiz (1925)	108+	123	119	
Mehmany (1943) #	80+	123		
Noor (1945) * #	109	123		
Field Day (1943) #	+	123	123	
Prince Taj (1954) *	112+	123		
Diableretta (1947) f * #	122+	105		
Sultan Mahomed (1934) #	114+	122	115	
Le Grand Duc (1934) * #	122+	120		
Anwar (1943) * #	+	122	119	
Dust Devil (1946) * #	95+	122	–	
Rivaz (1943) f *	122			
La Li (1935) f * #	95+	122		
Shikar II (1952) *		122	? 113	
Neron (1948)	104	121	119	
Kerkeb (1950) f		121		
Teresina (1920) f	90+	121	120	
Amante (1955) f *	100+	121		
Yla (1955) f *	108	121		
Paraguana (1956) f *	121	117		
Niceas (1920)	112	120	115	

Qurrat-Al-Ain (1927) f	117+	120	
Theresina (1927) f *	105+	120	
Khorsheed (1928) #	+	120	
Mrs Rustom (1931) f * #	120+	119	
Juldi (1922) f	85+	120	
Hakim (1925)	120+		
Nathoo (1945) * #	82	120	
Majideh (1939) f *	80?	120++	
Udaipur (1929) f * #		120	
Hindostan (1946) * #	100++	120	
Gino (1930) * #	112+	120	
Moondust (1946) * #	98++	120	120
Tambara (1947) f * #	112+	120	
Shamsuddin (1930) * #	90	120	
Skyraider (1950) *		120	
Masai King (1950) *	120+	116	
Noory (1950) f		120	
Ommeyad (1954)		116	120
Coeur Joie (1958) *		120	?
Paola (1920) f	119+	119	
Moti Mahal (1923) f *	119	118	
Bakshishi (1948) *	119	114	
Dark Japan (1923)		110	119
Vermilion Pencil (1922)		119	113
Tricky Aunt (1920) f	118	119	
Turtle Soup (1928) f *	119	103	
Stafaralla (1935) f * #	119+	105	
Bala Hissar (1933) * #	119+	104	
Cobetto (1952) *		119	
Fiere (1953)	119	?	
Ginetta (1956) f *	117	119	
Istanbul (1957) *		119	?
Foroughi (1935) * #	+	118	100
Khorassan (1947) *	+	118	
Ranjit Singh (1925)	118	115	
Tayeh (1949) f *	118	117	
Winterhalter (1937) #	95+	100	118
Tabriz (1947) * #	118+		
Princess Lora (1955) f *	?	118	
Teacup (1927) *	117	109	
La Phare (1926) *	95	117	116
Hindoo Holiday (1932) #	+	117	116
Nashua (1949) f *		117	
Charley's Mount (1921) f	101+	117	116
Khan Bahadur (1935) * #	117++	110	
Noble Venture (1954)	117	?	
Silver Hussar (1925)	90+	109	116

Shahali (1932) * #	116+	–
Ann Gudman (1927) f	116+	–
Pomme d'Api (1928) *	107+	116
Bulandshar (1929) * #	+	116
Taj Kasra (1929) * #	112+	116
Dhoti (1936) * #	116+	105
Yakimour (1936) * #	116	101
Pointis (1936) #	+	116
Neocracy (1944) #	116	
El Hawa (1945) #	116+	100
Kisaki (1947) * #	116+	–
Bari Bibi (1951) *	108	116
Tall Chief (1952) *		113	116
Poona (1951) *	116	112
Plume (1948) f		116	?
Imphal (1944) #		116
Rainbow Bloom (1943) #	116++	
Butiaba (1955) f *	?	116
La Coquenne (1956) f *		116
Lavandier (1955)	116	97
Sensualita (1954)	?	116

Big races won by the Aga Khan III

The following are the principal races won by the Aga Khan III and his family. Some have declined in value and importance while others have gained and some are no longer staged. In terms of value the five Classic races plus the Ascot Gold Cup, Coronation, St James's Palace, Jockey Club and the Eclipse Stakes were the most valuable. However, some handicaps carried huge prizes: The Hunt Cup, Cambridgeshire, Chester Cup, Lincolnshire, Ebor, City and Suburban, Cesarewitch and Newbury Autumn Cup were all worth more than the Coronation Cup, Champion and Sussex Stakes in 1935.

It should be remembered that The Aga and his trainers targeted different races between the wars than they would today. Many races from this period and just after the war have gradually been removed and replaced with maidens and handicaps. Important and valuable races for three-year-olds and up where all at a mile or further with sprinting considered of much lesser importance. Values have reduced drastically; it is impossible to imagine any racecourse today scheduling a race that was outside the pattern or was not a high-value handicap worth £50,000.

Races are listed approximately in order of importance and value with an indication of what each would be graded based on the current pattern. The grading today is given after. The values are average winning prize money for the period 1925 to 1939; during the war prize money was understandably well below what it was during peacetime. By the time that values had partially recovered after the war the Aga was no longer the force in England he had been before the war. It has been necessary to use the values of some races from after the war to indicate a true average. These values are converted into todays and compared with the winning prize money on offer in 2015. With the exception of the Derby, King George VI & Queen Elizabeth Stakes and, with the current vogue for promoting sprinting, several sprints which are all worth considerably more, the majority of races are worth less than they were between the wars.

Important races that the Aga Khan failed to win are included for the historical record. Some races are shown as "no longer run" although in some cases a different race is staged today under the same title. The distances given are those over which the race was run at the time. It should be remembered that until the Second World War the June meeting at Ascot, the May meeting at Chester and the July meeting at Goodwood comprised the only racing staged at those courses during the year. Epsom staged only the spring and Derby meetings.

Successful as the Aga Khan III was his record in the most significant races can be classed as slightly disappointing. He won the One Thousand Guineas only once and the Oaks just twice. When it is considered that he spent lavishly and bred so many good fillies it is surprising that he won only three fillies Classics. His record in the Two Thousand Guineas is not that impressive either with only three wins. However, in both the Derby and St Leger he was outstanding. The other two major races: the Ascot Gold Cup and Eclipse Stakes were won twice and three times respectively; again below the level that could have been expected.

The following are the Aga Khan III's Classic winners in Britain. These include those that ran in the colours of Aly Khan and other members of the family.

One Thousand Guineas (Group 1/Group1) – Newmarket one mile. (7,800) (390,000) (246,000)
1957 – Rose Royale III
1959 – Petite Etoile

Two Thousand Guineas (G1/1) – Newmarket one mile. (9,700) (485,000) (255,000)
1924 – Diophon
1935 – Bahram
1950 – Palestine
1959 – Taboun

Derby (G1/1) – Epsom about one mile and half. (10,500) (525,000) (782,000)
1930 – Blenheim
1935 – Bahram
1936 – Mahmoud
1948 – My Love
1952 – Tulyar

Oaks (G1/1) – Epsom about one mile and a half. (7,700) (385,000) (297,000)
1932 – Udaipur
1948 – Masaka
1959 – Petite Etoile

St. Leger (G1/1) – Doncaster about one mile six furlongs and 132 yards. (10,800) (540,000) (369,000)
1924 – Salmon-Trout
1932 – Firdaussi
1935 – Bahram
1940 – Turkhan
1944 – Tehran
1952 – Tulyar

In addition the Aga Khan bred, but had sold and did not own, Taj Mah who won the 1929 One Thousand Guineas.

The Aga Khan's wins in other principal races are shown below; these include those owned by Prince Aly Khan and other members of the family.

** Indicates a race not won by the Aga Khan III.

King George VI & Queen Elizabeth Stakes (G1/1) – Ascot one mile and a half. (First run in 1952) (23,300) (652,400) (604,000)
1952 – Tulyar

Eclipse Stakes (G1/1) – Sandown one mile and a quarter. (9,400) (470,000) (255,000)
1930 – Rustom Pasha
1947 – Migoli
1952 – Tulyar
1959 – Saint Crespin III

Ascot Gold Cup (G1/1) – Ascot two and half miles. (7,200) (360,000) (212,000)
1934 – Felicitation
1944 – Umiddad (substitute race at Newmarket; 2 ¼ miles)
1960 – Sheshoon

King George VI Stakes (G1/-) – Ascot Two miles (Run for only five years between 1946 & 1950) (7,500) (262,500) **

Jockey Club Stakes (G1/2) – Newmarket one mile and three quarters. (5,200) (260,000) (56,000)
1924 – Teresina
1932 – Firdaussi
1934 – Umidwar
1947 – Esprit de France
1949 – Dust Devil

Coronation Stakes (G1/1) – Ascot one mile. (4,900) (245,000) (212,000)
1923 – Paola
1926 – Moti Mahal
1930 – Qurrat-al-Ain
1932 – Udaipur
1950 – Tambara
1957 – Toro

St. James's Palace Stakes (G1/1) – Ascot one mile. (4,300) (215,000) (212,000)
1925 – Zambo
1935 – Bahram
1946 – Khaled
1950 – Palestine
1960 – Venture VII

Queen Elizabeth II Stakes (G1/1) – Ascot one mile (First run in 1955) (6,250) (162,500) (632,000)
1955 – Hafiz II

Royal Standard Stakes (G2/-) – Manchester one mile and a quarter. (No longer run) (3,200) (160,000) **

Gratwicke Stakes (G2/-) – Goodwood one mile and a half (No longer run) (3,150) (157,500)
1928 – Parwiz
1934 – Umidwar

Hardwicke Stakes (G2/2) – Ascot one mile and a half. (3,100) (155,000) (120,000)
1939 – Pointis

Princess of Wales's Stakes (G2/2) – Newmarket one mile and a half. (2,700) (135,000) (56,000)
1924 – Salmon-Trout
1936 – Taj Akbar
1955 – Cobetto

King Edward VII Stakes (G2/2) – Ascot one mile and a half. (2,500) (125,000) (113,000)
1932 – Dastur
1938 – Foroughi
1946 – Field Day
1947 – Migoli
1953 – Skyraider

White Rose Stakes (G2/-) – Hurst Park One mile and seven furlongs. (No longer run) (2,450) (122,500).
1948 – Migoli

Prince of Wales's Stakes (G2/-) – Ascot one mile and five furlongs (No longer run) (2,400) (120,000). **

Waterford Stakes (G3/-) – Ascot one mile (No longer run) (2,150) (107,500)
1934 – Badruddin

St. George's Stakes (G3/-) – Liverpool one mile and five furlongs. (No longer run) (2,150) (107,500). **

Atlantic Cup (G3/-) – Liverpool one mile and a quarter (No longer run) (2,150) (107,500)
1925 – Diophon
1934 – Alishah

Gold Vase (now Queens Vase) (G3/L) – Ascot two miles (2,100) (105,000) (48,000). **

John Porter Stakes – Newbury one mile and five furlongs. (G3/3) (Race discontinued in this form in 1935, race restarted in 1949 but worth only a fraction of its pre-war value). (2,050) (102,500) (34,000)
1929 – Silver Hussar
1934 – Felicitation
1952 – Neron

Great Yorkshire Stakes (G2/-) – York one mile and a half (No longer run) (1,950) (97,500)
1923 – Teresina
1925 – Zambo
1929 – Maggi
1937 – Mange Tout

Red Rose Stakes (G3/-) – Manchester 6 furlongs (No longer run) (1,925) (102,000).
1929 – Le Phare

Ormonde Stakes (G3/3) – Chester one mile five furlongs and 89 yards (1,900) (99,000) (42,000). Originally a race for two-year-olds and inaugurated in 1936 as a race for three-year-olds and up over one mile five furlongs and 75 yards. It was confined to three-year-olds for three years from 1955 and the distance cut to one mile two furlongs and ten yards. The original distance was restored in 1958 and the race confined to four-year-olds and up. The distance was extended in 1970.

1952 – Tulyar

Coronation Cup (G1/1) – Epsom about a mile and a half. (1,900) (95,000) (219,000)
1933 – Dastur
1941 – Winterhalter (substitute race run at Newmarket)
1952 – Nuccio
1960 – Petite Etoile
1961 – Petite Etoile

Newmarket Stakes (G2/-) – Newmarket one mile and a quarter (1,900) (95,000) (23,000). **

Jersey Stakes (G3/3) – Ascot seven furlongs and 155 yards (1850) (92,500) (42,000)
1935 – Theft

Ribblesdale Stakes (G3/-) – Ascot one mile. (1,850) (92,500). Was inaugurated in 1919 as a race for 3 & 4 y o over the old mile and was last run in 1939 and did not resume after the war. It became a race for 3 y o fillies over a mile and a half in 1950.

Gold Vase (G3/Listed) – Ascot Two miles (1,800) (90,000) (48,000)
1931 – Pomme d'Api

Liverpool Derby (G3/-) – Liverpool one mile and five furlongs (No longer run) (1,800) (90,000) **

Diomed Stakes (G3/3) – Epsom one mile and a half. (Staged only five times between 1947 and 1952 – it was run as a handicap in 1950) (2,600) (88,400) (40,000)
1947 – Imphal
1948 – Noor
1949 – Moondust
1952 – Nemrod

Champion Stakes (G1/1) – Newmarket one mile and a quarter (1,750) (87,500) (770,000)
1930 – Rustom Pasha
1932 – Dastur (dead heat)
1934 – Umidwar
1943 – Nasrullah
1947 – Migoli

1955 – Hafiz
1957 – Rose Royale
1959 – Petite Etoile

Nassau Stakes (G3/1) – Goodwood one mile and a quarter. (1,700) (85,000) (113,000)
1938 – Valedeh

Blue Riband Trial Stakes (Was Nonesuch Plate) (G3/-) – Epsom one mile and 155 yards. (1,650) (82,500) (31,000)
1929 – Buland Bala
1930 – Rustom Pasha
1936 – Taj Akbar

Princess Elizabeth Stakes (G3/-) – Epsom one mile and 155 yards. (Was the Ebbisham Stakes) (3,500) (94,500)
1954 – Bara Bibi
1958 – Princess Lora

Ebbisham Stakes (G3/3) – Epsom about one mile and 110 yards (First run in 1937 now Princess Elizabeth Stakes) (1,600) (80,000) (40,000)
1938 – La Li

Chester Vase (G2/3) – Chester about a mile and a half. (1,600) (80,000) (42,000)
1925 – Vermilion Pencil
1932 – Bulandshar
1936 – Taj Akbar

Queen Alexandra Stakes (G3/-) – Ascot two miles six furlongs and 85 yards. (1,600) (80,000) (37,000)
1926 – Vermilion Pencil
1953 – Lord Fox

Park Hill Stakes (G3/2) – Doncaster about one mile six furlongs and 132 yards. (1,550) (77,500) (51,000)
1924 – Charley's Mount
1925 – Juldi
1953 – Kerkeb
1954 – Bara Bibi

Goodwood Cup (G3/2) – Goodwood about two miles and five furlongs. (1,400) (70,000) (68,000)
1924 – Teresina
1927 – Dark Japan

King George Stakes (G2/2) – Goodwood 5 furlongs (1,400) (70,000) (56,000)
1924 – Mumtaz Mahal
1938 – Neuvy

Queen Anne Stakes (G3/1) – Ascot one mile. (1,350) (67,500) (230,000)
1936 – Hindoo Holiday
1951 – Neron

Cork & Orrery Stakes (G3/1) – Ascot 6 furlongs (was All-aged Stakes now Diamond Jubilee Stakes) (1,350) (67,500) (297,000)
1930 – Costaki Pasha
1937 – Pherozshah

Great Foal Stakes (L/-) – Newmarket one mile and a quarter (No longer run) (1,250) (62,500)
1934 – Alishah

King Stand Stakes (G3/1) – Ascot 5 furlongs (1,200) (60,000) (212,000)
1937 – Ticca Gari
1956 – Palariva

Heathcote Stakes (L/-) – Epsom one mile and a quarter. (First run in 1936 and no longer staged) (1,450) (58,750)
1947 – Esprit de France

Falmouth Stakes (G3/1) – Newmarket one mile. (1,100) (55,000) (113,000)
1930 – Theresina
1938 – La Li

Sussex Stakes (G2/1) – Goodwood one mile. (1,050) (52,500) (170,000)
1929 – Le Phare
1932 – Dastur
1934 – Badruddin
1935 – Hairan
1950 – Palestine
1959 – Petite Etoile
1960 – Venture VII

Column Produce Stakes (G3/-) – Newmarket one mile (No longer run) (1,050) (52,500)
1946 – Khaled

Newmarket St Leger (G3/-) – Newmarket one mile and three quarters. (No longer run) (1,050) (52,500)
1930 – Ut Majeur
1953 – Kerkeb

Limekiln Stakes (L/-) – Newmarket one mile and a quarter (1,025) (51,250) (No longer staged). **

Yorkshire Oaks (G3/1) – York one mile and a half. (1,020) (51,000) (187,000)
1953 – Kerkeb
1959 – Petite Etoile

Craven Stakes (G3/3) – Newmarket one mile. (1,000) (50,000) (37,000)
1947 – Migoli
1949 – Moondust

Rous Memorial (G3/-) – Ascot 7 furlongs and 166 yards. (No longer staged) (1,000) (50,000)
1934 – Alishah
1938 – Khan Bahadur
1961 – Petite Etoile

Newmarket Oaks (G3/-) – Newmarket one mile and three quarters. (950) (47,500) (No longer run)
1925 – Juldi
1932 – Udaipur

Lowther Stakes (L/-) – Newmarket one mile and three quarters. (950) (47,500) (No longer staged)
1938 – Sultan Mahomed

Nunthorpe Stakes (G2/G1) – York 5 furlongs (900) (45,000) (150,000)
1924 – Mumtaz Mahal

Dee Stakes (L/L) – Chester about one mile and half. (870) (43,500) (43,000)
1928 – Ranjit Singh
1934 – Alishah
1950 – Khorassan

Gordon Stakes (G3/3) – Goodwood one mile and a half. (870) (43,500) (45,000)
1930 – Ut Majeur (Dead-heat)
1932 – Firdaussi
1948 – Nathoo

Greenham Plate (Now Greenham Stakes) (G3/3) – Newbury one mile. (840) (42,000) (34,000)
1935 – Theft
1938 – Mirza

Princess Royal Stakes (G3/1) – Ascot one mile and a half (First run in 1946 now British Champions Fillies & Mares Stakes) (1,050) (37,000) (344,000)
1946 – Mehmany

July Cup (G3/1) – Newmarket 6 furlongs (750) (33,750) (289,000) * *

Jockey Club Cup (G3/2) – Newmarket two and a quarter miles. (Now British Champions Long Distance Cup) (700) (35,000) (178,000)

1934 – Felicitation

The following are Aga Khan III winners in principal juvenile races. These also include horses that ran in the colours of Aly Khan's and other members of the family. These were the most important races during the period 1922 to 1957. Plenty are no longer staged and others are not as valuable or important as for the period in question. Some races that have ceased have been subsequently run under a similar title but different conditions. No attempt has been made to classify each race as any meaningful categorisation is impossible. The distances given are those over which the race was run at that time.

National Breeders Produce Stakes – Sandown 5 furlongs. Ceased after 1959 and run as National Stakes since 1960 with reduced prize money. (6,500) (325,000) (15,000)
1923 – Mumtaz Mahal
1934 – Bahram
1939 – Stardust
1949 – Palestine

Imperial Produce Stakes – Kempton 6 furlongs. Ceased after 1959; run as the Imperial Stakes from 1960 – 1968 with reduced prize money. Run as Sirenia Stakes since 1969 (4,700) (235,000) (24,000)
1922 – Cos
1927 – Buland
1932 – Gino
1934 – Shahali
1949 – Kisaki
1958 – Saint Crespin III
1959 – Venture VII

Queen Mary Stakes – Ascot 5 furlongs. (3,500) (175,000) (56,000)
1922 – Cos
1923 – Mumtaz Mahal
1929 – Qurrat-al-Ain
1937 – Queen of Simla
1945 – Rivaz
1947 – Masaka
1949 – Diableretta

Lancashire Breeders Produce Stakes – Liverpool 5 furlongs ceased after 1939. (3,270) (163,500). **

Ham (Produce) Stakes – Goodwood 6 furlongs ceased after 1939. Run as New Ham Stakes since 1946 and ceased in 1980 (3,200) (160,000)
1925 – Moti Mahal
1929 – Ann Gudman
1932 – Moti Begum
1933 – Mrs Rustom
1934 – Theft
1937 – Tahir

Middle Park Stakes – Newmarket 6 furlongs. (3,150) (157,500) (123,000)
1923 – Diophon
1928 – Costaki Pasha
1932 – Felicitation
1934 – Bahram
1945 – Khaled
1946 – Saravan
1955 – Buisson Ardent
1959 – Venture VII

New Stakes (Now Norfolk Stakes) – Ascot 5 furlongs. (2,750) (137,500) (45,000)
1927 – Hakim
1929 – Blenheim
1936 – Le Grand Duc

Champagne Stakes – Doncaster 6 furlongs. (2,500) (125,000) (43,000)
1923 – Mumtaz Mahal
1935 – Mahmoud
1949 – Palestine

Coventry Stakes – Ascot 5 furlongs. (2,250) (112,500) (68,000)
1934 – Hairan
1937 – Mirza

1939 – Turkhan
1942 – Nasrullah (Substitution run at Newmarket).
1945 – Khaled
1949 – Palestine

Chesham Stakes – Ascot five furlongs (1,950) (97,500) (34,000)
1928 – Costaki Pasha
1934 – Shahali
1937 – Tahir
1938 – Dhoti
1950 – Bakshishi
1955 – Palariva

Sandown Park Stud Produce Stakes – Sandown 5 furlongs. Ceased after 1959. (1,900) (95,000)
1931 – Tarte Maison
1938 – Dasaratha
1947 – Masala
1949 – Palestine

Gimcrack Stakes – York 6 furlongs. (1,850) (92,500) Prize money for this race almost doubled in 1938 from 1,700 to 3,050. It reverted to about 2,200 after the war. (113,000)
1933 – Mrs Rustom
1934 – Bahram
1939 – Tant Mieux
1949 – Palestine

Molecomb Stakes – Goodwood – 5 furlongs. (1,825) (91,250) (28,000)
1923 – Mumtaz Mahal
1934 – La Gaiete
1937 – Ann of Austria
1949 – Diableretta
1951 – Tayeh
1955 – Palariva

Cheveley Park Stakes – Newmarket 6 furlongs. (1,800) (90,000) (117,000)
1922 – Paola
1937 – Stafaralla
1960 – Opaline

The Prince of Wales's Stakes – Goodwood 6 furlongs (ceased after 1933) (1,800) (90,000)
1928 – Le Voleur

Dewhurst Stakes – Newmarket 7 furlongs. (1,650) (82,500) (256,000)
1923 – Salmon-Trout
1924 – Zionist
1931 – Firdaussi
1933 – Mrs Rustom
1934 – Hairan
1935 – Bala Hissar
1936 – Sultan Mahomed
1942 – Umiddad
1946 – Migoli

Buckenham (Post Produce) Stakes – Newmarket 5 furlongs ceased after 1938. (1,600) (80,000)
1931 – Tarte Maison
1933 – Alishah
1934 – Theft

July Stakes – Newmarket 5 furlongs and 140 yards. (1,450) (72,500) (45,000)
1923 – Diophon
1929 – Teacup
1933 – Alishah
1934 – Hilla
1937 – Mirza
1945 – Rivaz
1947 – Masaka
1949 – Diableretta

Royal Lodge Stakes – Ascot one mile. First run in 1946 over 5 furlongs, run at a mile from 1948. (3,250) (90,000) (67,000).
1949 – Tabriz
1950 – Fraise du Bois II
1952 – Neemah
1956 – Noble Venture

Lavant Stakes – Goodwood 5 furlongs. Ceased after 1939. (1,650) (82,500)
1927 – Hakim
1937 – Mirza

Hurst Park Great Two-Year-Old-Stakes – Hurst Park 6 furlongs (1,550) (77,500) run as Hurst Park Two-Year-Old Stakes 1933 to 1937 with reduced prize money.
1930 – Turtle Soup
1933 – Umidwar
1937 – Dardanelles

Windsor Castle Stakes – Ascot 5 furlongs. (1,500) (75,000) (34,000)
1922 – Tricky Aunt
1929 – Teacup
1931 – Taj Kasra
1934 – Theft
1949 – Tabriz
1952 – Masai King

Rous Memorial Stakes – Goodwood 6 furlongs ceased after 1982 (1,400) (70,000)
1935 – Baber Shah
1947 – El Hawa

Lonsdale Stakes – Epsom 6 furlongs inaugurated in 1946 ceased after 1969. (2,050) (75,000)
1946 – Neocracy

Cherry Hinton Stakes – Newmarket 6 furlongs. (First run in 1948) (Now Duchess of Cambridge Stakes) (2,050) (65,600) (45,000)
1949 – Diableretta
1952 – Omelia

Great Surrey Foal Stakes – Epsom 5 furlongs ceased after 1957 (1,950) (65,000)
1955 – Palariva

Richmond Stakes – Goodwood 6 furlongs. (1,300) (65,000) (45,000)
1922 – Bombay Duck
1935 – Mahmoud
1939 – Moradabad
1949 – Palestine

Champagne Stakes – Salisbury 5 furlongs ceased after 1995 (1,250) (62,500)
1928 – Grand Terrace

Tattersall Sales Stakes – Doncaster 7 furlongs (no longer run) (1,200) (60,000)
1928 – Buland Bala

Woodcote Stakes – Epsom 6 furlongs. (1,200) (60,000) (23,000)
1931 – Dastur

Chesterfield Stakes – Newmarket 5 furlongs ceased after 1985) (1,050) (52,500)
1927 – Hakim
1937 – Mirza

Hopeful Stakes – Newmarket 5 furlongs ceased after 1960 (1,050) (52,500)
1925 – Moti Mahal
1928 – Costaki Pasha
1929 – Blenheim
1937 – Ann of Austria

Stud Produce Stakes – Newmarket 5 furlongs ceased after 1959 (975) (48,750)
1922 – Cos

Criterion Stakes – Newmarket 6 furlongs ceased after 1958. (625) (31,250)
1927 – Farhad
1934 – Shahali
** Indicates a race not won by the Aga Khan III.

The following are the Aga Khan's Classic winners in Ireland. These include horses that ran in Aly Khan's and other members of the families colours.

One Thousand Guineas – Curragh one mile.
1942 – Majideh
1952 – Nashua
1958 – Butiaba
1959 – Fiorentina

Two Thousand Guineas – Curragh one mile.
1946 – Claro

Derby – Curragh one mile and a half.
1925 – Zionist
1932 – Dastur
1940 – Turkhan
1948 – Nathoo
1949 – Hindostan
1951 – Fraise du Bois III

Oaks – Curragh one mile and a half.
1930 – Theresina
1940 – Queen of Shiraz
1942 – Majideh
1948 – Masaka
1953 – Noory
1958 – Amante

St Leger – Curragh one mile and six furlongs.
1947 – Esprit de France
1957 – Ommeyad

The following are the Aga Khan's Classic winners in France. These also include horses that ran in Aly Khan's and other members of the families colours.

Poule d'Essai des Poulains – Longchamp one mile.
1956 – Buisson Ardent

Poule d'Essai Pouliches – Longchamp one mile.
1957 – Toro
1958 – Yla
1959 – Ginetta

Prix du Jockey Club – Chantilly one mile and a half.
1924 – Pot-au-Feu
1960 – Charlottesville

The following are the Aga Khan's wins in other important French racing.

Prix du Moulin de Longchamp – Longchamp one mile
1957 – Rose Royale
1959 – Ginetta

Grand Prix de Paris – Longchamp – one mile and seven furlongs.
1947 – Avenger
1948 – My Love
1960 – Charlottesville

Grand Prix de Saint-Cloud – Saint-Cloud one mile and four and a half furlongs.
1924 – Pot-au-Feu
1960 – Sheshoon

Prix de l'Arc de Triomphe – Longchamp one mile and a half.
1948 – Migoli
1952 – Nuccio
1959 – Saint Crespin III

The following is the Aga Khan III's record as an owner in England. The figures are largely meaningless for the period after he decided in 1955 to have most of his horses trained in France. In addition some horses trained in England were owned by the Begum and are not included.

Year	Winners	Races	Value (£)	Position
1922	5	13	13,733	9th
1923	11	22	33,409	2nd
1924	11	19	44,377	1st

1925	13	28	32,974	3rd
1926	10	15	14,774	7th
1927	13	21	21,918	3rd
1928	11	14	20,570	4th
1929	20	35	39,886	1st
1930	16	23	46,259	1st
1931	17	27	19,484	5th
1932	14	28	57,778	1st
1933	16	24	19,311	3rd
1934	18	45	64,898	1st
1935	13	23	49,302	1st
1936	11	18	29,057	3rd
1937	17	30	30,655	1st
1938	14	19	20,964	4th
1939	7	10	10,797	8th
1940	3	5	2,427	7th
1941	3	7	2,503	12th
1942	7	12	5,063	3rd
1943	7	14	5,596	3rd
1944	13	22	13,984	1st
1945	12	28	13,465	3rd
1946	19	34	24,544	1st
1947	16	28	44,020	1st
1948	17	28	46,393	1st
1949	19	39	68,916	1st
1950	16	24	42,207	2nd
1951	16	23	12,647	12th
1952	14	29	92,518	1st
1953	16	28	26,070	2nd
1954	14	18	13,674	11th
1955	3	6	20,948	6th
1956	3	4	7,403	30th
1957	2	2	18,516	9th

In addition the Aga Khan III owned 65 winners of 104 races with a total value of £60,401 in Ireland. He also owned 133 winners of 173,466 FF (approximately £177,000) in France.

The Aga Khan III's record as a breeder in England.

Year	Winners	Races	Value (£)	Position
1925	1	5	6,357	–
1926	1	1	4,950	–
1927	–	–	–	–
1928	6	8	13,386	8th
1929	12	20	22,488	5th

1930	11	16	27,529	3rd
1931	15	24	18,590	7th
1932	15	30	62,644	1st
1933	13	19	17,436	5th
1934	15	41	57,733	1st
1935	13	23	49,285	1st
1936	14	26	29,920	2nd
1937	32	52	46,728	1st
1938	27	36	23,592	4th
1939	15	17	7,012	11th
1940	13	20	9,039	1st
1941	21	34	9,551	1st
1942	23	38	12,237	2nd
1943	15	22	8,153	3rd
1944	17	26	8,309	3rd
1945	21	41	18,328	2nd
1946	25	41	18,099	6th
1947	31	52	46,700	1st
1948	30	52	54,915	1st
1949	24	50	69,976	1st
1950	24	38	50,784	2nd
1951	20	31	16,391	9th
1952	27	45	97,204	1st
1953	16	27	18,219	7th
1954	17	22	19,952	6th
1955	10	16	23,459	5th
1956	14	23	13,323	20th
1957	9	18	30,247	4th
1958	6	7	17,953	12th
1959	8	14	102,489	1st
1960	4	6	20,672	7th
1961	1	4	7,604	–

All dead-heats count as a win and not ½ as some records show. Winnings are to the nearest pound with shillings and pence ignored.

Frank Butters

The following are the winners of Classic races and the most valuable and significant weight-for-age races trained by Frank Butters. Other races increased or decreased in value but these races were always the most valuable and important during the period from 1927 to 1949. It should be remembered that in 1939 the St Leger was not run and for the years 1940 to 1945 many other big races were also not staged. The Ascot Gold Cup was run as a substitute race at Newmarket from 1940 to 1944 inclusive.

2000 Guineas
1935 – Bahram

1000 Guineas
1930 – Fair Isle

Derby
1935 – Bahram
1936 – Mahmoud

Oaks
1927 – Beam
1928 – Toboggan
1932 – Udaipur
1934 – Light Brocade
1946 – Steady Aim
1948 – Masaka

St Leger
1928 – Fairway
1932 – Firdaussi
1935 – Bahram
1940 – Turkhan
1944 – Tehran

Eclipse Stakes
1927 – Colorado
1928 – Fairway
1947 – Migoli
1948 – Petition

Ascot Gold Cup
1930 – Bosworth
1934 – Felicitation
1944 – Umiddad

Jockey Club Stakes
1928 – Toboggan
1930 – Pyramid
1932 – Firdaussi
1934 – Umidwar
1949 – Dust Devil

Coronation Stakes
1928 – Toboggan

1932 – Udaipur
1938 – Solar Flower

St James's Palace Stakes
1935 – Bahram
1946 – Khaled

Gratwicke Stakes
1929 – Hunter's Moon
1934 – Umidwar
1938 – Solar Flower

Hardwick Stakes
1939 – Pointis

Princess of Wales's Stakes
1927 – Colorado
1929 – Fairway
1936 – Taj Akbar

King Edward VII Stakes
1932 – Dastur
1938 – Foroughi
1946 – Field Day
1947 – Migoli

Prince of Wales's Stakes
1934 – Achtenan

St George Stakes
1929 – Bosworth

Coronation Cup
1933 – Dastur
1941 – Winterhalter

Newmarket Stakes
1928 – Fairway
1929 – Hunter's Moon
1933 – Young Lover

Champion Stakes
1928 – Fairway
1929 – Fairway

1933 – Dastur
1934 – Umidwar
1943 – Nasrullah
1947 – Migoli

The following were the most valuable and important juvenile races for the period 1927 to 1949.

National Breeders Produce Stakes
1934 – Bahram
1939 – Stardust
1949 – Palestine

Imperial Produce Stakes
1932 – Gino
1934 – Shahali
1949 – Kisaki

Queen Mary Stakes
1937 – Queen of Simla
1938 – Belle Travers
1945 – Rivaz
1947 – Masaka
1949 – Diableretta

Ham (Produce) Stakes
1932 – Moti Begum
1933 – Mrs Rustom
1934 – Theft
1937 – Tahir

Middle Park Stakes
1927 – Pharamond
1932 – Felicitation
1934 – Bahram
1945 – Khaled
1946 – Saravan

New Stakes
1936 – Le Grand Duc
1946 – Petition

Champagne Stakes
1927 – Fairway
1935 – Mahmoud

1946 – Petition
1949 – Palestine

Coventry Stakes
1927 – Fairway
1934 – Hairan
1937 – Mirza
1939 – Turkhan
1942 – Nasrullah
1945 – Khaled
1949 – Palestine

Chesham Stakes
1934 – Shahali
1937 – Tahir
1938 – Dhoti

Gimcrack Stakes
1932 – Young Lover
1933 – Mrs Rustom
1934 – Bahram
1946 – Petition
1949 – Palestine

Molecomb Stakes
1933 – Light Brocade
1934 – La Gaiete
1937 – Ann of Austria
1949 – Diableretta

Cheveley Park Stakes
1933 – Light Brocade
1937 – Stafaralla

Dewhurst Stakes
1927 – Toboggan
1931 – Firdaussi
1933 – Mrs Rustom
1934 – Hairan
1935 – Bala Hissar
1936 – Sultan Mahomed
1942 – Umiddad
1944 – Paper Weight
1946 – Migoli

July Stakes
1927 – Fairway
1933 – Alishah
1934 – Hilla
1937 – Mirza
1945 – Rivaz
1947 – Masaka
1949 – Diableretta

The following is the year-by-year training record of Frank Butters in England.

Year	Horses In training	Winning	Races won	total value £	Position
1927	56	26	54	57,468	1st
1928	52	27	50	67,539	1st
1929	58	23	60	35,861	3rd
1930	54	28	60	41,418	3rd
1931	17+*	23	49	17,545	9th
1932	63	34	62	72,436	1st
1933	65	31	65	42,573	2nd
1934	68	33	79	88,884	1st
1935	72	30	48	59,687	1st
1936	66	19	31	35,153	4th
1937	61	37	57	48,609	3rd
1938	65	31	45	40,750	3rd
1939	63	24	36	26,186	4th
1940	23	11	13	4,757	6th
1941	11	7	14	5,149	7th
1942	23	13	23	8,239	3rd
1943	35	13	23	8,350	2nd
1944	40	18	34	17,585	1st
1945	41	16	34	15,652	4th
1946	53	31	60	56,140	1st
1947	60	27	43	57,911	2nd
1948	65	24	39	50,832	2nd
1949	58	20	42	71,721	1st
* Precise figure unknown			1,021	930,445	

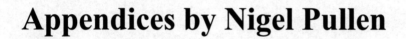

Appendices by Nigel Pullen

Appendix I

Bahram at stud

BAHRAM IN EUROPE

Bahram retired to Egerton House Stud, Newmarket at a fee of 500 guineas (£28,000). His initial book contained some of the Aga Khan's best mares including Theresina, Qurrat-Al-Ain and Mah Mahal.

1937

Bahram's first crop consisted of eight foals and of these, five went on to win races in England and Ireland, including one Classic and two further Irish Classics, while two of the other three won races abroad.

1938

Bahram's first yearlings were sold this year. At the Doncaster September sales twenty-four hours after Scottish Union had won the St. Leger, his half-brother by Bahram was sold as part of the Sledmere Stud's consignment of ten yearlings.

The St. Leger result heightened the appeal of this strongly-made colt, and after an opening bid of 5,000 guineas (£250,000), the bidding accelerated to 10,000 guineas (£500,000) and ended only after a bid of 13,000 guineas (£655,000). He was named The Druid and although only moderate on the race-course he was a successful stallion in Argentina.

The Newmarket First October Sales began at the end of September and, with War a possibility, more than half the lots submitted on the first two days failed to find buyers, and those that sold realised far below their real value. Bahram's yearling colt, out of Premiere Danseuse, was one of those led out unsold on the second day of the sale at 3,000 guineas (£476,000). Named Czadas, he would win one race worth £168.

Bahram's second crop of foals numbered twenty with a fertility rate of 81.4%; comprising up of fifteen fillies and five colts.

1938 Yearling Average 13,000 guineas (£655,000); Median 13,000 guineas (£655,000)

Yearling	Dam	Price (guineas)	Subsequent Career
The Druid [b c]	Trustful	13,000	Won 2 races worth £1,534. Successful stallion in Argentina.

1939

Bahram's progeny raced for the first time. From eight juveniles he was leading first season sire with three winners of four races worth £4,052 (186,000). His first winner was a filly: Great Truth won the Whitsuntide Plate at Manchester on her debut. She was unplaced in the Queen Mary Stakes, won the Fulbourne Stakes at Newmarket's July Meeting, before finishing third to Stardust in the National Breeders Produce Stakes at Sandown.

Bahram's first Ascot winner was Turkhan, who won the Coventry Stakes. At Goodwood he finished second to Hippius in the Ham Produce Stakes.

All three of Bahram's juvenile winners appeared in the Free Handicap at the end of the season, with Turkhan being allocated 9st.2lb. (5lbs. below top rated Tant Mieux) and both Great Truth and The Druid (winner of the Cranbourne Plate at Salisbury) being given a mark of 8st.10lb.

Bahram's third crop of foals numbered 22 with a fertility of 84.4%.

1939 Yearling Average 2,180 guineas (£105,000); Median 1,400 guineas (£67,500).

Yearling	Dam	Price (guineas)	Subsequent Career
Bukhara [gr f]	Una	3,500	Unplaced at 3
Bukumbi [b f]	La Douairiere	1,400	Won 3 races worth 37,950 lira in Italy at 3
Bura [b f]	Becti	1,200	Placed at 3
Queen of Bombay [br f]	Queen of Scots	3,300	Exported to USA as a foal. Unraced.
Shah Jehan [b c]	Trochee	1,500	Unplaced at 2 & 3

Winners in Great Britain and Ireland sired by Bahram
N.B. age and gender follow horses name in brackets.

1939	Dam	Dam Sire	Wins	Value in £
Great Truth [2 f]	Frankly	Franklin	5f. 5f.	1,420.00
The Druid [2 c]	Trustful	Bachelor's Double	5f.	132.00
Turkhan [2 c]	Theresina	Diophon	5f.	2,500.00
TOTAL			4	4,052.00

Principal winners: – **Great Truth** – Fulbourne Stakes (5f.); **Turkhan** – Coventry Stakes (5f.)

1940

Turkhan was second in the Derby and won the Irish Derby and St. Leger. Queen of Shiraz won the Irish Oaks. Bahram finished second to Hyperion on the list of winning sires.

Of the juveniles many of the fillies were unraced and the only colt to win was Nimrod, who won a minor event.

Bahram's foal crop for 1940 was 18 there were 15 mares that were barren, giving him a fertility of 58.33%

In July Bahram was sold and exported to North America.

1940 Foal Average 1,000 guineas (£46,000); Median 1,000 guineas (£46,000)

Yearling	Dam	Price (guineas)	Subsequent Career
Bahram Valdina [b c]	Love Tie	1,000	To USA 1941

1940 Yearling Average 130 guineas (£6,300); Median 130 guineas (£6,300)

Yearling	Dam	Price (guineas)	Subsequent Career
Balmoral (br c)	Flute	130	Placed at 3

Winners in Great Britain and Ireland sired by Bahram

1940 (2nd)	Dam	Dam Sire	Wins	Value in £
Czadas [3 c]	Premiere Danseuse	Phalaris	12f.	168.00
Nimrod [2 c]	Fireplace	Bruleur	8f.	206.00
Queen of Shiraz [3 f]	Qurrat-Al-Ain	Buchan	12f.	1,447.50
The Druid [3 c]	Trustful	Bachelor's Double	6f.	1,402.00
Turkhan [3 c]	Theresina	Diophon	12f. 14f.	3,480.00
TOTAL			6	6,703.50

Principal winners: – **Queen of Shiraz** – Irish Oaks (12f.); **Turkhan** – Irish Derby (12f.), St. Leger (14f.).

Bahram's British bred offspring with earnings abroad

1940	Dam	Dam Sire	Wins	Earnings	Country
Bukhara II [2 f]	Una	Tetratema	0	$300	USA

1941

None of Bahram's three-year-olds won a race. Nine of his juveniles won races, and Bahram was leading sire of two-year-olds. Their performances placed him third on the list of leading sires behind Hyperion and Colombo.

The best juvenile was Big Game whose career has already been covered. Bahram also sired a promising filly: Mah Iran, a three-quarter sister to Derby winner Mahmoud. The winner of two of her six starts, she also finished second to Watling Street in the Chesterfield Stakes.

Six of Bahram's two-year-olds were ranked in the top 42 of the Free Handicap; Big Game, 9st.6lb (1lb below top-rated Sun Chariot), Mah Iran; 9st.3lb, Birikan; 8st.9lb, Cheerful Annie; 8st.4lb, Paramount and Shah Rookh both 8st.1lb.

Bahram's final crop from his five year tenure in England was foaled. He sired 21 foals, 11 mares were barren and his fertility 68.57%.

1941 Yearling Average 1,200 guineas (£52,000); Median 1,200 guineas (£52,000).

Yearling	Dam	Price (guineas)	Subsequent Career
Dangerous Moonlight [b f]	Quadriga	1,200	Unplaced at 2 & 3

Winners in Great Britain and Ireland sired by Bahram

1941 (3rd)	Dam	Dam Sire	Wins	Value in £
Badr Bidi [2 f]	Becti	Salmon Trout	5f.	83.00
Big Game [2 c]	Myrobella	Tetratema	5f. 5f. 5f. 5f. 6f.	2,647.75
Birikan [2 c]	Carola	Tetratema	5f. 6f.	470.50
Cheerful Annie [2 f]	Anne of Brittany	Diligence	5f. 6f.	581.00
Hasty Shot [2 c]	Instantaneous	Hurry On	5f.	286.00
Mah Iran [2 f]	Mah Mahal	Gainsborough	5f. 5f.	780.25
Paramount [2 c]	Renate	Son and Heir	5f. 5f.	501.00
Shah Rookh [2 c]	Farmood	Phalaris	5f.	274.25
Valiant [2 f]	Trustful	Bachelor's Double	5f.	186.00
TOTAL			17	5,809.75

Principal winners: – **Big Game** – Coventry Stakes (5f.), Champagne Stakes (6f.); **Birikan** – Soltykoff Stakes (6f.).

Bahram's British bred offspring with earnings abroad

1941	Dam	Dam Sire	Wins	Earnings	Country
Bisharin [4 c]	La Voulzie	Teddy	2	6,430 Rs.	India
Golden Fawn [4 c]	Mah Mahal	Gainsborough	1	4,940 Rs.	India
Bukumai [3 f]	La Douairiere	Spearmint	3	37,950 Lira	Italy
Bukhara II [3 f]	Una	Tetratema	0	$1,455	USA
Ganges [3 f]	Gaillonelle	Gainsborough	0	$50	USA
Paladin [2 c]	Mah Mahal	Clarissimus	1	$1,125	USA

N.B. Golden Fawn was originally named Bashir

1942

Both Big Game and Mah Iran each won three races.
  1942 Yearling Average 1,775 guineas (£710,000); Median 1775 guineas (£710,000)

Yearling	Dam	Price (guineas)	Subsequent Career
Bahara [b c]	Hermia	1,550	Placed at 2
Nith [b f]	Alfane	2,000	Unplaced at 3

Winners in Great Britain and Ireland sired by Bahram

1942 (5th)	Dam	Dam Sire	Wins	Value in £
Big Game [3 c]	Myrobella	Tetratema	7f. 8f. 10f.	3,181.25
Birikan [3 c]	Carola	Tetratema	6f. 8f. 9f.	748.75
Brehon Law [2 c]	Constant Law	Portlaw	5f.	83.00
Bura [4 f]	Becti	Salmon Trout	8f.	298.50
Extravagance [2 f]	Spend A Penny	Apron	5f. 6f.	561.50
Isara [4 f]	Sultan Ranee	Hurry On	12f.	40.00
Mah Iran [3 f]	Mah Mahal	Gainsborough	5f. 6f. 6f.	1,154.00
Safari [2 f]	Solerina	Soldennis	5f.	83.00
Shah Rookh [3 c]	Farmood	Phalaris	8f.	186.00
Whirlaway [2 c]	Jury	Hurry On	6f.	167.00
TOTAL			17	6,503.00

Principal winners: – **Big Game** – 2000 Guineas (8f.), Champion Stakes (10f.).
Bahram's British bred offspring with earnings abroad

1942	Dam	Dam Sire	Wins	Earnings	Country
Brinda [3 f]	Herlinde	Asterus	2	126,940 frs.	France
Bisharin [5 c]	La Voulzie	Teddy	1	2,715 Rs.	India
Golden Fawn [5 c]	Mah Mahal	Gainsborough	4	80,126 Rs.	India
Paladin [3 c]	Mah Mahal	Clarissimus	2	$3,125	USA
Raj Kumar [3 c]	Quick Action	Happy Argo	0	$1,075	USA

N.B. Golden Fawn was originally named Bashir
Principal Winners: – **Golden Fawn** – Eclipse Stakes of India, Hughes Memorial Plate

1943

This year saw Bahram's final British crop race. Persian Gulf was still a maiden but would become Bahram's best progeny from this year.
  In India, Bahram's son Golden Fawn proved to be an outstanding performer, winning the Eclipse Stakes of India for the second year running. Racing as Bashir, he had failed to win when racing in England at two and three, although he had finished runner up in the Rous Memorial, Lancashire Breeders Produce, Red Rose and Union Jack Stakes, before being sold and renamed Golden Fawn. Golden Fawn was to stand at stud in England or Ireland after the war, but died of heat stroke on 2nd May 1943.
  Winners in Great Britain and Ireland sired by Bahram

1943	Dam	Dam Sire	Wins	Value in £
Babershah [3 c]	Taj Shirin	Gainsborough	8f.	197.00
Baman [3 c]	Una	Tetratema	6f.	197.00

1943	Dam	Dam Sire	Wins	Value in £
Dark Diana [2 f]	Gollywog	Pommern	5f.	234.50
Fair Aim [2 c]	Speedway	Fairway	5f.	347.50
Hasty Shot [4 c]	Instantaneous	Hurry On	8f	278.25
Kirman [2 c]	Scotia's Glen	Beresford	5f.	320.75
Pack Drill [2 f]	Light Sentence	Pharos	5f.	217.00
Rameses [2 c]	Mesa	Kircubbin	8f	487.25
Safari [3 f]	Solerina	Soldennis	9f.	256.50
TOTAL			9	2,535.75

Bahram's British bred offspring with earnings abroad

1943	Dam	Dam Sire	Wins	Earnings	Country
Bat's Tail [4 f]	Rat's Tail	Ramus	1	41,220 frs.	France
Brinda [4 f]	Herlinde	Asterus	1	116,000 frs.	France
Golden Fawn [6 c]	Mah Mahal	Gainsborough	2	57,956 Rs.	India
Brehon Law [3 c]	Constant Law	Portlaw	4	17,250 Ps.	Spain
Rangoon [3 c]	Silver Mist	Craig An Eran	1	$1,270	USA

N.B. Golden Fawn was originally named Bashir
Principal Winners: – **Golden Fawn** – Eclipse Stakes of India, Western India Cup

1944

Persian Gulf won four of his five starts, including the Coronation Cup (12f.). Bahram finished 14th place on the list of winning sires.
Winners sired by Bahram in Great Britain and Ireland

1944 (14th)	Dam	Dam Sire	Wins	Value in £
Baman [4 c]	Una	Tetratema	7f. 8f.	568.00
Bibibeg [3 f]	Mumtaz Begum	Blenheim	12f.	74.00
Bois de Rose [3 c]	La Moqueuse	Teddy	8f.	264.50
Doyenne [3 f]	Democratie	Epinard	8f.	221.00
Fair Aim [3 c]	Speedway	Fairway	6f.	420.00
Marinette [3 f]	My Pet	Son-in-Law	12f.	207.00
Persian Gulf [4 c]	Double Life	Bachelor's Double	11f. 12f. 12f. 16f.	2,123.00
Torch [3 f]	Gadabout	Gainsborough	8f.	177.25
TOTAL			12	4,054.75

Principal winners: – **Persian Gulf** – Coronation Cup (12f.)
Bahram's British bred offspring with earnings abroad

1944	Dam	Dam Sire	Wins	Earnings	Country
Paladin [5 h]	Kampala	Clarissimus	2	$3,035	USA
Raj Kumar [5 g]	Quick Action	Happy Argo	0	$50	USA
Rangoon [4 c]	Silver Mist	Craig An Eran	2	$3,925	USA
Valdina Leaf [3 c]	Gold Leaf II	Clarissimus	1	$1,250	USA

1945–1949

The final winner from Bahram's English-bred foals came on 22nd September 1947, when the six-year-old entire Bois De Rose won the Wolverhampton Handicap. However, it was not to be his last winner in England, for three of his American-bred offspring, namely Ballymacad, Florida Moon and Melisandre were later exported to race in Great Britain.

Florida Moon finished second to champion sprinter Abernant on her juvenile debut, was exported to Ireland at three where she won her only race, a minor event at Phoenix Park in August 1949.

Bahram's final winner in Europe was Ballymacad who won the Shire Handicap at Leicester, and his last runner, again Ballymacad; was unplaced in the Cambridgeshire.

Bahram's son Bandra became his only National Hunt winner; in the three mile United Border Hunt Steeplechase for amateur riders in the 1946/47 season. The following season Bandra won two more steeplechases: the Christmas Handicap Chase, over two and a half miles, at Wetherby on Boxing Day 1947, and Birmingham's Stayers Handicap Chase over half a mile further. He also finished runner-up in the Haydock Park National Trial Steeplechase.

Bahram's sired 36 individual winners in Great Britain and Ireland from 89 English-bred foals (40.4%). This is slightly disappointing as he covered many well-bred mares. His foals were limited by racing during the war years and in particular his second crop of twenty foals was sparingly raced. If these are removed from his figures the percentage improves to 47.8.

His stock contained plenty of quality; from five crops he sired the winners of two Classics and two Irish Classics plus a Champion Stakes, a Coronation Cup and two Coventry Stakes winners. Bahram's average stamina index in England was 8.69 furlongs.

1945

Winners sired by Bahram in Great Britain and Ireland

1945	Dam	Dam Sire	Wins	Value in £
Bahara [4 c]	Hermia	Hurry On	10f.	178.00
Torch [4 f]	Gadabout	Gainsborough	9f.	89.00
TOTAL			2	267.00

Bahram's British bred offspring with earnings abroad

1945	Dam	Dam Sire	Wins	Earnings	Country
Raj Kumar [6 g]	Quick Action	Happy Argo	1	$2,450	USA
Valdina Leaf [4 c]	Gold Leaf II	Clarissimus	2	$3,305	USA

1946

No winners in Great Britain or Ireland in 1946
Bahram's British bred offspring with earnings abroad

1946	Dam	Dam Sire	Wins	Earnings	Country
Valdina Leaf [5 g]	Gold Leaf II	Clarissimus	2	$4,050	USA

1947

Winners sired by Bahram in Great Britain and Ireland

1947	Dam	Dam Sire	Wins	Value in £
Bois de Rose [6 h]	La Moqueuse	Teddy	8f. 8f. 8f.	621.00
Nith [6 f]	Alfane	Asterus	10f.	138.00
TOTAL			4	759.00

Bahram's British bred offspring with earnings abroad

1947	Dam	Dam Sire	Wins	Earnings	Country
Byculla [6 g]	Theresina	Diophon	2	21,946 Rps	India

Principal winners: – **Byculla** – Byculla Club Cup

1948

Winners in Great Britain and Ireland sired by Bahram

1948	Dam	Dam Sire	Wins	Value in £
Melisandre [2 f]	Ancona	Toro	5f.	211.75
TOTAL			1	211.75

Bahram's British bred offspring with earnings abroad

1948	Dam	Dam Sire	Wins	Earnings	Country
Valdina Gwyn [7 h]	Gwyniad	Salmon-Trout	0	$300	USA

1949

Winners in Great Britain and Ireland sired by Bahram

1949	Dam	Dam Sire	Wins	Value in £
Ballymacad [3 c]	Irish Nora	Pharamond II	7f. 8f.	1,217.25
Florida Moon [3 f]	Yucca	Pharos	5f.	202.00
TOTAL			3	1,419.25

Summary of winners in Great Britain and Ireland sired by Bahram
Individual winners in England & Ireland – 39 (includes 3 sired in America)
Total races won in England & Ireland – 75
Value £32,315.75
19 fillies winning 28 races worth £8,662.75
20 colts winning 47 races worth £23,653
22 two-year-olds winners of 33 races worth £12,781
Bahram sired 1 winner of 3 steeplechases worth £555
Bahram sired 11 winners of 37 races overseas
Bahram's year-by-year record in Britain:-

Year	Winning horses	Races	Value of races won	Position in table of leading sires
1939	3	4	4,052	–
1940	5	6	6,703	2nd
1941	9	17	5,809	3rd
1942	10	17	6,503	5th
1943	9	9	2,535	20th
1944	8	12	4,054	14th
1945	2	2	567	–
1946	–	–	–	–
1947	2	4	759	–
1948	1	1	212	–
1949	1	2	1217	–

Winning distance of Bahram's offspring

	5f.	6f.	7f.	8f.	9f.	10f.	11f.	12f.	14f.	16f.	Total
2YO	26	5	0	2	0	0	0	0	0	0	33
3YO	2	6	2	8	2	1	0	5	1	0	27
4YO+	0	0	1	6	1	2	1	3	0	1	15

Analysis of Bahram's UK-bred crops

Year	Live foals	UK Winners	Overseas winners	% of winners to foals
1937	8	5	2	87.50
1938	20	3	1	20.00
1939	22	9	4	59.09
1940	18	7	2	50.00
1941	21	12	2	66.66
Total	89	36	11	52.81

BAHRAM IN USA

When Bahram arrived in America in August 1940 his health had been affected by an arduous sea voyage. He took up stallion duties for the 1941 covering season at Alfred G Vanderbilt's Sagamore Stud Farm in Maryland at a fee of $2,500 (£650) (23,400), making him the most expensive stallion in America alongside his paternal half-brother Blenheim and Sea Biscuit. In his first season Bahram covered 13 mares, 11 of which were tested in foal.

Bahram did not sell well at the sales: the highest price paid for one of his yearlings came at the 1945 Meadow Brook Sales, when his son out of the Peter Pan mare Flying Comet sold for $15,000 (£3,750) (140,000). A half brother to the 1937 Washington Futurity winner Teddy's Comet, he was subsequently named Bahrameter and won 5 races value $17,350 (£4,300) (142,000).

Yearlings by Bahram sold auction in America

Year	Yearling	Dam	Price in $	Subsequent Career
1940	Raj Kumar [c]	Quick Action	8,000	Won 1 race earning $3,575
1943	Super Duper [c]	Bride Elect	1,300	Won 4 races earning $13,815. Stood as stallion
1944	Crowflight [f]	Flyaway Home	2,700	Won 10 races earning $22,600
1944	Darjeeling [c]	Chin Up	3,500	Won 10 races over hurdles and fences earning $42,165
1944	Persian Light [f]	Swift Light	4,000	Unraced
1944	Strafford [f]	Cherry Orchard	1,200	Unplaced at 2
1944	Whatuknow [f]	Salvation	1,000	Unplaced at 2
1945	Bahrameter [c]	Flying Comet	14,000	Won 5 races earning $17,350
1945	Extrovert [f]	Watch Her	11,000	Unraced
1945	Graciousme [f]	Floradora Girl	5,500	Unraced
1945	Homing [f]	Flyaway Home	2,100	Won 6 races earning $21,705
1945	Rappahanock [c]	Nouveau Riche	2,600	Won 4 races earning $13,025
1945	Tappahannock [c]	Tee Totum	4,300	Won 2 races earning $4,500
1947	Master Harold [c]	Karell	1,200	Won 11 races earning $14,500

Bahram's American bred offspring with earnings foaled in 1942

Horse	Dam	Dam Sire	Career Wins	Earnings
Ardashir [c]	Natica	Stefan The Great	6	5,077
Liberty Head [c]	Silver Lady	Sir Gallahad III	1	2,625
Super Duper [c]	Bride Elect	High Time	4	13,815
The Shah [c]	Astralobe	Sir Gallahad III	2	5,721
			13	27,238

For the 1942 covering season Bahram was moved to Mr Walter J Chrysler junior's North Wales Stud Farm about three miles from Warrenton, Virginia. This 1,000 acres property included 70 buildings for livestock, a training stable and a six furlongs track. Records for this historic property go back to 1719. By this time Bahram's health had been restored and he covered a full book of mares.

Bahram's second US-bred crop contained his highest earner: Stud Poker. He raced 130 times and won 14 races including the $50,000 (£12,500) (425,000) Arlington Handicap.

Bahram's American bred offspring with earnings foaled in 1943

Horse	Dam	Dam Sire	Career Wins	Earnings
Barval [c]	Valdina Myth	Sortie	5	11,800
Cedar Creek [c]	Green Fee	Fairway	4	18,990
Crowflight [f]	Flyaway Home	Display	10	22,600
Darjeeling [c]	Chin Up	Mad Hatter	10	42,165
Glyndon Mac [c]	Floradora Girl	Display	4	16,135
Hamull [c]	Portever	The Porter	15	34,925
Lady Bahram [f]	Lady Wisdom	Sir Gallahad III	2	4,330
Lombock [c]	Monel	Sir Greysteel	4	5,865
Majalis [c]	Lily of the Valley	Tetratema	4	11,260
Menu [c]	Dinner Date	Stimulus	19	80,275
Monstrance [c]	Sunlygret	Sun Briar	6	8,425
Mother India [f]	Maradadi	Stimulus	2	4,825
Next [c]	Now What	Chance Play	6	11,035
Perfect Bahram [c]	Perfect Love	Man O'War	15	57,265
Stud Poker [c]	Betagain II	Gainsborough	14	192,460
Visor [c]	Lampshade	Whichone	0	1,200
War Ballad [c]	War Plumage	On Watch	1	3,450
Whatuknow [f]	Salvation	Sandwich	0	50
			121	527,055

Principal winners: – **Cedar Creek** – 1946 Bahamas Handicap; **Darjeeling** – 1947 Amagansett Handicap Hurdle, 1950 Meadow Brook Handicap Steeplechase, 1950 Charles L Appleton Steeplechase; **Menu** – 1948 Governor's Handicap, Speed Handicap; **Stud Poker** – 1947 Illinois Owners Handicap, 1948 Arlington Handicap, Meadowlands Handicap, Miami Beach Handicap, 1949 Belle Isle Handicap

Bahram's American bred offspring with earnings foaled in 1944

Horse	Dam	Dam Sire	Career Wins	Earnings
Aboko [c]	Blast Furnace	Sir Greysteel	8	19,412
Angelus Bell [f]	Vesper Bells II	Stefan the Great	2	5,210
Bahrameter [c]	Flying Comet	Peter Pan	5	17,350
Balbar [c]	Knight's Nurse	Bright Knight	20	20,447
Cherish [f]	Cherachin	Stimulus	7	29,450
Cuisine [f]	Dinner Date	Stimulus	2	11,050
Cutty Hunk [c]	War Plumage	On Watch	8	33,300
Gallalad [c]	Gallalice	Sir Gallahad III	22	60,545

Horse	Dam	Dam Sire	Career Wins	Earnings
Grindelia [f]	Marsh Marigold	Sir Gallahad III	0	600
Homing [f]	Flyaway Home	Display	6	21,705
Imperil [f]	Peril	Sir Gallahad III	3	8,675
Irish Pennant [f]	Minnant	Pennant	4	11,365
Manchac [c]	Sassaby	Broomstick	26	72,222
Mayram [f]	Plain Mary	Discovery	16	52,361
Mr Greek [c]	Greek Goddess	Hyperion	1	3,025
Now And Again [f]	Now What	Chance Play	2	6,297
Rampano [c]	Evening Light	Jack High	1	2,550
Raol [c]	Monel	Sir Greysteel	3	9,050
Rappahannock [c]	Nouveau Riche	Display	4	13,025
Reckon [c]	Reckless	Stimulus	9	51,290
Spare A Dime [f]	The Spare	John P Grier	1	1,550
Tappahannock [c]	Tee Totum	Display	2	4,500
Warrenton [c]	Lily of the Valley	Tetratema	0	5,675
Yankee Hill [c]	The Beasel	Sunspot	17	67,450
			169	528,104

Principal winners: – **Cutty Hunk** – 1947 Golden Gate Derby; **Raol** – 1946 Eastern Shore Handicap; **Reckon** – 1947 Daingerfield Handicap; **Yankee Hill** – 1948 Oceanport Handicap.

Bahram sired only on horse to earn a place in one of North America's Triple Crown races. In 1948 Bovard finished third in the Preakness Stakes to the American Triple Crown winner Citation in a field of four.

Bahram's American bred offspring with earnings foaled in 1945

Horse	Dam	Dam Sire	Career Wins	Earnings
Aviation [c]	Canfli	Campfire	1	3,725
Basis [c]	Oasis	Lucullite	19	57,549
Bovard [c]	Knight's Nurse	Bright Knight	6	48,855
Brass Band [c]	Parade Girl	Display	4	15,175
Caltha [f]	Marsh Marigold	Sir Gallahad III	3	20,700
Dime [c]	Spare Change	Discovery	15	27,510
Filament [f]	Ky Flash	Sun Teddy	5	14,600
Four Leaves [f]	Four Stars	Quatre Bras II	0	225
Ramadan [c]	Arden Lass	Ariel	4	10,325
Ringside Table [f]	Nouveau Riche	Display	4	5,750
Rogue [c]	Reckless	Stimulus	20	41,315
Sassanid [c]	Therm	Hyperion	10	22,567
Sinsin [f]	Blue Ensign	Blue Larkspur	1	4,200
The Begum [f]	Responsive	Foray II	0	1,585
Trumpeter [c]	Army Flirt	Man O'War	8	21,465
			100	295,546

Principal winners: – **Basis** – 1949 Quaker City Handicap; **Bovard** – 1948 Louisiana Derby, Survivor Strakes; **Caltha** – 1947 Fashion Stakes; **Rogue** – 1950 Fred S Livingston Handicap.

At the end of the 1945 covering season Bahram was sold for a reputed $130,000 ($32,500) (£1,200,000) to an Argentine syndicate. Bahram's tenure in North America was not a success and he failed to sire anything to compare with the best of his English stock.

He finished in the top 20 leading sires three times; his best was a 6th place in 1948. This was in contrast to two other stallions sold by the Aga Khan to America at around the same time: Blenheim and Mahmoud, while another Aga Khan sale to America, Nasrullah, proved an even bigger success.

Bahram's progeny may not have been high class but they were tough and durable. His five American bred crops winning between them almost 600 races worth almost on $2 million. Indeed, in each of the seasons 1947, 1948 and 1949 Bahram's US-bred offspring won more races than his UK-bred offspring won in total.

Bahram's American bred offspring with earnings foaled in 1946:-

Horse	Dam	Dam Sire	Career Wins	Earnings
Ballymacad [c]	Irish Nora	Pharamond II	1	2,600
Bar Sinister [c]	Savage Beauty	Challenger II	2	10,250
Demavend [c]	Gallalice	Sir Gallahad III	14	32,562
False Front [f]	Superficial	Supremus	17	41,860
Fugitive [c]	Escapade II	Tetratema	21	67,185
Indian Jewel [c]	War Jewel	War Whoop	4	9,490
Lady Alice [f]	Princess Alice	Teddy	12	46,225
Master Harold [c]	Karell	Kantar	11	14,500
Open Question [f]	Now What	Chance Play	1	2,600
Outland [c]	Maradadi	Stimulus	23	52,810
Parting Shot [f]	That's That	High Time	0	1,000
Pibroch [c]	Martial Air	Man O'War	14	31,830
Pro [c]	Golf Widow	Fairway	12	17,900
Ratine [f]	Monel	Sir Greysteel	1	2,755
Speaking Rock [f]	Atonement II	Achtoi	1	1,790
Stone Age [c]	Petrify	Identify	6	53,550
Sub [f]	U-Boat	Man O'War	6	21,125
Sun Bahram [c]	Suntica	Sun Briar	12	112,330
Taran [c]	Trina	Sickle	14	49,245
Wild Pitch [f]	Balking	Balko	1	2,850
Yazdegerd [c]	The Beasel	Sunspot	15	27,340
			188	601,797

Principal winners: – **Outland** – 1950 Governor's Handicap; **Stone Age** – 1948 Walden Stakes; **Sun Bahram** – 1949 Leonard Richards Stakes, Saranac Handicap.

The best progeny of Bahram's final American-bred crop was Sun Bahram. He won 12 races and over $100,000, and finished fourth in both the Preakness and Belmont Stakes behind Capot.

Bahram's record as a sire in America

Year	Runners	Earners	1st.	2nd.	3rd.	Earnings in $
1940	1 (1)	1 (1)	0	1 (1)	0	300
1941	3 (1)	3 (1)	1 (1)	5 (0)	3 (1)	2,630 (1,125)
1942	3 (1)	2	2	3	6	4,200
1943	5 (1)	1	1	0	1	1,270
1944	10 (5)	5 (1)	6 (1)	5 (1)	11 (0)	10,725 (2,465)
1945	20 (14)	12 (6)	11 (7)	9 (5)	15 (5)	24,600 (17,410)
1946	43 (20)	32 (11)	46 (21)	32 (11)	48 (13)	139,942 (53,672)
1947 (18th)	53 (15)	43 (7)	85 (15)	81 (7)	71 (6)	348,926 (42,610)
1948 (6th)	67 (19)	60 (12)	108 (23)	132 (28)	78 (16)	497,857 (98,425)
1949 (16th)	63	49	93	108	93	378,087
1950	43	38	65	55	69	195,246
1951	31	25	59	52	51	152,986
1952	25	24	58	37	40	130,238

Year	Runners	Earners	1st.	2nd.	3rd.	Earnings in $
1953	19	18	49	48	42	80,563
1954	12	9	33	21	21	42,027
1955	11	8	9	11	7	11,703
1956	4	3	5	4	1	23,305
1957	4	4	3	4	7	3,482
1958	3	3	10	4	1	17,955
1959	3	1	0	0	1	525
1960	2	2	2	4	1	4,180
1961	3	3	3	5	5	4,321
1962	1	1	1	0	3	1,086
1963	3	3	0	0	2	1,793
1964	2	2	0	0	0	81
Total			650 (68)	620 (52)	577 (41)	2,078,028
						(215,807)

N.B. Figures in brackets refer to two-year-olds
Summary of earners and winners in USA sired by Bahram

Fillies	Earners	Winners	Wins	Earnings
USA bred	54	52	482	1,632,407
UK bred	5	4	14	24,960
Argentine bred	8	7	45	71,523
Total	67	63	541	1,728,890

Colts	Earners	Winners	Wins	Earnings
USA bred	28	23	109	347,333
UK bred	2	0	0	1,805
Argentine bred	0	0	0	0
Total	30	23	109	349,138

BAHRAM IN ARGENTINA

Bahram stood at the Haras Chapadamala, owned by the brothers Jose A and Miguel Martinez de Hoz. It was one of the leading studs in Argentina, but despite covering many well-bred mares, Bahram's stallion career mirrored that of his period in America.

His initial crops in both England and America had been small, but he appeared to settle in well, his first Argentinian crop foaled in 1947 amounted to 11 colts and 13 fillies and his second 15 colts and 12 fillies. However there were no really important winners from his 8 crops, and he was retired from stallion duties after the 1953 covering season.

Bahram's first crop of two-year-olds proved popular at the sales with his son Grantico (later renamed Royal Bahram) fetching a price of 160,000 pesos in 1949, beating the previous record by 40,000 pesos. Over the years his results proved consistent but less spectacular, with 1952 being the only year in which at least one of his two-year-olds failed to fetch at least 100,000 pesos.

Summary of Bahram's offspring sold at the two-year-old sales

Year	Sold	Average	Median	Highest
1949	10	67,500	65,500	160,000
1950	14	75,786	76,000	110,000
1951	14	82,857	65,000	160,000
1952	11	51,182	47,000	90,000
1953	19	53,368	50,000	100,000
1954	14	66,143	60,000	170,000
1955	8	79,875	77,500	115,000
1956	5	93,400	100,000	120,000

Bahram's Argentine bred offspring foaled in 1947 with their career earnings

Horse	Dam	Dam Sire	Sale price	Wins	Earnings
Anubis [c]	Anapa	Copyright	72,000	3	65,650
Bahranell [c]	Tetra Nell	Tetratema		3	53,000
Bahuda [f]	Candonga	Copyright		0	5,500
Barbecue [c]	Omaha	Picacero	65,000	0	0
Barheim [c]	Futulity	Solario	55,000	0	650
Bellissima [f]	La Elisa	Captain Cuttle		4	87,150
Bertrande [f]	Clotilda	Papyrus	37,000	0	0
Bisono [c]	Bimba	Congreve	66,000	1	20,800
Bitter Orange [f]	Orangerie	Parlanchin		0	1,500
Brahman [c]	Ridere	Master Vere		3	43,750
Cara Mia [f]	Cara	Bosworth		1	12,950
Cruz de Acero [c]	Cruz de Malta	Macon	70,000	0	11,550
Enjambre [f]	Honey Queen	Hunter's Moon	20,000	0	0
Granitico [c]	Cantera	Copyright	160,000	0	0
Lady Jean [f]	Lorlotte	Polemarch		4	95,850
Nevazon [c]	Snow Boots	Mahmoud	40,000	0	0
Partidaria [f]	Sufragista	Parlanchin		4	53,000
Shahpur [c]	Shiva	Rustom Pasha	90,000	2	37,450
				25	488,800

N.B. Grantico was later renamed Royal Bahram

Bahram's Argentine bred offspring foaled in 1948 with their career earnings

Horse	Dam	Dam Sire	Sale Price	Wins	Earnings
Arbois [c]	La Mission	Congreve	65,000	3	92,950
Atbarah [c]	Tetra Nell	Tetratema	52,000	1	23,650
Bahent [c]	Chuza	Madrigal		1	14,400
Bahram Son [c]	Foxiole	Foxhunter		4	112,250
Barranca Yaco [c]	Barranquilla	Alan Breck	30,000	3	32,750
Bethel [c]	Betsabe	Congreve		1	25,000
Bluesmoke [c]	Blue Haze	Blue Peter	80,000	0	0
Bramble [c]	Maleza	Parlanchin		3	58,400
Bribon [c]	Betty	Teddy	95,000	3	78,000
Brush Up [f]	Taloche	Parlanchin	80,000	0	0
Bumble Bee [f]	Honey Queen	Hunter's Moon	110,000	2	38,500
Carlomagno [c]	Cara	Bosworth	52,000	6	131,450
Dinamitero [c]	Cantera	Copyright	60,000	3	88,850
Farouk [c]	Fachosa	Full Sail	95,000	0	0
Gin Gala [f]	Lady Buchan	Buchan	72,000	0	0
His Honor [c]	Her Sister	Full Sail	125,000	0	0
Lulit [f]	Lilaila	Parwiz		3	68,800
Lusto [c]	Lastimera	Lombardo	85,000	0	750
Maritchou [f]	Madrona	Alan Breck		1	15,800
Mosqueton [c]	Margarita	Full Sail	60,000	0	0
Raza [f]	Estirpe	Congreve		1	25,400
Vanguard [c]	Lady Divine	Sandal		1	21,550
				36	828,500

Bahram's Argentine bred offspring foaled in 1949 with their career earnings

Horse	Dam	Dam Sire	Sale Price	Wins	Earnings
Baccarat [c]	Fortuna	Full Sail	65,000	1	6,000
Barcarolle [f]	Evening Lullaby	Hurry On	160,000	0	0
Bataille [f]	Conquete	Congreve	150,000	1	15,875
Baxar [c]	Inglesa	Loaningdale		1	21,000
Bengala [f]	Betty	Teddy	55,000	2	55,300
Betharran [c]	Her Sister	Full Sail	75,000	0	1,800
Biweh [f]	Whisper	Full Sail	150,000	0	0
Blackwood [c]	Tinga-Linga-Ling	Sansovino	45,000	3	76,400
Bookmaker [c]	Borrasquera	Tresiete	55,000	2	34,410
Borderlaise [f]	Nuits	Congreve	90,000	0	0
Brumazon [c]	Blue Haze	Blue Peter	95,000	0	0
Buisson [c]	Maleza	Parlanchin	45,000	3	32,400
Carice [f]	Cosmobelle	Sir Cosmo		4	38,600
Eastern Legend [c]	Indian Legend	Rustom Pasha	60,000	0	0
Farida [f]	Fachosa	Full Sail		2	66,450
Magister [c]	Madrona	Alan Breck	50,000	0	0
Persian Legend [c]	Rustom's Legend	Rustom Pasha	65,000	0	12,700
				19	360,935

Bahram's Argentine bred offspring foaled in 1950 with their career earnings

Horse	Dam	Dam Sire	Sale Price	Wins	Earnings
Bachiller [c]	Undergaruette	Rhodes Scholar	47,000	0	0
Bahrein [c]	White Rose	Papirote		0	1,000
Baradine [f]	Irancy	Master Vere		3	83,550
Benaresa [f]	Betty	Teddy		2	24,000
Birra [f]	Nuits	Congreve		2	54,200
Blue Sky [c]	Blue Haze	Blue Peter	60,000	2	64,100
Canturrero [c]	Canzonetta	Parwiz	42,000	0	0
Cherbourg [c]	Cote D'Argent	Rustom Pasha	47,000	0	0
Complot [c]	Caudilla	Parwiz	50,000	0	0
Curry [c]	Bombay	Badruddin	90,000	5	76,050
Entusiasta [f]	Sufragista	Parlanchin	28,000	2	51,764
Hold On [c]	Holda	Hunter's Moon		4	230,005
Legend Prince [c]	Indian Legend	Rustom Pasha	47,000	3	39,150
Manipour [c]	La Boba	Tonto		2	83,200
Monseigneur [c]	Mam'zelle	Adam's Apple	32,000	1	57,100
Nayahue [f]	Naihati	Strip The Willow	45,000	1	32,750
Orange Tree [c]	Orangerie	Parlanchin		0	1,000
Velera [f]	Umyak	Rustom Pasha		4	192,750
Zingaro [c]	Zaza	Congreve	75,000	2	14,400
				33	1,005,019

Bahram's Argentine bred offspring 1951 with their career earnings

Horse	Dam	Dam Sire	Sale Price	Wins	Earnings
Avro [c]	Aleta	Strip The Willow	46,000	4	255,511
Bengazi [c]	Betty	Teddy	43,000	1	26,250

Horse	Dam	Dam Sire	Sale Price	Wins	Earnings
Bimbi [f]	Brenda	Alan Breck		1	24,000
Bizarria [f]	Caudilla	Parwiz	100,000	0	0
Blaque [f]	Waggish	Embrujo		1	17,750
Brigantine [f]	Umyak	Rustom Pasha	60,000	1	41,950
Cote Bretonne [f]	Cote D'Argent	Rustom Pasha		0	43,350
Ding Dong [c]	Tinga-Linga-Ling	Sansovino	23,000	1	23,500
Doremi [f]	Mistigri	Foxhunter	95,000	1	41,450
Espartillo [c]	Maleza	Parlanchin	48,000	2	88,200
Flavia [f]	Fachosa	Full Sail	67,000	0	0
Fox Cry [f]	Hasty Vixen	Foxlaw		5	204,000
Hermandad [f]	Her Sister	Full Sail	52,000	1	28,900
Heroina [f]	Holda	Hunters Moon	60,000	0	7,200
Lord Bahram [c]	Milady	Parlanchin	25,000	2	48,300
Marisconea [c]	Merry Girl	Full Sail	50,000	3	141,800
Monilla [f]	Ma Belle	Rustom Pasha	50,000	6	201,800
Mysore [f]	Praline	Master Vere		2	56,550
Ouvidor [c]	Ortygia	Foxhunter	42,000	0	14,650
Oxonian [c]	Undergraduette	Rhodes Scholar	50,000	3	105,750
Radiancy [f]	Relumbrosa	Alan Breck	53,000	0	0
Rival [c]	Sufragista	Parlanchin	45,000	2	22,900
Signore [c]	Mam'zelle	Adams Apple	45,000	2	45,000
Star Legend [c]	Rustom's Legend	Rustom Pasha	60,000	0	3,600
				38	1,442,411

Bahram's Argentine bred offspring foaled in 1952 with their career earnings;

Horse	Dam	Dam Sire	Sale Price	Wins	Earnings
Arcachon [c]	Cote D'Argent	Rustom Pasha	25,000	0	0
Banner [c]	Caudilla	Parwiz	37,000	0	850
Berberisca [f]	Brownie	Rustom Pasha		2	70,800
Blackburn [c]	Aleta	Strip the Willow	170,000	0	0
Blazing Sun [c]	Sunna	Rustom Pasha		0	600
Bracken [c]	Maleza	Parlanchin	100,000	3	123,200
Burma [f]	Irancy	Master Vere		6	276,200
Buster {c]	Big Sister	Rustom Pasha	30,000	0	0
Cantab [c]	Undergraduette	Rhodes Scholar	55,000	1	49,300
Galonado [c]	Gaillarde	Parwiz	75,000	5	68,300
Hermance [f]	Her Sister	Full Sail		1	40,300
Honra [f]	Holda	Hunter's Moon		4	186,800
Lahore [c]	Lilaila	Parwiz	37,000	2	188,600
Moonray [c]	Crescent	Rustom Pasha	75,000	1	64,600
Mountbatten [c]	Queen Elizabeth	Embrujo	60,000	1	49,700
Musulmana [f]	Madrona	Alan Breck	80,000	3	115,800
Tigris [c]	Tillyke	Foxhunter		0	9,700
Trirreme [c]	Umyak	Rustom Pasha	60,000	0	0
Votante [c]	Sufragista	Parlanchin	60,000	2	54,000
Whacking [c]	Cravache	Parwiz	62,000	4	188,200
				35	1,486,950

Bahram's Argentine bred offspring foaled in 1953 with their career earnings;

Horse	Dam	Dam Sire	Sale Price	Wins	Earnings
Aeronauta [f]	Aleta	Strip The Willow		1	42,000
Apagaluz [f]	Night Cap	Rustom Pasha	80,000	0	0
Belmonte [c]	Cantabrica	Parlanchin	80,000	0	0
Campaneo [c]	Crecelle	Parwiz	75,000	2	113,225
Confederada [f]	Caudilla	Parwiz	47,000	1	27,000
Exhorto [c]	Excelencia	Diadoque	85,000	7	55,000
Goleta [f]	Umyak	Rustom Pasha		1	61,100
Heraldico [c]	Her Sister	Full Sail	100,000	0	0
Horaciana [f]	Horatia	Pont L'Eveque		2	28,850
Privet [f]	Ligustrina	Embrujo	57,000	0	0
Romanova [f]	Troika	Embrujo	115,000	6	111,600
Rondeno [c]	Anglofila	Madrigal		1	29,000
				21	467,775

Bahram's Argentine bred offspring foaled in 1954 with their career earnings;

Horse	Dam	Dam Sire	Sale Price	Wins	Earnings
Arome [c]	Cute She	Cute Eyes	110,000	3	437,150
Charmee [f]	Adoree	Embrujo	120,000	1	77,450
Cointreau [c]	Night Cap	Rustom Pasha	77,000	0	31,050
Dior [c]	New Look	Embrujo	60,000	7	313,250
Hassan [c]	Huina	Hunter's Moon	100,000	0	22,300
Melena [f]	Manotada	Parlanchin		1	122,200
				12	1,003,400

Bahram's record as a sire in Argentine;

Year	Winners	Wins	Win & place earnings (pesos)
1950	5	9	153,200
1951 (17th)	15	25	504,850
1952 (21st)	13	24	534,475
1953 (21st)	15	23	575,314
1954 (11th)	16	26	891,105
1955 (6th)	23	36	1,266,650
1956 (25th)	18	27	945,800
1957	13	20	831,121
1958	10	19	747,300
1959	3	8	357,175
1960	2	2	276,800
Total		219	7,083,790

Summary of earners and winners in Argentine sired by Bahram;

Colts	Earners	Winners	Wins	Earnings
Argentine bred	63	49	126	4,237,051

Fillies	Earners	Winners	Wins	Earnings
Argentine bred	43	39	93	2,846,739

Bahram's Argentine bred offspring with earnings in Brazil;

Horse	Dam	Dam Sire	Wins	Earnings in Crs
Bethel (1948) [c]	Betsabe	Congreve	1	70,500
Anubis (1947) [c]	Anapa	Copyright	2	105,500
Ravel (1949) [c]	Radiant Princess	Hyperion	9	1,280,500
Silver Lass (1947) [f]	Silver Star	Fox Cub	1	94,000
Atbarah (1948) [c]	Tetra Nell	Tetratema	2	156,000
Bahranell (1947) [c]	Tetra Nell	Tetratema	0	4,000
Bisono (1947) [c]	Bimba	Congreve	0	20,200
Bumble Bee (1948) [f]	Honey Queen	Hunter's Moon	1	73,000
Shahpur (1947) [c]	Shiva	Rustom Pasha	5	233,000
Mayfair (1949 [c]	Mab	Winalot	3	154,500
Blackie (1949 [f]	Blue Lotus	Cameronian	0	15,000
Eaglewood (1949) [c]	East Glen	Easton	1	78,750
El Banderin (1948) [c]	Lady Divine	Sandal	3	330,400
Envidia (1950) [f]	Enamel Eyes	Precipitation	3	323,750
Snooker (1952) [c]	Snobless	Rustom Pasha	6	1,421,500
			37	4,360,600

N.B. Mayfair later renamed Gaturama; N.B. £1 = 176 Cruzeiro

Principal performers: – **Ravel** – Won 1954 Gran Premio Salgado Filho (12f.); **Snooker** – 2nd in 1956 Cruzeiro do Sul (Brazilian Derby) (12f.)

Bahram's Argentine bred offspring with earnings in Mexico;

Horse	Dam	Dam Sire	Wins	Earnings
Hold On (1950) [c]	Holda	Hunter's Moon	2	

Principal Winner: – **Hold On** – 1956 Handicap de las Americas (10f.), 1956 Clasico Copa de Oro (Gold Cup) (12f.). Voted Mexican 'Horse of the Year".

Bahram's Argentine bred offspring with earnings in USA;

Horse	Dam	Dam Sire	Wins	Earnings in $
Cantab (1952) [c]	Undergraduette	Rhodes Scholar	2	2,218
Cointreau (1954) [c]	Night Cap	Rustom Pasha	5	8,195
Dior (1954) [c]	New Look	Embrujo	0	1,308
Hold On (1950) [c]	Holda	Hunter's Moon	6	20,463
Lahore (1952) [c]	Lilaila	Parwiz	0	1,757
Naranja (1949) [c]	Orangerie	Parlanchin	21	18,453
Tigris II (1952) [c]	Tillyke	Foxhunter	2	2,949
Whacking (1952) [c]	Cravache	Parwiz	9	16,180
			45	71,523

Bahram's Argentine bred offspring with earnings in Venezuela;

Horse	Dam	Dam Sire	Wins	Earnings in Bolivars
Senegal (1953) [c]	Brownie	Rustom Pasha	12	466,560

N.B.: – £1 = 9.40 Bolivars

Principal winner: – **Senegal** – 1956 & 1957 Clasico Simon Bolivar (10f.), 1957 Clasico Los Sprinters (6f,), Clasico Gobernacion del Districto Federal (10f.), Clasico Fuerzas Armadas (16f.)

INBREEDING TO BAHRAM

The best horse inbred to Bahram was the 1968 Prix de l'Arc de Triomphe winner Vaguely Noble who was bred by Major Lionel Holliday. The Major or his son bred many of the best racehorses inbred to Bahram. Verdura, whose dam was the Bahram mare Bura, produced both classic trial winners Heathen and Highest Hopes when covered by Major Holliday's St. Leger winner Hethersett (dam by Bahram's son Big Game). Hethersett also covered Verdura's daughter Pharsalia (by Panorama), and produced the Chesterfield Cup winner Harken. In addition Hethersett's half brother Proud Chieftain, who was placed in the Coronation Cup, Eclipse and Champion Stakes, was by Bahram's son Persian Gulf.

Bahram occurs 5x4 via Big Game and Babylon in the pedigree of the mare Allegretta, who produced the Two Thousand Guineas winner King's Best and Prix de L'Arc de Triomphe winner Urban Sea. The latter was the dam of Galileo and Sea The Stars. Bahram's influence is reinforced in Galileo's daughter, the One Thousand Guinness and Oaks winner Minding. She has as her fourth dam Alathea, who was 5x5x5 Bahram, twice via Big Game and once via Turkhan.

In Australia, the Cox Plate winner Sir Dane was inbred 3x3 to Bahram, via Great Truth and Treasure Hunt, he sired his best winner: Group 2 Phar Lap Stakes winner Blue Dane, from a mare by Regal Light, who was inbred 3x3 to Bahram and his half brother Dastur.

Grounded was intensely inbred: he was by Migoli out of the Bibibeg, and both the latter and Migoli's dam Mah Iran were by Bahram out of a daughter of Mumtaz Mahal. In addition Migoli was by Bois Roussel; whose dam Plucky Liege was a half-sister to the grand dam of Bahram. Grounded won the second of his three starts as a juvenile, the Fenwolf Stakes at Ascot, by five lengths, before being exported to America where he stood as stallion. His best offspring was the Grade 1 Hopeful Stakes winner The Bagel Prince, who dam was inbred 4x4x4 to Bull Dog, a half-sister to Bois Roussel.

Winners of major races with a duplication of Bahram within their first four generations

Horse	Inbreeding via	Major Races won
Aquarelle	3x4 Big Game/Great Truth	1968 New Zealand Oaks (12f.)
Beja	4x4 Bura/Big Game	1970 Linda Vista Handicap (8.5)
		1970 Del Mar Oaks (9f.)
Carry Off	4x4 Big Game/Persian Gulf	1971 County Hurdle (16f.)
Doleswood	4x4 Persian Gulf/Cheerful Annie	1973 Coventry Stakes (6f.)
Foothill	4x4 Big Game/Mah Iran	1964 Horris Hill Stakes (7f.)
Harken	4x4 Big Game/Bura	1970 Chesterfield Cup (10f.)
Heathen	4x3 Big Game/Bura	1968 Greenham Stakes (7f.)
Highest Hopes	4x3 Big Game/Bura	1970 Ascot 1000 Guineas Trial (7f.)
		1970 Fred Darling Stakes (7f.)
		1970 Prix Eugene Adam (10f.)
		1970 Prix Vermeille (12f.)
Kilbegan	4x4 Big Game/Turkhan	1968 Nellie Morse Stakes (.)
Kursaal	4x5x4 Turkhan/Bura/Big Game	1968 Strensall Stakes (7f.)
Mesopotamia	3x4 Persian Gulf/Big Game	1963 Chesham Stakes (6f.)
		1963 Railway Stakes (6f.)
Proud Chieftain	2x3 Persian Gulf/Big Game	1960 Column Produce Stakes (8f.)
		1961 Rosebery Handicap (10f.)
		1961 John Smiths Cup (10f.)
Red Nose	4x4 Queen of Shiraz/Big Game	1981 Apollo Stakes (7f.)
Sandy's Hope	4x4 Birikan/Big Game	1968 Doomben Cup (10f.)
Sir Dane	3x3 Great Truth/Treasure Hunt	1964 Turnbull Stakes (12f.)
		1964 W S Cox Plate (10f.)
Terminal	4x3 Flowerdale/Avro	1971 Grand Premio Brasil (15f.)

Horse	Inbreeding via	Major Races won
Turkish Trousers	4x4 Bura/Big Game	1971 Del Mar Oaks (9f.)
		1971 Hollywood Oaks (9f.)
		1971 Santa Susana Stakes (8.5f)
		1971 Santa Ynez Stakes (7f.)
		1971 Railbird Stakes (7f.)
		1971 Princess Stakes (7.5f.)
		1972 Santa Maria Handicap (8.5f.)
		1972 Santa Margarita Handicap (9f.)
Vaguely Noble	4x4 Turkhan/Big Game	1967 Observer Gold Cup (8f.)
		1968 Prix de Guiche (9.5f.)
		1968 Prix de Chantilly (10f.)
		1968 Prix du Lys (12f.)
		1968 Prix de L'Arc de Triomphe (12f.)
Zap	4x4 Queen of Shiraz/Big Game	1981 T S Carlyon Cup (9f.)

Appendix II

Big Game, Turkhan and Persian Gulf at Stud.

Big Game

Big Game retired to Aislabie Stud, Newmarket, in 1943 at a fee of £250 (9,500). With his excellent breeding, impressive physique and successful racing career it must be conceded that he was a disappointing sire. He was a heavy-topped horse as were many of his progeny; some, particularly the colts were difficult to train and as a consequence they were not popular with trainers. Generally his fillies proved to be better than his colts.

His best colts were full-brothers. Combat, was from Big Game's first crop and out of the Oaks winner Commotion, by Mieuxce. He won all four of his starts as a juvenile including the Windsor Castle and the Champagne Stakes at Salisbury. He was ranked fifth in the Free Handicap with a weight of 8st. 12 lbs. seven pounds behind Tudor Minstrel. He was a medium-sized, attractive, good moving sort as a juvenile; still slightly on the leg. He did not win his races easily but showed the right attitude.

As three-year-old Combat made up into a fine sort with strong quarters and he won all five of his starts, including the Rous Memorial Stakes at Ascot and the Sussex Stakes; beating Petition in the latter when receiving five pounds. He also beat the subsequent St Leger winner: Sayajirao, in the Blue Riband Trial Stakes at Epsom; conceding him 10 lbs.

Combat was retired at the end of his three-year-old career and syndicated to stud. So he retired unbeaten in nine races having demonstrated considerable determination in a battle and, in the view of Phil Bull, would have won the 2000 Guineas in most years. However, with Tudor Minstrel in the same stable and ownership there was no prospect of them opposing one another. Combat raced beyond eight and a half furlongs only once; when winning a minor three runner event easily over ten furlongs at 15/2 on.

Combat was a good horse; probably about a Timeform rating of 123. At stud he sired the King George VI & Queen Elizabeth Stakes winner Aggressor, but as with Big Game himself his best winners were fillies such as Aggravate (Park Hill Stakes) and Dibidale (Irish Oaks).

Among Aggressor's sons were Streetfighter, who won three traces as a juvenile and took up stallion duties in Australia with minor success. Another of Aggressor's sons, Pry, a winner in France, stood as a National Hunt sire in Ireland where his best offspring were Gay Return (Charlie Hall Chase) and Bold Agent (Troytown Chase).

Two years after Combat his brother Faux Tirage was foaled. He was also unbeaten as a juvenile winning the Granville Stakes at Ascot and then the Rous Memorial Stakes at Newmarket. Described as "half a size bigger than his brother and, like his sibling, he had "tremendous power". However, it would seem he did not share his brother's action, Faux Tirage being powerful but not as good moving. Faux Tirage was allotted 9 st. 2 lbs. in the Free Handicap. He was rated 121 by Timeform.

As a three-year-old he won his first three races: a minor stakes race, the Newmarket and St James's Palace Stakes. He missed the Derby as he was jarred up and after finishing third in the Eclipse Stakes to Djeddah he was sold as a stallion to New Zealand. He was rated 126 by Timeform as a three-year-old.

Faux Tirage became leading stallion in New Zealand for the 1957/58 season and sired two New Zealand Oaks winners in Froth and Aquarelle, while his son Straight Draw won the 1957 Melbourne Cup. Faux Tirage was also leading broodmare sire in New Zealand for 1971/72.

Big Game's first Classic winner came from his second crop with Queenpot. As a juvenile she won three of her four races and given 8st. 8lbs. in the Free Handicap. As a three-year-old she won a minor stakes race and the 1000 Guineas but was unplaced in the Jersey Stakes at Royal Ascot on her only other start. She was rated 121 by Timeform.

In that season: 1948, Big Game finished second on the list of winning sires, his highest ever position, and with 17 of his juveniles winning 29 races that year. In addition to Faux Tirage the best of the others would have been Bignonia, Gigantic and Makarpura. Big Game was leading two-year-old sire.

Bignonia, a big filly out of Gold Lily by Gold Bridge only stayed five and a half furlongs but was speedy as a juvenile and rated 112 by Timeform; however, kept to five furlongs she failed to win as a three-year-old and her Timeform rating dropped to 100.

Gigantic out of Sun Chariot by Hyperion was a heavy topped colt and could hardly have been better bred; between them his sire and dam won four of the five Classics. As a juvenile he won two races; including the Imperial Produce Stakes at Kempton and earned a *Timeform* rating of 109. As a three-year-old he failed to win in five starts and his rating dropped to 101.

At stud in England Gigantic was a failure and was exported to New Zealand. When aged fourteen in 1960, he sired New Zealand Derby winner Royal Duty, and two New Zealand St. Leger winners: Empyreus, Terrific and Not Again.

Makarpura out of Cap d'Or by Gold Bridge was a well-developed and striking yearling and cost the Maharaja of Baroda 14,000 guineas (£530,000) at the Doncaster September sales; he was the highest priced yearling of 1947.

As a juvenile Makarpura was physically impressive, powerful colt with strong quarters. He won three of his six races and was placed in the other three; third in a plate race at Windsor, second in stakes race at Epsom, won the New Stakes at Royal Ascot, a plate race at Sandown, second in the Gimcrack Stakes and finally he finished the season by winning the Rous Stakes at Doncaster. He was allocated 9 st. 0 lbs. in the Free Handicap; he was rated 124 by *Timeform*.

As a three-year-old Makarpura failed to win in from eight starts. He did not stay a mile and did no better when he reverted to sprinting. As a stallion in Australia he sired 16 stakes winners.

Khorassan out of Naishapur by Nearco was bred by the Aga Khan ran unplaced on his only juvenile start. But as three-year-old this well-made colt won two of his six races: the Dee Stakes at Chester and a Derby trial at Kempton. But he was unplaced in the Derby and Jersey Stakes and then sold as a stallion to Australia where he was a success. He was rated 118 by *Timeform*.

Khorassan was leading sire in Australia for 1957/58 before being exported to New Zealand where he Tulloch. He won 36 races including 21 at the highest level; the AJC Derby, W S Cox Plate and Caulfield Cup. Khorassan was later exported to America.

Big Game's dam Myrobella had been a fast two-year-old and a sprinter, so it was probably no surprise to see that some of Big Game's progeny were speedy as juveniles. Plenty won many of the better juvenile events over five and six furlongs, including the Queen Mary Stakes, Windsor Castle Stakes, Cherry Hinton Stakes, July Stakes, Lowther Stakes, Imperial Produce Stakes (twice) and Molecomb Stakes (three times). At this time many observers felt that Big Game would never sire a top-class winner over twelve furlongs and beyond.

However, in 1953 Big Game's sired his second and final Classic winner. Ambiguity, out of Amber Flash by Precipitation, showed little on her only juvenile appearance. As a three-year-old she raced ten times winning on three occasions. A bay filly with four white legs and a white blaze Ambiguity was not quite top-class; she was second in the Cheshire Oaks before winning the now defunct White Rose Stakes at Ascot and the Oaks showing strong stamina to prevail. However, she lacked speed and needed further than 12 furlongs to beat good horses and it was not until she was able to race over extreme distances that she won again; winning the Jockey Club Cup over two miles and two furlongs; emulating her dam who also won the same race. It is almost certain that Ambiguity received her stamina from her dam.

Big Game's other principal winner over further than twelve furlongs was the Park Hill Stakes (14f.) winner Kyak, out of Felucca by Nearco, whose family was a strong influence for stamina.

With few top-class colts to his name it was always going to be difficult for Big Game to establish a lasting male line. The principal sire lines descending from Big Game, with country where they stood in brackets are shown below:-

Big Game (UK)
| Makarpura (Australia)
| Khorassan (New Zealand & USA)
| Stockade (Australia)
| Gigantic (UK & New Zealand)
| Head Hunter (New Zealand)
| Faux Tirage (New Zealand)
| Combat (UK)
| | Aggressor (UK)
| | | Pry (Ireland)
| | | Streetfighter (Australia)

Big Game was a disappointing sire but was better as a broodmare sire. Between 1957 and 1967 he was only twice outside the top four, and in those eleven seasons was leading broodmare sire in 1961, 1962 and 1966.

During that time his daughters produced two winners of the Irish 1000 Guineas in Even Star and

Gazpacho, and two winners of the St. Leger in Hethersett and Sodium, while the later also won the Irish Derby. Hethersett was made the favourite for the Derby, but was one of six horses brought down when Romulus fell.

Big Game was destroyed on 3rd July 1963.

Principal winners sired by Big Game

Horse with maternal grandsire in brackets	Principal races won
African Patrol (Djebel)	1966 Scottish Grand National Chase (33f.)
Ambiguity (Precipitation)	1953 Oaks (12f)
	1953 Jockey Club Cup (18f.)
Baba Au Rhum (Bois Roussel)	1958 Prix Quincey (8f.)
Bear Dance (Colombo)	1951 Eclipse Stakes of India (10f.)
Big Berry (Owen Tudor)	1954 Ebbisham Stakes (8.5f.)
Brave Venture (Deiri)	1954 Molecomb Stakes (5f.)
Bride Elect (Nearco)	1954 Queen Mary Stakes (5f.)
Combat (Mieuxce)	1946 Windsor Castle Stakes (5f.)
	1947 Blue Riband Trial Stakes (8.5f.)
	1947 Rous Memorial Stakes (7f.)
	1947 Sussex Stakes (8f.)
Crawley Beauty (Dastur)	1950 Molecomb Stakes (5f.)
Fair Dinah (Gold Bridge)	1947 Princess Margaret Stakes (5f.)
Faux Tirage (Mieuxce)	1949 Newmarket Stakes (10f.)
	1950 St. James's Palace Stakes (8f.)
Gamble in Gold (Gold Bridge)	1950 Lowther Stakes (5f.)
Game Book (Fair Trial)	1949 St. Hugh's Fillies Stakes (5f.)
Gigantic (Hyperion)	1948 Imperial Produce Stakes (6f.)
Great Fun (Colombo)	1947 Cherry Hinton Stakes (6f.)
Henley-in-Arden (Caerleon)	1947 Imperial Produce Stakes (6f.)
Instow (Harroway)	1957 Sandringham Handicap (8f.)
Key (Winalot)	1954 Kempton 1000 Guineas Trial (7f.)
	1954 Cork & Orrery Stakes (6f.)
	1954 Nassau Stakes (10f.)
Khorassan (Nearco)	1950 Kempton 2000 Guineas Trial (7f.)
	1950 Dee Stakes (12f.)
Kyak (Nearco)	1956 Park Hill Stakes (14f.)
Makarpura (Gold Bridge)	1948 New Stakes (5f.)
Masai King (Vatellor)	1952 Windsor Castle Stakes (5f.)
	1953 Kempton 2000 Guineas Trial (7f.)
Miss Stripes (Pharos)	1946 July Stakes (5f.)
Murrayfield (Solario)	1952 J&B Metropolitan (10f.)
Nosey (Tiberius)	1964 Spa Hurdle (24f.)
Queenpot (The Recorder)	1947 Lavant Stakes (5f.)
	1948 1000 Guineas (8f.)
Rally (Mieuxce)	1956 & 1957 Brown Jack Handicap (22f.)
	1958 Queen Alexandra Stakes (22f.)
Rowland Ward (Solario)	1957 Chesterfield Cup (10f.)
Rule Britannia (Gainsborough)	1944 Molecomb Stakes (5f.)
Square Dance (Foxhunter)	1956 Triumph Hurdle (16f.)
Whipsnade (Felstead)	1959 Ebbisham Stakes (8.5f.)
Winged Foot (Bosworth)	1952 Athasi Stakes (7f.)
Yoyo (Solario)	1949 Great Metropolitan Handicap (18f.)

Principal winners produced by daughters of Big Game

Horse with maternal grandsire in brackets	Principal races won
Abelia (Abernant)	1957 Queen Mary Stakes (5f.)
	1957 July Stakes (5f.)
	1957 Molecomb Stakes (5f.)
	1957 Cornwallis Stakes (5f.)
Aiming High (Djebe)	1961 Coronation Stakes (8f.)
Arctic Explorer (Arctic Prince)	1957 King Edward VII Stakes (12f.)
	1957 Eclipse Stakes (10f.)
	1958 Sandown Coronation Stakes (10f.)
Arnica (Alcide)	1964 Prix Fille de L'Air (10.5f.)
Artania (Arbar)	1962 Prix Fille de L'Air (10.5f.)
Barbwolf (Double Jay)	1963 Test Stakes (7f.)
Beauseant (Pinza)	1967 Union Jack Stakes (8f.)
Belle Geste (The Scoundrel)	1971 Woodbine Breeders Stakes (12f.)
	1971 & 1972 Woodbine Nassau Stakes (8.5f.)
	1972 Niagara Handicap (12f.)
Beta (Alycidon)	1960 Royal Lodge Stakes (8f.)
Bluefin (Nearco)	1952 Imperial Produce Stakes (6f.)
Bunker (Kalydon)	1967 Great Yorkshire Handicap (14f.)
Burning Torch (Tropique)	1964 Union Jack Stakes (8f.)
Caerphilly (Abernant)	1961 Lavant Stakes (5f.)
Campaign (Aureole)	1963 William Hill Gold Cup Handicap (8f.)
Carnoustie (Dante)	1958 Windsor Castle Stakes (5f.)
	1958 Rous Memorial Stakes (6f.)
Casque (Vatellor)	1959 Royal Stakes (10f.)
Charlton (Charlottesville)	1970 Predominate Stakes (10f.)
	1971 Henry II Stakes (16f.)
Eudaemon (Pardal)	1956 Gimcrack Stakes (6f.)
	1956 Champagne Stakes (6f.)
	1957 Column Produce Stakes (8f.)
Even Star (Abernant)	1957 Kempton 1000 Guineas Trial (7f.)
	1957 Irish 1000 Guineas (8f.)
Fear Naught (Connaught)	1978 Royal Hunt Cup (8f.)
Ferneley (Aureole)	1962 Royal Stakes (10f.)
Foot Note (Narrator)	1961 Meld Stakes (10f.)
Futurama (Borealis)	1961 Ribblesdale Stakes (12f.)
Gaul (Alycidon)	1962 King Edward VII Stakes (12f.)
	1962 Jockey Club Stakes (14f.)
	1963 Jockey Club Cup (16f.)
	1963 Henry II Stakes (16f.)
Gazpacho (Hard Sauce)	1963 Fred Darling Stakes (7f.)
	1963 Irish 1000 Guineas (8f.)
General Gordon (Never Say Die)	1966 Chester Vase (13f.)
Good Match (Match)	1967 Queen Anne Stakes (8f.)
Gustav (Grey Sovereign)	1961 Middle Park Stakes (6f.)
Hambleden (Elopement)	1966 Chesham Stakes (6f.)
	1966 Richmond Stakes (6f.)
Hardiesse (Hornbeam)	1968 Cheshire Oaks (12f.)
	1968 Prix de Mallaret (11f.)
Hethersett (Hugh Lupus)	1962 Great Voltigeur Stakes (12f.)
	1962 St. Leger (14f.)
Hidden Meaning (Woodcut)	1961 Solario Stakes (7f.)
	1962 Kempton 1000 Guineas Trial (7f.)
	1962 Cambridgeshire Handicap (9f.)
Light Harvest (Signal Light)	1956 Wokingham Handicap (6f.)
Lovestone (Amour Drake)	1958 Hungerford Stakes (7f.)

Horse with maternal grandsire in brackets	Principal races won
Lowna (Princely Gift)	1967 Molecomb Stakes (5f.)
Loyal Lady (Preciptic)	1958 Woodcote Stakes (6f.)
Lynch Law (Court Martial)	1959 Esher Cup Handicap (8f.)
Maina (St. Paddy)	1971 Lingfield Oaks Trial Stakes (12f.)
	1971 Lancashire Oaks (12f.)
Mandamus (Petition)	1965 William Hill God Cup Handicap (8f.)
Mariner (Acropolis)	1967 King Edward VII Stakes (12f.)
Memorandum (Mat de Cocagne)	1959 Prix Jean Prat (9f.)
	1959 Prix Eugene Adam (10f.)
	1959 Prix du Lys (12f.)
Moonbeam (Hornbeam)	1972 Danish Derby (12f.)
	1972 Swedish Derby (12f.)
	1972 Swedish St. Leger (14f.)
Moonlight Bay (Floribunda)	1973 Triumph Hurdle (16f.)
Moss Bank (Mossborough)	1956 Queen Alexandra Stakes (22f.)
Newbus (Nimbus)	1959 Chesham Stakes (5f.)
Noble Lassie (Nearco)	1959 Lancashire Oaks (11f.)
None Fairer (Nearco)	1956 Fred Darling Stakes (7f.)
Off Key (Nearco)	1961 Vaux Gold Tankard Handicap (14f.)
Ole Fols (Tudor Minstrel)	1959 Sports Page Handicap (6f.)
	1959 Will Rogers Handicap (8f.)
	1960 Palos Verdes Handicap (6f.)
Olympiad King (Curragh King)	1960 Debonair Stakes (8.5f.)
	1960 Del Mar Derby (9f.)
Pan's Surprise (Panaslipper)	1964 Esher Cup Handicap (8f.)
Pandour (Petition)	1958 Dee Stakes (10f.)
Panga (My Babu)	1959 Cherry Hinton Stakes (6f.)
Pappagena (Pappageno II)	1955 Princess Elizabeth Stakes (8.5f.)
Pardao (Pardal)	1961 Lingfield Derby Trial Stakes (12f.)
	1961 Gordon Stakes (11f.)
	1962 Jockey Club Cup (12f.)
	1963 San Juan Capistrano Handicap (14f.)
Parquetta (Pardal)	1961 Princess Margaret Stakes (5f.)
Pasha (Prince Taj)	1966 Prix Daru (10.5f.)
Peroxide (Never Say Die)	1962 Sandringham Handicap (8f.)
Philemon (Never Say Die)	1962 Anglesey Stakes (6f.)
	1964 Great Yorkshire Handicap (14f.)
	1965 Brown Jack Handicap (22f.)
Plump (Pinza)	1960 Princess Elizabeth Stakes (8.5f.)
Princillon (Prince Bio)	1958 Prix de la Salamandre (7f.)
Private Side (Tudor Melody)	1968 Esher cup Handicap (8f.)
Proud Chieftain (Persian Gulf)	1960 Column Produce Stakes (8f.)
	1961 Rosebery Handicap (10f.)
	1961 John Smith's Cup Handicap (10f.)
Raft (Ragusa)	1969 Princess Elizabeth Stakes (8.5f.)
Riverside (Sheshoon)	1969 Prix Royallieu (12.5f.)
Romantic (Princely Gift)	1962 July Stakes (6f.)
	1962 Richmond Stakes (6f.)
Royal Prerogative (Relko)	1973 Victoria Cup Handicap (7f.)
	1973 William Hill Gold Cup Handicap (8f.)
Royal Ridge (Vimy)	1967 Queen's Prize Handicap (16f.)
Rue de Romance (Watling Street)	1957 & 1960 Newbury Summer Cup (12f.)
Samson (Nilo)	1962 Doomben Cup (10f.)
	1964 All Aged Stakes (8f.)

Horse with maternal grandsire in brackets	Principal races won
Sea Music (Atan)	1971 Rous Memorial Stakes (6f.)
	1971 Firth of Clyde Stakes (6f.)
Seam (Nearula)	1961 Union Jack Stakes (8f.)
Shibafuji (Admiral Byrd)	1967 Kisaragi Sho (8.5f.)
	1968 Kyoto Kinen Autumn (11f.)
Short Sentence (Court Martial)	1958 St. Hugh's Fillies Stakes (5f.)
Sodium (Psidium)	1966 Irish Derby (12f.)
	1966 St. Leger (14f.)
Sparrow Hawk (Honeyway)	1967 Gladness Stakes (7f.)
Tender Annie (Tenerani)	1962 Ribblesdale Stakes (12f.)
The Elk (Only For Life)	1968 Observer Gold Cup (8f.)
	1969 Lingfield Derby Trial Stakes (12f.)
Three Fire (Tesco Boy)	1978 Hankyu Hai (8f.)
	1978 Kinko Sho (9f.)
	1979 Kitakyushu Kinen (10f.)
Tudor Era (Owen Tudor)	1959 Man O'War Stakes (11f.)
	1959 Hialeah Turf Cup (12f.)
Twelfth Man (Fidalgo)	1965 Ebor Handicap (14f.)
	1966 Bessborough Handicap (12f.)
Tzigane (Tudor Minstrel)	1962 Cherry Hinton Stakes (6f.)
Whitefoot (Relko)	1970 Musidora Stakes (10.5f.)

Turkhan

Turkhan retired to stud in Ireland in 1941 at Old Connell, Newbridge, County Kildare. His initial fee of £75 (3,075) reflected the war situation but by 1944 when the position had improved it had risen to £98 (3,625) and £198 (7,325) a year later. In late November 1945 it was announced that a syndicate of breeders had been formed to purchase Turkhan from the Aga Khan.

The ownership of the horse was divided into 40 shares of £1,250 (46,250) each, making a capital value of £50,000 (1,850,000). Turkhan continued to stand at Old Connell, at a fee of 300 guineas (10,800) for 1946, with the Aga Khan and Prince Aly Khan retaining the right to take up ten shares between them. Preference to purchase shares was given to those breeders who had booked nominations to Turkhan for the 1946 season. The purchase took effect from midnight on 17th December 1945, with the Committee of Management consisting of Prince Aly Khan, Earl Fitzwilliam and Messrs Frank Butters, Peter Burrell and R.P.C Griffin.

Turkhan had two winners with his first crop of juveniles in 1944. His second crop did better and progressed well when racing as three-year-olds.

Turkhan's daughters featured prominently in the Irish fillies Classics of 1946. In the One Thousand Guineas his daughters occupied the first two positions with Ella Retford beating Turkish Tune. In the Irish Oaks his daughters finished first, second and third; Linaria, Turkish Tune and Ella Retford. In the Irish St. Leger, Turkish Tune and Linaria finished second and third respectively behind Cassock. Turkhan was leading sire in Ireland for 1946, but whilst the winners continued to come, it was to be the high point of his stallion career.

The following season Turkish Blood finished third in the Irish Oaks; she would return to prominence a few years later as a broodmare.

In 1952 the syndicate that owned Turkhan was dissolved, and on 3rd December of that year Turkhan was entered in the Tattersall's' December Sale. Purchased by Comte de Beauregarde on behalf of the French breeder Maurice Olivier for 610 guineas (£17,950), Turkhan took up stallion duties in France and died there he died a few years later. Turkhan sired the winners of 240 races worth £81,233.50 (2,112,000), his average stamina index was 10.66 furlongs.

Principal winners sired by Turkhan

Horse with maternal grandsire in brackets	Principal races won
Clockwise (Horus)	1949 Fern Hill Stakes (7.5f.)
Eastern City (Hyperion)	1950 Whitehall Stakes (8f.)
Eastern Gem (Fairford)	1949 Royal Whip Stakes (12f.)
Ella Retford (The MacNab)	1946 Irish 1000 Guineas (8f.)
Linaria (Buen Ojo)	1945 Railway Stakes (6f.)
	1945 Beresford Stakes (8f.)
	1946 Irish Oaks (12f.)
Strathmore (Winalot)	1947 Goodwood Stakes (19f.)
Turkaris (Salamis)	1947 Great Northern Stakes (10.5f.)
Turkish Blood (Manna)	1946 Marble Hill Stakes (5f.)
Turkish Prince (Tai-Yang)	1950 Ulster Derby (12f.)
Turkish Spice (Fairway)	1954 Irish Cambridgeshire (8f.)
Turkish Tune (Prince Galahad)	1946 Aintree Derby (13f.)
	1947 Ormonde Stakes (13f.)

Turkhan's sons made little impact at stud. The 1948 Ebor Handicap runner-up Davistan was exported to Uruguay, where he had some success, while Turks Reliance, second in both Richmond and Cornwallis Stakes at two and a winner at twelve furlongs at three, did reasonably well in Japan, siring classic winners Kazuyoshi (Japanese 2000 Guineas) and Miss Marusa (Japanese Oaks).

Turkhan's daughters produce one European Classic winner: Pantomime Queen, who won both Irish 1000 Guineas and Irish Oaks. She was sired by Stardust who had stood alongside Turkhan at Old Connell Stud, and had also finished runner-up to him in the St. Leger.

Turkhan's daughter Vale of Towy produced the 1954 One Thousand Guineas third Welsh Fairy, and in the 1956 Irish St. Leger Jongleur finished second. He was a son of Turkhan's daughter Turkish Tune and later finished third in the Champion Stakes and second in the Doncaster Cup, before standing as a stallion in Poland.

Turkhan's daughter: Turkish Blood was the dam of Vienna (by Aureole) and would turn out to be the most important product of a Turkhan mare. A good, but not outstanding racehorse, Vienna won the Prix D'Harcourt, finished third in the St. Leger and runner-up in successive Coronation Cups, before taking up stallion duties where he sired Vaguely Noble. His breeder: Major Lionel Holliday died before he could see him race. Vaguely Noble won the Sandwich Stakes at Ascot by twelve lengths on his third start and two weeks later he won the Observer Gold Cup by seven lengths.

Death duties forced the sale of Vaguely Noble and he fetched a record 136,000 guineas (£2,450,000) at the Newmarket December sales. He had no Classic engagements and, as he could not be supplemented, to justify such a price would need to win either or both of the King George the VI & Queen Elizabeth Stakes or the Prix de l'Arc de Triomphe. He won the latter to establish his credentials as a great horse.

Vaguely Noble's grand dam Belle Sauvage was by Bahram's son Big Game, so Vaguely Noble was inbred 4x4 to Bahram.

Turkhan's daughter Turkish Tourist became the dam of 1970 Aintree Grand National winner Gay Trip.

Principal winners produced by daughters of Turkhan

Horse with sire in brackets	Principal races won
Arcandy (Archive)	1955 Lavant Stakes (5f.)
	1957 Steward's Cup Handicap (6f.)
	1957 Diadem Stakes (6f.)
Blessing (Devil's Thumb)	1955 Queen Stakes (9f.)
	1958 Keio Hai Spring Cup (8f.)
	1958 Chukyo Kinen (9f.)
Blood Test (Fair Trial)	1953 Cork & Orrery Stakes (6f.)
Carezza (Rockefella)	1955 Beresford Stakes (8f.)
	1956 Princess Royal Stakes (12f.)

Horse with sire in brackets	Principal races won
Courageuse (Cranach)	1955 Grand Premio Herique Possolo (8f.)
	1955 Gran Premio Marciano de Aguiar Moreira (12f.)
	1955 Gran Premio Cruzeiro do Sul (12f.)
	1955 Grande Premio Diana (12f.)
Gay Trip (Vulgan)	1969 & 1971 Mackeson Gold Cup Chase (20.5f.)
	1970 Aintree Grand National Chase (36f.)
Hardy Scot (Hard Sauce)	1972 Rose of York Handicap (8f.)
Idler (The Cobbler)	1957 Prendergast Stakes (5f.)
Jongleur (Sayajirao)	1956 Desmond Stakes (8f.)
	1956 Blandford Stakes (12f.)
	1956 Royal Whip Stakes (12f.)
Lock Hard (Hard Tack)	1963 Player's 2000 Guineas Trial Stake (8f.)
Minou (Court Martial)	1958 Athasi Stakes (7f.)
Minute Gun (Mossborough)	1962 Queen's Prize Handicap (16f.)
My Smokey (Signal Light)	1954 Dewhurst Stakes (7f.)
Pantomime Queen (Stardust)	1954 Irish 1000 Guineas (8f.)
	1954 Irish Oaks (12f.)
Spice (Arctic Prince)	1959 Kempton 1000 Guineas Trial Stakes (7f.)
Su Ka Wa (Barbizon)	1961 Kentucky Jockey Club Stakes (9f.)
	1961 Youthful Stakes (8f.)
Tudor Harmony (Tudor Melody)	1971 Rosebery Handicap (10f.)
Tudor Treasure (King of the Tudors)	1961 St. James's Palace Stakes (8f.)
	1963 Victoria Cup Handicap (7f.)
Turf (Historic)	1950 Polish 2000 Guineas (8f.)
Turko (Black Tarquin)	1961 Prix Daphnis (9f.)
Vienna (Aureole)	1960 Blue Riband Trial Stakes (8.5f.)
	1962 Prix D'Harcourt (10f.)
Welsh Fairy (Fair Trial)	1953 St. Hugh's Fillies Stakes (5f.)

Persian Gulf

Persian Gulf took up stallion duties at the Wernher family's Someries Stud, Newmarket in 1946, standing alongside his half-brother, the Ascot Gold Cup winner Precipitation. His fee of 300 guineas (£11,650) put him alongside Fair Trial and Fairway, and 100 guineas (£3,880) below the top priced stallions: Bois Roussel, Dante, Hyperion and Rockefella. Despite being a late maturing horse Persian Gulf sired a number of fast performers.

His first crop produced Abadan, winner of the five furlongs Phoenix Stakes at two, and the Cork & Orrery and Diomed Stakes over six furlongs at three. Abadan also finished second in the Irish Two Thousand Guineas, and when retired to stud in Ireland became the leading first season sire in Great Britain in 1956. His winners included the Irish Two Thousand Guineas winner Jack Ketch. Abadan spent one season at stud in Ireland before he was exported to South Africa, where he became Champion Sire for the 1960/61 season.

Persian Gulf's first European Classic winner came from his second crop; daughters Queen of Sheba and Engulfed were first and second in the Irish One Thousand Guineas. Queen of Sheba was also second in the Irish Oaks. His first Classic success in England came from his third crop: Cheveley Park Stakes winner Zabara won the 1952 One Thousand Guineas. She also won the Coronation Stakes at Royal Ascot.

These early successes were achieved with progeny that had speed as their prominent feature. However, Zarathustra, from Persian Gulf's fifth crop, was a strong stayer; winning the Irish Derby and Irish St. Leger. Zarathustra progressed with age and won the Ascot Stakes (20f.) and Goodwood Cup (21f.) at five; and the following year the Ascot Gold Cup.

Persian Gulf continued to transmit speed with his next two crops which featured Tamerlane, winner of the New and July Stakes over five furlongs, and Zabara's full brother Rustam, who won the National Breeders Produce Stakes (5f.) and Champagne Stakes (6f.) at Doncaster.

Tamerlane developed into a very useful miler at three, winning the St. James's Palace Stakes, and was beaten only once that year by Our Babu in the Two Thousand Guineas. Rustam was later to sire another fast juvenile in Double Jump.

Persian Gulf's son Agreement was a good stayer winning the Chester Cup (18f.) and successive Doncaster Cups (18f.). Arabian Night finished second to Never Say Die in the 1954 Derby after finishing fourth in the in the Two Thousand Guineas.

In 1959 Parthia won the Derby plus the White Rose, Dee and Lingfield Derby Stakes before finishing fourth in the St Leger. At four he won the Jockey Club Cup and Paradise Stakes was second to Petite Etoile in the Coronation Cup and also to Aggressor in the Hardwicke Stakes. In Parthia's final appearance he was unplaced in the King George VI & Queen Elizabeth Stakes. Parthia's dam was by Hyperion, and was therefore linebred 6x6 to Black Duchess via Black Cherry and Dark Ronald.

Parthia's Derby win in 1959 helped Persian Gulf to finish third in the list of leading sires that year, his highest position, and he also finished fourth in 1952 and 1955 and fifth in 1954.

Persian Gulf died of heart failure on 22nd July 1964, but a year before that he sired Persian War. A useful stayer on the flat Persian War was an outstanding hurdler; he won the Triumph Hurdle at Cheltenham in 1967 and the Champion Hurdle three times in a row between 1968 and 1970.

Overall Persian Gulf can be considered a consistent but not outstanding stallion; he sired the winners of 470 races worth £411,937 and his Average stamina index was 11.25 furlongs.

Principal races won by the offspring of Persian Gulf:-

Horse with maternal grandsire in brackets	Principal races won
Abadan (Fair Trial)	1949 Phoenix Stakes (5f.)
	1950 Cork & Orrery Stakes (6f.)
	1950 Diadem Stakes (6f.)
Agreement (Borealis)	1958 & 1959 Doncaster Cup (18f.)
	1959 Chester Cup (18f.)
Arabian Night (Rhodes Scholar)	1954 Column Produce Stakes (8f.)
Ashavan (Nepenthe)	1964 Prix Kergorlay (15f.)
Beau Persan (Ticino)	1963 Prix Daru (10.5f.)
Clarification (Blue Peter)	1955 Horris Hill Stakes (7f.)
Double Luck (fair Trial)	1955 Prix de Flore (10.5f.)
Engulfed (Xandover)	1951 Anglesey Stakes (6f.)
Green Opal (Ocean Swell)	1960 Falmouth Stakes (8f.)
	1960 Princess Royal Stakes (12f.)
Gulf Pearl (Nearco)	1964 Imperial Stakes (6f.)
	1965 Chester Vase (13f.)
Khor-Mousa (Hyperion)	1951 Royal Lodge Stakes (8f.)
King Cardinal (Caerleon)	1952 Liverpool Autumn Cup (11f.)
Olga (Easton)	1953 Hungerford Stakes (7f.)
Parthia (Hyperion)	1959 Dee Stakes (10f.)
	1959 Lingfield Derby Trial (12f.)
	1959 Derby (12f.)
	1960 Paradise Stakes (14f.)
	1960 Jockey Club Cup (12f.)
Penitent (Nearco)	1954 Old Newton Cup Handicap (12f.)
	1957 Liverpool Spring Cup (11f.)
Persian Lancer (Nearco)	1961 Melrose Handicap (14f.)
	1966 Cesarewitch Handicap (18f.)
Persian Road (Watling Street)	1958 Melrose Handicap (14f.)
	1959 Great Yorkshire Handicap (14f.)
	1959 Manchester Cup (12f.)
	1960Bessborough Handicap (12f.)
	1960 Ebor Handicap (14f.)

Horse with maternal grandsire in brackets	Principal races won
Persian War (Chanteur II)	1967 Triumph Hurdle (16f.)
	1967 Challow Hurdle (16f.)
	1968 Schweppes Gold Trophy Hurdle (16f.)
	1968, 1969 &1970 Champion Hurdle (16f.)
	1970 Irish Sweeps Hurdle (16f.)
Persian Wonder (Petition)	1967 Dee Stakes (10f.)
Philos (Nearco)	1953 Warren Stakes (12f.)
Proud Chieftain (Big Game)	1960 Column Produce Stakes (8f.)
	1961 Rosebery Handicap (10f.)
	1961 John Smith's Cup Handicap (10f.)
Queen of Sheba (Buen Ojo)	1951 Irish 1000 Guineas (8f.)
	1951 Cheshire Oaks (12f.)
	1952 Royal Hunt Cup (7f.)
Restoration (Hyperion)	19598 King Edward VII Stakes (12f.)
Rhythmic Light (Gold Bridge)	1957 Old Newton Cup Handicap (12f.)
Rustam (Caerleon)	1955 National Breeders Produce Stakes (5f.)
	1955 Champagne Stakes (6f.)
Star Magic (Link Boy)	1956 Cornwallis Stakes (8f.)
Tahiri (Nearco)	19 63 City & Suburban Handicap (10f.)
Tamerlane (Nearco)	1954 New Stakes (5f.)
	1954 July Stakes (5f.)
	1955 St. James's Palace Stakes (8f.)
Valdesta (Sir Cosmo)	1965 Kempton 1000 Guineas Trial (7f.)
Wake Up! (Fairway)	1957 Princess of Wales Stakes (12f.)
Zabara (Caerleon)	1951 Imperial Produce Stakes (6f.)
	1951 Cheveley Park Stakes (6f.)
	1952 1000 Guineas (8f.)
	1952 Lingfield Oaks Trial (12f.)
	1952 Coronation Stakes (8f.)
Zarathustra (Sansovino)	1954 Desmond Stakes (8f.)
	1954 Irish Derby (12f.)
	1954 Irish St. Leger (14f.)
	1955 Royal Whip Stakes (12f.)
	1956 Ascot Stakes (20f.)
	1956 Goodwood Cup (21f.)
	1957 Ascot Gold Cup (20f.)
Zimone (Nearco)	1957 Premio Chiusura (7f.)

Persian Wonder was exported to South Africa and became a most successful stallion. In nine seasons between 1972/73 and 1980/81 he was Champion South African Sire six times and finished second in the other three seasons. His progeny included the 1971 South African Derby winner Pedlar, two winners of the South African Oaks in Avila and Siberian Wonder, together with Force Ten and Sunshine Man, who both won the important J&B Metropolitan.

Persian Wonder, inbred 3x4 to Blandford, won the ten furlongs Dee Stakes, before finishing third in both Lockinge and Queen Anne Stakes.

In 1961 Tamerlane sired a colt: Dschingis Khan out of Donna Diana by Necktar. Dschingis Khan won twelve of his thirty-three starts including the German Two Thousand Guineas, and stood as a stallion there in Germany with considerable success. He was Champion Sire in 1981 and sired two colts who both won the German Derby and Two Thousand Guineas: Orofino and Konigsstuhl. The latter completed the German Triple Crown; the only horse ever to do so.

At stud Konigsstuhl became Champion German Stallion in 1994 and 1996, and also sired two German Derby winners: Lavirco and Pik Konig. Konigsstuhl's son Monsun finished second in the German Derby was a high-class racehorse but a better sire. He was leading sire in Germany in 2000, 2002 and 2004. This success resulted in his covering fee increasing from 20,000 euros (£24,000) to 150,000 euros (£180,000) by 2008. Monsun has sired three German Derby winners: Samum,

Schiaparelli and Shirocco, who all now stand as stallions; Samum has sired the 2008 German Derby winner Kamsin. Monsun's influence looks set to continue as he is maternal grandsire to three further German Derby winners: Pastorius, Lucky Speed and Sea The Moon.

Monsun's influence continues to spread; Shirocco won the Breeder's Cup Turf in 2005 and his sons Fiorente and Protectionist won consecutive runnings of the Melbourne Cup in 2013 and 2014. Monsun's daughter Estimate won the Ascot Gold Cup in 2013 and his son Novellist the King George VI & Queen Elizabeth Stakes the same year.

Two other sons of Monsun: Getaway and Network stand as National Hunt stallions; Network has sired steeplechasers Rubi Ball and Sprinter Sacre.

Principal sire lines descending from Persian Gulf, with country where they stood in brackets
Persian Gulf (UK)
| Parthia (UK & Japan)
| Gulf Pearl (UK)
| Zarathustra (UK & Japan)
| Clarification (New Zealand)
| Zimone (Italy)
| Persian Road (USA)
| Istanbul (Australia)
| Idle Hour (Argentine)
| | Figonero (USA)
| | Farley (Argentine)
| Proud Chieftain (UK)
| | Owen Anthony (UK)
| Abadan (Ireland & South Africa)
| | My Pal (New Zealand)
| | Kings Agree (South Africa)
| | Jack Ketch (Australia)
| Persian Wonder (South Africa)
| | Pedlar (South Africa)
| | Big Swinger (South Africa)
| Tamerlane (UK)
| | Eucalpytus (Australia)
| | Indian Conquest (Australia)
| | Lanesborough (Australia)
| | Alpenkonig (Germany)
| | Dschingis Khan (Germany)
| | | Cagliostro (Germany)
| | | Orofino (Germany)
| | | Konigsstuhl (Germany)
| | | | Lavirco (Germany & France)
| | | | Alkalde (Germany)
| | | | Monsun (Germany)
| | | | | Gentlewave (France)
| | | | | Getaway (France)
| | | | | Manduro (Ireland)
| | | | | Network (France)
| | | | | Samum (Germany)
| | | | | Schiaparelli (UK)
| | | | | Shirocco (UK)
| | | | | Speedmaster (Germany & France)

Persian Gulf's record as broodmare sire was consistent but average. His daughters produced three European Classic winners: Zenobia, who won the 1960 Irish One Thousand Guineas, Craighouse, 1965 Irish St. Leger winner and Intermezzo, 1969 St. Leger winner. Intermezzo helped Persian Gulf to finish second in the list of leading broodmare sires in 1969; his best position. His daughters produced plenty of winners but Persian Gulf did not finish higher than seventh before or after.

The progeny of Persian Gulf's daughters had success in staying events; they included two Ascot Stakes winners: Crash Course and Full of Beans. Crash Course also won the Doncaster Cup (18f.), while Acharacle, Great Rock and Arctic Kanda respectively won handicaps such as the Goodwood Stakes (19f.), Northumberland Plate (16f.) and Irish Cesarewitch (16f.).

The leading National Hunt stallions, Carmarthen and Menelek, were also the product of Persian Gulf mares. Carmarthen was a useful performer in France winning the Prix Ganay, and was later leading French jumping stallion six times between 1980 and 1987.

Menelek, a son of Derby winner Tulyar and Irish One Thousand Guineas winner Queen of Sheba, won eleven races on the flat over distances varying from ten to sixteen furlongs, and became the leading National Hunt sire in Great Britain for the 1975/76 season, when his progeny included Grand National winner Rag Trade.

But the progeny of Persian Gulf mares were not exclusively stayers, and his daughters produced some fast juveniles: Another Realm, Glen Strae, Golden Horus and My Goodness Me.

Persian Gulf's most influential daughter was his One Thousand Guineas winner Zabara. She produced three minor winners and her descendants included Group 1 winners Belele (Western Australian Derby, Blue Canari (Prix du Jockey Club), Circus Plume (Oaks, Yorkshire Oaks), Mtoto (King George VI and Queen Elizabeth Stakes, Eclipse Stakes twice) and Mutamam (Canadian International).

Principal winners produced by daughters of Persian Gulf:-

Horse with sire in brackets	Principal races won
Acharacle (Alcide)	1968 Goodwood Cup (19f.)
Another Realm (Realm)	1980 Richmond Stakes (6f.)
	1981 Greenham Stakes (7f.)
Arctic Kanda (Arctic Star)	1963 Irish Cesarewitch (16f.)
Ashiya Fuji (Tosa Midori)	1968 Tokyo Daishoten (15f.)
	1969 Kawasaki Kinen (10.f)
Bunkered (Entanglement)	1972 Whitehall Stakes (8f.)
Carmarthen (Devon)	1967 Prix Daru (10.5f.)
	1967 Prix du Prince D'Orange (10f.)
	1968 Prix D'Harcourt (10f.)
	1969 Prix Exbury (8f.)
	1969 Prix Ganay (10.5f.)
Catherine Wheel (Roan Rocket)	1971 Musidora Stakes (10.5f.)
	1971 Nassau Stakes (10f.)
Craighouse (Mossborough	1965 Irish St. Leger (14f.)
Crash Course (Busted)	1975 Ascot Stakes (20f.)
	1975 Doncaster Cup (18f.)
Date Horai (Wildeal)	1968 Mainichi Hai (10f.)
	1969 Sankei Osaka Hai (9.5f.)
	1969 Asahi Challenge Cup (10f.)
	1969 Nikkei Shinshun Hai (12f.)
	1969 Takarazuka Kinen (11f.)
Flamboyante (Reliance)	1971 Prix Vanteaux (9f.)
Follow Suit (Ballymoss)	1962 Dewhurst Stakes (7f.)
Full of Beans (Con Brio)	1973 Ascot Stakes (20f.)
Gambola (Exbury)	1969 Lancashire Oaks (12f.)
Glen Strae (Reform)	1973 Lavant Stakes (5f.)
	1974 Greenham Stakes (7f.)
Golden Horus (Tudor Melody)	1966 July Stakes (6f.)
	1966 Gimcrack Stakes (6f.)
Great Rock (Black Rock)	1957 Northumberland Plate (16f.)
	1958 Manchester Cup (12f.)
Grey Lord (Quorum)	1965 Bunbury Cup Handicap (7f.)
Harmony Hall (Tudor Melody)	1969 Princess of Wales Stakes (12f.)
	1969 Gordon Stakes (12f.)
	1969 Great Voltigeur Stakes (12f.)
Intermezzo (Hornbeam)	1969 St. Leger (14f.)

Horse with sire in brackets	Principal races won
Jibuti (Djebe)	1962 Ebbisham Stakes (8.5f.)
Little Iron (Palestine)	1963 Premio Bimbi (5f.)
Look Sharp (Crepello)	1965 Dee Stakes (10f.)
Menelek (Tulyar)	1961 Old Newton Cup (12f.)
My Goodness Me (Abernant)	1962 St Hugh's Fillies Stakes (5f.)
	1962 Cheveley Park Stakes (6f.)
Patti (Chanteur II)	1964 Galtres Stakes (12f.)
Petronelle (O'Grady)	1970 Prix Cleopatre (10.5f.)
Ranimer (Relko)	1976 Sun Chariot Stakes (10f.)
Rasgavor (Reliance)	1973 Prix de L'Esperance (15f.)
Ruantallan (Ribot)	1964 Newbury Autumn Cup (16f.)
Satan (Buisson Ardent)	1961 Diadem Stakes (6f.)
Silly Talk (Quorum)	1972 Liverpool Spring Cup (11f.)
Solomon II (Aureole)	1970 Kingwell Hurdle (16f.)
	1970 Imperial Cup Hurdle (16f.)
Stupor Mundi (Tulyar)	1960 Newmarket Stakes (10f.)
	1961 Chesterfield Cup (10f.)
Sunny Cove (Nearco)	1960 Park Hill Stakes (14f.)
	1960 Newmarket Oaks (14f.)
Tierra del Fuego (Buisson Ardent)	1962 Woodcote Stakes (6f.)
Zenobia (Sayajirao)	1960 Irish 1000 Guineas (8f.)

Appendix III

Other sons at stud

ANUBIS (1947 b c Bahram – Anapa by Copyright)

Anubis' older half-brother Aden (by Rustom Pasha) had won Argentine's Gran Premio Polla de Potrillos in 1944, but the main attraction in Anubis' pedigree was that his dam Anapa was a three – quarter sister to the dam of Postin. The latter won 13 races in Peru, including the Clasico Presidente de la Republica twice, and then became Champion Sire there six times in succession from 1954 and 1959. He sired five Peruvian Derby winners, among whom were the Peruvian Triple Crown winning filly Pamplona, who went on to become the dam of two European Classic winners in Pampered Miss (French 1000 Guineas) and Empery (Derby). It is interesting to note that Anubis' dam Anapa, with a cross of Cyllene with St. Simon's son William the Third and Persimmon was bred on very similar lines to Bahram's own dam Friar's Daughter.

Purchased for 72,000 pesos as a two-year-old and unraced at two, Anubis made a winning debut at San Isidro on 2nd September 1950, winning the Premio Guapo (1500m.). He followed this up with four third places over distances ranging from 1500 to 2000 metres, before winning the Premio Stiletto (2000m.) and the Premio Ivaro (2400m.).

Anubis was never out of the first three in nine starts with earnings of 65,650 pesos. He was then exported to Brazil, where he won twice more.

Principal winners sired by Anubis

Horse with maternal grandsire in brackets	Principal Races Won
Duraque (My Prince)	1967 Grande Premio Brasil (15f.)

AVRO (1951 b c Bahram – Aleta by Strip the Willow)

Avro's dam Aleta was a useful performer in Argentine where she won the Gran Premio Eliseo Ramirez (7f.) and Gran Premio Jorge de Atucha (7.5f.) in 1943. At stud she produced, in addition to Avro, two colts of above average ability in Carlinga, whose wins included the Gran Premio Seleccion (11f) and Gran Premio 25 de Mayo (12f.), along with Panair, winner of the 1959 Gran Premio Polla de Potrillos (8f).

Purchased for 46,000 pesos as a two-year-old, Avro won his first race aged four when winning on his tenth start in the Premio Sicuani (1600m.). His first nine starts had yielded two second places over distances as varied as 1200 and 2500 metres, and he also finished third twice over 1600 metres. He won twice more from five starts: the Premio Sidera (1800m.) and the Premio Gulf Stream (2000m.).

Avro had little success as a stallion in Argentine, and his only winner of note came in Chile, where his daughter Rayita won their equivalent of the 1000 Guineas (Polla de Potrancas) and Derby (El Ensayo) in 1966. Interestingly, Rayita's dam Yalu had the same cross of Blandford, Cyllene and Persimmon found in Bahram.

Among Avro's daughters was the mare Extravagancia, whose daughter Eternity produced the full brothers Espontaneo, winner of the 1983 Group 3 Cotejo de Potrillos (6f.) and Endiosado, who won the 1987 Group 2 Clasico Seleccion de Velocistas (5f.) in Chile. Their sire, El Oriental, a Group 3 winner in Argentine, was linebred 5x5x4 to three offspring of the mare Plucky Liege in Sir Gallahad II, Marguerite de Valoir and Bois Roussel. Plucky Liege, of course, was a half sister to Bahram's granddam Garron Lass.

Principal winners sired by Avro

Horse with maternal grandsire in brackets	Principal Races Won
Rayita (Closworth)	1966 Polla de Potrancas (8.5f.)
	1966 El Ensayo (12f.)

Principal winners produced by daughters of Avro

Horse with sire in brackets
Terminal (Maniatico)

Principal Races Won
1971 Grande Premio Brasil (15f.)

BAHERSHAH (1940 b c Bahram – Taj Shirin by Gainsborough)

Taj Shirin's dam: Taj Mah was sold for 250,000 francs (about £2,000) for Taj Mah, who later won the 1000 Guineas.

Taj Shirin won minor race as a juvenile worth £250. However, at stud she bred two useful performers in the 1936 Chester Vase winner and Derby runner-up Taj Akbar, and the 1948 Irish Derby winner Nathoo. Bahershah won one minor race and was placed twice from 26 starts over 3 seasons.

Bahershah was sold and took up stallion duties in New Zealand.at his newly founded Tudor Lodge Stud in Otaki. He later moved to Mr. S. Fabish's New Plymouth Stud, before his death in 1960.

Bahershah had few opportunities at stud and produced only one black-type winner: Queen's Navy, whose son was the stayer Guest Star (by Crest of the Wave), who won the New Zealand St. Leger and, in Australia, the 1975 Caulfield Stakes, and back in New Zealand the Wellington Cup, a race he had previously finished second in.

A daughter of Bahershah: Shahnoon, her daughter: Noonlight produced the 1973 USA Grade 3 Autumn Days Handicap (6.5f.) winner New Moon II, while New Moon's half-sister: Dark Moon, became the dam of Our High Noon, who won the 1990 Group 3 Awapuni Metric Mile (8f.).

A daughter of Noonlight: Moon Tide, produced Lord Triad, who stood with minor success as a stallion in New Zealand, where his best offspring was Group 2 Travis Stakes and New Zealand 1000 Guineas runner-up Covered N' Grey. The latter's grandson: President Lincoln won the 2011 Wellington Guineas (8f.).

Finally, Bahershah's daughter Karessa appeared as the fifth dam of Voting, winner of the 1993 Group 2 Sandown Guineas (8f.) and 1997 G3 Tokyo City Cup (8f.) in Australia.

Principal winners produced by daughters of Bahershah

Horse with sire in brackets
Guest Star (Crest of the Wave)

Principal Races Won
1974 New Zealand St. Leger (14f.)
1975 Caulfield Stakes (10f.)
1976 Wellington Cup (16f.)

BAHRAM SON (1948 b c Bahram – Foxiole by Foxhunter)

Bahram Son traced back in direct female line to Zariba, one of Marcel Boussac's foundation mares. His granddam Iole was also Boussac-bred and a three-quarter sister to Middle Park Stakes winner Abjer, but she failed to win, and was exported to Argentine in 1941, in foal to Foxhunter, where she produced the filly Foxiole, the dam of Bahram Son, in 1942. Foxiole raced twice, finishing third over 1000 metres on her final start.

Bahram Son's half-brother Foxtrap (by Don Mac) did finish third in Argentine's Premio Saturino J Unzue in 1962, while Foxtrap's full brother: Turin was exported to America where he finished third in both Sunset and San Luis Rey Handicaps.

Bahram Son won the Premio Sicuani (1600m.) and following two fourth places over the same distance, either side of a second over 1500 metres, he won in consecutive races the Premio Ventisquero (1600m.), Premio Crucero (1400m.) and Premio Receloso (1800m.) in the space of five weeks. It was to be his final victory, but he finished out of the first four only once more in his remaining nine starts winning 112,250 pesos.

Retired to stud in Argentine, Bahram Son's best offspring was Poliyense, winner of the Clasico Ramon Biaus.

Principal winners sired by Bahram Son

Horse with maternal grandsire in brackets	Principal Races Won
Poliyense (Advocate)	1962 Clasico Ramon Biaus (11f.)

BAMAN (1940 b c Bahram – Una by Tetratema)

Baman was a half-brother to the top-class juvenile and miler Palestine (by Fair Trial). Baman was bred on similar lines to the full-brother and sister Umidwar (winner of 1934 Champion Stakes) and Udaipur (winner of 1932 Oaks), who were by Bahram's sire Blandford out of Baman's granddam Uganda. Another horse with a similar pedigree background to Baman was the 1950 Dee Stakes winner, and later Champion Sire in Australia, Khorassan. His pedigree featured Bahram, Tetratema and Uganda close up, just line Baman

As a juvenile Baman failed to win any of his five races, but was second three times. He was disappointing as he had been favourite four times. As a three-year-old he won one of his six races: a six furlong maiden at Newmarket. He ran in the 2000 guineas but was out-classed. As a four-year-old he won two of his six races:

Baman retired to stud in 1945, at Knockeeven Stud, Clonmel, Ireland at a fee of 48 guineas, Baman spent four seasons there before being exported to Argentine in 1948. He sired the winners of 45 races worth £10,206 (£367,500) in Great Britain and Ireland. Baman's progeny were slightly better over jumps, with his son Boys Hurrah winning a division of the 1956 Gloucester Hurdle at the 1956 Cheltenham National Hunt Festival.

Among Baman's second crop was a filly: Clear Bay, whose son Merry Court won the 1968 Mildmay of Flete Steeplechase (20f.), her daughter Treize later became the third dam of both The Bushkeeper, winner of the 2002 Kim Muir Handicap Chase (24f.), and Cue Card, who won the 2010 Champion Bumper (16f.).

Baman's final Irish crop contained two other fillies: Merry Optic and Viviparus. Merry Optic was the fifth dam of 2006 Becher Chase (26f.) winner Eurotrek, while the descendants of Viviparus won on the flat.

Viviparus won 3 times from 14 starts as a three-year-old over six and eight furlongs, and at stud produced 7 winners of 13 races worth £9,718 (184,500). Her first three foals were; Viviptic (by Preciptic) winning the Beresford Stakes; Vivi Tarquin (by Black Tarquin) winning Royal Ascot's Queen's Vase. Paris Princess (by Prince Chevalier) won both the National Stakes and Beresford Stakes at two, before finishing third both the Ribblesdale and Princess Royal Stakes at three. Paris Princess' full brother Fuengirola later finished second in the 1965 Irish Cesarewitch.

At stud Paris Princess became the granddam of two contrasting performers in the sprinter/miler Tender King, winner of the 1981 Windsor Castle (5f.) and Richmond Stakes (6f.) at two and placed in both 2000 Guineas and Irish 2000 Guineas at three, together with the stayer Weavers' Pin, who won the 1983 Northumberland Plate Handicap (16f.). Paris Princess was also the third dam of Kemago, winner of the 1986 Athasi Stakes (7f.).

One final descendant of Viviparus who merits a mention is her great granddaughter Inis-Gloire, winner of the 1975 Irish Cambridgeshire Handicap (8f.).

Baman stood in Argentina in 1948. He sired the winners of 210 races worth 8,578,182 pesos, with his best season in 1957 when he finished 15th. His best colt was probably Bucentauro who won the 1959 Clasico General Pueyrredon (20f.), while three of his daughters were to make their mark as broodmares in other South American countries.

Bamanella, a daughter from his first Argentine crop, later became the third dam of Maye, winner of the 1987 G1 Clasico Ernesto Ayulo Pardo (10.5f) in Peru, as well as the fifth dam of Electa, who won the 2003 G3 Clasico Cesar del Rio Suito (10f.) also in Peru. Maye's dam was inbred 3x4 to Bahram and his half brother Dastur.

Also from the first South American crop was Kankanette who had descendants who made their mark in Chile. Her granddaughter Moonstone won the 1971 Chilean 1000 Guineas (8.5f.), and Moonstone's daughter: Moonfree, produced two useful performers in 2000 Chilean Derby (12f.) winner El Aragones, along with Mayorcita who won both the 1988 G3 Premio Seleccion de Potrancas (6f.) and 1988 G3 Premio Juan Cavieres Mella (6.5f.).

A further daughter of Baman whose descendants did well in Chile was La Begum. She became the fourth dam of Musica Si, the winner of both 2004 G1 Clasico Haras de Chile (10f.) and 2004 G1 Clasico Alberto Solari Magnasco (10f.). Meanwhile, back in Argentine, La Begum was also the grand-dam of L'Existence, who won the 1977 G3 Clasico Marcos Lavelle (8f.) and 1977 G3 Clasico Carlos Tomkinson (13.5f.).

Principal winners sired by Baman

Horse with maternal grandsire in brackets	Principal Races Won
Boys Hurrah (Pactolus)	1956 Gloucester Hurdle (16f.)
Bucentauro (Quick Ray)	1959 Clasico General Pueyrredon (20f.)

Principal winners produced by daughters of Baman

Horse with sire in brackets	Principal Races Won
Dante's Hope (Dante)	1960 Whitehall Stakes (9f.)
Merry Court (Buckhound)	1968 Mildmay of Flete Steeplechase (20f.)
Paris Princess (Prince Chevalier)	1960 National Stakes (7f.)
	1960 Beresford Stakes (8f.)
Vivi Tarquin (Black Tarquin)	1959 Queen's Vase (16f.)
Viviptic (Preciptic)	1956 Beresford Stakes (8f.)

BASIS (1945 b c Bahram – Oasis by Lucullite)

American bred Oasis won 11 of her 21 starts over two seasons winning earnings of $11,985. She was a full-sister to the useful performer Only One, a colt who ran 56 times winning 13 times and was placed 26 times worth $39,495, including victories in both Dixie and Baltimore Handicaps, as well as finishing third in the Suburban Handicap.

Oasis' half-brother: Donor won 20 races over six seasons worth $367,560. Donor won important races such as the Champagne, Sanford and Sapling Stakes as a juvenile and also valuable race at three, four and five, including the Jerome, Butler and Saratoga Handicaps.

Basis raced for 6 seasons and won 19 of his 68 starts worth $57,549. His best victory came as a four-year-old, when he won the 1949 Quaker City Handicap. His dam Oasis produced 8 other winners of 43 races with the best being Landmark and Landlocked, the latter winning the Sapling Stakes at two.

Retired to stud in America, Basis sired the winners of 84 races with earnings of $199,770, but made a surprise appearance in pedigrees again in 1984, when Wagoner won the Group 3 Doncaster Cup (18f.). Wagoner's grand dam Mill House won 15 of her 95 starts being a daughter of Basis.

BAXAR (1949 br c Bahram – Inglesa by Loaningdale)

At the 1939 Newmarket December Sales, the five-year-old Blandford mare Wilma's Ford, the winner of a minor race worth £132 (6,500) as a juvenile, and her unnamed filly foal by Loaningdale were sold for 300 guineas (£14,500) and 90 guineas (£4,350) respectively. A moderate family that had not produced much for a while; Wilma's Ford's grandam: William's Pride and her offspring including Town Guard (winner of 1922 Gimcrack and Molecomb Stakes), Will o' the Wisp (winner of the 1932 Yorkshire Oaks) and Walter Gay (runner-up in the 1929 Derby).

The pair was exported to Argentine, where the Loaningdale filly was named Inglesa. Inglesa raced four times, finishing third once over 1000 metres. In 1948 she was covered by Bahram, and the resulting foal named Baxar, was thus inbred 2x3 to Blandford.

Baxar's racing career was limited to just two starts, and after finishing runner-up on his debut he won the Premio Smirna (1100m.) at Palermo.

Principal winners sired by Baxar

Horse with maternal grandsire in brackets	Principal Races Won
Bonete (Misero)	1959 G.P. Raul Y Raul E Chevalier (7f.)
	1959 Premio Santiago Luro (6f.)

BIRIKAN (1939 br c Bahram – Carola by Tetratema)

Birikan's dam Carola won the Rous Memorial Stakes (5f.) at Newmarket in 1930 and her full brother Trivit following year won the Champion Breeders Foal Stakes (5f.) at Derby.

Five years before the arrival of Birikan, Carola had produced a filly by Bahram's sire Blandford named Daring Duchess. She was placed in both Chesham and Cheveley Park Stakes as a juvenile and won two minor five furlongs races at three. It is interesting to note the Birikan was bred on the same Bahram/Tetratema cross as his contemporary, 2000 Guineas winner Big Game.

Birikan won two of his six starts as a juvenile: both at Newmarket; the Granby Plate (5f.) and the Soltykoff Stakes (6f). He was also second to Watling Street and allocated 8st.9lb. in the Free Handicap, 12lb. behind Sun Chariot.

As a three-year-old Birikan won three of his eight starts; the Risby Handicap, the Cherry Hinton Stakes (not to be confused with the current race of the same name for juvenile fillies) and the Bluntisham Stakes (8f.). As a four-year-old Birikan failed to win any of his four starts.

Birikan retired to stud in 1944 and despite his first crop numbering just 13 individuals from the 25 mares he covered, it contained a useful colt in Barfelt, who won the Beresford Stakes (8f.) at two and finished third in the Irish St. Leger the following year. In total Birikan sired the winner of 96.5 races worth £30,110 (903,000) before his death on the 5th November 1955.

Stamina seemed to be the strong suit of Birikan offspring and from his third crop a colt out of Ecilace: Umm won the Irish Grand National Steeplechase (26f.) the Galway Plate Handicap Chase (21f.) under 12st.2lb. He fell fatally at the final hurdle at Baldoyle.

Birikan also sired Westinform, the winner of 8 races from 12 to 16 furlongs, including the Geoffrey Freer Stakes, together with the filly Sinna.

Sinna won twice from three starts over 6 and 7 furlongs at two, and the following year twice at 12 and 15 furlongs, including the Trigo Stakes. Sinna would also prove to be one of Birikan most important broodmares; producing El-Al (by Palestine), who won the 1967 Firth of Clyde Stakes (6f.), and became the first of four winners produced by Sinna.

El-Al's name reappeared in pedigrees in 2001 as the fourth dam of the filly Forty On Line, winner of the Grade 3 Miesque Stakes (8f.) in America. El-Al produced two further full sisters: Paltrasse, winner over a mile maiden at three, and the maiden Pal Sinna.

At stud Paltrasse produced the G2 Mill Reef Stakes (6f.) winner Anax together with the maiden filly Glen Cottage. Exported to New Zealand as a five-year-old, the latter became the dam of the 1994 G3 Waikato Guineas (8f.) winner Cottage View.

Pal Sinna's first foal Bay Express developed into an above average sprinter winning the Group 3 Temple Stakes (5f.) and Group 1 King's Stand Stakes (5f.) at three, plus the Group 2 Nunthorpe Stakes (5f.) the following year. He later became a useful sire with his Group 3 winners including Poets Cove (Molecomb Stakes 5f.), Shoot Clear (Prestige Stakes 7f.), Littlefield (Fred Darling Stakes 7f.) and All Systems Go (Seaton Delaval 5f.) and Vintage Stakes 7f.). Pal Sinna was also the third dam of Italian Group 3 winner Development, whose wins in 2000 included the Premio Umbria (6f.) and Premio Omenoni (5f.).

Among Sinna's other winner was Klairenne (by Klairon), produced two useful colts by the sprinter Polyfoto: Clear Picture, winner the 1977 G3 Prix des Reservoirs (8f.) and 1978 G3 Prix D'Astarte (8f.) Negresco, who won the one of Venezuela's major races, the 1979 G1 Clasico Simon Bolivar (12f.).

Mares by Birikan had some success in Australia and New Zealand. His third crop contained the 5 furlongs winning juvenile Lavender, whose second foal London Cry developed into a good handicapper winning the Chesterfield Cup and Cambridgeshire Handicaps at four. At stud in Australia he sired the 1968 Doomben Cup (10f.) winner Sandy's Hope and became maternal grandsire of the 1974 Western Australian Oaks (12f.) winner Vatilla and her half-brother, the 1981 Australian Derby winner Quadtilla.

Another mare by Birikan whose descendants proved successful in Australia was Bareme, a half sister to the 1956 Nunthorpe Stakes winning sprinter Ennis. Bareme was exported to Australia, where her daughter Bareme's Image became the third dam of Hot to Race, winner of the 1985 Group 3 Lightning Handicap (5f.), and the fourth dam of Integrate who won the Group 2 Japan/New Zealand International Trophy (8f.) in 1999 and followed this up the next year with wins in both Group 2 Travis Stakes (8f.) and Group 3 Lord Mayor's Cup (10f).

Finally, the1987 Cheltenham Gold Cup Chase (26f.) winner The Thinker, had Birikan's daughter Meadowbrook as his third dam, while another good steeplechaser, Somersby, winner of both the 2009 Henry VIII Novice Chase (16f.) and the 2012 Clarence House Chase (16f.) traced back in female line to Birikan's daughter Rock of Iron.

Principal winners sired by Birikan

Horse with maternal grandsire in brackets	Principal Races Won
Barfelt (Felstead)	1947 Beresford Stakes (8f.)
Sinna (Devonian)	1959 Trigo Stakes (12f.)
Umm (Yutoi)	1955 Irish Grand National Steeplechase (26f.)
Westinform (Buen Ojo)	1952 Geoffrey Freer Stakes (13f.)

Principal winners produced by daughters of Birikan

Horse with sire in brackets	Principal Races Won
Black Patch (Solar Slipper)	1955 National Stakes (7f.)
El-Al (Palestine)	1967 Firth of Clyde Stakes (6f.)
London Cry (Pardal)	1958 Chesterfield Cup (10f.)
	1958 Cambridge shire Handicap (9f,)

BOIS DE ROSE (1941 b c Bahram – La Moqueuse by Teddy)

Darshaan's dam Delsy was by the Boussac-bred Abdos, whose dam Pretty Lady was a daughter of the mare La Moqueuse.

La Moqueuse finished second in the French 1000 Guineas and won the Prix de la Foret, while at stud her first foal La Circe went on to win the Prix Vermeille.

Bois de Rose was unplaced in all four of his juvenile races. As a three-year-old he won one of his three starts, but did not race as a four-year-old. He returned as a five-year-old but was unplaced in three races. As a six-year-old he won three of his nine starts.

Bois de Rose was exported to Australia in 1948, and stood at the Puen Buen Stud, New South Wales. He had only limited success with his best offspring the Rosehill Guineas winner Idlewild; a horse inbred 3x4 to Bahram's sire Blandford.

Among Bois de Roses' daughters, Rosetum merits a mention. She was inbred 3x4 to Friar's Daughter via Bahram and his half-brother Dastur, and later produced the George Adams Handicap winner Brandy Lad. Interestingly, another mare inbred this time 4x4 to Friar's Daughter via Dastur and Bahram named Jambo Rose (a daughter of the Bois de Rose mare Bed of Roses), produced the colt Rosie Heir, winner of the AJC Champagne Stakes, Hobartville Stakes and Canterbury Guineas

Bois de Rose's daughter Dollarate also featured as the third dam of the 1986 Group 2 Dalgety Handicap winner Silver Award, a colt who also finished third in the Group 1 AJC Derby.

Also of interest was the filly Magnifique, who was by Alcimedes out of the Bois de Rose mare Rosebelle, and thus inbred 5x4 to Blandford. She finished second in the 1972 Melbourne Cup, ironically beaten by a male line descendant of Bahram in Piping Lane, who was by Lanesborough, a grandson of Bahram's son Persian Gulf.

Principal winners sired by Bois de Rose

Horse with maternal grandsire in brackets	Principal Races Won
Idlewild (Le Grand Duc)	1952 Rosehill Guineas (10f.)

Principal winners produced by daughters of Bois de Rose

Horse with sire in brackets	Principal Races Won
Brandy Lad (Good Brandy)	1964 George Adams Handicap (8f.)
Ridicule (Good Brandy)	1966 Standish Handicap (6f.)

BREHON LAW (1940 gr c Bahram – Constant Law by Portlaw)

Brehon Law was inbred 3x4 to Friar Marcus but also his grandam Constant Lady was by a son of Chaucer out of the mare Baronin, the latter being by Isinglass out of the outstanding racemare La Fleche. Baronin was thus a three-quarter sister to John O'Gaunt. Bahram's grandsire Swynford was bred on very similar lines to Constant Lady, not only a son of John O'Gaunt, but also a half-brother to Chaucer.

Brehon Law won one of his six starts as a juvenile in Ireland but only once at three when he was unplaced; again in Ireland.

Brehon Law was exported to Spain in 1944 where he won four races value 17,250 pesetas.

At stud in Spain Brehon Law was champion sire posthumously in 1952 and 1953 having died in 1949. His final crop monopolised the Spanish Classic races in 1953; his son Narrichkin won the Spanish 2000 Guineas, and later finished second in the Spanish Derby. In the Spanish Oaks, daughters of Brehon Law filled the first three places; Ascar, Calesa and Nelia, with Ascar later finishing third in the Spanish Derby. At the end of the season Brehon Law had five of the top six in the three-year-old Free Handicap, and as well as the above classic success his son Naranco won the Gran Premio de Madrid, the top weight-for-age race in the Spanish racing.

One of Brehon Law's most consistent performers was the colt Pumba. The leading Spanish juvenile of 1949, Pumba raced until he was six, winning one of Spain's top staying races the Premio Corpa in both 1951 and 1953, before taking up stallion duties. His daughter Zumba later became the granddam of 1986 Spanish 2000 Guineas winner Orbital.

Principal winners sired by Brehon Law

Horse with maternal grandsire in brackets	Principal Races Won
Ascar (Embargo)	1953 Spanish Oaks (10f.)
Calesa (Pharian)	1953 Premio Villamejor (11f.)
	1953 G. P. Memorial Duque de Toledo (12f.)
Grey Eagle (Colombo)	1951 G.P. Memorial Duque de Toledo (12f.)
Jabato (Sans Le Sou)	1949 Spanish 2000 Guineas (8f.)
Murillo (Ksar)	1952 Premio Villamejor (11f.)
Naranco (Colindres)	1953 Gran Premio de Madrid (12f.)
Narrichkin (Ksar)	1953 Spanish 2000 Guineas (8f.)
Pumba (Sans Le Sou)	1949 Criterium Internacional (7f.)
	1951 & 1953 Premio Corpa (15f.)

Principal winners produced by daughters of Brehon Law

Horse with sire in brackets	Principal Races Won
Sultan El Yago (Goyaz)	1957 Spanish Derby (12f.)

BRUMAZON (1949 b c Bahram – Blue Haze by Blue Peter)

Brumazon's third dam: Vesper Bell had already produced the 1934 1000 Guineas winner Campanula, and not only was Brumazon a son of a Derby winner, but so too were his first three dams, who were respectively daughters of Blue Peter, Coronach and Pommern.

Neither Brumazon's dam nor grandam was able to win a race. Blue Haze was sold at the 1944 December Sales, at the end of her unsuccessful juvenile career for 1,000 guineas, and exported to Argentine.

A 95,000 pesos purchase as a two-year-old, Brumazon failed to win a race.

Principal winners sired by Brumazon

Horse with maternal grandsire in brackets	Principal Races Won
Soldera (Peter's Choice)	1965 Clasico Ministerio da Agricultura

FAIR AIM (1941 b c by Bahram – Speedway by Fairway)

Fair Aim's third dam: Pompadour was a useful filly winning three races including the Imperial Produce Stakes at two and Nassau Stakes at three.

At stud Pompadour's best offspring was the 1929 Craven Stakes winner Cragadour, who was also second in the 2000 Guineas and third in the Irish Derby. Her second foal: a filly Pretty Swift won a minor event as a three-year-old and produced one winner at stud: a colt Bright Bird won two races worth £3,280 (£170,500): the Princess of Wales and Gordon Stakes over twelve furlongs. In 1936 Pretty Swift's yearling daughter by Fairway, was sold for 3,100 guineas (£166,000). Subsequently named Speedway she raced only at two, but was never placed.

Fair Aim's grand dam Pretty Swift was bred on quite similar lines to Bahram's sire Blandford. Both were by Swynford, making Fair Aim inbred 3x3 to that stallion, while Blandford's dam Blanche and Pretty Swift's maternal grandsire Bayardo shared a similar background of Galopin, Isonomy and Black Duchess.

As a juvenile Fair Aim won one of his two starts: a minor stakes race over 5 furlongs. At three he won one of his six races: a minor six furlong handicap.

Fair Aim was exported to Australia in 1945, where he took up stallion duties at the Streaky Bay Stud, in South Australia. An attraction to Australian breeders was the fact that Fair Aim was from the same female family as both Magpie, the Champion Sire in Australia in 1928/29, and Law Maker who finished in the top ten of Australia's leading sires six times, including third place in 1943/44.

Fair Aim wasn't a success and it was his daughter: Fair Dashwood who, via her own daughter: Miss Cal, who produced the Group 1 Caulfield Futurity Stakes (7f.) winner Bonfield (by Holborn). He also won the Group3 Port Adelaide Guineas. Bonfield's half-sister: Dark Dashwood was covered by Holborn later in 1977 and the result was Bonwood, winner of the 1982 G3 Adelaide Guineas (8f.).

HASTY SHOT (1939 b c by Bahram – Instantaneous by Hurry On)

Hasty Shot's dam Instantaneous was a close relative to the 1929 1000 Guineas winner Pennycomequick, and at stud Instantaneous produced a Classic winner in Court Martial, who won the 1945 2000 Guineas, and later became a top-class stallion. Instantaneous was also the dam of 2000 Guineas third Way In, a three-quarter brother to Court Martial.

As a juvenile Hasty Shot won one of his three starts; a minor plate over five furlongs. As a three-year-old he failed to win any of his six races but was second three times. As a four-year-old Hasty Shot won one of his eight races; a stakes race at Ascot.

Hasty Shot was sold at the 1943 Newmarket December Sales to stand in Uruguay. Due to problems with shipping he missed the 1944 covering season and was ultimately not a success. He did however sire a filly Lucky Shot who was the fifth dam of the Brazilian Group winning half-brothers Karlo Guitar, who won the 2007 Group 2 Gran Premio 11 de Julho (5f.), and Quality Guitar, winner of the 2010 Group 2 Gran Premio General Couto de Magalhaes Taca de Ouro (16f.). It is interesting to note that Karlo Guitar was inbred 4x6 to Hasty Shot's half brother Court Martial.

MANIPOUR (1950 b c Bahram – La Boba by Tonto)

Two French Classic winners: Madrigal and Poesie who won respectively the French Derby and 1000 Guineas produced a filly: Romanza. She was exported to Argentina where she produced La Boba, who won once over 1,500 metres.

Manipour won two races both over 1,600 metres: the Premio Jose Mariano Serrano and the San Isidro's Premio Jose Hernandez.

Manipour stood as a stallion in Chile, where his daughter Jordania produced two winners of Chile's most important races: the El Ensayo in Zenith and El Tiron. Jordania was also the granddam of Mapalo, winner of the 1982 Chilean St Leger (15f.).

Principal winners produced by daughters of Manipour

Horse with sire in brackets   **Principal Races Won**
El Tiron (Silver Moon III)   1971 El Ensayo (12f.)
Zenith (Ghirlandaio)   1968 El Ensayo (12f.)

ROYAL BAHRAM (1947 b c by Bahram – Cantera by Copyright)

Royal Bahram was inbred 5x4 to William the Third and 5x5 to Persimmon, both sons of St. Simon, and in all had seven strains of St. Simon in the first six generations of his pedigree, together with eleven strains of St. Simon's sire Galopin in the first seven. His dam Cantera won once.

Originally named Granitico, and from Bahram's first crop of Argentinian foals, he was sold as an unraced juvenile for a record $160,000; the previous one had been $120,000.

Royal Bahram was unraced and a failure as a stallion. He did produce a daughter: Monotona who appeared as the third dam of Dalaba, the winner of the 1988 Group 1 Gran Premio Major Suckow (5f.) in Brazil.

He sired the winners of 48 races worth 1,865,494 pesos.

SENEGAL (1953 b c by Bahram – Brownie by Rustom Pasha)

Senegal's dam Brownie won once over 1400 metres and was a full sister to the 1943 Argentine 2000 Guineas: (Gran Premio Polla de Potrillos) winner Black Out, and a half sister to Blackie, who won both the 1941 Argentine 1000 Guineas: (Gran Premio Polla de Potrancas) and Argentine Oaks (Gran Premio Seleccion). Blackie emulated her dam Black Arrow, who won both those classics in 1934.

Foaled in Argentina, Senegal was sold as a yearling and exported to Venezuela in November 1955. As a juvenile he won six of his eight starts; including the Venezuela's most important race the Clasico Simon Bolivar. As a three-year-old he won all his six starts over distances ranging from 1200 to 3200 metres. Senegal was an outstanding racehorse; a front-runner, difficult to pass, and all his wins came by two lengths or more. He often conceded up to 22lb. Senegal's victories in 1957 included the Clasico Los Sprinter (1200m.), the Clasico Fuerzas Armadas (3200m.), in record time, and the Clasico Gobernacion del Districto Federal (2000m.). In addition he won a second victory in the Clasico Simon Bolivar beating the previously unbeaten McKinley. The race was run on heavy ground but his sectional times give some indication of his excellence; 47.80 (800m.), 1:12 (1200m.), 1:38 (1600m.) and 2:05 (2000m.).

By winning the Clasico Simon Bolivar for a second time he out-performed his older half-brother Prendase, who won the race in 1955. Prendase also finished runner-up in the Washington D. C. International in America, beating another Venezuelan challenger in El Chama.

Senegal received an invitation from Laurel Park for the 1957 Washington D.C International. However, he did not run due to a windgall, a swelling caused by wear and tear, on his near knee. McKinley took his place in the race and finished sixth

Senegal won 12 races earning 466,560 Bolivars (approx. £49,634) (1,340,000). He was retired to stud in Venezuela with only moderate success, his best season was 1964 when his progeny won 15 races worth 490,335 Bolivars, this placed him sixth place on the list of leading sires.

Principal winners sired by Senegal

Horse with maternal grandsire in brackets   **Principal Races Won**
Antar (Petition)   1963 Clasico Comparacion (8f.)

STONE AGE (1946 br c Bahram – Petrify by Identify)

Petrify was a leading juvenile filly in North America in 1941, but was troubled all season by unsoundness. She won six of her races as a juvenile including the Arlington Lassie Stakes and the Matron Stakes

(6f.). She was beaten by subsequent Kentucky Oaks winner Miss Dogwood (later to earn fame as the third dam of Mr Prospector). As a three-year-old she ran twice unplaced both times.

Stone Age was the first and best of Petrify's foals, winning 6 of his 30 starts, worth $53,550, over four seasons. Like his dam he showed his best form at two winning the $15,000 Walden Stakes, and finishing second in the $25,000 Champagne Stakes.

Stone Age stood as a stallion in Puerto Rico, where he sired two of their leading winners: Red Salvage and Speedy. In America, where his offspring won 276 races with earnings of $771,581, his best son was Hard Rock Man, the winner of 17 of his 80 races worth $155,663, including two $30,000 events, the Swaps Handicap and Star and Stripes Handicap.

Stone Age's daughter Vina was covered by Reneged, a stallion who was inbred 3x3 to Sir Gallahad III (a horse from Bahram's family), and produced Renewed Vigor, who won the Equipoise Mile. Two more of Stone Age's daughters whose descendants won at Graded level were Stumbling Block and Las Olas. The winner of the 1994 Grade 3 California Derby (9f.), Screaming Don, had Stumbling Block as his third dam, while dual Grade 1 winner Stocks Up, winner of both 1988 Grade 1 Hollywood Starlet Stakes (8.5f.) and Grade 3 Sorrento Stakes (7f.) traced in female line to Las Olas.

Principal winners sired by Stone Age

Horse with maternal grandsire in brackets	Principal Races Won
Red Salvage (Challendon)	1968 Antonio R Barcelo ( )
Speedy (Count Speed)	1966 Clasico Luis Munoz Rivera Memorial (6f.)
	1966 Clasico Navidad (8.5f.)

Principal winners produced by daughters of Stone Age

Horse with sire in brackets	Principal Races Won
Renewed Vigor (Reneged)	1967 Equipoise Mile Handicap (8f.)

SUN BAHRAM (1946 b c Bahram – Suntica by Sun Briar)

Sun Bahram's dam Suntica won 12 of her 23 starts worth $31,345, included the 1932 Illionis Oaks, Kentucky Oaks and Test Stakes.

At stud the best of Suntica's four winners was her final foal, Sun Bahram. Racing for 5 seasons Sun Bahram won 12 races from 50 starts worth $112,330, winning the Leonard Richards Stakes (on a disqualification) and Saranac Handicap, as well as finishing third in the Travers Stakes at three.

As with all of Bahram's American based stallion sons he made little impact when taking up stallion duties, and his best winner was probably the $50,000 Tropical Park Handicap winner Trans-Way, who was inbred 3x4 to Sun Briar. Other useful performers were the colt Hussar, who won the $23,000 Maryland Futurity as a juvenile, and the filly Sue Baru, whose biggest win came in the $20,000 Black Eyed Susan Stakes. In total Sun Bahram sired the winners of 342 races worth $1,137,160.

Principal winners sired by Sun Bahram

Horse with maternal grandsire in brackets	Principal Races Won
Hussar (Grand Slam)	1963 Maryland Futurity
Sue Baru (Escadru)	1965 Black Eyed Susan Stakes (8.5f.)
Trans-Way (Nedayr)	1962 Tropical Park Handicap (9f.)

SUPER DUPER (1942 b c Bahram – Bride Elect by High Time)

Super Duper's grandam: High Born Lady produced several winners including Bride Elect, who won one minor race.

At stud she produced two above-average colts by Discovery: Knockdown and First Glance. As a juvenile Knockdown won the Cowdin Stakes and finished second in the Arlington Futurity.

As a three-year-old he won the Santa Anita Derby Knockdown was kept in training for a further four years winning the Excelsior Handicap as a five-year-old to give him a career total of 8 wins from 33 starts worth $165,545.

Knockdown's younger full-brother First Glance also won the Excelsior Handicap, and in 9 seasons of racing won 21 races from 100 starts worth $154,040.

Foaled a year before Knockdown, in 1942, Super Duper won one of his three stars as a juvenile in 1944. He did not race in 1945 and 1946 but in 1947 and 1948 he won 3 more races to bring his career earnings to $13,815 from 16 starts.

He sired little of note at stud; his best progeny was the 1948 Sanford Stakes runner-up Keep Right, and 1954 Arkansas Derby third Super Devil. In total Super Duper sired the winners of 307 races with earnings of $700,472.

Two daughters of Super Duper made their mark on the Puerto Rico racing and breeding. Foaled in 1947, Super Duper's daughter Lyric Words was un-raced, but her own daughter Lady Lyric (by Lord Boswell) won 4 races in 3 seasons, and finished third in the $15,000 Fashion Stakes at two. Exported to Puerto Rico in 1965, she produced Biopolis (by New Outlook), winner of the Clasico Segundo Ruiz Belvis in 1975.

Lady Lyric later became the third dam of US Grade 2 winner Pine Tree Lane (by Apalachee), who won the Bold Ruler Stakes and the Carter and Santa Monica Handicaps in 1987. The following year he won a second Santa Monica, to bring his career earnings to $1,150,561. Lady Lyric's year younger full sister Canita was exported to Puerto Rico as a juvenile, where she became a useful performer.

Lyric Words' final foal: Charles Center (by Saggy), won 9 races with earnings of $29,588, including a third place in the Pimlico Breeders Stakes at two. He later sired the grandam of Oferu Bird (by Court Road), winner of the 1987 Group 1 Gran Premio Matias Machline in Brazil.

In 1958 the six-year-old Super Duper mare Benalee was another export to Puerto Rico. The first two foals she produced there: King Kong (by Combat Boots) and Don Nepo (by Guitarrero), developed into leading performers; King Kong becoming Puerto Rico's champion three-year-old of 1962. King Kong's younger full sister Bizcocho also made her mark, for her daughter Panadera (by Pole Vault) became the leading juvenile in Puerto Rico in 1975, and her son Tahonero (by Special Assignment) was the country's champion three-year-old in 1983. Panadera was linebred 5x4 to Bahram via Big Game and Super Duper

Principal winners produced by daughters of Super Duper

Horse with sire in brackets	Principal Races Won
Canita (Lord Boswell)	1958 Clasico Accion de Gracias
	1958 Clasico Naciones Unidas
	1959 Clasico Porvenir
Don Nepo (Guitarrero)	1965 Constitution E L A
King Kong (Combat Boot)	1962 Segundo Ruis Belvis
	1962 Santiago Iglesias Pantin

THE DRUID (1937 b c Bahram – Trustful by Bachelor's Double)

Trustful's dam: Credenda produced 12 winners of 41.5 races, and r Trustful produced 13 individual winners of 31.5 races. Trustful's offspring won over a variety of distances, the best were Coroado, winner the Wokingham Handicap (6f.) and July Cup (6f.); Buoyant, winner of the Ebbisham Stakes (8.5f.); and Scottish Union, winner of the Middle Park Stakes (6f.), St. James's Palace Stakes (8f.), St. Leger (14f.) and Coronation Cup (12f.).

The Druid was sold as a yearling for 13,000 guineas (£628,000) and raced un-named as a juvenile when he won one of his three starts: Cranbourne Plate (5f). As a three-year-old and now racing as The Druid he won one of his four races: The Red Rose Stakes (6f). He was tried in the highest company but was well below the top level. As a four-year-old he failed to win any of his nine races. However, he was only once out of the first four and generally ran to form; his form was simply not that good and of course well below the level his breeding and price tag would have hoped for.

Exported to Argentine in 1942, The Druid proved to be Bahram's most successful stallion son in South America, and, although he was never champion sire in Argentine, he finished in the top eight for four consecutive years between 1947 and 1950 inclusive, with a best placing of fifth in 1948. In total he sired the winners of 283 races worth 4,580,106 pesos in Argentine.

The Druid' best progeny won over a variety of distances: Baturro, a sprinter, winner of the Gran Premio Maipu (5f.) to Gualicho, champion three-year-old and older horse in Brazil who won consecutive runnings of three of the country's important events: the Gran Premio Brasil (15f.), Gran Premio Sao Paulo (15f.) and Gran Premio Derby Sul Americano (12f.) in 1952 and 1953.

In Chile The Druid's son El Gaucho won the 1947 Nacional Ricardo Lyon (10f.), and went on to become champion stallion in Chile in 1954, when his winners included Provita (El Ensayo and Premio Las Oaks) and Vlasov (Premio El Derby). Two other sons of The Druid to have some success as stallions were the Chilean based Bayano, and Luchado, who in Puerto Rico sired one of their best horses: El Aguila.

Two of The Druid's most successful broodmares were Orlowa and Thermidor. Orlowa's daughter Otomana won the 1956 Clasico Carlos Tomkinson (13.5f.), while another of her daughters: Orlinda became the ancestress of Jim West (2005 G3 Clasico Carlos Bello Silva (8f.) in Chile); Know (2004 G3 Clasico Fortunato Damiani (5f.) in Argentine); Odalea (1989 G1 Gran Premio Internacional Joaquin S de Anchorena (8f.) in Argentine); and Pionero Tal (2002 G1 Gran Premio Internacional Ciudad de la Plata (6f.) in Argentine),

Thermida proved influential through her granddaughter: Infidele. It is worth noting too that Infidele's dam Flegma was by Flexton, a stallion whose dam Silver Birch was bred on a similar cross of Blandford and Bachelor's Double to The Druid the pair appearing 2 x 2 in Flegma's pedigree. Infidele's influence was restricted mostly to Chile where her progeny included Ganancia winner of the 1973 Group 2 Cotejo de Potrancas (6.5f.); Infanzon, who won the 1980 Group 2 Premio Geoffrey Bushell (9f.) together with the 1981 and 1982 Group 1 Clasico Seleccion de Velocistas (5f.); and Infinidad.

Infinidad won the 1985 Group 1 Mil Guineas (8f.) in Chile before being exported to America when he won both the Grade 1 Vanity Handicap (10f.) and Grade 3 Chula Vista Handicap (8.5f.) in 1987.

Ganacia later produced First Norman, the winner in North America of 6 races worth $570, 750, including the Del Mar Derby (9f.). He was exported to New Zealand as a five-year-old, where he became a reasonably successful sire numbering the Group 1 Rawson Stakes winner Electronic among his Progeny.

Two other Group 1 winners with Infidel as their third dam were Light Green, who won the 2007 G1 Premio Henrique de Toledo Lara (9f.) and 2007 G1 Gran Premio Barao de Piracicaba (8f.) in Brazil, and Athenea, who won Chile's G1 Clasico Haras de Chile (10f) in 1998.

The influence of The Druid's daughters also extended to Uruguay. Amodeo, the winner of four Group 1 events in Uruguay in 1988: the Group 1 Uruguay 2000 Guineas (8f.), Group 1 Uruguay Derby (12.5f.), Group 1 Gran Criterium, and Group 1 Gran Premio Jose Pedro Ramirez (12f.) had The Druid's daughter Arcaica as his third dam; while 1971 Uruguay Derby (12.5f.) winner Chocon was a grandson of The Druid's daughter Enfantica.

Principal winners sired by The Druid

Horse with maternal grandsire in brackets	Principal Races Won
Baturro (Amsterdam)	1949 Gran Premio Maipu (5f.)
El Gaucho (Movedizo)	1947 Nacional Ricardo Lyon (10f.)
Gualicho (Congreve)	1952 & 1953 Gran Premio Brasil (15f.)
	1952 & 1953 Gran Premio Sao Paulo (15f.)
	1952 & 1953 Gran Premio Derby Sul Americano (12f.)
Tespia (Congreve)	1953 Seleccion de Potrancas

Principal winners produced by daughters of The Druid

Horse with sire in brackets	Principal Races Won
Otomana (Timor)	1956 Clasico Carlos Tomkinson (13.5f.)
Pahua (Le Petit Prince)	1962 Gran Premio General San Martin (12f.)

TREASURE HUNT (1940 br c Bahram – Amuse by Phalaris)

Amuse's dam: Gesture won one of her eight starts; Ham Stakes (6f.) at Goodwood on her juvenile debut.

Amuse raced twice finishing second in the Kennet Stakes at Newmarket on her debut. At stud Amuse was fourteen before she produced her one and only winner: a filly named Picture Play, who won the 1944 1000 Guineas. She broke down in the Oaks.

Treasure Hunt ran three times as a juvenile failing to win but finishing third on his debut when running as Amuse colt.

Treasure Hunt was sold in 1943 for 90 guineas (£35,000). He was sold again the following year to stand at the Mardella Stud, in Otahuhu, New Zealand. Treasure Hunt was fortunate to survive the sea journey; the ship ran into a storm and his box was damaged and he broke loose. Apart from a damaged hock and considerable bruising he escaped serious injury.

Treasure Hunt's attraction to New Zealand was probably due to his family recently producing two of New Zealand's champion sires: Absurd and Chief Ruler; the leading New Zealand stallion for five years out of six between seasons 1921/22 and 1926/27,

Absurd was a three-quarter brother to Treasure Hunt's granddam Gesture, while the mare Jest, Absurd's full sister, was the dam of Chief Ruler; champion New Zealand sire in 1929/30 and 1931/32.

Principal winners sired by Treasure Hunt

Horse with maternal grandsire in brackets	Principal Races Won
Copper Beech (Autopay)	1952 Karrakatta Plate (5f.)
	1952 Western Australian Oaks (12f.)
	1953 Champion Fillies Stakes (8f.)
	1953 Lee Steere Stakes (7f.)
Mighty Dollar (Nightly)	1954 CJC Challenge Stakes (7f.)
	1955 WRC Thompson Handicap (8f.)

Treasure Hunt's son: Regal Diamond achieved little until his daughter: Royal Souci appeared as the third dam of a colt; Strawberry Road. He was Champion three-year-old colt in Australia and subsequently proved to be a tough high-class performer in Europe and North America. He was a successful sire in North America where he sired the winners of three Breeders Cup events: Ajuina, Escina and Fraise.

The two best horses produced by Treasure Hunt mares were Apollo Eleven and Sir Dane. Apollo Eleven, a son of Treasure Hunt's daughter Lady Rizzio, and inbred 4x3 to the half brothers Dastur and Bahram, won over a wide variety of distances, from one mile up to two when winning successive Chipping Norton Stakes (8f.), and Auckland and Sydney Cups (16f.).

Sir Dane, winner of the Cox Plate, was out of Summertime and the Treasure Hunt mare Casa, and since Summertime was a son of the Bahram mare Great Truth, Sir Dane was inbred 3x3 to Bahram. Two daughters of Casa: Cassowary and Tesa respectively becoming the dams of Azaway, winner of the 1982 Group 1 Sydney Cup (16f.), and Millefleurs, winner of the 1973 Queen of the Turf Stakes (7.5f.).

Principal winners produced by daughters of Treasure Hunt

Horse with sire in brackets	Principal Races Won
Apollo Eleven (Cyrus)	1973 AJC Queen Elizabeth Stakes (12f.)
	1973 Auckland Cup (16f.)
	1973 & 1975 Chipping Norton Stakes (8f.)
	1973 H E Tancred Stakes (12f.)
	1973 Sydney Cup (16f.)
	1975 Trentham Stakes (12f.)
Arama (Oncidium)	1974 John F Feehan Stakes (8f.)
Artello Bay (Martello Towers)	1969 Perth Cup (16f.)
Bel Cavallo (Fountainhead)	1973 CJC George Adams Handicap (10f.)

Horse with sire in brackets	Principal Races Won
Rochdale (Alpheus)	1962 AJC Epsom Handicap (8f.)
	1962 George Adams Handicap (8f.)
	1962 WRC Thompson Handicap (8f.)
Royal Dee (Royal Arch)	1960 Newmarket Handicap (6f.)
Sir Dane (Summertime)	1964 Alister Clark Stakes (8f.)
	1964 Craiglee Stakes (8f.)
	1964 LKS MacKinnon Stakes (10f.)
	1964 Turnbull Stakes (12f.)
	1964 W S Cox Plate (10f.)
	1964 Blamey Stakes (10f.)

The following is a list of other Treasure Hunt mares whose descendants won Group races:-
Copper Beech (Treasure Hunt) (Karrakatta Plate, Lee Steere S, Champion Fillies S)
| **Artello Bay** (Martello Towers) (Perth Cup)
| Star Beech (Asteroid)
| | Beech Gold (Haymaker)
| | | **Calypso** (Cheraw) (G3 A J Scarhill S)
| | Beech Mast (Martello Towers)
| | | **Blonde Jev** (Jevington) (G3 Belmont Sprint)
Both Calypso (6x6x5) and Blonde Jev (6x5) were inbred to Bahram.
Eutropie (Treasure Hunt)
| Microwave (Crest Of The Wave)
| | Tiger Lily (Sovereign Edition)
| | | Wave To Lottie (Crested Wave)
| | | | **Veloce Bella** (Volksraad) (G1 Te Rapa International S)
Group 1 winner Veloce Bella also won the G2 Avondale Guineas, G2 Dulcie Stakes, G2 Sir Tristram Fillies Classic, G2 Eight Carat Stakes and G3 Trentham Stakes.
Foxtrot (Treasure Hunt)
| Miss Hagen (Copenhagen II)
| | I'm A Charmer (Trictrac)
| | | Kaoru Kate (Kaoru Star)
| | | | Kate Be Good (Semipalatinsk)
| | | | | **Another Warrior** (Brave Warrior) (G2 Moonee Valley Gold Cup)
| | | | | Windy Kate (Air Express)
| | | | | | **Real Saga** (Tale Of The Cat) (G2 Todman Slipper Trial)
Another Warrior also won the G3 Chairman's Handicap and G3 Newcastle Gold Cup. Real Saga won the G3 Blue Diamond Prelude. Both later stood as stallions in Australia. Their ancestor Kaoru Kate was inbred 5x5 Bahram, for her sire Kaoru Star was out of a mare by Emperor, whose dam was the Bahram mare Liberation.
Hunting Melody (Treasure Hunt)
| Kimbell (Jeckyll)
| | Lady Camille (Greek God)
| | | April Dazzler (Tarrago)
| | | | **Tartan Belle** (Kreisler) (G3 Desert Gold S)
Tartan Belle's dam April Dazzler had an interesting pedigree: she was inbred 4x5x4 to Bahram, two of the strains coming via the full brothers Persian Gulf and Doubleton.
Isma's Treasure (Treasure Hunt)
| Gay Party (Gay Saint)
| | Forever Gay (Lucky Finish)
| | | Rompalong (Lord Helpus)
| | | | Out In Style (Brave Regent)
| | | | | **Like It Is** (Distorted Humor) (G2 Diamond Jubilee S)
Like It Is also won the G3 VATC Eclipse Stakes, G3 Flemington Matron Stakes and G3 Easter Cup.
Murietta (Treasure Hunt)
| Suppi-Yawlet (Eastern Nip)
| | Almabar (Kazakstaan)

||| **Bar Landy** (Aurilandy) (G1 Winfield S, G2 Alister Clark S, G3 Tasmanian Derby)

There is inbreeding to Bahram: Bar Landy has Bahram appearing 5x6x6x5 in his pedigree, via Big Game, Mah Iran, Persian Gulf and Treasure Hunt.

Smuggles (Treasure Hunt)
| Smuggler's Bank (Dogger Bank)
|| I Spy (Mystery)
||| **Peach Melba** (Palatable) (G3 Race Images H)
||| **Eye Full** (Palatable) (G3 Hawkes Bay Cup)
|||| **Gaze** (Cape Cross) (G1 Second Century S)

Gaze also won the G2 Auckland Thoroughbred Breeders Stakes and G3 Doomben Roses.

Treasure Mine (Treasure Hunt)
| Fair Treasure (Fair's Fair)
|| Kandy Treasure (Candid Picture)
||| Valley Of Treasure (Brigand)
|||| Pampas Dancer (Laudham Star)
||||| **Bedouin** (Snadee) (G1 Metropolitan Handicap, G3 Canterbury Cup)
||||| **Rockford Bay** (Flying Spur) (G3 Adelaide Guineas, G3 Chatham S)
||||| **Slavonic** (Cossack Warrior) (G1 Railway S, G2 Lee Steere S)

Slavonic also won the G2 Norman Carlyon Stakes.

Treasure Bond (Treasure Hunt)
| Quake (Pictavia)
|| **Gallipoli** (Palatable) (G1 New Zealand Cup)

WHIRLAWAY (1940 b c Bahram – Jury by Hurry On)

Whirlaway was a three-quarters brother to The Druid; his dam Jury was a daughter of The Druid's dam Trustful. He won one of his four races as a juvenile: a six furlong maiden at Salisbury. As a three-year-old he failed to win any of his eight races and as a four-year-old any of his five races. He did achieve four seconds and two thirds.

In 1944 Whirlaway was sold to stand as a stallion at the Widden Stud in New South Wales, Australia, alongside the successful stallion Breughel. He made an immediate impact with his first crop containing the exceptionally fast filly Rhumba and AJC Champagne Stakes winner Lady Pirouette. This was quickly followed by AJC Derby and Cox Plate winner Alister, the leading there-year-old of the 1950/51 season, who was from his second crop.

Lady Pirouette later produced another speedy sort in Kilshery, while the latter's half-sister: Waltz founded a successful family via her own daughter Party. Party became the dam of both Festal, winner of the 1989 Group 1 Elders Handicap in New Zealand and later sire of a Group 1 winner in Railway Handicap winner Kailey, along with Masked Party, who won the Group 2 Angas Brut (6f.) in 1996 and both G1 The Galaxy (5.5f.) and G2 Premiere Stakes (6f.) in 1998.

Two other daughters of Party: Awards Party and La Bamba produced Group 1 winners in Australia and Hong Kong. Awards Party became the dam of both multiple Group 1 winner Dracula, who won the Group 1 AJC Champagne Stakes (8f.), Group 1 George Main Stakes (8f.), Group 1 Queensland Sires Produce Stakes (7f.) and Group 3 Fernhill Handicap (8f.) in 1998, before becoming a reasonably successful stallion, while La Bamba's son Inspiration won the Group 1 Hong Kong Sprint (5f.) in 2008, and both Group 3 Premier Bowl Handicap (6f.) and G1 Centenary Sprint Cup (5f.) in 2009.

Finally, Awards Party's daughter Thespian produced Screen, the 2011 Group 3 Golden Pendant (6f.) winner.

Principal winners sired by Whirlaway

Horse with maternal grandsire in brackets	Principal Races Won
Alister (Nuffield)	1950 AJC Derby (12f.)
	1950 Victoria Derby (12.5f.)
	1950 W S Cox Plate (10f.)
Lady Pirouette (Brueghel)	1949 AJC Champagne Strakes (8f.)
Rhumba (Medieval Knight)	1949 AJC Gimcrack Stakes (5f.)

Principal winners produced by daughters of Whirlaway

Horse with sire in brackets	Principal Races Won
Kilshery (Edmundo)	1961 Canterbury Guineas (9f.)
	1962 & 1963 All Aged Stakes (8f.)
	1963 Oakleigh Plate (5.5f.)
	1963 Stradbroke H (7f.)

YANKEE HILL (1944 b c by Bahram – The Beasel by Sunspot)

Yankee Hill was from an undistinguished family his grandam: an unraced mare Antipodes by Roi Herode foaled The Beasel who won 26 of her 49 starts over four seasons. As a juvenile her victories included the Beldame and Baldwin Handicaps and Demoiselle Stakes, and she later won the Fleetwing Handicap at both three and five. Her total earnings were $52,825.

At stud The Beasel's first three foals failed to win. She then produced Boom On who won 11 of his 174 starts, Arthur J; 18 wins from 80 starts and Gainer; 15 wins from 188 starts.

Yankee Hill was foaled when The Beasel was 17 years old, and he was her best offspring. Racing for 6 seasons he won 17 of his 87 starts, winning $67,450, his best year was as a five-year-old when he won the $10,000 Oceanport Handicap (8.5f.).

Retired to stud, Yankee Hill had little success, his offspring winning 186 races with earnings of $418,984. His daughter Louise Bell finished second in the $20,000 1953 Miss Woodford Stakes. Twenty-five years later Louise Bell would reappear as the granddam of the 1978 Grade 3 Discovery Handicap (9f.) winner Sorry Lookin. Probably Yankee Hill's best winner was Pamet, winner of 15 of his 102 starts worth $56,315, including the $5,000 George Wolfe Handicap in 1963.

Other sons of Bahram to stand as stallions, but who produced nothing of note:-
Bar Sinister (1946 b c Bahram – Savage Beauty –by Challenger II) – USA
Barranca Yaco (1948 b c Bahram – Barranquilla by Alan Breck) – Argentine
Bethel (1948 b c Bahram – Betsabe by Congreve) – Brazil
Bisono (1947 b c by Bahram – Congreve) – Argentine
Carlomagno (1948 b c by Bahram – Cara by Bosworth) – Argentine
Cedar Creek (1943 b c by Bahram – Green Fee by Fairway) – USA
Curry (1950 b c by Bahram – Bombay by Badruddin) – Argentine
Espartillo (1951 b c by Bahram – Maleza by Parlanchin) – Argentine
Fugitive (1946 b c by Bahram – Escapade II by Tetratema) – Argentine
Hern the Hunter (1939 b c by Bahram – Panic by Hurry On) – France
His Honour (1948 b c by Bahram – Her Sister by Full Sail) – Argentine
Hold On (1950 b c by Bahram – Holda by Hunters Moon) – USA
Lahore (1952 b c by Bahram – Lilalia by Parwiz) – Argentine
Manchac (1944 b c by Bahram – Sassaby by Broomstick) – USA
Menu (1943 b c by Bahram – Dinner Date by Stimulus) – USA
Mosqueton (1948 b c by Bahram – Margarita by Full Sail) – Argentine
Naranjal (1949 b c by Bahram – Orangerie by Parlanchin) – Argentine
Next (1943 b c by Bahram – Now What by Chance Play) – USA
Perfect Bahram (1943 b c by Bahram – Perfect Love by Man O'War) – USA
Ramadan (1945 b c by Bahram – Arden Lass by Ariel) – USA
Rangoon (1940 b c by Bahram – Silver Mist by Craig An Eran) – USA
Reckon (1944 b c by Bahram – Reckless by Stimulus) – USA
Rogue (1945 b c by Bahram – Reckless by Stimulus) – USA
Sassanid (1945 b c by Bahram – Therm by Hyperion) – Australia
Shah Rookh (1939 b c by Bahram – Pharmood by Phalaris) – Brazil
Snooker (1952 b c by Bahram – Snobless by Rustom Pasha) – Brazil
Taran (1946 b c by Bahram – Trina by Sickle) – USA
Yazdegerd (1946 b c by Bahram – The Beazel by Sunspot) – USA

Appendix IV

Daughters as broodmares

With only five British-bred crops to represent him, Bahram was unlikely to sire enough daughters to a make real impact as a broodmare sire. Despite this 32 of his 35 English or Irish bred mares registered in Volume 33 of the General Stud Book produced winners. Bahram never finished higher than ninth on the list of leading broodmare sires in Great Britain, and his daughters failed to produce a European Classic winner.

They came close with Migoli (2nd Derby, 3rd St.Leger), Noor (3rd Derby), Double Eclipse (3rd Derby), Poona (3rd 2000 Guineas), Doubleton (3rd 1000 Guineas) and Uptala (3rd French 1000 Guineas). The two best winners produced by Bahram mares were Migoli, winner of the Eclipse and Champion Stakes in 1947 and the Prix de l'Arc de Triomphe in 1948, and the stayer Elpenor. He won the Ascot Gold Cup in 1954 and the Prix du Cadran in 1955. In 1954 Elpenor finished second in the Prix du Cadran, and third in both the 1955 Ascot Gold Cup and Goodwood Cup.

Winners in Great Britain and Ireland by year produced by Bahram mares;

1944	Races Won	Value in £
Dilawarji (by Dastur – Queen of Baghdad)	0.5	220.00
Porza (by Stardust – Queen of Shiraz)	2	809.00
TOTAL	2.5	1,029.00

1945	Races Won	Value in £
Daily Double (by Fair Trial – Doubleton)	1	323.00
Dilawarji (by Dastur – Queen of Baghdad)	2	618.00
TOTAL	3	941.00

1946	Races Won	Value in £
Cadenazzo (by Felicitation – Queen of Shiraz)	2	1,445.00
Daily Double (by Fair Trial – Doubleton)	3	1,330.25
Didima (by Nearco – Doubleton)	1	435.00
Migoli (by Bois Roussel – Mah Iran)	1	1,002.75
Norman Prince (by William of Valence – Jovial Lady)	3	1,902.00
TOTAL	10	6,115.00

Principal winners: – **Migoli** – Dewhurst Stakes (7f.)

1947 (9th)	Races Won	Value in £
Lake Placid (by Bobsleigh – Pallida)	1	650.50
Mallowry (by Solferino – Cubhunter)	1	483.00
Migoli (by Bois Roussel – Mah Iran)	6	17,215.00
Mistress Ann (by Nearco – Cheerful Anne)	1	505.25
Nairn Street (by Panorama – Miss Melissa)	1	237.00
Noor (by Nasrullah – Queen of Baghdad)	2	1,395.75
Shieldaig (by Solario – Flowerdale)	1	138.00
TOTAL	13	20,624.50

Principal winners: – **Migoli** – Craven Stakes (8f.), King Edward VII Stakes (12f.), Eclipse Stakes (10f.), Aintree Derby (13f.), Champion Stakes (10f.)

1948 (9th)	Races Won	Value in £
Cabot (by Fair Trial – Safari)	2	572.00
Civil Lord (by Lay Lord – Dark Diana)	1.5	487.00
Duplicity (by Nearco – Doubleton)	2	1,438.25
Florescent (by Hyperion – Safari)	2	1,143.50
Houmyra (by Stardust – Bibibeg)	2	1,115.25
Lake Placid (by Bobsleigh – Pallida)	3	4,534.50
Mallowry (by Solferino – Cubhunter)	2	744.00
Migoli (by Bois Roussel – Mah Iran)	3	4,733.00
Neolanta (by Nearco – Valiant)	1	276.00
Noor (by Nasrullah – Queen of Baghdad)	2	3,308.75
Queen of Basrah (Fair Trial – Queen of Baghdad)	1	615.25
Salfax (by Fairfax – Princess Sally)	2	302.00
TOTAL	23.5	19,269.50

Principal winners: – **Duplicity** – Scarborough Stakes (8f.), **Houmyra** – Acorn Plate (5f.); **Lake Placid** – Great Yorkshire Handicap (14f.), King George V Handicap (12f.); **Migoli** – White Rose Stakes (15f.); **Noor** – Diomed Stakes (12f.)

1949 (9th)	Races Won	Value in £
Anna Lucasta (by Bois Roussel – Cheerful Anne)	1	491.25
Emperor II (by Djebel – Liberation)	1	2,136.00
French Squadron (by Mieuxce – Pack Drill)	3	1,601.75
Garden City (by Mieuxce – Babylon)	2	552.00
Kinlochewe (by Mieuxce – Flowerdale)	1	599.00
Mallowry (by Solferino – Cubhunter)	2	719.50
Moondust (by Stardust – Mah Iran)	2	4,961.25
Royal Deal (by His Highness – Brave Deal)	1	100.00
Salfax (by Fairfax – Princess Sally)	1	202.00
Seventh Wonder (by Watling Street – Babylon)	1	198.00
Strange Lady (by Stardust – Bibijan)	3	690.00
Summertime (Precipitation – Great Truth)	5	3,864.75
TOTAL	23	16,115.50

Principal winners: – **Emperor II** – Dewhurst Stakes (7f.); **Moondust** – Craven Stakes (8f.), Diomed Stakes (12f.); **Summertime** – Classic Trial Stakes (12f.)

1950 (12th)	Races Won	Value in £
Astrida (by Court Martial – Bibibeg)	1	100.00
Double Eclipse (by Hyperion – Doubleton)	2	4,557.75
Drury Lady (by William of Valence – Drury Lane)	1	138.00
Excessive (by Straight Deal – Extravagance)	2	689.75
French Squadron (by Mieuxce – Pack Drill)	2	562.75
Game Star (by Stardust – Extravagance)	1	207.00
Happy William (by Casanova – Cheerful Anne)	1	246.00
Kermanshah (by Tehran – Mah Iran)	2	397.50
Lake Placid (by Bobsleigh – Pallida)	1	1,781.25
Moondust (by Stardust – Mah Iran)	1	2,216.25
Nahar (by Stardust – Queen of Baghdad)	1	276.00
Pantomine (by Stratford – Drury Lane)	1	207.00
Queen of Karachi (by Nearco – Queen of Shiraz)	2	200.00
Rockery (by Full Bloom – Babylon)	1	317.50
Soubrette (by Colombo – Jovial Lady)	1	207.00
Strange Lady (by Stardust – Bibijan)	1	198.00

1950 (12th)	Races Won	Value in £
Summertime (by Precipitation – Great Truth)	2	867.75
Verdura (by Court Martial – Bura)	2	1,750.75
TOTAL	25	14,920.25

Principal winners: – **Double Eclipse** – Jersey Stakes (7.5f.), Princess of Wales Stakes (12f.); **Lake Placid** – Manchester Cup (12f.); **Mountain Ash** – Warwickshire Breeders Foal Stakes (5f.).

1951	Races Won	Value in £
Bibi Toori (by Owen Tudor – Bibibeg)	2.5	976.75
Fair Justice (by Fair Trial – Jovial Lady)	1	138.00
Lake Placid (by Bobsleigh – Pallida)	1	1,034.00
Mountain Ash (by Owen Tudor – Flowerdale)	1	1,304.75
Rose of Baghdad (by Blue Peter – Queen of Baghdad)	1	100.00
Verdura (by Court Martial – Bura)	1	276.00
Way Side (by Way In – Marinette)	1	100.00
TOTAL	8.5	3,929.50

Principal winners: – **Bibi Toori** – Princess Royal Stakes (5f.); **Lake Placid** – Burwell Stakes (12f.); Mountain Ash – Warwickshire Breeders' Foal Stakes.

1952	Races Won	Value in £
Banri Calma (by Royal Charger – Valiant)	3	1,998.25
Brogan (by Ballyogan – Brave Deal)	2	233.00
Eastern Moonlight (by Nasrullah – Dangerous Moonlight)	1	276.00
Emmanuel (by Tehran – Am Allana)	1	370.75
French Squadron (by Mieuxce – Pack Drill)	2	1,480.75
Italia (by Nearco – Marinette)	1	207.00
Kameran (by Tehran – Bibibeg)	1	138.00
Lake Pleasant (by Bobsleigh – Pallida)	1	276.00
Royal Coach (by Royal Charger – Four In Hand)	2	370.00
Sleeping Warrior (by Nepenthe – Nith)	2	493.50
Sporter (by Fair Trial – Safari)	2	483.00
TOTAL	18	6,326.25

Principal winners: – **Banri Calma** – Curragh Stakes (5f.); **French Squadron** – Great Metropolitan Handicap (18f.).

1953	Races Won	Value in £
Babirus (by Precipitation – Babylon)	1	138.00
Babylonian (by Prince Chevalier – Babylon)	3	690.00
Fairy Book (by Stardust – Jovial Lady)	1	193.00
Finn Calma (by Fair Trial – Valiant)	1	133.00
Gala Performance (by Stardust –Extravagance)	2	1,384.00
Lake Pleasant (by Bobsleigh – Pallida)	2	503.25
Mountain Ash (by Owen Tudor – Flowerdale)	1	276.00
Pamela (by Panorama – Miss Melissa)	3	641.00
Poona (by Tudor Minstrel – Queen of Shiraz)	2	1,263.50
Sleeping Warrior (by Nepenthe – Nith)	3	2,850.75
TOTAL	19	8,072.50

Principal winners: – **Gala Performance** – Diomed Handicap (10f.); **Poona** – Rous Memorial Stakes (6f.); **Sleeping Warrior** – Bessborough Handicap (12f.).

1954 (15th)	Races Won	Value in £
Babylonian (by Prince Chevalier – Babylon)	3	834.00
Daoud Pasha (by Dante – Bibibeg)	1	360.25
Defender (by Devonian – Pallida)	1	524.50
Elpenor (by Owen Tudor – Liberation)	1	11,672.50
Feragamo (Windsor Slipper – Extravagance)	1	280.00
Gala Performance (by Stardust –Extravagance)	3	3,388.00
Las-Innia (by Hindostan – Torch)	1	133.00
Nahar (by Stardust – Queen of Baghdad)	1	2,824.50
Pamela (by Panorama – Miss Melissa)	1	420.00
Queen of Hind (by Nearco – Queen of Baghdad)	0.5	158.50
TOTAL	13.5	20,595.25

Principal winners : – **Elpenor** – Ascot Gold Cup (20f.); **Gala Performance** – Brighton Cup Handicap (12f.), Brocas Handicap (12f.); **Nahar** – Lincoln Handicap (8f.)

1955	Races Won	Value in £
Alibi (by Alycidon – Bura)	2	573.00
Babylonian (by Prince Chevalier – Babylon)	1	1,319.50
Captain Courageous (by Amour Drake – Valiant)	1	202.00
Feragamo (Windsor Slipper – Extravagance)	1	207.00
Jacks Choice (by Owen Tudor – Babylon)	2	432.00
Melody Fair (by Fair Copy – Miss Melissa)	1	138.00
Past Master (by My Love – Jovial Lady)	3	1,188.00
TOTAL	11	4,059.50

Principal winner: – **Babylonian** – Great Metropolitan Handicap (18f.)

1956	Races Won	Value in £
Babogeen (by My Babu – Brave Deal)	1	207.00
Exclamation (by Escamillo – Bura)	1	100.00
Grounded (by Migoli – Bibibeg)	1	861.25
Lunar Way (by Solonaway – Florida Moon)	2	1,495.25
Melody Fair (by Fair Copy – Miss Melissa)	3	744.50
Trovato (by Nearco – Bura)	1	276.00
War Togs (by General Staff – Tabard)	1	207.00
TOTAL	10	3,891.00

Principal winner: – **Lunar Way** – Seaton Delaval Stakes (5f.)

1957	Races Won	Value in £
Hue and Cry (by Tenerani – Babylon)	1	188.00
Jacks Choice (by Owen Tudor – Babylon)	3	730.00
Lunar Way (by Solonaway – Florida Moon)	1	276.00
Melody Fair (by Fair Copy – Miss Melissa)	3	926.75
Pyrford Court (by Court Martial –Nith)	1	133.00
TOTAL	9	2,253.75

1958	Races Won	Value in £
Floral Park (by Cagire II – Babylon)	1	276.00
Florida Court (by Court Martial – Florida Moon)	1	347.25
Gallant Scholar (by Vilmorin – Hunt the Slipper)	1	375.00
Harry Goldmine (by Golden Cloud – Am Allana)	1	389.75

1958	**Races Won**	**Value in £**
Himself (by Supreme Court – Bura)	1	350.25
Jacks Choice (by Owen Tudor – Babylon)	3	803.50
Melody Fair (by Fair Copy – Miss Melissa)	1	276.00
TOTAL	9	2,817.75

1959	**Races Won**	**Value in £**
Babel (by Cagire II – Babylon)	3	1,144.75
Gallant Scholar (by Vilmorin – Hunt the Slipper)	1	256.25
Jacks Choice (by Owen Tudor – Babylon)	2	512.00
Melody Fair (by Fair Copy – Miss Melissa)	1	317.25
Sallymount (by Tudor Minstrel – Queen of Shiraz)	1	3,824.50
TOTAL	8	6,054.75

1960	**Races Won**	**Value in £**
Espresso (by Acropolis – Babylon)	1	438.75
Harry Goldmine (by Golden Cloud – Am Allana)	2	650.00
TOTAL	3	1,088.75

1961	**Races Won**	**Value in £**
Double Exposure (by Prince Chevalier – Doubleton)	2	696.50
Espresso (by Acropolis – Babylon)	2	1,590.00
Harry Goldmine (by Golden Cloud – Am Allana)	1	292.00
Total	5	2,578.50

1962	**Races Won**	**Value in £**
Babble On (by Acropolis – Babylon)	2	533.00
Espresso (by Acropolis – Babylon)	3	3,774.00
Harry Goldmine (by Golden Cloud – Am Allana)	1	265.00
King of Babylon (by King of the Tudors – Babylon)	2	5,957.50
Total	8	10,529.50

Principal winners: – **Espresso** – Newbury Summer Cup (12f.); **King of Babylon** – Champagne Stakes (7f.)

1963	**Races Won**	**Value in £**
Espresso (by Acropolis – Babylon)	2	14,619.00
King of Babylon (by King of the Tudors – Babylon)	1	1,973.00
TOTAL	3	16,592.00

Principal winners: – **Espresso** – Vaux Gold Tankard Handicap (14f.), Manchester Cup (11f.), **King of Babylon** – Thirsk Classic Trial (8f.)

1964	**Races Won**	**Value in £**
French Baby (by French Beige – Babylon)	1	351.00
On Safari (by King Hal – Safari)	1	168.00
TOTAL	2	519.00

1965	**Races Won**	**Value in £**
On Safari (by King Hal – Safari)	1	1,063.00
TOTAL	1	1,063.00

Bahram mares produced 98 individual winners of 228 races worth £169,385.75 in Great Britain and Ireland

Bahram's record as a broodmare sire in France

Year	Horses	Wins	Places	Earnings in Francs
1946	1	1	1	124,000
1947	0	0	0	0
1948	4	2	7	5,489,500
1949	5	9	12	2,636,000
1950	2	1	5	349,500
1951	5	4	6	1,433,300
1952	4	7	13	2,212,500
1953	8	10	24	6,590,600
1954	3	3	15	4,089,300
1955	6	6	11	8,506,250
1956	4	7	8	4,039,200
1957	4	5	3	1,457,950
1958	3	2	5	1,353,000
1959	2	1	4	7,343,900
1960	1	2	2	39,930
1961	1	0	2	5,500
1962	1	0	4	4,550
1963	2	0	2	1,300
1964				0
1965				0
1966	1	1	2	6,200

Principal winners: – **Migoli** (by Bois Roussel – Mah Iran) – 1948 Prix de L'Arc de Triomphe (12f.); **Emperor II** (by Djebel – Liberation) – 1949 Prix Robert Papin (6f.); **Bibi Toori** (by Owen Tudor – Bibibeg) – 1952 Prix de Meautry (6f.); **Nahar** (by Stardust – Queen of Baghdad) – 1953 Grand Handicap de Deauville; **Elpenor** by Owen Tudor – Liberation) – 1955 Prix du Cadran (20f.); **Sallymount** (by Tudor Minstrel – Queen of Shiraz) – 1959 Prix Jacques Le Marois (8f.)

Other principal winners in Europe produced by Bahram mares:-

Jini (by Nosca – Silver Lass)– 1956 Grand Criterium D'Ostend (5f.); **Espresso** (by Acropolis – Babylon) – 1963 & 1964 Grosser Preis Von Baden (12f.)

Bahram mares that produced horses with earnings in North America

Broodmare	Earners	Winners	Races Won	Earnings $	Principal earner
Alarma	1	1	1	1,344	Pasmoso
Angelus Bell	4	2	3	5,110	Merope
Babylon	1	0	0	10,000	Espresso
Bataille	1	1	6	64,320	Azincourt
Bauble	3	3	31	34,682	Enthusiastic
Benaresa	1	1	18	35,981	Bengal
Bengala	1	0	0	295	Bric-Brac
Bibibeg	4	2	38	42,283	Bura
Bibijan	2	2	20	255,251	Mail Order
Bimbi	1	1	1	6,630	Bibijagua
Bitter Orange	4	2	3	18,463	Cidra II
Blague	1	1	3	4,497	Guaicapiuro
Brave Deal	1	1	1	1,225	Tiger Shark
Brigantine	1	1	4	13,652	Ni Modo
Brush Up	1	1	15	38,660	Pepe El Zorro

Broodmare	Earners	Winners	Races Won	Earnings $	Principal earner
Bukhara II	4	4	33	62,554	Foreign Affair
Bura	1	0	0	1,425	Alibi II
Burma	1	1	2	15,725	Buxa
Caltha	5	4	46	99,812	Palustris
Chaperone	1	1	4	8,140	Busherone
Charmee	1	1	1	5,110	Charmer II
Cheerful Annie	2	2	11	17,657	Alcindor
Cherish	4	4	46	65,604	Driving
Cote Bretonne	2	1	9	25,706	Celtic-Song II
Crowflight	1	1	26	45,962	Danger Flight
Cuisine	2	2	23	102,067	Jimminy Baxter
Dallas	1	1	11	32,235	Glen Roy II
Doremi	1	1	1	4,858	Dosila
Doubleton	1	1	28	103,017	Nivrag
False Front	2	2	18	36,039	Falsun
Filament	2	2	18	67,441	Lament
Flavia	2	2	3	13,304	Tito Druso
Florida Moon	6	6	23	44,361	Mystery Moon
Flowerdale	1	1	2	3,230	Blue Repeater
Ganges	3	2	13	35,173	Jhansi
Gigolette	1	1	2	6,413	Sebasto
Goleta	1	1	7	12,293	Vigia II
Grindelia	2	2	17	51,500	Djebah
Hermance	1	1	1	4,925	Seducido
Homing	4	4	25	42,619	Sweet Mimi
Honra	2	0	0	4,626	Aprobacion
Horaciana	1	1	7	28,507	Homero
Hunting Party	6	5	72	209,334	Fleet Argo
Hunting Scene	4	3	34	87,445	Woodlands
Irish Pennant	3	2	15	35,604	North Irish
Lady Alice	2	2	16	62,058	Count Summit
Lady Bahram	4	3	11	44,934	Prince of Paris
Lilabeth	3	2	8	27,975	Lil's Joy
Lulit	1	1	10	24,245	Iranio
Mah Iran	1	1	1	2,460	Persian Garden
Melisande	6	6	74	175,579	Miss Melisande
Meritory	9	7	67	139,632	Behead
Miss Melissa	1	1	5	4,090	Ventura Point
Mother India	8	3	23	206,053	Goyamo
My Lassie	4	4	54	99,161	My King
Nith	5	5	27	45,645	Persian Tune
Now and Again	5	5	36	175,264	Something Thing
Open Question	7	5	30	90,154	Prank
Parting Shot	2	2	20	46,515	Last Word
Patna	3	3	11	67,914	Guay
Persian Light	1	1	4	10,027	Geembea
Presentation	8	8	37	104,543	Goforward
Proud Lady	3	3	33	124,265	Clatterbox
Queen of Baghdad	2	2	9	360,775	Noor
Queen of Shiraz	1	1	6	184,250	Poona
Ratine	9	9	74	519,196	He's a Smoothie
Ringside Table	1	1	2	2,575	Ringside Song

Broodmare	Earners	Winners	Races Won	Earnings $	Principal earner
Riskless	5	4	36	48,594	Fuel
Romanesque	2	1	1	24,745	Rumoto
Romanova	1	1	1	33,730	Denegri
Salaria	2	1	5	16,769	Inquisidor
Silver Lass	2	2	39	97,119	Rodeo Hand
Sinsin	8	8	44	84,911	Briefsin
Skeet	5	7	18	76,009	Contest
Spare A Dime	5	5	57	98,317	Oalo
Speaking Rock	4	4	32	50,279	Chicago Style
Stark Ravin	6	6	90	204,632	Hone
Sub	2	2	21	79,285	Jet Sub
Symbolism	1	1	7	21,405	Sacred Cow
Tabard	8	8	57	116,550	Tassel
The Begum	6	4	50	160,320	Frog Hair
Twi	2	2	7	21,305	Royal Anzac
Valiant	5	3	11	28,343	Precept
Whatuknow	4	4	29	41,910	Fighting Home
	249	216	1,705	5,526,612	

Principal winners in North America produced by Bahram mares

Horse (breeding)	Principal races won
Dizzy Dora (by Black Tarquin – Ratine)	1955 Clarendon Stakes (5.5f.) 1955 My Dear Stakes (5f.)
Hidden Treasure (by Dark Star – Ratine)	1959 Summer Stakes (8f.) 1960 Kingarvie Stakes (8.5f.) 1960 Toronto Cup Handicap (9f.) 1960 Woodbine Breeders Stakes (12f.) 1961 Connaught Cup Stakes (8.5f.) 1961 Durham Cup (9f.)
Goyamo (by Goya – Mother India)	1954 Blue Grass Stakes (9f.)
Mail Order (by One Count – Bibijan)	1959 Saranac Handicap (8f.) 1960 Vosburgh Handicap (7f.) 1961 Excelsior Handicap (9f.) 1961 Grey Lag Handicap ((10f.) 1961 Westchester Handicap (8f.)
He's A Smoothie (by Round Table – Ratine)	1966 & !967 Seagram Cup (8.5f.) 1966 Canadian Prince of Wales Stakes (11f.) 1967 Durham Cup (9f.) 1967 Canadian International (13f.)
Noor (by Nasrullah – Queen of Baghdad)	1950 Golden Gate H (9.5f.) 1950 Hollywood God Cup H (10f.) 1950 San Juan Capistrano H (14f.) 1950 Santa Anita H (10f.)
Poona (by Tudor Minstrel – Queen of Shiraz)	1955 Santa Anita H (10f.)

Bahram's record as a broodmare sire in Argentine

Year	Winners	Races Won	Earnings in Pesos
1954	2	5	90,000
1955	2	2	46,100

Year	Winners	Races Won	Earnings in Pesos
1956	6	14	498,200
1957	6	7	338,440
1958	8	12	817,185
1959 (16th)	10	19	2,460,758
1960 (8th)	16	32	5,234,888
1961 (12th)	23	44	4,943,625
1962 (11th)	26	47	6,035,650
1963 (12th)	20	33	6,180,168
1964 (17th)	20	40	7,447,673
1965 (16th)	27	44	8,594,600
1966 (13th)	25	48	12,971,875
1967 (6th)	24	51	29,528,935
1968 (7th)	17	37	38,902,000
1969	14	25	17,549,000
1970	7	16	123,195
1971	12	33	206,729
1972	15	33	252,455
1973	14	22	291,750

Principal winners in Argentine produced by Bahram mares

Horse (breeding)	Principal races won
Imbroglio (by Again II – Chtiglia)	1959 & 1960 Clasico Ayacucho (12.5f.)
	1959 & 1960 Clasico Chacabuco (15f.)
	1959 & 1960 Gran Premio de Honor (12.5f.)
	1961 Clasico Jockey Club del Peru (12f.)
Bucarest (by Birikil – Bumble Bee)	1959 Gran Premio Major Suckow (5f.)
Azincourt (by Rianco – Bataille)	1968 Gran Premio 25 de Mayo (12f.)

The following daughters of Bahram had descendants who won Group1 /Grade 1 races:-

ALARMA (1947 b f Bahram – Halte-La by Congreve)

Although she was unraced Alarma's immediate female line included two Argentine Classic winners, with her dam Halte-La being a three-quarter sister to 1935 Argentine Derby and St. Leger winner Ix, and her granddam Hache a three-quarter sister to Omega, who won the 1919 Argentine Oaks and St. Leger. Alarma was inbred 5x5x4 to Persimmon and 5x5 to William The Third, both sons of St. Simon, and she was thus bred on quite similar lines to two sons of Bahram who stood as stallions in South America: Anubis and Royal Bahram.

After winning once over 1600 metres in 1939, Halte-La won her first 6 races in 1940 before finishing fourth twice and then winning twice more. Raised in class for her final three starts she finished third in the Premio Francisco J Beazley and runner-up in both Premio Arturo R Bullrich and Premio Chile, races now accorded Group 2 or Group 3 status.

Principal winners descending from Alarma:-
Alarma (Bahram)
| Angustia (Advocate)
| | Always Sun (Solazo)
| | | Always Tracks (Make Tracks)
| | | | Aquarelle (Logical)
| | | | | **La Galerie** (Southern Halo) (G1 G.P. Saturino J Unzue)
| | | | | **Gouache** (Southern Halo) (G1 G.P. Saturino J Unzue)
| | | | | | **Guernika** (Luhuk) (G1 G.P. Palermo, G1 Argentine 1000 Guineas)
| | | | | | | **Eishin Oman** (Rock of Gibraltar) (G2 New Zealand Trophy)
| | | | | **Apeles** (Senor Pete) (G1 G.P. Palermo)

| | | | | Art Deco (Lookinforthebigone)
| | | | | | Bellas Artes (Rainbow Corner)
| | | | | | | **Art Attack** (Russian Blue) (G3 Clasico Congreve)
| | | | | | Arteba (Southern Halo)
| | | | | | | **Arte Pop** (Mutakddim) (G1 G.P. Santiago Luro, G2 Clasico Umberto F Vignart)
| | Zozobra (My Love)
| | | East Sun (Solazo)
| | | | Matricula (Logical)
| | | | | Eastern Forli (Forlitano)
| | | | | | | **Sam Forli** (Sam M) (G1 Premio Alberto Vial Infante)
| | | Alarmingly (Mount Athos)
| | | | Auckland (Salt Marsh)
| | | | | Australian Girl (Lode)
| | | | | | **Refuge Cove** (American Gipsy) (G1 G.P. Assoc. Cavalo de Corrida)
| | | Zodiac Sun (Solazo)
| | | | Alarm Bell (Salt Marsh)
| | | | | Lareira (Gem Master)
| | | | | | **Slara** (Slack) (G3 Clasico Ocurrencia)

APAGALUZ (1953 b f Bahram – Night Cap by Rustom Pasha)

Bought for 380 guineas (£18,000) as a yearling at the 1930 Newmarket October Sales, Apagaluz's granddam Lady Buchan was unplaced in all her races as juvenile and was subsequently exported to Argentine in 1932, where her offspring included a filly by Rustom Pasha named Night Cap. The price reflected the fact that it was an unremarkable family, and after winning once over 1500 metres, Night Cap was covered by Bahram and produced Apagaluz.

One point of interest in Apagaluz pedigree is that her sire Bahram was by Blandford, whose grandsire John O'Gaunt was a son of La Fleche, and granddam Black Cherry was a daughter of Black Duchess. Both La Fleche and Black Duchess were important broodmares, and in the pedigree of Apagaluz's dam Night Cap there is the reverse cross of the pair; as she traced back in direct male line to Black Duchess' son Bay Ronald, and back in direct female line to La Fleche.

An 80,000 pesos purchase as a two-year-old, Apagaluz was unplaced on her two starts in 1942, but the following year recorded a win over 1500 metres.

Principal winners descending from Apagaluz:-
Apagaluz (Bahram)
| Argidia (Branding)
| | Tropical Rose (Tropical Sun)
| | | **Luna Rose** (Ahmad) (G1 Argentine 1000 Guineas)
| | | Snow Tropical (Snow Festival)
| | | | **Snow Troy** (Cautin) (G2 Clasico Marcos Levalle, G2 Clasico Los Criadores)

BABYLON (1940 b f Bahram – Clairvoyante by Clarissimus)

Babylon was from a family that had limited success in France. Her granddam Doddles was a full sister to King Arthur, winner of the 1927 Prix Edmond Blanc, while her dam Clairvoyante won three races worth 235,070 francs as a three-year-old in 1935. Her wins included the Prix Penelope (10f.), and she also finished second in the Prix Jacques Le Marois and third in the French Oaks. This earned her a rating of 55.5 kilos on the French Free Handicap, 4.5 kilos behind the top rated Peniche and Samos, the two fillies who had beaten her in the French Oaks.

Further back, Babylon's fourth dam Blue Cap was a half sister to two Gimcrack Stakes winners in Colonia and Royal Realm, the latter developing into a useful stayer, as was another half-brother: Sandboy, who won the Ascot Stakes and Chester Cup.

In July 1935, Clairvoyante was sold privately to Mr. H. E. Morriss, and sent to the Banstead Manor Stud in Newmarket. Babylon was her second foal, and, racing in the colours of Sir Richard Brooke, she failed to win from twelve starts at two and three. She finished second once and third five times.

Babylon did much better at stud producing 13 winners from 16 foals including three above average sorts: Babylonian, Espresso and King of Babylon

Babylon was by a son of Blandford out of a daughter of Clarissimus, a pattern reflected in Espresso's paternal grandsire Donatello II, who was also by a son of Blandford out of a daughter of Clarissimus. Espresso later sired the triple Ascot Gold Cup winner Sagaro.

Principal winners descending from Babylon via Babble On:-

Babylon (Bahram)
| **Babylonian** (Prince Chevalier) (Great Metropolitan Handicap)
| **King of Babylon** (King of the Tudors) (Champagne S)
| **Espresso** (Acropolis) (Grosser Preis von Baden (x2))
| Babble On (Acropolis)
| | Christmas (Santa Claus)
| | | Crest (Klairon)
| | | | Kessel-Loo (Lunard)
| | | | | **Steff Graf** (Executioner) (G3 Golden Poppy H)
| | | | | **Really Welcome** (Midnight Tiger) (G1 G.P. Presidente da Republica)
| | | | Income Tax (Lunard)
| | | | | Prizzi's Honour (Executioner)
| | | | | | All American (Midnight Tiger)
| | | | | | | **Knightsbridge** (Yagli) (G2 G.P. Immensity)
| | Glen Devon (Klairon)
| | | **Executive Man** (Nebbiolo) (G3 Premio Primi Passi)

Babylon's second foal Garden Party was her first winner when winning twice over 5 furlongs in early 1949, and she would become the third dam of the top-class filly Madam Gay. Winner of the French Oaks, Madam Gay also finished runner-up in the Oaks and King George VI & Queen Elizabeth Stakes, when second to Derby winner Shergar, as well as finishing third in both Arlington Million and Prix Vermeille.

Principal winners descending from Babylon via Floral Park and Garden City:-

Babylon (Bahram)
| Floral Park (Cagire II)
| | Eden (Gulf Pearl)
| | | Apple Peel (Pall Mall)
| | | | **Eve's Error** (G2 Grosser Preis von Dusseldorf, G3 Oettingen-Rennen)
| | | | Apples of Gold (Godswalk)
| | | | | Averogold (Averof)
| | | | | | **Golden Apple** (Northern Guest) (G2 Gosforth Fillies Guineas)
| | | | | | | **Golden Chariot** (Caesour) (G2 Greyville Astrapak 1900)
| | | | | | | **Pomodoro** (Jet Master) (G1 South African Derby, G1 July H)
| Garden City (Mieuxce)
| | Picnic Party (Honeyway)
| | | Saucy Flirt (King's Troop)
| | | | **Madam Gay** (Star Appeal) (G1 Prix de Diane)
| | | | Arminda (Blakeney)
| | | | | Woodbeck (Terimon)
| | | | | | **Franklins Gardens** (Halling) (G2 Yorkshire Cup, G3 Lingfield Derby Trial S)
| | | | | | **Polar Ben** (Polar Falcon) (G3 Park S, G3 Joel S)
| | | Real Party (Realm)
| | | | Really Sharp (Sharpen Up)
| | | | | **Carol's Treasure** (Balidar) (Windsor Castle S)
| | | | | | Flame Violet (Fairy King)
| | | | | | | Silken Sash (Danehill)
| | | | | | | | **Raw Silk** (G2 Sands Point S)

BATAILLE (1949 b f Bahram – Conquete by Congreve)

Bataille was a half sister to the useful Argentine filly La Rubia, who won the 1960 Gran Premio Ignacio E Ignacio F Correra (12.5f.) and 1961 Gran Premio 25 de Mayo (12f). La Rubia later produced an Argentine 1000 Guineas winner in Tutta Bionda. Her dam Conquete won three races over 1400 and 1600 metres.

Bataille was sold for 150,000 as a two-year-old, making her the second most expensive filly by Bahram ever sold in Argentine. Bataille won one of her four races: the Premio Provincia de Tucuman (1500m.) at San Isidro.

At stud Bataille produced the winner of the Gran Premio 25 de Mayo (12f): the 1968 winner Azincourt. Later exported to America, Azincourt raced there for five seasons winning 6 of his 612 starts and earning $64,230.

Principal winners descending from Bataille:-

Bataille (Bahram)
| **Azincourt** (Rianco) (G.P. 25 de Mayo)
| Ramba (The Champ)
| | Maria Bueno (Babu's Pet)
| | | Masai Mara (Niarkos)
| | | | **Boran** (Mariache) (G1 G.P. Gran Criterium)

BENGALA (1949 b f Bahram – Betty by Teddy)

Bengala was from a strong female family; her third dam Sunny Jane won the 1917 Oaks, and her dam Betty, won the 1933 Coronation Stakes. Betty also won the Molecomb Stakes at two, and was a half-sister to two useful performers in Chester Vase winner Cave Man and Crème Brulee, whose 10 victories included the Liverpool, Newmarket, Welsh and Breeders St. Legers at three, the Manchester Cup at four and Newbury Summer Cup at five.

Betty produced just 3 minor winners of 4 races worth £1,668.25 (73,400) in England before being sold at the 1944 Newmarket December Sales for 2,500 guineas (£97,100) in foal to Foxhunter, and after being exported to Argentine, she produced Bengala; as a 19 year-old. Bengala's full brother and sister, Bribon and Bonaresa, were useful performers in Argentine, Bribon winning three races and earning 71,050 pesos and Benaresa amassing 24,000 pesos and two victories.

Purchased for 55,000 pesos as a two-year-old, Bengala won twice from 24 starts. She did not gain her first win until her 17th race, winning the Premio Panther (1600m.) at San Isidro in 1954. A further victory followed on her penultimate start, when she won the Premio La Cuarta (1400m.).

Principal winners descending from Bengala:-

Bengala (Bahram)
| Ballerine (Timor)
| | Ballecla (Claro)
| | | **Clear Sun** (Solazo) (G.P. Major Suckow)
| | | Grand Soleil (Solazo)
| | | | Shangri-La (Logical)
| | | | | Kavalla (Southern Halo)
| | | | | | **Xua de Crack** (Ojotabe) (G2 G.P. 25 de Janeiro)

BIBIBEG (1941 b f Bahram – Mumtaz Begum by Blenheim)

Bibibeg's dam Mumtaz Begum was a daughter Mumtaz Mahal and was inbred 2x3 to Blandford, the fifth foal of Mumtaz Begum, and a year younger than her half-brother Nasrullah (by Nearco). Unraced at two, Bibibeg raced only at three winning one of her nine starts and finishing third once.

At stud Bibibeg produced 7 winners from 9 foals before she was exported to North America. Her best colt was Kameran Khan (by Tehran), who was runner-up in the St. James's Palace Stakes and later stood as a stallion Brazil. Among her fillies Bibi Toori was probably the best racehorse, she won the Princess Royal two-year-old Stakes, and the most influential at stud, where she produced Mabina, the dam of Chester Cup winner Mahbub Aly, and Tina II.

Tina II, who was inbred 4x4x5 to Blandford and 5x6 Concertina, founded a very successful family, her son Ovaltine developing into a useful stayer and won both the Ebor Handicap and Goodwood Cup. Her daughters Guillotina and Pristina became excellent broodmares.

The descendants of Guillotina, who won the Group 3 Prix Royallieu over 12.5 furlongs and was sired by stamina influence Busted, proved best over middle distances. However, Pristina's daughters were principally sprinters; her first three foals, the fillies Mange Tout, Hecla and Rose Dubarry, were exceptionally fast, and as well as their victories recorded below,

Mange Tout finished second in the Prix de l'Abbaye, against older horses, as a juvenile, Hecla was third in the July Cup at three and Rose Dubarry finished third in the 1000 Guineas.

Bibibeg was covered by Owen Tudor and exported to America, where she produced Quaheri. Although a maiden from three starts Quaheri became the third dam of Grade 1 Preakness and Belmont Stakes winner Risen Star. The latter was a son of Secretariat, whose grandsire Nasrullah was a half-sister to Bibibeg. Bibibeg's principal earner in America was Bura, a gelding by Count Fleet, and not to be confused with the daughter of Bahram of the same name. Racing for 6 seasons Bura won 16 of his 99 starts, earning $22,038. Bura's younger half-brother Dark Tide (by Tehran) proved even tougher winning 22 of his 145 starts, winning $19,585 in the process.

Principal winners descending from Bibibeg via Bibi Toori:-

Bibibeg (Bahram)
| **Bibi Toori** (Owen Tudor) (Prix de Meautry)
| | Mabiba (Vieux Manoir)
| | | **Mahbub Aly** (Worden II) (Chester Cup H)
| | Tina II (Tulyar)
| | | **Guillotina** (Busted) (G3 Prix de Royallieu)
| | | | Headrest (Habitat)
| | | | | **Polaire** (Polish Patriot) (G2 Pretty Polly S)
| | | | **One Way Street** (Habitat) (G2 Princess Royal S)
| | | | | **Grape Tree Road** (Caerleon) (G1 Grand Prix de Paris)
| | | | | **Red Route** (Polish Precedent) (G2 Geoffrey Freer S)
| | | | | **Windsor Castle** (Generous) (G3 Queen's Vase, Northumberland Plate H)
| | | | | Street Opera (Sadler's Wells)
| | | | | | **Stretarez** (Saumarez) (G2 Prix Vicomtesse Vigier, G3 Ormonde S)
| | | | | | **Street Shaana** (Darshaan) (G3 Prix de Lutece)
| | | | | Ombrie (Zafonic)
| | | | | | **Watar** (Marju) (G2 Prix Hubert de Chaudenay, G2 Prix Maurice de Nieuil)
| | | | Shorthouse (Habitat)
| | | | | **Ever Genial** (Brigadier Gerard) (G3 May Hill S, G3 Hungerford S)
| | | **Ovaltine** (Match III) (Ebor H, Goodwood Cup)
| | | Pristina (Petition)
| | | | **Hecla** (Henry The Seventh) (Cherry Hinton S)
| | | | | **Famous Star** (Sharpen Up) (Ayr Gold Cup H)
| | | | **Mange Tout** (Galivanter) (Windsor Castle S, Molecomb S, Prix D'Arenberg)
| | | | **Rose Dubarry** (Klairon) (G1 Flying Childers S, G3 Lowther S)
| | | Tenzone (Aggressor)
| | | | Combattente (Reform)
| | | | | **Coastal Bluff** (Standaan) (Stewards Cup H, Ayr Gold Cup H, G1 Nunthorpe S)
Principal winners descending from Bibibeg via Quaheri:-
Bibibeg (Bahram)
| Quaheri (Olympia)
| | Break Through (Hail To Reason)
| | | **Ribbon** (His Majesty) (G3 Pucker Up S)
| | | | **Risen Star** (Secretariat) (G1 Preakness S, G1 Belmont S, G2 Lexington S)
| | Foreign Strand (Ribot)
| | | | **Montagnet** (To The Quick) (G2 Round Table H)

BITTER ORANGE (1947 b f Bahram – Orangerie by Parlanchin)

Bitter Orange's third dam Freesia won nine races including the 1917 Cheveley Park Stakes.

At stud she produced the Coventry Stakes winner Iceberg, as well as Bitter Orange's granddam Orange Flower, a maiden who was sold for 320 guineas ((£14,750) as a three-year-old at the 1929 Newmarket December Sales, and was exported to Argentina.

At stud Orange Flower's best offspring was a colt: Okay, winner of the 1938 Gran Premio de Mayo and 1939 Gran Premio Comparacion. Four years later Orange Flower produced Bitter Orange's dam Orangerie, the winner of three races over 1500 and 1600 metres.

Bitter Orange did not make her racecourse debut until she was a four-year-old and managed a second and a third from three races.

Principal winners descending from Bitter Orange:-

Bitter Orange (Bahram)

| Valencia (Seductor)

| | Ayora (Cipol)

| | | Mayoras (Mountdrago)

| | | | Maya Toss (Egg Toss)

| | | | | **Storm Mayor** (Bernstein) (G1 G.P. Honor, G1 G.P Carlos Pellegrini (x2))

BOUILLETTE (1949 b f Bahram – Brulee by Fairway)

In 1924 a mare Seaweed went from England to France to be covered by Bruleur. The result was a colt: Hotweed, winner of the 1929 French Derby and Grand Prix de Paris and in 1930 the Prix du Cadran. The same mating two years later produced a filly: Brulette, who won the Oaks in 1931. She was sold as a three-year-old and at four won the Goodwood Cup, Jockey Club Cup and the Prix du Cadran.

Brulette bred 7 minor winners, however, Brulee was not one of them, and she was exported to Argentine in 1941 where she produced Bouillette, who did not race.

There is an interesting postscript to this mating with Bahram; 16 years later Vaguely Noble was foaled, a horse inbred 4x4 to Bahram, and whose third dam Tropical Sun was a half sister to Bouillette's dam Brulee.

Principal winners descending from Bouillette:-

Bouillette (Bahram)

| Javotte (Again II)

| | Taqueada (The Yuvaraj)

| | | **Tayaquito** (Amateur) (G.P. Internacional Joaquin V Gonzalez)

BRAVE DEAL (1941 b f Bahram – Good Deal by Apelle)

Brave Deal's dam: Good Deal was a 260 guineas (£14,200) yearling, who won seven races over three seasons, including the Atalanta Stakes (10f.), Brighton Autumn Cup (10f.) and Duke of Cambridgeshire Handicap (8f.). After the death of her owner, Good Deal was offered at the 1936 Newmarket December Sales, and purchased for 1,800 guineas (£98,200) for Miss Dorothy Paget. Good Deal's third foal: Straight Deal (by Solario), won the 1943 Derby and finished third in the St. Leger.

A year after the arrival of Straight Deal, Good Deal produced Brave Deal, but died in Ireland in early 1943 without producing another winner. Brave Deal was actually bred on quite similar lines to the mare Yasna, the dam of 2000 Guineas and Eclipse winner Darius, for she was by Bahram's half brother Dastur, out of a three-quarter sister to the successful dam Weeds.

Unraced at two, Brave Deal failed to win and was third twice from six starts.

At stud Brave Deal produced 3 minor winners of 4 races worth £523.25 (18,750). Her influence would come through Princely Maid, who had Brave Deal as her fourth dam. A winner over five furlongs as a juvenile, Princely Maid produced another speedy individual in Forzando. Winner of the Premio Melton in Italy at three, Forzando raced in America at four, winning the Metropolitan, Fort Macy and Sierra Madre Handicaps. He took up stud duties in England and sired useful sprinters Easycall (Richmond, Flying Childers Stakes), Great Deeds (Ballyogan Stakes), High Premium (Lincoln Handicap) and Superior Premium (Stewards Cup Handicap, Cork & Orrery Stakes).

Another Group winning sprinter to descend from Princely Maid was Majestic Missile, who had Princely Maid as his fourth dam. At two he won the Group 3 Molecomb and Cornwallis Stakes, and at four the Group 3 Prix du Petit Couvert, all over five furlongs. Majestic Missile's half-brother Santo Padre won the 2009 Portland Handicap (5.5f.).

Finally, Brave Deal's daughter Royal Deal was exported to Japan as a nine-year old, was covered by Turkhan's son Turks Revenge, and produced a filly: Kimarasu. Since Turkhan was a son of Bahram, Kimarasu was inbred 3x3 to Bahram and later became the granddam of Japanese Group 2 winner and sire C B Cross.

Principal winners descending from Brave Deal:-

Brave Deal (Bahram)

| Royal Deal (His Highness)

| | Kimarasu (Turks Reliance)
| | | Zuisho (Partholon)
| | | | **C B Cross** (Fortino II) (G2 Meguro Kinen Autumn)
| | Jules Magic (Magic Red)
| | | Moss Maid (Mossborough)
| | | | Princely Maid (King's Troop)
| | | | | **Forzando** (Formidable) (G1 Metropolitan H, G3 Premio Melton)
| | | | | Alteza Real (Mansingh)
| | | | | | Infanta Real (Formidable)
| | | | | | | **Informant** (Kris) (Taby Open Sprint Championship)
| | | | | | | Tshusick (Dancing Brave)
| | | | | | | | **Majestic Missile** (Royal Applause) (G3 Molecomb S, G3 Cornwallis S)
| | | | | | | | | **Santo Padre** (Elnadim) (Portland H)
| | | | | Lady Constance (Connaught)
| | | | | | Bahrain Star (Star Appeal)
| | | | | | | **Hikoko Gumo** (Keen) (G3 Kisaragi Sho)
| | | | | Aonia (Mummy's Pet)
| | | | | | Urania (Most Welcome)
| | | | | | | **Lucky Strike** (Petong) (G3 Benazet-Rennen (x3))

BRIGANTINE (1951 b f Bahram – Umyak by Rustom Pasha)

Brigantine was from a family that had produced little of note for some years. Her second dam, Mosquita, produced 1939 Hollywood Gold Cup and Santa Anita Handicap winner Kayak II. Mosquita is also of interest as she was bred on similar lines to the mare Dogresa, the third dam of Argentine Champion Forli. Both were sired by His Majesty, and respectively out of the half sisters La Mouche and Casiopea. Brigantine's dam Umyak won twice in Argentina over 1600 metres,

Bought for 60,000 pesos as a two-year-old, Brigantine won one race on her sixth start, when winning the Premio Segonzac (2200m.). In her final five starts she finished fourth three times over distances ranging from 1500 to 2200 metres,

Brigantine's daughter Bride later became the dam of multiple Argentine Group 1 winner Brilliantly. Principal winners descending from Brigantine:-
Brigantine (Bahram)
| Bride (Bristol)
| | **Brilliantly** (Major Gundry) (G1 G.P. Ignacio E Ignacio F Correas G1 G.P Copa de Oro)

BRINDA (1939 br f Bahram – Herlinde by Asterus)

Brinda's granddam Althea was a three-quarter sister to the 1926 Derby and St. Leger winner Coronach. Sold for 3,300 guineas (£152,500) as a three-year-old at the 1928 Newmarket December Sales, Althea produced the 1939 Premio Principe Amadeo winner Aquaforte, whose son Antonio Canale was a useful performer in Italy, where he won the 1949 Gran Premio di Milano and Italian St. Leger.

Bred in Italy Herlinde was later exported to France where she produced a quartet of useful performers, including two winners of the Grand Prix de Compiegne: Assam and Pharaon, the latter also winning the Prix Edgard Gillois and finishing second in the French Champion Hurdle. Herlinde's offspring also included French Derby third Laborde, and his full-sister La Capitane, who finished second in the Prix de la Salamandre.

Brinda was unplaced in two races as a juvenile but won twice: the Prix Verlion (1600m.) at Le Tremblay and the Prix des Brolins (1600m.) at Maisons-Laffitte, and was placed three times in France as a three-year-old from eleven starts. As a four-year-old Brinda won one race: the Prix du Sources (1600m.) at Vichy, from nineteen starts, when she was also placed eleven times.

At stud Brinda had some influence after her granddaughter Idaliza, the daughter of dual French winner Pearl Fishing, was exported to America, where she produced Sister Shannon, the dam of Belmont Stakes winner Temperence Hill. Sister Shannon's daughter Populi produced another multiple US Grade 1 winner in Vanlandingham, and Populi's descendants included Group 1 winners African Rose, Distant Music, Funny Moon and Termagent as well as other Group winners such as Helleborine

(G3 Prix D'Aumale), Kirkwall (G2 Prix Eugene Adam & Keeneland Turf Mile), Northern Fleet (G3 San Diego Handicap) and Top Hit (G3 Oklahoma Derby).

Principal winners descending from Brinda:-

Brinda (Bahram)
| Pearl Fishing (Fair Copy)
| | Idaliza (Princely Gift)
| | | Sister Shannon (Etonian)
| | | | **Temperence Hill** (Stop The Music) (G1 Belmont S, G1 Travers S, G1 Suburban H)
| | | | Populi (Star Envoy)
| | | | | **Vanlandingham** (Cox's Ridge) (G1 Suburban H, G1 Washington D C International)
| | | | | Fun Crowd (Easy Goer)
| | | | | | **Funny Moon** (Malibu Moon) (G1 Coaching Club American Oaks)
| | | | | Musicanti (Nijinsky)
| | | | | | **Distant Music** (Distant View) (G1 Dewhurst S)
| | | | | | New Orchid (Quest For Fame)
| | | | | | | **African Rose** (Observatory) (G1 Haydock Sprint Cup)
| | | | | | | **Helleborine** (Observatory) (G3 Prix D'Aumale)
| | | | | Kamkova (Northern Dancer)
| | | | | | **Kirkwall** (Selkirk) (G2 Prix Eugene Adam, G2 Keeneland Turf Mile S)
| | | | | | **Northern Fleet** (Slip Anchor) (G3 San Diego H)
| | | | | | Rock Salt (Selkirk)
| | | | | | | **Termagant** (Powerscourt) (G1 Moyglare Stud S)
| | | | | Popular Tune (Stop The Music)
| | | | | | **Top Hit** (Twining) (G3 Oklahoma Derby)

BUKHARA II (1938 gr f Bahram – Una by Tetratema)

Bukhara II was a full sister to Baman and was exported to America where she failed to win a race in 14 attempts.

Bukhara II's best offspring was Foreign Affair (by Discovery), who won 14 of his 83 starts earning $28,572, including the Maryland Futurity at two. His year younger half-sister: Foreign Star (by By Jimminy) won once from 13 starts, and later produced some tough performers including the full siblings by River War: Wise Command (14 wins from 103 starts) and War Star (8 wins from 84 starts). The latter produced an equally tough racehorse in Strong Strong, whose 8 wins from 88 starts include the $150,000 Washington Futurity.

Principal winners descending from Bukhara II:-

Bukhara II (Bahram)
| Foreign Star (By Jimminy)
| | War Star (River War)
| | | **Strong Strong** (Traffic Judge) (Washington Futurity)
| | | Door Star (Stage Door Johnny)
| | | | **Dawn Johnny** (Grey Dawn II) (Chester Cup H, Northumberland Plate H)

BUMBLE BEE (1948 b f Bahram – Honey Queen by Hunter's Moon)

Bumble Bee's fourth dam Princess Sterling produced the 1922 2000 Guineas winner St. Louis. Another Classic winner from this female family was the 1941 Irish Derby winner Sol Oriens, a close relative to Bumble Bee's dam Honey Queen. The latter was by Hunter's Moon out of Silver Queen's daughter Silver Wedding, while Sol Oriens was by Hunter's Moon's half brother Hyperion out of Silver Wedding's half sister Silver Mist.

Silver Wedding won two minor races in England at three in 1928, and three years later she was covered by Manna, before being sold at the 1931 Newmarket December Sales for 150 guineas (£7,400). Exported to Argentine, she later produced Bumble Bee's dam Honey Queen; a daughter of Hunter's Moon, and winner of one race over 1100 metres.

Purchased for 110,000 pesos as a two-year-old, Bumble Bee won two of her six starts: the Premio Palanca (1200m.) and the Premio Blackie (1600m.). She was subsequently exported to Brazil where she one further race

When Bumble Bee retired to the paddocks she produced the sprinter Bucarest, winner of the Gran Premio Major Suckow (5f.), a race now accorded Group 1 status.

Principal winners descending from Bumble Bee:-

Bumble Bee (Bahram)

| **Bucarest** (Birikil) (G.P. Major Suckow)

BURA (1938 b f Bahram – Becti by Salmon-Trout)

Becti's dam: Mirawala, from the family of Pretty Polly was brought as a yearling first for 1,500 guineas (£67,750) and secondly by the Aga Khan, also as a yearling for 2,900 guineas (£128,000).

Mirawala won four of her twelve races at two and three. At stud she produced seven winners from eleven live foals. Becti was her first and amongst her other produce were two useful juveniles: Moradabad (Richmond Stakes) and Stafaralla (Cheveley Park Stakes). Stafaralla became the dam of St. Leger winner Tehran. Moradabad was bred on similar lines to Becti, being by Blandford's son Blenheim, and when Blenheim was mated with Bura's dam Becti the result was Bouillabaisse, the dam, of the 1953 Eclipse Stakes winner Argur.

Becti won two of her six starts as a juvenile: both nurseries at Newmarket; one over a mile the other over six furlongs. At three she won one race: the Haverhill Stakes at Newmarket over nine furlongs, from nine starts.

At stud she produced six winners form seven live foals. Bura was her fourth foal and in 1939, Bura became one of a dozen yearlings sold by the Aga Khan. She made 1,200 guineas (£58,000), was unraced at two and at three she failed to win any of her eight starts.

At stud Bura produced 5 winners of 8 races worth £3,326 (120,000), with her daughter Verdura earning second place in the Princess of Wales's Stakes.

Verdura became Bura's most influential daughter at stud, producing five above average winners over a vast range of distances. In 1955 her first foal: Gratitude, won the New Stakes and later the Nunthorpe Stakes, before becoming the sire of sprinters.

Verdura's second foal; Pharsalia, was unbeaten in four races as a juvenile, including the Queen Mary, Molecomb and Lowther Stakes, before retiring to the paddocks.

Verdura's daughter: Highest Hopes, finished runner-up in the French Oaks and Yorkshire Oaks, while her son: Avon's Pride won the 1961 Cesarewitch Handicap (18f.).

Another daughter of Verdura: her third foal Patroness was runner-up in the Queen Mary Stakes, and at stud produced Grade 1 winners Archdeacon, White Heart and Tempera.

Finally, Bura's second foal Bazura, was the dam of Bagdad, winner of the Hollywood Derby and runner-up in the Belmont Stakes, and became a successful stallion.

Principal winners descending from Bura:-

Bura (Bahram)

| Bazura (Blue Peter)

| | **Bagdad** (Double Jay) (Hollywood Derby)

| Verdura (Court Martial)

| | **Avon's Pride** (Arctic Prince) (Cesarewitch Handicap)

| | **Gratitude** (Golden Cloud) (New S, Nunthorpe S)

| | **Heathen** (Hethersett) (Greenham S)

| | **Highest Hopes** (Hethersett) (Fred Darling S, Prix Vermeille)

| | Patroness (Prince Chevalier)

| | | Auburn's Pride (Aureole)

| | | | Hangin Round (Stage Door Johnny)

| | | | | **Archdeacon** (Dancing Champ) (G1 Canadian Prince of Wales S)

| | | | | **Mr Macho** (G2 King Edward H)

| | | | | **Rainbow Connection** (Halo) (G2 Demoiselle S)

| | | | | | **Always a Rainbow** (Mr Prospector) (Cup & Saucer S)

| | | | | | Barari (Blushing Groom)

| | | | | | | **White Heart** (Green Desert) (G1 Turf Classic, G1 Charles Whittingham H)

| | | | | | **Colour Chart** (Mr Prospector) (G2 Prix de L'Opera)

| | | | | | | **Equerry** (St Jovite) (G3 Prix du Prince D'Orange)

| | | | | | | **Tempera** (A P Indy) (G1 Breeders Cup Juvenile Fillies)

| | | | | | **Rainbows For Life** (Lyphard) (G2 Connaught Cup, G3 Hawthorne Derby)

||||| **Hangin on a Star** (Vice Regent) (G1 Woodbine Breeders S)
||||| Rainbow Two (Halo)
|||||| Stormbow (Storm Cat)
||||||| **City To City** (City Zip) (G2 Palomar H, G2 Buena Vista H)
|| **Pharsalia** (Panorama) (Queen Mary S, Molecomb S, Lowther S)
||| **High Powered** (Hugh Lupus) (Princess Margaret S, Ebbisham S)
|||| **Coltinger** (Relko) (G2 Premio Ellington)
||| Too Cute (Tenerani)
|||| Abbot's Isle (Welsh Abbott)
||||| Welsh Jane (Bold Lad)
|||||| **Only Yours** (Aragon) (G2 Lowther S, G2 Falmouth S, G3 Hungerford S)
|||||| **Osario** (Kind of Hush) (G3 Supreme S)
|| Pampas Flower (Pampered King)
||| **Evita** (Reform) (G3 Nell Gwyn S)

CARA MIA (1947 b f Bahram – Cara by Bosworth)

Cara Mia was from a high-class family; her dam Cara was a full-sister to Coronation Cup winner Plassy. Furthermore Cara's dam Pladda was a close relative to Pharos and Fairway. All three were by Phalaris and Pladda's dam Rothesay Bay was a half sister to Scapa Flow, the dam of Pharos and Fairway.

Cara failed to win as a juvenile and was sold at the 1939 Newmarket December Sales for 500 guineas (£24,000) and was exported to Argentina where she produced Cara Mia and her full brother Carlomagno, who won 6 races and earned 131,450 pesos before standing as a stallion in Argentina.

Cara Mia won one of her ten starts: the Premio Gandoura (1300m.).

At stud Cara Mia's daughter Catedratica (by Gulf Stream) produced two daughters in Cromada and Castana who would later be the source of Group 1 winners; Cromada becoming the fourth dam of Recordado and Castana the fifth dam of Viva-Raz.

Principal winners descending from Cara Mia:-
Cara Mia (Bahram)
| Catedratica (Gulf Stream)
|| Cromada (Guatan)
||| Cromante (Practicante)
|||| Ruscromada (Rustler)
||||| Russian Lady (Farnesio)
|||||| **Recordado** (Candy Spots) (G1 G.P 2000 Guineas Consagracion de Potrillos)
|| Castana (Magabit)
||| Rosa Inca (Incaico)
|||| Gluma (Gemini Six)
||||| Glumela (Muneco Bravo)
|||||| Choir Glum (Choir Prospect)
||||||| **Viva-Raz** (Cutias) (G1 G.P. Internacional Ciudad de la Plata)

CHEERFUL ANNE (1939 b f Bahram – Anne of Brittany by Diligence)

Cheerful Anne's female family had produced little of note for some time. Her fourth dam Scene was the granddam of the 1919 Argentine 2000 Guineas and Gran Premio Jockey Club winner Buen Ojo, and the fourth dam of 1927 French Derby and Prix de L'Arc de Triomphe hero Mon Talisman.

Anne of Brittany was bought at the 1933 Newmarket Second July Sales as a seven-year-old mare in foal to Winalot for 1,150 guineas (£62,750). She had already produced the useful filly Miss Elegance, winner of eight races over three seasons.

Cheerful Anne won two of her six races as a juvenile: Bartlow Plate (5f.), and the Manchester's Forces Plate (6f.). She was allocated 8st.4lb. in the Free Handicap, 17lb. below Sun Chariot. Cheerful Anne was bred on very similar lines to Sun Chariot's dam Clarence. The latter was by Diligence out of Nun's Veil by Friar Marcus out of Blanche, while Cheerful Anne was by Bahram (by a son of Blanche out of a daughter of Friar Marcus) out of a mare by Diligence.

As a three-year-old Cheerful Anne failed to win any of her five starts managing only one second.

At stud Cheerful Anne produced 3 winners of 3 races worth £1,242.50 (47,000) in Great Britain, and

6 winners of 10 races in France. In 1961 Anne La Douce, a granddaughter of Cheerful Anne finished third in the Oaks, and dead-heated for first place in the Prix Vermeille. Anne La Douce's two younger half brothers, Le Biene Amie and Chevalier Bayard, each finished runner-up in successive runnings of the Prix de Longchamp. Anne La Douce later produced the Grade 1 winner Anne's Pretender, a front-runner who also finished fourth in the Derby and third in the Irish equivalent.

Principal winners descending from Cheerful Anne:-
Cheerful Anne (Bahram)
| Anna Lucasta (Bois Roussel)
| | Shirley Pat (Roi de Navaarre II)
| | | **Janeat** (Grey Sovereign) (Ayr Gold Cup H)
| | **Courtesan** (Supreme Court) (Cheshire Oaks)
| | | **Court Gift** (Tanerko) (Geoffrey Freer)
| | Sailanna (Sailing Light)
| | | Pixie Jet (Polly's Jet)
| | | | Margaret's Ruby (Tesco Boy)
| | | | | Midnight's Reward (Night Shift)
| | | | | | **Somnus** (Pivotal) (G1 Haydock Sprint, Prix Maurice de Gheest, Prix de la Foret)
| Mistress Ann (Nearco)
| | Alley Cat (Alycidon)
| | | **Doleswood** (Double Jump) (G3 Coventry S)
| Sweet Anne (Tehran)
| | **Anne La Douce** (Silnet) (Prix Vermeille)
| | | **Anne's Pretender** (Pretense) (G1 Century H, G2 Prince of Wales's S)
| | | Noblanna (Vaguely Noble)
| | | | **Baylis** (Sadler's Swells) (G3 Lawrence Realization H)
| | | | Annie Girl (Danehill)
| | | | | **Noll Wallop** (High Chaparral) (G3 Leopardstown 2000 Guineas Trial)

CHTIGLIA (1950 b f Bahram – Kiglia by Biribi)

Chtiglia's dam Kilkerley produced two winners of the Prix Jean Prat in Roi de Trefle and Galloway. Her granddam Kill Lady was sired by the leading hurdler Trespasser, winner of the Imperial Cup Hurdle three years in succession between 1920 and 1922, in the days before the Champion Hurdle itself had been instigated.

Kill Lady produced the Grand Prix de Deauville winner Birikil, and Chtiglia's dam Kiglia, who become the dam of 1950 Prix Vermeille heroine Kilette. Kiglia raced 28 times at three and four. At three she won three races: the Prix Perdita (1400m.), Prix des Lilas (2000m.) and the Prix de Chantilly (3100m.). The following season her only win came in the Prix Salverte (4000m.).

Kiglia was exported to Argentina in 1948 where she produced the unraced filly Chtiglia, whose first foal Imbroglio (by Again II) was a multiple big race winner in Argentina and Peru, before taking up stallion duties. Two of Imbroglio's full sisters: Nantua and Rolleboise, also produced Group race performers.

Nantua was exported to America and produced the tough performer Card King, who raced until he was seven, winning the Group 2 Grand Prix de Deauville and Group 3 Prix D'Harcourt.

Rolleboise was unraced, but her first foal Yvetot, raced 70 times raced successfully in North America, winning the Grade 3 Niagara Handicap in Canada at seven.

A third full sister to Imbroglio: Long Beach, the fourth dam of the 2011 Grade 3 Native Diver Handicap winner Kettle Corn.

It is worth noting that Imbroglio and his full sisters were all sired by Again II, whose own sire Foxhunter had a similar background of Gallinule, William The Third, Cyllene and Black Duchess to Bahram.

Principal winners descending from Chtiglia:-
Chtiglia (Bahram)
| **Imbroglio** (Again II) (G.P. de Honor (x2), Clasico Ayacucho (x2), Clasico Chacabuco (x2))
| Nantua (Again II)
| | **Card King** (Cardington King) (G2 Grand Prix de Deauville, G3 Prix D'Harcourt)
| Rolleboise (Again II)

|| **Yvetot** (Tournevent) (G3 Niagara Handicap)
| Long Beach (Again II)
|| Longhill (Rigolo)
||| Bubali (Bdashd)
|||| Somethingbeautiful (Lil E Tee)
||||| **Kettle Corn** (Candy Ride) (G3 Native Diver H)

DOUBLETON (1938 b f Bahram – Double Life by Bachelor's Double)

Double Life was the second foal of Saint Joan who won twice as a juvenile and at stud produced four winners. Her second foal: Double Life, was rather small and lightly made, but was purchased as a yearling at the 1927 Newmarket October Sales for 600 guineas (£27,000).

Double Life won two minor races from six starts as a juvenile. At three she won four of her six races, and was disqualified from another: the Bendigo Handicap at Kempton. The four races she won were in succession: the Perkins Memorial at Newcastle, Chesterfield Cup at Goodwood and Duke of York Handicap at Kempton. This victory resulted in a ten pound penalty for the Cambridgeshire Handicap, raising her weight to 7st.12lb. However, in a close finish, Double Life won by a neck from Vatout with Palais Royal a head away in third. The three-year-old Vatout was conceding Double Life three pounds but had won the French 2000 Guineas earlier in year. Double Life was retired afterwards.

At stud Double Life produced four winners, three of whom can be considered above average.

Double Life's second foal Precipitation (by Hurry On) won seven races value £18,419 (921,000) including the 1937 Ascot Gold Cup, a race won by his own son Sheshoon in 1960, Precipitation also won the Jockey Club Stakes. At stud Precipitation sired three St. Leger winners: Premonition, Chamossaire and Airborne, who also won the Derby.

In 1938 Double Life's son Casanova (by Hyperion) won the Dewhurst Stakes. Double Life also produced Persian Gulf (by Bahram) who has a chapter devoted to him.

Persian Gulf's full-sister Doubleton was foaled in 1938, and although unraced, produced four winners of 9 races worth £8,084.25.

Doubleton's first foal was a filly: Daily Double (by Fair Trial). At two she won one of her three races and as a three-year-old, three of her eight starts. At stud Daily Double was the most influential of Doubleton's produce. Her second foal Chione (by Borealis) won the Galtres Stakes (12f.) and finishing third in the Newmarket Oaks (14f.). When retired to stud Chione founded a successful family that included speedy individuals such as Amigo Sucio, Rolly Polly and Standaan, while one branch had Group 1 success in South Africa.

Doubleton's second foal: Didima (by Nearco) won one of her two starts at two but at three failed to win either of her starts.

At stud Didima produced two foals, her unraced first foal Double Charm and the maiden Rothia. At stud Double Charm produced the useful stayer Sagacity, the winner of both Yorkshire and Goodwood Cup, as well as finishing runner-up in the Ascot Gold Cup, and second and third in successive Doncaster Cups. Sagacity was inbred 3x3 to Precipitation and his half-sister Doubleton.

Doubletons third foal: Duplicity (by Nearco) did not race as a juvenile but won two of her seven starts at three and was disqualified in another; the Coronation Stakes. She was second Falmouth Stakes and third in the 1000 Guineas.

At stud Duplicity's descendants included the Oaks winner Shahtoush, and excellent racehorse and sire Kalaglow.

Duplicity's half-brother and Doubleton's fourth foal to survive: Double Eclipse (by Hyperion), finished third to Galcador in the Derby, and won the Jersey and Princess of Wales's Stakes.

Daily Double best produce was her fifth foal: Meld (by Alycidon), a three-quarter sister to Chione, as their respective sires were half-brothers. Meld won the fillies Triple Crown: 1000 guineas, Oaks and St. Leger, plus the Coronation Stakes.

At stud Meld became only the eighth Oaks winner to produce a Derby winner when her son Charlottown won the race in 1966.

Principal winners descending from Doubleton via Duplicity:-

Doubleton (Bahram)
| Duplicity (Nearco)
|| **Dual** (Chanteur II) (Solario S)
|| **Duplation** (Vimy) (Lingfield Derby Trial)

| | **Sonsa** (Hyperion) (Ebbisham S)
| | | Sonia (Worden II)
| | | Rossitor (Pall Mall)
| | | | **Kalaglow** (Kalamoun) (G1 Eclipse S, G1 King George VI & Queen Elizabeth S)
| | | | **Armarama** (Persian Bold) (G2 Ribblesdale S)
| | | | | **Artistique** (Linamix) (G3 Prix Berteux)
| | | | | | **Montmartre** (Montjeu) (G1 Grand Prix de Paris)
| | | **Sunspeck** (Nearula) (Ebbisham S)
| | | | Radiant Beam (Sicambre)
| | | | | Mrs Vee Vee (Ridan)
| | | | | | Fabulous Vee (Somethingfabulous)
| | | | | | | Vee Vee Star (Norquestor)
| | | | | | | | | **Declan's Moon** (Malibu Moon) (G1 Hollywood Futurity)
| | Two Fold (Hyperion)
| | | Tabulator (Never Say Die)
| | | | **Formulate** (Reform) (G3 Prestige S, G3 May Hill S, G3 Fillies Mile)
| | | | | **Shahtoush** (Alzao) (G1 Oaks)
| | | | | **Game Plan** (Darshaan) (G2 Pretty Polly S)
| | | | | | **Sobieski** (Polish Precedent) (G2 Prix Eugene Adam)
Principal winners descending from Doubleton via Daily Double and Chione:-
Doubleton (Bahram)
| **Double Eclipse** (Hyperion) (Princess of Wales's S, Jersey S)
| Daily Double (Fair Trial)
| | **Chione** (Borealis) (Galtres S)
| | | Chios (Nearco)
| | | | Castania (Orsini)
| | | | | **Standaan** (Zeddaan) (Steward's Cup H, G3 Palace House)
| | | Grey Speck (Grey Sovereign)
| | | | Grey Fleck (Sing Sing)
| | | | | Haunting (Lord Gayle)
| | | | | | **Amigo Sucio** (Stanford) (G2 Zukunfts-Rennen)
| | | | | | Rare Sound (Rarity)
| | | | | | | **Rolly Polly** (Mukaddamah) (G2 Prix Robert Papin)
| | | | | | | Rumba Azul (Fabulous Dancer)
| | | | | | | | **Rumba Loca** (Sri Pekan) (G2 Italian 1000 Guineas)
| | | | | | Mrs Gray (Red Sunset)
| | | | | | | Woodcock Moon (Kyllachy)
| | | | | | | | **Moonstone Magic** (G3 Fred Darling S)
| | | Maricopa (The Phoenix)
| | | | Mashka (New South Wales)
| | | | | **Dancing Duel** (Dancing Champ) (G1 South African Guineas, G1 July H)
| | | | | **Olympic Duel** (Dancing Champ) (G1 J&B Metropolitan S, G1 Paddock S (x2))
| | | | | | **Flying Duel** (Foveros) (G1 Daily News 2000 S)
| | | | | | Lightning Duel (Foveros)
| | | | | | | **Thundering Star** (Fort Wood) (G1 Greyville Gold Cup)
| | | | | | Supreme Duel (Royal Chalice)
| | | | | | | **Northern Heritage** (Western Winter) (G3 Kenilworth Champagne S)
Principal winners descending from Doubleton via Daily Double and Meld:-
Doubleton (Bahram)
| Daily Double (Fair Trial)
| | **Meld** (Alycidon) (1000 Guineas, Oaks, St. Leger, Coronation S)
| | | **Charlottown** (Charlottesville) (Derby, Coronation Cup)
| | | **Intaglio** (Tenerani) (Meld S)
| | | | Engraving (Crepello)
| | | | | La Locandiera (Alleged)
| | | | | | Fosca (El Gran Senor)
| | | | | | | **Ramonti** (Martino Alonso) (G1 Queen Anne S, G1 Sussex S, G1 QE II S)

| | | | Hants (Exbury)
| | | | | Gerardmer (Brigadier Gerard)
| | | | | | **Bengal Fire** (Nishapour) (G2 Royal Lodge S)
| | | | | | **Kings Island** (G1 Sunset H)
| | | | | **Tants** (Vitiges) (G3 Lingfield Oaks Trial)
| | | | | | Lady of Persia (Persian Bold)
| | | | | | | Christchurch (Caerleon)
| | | | | | | | | **Cheeky Choice** (Redoute's Choice) (G1 Flight S)
| | | | | | | Danasia (Danehill)
| | | | | | | | **Zabrasive** (Zabeel) (G1 Rosehill Guineas)
| | | | Seedling (Exbury)
| | | | | **Easy Regent** (Prince Regent) (G2 Criterium de St-Cloud, 2 Prix Daru)
| | | | Double Type (Behistoun)
| | | | | Dressed In Red (Red Alert)
| | | | | | **Tinterosse** (Kenmare (G2 Premio Melton)
Principal winners descending from Doubleton via Didima:-
Doubleton (Bahram)
| Didima (Nearco)
| | Double Charm (Epigram)
| | | **Sagacity** (Le Sage (Yorkshire Cup, Goodwood Cup, Geoffrey Freer S)

FALKIRK (1952 b f Bahram – Matyoka by Winterhalter)

The unraced Falkirk possessed an interesting pedigree, for her third dam Compromise was a three-quarter sister to Blanche, the dam of Bahram's own sire Blandford, thus making Falkirk inbred 3x3 to that pair of close relatives.

Falkirk's granddam Sickle Moon was sold at the 1944 Newmarket December Sales, in foal to 1941 Coronation Cup winner Winterhalter, for 1,800 guineas (77,500), and exported to Argentine. The mating produced Matyoka, and the following year Sickle Moon produced a filly by Rustom Pasha named Crescent, who developed into a useful performer in Argentine, winning both Premio Buenos Aires and Premio Suipacha.

Principal winners descending from Falkirk:-
Falkirk (Bahram)
| Impertinente (Again II)
| | Lola Montes III (Birikil)
| | | **Acclimatization** (Clem) (G1 United Nations H)
| | | Gussie (Gustav)
| | | | Gussie's Appeal (Valid Appeal)
| | | | | **Stormy Blues** (Cure The Blues) (G3 Sorority S, G3 Selima S)
| | | | | | Capote Blues (Capote)
| | | | | | | **Blues Street** (Street Cry) (G2 Mervyn Muniz Jr. Memorial S)

FLOWERDALE (1940 b f Bahram – Fair Diana by Hurry On)

Flowerdale's dam Fair Diana was out of Daughter-in-Law (by Son-in-Law) who was a three-quarter sister to the 1924 Oaks winner Straitlace.

Fair Diana won two of her four races as a juvenile: a plate and the Champagne Stakes where she beat the following year's Derby winner Blenheim. She also finished second to Fair Isle, who later won the 1000 Guineas. At three she was unplaced in two starts.

At stud Fair Diana produced 5 winners, including the 1940 Dewhurst Stakes winner Fettes (by Felstead), while her first foal, Ben Marshal (by Gainsborough) finished runner-up in the same race six years earlier.

Flowerdale only raced at two and failed to win any of her five races.

At stud Flowerdale produced 3 winners of 4 races worth £2,317.75 (74,000), the best being Mountain Ash (by Owen Tudor), who won the Warwickshire Breeders' Foal Stakes and finished third in the Horris Hill Stakes. Her third foal Cairngorm (by Hyperion), a maiden, was exported to Argentine where he had minor success as a stallion, siring Maniatico, who won the Gran Premio Miguel A Martinez de Hoz, and Le Trayas, winner of the Gran Premio Comparacion.

Flowerdale's first foal, a filly: Shieldaig (by Solario), won a minor race over five furlongs at Bath from five juvenile starts. At stud her descendants ranged from a couple of Italian 1000 winners: Dir El Gobi (also third in Italian Oaks) and Danzica (also second in the Italian Oaks), to the Irish Champion Hurdle winner Prominent King.

Principal winners descending from Flowerdale:-

Flowerdale (Bahram)
| Shieldaig (Solario)
| | Diabaig (Dante)
| | | Ben Alligin (Abernant)
| | | | Blooming Hills (Hillsdale)
| | | | | **Mark's Place** (Stoic) (G3 Caballero H)
| | | Dessie (Pinza)
| | | | Dorilea (Tissot)
| | | | | **Dir El Gobi** (Aureole) (G2 Italian 1000 Guineas)
| | | | | Duppel (King Emperor)
| | | | | | **Danzica** (Rusticaro) (G1 Italian 1000 Guineas)
| | Mallaig (Owen Tudor)
| | | Christmas Gift (Princely Gift)
| | | | **Prominent King** (Prominer) (Irish Cesarewitch H, Irish Champion Hurdle)

GOLETA (1953 b f Bahram – Umyak by Rustom Pasha)

Goleta was a full sister to Brigantine and unraced. At stud she became the third dam of Peru's Champion sprinter La Chaposa. At stud in North America La Chaposa produced two above average performers in the Grade 1 winners Chaposa Springs and You And I.

One of Chaposa Springs' victories came in the Grade 1 Test Stakes; a race also won by You And I's best offspring, the multiple Grade 1 winner You. Some of La Chaposa's descendants later returned to Peru, including Palestino, who finished third in the Group 1 Peruvian Derby.

Principal winners descending from Goleta:-

Goleta (Bahram)
| Goelette (Seductor)
| | Belinda (Nyangai)
| | | **La Chaposa** (Ups) (G1 Clasico America, G1 Premio Velocidad)
| | | | **Chaposa Springs** (Baldski) (G1 Ballerina H, G1 Test S)
| | | | **You And I** (Kris S) (G1 Metropolitan H, G2 Cowdin S, G2 Brooklyn H)
| | | | Peruvian Pride (Baldski)
| | | | | **Palestino** (Stash) (G3 Clasico Luis Olaechea Bois)
| | | | | Mas Sabrosa (L'Emigrant)
| | | | | | **Mayorazgo** (Prospector's Cap) (G2 Clasico Santorin)

GREAT TRUTH (1937 b f Bahram – Frankly by Franklin)

Great Truth's dam was a half sister to three top-class colts: Blenheim (Derby), His Grace (Coronation Cup) and King Salmon (Coronation Cup & Eclipse Stakes). Both Blenheim and His Grace were sired by re Blandford, making Great Truth a close relative.

Great Truth was the first winner sired by Bahram, when winning Manchester's Whitsuntide Foal Plate (5f.). She also won at Newmarket's First July meeting; the Fulbourne Stakes (5f.). She was also third in the National Breeders Produce Stakes (promoted from fourth).

Great Truth was given 8st.10lb. in the Free Handicap, 11lb. behind the top rated colt Tant Mieux, and 7lb. behind the leading filly Golden Penny.

Great Truth's only race at three was in the 1000 Guineas, when she was unplaced. In December 1940 Great Truth was sold for 1,300 guineas and retired to stud (£60,000).

Great Truth sired one winner: Summertime (by Precipitation). At stud Summertime was a success and Great Truth's importance became clear.

Summertime was unplaced from two starts as a juvenile. At three he won five of his ten races: the

Chaplin Stakes (10f.) at Lincoln, Risby Handicap (10f.) at Newmarket, Classic Trial Stakes (12f.) at Kempton Park, King's Stakes (12f.) at Windsor and Lowther Stakes at Newmarket (14f).

As a four-year-old he won two of his three starts: a plate at Windsor (12f) and the Chippenham Stakes (12f) at Newmarket. He was then exported to New Zealand where he stood for 150 guineas (£4,750) at the Te Rapa Stud Frankston Junction, near Hamilton.

At stud Summertime was a success in the eight seasons between 1959/60 and 1966/67 and was only outside the top three leading New Zealand sires twice, winning the title in 1959/60, 1960/61 and 1964/65.

He also won the Dewar Stallion Trophy award four times – being the leading New Zealand based sire on the combined Australian and New Zealand stakes earnings list in seasons 1959/60, 1962/63, 1963/64 and 1964/65. Summertime continued to do well when transferred to the Kinross Stud, Te Kauwhata. His fee had risen to 1,000 guineas (£18,900) by 1966, and at his death in May 1969 he had sired the winners of $2.5 million, including 59 stakes winners.

Summertime's offspring included the winners of three consecutive AJC Derbys (Summer Fair, Summer Prince & Summer Fiesta), two Caulfield Cups (Summer Fair, Sometime) and two consecutive Cox Plates (Summer Regent & Sir Dane). One of his best fillies was the New Zealand Oaks winner Star Belle.

Sir Dane is of particular interest; he was inbred 3x3 to Bahram; his maternal grandsire was Bahram's son Treasure Hunt.

Summertime sired three important sire sons: Broker's Tip, Sir Dane and Sobig. Broker's Tip became a successful sire in Chile, where in 1983 he sired the Chilean Derby winner Musico Brok. In Australia Sobig's offspring included the dual Melbourne Cup winner Think Big.

Sobig ranks as one the greatest New Zealand-bred stallions, and did much to shatter the traditional stigma against the home-grown sire. The winner of 12 races from 40 starts at distances ranging from six to twelve furlongs; he was well-bred for his dam Passive had won thirteen races, including the New Zealand Derby, Oaks and St. Leger plus the Great Northern Derby and Wellington Guineas.

The nearest Summertime's year older full sister Hasten came to winning from six starts was when third as a three-year-old over a mile. At stud Hasten produced Our Boy, winner of Newmarket's Rous Memorial Stakes as a juvenile.

Great Truth was later exported to Brazil in 1949, where she became the sixth dam of Group 1 winner Belo Acteon.

Principal winners descending from Great Truth:-
Great Truth (Bahram)
| **Summertime** (Precipitation) (Kempton Classic Trial)
| Hasten (Precipitation)
| | **Our Boy** (Palestine) (Rous Memorial S)
| Sans Pareil (Heron)
| | Galilea (Fort Napoleon)
| | | Gold Stern (Karabas)
| | | | **All Gold** (Midnight Tiger) (G3 G.P. Jose Carlos E Joao Jose E Figueiredo (x2))
| | | | Royale (Itajara)
| | | | | Back For Good (Ghadeer)
| | | | | | **Belo Acteon** (Acteon Man) (G1 G.P. Brasil)

HONRA (1952 b f Bahram – Holda by Hunter's Moon)

Honra's third dam: En Guardia had already had success in Argentine, her daughter; Anapa produced the 1944 Argentine 2000 Guineas winner Aden. Another Argentine 2000 Guineas winner from this family the 1962 winner Ukase, whose dam Parapet was a half sister to Honra's dam Holda. Holda produced two winners of the Argentine 1000 Guineas in Hold Her and Himera, who won the race in 1961 and 1966 respectively. En Guardia was by Cyllene out of a mare by Persimmon so was bred on a similar cross to Bahram's maternal grandsire Friar Marcus, who was by a son of Cyllene out of a daughter of Persimmon. Holda won twice over 1100 and 1500 metres.

Honra won four races from thirteen starts: the Premio Eden (1400m.) at Palermo, and won the Premio Yatasto (1600m.) the Premio Ensayo (2000m.) and Premio Solitaria (2000m.).

At stud Honra's was the fourth dam of dual Brazilian Group 1 winner Severado
Principal winners descending from Honra:-

Honra (Bahram)
| Integridad (Sideral)
| | Eclat (Cambremont)
| | | Requerida (Hang Ten)
| | | | **Severado** (Clackson) (G1 G.P. Matias Machline, G.P. Francisco de Paula Machado)

HUNT THE SLIPPER (1940 br f Bahram – Premiere Danseuse by Phalaris)

Premiere Danseuse was bought for 1,800 guineas (£81,250) at the 1927 Newmarket First July Sales. She won once as a juvenile,

At stud Premiere Danseuse's two best offspring: the 1935 Falmouth and Nassau Stakes winner Coppelia, and 1946 Ebor Handicap winner Foxtrot. Coppelia's offspring included Golovine (Chester Cup) and Danse D'Espoir (Galtres Stakes), while Foxtrot's son Square Dance won the Triumph Hurdle.

Hunt The Slipper neither raced nor produced a winner at stud, so by the time her own unraced daughter: Badminton, was exported to Japan as a seven-year-old in 1960, this branch of the family looked to be heading for obscurity. However in the early 1990's Badminton made an appearance in pedigrees as the fourth dam of the leading Japanese Horse Yamanin Zephyr, winner the Group 1 Tenno Sho Autumn, and consecutive runnings of the Group 1 Yasuda Kinen.

Principal winners descending from Hunt The Slipper:-
Hunt The Slipper (Bahram)
| Badminton (Epigram)
| | Miss Tarumae (Hakuryo)
| | | Yamahoyou (Guersant)
| | | | Yamnin Polish (Blushing Groom)
| | | | | **Yamanin Zephyr** (Nihon Pillow Winner) (G1 Yasuda Kinen (x2))

HUNTING PARTY (1943 b f Bahram – Third Party by Teddy)

Hunting Party was from a moderate American family. Her dam Third Party had won 4 of her 22 starts over 4 seasons, earning $8,265. Her biggest win came as a juvenile when winning the $5,000 Boston American Pink Final Juvenile, and she also finished third that same year in the Betsy Ross Stakes.

Hunting Party was bred on similar lines to the 1965 Black-Eyed Susan Stakes winner Sue Baru, for the latter was by Bahram's son Sun Bahram, and her granddam was a half sister to Third Party.

Hunting Party was unplaced in her only two starts as a juvenile. Her older half-brother: Mightiest (by Man O'War), raced over 10 seasons and 248 races, winning 24 races and earning $31,230.

Covered by Happy Argo as a three-year-old, Hunting Party produced her best offspring: a colt Fleet Argo. He raced 243 times in a 12 year racing career, Fleet Argo's 52 wins were worth$149,000, with his biggest win coming as three-year-old in the $7,500 Laurel Stakes.

In total Hunting Party produced 5 winners, among them being her third foal Safari, the winner of one race worth $3,300 from her 6 starts. At stud Safari produced a performer much better than herself in Oink, the winner of 16 races worth $268,227, including the $100,000 United Nations Handicap.

Principal winners descending from Hunting Party:-
Hunting Party (Bahram)
| Safari (Jacopo)
| | **Oink** (To Market) (United Nations H)

LIBERATION 1941 b f Bahram – Carissima by Clarissimus)

Carissima won the Prix Minerve and Prix de Mallaret and was second in the French Oaks.

At stud she produced Pharis (by Pharos) who was unbeaten. Unraced at two, Pharis won the Prix Noailles, Prix du Jockey Club (French Derby) and Grand Prix de Paris.

Liberation raced in England but failed to win or be placed in three starts.

At stud Liberation five winners: Emperor, Elpenor, Alto, Celtiber and Liberator. Emperor won the Prix Robert Papin and Dewhurst Stakes as a juvenile and at three finished runner up in both the Jersey Stakes and Prix Jacques Le Marois. He then stood as a stallion in Australia.

Elpenor won the Ascot Gold Cup and Prix du Cadran and later took up stallion duties in Brazil.

Principal winners descending from Liberation:-

Liberation (Bahram)
| **Elpenor** (Owen Tudor) (Ascot Gold Cup, Prix du Cadran)
| **Emperor** (Djebel) (Prix Robert Papin, Dewhurst S)
| Aldaya (Marsyas)
| | Oitiva (Caporal)
| | | **Xengo** (Gabari) (G3 G.P.Prefeitura da Cidade do Rio Janeiro)
| | | Bita (Silver)
| | | | Farsada (Figuron)
| | | | | Fair Lane (Executioner)
| | | | | | Carol Fast (Fast Gold)
| | | | | | | **Gold Tango** (Khatango) (G3 G.P. Presidente Silvio Alvares Penteado)
| | | | | | | **Lady Carol** (Our Captain Willie) (G3 G.P. Presidente Jose Nogueira)

MAH IRAN (1939 gr f Bahram – Mah Mahal by Gainsborough)

Mah Iran was Bahram's most influential daughter. Her dam: Mah Mahal was the second foal of Mumtaz Mahal. Mah Iran won two of her seven races as a juvenile; the Denston Stakes at Newmarket and a nursery at Newbury, both over five furlongs. She was also second in both the Molecomb and Chesterfield Stakes.

As a three-year-old Mah Iran won three of her six races all at Newmarket; the Soham Stakes (5f.140yds.), Barnham Stakes (6f.) and Hildersham Stakes (6f.). She also finished third in the Severals Stakes.

At stud Mah Iran produced seven winners from nine foals before she was exported to North America. Her first foal: Migoli was by Bois Roussel and won 11 races, including the Dewhurst Stakes at two, the Eclipse and Champion Stakes at three and Prix de L'Arc de Triomphe at four. In addition he finished second in the Derby and third in the St. Leger.

Migoli had an interesting pedigree; his sire Bois Roussel traced tail male to Chaucer and was out of a daughter of the mare Concertina. This was very similar pattern to Mah Iran's sire Bahram, who was tail male to Chaucer's half brother Swynford, out of a granddaughter of Concertina.

Migoli's full sister: Mah Behar, won only one race and was fourth in the Irish Oaks. At stud her descendants included the Classic winners Alandi, Almashar, Nishapour, Aussie Rules and Yesterday.

Mah Iran produced the winners of 15 races in England, namely Migoli, Moondust and Kermanshah, while five of her offspring; Migoli, Danira, Star Of Iran, Mah Pak and Mah Behar, won 8 races in France.

Persian Garden, another full sister to Migoli, was sold to America, but her descendants later returned to Europe where Prince Arthur won the Italian Derby and In A Tiff won the Italian 1000 Guineas. In A Tiff's half-brother: Pennine Walk was a useful miler, and at stud sired Nicer who won the Irish 1000 Guineas.

Another full sister to Migoli; Star of Iran produced three winners from as many foals before she was exported to North America. The best of these was Petite Etoile, a great racehorse that won 14 of her 19 starts. However she was highly strung as well as brilliant and also difficult to get into foal and she produced only three foals of which one was a winner. She was barren seven times produced dead twins and another foal born dead and once she slipped twins. All this from thirteen years at stud, she was not covered one year, and was retired in 1976.

Petite Etoile's three foals: colts Afaridaan (by Charlottesville) and Kazakstaan (by Never Say Die), stood as stallions in South Africa and New Zealand respectively, and the filly Zahra (by Habitat), who was produced by Petite Etoile when she was eighteen.

Zahra failed to win but produced five winners from eight foals; seven of which were fillies. Her descendants included the South African performer Igugu, together with another champion in the unbeaten filly Zarkava, winner of the French 1000 Guineas, French Oaks and Prix de l'Arc de Triomphe.

Principal winners descending from Mah Iran via Danira & Mah Behar:-
Mah Iran (Bahram)
| **Migoli** (Bois Roussel) (Dewhurst S, Eclipse S, Prix de L'Arc de Triomphe)
| Danira (Dante)
| | **Darannour** (Sunny Boy) (Prix Morny)
| Mah Behar (Bois Roussel)

| | Nucciolina (Nuccio)
| | | Alama (Aureole)
| | | | **Nassipour** (Blushing Groom) (G1 Canadian International)
| | | | **Nishapour** (Zeddaan) (G1 French 2000 Guineas)
| | | Alannya (Relko)
| | | | Alaviya (Kalaglow)
| | | | | Lilac Fairy (Rainbow Quest)
| | | | | | Fuji Fairy (Fuji Kiseki)
| | | | | | | **Yosei** (Invincible Spirit) (G1 Caulfield 1000 Guineas, G1 AJC Sires Produce S)
| | | | Aliya (Darshaan)
| | | | | **Alandi** (Galileo) (G1 Irish St. Leger, G1 Prix du Cadran)
| | | | **Aliysa** (Darshaan) (Lingfield Oaks Trial)
| | | | | Alaiyda (Shahrastani)
| | | | | | **Alamshar** (Key of Luck) (G1 Irish Derby, King George VI & Queen Elizabeth S)
| | | Allara (Zeddaan)
| | | | Alruccaba (Crystal Palace)
| | | | | Alouette (Darshaan)
| | | | | | **Alborada** (Alzao) (G1 Champion Stakes (x2), G2 Nassau S, G2 Pretty Polly S)
| | | | | | **Albanova** (Alzao) (G1 Preis von Europa, G1 Deutschland Preis)
| | | | | Jude (Darshaan)
| | | | | | **Quarter Moon** (Sadler's Wells) (G1 Moyglare Stud S)
| | | | | | **Yesterday** (Sadler's Wells) (G1 Irish 1000 Guineas)
| | | | | **Last Second** (Alzao) (G2 Nassau S, G2 Sun Chariot S)
| | | | | | **Aussie Rules** (Danehill) (G1 French 2000 Guineas, G1 Keeneland Turf Mile S)
| | | | | **Allelula** (Caerleon) (G3 Doncaster Cup)
| | | | | | **Allegretto** (Galileo) (G1 Prix Royal Oak, G2 Lancashire Oaks)
| | | Ariann (Silver Shark)
| | | | Kyoei Shirayuki (Crowned Prince)
| | | | | Keishu Herb (Mississipian)
| | | | | | **World Cleek** (Magic Mirror) (G1 Tokyo Daishoten)
Principal winners descending from Mah Iran via Mah Pak & Persian Garden:-
Mah Iran (Bahram)
| Mah Pak (Nearco)
| | Tanhausa (Summer Tan)
| | | Meryta (Mourne)
| | | | Royal Mahal (Charlton)
| | | | | Amanda Mahal (March Legend)
| | | | | | **The Guida** (All Glory) (G1 Queensland Sires Produce S)
| Persian Garden (Bois Roussel)
| | Garden of Delight (Tom Fool)
| | | Daniela Samuel (No Robbery)
| | | | **Prince Arthur** (Fairy King) (G1 Italian 2000 Guineas)
| | Persian Apple (No Robbery)
| | | Tifrums (Thatch)
| | | | **In A Tiff** (Caerleon) (G1 Italian Derby)
| | | | **Pennine Walk** (Persian Bold) (G2 Queen Anne S, G3 Jersey S, G3 Diomed S)
| | | | **Perfect Imposter** (Persian Bold) (G2 Tattersall's Gold Cup, G3 Derby Trial S)
| | | Exactly Like You (Sassafras)
| | | | Like (Al Nasr)
| | | | | **Indirecto** (Exile King) (G1 G.P. Consagracao)
| | | | Topsa (Topsider)
| | | | | Brisk Walk (Easy Goer)
| | | | | | Calunga (Sea of Secrets)
| | | | | | | **Calling Elvis** (Romarin) (G2 G.P. Antenor Lara Campos)
Principal winners descending from Mah Iran via Star of Iran:-
Mah Iran (Bahram)
| Star of Iran (Bois Roussel)

|| **Petite Etoile** (Petition) (1000 Guineas, Oaks, Sussex S, Champion S, Coronation Cup (x2)
|| Star of Shiraz (Nuccio)
||| Esmerald (Sunny Boy)
|||| Gulab (Prince Bio)
||||| Gulanar (Val de Loir)
|||||| **Magnificent Star** (Silver Hawk) (G1 Yorkshire Oaks)
|||| Stellita (Petition)
||||| Docent R (Czar Alexander)
|||||| Faulkland's Folly (Frejus)
||||||| Hufeisen (Never Cye)
||||||||| Naoki (Kenetico)
|||||||||| **Norton** (Allied Forces) (G1 G.P 2000 Guineas Consagracion de Potrillos)
|||| Persian Princess (Prince Taj)
||||| Persian Tale (Le Haar)
|||||| **Rugby Ball** (Nice Dancer) (G2 Takamatsunomiya Kinen)
||| Mumtaz (Sheshoon)
|||| Naveen (Sir Gaylord)
||||| **Nayrizi** (Riverman) (G2 Herbert Power H)
Principal winners descending from Mah Iran via Petite Etoile:-
Petite Etoile (Petition) (1000 Guineas, Oaks, Sussex S, Champion S, Coronation Cup (x2)
| Zahra (Habitat)
|| Zaila (Darshaan)
||| **Zainta** (Kahyasi) (G1 Prix Saint-Alary, G1 Prix de Diane)
|| Zariya (Blushing Groom)
||| **Zayyani** (Darshaan) (G3 Greenham S)
||| Zerzaya (Beldale Flutter)
|||| **Zerpour** (Darshaan) (G2 VRC Queen Elizabeth S)
||| Zariliya (Darshaan)
|||| Zarinia (Intikhab)
||||| **Igugu** (Galileo) (G1 July H, G1 J&B Metropolitan S, G1 Woolavington S)
|| Zarzaya (Caro)
||| Spring Morning (Ashkalani)
|||| **French Fifteen** (Turtle Bowl) (G1 Criterium International, G3 Prix Djebel)
||| Zaydiya (Shernazar)
|||| Zayraba (Doyoun)
||||| **Zarewitsch** (Night Shift) (G3 Badener Meile, G3 Oettinger Rennen)
|||| Zayana (Darshaan)
||||| Zayanida (King's Best)
|||||| **Ziyarid** (Desert Style) (G3 Prix Daphnis)
|| Zarna (Shernazar)
||| Zarkana (Doyoun)
|||| Zarkasha (Kahyasi)
||||| **Zarkava** (Zamindar) (G1 French 1000, Prix de Diane, Prix de L'Arc de Triomphe)
|| Zarafa (Blushing Groom)
||| Zafadola (Darshaan)
|||| Zelanda (Night Shift)
||||| **Time Prisoner** (Elusive Quality) (G3 Prix de Ris-Orangis)
||||| **Emily Bronte** (Machiavellian) (G3 Prix de Reservoirs)
||||| **Lockwood** (Invincible Spirit) (G3 Prix de Ris-Orangis)

MOTHER INDIA (1943 b f Bahram – Maradadi by Stimulus)

Mother India's dam Maradadi was a half-sister to three American Stakes winners: Canter (1923 Kentucky Jockey Club Stakes), Single Foot (1926 Brooklyn Handicap) and Teufel (1936 Wood Memorial).

At stud Maradadi produced two Stakes winners: Ellis, the winner of 14 races worth $63,101, and Brabancon, whose 9 wins were worth $114,755. Brabancon's best performance was in defeat when second to the Preakness Stakes winner Faultless in the $25,000 Withers Stakes. Mother India won 2 races from 17 starts worth $4,825 over 3 seasons.

At stud Mother India produced Goyamo, the winner of 9 races worth $157,099, including winning the Blue Grass Stakes and finishing fourth in the Kentucky Derby. She produced just two more minor winners from her other 9 foals to race. One of these was her daughter Polinique who later became the dam of the Grade 3 Oil Capitol Handicap winner Polito.

Principal winners descending from Mother India:-

Mother India (Bahram)
| **Goyamo** (Goya) (Blue Grass S)
| Polinique (Polynesian)
| | **Polito** (Crozier) (G3 Oil Capitol H)

OPEN QUESTION (1946 b f Bahram – Now What by Chance Play)

Now What's best produce was her daughter Next Move (by Bull Lea), the winner of 17 of her 46 starts worth $398,550 with victories in the Coaching Club American Oaks and Beldame Handicap, both $50,000 events.

Open Question was foaled a year before Next Move, and managed just one win from 7 starts over two seasons, earning $2,600.

At stud Open Question produced just 6 minor winners, among them the filly Foolish Question, the winner of one race from 7 starts with earnings of $2,865. However, Foolish Question's daughter Precious Promises, the winner of one of her 32 starts, was exported to Argentine as a five-year-old in 1978, where she later produced the Group1 winner Preciosura.

Principal winners descending from Open Question:-

Open Question (Bahram)
| Foolish Question (Tom Fool)
| | Precious Promises (Pieces of Eight)
| | | **Preciosura** (Laramie Trail) (G1 G.P.Internacional Felix de Alzaga Unzue)

QUEEN OF BAGHDAD (1937 br f Bahram – Queen of Scots by Dark Legend)

Queen of Scots was the leading three-year-old filly in France in 1933. As a juvenile Queen of Scots won one race. At three she won three races in succession including the Prix de Pomone and Grand Prix de Deauville. She subsequently finished second in the Grand Prix de Marseille.

Queen of Scots produced seven winners from eleven foals; however, Queen of Baghdad was not one of them; failing to win from two starts. However, at stud she produced seven winners from ten foals, including two good performers: Noor and Nahar.

Queen of Baghdad had an interesting pedigree being inbred 5x5 to the mare Black Duchess and 6x6x6x5x6x6x6 to St. Simon.

Noor won the Diomed Stakes and finished third in both the Derby and Eclipse Stakes. Then transferred to America, where he raced for two more seasons, he won two $100,000 events: the Hollywood Gold Cup and Santa Anita Handicap and won a total of eight races there.

Nahar won five races including the Grand Handicap de Deauville as a six-year-old. The following season he won the Lincolnshire Handicap.

Queen of Baghdad later became the grand dam of Taboun, who won the Prix Robert Papin and finished second in the in both Prix Morny and Coventry Stakes. The following season Taboun won the 2000 Guineas before finishing runner-up in the French equivalent.

Principal winners descending from Queen of Baghdad:-

Queen of Baghdad (Bahram)
| **Noor** (Nasrullah) (Santa Anita H, San Juan Capistrano H, Hollywood Gold Cup H)
| **Nahar** (Stardust) (Lincolnshire H)
| Queen of Basrah (Fair Trial)
| | **Taboun** (Tabriz) (Prix Robert Papin, 2000 Guineas)

QUEEN OF SHIRAZ (1937 b f Bahram – Qurrat-Al-Ain by Buchan)

Qurrat-Al-Ain was a half-sister to four winners: Gainsharp, Royal Minstrel, and after her, Havelock and Hairan. She won the Queen Mary and Coronation Stakes at successive Ascots, as well as finishing fourth in the 1000 Guineas.

At stud Qurrat-Al-Ain produced two Irish Oaks winners: Queen of Shiraz and Majideh (by Mahmoud), the latter also won the Irish 1000 Guineas, and later produced the Oaks and Irish Oaks winner Masaka and Belmont Stakes winner and sire Gallant Man.

Queen of Shiraz won only the Irish Oaks from seven starts; failing to gain even a place in the other six. However, as Bahram also sired the winner of the Irish Derby: Turkhan, he had an Irish Classic double from his first crop.

At stud Queen of Shiraz produced the 2000 Guineas third and Santa Anita Handicap winner Poona II and Prix Jacques Le Marois winner Sallymount.

Queen of Shiraz's daughter: Reine des Bois was a maiden who was placed six times as a three-year-old before being sold for 5,600 guineas (£217,500). Reine des Bois produced three Irish Classic winners in four years: Atherstone Wood, Reindeer and Santa Tina. The latter produced the Group 1 Prix Vermeille winner Young Mother, in addition to becoming the granddam of Equalize, a US Grade 1 winner and successful sire in Argentine.

Another branch of the Queen of Shiraz family flourished in America via her unraced first foal Porza; the latter's descendants including the mare Ava Knowsthecode, the dam of four US Graded Stakes winners.

Principal winners descending from Queen of Shiraz:-
Queen of Shiraz (Bahram)
| **Poona II** (Tudor Minstrel) (Rous Memorial S, Santa Anita H)
| **Sallymount** (Tudor Minstrel) (Prix Jacques Le Marois)
| Bamira (Bois Roussel)
| | Bajideh (Supreme Court)
| | | Golden Princes (Blanc Bleu)
| | | | Golden Crown (Mondragon)
| | | | | **Goldenley** (Farley) (G1 G.P. Seleccion)
| Porza (Stardust)
| | Summer Blossom (Sun Again)
| | | Noble Blossom (Noble Commander)
| | | | **Sunny Blossom** (Sunny Chime) (G3 Palos Verdes H, G3 Toboggan H)
| | | Sundestine (Clandestine)
| | | | Sunny Romance (Gallant Romeo)
| | | | | Ava Romance (Avatar)
| | | | | | Ava Knowsthecode (Cryptoclearance)
| | | | | | | **Keyed Entry** (Honour and Glory) (G2 Hutcheson S)
| | | | | | | **Successful Mission** (Successful Appeal) (G3 Miami Mile H)
| | | | | | | **Justin Phillip** (First Samurai) (G2 Woody Stephens S)
| | | | | | | **Algorithms** (Bernardini) (G3 Holy Bull S)
| Reine Dees Bois (Bois Roussel)
| | **Atherstone Wood** (Buisson Ardent) (Irish 2000 Guineas, Gallinule S)
| | **Reindeer** (Santa Claus) (Irish St. Leger, Desmond S, Prix Kergorlay)
| | **Santa Tina** (Santa Claus) (Irish Oaks, Prix de Pomone, Prix de Royaumont)
| | | **Young Mother** (Youth) (G1 Prix Vermeille, G2 Prix de Malleret)
| | | Zonta (De Fager)
| | | | **Equalize** (Northern Jove) (G1 United Nations H, G2 Canadian Turf H (x2))
| | | | **Maudlin** (Foolish Pleasure) (G3 Forego H, G3 Bold Ruler S)

RATINE (1946 b f Bahram – Monel by Sir Greysteel)

Ratine's family had been in obscurity for many years; five generations. Ratine was among 7 minor winners produced by the mare Monel, and racing over two seasons she won once from 19 starts, earning $2,755. As a broodmare in Canada, Ratine, produced 9 winners of 74 races worth $519,196.

Her first foal Dizzy Dora won both the My Dear and Clarendon Stakes in 1955, important juvenile events. Her chief progeny were Hidden Treasure, 24 wins from 65 starts worth $187,734, and He's A Smoothie, 18 wins from 38 starts worth $258,410. In addition her daughter Dangerous Dill finished runner-up in the 1961 Canadian Oaks, while another daughter, Sassy Sarah was exported to France where she produced the Group 3 winner Shari.

It is worth noting that Hidden Treasure's sire Dark Star traced back in direct male line to Bahram's half brother Dastur, and was also out of a mare by Bull Dog who was from Bahram's female family.

Principal winners descending from Ratine:-
Ratine (Bahram)
| **Dizzy Dora** (Black Tarquin) (My Dear S, Clarendon S)
| **He's A Smoothie** (Round Table) (Canadian Prince of Wales S, Canadian International)
| **Hidden Treasure** (Dark Star) (Toronto Cup H, Connaught Cup S, Durham Cup)
| Sassy Sarah (Hill Prince)
| | **Shari** (Mossborough) (G3 Prix Exbury)

RAZA (1948 b f Bahram – Estirpe by Congreve)

Raza's dam Estirpe was a full brother to Embrujo, who was the leading three-year-old in Argentine in 1939, winning their Triple Crown, the Polla de Potrillos (Argentine 2000 Guineas), Gran Premio Jockey Club, and Gran Premio Nacional (Argentine Derby). He was lame when fourth in the Gran Premio Carlos Pellegrini. At four Embrujo won the Clasico General Pueyrredon in record time, but in his final race he broke down in the Gran Premio de Honor. Retired to stud, Embrujo became an instant success, and although never champion sire, finished second twice in 1951 and 1953.

Estirpe won once over 1600 metres in 1945 and twice more over the same distance the following year and once over 2000 metres.

Raza won once from four starts: the Premio Sospiro over 1000 metres.

Raza's female line survives principally through her great granddaughter Nipona. She produced the Argentine Group 2 winner Stormy Nirvana; while her own daughter, South Nina, became the dam of a trio of Group 1 winning full sister by Bernstein named Stormy Nina, Stormy Nimble and Stormy Ninguna.

Principal winners descending from Raza:-
Raza (Bahram)
| Anamita (Cardanil)
| | Mauritana (Good Manners)
| | | Nipona (Babas Fables)
| | | | **Stormy Nirvana** (Bernstein) (G2 Clasico Ricardo Y Ezequiel F Guerrico)
| | | | South Nina (Southern Halo)
| | | | | **Stormy Nina** (Bernstein) (G1 G.P. Eliseo Ramirez)
| | | | | **Stormy Nimble** (Bernstein) (G1 G.P. Eliseo Ramirez, G1 G.P. 1000 Guineas)
| | | | | **Stormy Ninguna** (Bernstein) (G1 G.P. 1000 Guineas)
| | Persane (Right of Way)
| | | Iberienne (Treviglio)
| | | | **Ibero** (Cinco Grande) (G1 G.P.Montevideo, G1 NYRA Mile H, G1 Metropolitan H)
| | | | **Ski Iberia** (Political Ambition) (G1 G.P.Seleccion)
| | | | **Ski Portugues** (Sings) (G3 Clasico Augustin B Gambier)
| | | Iranienne (Master Bold)
| | | | Iraqui (Halpern Bay)
| | | | | **Ghazix** (Lode) (G3 Premio Luis Maria Doyhenard)
| | Chinoise (Aristophanes)
| | | China Town (Rey Claro)
| | | | China Libre (Petrarque)
| | | | | **Barrio Chino** (Roy) (G1 Chile 2000 Guineas, G1 Chile St.Leger, G1 Copa de Plata)
| | La Anamita (Good Manners)
| | | La Nordica (Ringaro)
| | | | La Gran Portada (Hidden Prize)
| | | | | **Life of Victory** (Incurable Optimist) (G1 G.P. Carlos Pellegrini, Copa de Oro (x2))
| | | | | **Leading The Way** (Brancusi) (G1 G.P. Premio de Potrancas)
| | | | | **Lloyd** (Val Royal) (G2 Clasico Provincia de Buenos Aires)

SINSIN (1945 b f Bahram – Blue Ensign by Blue Larkspur)

Sinsin was from a modest American family that had been in the doldrums for many years; nothing of note for seven generations. Lady Reel, the dam of Champion US Sire Hamburg. Sinsin won just once from 16 starts over 2 seasons earning $4,200 and was half-sister to Supersonic (by Devil Diver), who won 3 races and put up her best performances when third as a three-year-old in the Diana Handicap and Test Stakes. At stud Supersonic produced the best horse from this family for many generations; her first foal Outer Space, winner of the $25,000 Mother Goose Stakes at two, and $50,000 Beldame Stakes at three.

At stud Sinsin produced 8 foals, each were winners winning 44 races and earning $84,910 in minor company. They included her second foal: Laurel Wreath, who was the dam of the leading American Steeplechaser Inkslinger. A $5,500 yearling, Inkslinger won 10 races including the 1971 Colonial Cup Steeplechase as a four-year-old. Trained by Dan Moore in Ireland two years later Inkslinger won both the Champion Chase and the Cathcart Chase at the 1973 Cheltenham. Although he only won once more in Europe, Inkslinger also finished second in the 1973 King George VI Chase, third in the 1974 Whitbread Gold Cup Chase and fourth in the 1973 Irish Grand National.

Inkslinger's half-sister Toyoto Rose, the winner of one minor event from 9 starts, later became the granddam of multiple Grade 1 winner Avigaition, the winner of 8 races and earnings of $688,625.

Principal winners descending from Sinsin:-
Sinsin (Bahram)
| Laurel Wreath (Ardan)
| | **Inkslinger** (Bronze Babu) ((Colonial Cup Chase, Champion Chase, Cathcart Chase)
| | Toyoto Rose (North's Rullah)
| | | Daddy's Datsun (Pappa's All)
| | | | **Avigaition** (Windy Sands) (G1 Santa Barbara H, G1 La Canada S, G1 Santa Ana H)
VALIANT (1939 b f Bahram – Trustful by Bachelor's Double)
Valiant was a full-sister to The Druid and won one of her five races; a five furlong plate at Ripon. At stud she produced 4 winners of 6 races worth £2609 (96,500) in Great Britain, with the best being Banri Calma, a useful juvenile filly in Ireland, where she won both the Curragh Foal Plate and Leopardstown Produce Stakes.

At stud Banri Calm's offspring also did well as juveniles with her daughters Tula Ban and Cuaran Biona being placed in the Railway and Beresford Stakes respectively. Tula Ban was exported to Brazil as a three-year-old in 1960, and her descendants there included the Group 1 winner Sorrentino. Towards the end of her career Valiant was export to America, where 3 of her offspring won 11 minor races.

Principal winners descending from Valiant:-
Valiant (Bahram)
| **Banri Calma** (Royal Charger) (Curragh Foal Plate)
| | Tula Ban (Tulyar)
| | | Recusa (Adil)
| | | | Adecusa (Silver)
| | | | | Birot (Thundering Force)
| | | | | | **Bukebele** (Punk) (G3 G.P. Luiz Fernando Cirne Lima)
| | | | | | | **Sorrentino** (Wild Event) (G1 G.P. Ipiranga, G1 G.P Jockey Club de Sao Paulo)
| Roman Triumph (Watling Street)
| | Rhoma (Combat)
| | | **Tama Shuho** (Sound Track) (Sapporo Kinen, Yayoi Sho)

Sources

The Sporting Life

The Sporting Chronicle

The Times

The Daily Mirror

The Morning Post

The Daily Telegraph

The Illustrated Sporting and Dramatic News

The British Racehorse

The Bloodstock Breeders Review

Phil Bull – Best Horses 1943 – 1947

Timeform Racehorses 1948 to date.

Ruffs Guide to the Turf

Racing Calendar

Raceform 1936 – to date.

Racing and Breeding

General Stud Book

Dams of Winners

Baerlein Richard – Shergar

Barry Quintin – Lord Derby and his Horses.

Binns Matthew & Morris Tony – Thoroughbred Breeding

Bland Ernest – Flat Racing Since 1900

Bose Mihir – The Aga Khans

Browne T. H. – A History of the Turf

Coaten Arthur – Famous Horses of the British Turf

Church Michael – The Derby Stakes

Church Michael – Eclipse

Church Michael – Dams of Classic Winners

Churchill Jennifer,

Reichard Andrew & Rogers Byron – Great Thoroughbred Sires of
    the World

Corbett Peter – Bayardo; the Life Times and

Legacy of an Edwardian Champion

Edwards Anne – Throne of Gold

Felstead Theodore – Racing Romance

Frischauer Willi – The Aga Khans

Galtrey Sidney – Memoirs of a Racing Journalist

Gilbey Quintin – Racing For Fun

Gilbey Quintin – Fun Was My Living

Good Meyrick – The Lure of the Turf

Good Meyrick – Good Days

Greenwall Harry – The Aga Khan

Hislop John – Of Horses and Races

Hislop John – Racing Reflections

Jackson Stanley – The Aga Khan

Jodidio Philip – A Racing and Breeding Tradition; The Horses of the
   Aga Khan

Khan Aga – The Memoirs of the Aga Khan

Lambton George – Men and Horses I have Known

Lange Georg – 75 Years The Aga Khan's Racing and Breeding Studs

Leicester Sir Charles – Bloodstock Breeding

Lyle R. C. – The Aga Khan's Horses

Marsh Marcus – Racing with the Gods

Melton George – The Derby

McLean Ken – Genetic Heritage

Mitchell Frank – Racehorse Breeding Theories

Mortimer Roger – The Flat

Mortimer Roger – The History of the Derby Stakes

Mortimer Roger – Twenty great racehorses

Mortimer Roger & Willett Peter – More Great racehorses of the
   World

Mortimer Roger,

Onslow Richard & Willett Peter – Biographical Encyclopedia of
   British Flat Racing

Onslow Richard – The Heath and the Turf

Orchard Vincent – The Derby Stakes

Randall John & Morris Tony – A Century of Champions

O'Sullevan Peter – Calling the Horses

Richards Gordon – My Story

Seth-Smith Michael – Knight of the Turf
Seth-Smith Michael – A Classic Connection.
Seth-Smith Michael & Mortimer Roger – Derby 200
Rickman Eric – On and Off the Racecourse
Rickman Eric – Come Racing With Me
Seth-Smith Michael – The Head Waiter
Seth-Smith Michael – A Classic Connection
Smirke Charlie – Finishing Post
Swaffer Percy – Fleet Street Goes Racing
Tanner Michael & Cranham Gerry – Great Jockeys of the Flat
Thompson Laura – Newmarket
Ulbrich Richard – The Great Stallion Book
Various – Lonsdale Library; Flat Racing
Weston Tommy – My Racing Life
Willett Peter – An Introduction to the Thoroughbred
Wright Howard – Bull; the Biography
Wynn Jones Michael – The Derby

General Index

Adamson, Sir Harvey 18
Aga Jangishah 6
Aga Khan I, Shah Hasan Ali
    Shah 1–2
Aga Khan II, Aga Ali Shah 1, 3
Aga Khan III, Prince Sultan
    Mohammed: and Adolf
    Hitler 52–3; in America
    19–20; appearance 11,
    37, 61; assassination
    attempt 28–9; charitable
    work 15–17, 51, 80; early
    years 1–6; England, visit to
    8–10; evaluation of 78–81;
    eye-sight 4, 5; Germany,
    visit to 11; golf 32, 67–8;
    health 26, 29, 30, 37–8,
    69–70, 71, 74–5; honours
    awarded 11, 12, 26, 28,
    64, 71; income and wealth
    2, 34–5; Indian territory
    request 46–7; Jubilees
    51, 59–60, 70, 71; luxury
    lifestyle 63; marriage to
    Ginetta (Theresa) Magliano
    20–4, 32–3, 39–40; marriage
    to Jane (Andrée) Carron
    33, 41, 42–3, 54–5, 57–8;
    marriage to Shahzadi 6–7,
    13, 21–2; marriage to
    Yvette (Yvonne) Blanche
    Labrousse 57–9, 63, 64,
    70, 76; memoirs 65–7;
    Muslim faith 14, 25;
    Muslim leadership 2–3, 7,
    10, 15–18, 19, 25, 79; Nobel
    Peace Prize nomination
    35–6; personality 77–8;
    political career 6, 12,
    18–19, 24–5, 43–5, 46,
    64–5; and Queen Victoria 7,
    8, 12; and Sir Walter Roper-
    Lawrence 13–15; and
    women 9, 15, 23; World
    War I 26–31; World War II
    55–6, 160–1
Aga Khan III, Prince Sultan
    Mohammed and horse
    racing: attends Derby
    for first time 9–10, 84;
    attitude to racing 202–4;

and Bahram 203, 427;
    benefit to British racing
    and breeding 216–17; and
    breeding theories 87–8,
    95, 122, 217; could not
    distinguish one horse from
    another 136–7; decision to
    build racing stable 84–5,
    89–90; early retirement of
    good horses 207–8; France,
    training moved to 174;
    on Frank Butters 282–3;
    Gimcrack Dinner speeches
    148; greatest horses 202;
    India, horses owned in
    83; Ireland, stud farms in
    121–2; purchases of horses,
    early 92–100, 108–17;
    purchases of horses, later
    125–8, 131, 135, 146–7;
    purchases of horses,
    wartime 158–60; purchases
    of horses, post-war 167;
    racing colours 84; results
    (1922-1925) 110, 113, 119,
    121, 123; results (1926-
    1930) 128–9, 131–2, 139;
    results (1931-1938) 144,
    149–50, 152–3, 243, 255,
    255–6, 257; results (1940-
    1945) 156, 158, 160, 257;
    results (1946-1952) 161,
    173; results compared to
    Lord Derby 193–4; results,
    summary 153, 183; rift
    with Dick Dawson 142–4;
    sales of best horses 150–2,
    211–12, 213–16; sales of
    horses, pre-war 118, 133,
    136, 147, 150, 153; sales of
    horses, wartime 154, 156–8,
    159, 159–60, 216; sales of
    horses, post-war 170, 180;
    on training of horses 277
Aga Khan IV, Shah Karim
    al-Husseini: family
    background 49, 62–3;
    and horse racing 182–3,
    208–11, 218; inheritance
    75, 80, 181; tour of East
    Africa 70

Aga Shamsuddin 83, 88
Aitken, Max, 1st Baron
    Beaverbrook 31–2, 34, 67
Ajax (*Evening Standard*) 415
Ali Shah, Lady: and Aga Khan
    III 4, 6, 12, 13, 33; and
    Aly Khan 50; death of 54;
    death of husband 3; visits to
    Europe 15, 44
All India Muslim League
    16–17
Allison, William 187
Allnatt, Alfred E. 157–8, 216,
    264
Aly Khan, Prince: early
    years 24, 39–42; and
    Jane (Andrée) Carron 43;
    and Joan Guinness 49,
    432; lifestyle of 47–8,
    50; marriage to Rita
    Hayworth 62; obituary
    50–1; personality 71–4;
    presentation at court 42;
    visits to India 33–4, 44–5;
    and women 48–50; World
    War II 56–7
Aly Khan, Prince, and horse
    racing: attends 1950 Two
    Thousand Guineas 168–9;
    attitude to racing 203; bets
    171, 273, 412; and breeding
    181–2; and conformation
    50, 163, 217; as jockey
    142–3; and Marcus Marsh
    173; on Nasrullah 263;
    partners Aga Khan III 161;
    purchases of horses 147–8,
    152, 153–4, 162–3, 167,
    170; retrieves horses from
    Germany 161; successes
    218, 275
"American invasion" of British
    racing 396, 422
*An Introduction to the
    Thoroughbred* (Willett) 192
Antony, Ivor 305
Arcaro, Eddie 167
Archer, Fred 83–4, 285
Armstrong, Fred 162
Arthur, Prince, 1st Duke of
    Connaught 9–10

Asquith, Mrs. 89
Astor, Nancy, Viscountess 47
Astor, Waldorf, 2nd Viscount:
 horses raced 225, 291, 306,
 307, 308, 363, 384, 387,
 400, 419; racing successes
 123
Astor, William, 3rd Viscount
 50–1, 73–4
Augur (Capt. Long) 352, 366,
 388–9, 395, 402–3, 416

Baerlein, Richard 171–2, 280
Bahram, Prince of Persia 344
Bailey, Abraham, 1st Baronet
 131, 289, 347, 384
Baird, E. W. 404
Ballymany stud, Ireland 122,
 153, 174
Basset, A. F. 366
Beary, John 142–3
Beary, Michael: and Aga Khan
 III 144, 163, 303–4; and
 Aly Khan 47, 142–3; and
 Dick Dawson 302; and
 Frank Butters 243; and
 Harry Wragg 138–9; horses
 ridden 132, 136, 138–41,
 143; personality 130
Beatty, Peter 154
Beaverbrook, Max Aitken, 1st
 Baron 31–2, 34, 67
Benson, Martin 299
Beresford, Lord William 83,
 130
Bernard, Jeffrey 65
The Best Horses of 1945 (Bull)
 185–6, 187–8
betting industry 165, 175
Bewicke, Percy 102
Binns, Matthew 190–1
Blain, Freda 45–6, 61
bloodlines 185–9
bookmaking industry 165, 175
Bostwick, A. C. 305–6
Bouillon, Christophe 328
Bouverie (*Daily Mirror*) 433
Boyd-Rochfort, Cecil 303, 480
Brabazon, Aubrey 273
Bradley, James Cox 156
breeding of horses 439–42
breeding systems 185–218;
 Dosage System 185,
 191–2, 195–7, 201–2;
 early retirement of good
 horses 207–8; failures
 of 198–9; fashionable

breeding 188–9; figure
 system 187–8; genetics and
 190–1; luck in 201; mares,
 use of 200; North American
 206; recent trends 208–10;
 stallions, use of 199–200;
 understanding strengths and
 weaknesses 197–8
Briscoe, Basil 146–7
Britain, racing in 165, 175–6
Brook Stud, Newmarket 290
Brookes, Sir Richard 307
Bruce, Victor Alexander, 9th
 Earl of Elgin 7
Buchanan, James, 1st Baron
 Woolavington 242, 295–6,
 299, 324, 385
Buchanan, Mrs. Macdonald
 107
Bull, Phil 185–9, 262–3,
 455–6, 479, 481–3
bullfighting, horses used in
 311–12
Bullock, Frank 286–7
Bullough, Sir George 225,
 352–3
Burrell, Peter 448
Butler, R. A. (Rab) 46
Butler, Sir Harcourt 18
Butt, Sir Alfred 167, 234, 236,
 240, 244–5, 269–70, 302,
 382–4
Butters, Frank 219–34,
 235–83; and Bahram 348,
 399, 426, 429–30, 432–3,
 457; and betting 279; and
 Charlie Smirke 163–4,
 250–2; and conformation
 281; daily routine 254–5;
 early employment 221–2;
 end of training career 276;
 family background 219–21;
 hobbies and interests 282;
 horses trained for Aga Khan
 III 106, 131, 153–4, 169,
 236–49, 252, 254–76, 327,
 346, 356, 363, 377; horses
 trained for Aly Khan 465;
 horses trained for Lord
 Derby 222–34; horses
 trained for Sir Alfred Butt
 244–5; horses trained for
 other owners 242, 256,
 302, 309, 356, 377; leading
 trainers (1927-1933) 223,
 225, 230, 233, 240, 243;
 leading trainers (1944-1949)

265, 269, 273; meets with
 Aly Khan 162; and Michael
 Beary 139, 243; and
 newspapers 280; successes,
 summary of 254, 276;
 training methods 252–4,
 277, 280–1
Butters, Fred 219, 221–2
Butters, Isobel 219
Butters, Janet 219
Butters, Jim 219, 222
Butters, Joseph (Joe) 219–21
Butters, Oliver 219, 222
Butters, Victor 255, 257

Carnarvon, Henry Herbert, 6th
 Earl of: bidding for horses
 125; horses bred by 135;
 horses raced 101, 105, 137,
 305, 318, 323, 324, 349
Carron, Jane (Andrée) 33, 41,
 42–3, 53, 54–5, 57–8, 64
Carslake, Brownie 120, 287
Carson, William (Willie) 444
Carver, Richard 166
Castle, Barbara 53–4
Cayzer, Harold 289–90
Cayzer, Mrs Harold 291
Cecil, Sir Henry 253
Chamberlain, Neville 52
Champagne Stakes, Doncaster
 361, 377
Champagne Stakes, Goodwood
 356
Champion Sires 194, 204–6
cheeses, prize 180
Childs, Joe 290, 299–300,
 311
Cholmondeley, Henry 101
Chrysler, Walter J. 156
Churchill, Sir Winston 53, 60
Clayton, H. F. 297
Clements, A. B. 214
Clifford, R. 296
Cochrane-Baillie, Charles, 2nd
 Baron Lamington 14, 16
Colling, George 253
comparison of horses 370–4,
 435–6
conformation 50, 95, 163, 211,
 217, 281, 283
Connaught, Prince Arthur, 1st
 Duke of 9–10
Coolmore stud, Ireland 209,
 434, 440, 442–3
Cooper, Diana, Viscountess
 Norwich 31, 77

Cooper, Duff, 1st Viscount
Norwich 59
Cornell, John 65
Cosgrave, Joe 460–1
coughing epidemics 424–5
Courtauld, J. S. 384
Crawford, J. H. 234
criteria for great horses 450
Criticos Fafoutakis, George
145–6
*Croisements Rationnels dans la
Race Pure* (Vuillier) 89
Croker, Mr. R. 100, 404
Cundell, F. H. W. 301
Curzon, George, 1st Marquess
Curzon 12–13, 60

D'Abernon, Edgar Vincent, 1st
Viscount 113–14
Daily Mail 383
Daily Mirror (Bouverie) 433
Daily Telegraph (Hotspur) 433
Dale, Raymond 125, 150
Darling, Fred: and Freddie Fox
296–8, 301; in Germany
286; and Gordon Richards
149, 164, 251, 301; horses
raced 107, 154, 299–300,
457, 470–1, 473–9; and
Lady de Bathe (Lillie
Langtry) 286; and Lord
Woolavington 295–6;
purchases of horses 112–14,
117; successes 225, 240,
269; and Walter Gay 295
Dawson, Richard Cecil (Dick):
and Blandford 318, 323–4;
and Blenheim 139; and
doping of horses 90–1; and
Duke John 349, 399; and
Feridoon 116; and Frank
Butters 433; and Friar's
Daughter 142, 336; and
jockeys 144, 251, 302; and
Mumtaz Mahal 103–5;
purchases of horses 99–100,
117; and Qurrat-al-Ain 140;
riders and jockeys 279; rift
with Aga Khan III 142–4;
and Salmon-Trout 120;
successes 119, 133; and Ut
Majeur 140–1
Day, Reg 289
de Bathe, Lillie, Lady (Lillie
Langtry) 286
Derby, Edward Stanley, 17th
Earl of: antipathy towards

Aga Khan III 149, 160,
211–12, 214, 215–16;
on Epsom Derby (1935)
408–9; and Frank Butters
222–5, 230–3; horses raced
268, 286, 320–1, 347,
355, 361, 367, 404, 474;
successes compared to Aga
Khan III 193–4
Dewar, John Arthur 297, 299
Dewar, Thomas, 1st Baron 299
Dewhurst Stakes, Newmarket
363–5
Diaghilev, Sergei 23
Dimitri, Prince Soltykoff 220
Doncaster: Champagne Stakes
361, 377; St Leger Stakes
430, 443–4; Tattersall Sale
Stakes 361; *Timeform* Gold
Cup 455–6
Donoghue, Steve 287, 414
doping of horses 90–1, 300
Dosage System: comparisons
of 195–6; criticisms of 185,
191–2; and Friar's Daughter
336; method of 194, 197;
origin of 88–9; use by Aga
Khan III 92, 122, 194,
201–2; use by Aga Khan
IV 211
Douglas, James, Lady 228
Duke, William: and Aga Khan
III 84, 90, 94, 121; and
conformation 281, 283;
and Maintenon and Prestige
202; training methods 253
Durbars 13, 26
Durham, John Lambton, 5th
Earl of 224–5

Earl, Walter 474, 477
Eclipse Stakes, Sandown Park
381–2
Edward VII, King 8, 9, 12,
23, 285
Edward VIII, King ('David';
formerly Prince of Wales;
later Duke of Windsor) 42,
51–2
Edwardes, George 286
Egerton, John, 4th Earl of
Ellesmere 295, 299
Egypt 27–8
Eley, Sir Frederick 360
Elgin, Victor Alexander Bruce,
9th Earl of 7
Elizabeth II, Queen 165–6

Ellesmere, John Egerton, 4th
Earl of 295, 299
Elliot, Charlie 299
Elliot-Murray-Kynynmound,
Gilbert, 4th Earl of Minto
16
Ellsworth, Rex 180, 212
Epsom: Spring Meeting 84
Esmond, Edward 153
Estes, Joe 201
Evans, Montague 305
exports of horses to Spain
311–12
Eyrefield stud, Ireland 174

Fairchild, Norman 274
Felstead, Theodore 226, 280–1
Fields, M. 324
figure system 187–8
firing, horse treatment 123
FitzGerald, Mrs. Derek 346
Fitzroy House stables 234,
242, 247, 261
Fontarce, Vicomte de 346
Foster, T. A. 293
four-year-old racing 434–5
Fox, Freddie 285–316; and
Aga Khan III 292–3, 302–4,
433; appearance 312; and
Bahram 366, 414–17, 420,
445–6, 448–9; and Danny
Maher 313; death of 314;
early years 285–7; and Fred
Darling 301; and George
V 303–4; on horses 314;
injuries 294, 310, 406,
429; personality 311–12;
protection of old horses
311–12; racing career 132,
143, 289–310; retirement
of 310–11; successes 287,
296–7, 309, 314–15
Fox, Michael 314
France, studs owned by Aga
Khan III 123
Franz Josef I, Emperor of
Austria-Hungary 220
Fry, C. B. 52–3
Furness, Thelma, Viscountess
48

Galtrey, Sidney 130, 217
Garton, Sir Richard 303
genetics and breeding 190–1
George V, King: and Aga Khan
III 28, 51, 137, 237, 417;
coronation 24, 26; at Epsom

Derby (1935) 411; horses bred by 333; and Lady Ali Shah 44; visit to India 15
George VI, King 473, 475
German East Africa 11
Ghandhi, Mohandas (Mohatma) 35, 43–4
Gilbey, Geoffrey 237
Gilbey, Quintin: and Aly Khan 48–9, 412; on Frank Butters 280; on horses 197, 392, 421, 458–9; sale of Aga Khan's horses 214
Gilbey, Sir Walter 404
Gilltown stud, Ireland 122, 153, 174
Gilpin, Peter 277
Gimcrack Dinner 148, 215, 359
Gimcrack Stakes, York 358–9
Ginistrelli, Edoardo 198
Glanely, William Tatem, 1st Baron Glanely: attempt to buy Teresina 96; and Gordon Richards 301; horses raced 296–7, 304, 323, 361–2, 384–5; sold bloodstock to Maj. Allnatt 157
Glorney, Corlette 346
Gooch, Richard 290–1, 294
Good, Meyrick: on Bahram 417, 430, 432; on Big Game 477; on Derby (1935) 400, 409–11, 414; on Middle Park Stakes (1934) 365–7; on National Breeders Produce Stakes (1934) 350–1; on Two Thousand Guineas Stakes (1935) 391–3
Goodfellow, Robin 383
Goodwood races, status of 356
Goold, D. 296
Gordon, A. W. 234
Gordon, C. W. 385
Graziani, Bettina 75
great horses, criteria for 450
Great War *see* World War I
Greenwall, Harry J. 65
Greer, Sir Henry 121–2, 131, 317, 404
Grey, Edward, 1st Viscount Grey of Fallodon 29
Griffin, Thomas 317
Gubbins, J. 403–4
Guinness, Joan 49

Guinness, Loel 49
Guthmann, Simon 109, 118

Haffkine, Waldemar 7
Halifax, Edward Wood, 1st Earl of (formerly Lord Irwin) 43
Hall, Cyril 174
Hall-Walker, William, 1st Baron Wavertree of Delamere 84–7, 185
Hamilton, Lord George 15
Hancock, Arthur (Bull) 150, 213, 263
handicap system 148, 278, 370–2
Haras de Coquenne stud, France 163
Haras de Marly-la-Ville stud, France 123
Harmsworth, Harold, 1st Viscount Rothermere 67
Harmsworth, Mrs. Esmond 348
Hartigan, Hubert 258, 269, 273
Harvey, Wilfred 170
Hashim Shah 11
Hawkins, Mrs Henry 386
Hayworth, Rita 62
Head, Alec 75, 170, 174–7, 180–1, 218, 251
Heathorn, Ted 105
Herbert, Henry, 6th Earl of Carnarvon: bidding for horses 125; horses bred by 135; horses raced 101, 105, 137, 305, 318, 323, 324, 349
Herbert, Reginald, 15th Earl of Pembroke 137
Hill, Warren (Willie Standring): on Bahram 407–8, 411, 421–2, 428; on Bobsleigh 388, 392–3, 397–8, 401–2; on Windsor Lad 422–3
Hindus in India 16
Hirst, Sir Hugo 297
Hirtzel, Sir Arthur 35
His Highness the Aga Khan (Greenwall) 65
Hislop, John 171, 186, 191, 459
Hitler, Adolf 52–3, 54
Hogg, Capt. 428
Horlock, F. W. 390
horse pedigrees 88–9, 92, 118–19, 122; *see also* breeding systems; Dosage System

horse price value 128
horse racing in Britain 165, 175–6
Hotspur (*Daily Telegraph*) 433
Howard de Walden, Thomas Scott-Ellis, 8th Baron 324
Hulme, George 103, 105
Hydari, Sir Akbar 46
Hyde, Sir Charles 293–4, 361, 377

Illustrated Sporting and Dramatic News 359, 383
India 10, 43–4, 60
India in Transition (Aga Khan III) 31
Indian Congress Party 12
Iran (Persia) 29
Ireland, studs owned by Aga Khan III 121–2
Irwin, Edward Wood, Lord (later 1st Earl of Halifax) 43

Jackson, Stanley 65
James, Mrs. Arthur 310, 346
Jarvis, Bridget 219
Jarvis, C. 346
Jarvis, Isobel 219
Jarvis, Jack 292, 477
Jarvis, Ryan 219
Jarvis, William 219
Jarvis, William Rose 219
Jelliss, Henri 309
Jersey, George Child-Villiers, 8th Earl of 288, 323
Jersey, Margaret Elizabeth Child-Villiers, Countess of 4
Jockey Club: and doping of horses 91; membership of 149, 214; Rule 86 change 299; running of racing 175, 308, 456, 467
Jockey Club Stakes, Newmarket 308, 381–2
Joel, Jack 286, 293
Joel, Solly 120, 123, 292–3, 295
Johnson, Dr. 30
Johnson, Noble 317
Johnstone, Rae 166, 305, 313
Jones, Bobby 138, 482–3
Jooma, Jiva 11
Juddmonte Farms, USA 206–7, 443
July Cup, Newmarket 388

juvenile races 356–7

Kann, Edouard 123
Karim, Abdul (the Munshi) 8
Karsavina, Tamara 23
Kenny, Mr. 5
Keylock, Harry Edward 191–2
Khalid bin Abdullah Al Saud 209
Khan, Aly Salman *see* Aly Khan, Prince
Kingsclere stables, Newbury 222
Kitchener, Herbert, 1st Earl 27
Kohalevska, Josefina 23

La Coquenne stud, France 123
Labrot, Sylvester W. 156
Labrousse, Yvette (Yvonne) Blanche: and Aga Khan III 57–9, 63, 64, 70, 76; buys horses 167–8; wins cheese 180
Lambton, George: background 89–92; and doping 91–2; and Mumtaz Mahal 101–2; purchases of horses 92–5, 97–9, 108–15, 125; and Swynford 319–20; and Teresina 95–6; work for Lord Derby 223–33
Lambton, John, 5th Earl of Durham 224–5, 242
Lamington, Charles Cochrane-Baillie, 2nd Baron 14, 16
Langtry, Lillie (Lady de Bathe) 286
Lant, Thomas 242, 256, 307, 401
Lassy stud, France 163
Lawson, Joe 152, 236, 306–7, 427
Leader, Colledge 289, 355, 398–9, 401, 404
Ledlie, Mr. A. H. 100
Leicester, Sir Charles 460
Livock, Mr. 320
Lloyd George, David 31–2, 52
Loder, Giles 324, 350
Loder, John 187
Long, Capt. (Augur) 352, 366, 388–9, 395, 402–3, 416
Lonsdale, Hugh Lowther, 5th Earl of 293
Lort Phillips, F. 336
Lottery System *see* Dosage System

Lowe, Bruce 187–8
Lowther, Hugh, 5th Earl of Lonsdale 293
Luro, Horatio 205
Lyle, R. C. 432

Machell, Capt. 382
Mackean, Mrs. C. L. 303
Magliano, Rosa 22
Magliano, Theresa (Ginetta) 20–4, 32–3, 39–40
Mahdi Khan, Giuseppe (Mohammed) 23–4
Maher, Danny 313
Mankato (J. B. Robertson) 101
Mansfield, H. 187–8
Marly-le-Ville stud, France 163
Marsh, Marcus: and Aga Khan III 69, 151, 160, 168, 170–3, 213; and Aly Khan 173; and Freddie Fox 304; successes 243
Marsh, Richard 333–4
Mary of Teck, Queen 15, 42, 44, 417
Mason, P. 323
Massard, Jean 177
Massenet, Jules 20
Maugham, Somerset 66–7, 76–7
Mautner-Markhof, Herr Von 221
McAlpine, Sir Malcolm 427
McCalmont, Dermot 289, 345, 352
McCalmont, Harry 308
McCann, Pete 205–6
McGrath, Joe 213
McLeod, Sir Charles 359, 366
McPhail, L. S. 177
Meux, Sir Hedworth 291
middle distance races 306–7, 418, 441–2
Middle Park Stakes, Newmarket 363–5, 455–6
Miller, Mrs. G. B. 309
Mills, Mrs. Ogden 19
miners' strike (1920) 290
Minto, Gilbert Elliot-Murray-Kynynmound, 4th Earl of 16
Mohammed bin Rashid Al Maktoum, Sheikh 207, 209
Montagu, Edwin 35–6
Montagu, Venetia 31–2, 89
Morley, John 16

Morris, Tony 190–1
Mountbatten, Louis, 1st Viscount Mountbatten of Burma 60
Muller, Robert 145, 161–3
Munnings, Sir Alfred 221
Murless, Noel 173–4, 178
Muslims in India 16
Mussolini, Benito 53–4, 216

National Breeders Produce Stakes, Sandown Park 348–9, 455
National Strike (1926) 291
Nehru, Jawaharlal 60, 79
Nesbit, Evelyn 19–20
Nevett, Billy 272
New Dosages of the Thoroughbred (Varola) 192
Newmarket: Dewhurst Stakes 363–5; Jockey Club Stakes 308, 381–2; July Cup 388; Middle Park Stakes 363–5, 455–6; Princess of Wales's Stakes 381; Two Thousand Guineas 387–8
Nightingale, Florence 9
Nobel Peace Prize 35–6
Noble, Sir George 298
North American racing 206, 440–1
North American Triple Crown race wins 441, 446–7
Northcote, Henry Stafford, 1st Baron Northcote 11, 12

O'Brien, Aiden 209
O'Brien, Vincent 444
O'Neill, Frank 220
Ongar stud, Ireland 122, 153, 174
Oppenheimer, Anthony 440

Paget, Dorothy 146–7, 347
Park, James H. (Jimmy) 245
Parkinson, J. J. 131
Parkinson, Jim 460
Pattern system 165
Patton, George S. 161
Peacocke, Colonel 343
Pedigree Theories and the Science of Genetics (Binns and Morris) 190–1
pedigrees of horses 88–9, 92, 118–19, 122; *see also* breeding systems; Dosage System

Pembroke, Reginald Herbert, 15th Earl of 137
Perryman, Dick 307, 348, 359, 392
Persia 29
Philipps, Sir Laurence 360
Piggot, Lester 444
Pius XI, Pope 53
Pledge, W. T. de 323
Plummer, Mrs E. 99, 336, 405–6
Porter, John 222
Pratapsinhrao, Maharaja of Baroda 162
Pratt, Fred 285–6
Prevost, Andre 122
prices of horses, relative 128
Primrose, Harry, 6th Earl of Rosebery 214–16, 292, 360, 361–2, 477
Prince, Prophet and Sportsman (Jackson) 65
Princess of Wales's Stakes, Newmarket 381
prize cheeses 180
prize money system: Aga Khan III discussed 148, 164; middle distance races 306, 418; values 128, 175, 348–9, 369–70, 379–81, 387–8, 455
Pryor, T. 108
Puccini, Giacomo 20

race experience for juvenile horses 356–7
race times 454
Racing Post Trophy (*Timeform Gold Cup*), Doncaster 455–6
racing speed 396, 422
Rafael, Ralph 68
Rajpipla, Maharaja of 304
Rapier (*Illustrated Sporting and Dramatic News*) 359, 383
rating of horses 370–4, 435–6
Ratliffe, Mrs. T. H. 336
Razza Bellata stable, Italy 222
Read, W. A. 293
Redman, A. J. 347
Reynolds, Brayley 328
Richards, Clifford 296
Richards, Gordon: and Big Game 473, 477–8; and Buckleigh 385; champion jockey 294–5, 296–7; and

Felicitation 240; and Fred Darling 301; and Joe Childs 311; and Lady Marjorie 299–300; and Nahar 177; and Nasrullah 261–2; and Palestine 273; and Persian Gulf 482; retained by Aga Khan III 149, 164, 251; and Roi de Paris 305; and Rustom Mahal 107; and Taj Akbar 240, 250; and Tehran 265, 267; and Theft 348, 387; and Turkhan 259, 468–9; and Ujiji 264; and Umiddad 265–6, 482; and Up Rivers 308
Richmond Stakes, Goodwood 356
Rickaby, Bridget 219
Rickaby, William (Bill) 219
Rickman, Eric 227, 247, 277, 279–80, 405–6
Rivaud, Comte de 118, 426
Robert, Lucien 328
Robertson, J. B. (Mankato) 101
Robinson, Mrs. C. B. 367
Robinson, Peter 179–80
Robinson, W. T. (Jack) 86
Roosevelt, Theodore 19, 53
Roper-Lawrence, Sir Walter 13–15
Rosebery, Harry Primrose, 6th Earl of 214–16, 292, 360, 361–2, 477
Rothermere, Harold Harmsworth, 1st Viscount 67
Rothschild, Anthony de 228
Rothschild, Edouard de 326
Rothschild, James de 285–6
Rothschild, Nathaniel de, 1st Baron 220
Rous Memorial Stakes, Goodwood 356
Russia 26
Rutherford, Sir John 112–13, 131, 236, 300

Sadruddin, Prince 45, 63, 409
Saint Crespin stud, France 123, 163
Sallymount stud, Ireland 122, 153, 174
Sanders, Horace 179
Sandown Park: Eclipse Stakes

381–2; National Breeders Produce Stakes 348–9, 455
Sandwich Stud 170, 213
Sanford, John 220
Sassoon, Sir Victor 234
Savill, Mr. W. M. 100–1
Scobie, Norman 294
Scott-Ellis, Thomas, 8th Baron Howard de Walden 324
Scott, John 219
Semblat, Charles 180
Shaffer, Mr. C. B. 121
Shah, Lady Ali *see* Ali Shah, Lady
Shahzadi Begum 6–7, 13, 21–2
Shaw, George Bernard 53
Sheshoon stud, Ireland 121–2, 153, 170, 174
Simpson, Wallis (later Duchess of Windsor) 48
Sirett, Jackie 143, 433
Smirke, Charlie: and Aga Khan III 144, 163–4, 292–3; and Bahram 429, 432, 433, 449; and Frank Butters 250–2; and Marcus Marsh 174; and Michael Beary 138, 302; at Newbury 360; and other horses 106, 124, 168–9, 171–2, 179, 252, 256, 314, 467; personality 249–52; on riders and jockeys 279; and Windsor Lad 244, 304, 307, 449
Smith, Doug 279
Soltykoff, Prince Dimitri 220
Spear, Nathan 220
speed, breeding for 439–43, 447–8
Spencer, A. W. B. 323
St Leger Stakes, Doncaster 430, 443–4
Stalin, Joseph 53–4
stamina, breeding for 439–43
Standring, Willie (Warren Hill): on Bahram 407–8, 411, 421–2, 428; on Bobsleigh 388, 392–3, 397–8, 401–2; on Windsor Lad 422–3
Stanley, Edward, 17th Earl of Derby: antipathy towards Aga Khan III 149, 160, 211–12, 214, 215–16; on Epsom Derby (1935) 408–9; and Frank Butters 222–5, 230–3; horses raced 268, 286, 320–1, 347,

355, 361, 367, 404, 474;
successes compared to Aga
Khan III 193–4
Stanley House, Newmarket
222–3, 232–3
Stern, Sir Albert 349
Stevenson, Frances 31–2
Story, W. F. 346
Stoute, Sir Michael 253
Sullivan, D. 363

Tatem, William, 1st Baron
Glanely: attempt to buy
Teresina 96; and Gordon
Richards 301; horses raced
296–7, 304, 323, 361–2,
384–5; sold bloodstock to
Maj. Allnatt 157
Tattersall Sale Stakes,
Doncaster 361
Tattersall, Somerville 291
Taylor, Alec 119, 223
Taylor, John Henry 32, 68
Templeman, Fred 297, 311
Thaw, Harry K. 19–20
thermocautery 123
thunderstorm at Ascot (1930)
297–8
Tierney, Gene 62
Timeform Gold Cup, Doncaster
455–6
Timeform ratings 371–4
times of races 454
Topper, Charles 38
training methods 252–4, 277–8
Triple Crown race wins 439,
441, 442, 446–7, 455
Tully Stud, Ireland 86–7, 317
Tuyll, Baron de 296
Two Thousand Guineas,
Newmarket 387–8

Valiani, Zulfikarali 63–4
Vanderbilt, Alfred G. 156
Vanderbilt, William K. 84
Varola, Franco 192, 459
Victoria, Queen and Empress of
India 7, 8, 12

Villaneuva, Benito 132
Villiers, George Child-, 8th
Earl of Jersey 288, 323
Villiers, Margaret Elizabeth
Child-, Countess of Jersey 4
Vincent, Edgar, 1st Viscount
D'Abernon 113–14
Volterra, M. 166
Vuillier, John-Joseph 88–9,
101, 112, 122–3, 145, 194;
see also Dosage System
Vuillier, Madame 145, 162–3

Waddington, Charles 42
Waddington, Nesbit: and
Friar's Daughter 337; and
Marcus Marsh 173; on
pedigree systems 163, 191;
purchases of horses 122,
153, 158; retirement 174;
on thoroughbred race horses
447–8
Walker, George 206
Walker, Sir William Lee 11
Wallace, Edgar 299
Waugh, Charles 219, 234
Waugh, Dawson 219
Waugh, Evelyn 71–2
Waugh, James (Jimmy) 219
Waugh, Janet 219
Waugh, Tom 219
Waugh, Willie 219
Wavell, Archibald, 1st Earl
Wavell 59–60
Wavertree, William Hall-
Walker, 1st Baron 84–7,
185
Wellesley, Gerald 258, 260
Wernher, Sir Harold A. 305
Wernher, Zia, Lady 303, 350,
480
Weston, Tommy 224–7, 229,
232, 355, 414
Whatcombe Stables, Wantage,
Oxon.: horses at 103–4,
108–9, 116, 129, 323–4,
328, 349; Richard Dawson
at 90, 142; stud at 326, 331

Whigham, Margaret 48
White, James 287
White, Sandford 19–20
Whitford, Dick 187
Whitney, Cornelius Vanderbilt
156–7
Whitney, "Jock" 295, 350
Widener, J. E. 303
Wilhelm II, Emperor of
Germany 11
Willett, Peter 192
Williamstown stud, Ireland
174
Wills, Arnold 302
Wilson, A. Stanley 298
Wood, Edward, 1st Earl of
Halifax (formerly Lord
Irwin) 43
Woodward, William 366, 404
Woolavington, James
Buchanan, 1st Baron 242,
295–6, 299, 324, 355, 385
Wootton, Frank 286, 313
World War I 26–31
World War II: Aga Khan III
during 55–6, 160–1; racing
during 257–67, 467–8, 474
Wragg, Harry: and Aga Khan
III 34, 174, 178; and
Big Game 473, 475; and
Blenheim 136–7; and
Charlie Smirke 251; and
Glommen 292; and Khaled
212; and Michael Beary
138–9; and Mirza 252;
purchases of horses 167–8;
and Rustom Pasha 138–9;
and Sir Alfred Butt 245;
and Stardust 259; and Sun
Chariot 476; and Theft
414–15, 447; and Umidwar
304; and Watling Street 477
Wragg, Marjorie 180

York, Gimcrack Stakes 358–9

Index of Horses

Abernant 107, 453
Achtenan 401
Adept 307
Admiral Drake 335
Affirmed 446–7
African Boy 340
Aftab 117, 126
Afterthought 478
Airborne 251
Al Dakhil 212–13
Al Nasser 212
Al Wassat 212
Alaric 323
Alcazar 404, 446
Alibhai 97, 155
Alishah 97, 242, 244, 305, 307
All Joy 158
Alleged 444
Alondite 340
Alrabia 340
Alycidon 193–4
Alydar 446–7
Alykhan (Tereson) 307, 347
American Pharoah 200, 441
Americus 100
Americus Girl 100
Amilcar 113–14
Amina 273
Ankaret 309
Ann Gudman 133, 158
Ann of Austria 256
Antar II 399
Anwar 251
Apollo 390–1
April the Fifth 237
Ard Patrick 202
Arion 288
Assignation 403, 412
Assuerus 327
Astrakhan 165–6
Astre d'Or 130
Athasi 329
Athens Wood 453
Athford 325
Athnus 329
Atmah 286
Auf Weidersehen 390
Aurium 335
Australia 200–1, 209
Avena 329

Avenger II 162
Azamour 210

Baba Au Rhum 341, 350–1
Bad Joke 99
Badruddin: and Freddie Fox
  304–5, 307; handicap 384;
  pedigree of 106, 330; races
  of 106, 242, 304, 307; sale
  of 153
Bagman 346
Bahram: Aga Khan III attitude
  to 203; appearance 344–5,
  389–90, 410, 412, 430;
  breeding of 193, 201–2;
  claims to greatness 453–5,
  457–60; compared to best
  horses 450–2; compared to
  Bobsleigh 446; compared
  to criteria for great horses
  450–1; compared to
  other horses 374, 421–3;
  compared to Windsor Lad
  422–3, 453; contribution to
  Blandford's achievements
  326; coughing of 424–5,
  458; early years 343;
  and Freddie Fox 307–9;
  handicap 370; intelligence
  of 448; as juvenile 374–5;
  name 343–4; pedigree of
  316; see also Blandford;
  Friar's Daughter; ;
  personality 445; prize
  money 377, 462; race value
  339; rating of 370–2, 374,
  462; sale of 156–7, 211,
  215, 460–1; at stud 436–7,
  460, 461; training of: (1934)
  348, 355, 358, 362–3;
  (1935) 382–4, 386, 395,
  398–9, 401, 418, 424–6;
  Ascot (1935): St. James's
  Palace Stakes 419, 448–9,
  454; Doncaster (1935): St
  Leger Stakes 426–33, 449;
  Epsom (1935): Derby 398–
  403, 405–17; Goodwood
  (1934): Rous Memorial
  Stakes 357–8, 454;
  Lingfield (1935): Derby

Trial 400; Newmarket
  (1934): Boscawen (Post)
  Stakes 362–3, 454; Middle
  Park Stakes 308, 360,
  365–7, 454–5; Newmarket
  (1935): Two Thousand
  Guineas 308, 386–93,
  408; Sandown Park (1934):
  National Breeders Produce
  Stakes 348–52, 454–5; York
  (1934): Gimcrack Stakes
  358–9, 454
Bakhtawar 155, 340
Bala Hissar 99, 247–50
Bannaby 341
Bara Bibi 173–4
Barberry 412–13
Barrage 305
Bartaville 127
Battle Note 357
Bayardo 313, 430, 453, 454–5
Baytown 293–4
Beam 224–5
Beeswing 204
Begum 150
Behkabad 210
Belle Travers 256–7
Ben Marshall 355, 363, 375
Beresford 335
Bernardini 207
Bessborough 285
Bettina 321
Betty 471
Bhuidhaonach 290
Big Game 470, 473–9
Birikan 475
Birth Control 293
Black Arrow 322
Black Cherry 322, 325
Blanchailles 126
Blanche 322–3
Blandford 317–32; death
  of 328; and Dick Dawson
  90; early years 317, 323;
  pedigree of 317, 318–19,
  322, 323; races 323–5; at
  stud 201–2, 247, 325–32
Blanding 146–7
Blenheim: pedigree of 201–2,
  325; purchase of 126, 135;
  quality of 128, 330; races

of 132–3, 136–9; sale of 150–2, 211
Blondel 221
Blue Peter 442
Blue Skies 330
Blue Vision 305
Bobsleigh: appearance 385–6, 404; compared to Bahram 374, 421–2, 446; handicap 370–1; potential 377, 388–9, 404–5; Ascot (1934): *Windsor Castle Stakes* 347; Epsom (1935): *Derby* 398–404; Goodwood (1934): *Richmond Stakes* 352, 355–6; Newmarket (1935): *Limekiln Stakes* 404, 446; *Newmarket Stakes* 396–7; *Two Thousand Guineas* 387, 390–2, 396; Newmarket (1936): *Chippenham Stakes* 404; *Dullingham Stakes* 404
Bois Josselyn 313
Bois Roussel 154, 163, 335
Bold Ruler 213
Bold Venture 321
Bomba 286
Bombay Duck 93
Bongrace 291–2
Book Law 225
Boswell 246
Bosworth 229–30, 232–3
Bouldnor 390
Bower of Roses 335
Brantôme 326–8, 330
Brigadier Gerard 186–7, 448, 453
Brigand 285
Bright Bird 306
Bright Knight 119
Bright Lady 266
Brise Bise 111
British Empire 257
Bronzino 286, 313, 319
Brown Betty 335, 471
Brown Jack 186, 305
Buchan 111, 321–2
Buckleigh: Doncaster (1935): *St Leger Stakes* 426, 428, 430–2; Newmarket (1935): *Champion Stakes* 446; *Craven Stakes* 384–5; *St Leger* 435; *Two Thousand Guineas* 387, 390–1
Buisson Ardent 180
Bukhara 155

Bukumbi 155
Buland 129, 325
Buland Bala 126
Buland Bibi 127
Buland Dar 127
Bulandshar 239, 302, 330
Bull Dog 335
Bunker 361–2
Bura 155
Burnt Brown 341

Caerleon 232
California Chrome 206
Call Boy 455
Camelot 209, 434–5, 442–3
Cameronian 238, 298–301
Campanula 326
Canfield 296
Cap d'Ail 127
Cape Cross 200, 440
Captain Cuttle 324
Captain Fracasse 324
Caretta 371, 375
Cavalcade 321
Centeno 329
Chaleureux 198
Challedon 322
Challenger II 322
Charley's Mount 108
Cherry Lass 322
Chico 329
Chivalry 170
Choclo 329
Cimiez 116
Citation 167
Clarissimus 220
Claro 269–70
Claudius 467
Clovelly 155
Cobetto 270–1
Cobra 126
Colombo 157, 243, 304–5, 313, 422–3, 479
Colorado 223–4, 280
Comic Song 335
Common 238
Concertina 335
Concerto 471–2
Concordat 247
Consequential 359–60, 365–7, 371, 377, 387, 390–1
Conversion 401
Corejada 274
Coronach 224, 456–7
Cos 97–8, 109–10
Costaki Pasha 98, 130–1, 132, 139

Crawley Beauty 341
Crepello 442, 448
Cygnus 329
Cyrus 348

Daily Busy 341
Dalmary 330
Dancing Brave 448
Dandyprat 109
Danehill 199
Dante 453, 455
Dara 167
Dark Angel 440
Dark Japan 129
Darranour 341
Dastur 137, 145, 236–8, 301, 339
Dean Swift 320
Desert Cloud 387, 390
Deux Pour Cent 116
Dhoti 98–9, 256
Diableretta 169, 273–4
Diacquenod 112
Dialia 159
Dictator 349
Diolite 297
Diophon 99–100, 113, 119, 124–5, 150
Dix Pour Cent 116
Djebel 259, 466
Do Well 170
Dolabella 323, 470
Donatello II 330
Donzelon 291
Dorigen 241
Double Event 308
Double Life 480
Drake's Drum 323
Drogheda 90
Dubai Millennium 210, 448
Duke John 349–52, 398–9
Dunfermline 444
Dust Devil 169, 275–6

Eagle Snipe 99
Eastern Joy 341
Easton 385
Easy Goer 206, 447
Éclair 159, 212
Éclat 169, 275
Edward Tudor 251
El Condor Pasa 330
El Hawa 212
Empire Maker 207
Esprit du Nord 341
Esquire 340
Etiqueta Negra 341

Eton Blue 359–60
Eurydice 127

Fair Diana 295–6, 298
Fair Isle 228, 232
Fairbairn: appearance 350;
  Ascot (1935): *Prince
  of Wales's Stakes* 427;
  Waterford Stakes 427;
  Doncaster (1935): *St Leger
  Stakes* 426, 430–1; Epsom
  (1935): *Derby* 400, 403,
  407, 411–12; Goodwood
  (1935): *Sussex Stakes*
  427; Newmarket (1934):
  Two Thousand Guineas
  390; Newmarket (1935):
  Princess of Wales's Stakes
  427; Redcar (1935): *Great
  National Breeders Foal
  Plate* 427; Sandown Park
  (1934): *National Breeders
  Produce Stakes* 350–2; York
  (1935): *Great Yorkshire
  Stakes* 427
Fairhaven 403, 407, 411–12,
  435
Fairway: achievements 128,
  328–9; and Frank Butters
  232–3, 279–80; and Lord
  Derby 193–4; races of 129,
  225–7, 294
Falko 126
Farhad 126
Faris II 152
Farman Farma 126
Farmood 158
Faster Still 127
Fearless Fox 246
Felicitation: races of 239,
  240–1, 304, 306, 308–9,
  327; sale of 159
Felstead 329
Feola 310
Feridoon 116, 126
Ferry 321
Field Trial: compared to Theft
  447; Ascot: *King Edward
  VII Stakes* 427; Doncaster
  (1935): *St Leger Stakes*
  426–7, 430–3; Epsom
  (1935): *Derby* 403, 407,
  411–17; Lingfield (1935):
  Derby Trial 400
Fifinella 220
Fille D'Amour 339
Fille de Salut 158, 339

Fille D'Espoir 338
Firdaussi 137, 143, 145,
  236–7, 238–9, 302
Fironze Mahal 111
Firoze Din 155
First Son 403, 407, 412–15,
  417
Flash Bye 362–3, 426–8,
  430–1
Floreat Etona 127
Flying Orders 371, 376–7
Four Course 299
Foxglove II 153–4
Foxlaw 129
Fraise du Bois 179
Frankel 199, 209, 434, 443,
  448
Franklin 324
Fresh Fox 365–7, 419
Friar Marcus 333–5, 336
Friar's Daughter 333–42;
  bought by Dick Dawson 99,
  142; character 338; death
  of 338; descendents of 158;
  at gallops 103; pedigree of
  333–6; races of 334, 336–7;
  stud career 338–40
Frivolity 335
Full Ripe 322
Furrokh Siyar 106

Gainsborough 201, 228,
  423–4
Galicia 338
Galileo 199, 442–3
Gallinule 121
Gallorette 322
Galtee More 403–4
Ganga Singh 126
Garron Lass 335–6
Gay Baby 127
Gay Crusader 220, 423–4
Gino 97, 239–40, 304
Glommen 292
Glorious Devon 296
Godiva 466
Godolphin 348, 365–7, 371,
  375–6
Gold Bridge 472
Golden Araby 351
Golden Corn 324
Golden Horn 200, 440
Golden Knight 336
Golden Tiger 467–8
Golovine 179–80
Good Morning 330
Good Sport 296–7

Goyama 272
Grand Weather 330
Grande Vitesse 225
Great Bear 341
Grison 341
Grittar 329
Guadanini 341
Guest of Honour 386
Gynerium 346

Hafiz 176–7
Hairan: purchase of 147;
  rating of 370–1; Ascot
  (1934): *Coventry Stakes*
  346; Doncaster (1934):
  Champagne Stakes 361–2,
  375; Doncaster (1935): *St
  Leger Stakes* 426; Epsom
  (1935): *Derby* 398, 400,
  403, 405, 407, 409, 411–15;
  Goodwood (1935): *Sussex
  Stakes* 427; Newmarket
  (1934): *Dewhurst Stakes*
  309, 375; Newmarket
  (1935): *Newmarket Stakes*
  396
Hajibibi 109
Hakem 127
Hakim 127–9, 335
Half Caste 322
Halim 126
Hamoaze 321–2
Happi 359–60
Happy Knight 269
Hard Ridden 188
Harina 329
Harinero 329
Harzand 183, 443
Hastra 159, 165–6
Heronslea 472
Herringbone 481
High Chancellor 482–3
Highland Lament 351, 352–3
Hilla 347
Hindoo Holiday 348, 384,
  399
Hippius 466
Holmbush 170
Honeydew 204
Honeysuckle 204
Hunter's Moon 229
Hurstwood 291
Hyder Ali 159, 212
Hyderabad 158–9, 212
Hyperides 477–8
Hyperion 111, 193–4, 212–13,
  240, 302, 304

Imphal 251
Innes of Court 323
Iran 127
Irish Elegance 287–9
Isfandiar 143
Isinglass: compared to later
    horses 422; descendents of
    319, 322; laziness of 408;
    prize winnings 172; races
    of 308, 381–2, 417
Isthmus 297

Jan Mahal 114
Jan Renee 114
Japetus 412–13
Jean's Folly 322
Jeddah 9, 84
The Jesuit 346
Jet Pilot 330
Jindani 114, 465
John Amendall 322
John O'Gaunt 319
Joy Boy 158

Kalamoun 178
Keenan 130
Kennymore 319
Keysoe 321
Khairunissa 178
Khaled 159, 212, 268–9
Khalif 341
Khorassan 169
Khorsheed 131, 143
Khoshbood 155
Kinchinjunga 313
King of Clubs 124
King Salmon 244, 307
Kingsem 360, 361, 371, 377
Kingston Black 322
Kisaki 169, 275
Knight Error 298, 302
Knighted 346
Kopi 295
Kwang-Su 220
Kyoei Promise 341

La Boni 110
La Furka 330
La Gaiete 356
La Li 110–11
La Mauri 110
La Voleur 99
Lady Gabriel 363
Lady Josephine 100–1, 102
Lady Juror 101, 102
Lady Lawless 114
Lady Marjorie 299–300

Lady Peregrine 323
Lady Sybil 264
Lambert Simnel 330
Lancegaye 321
Landsong 296
Lashkari 210
Le Capucin 113
Le Grand Duc 255–6
Le Phare 136, 140, 141–2, 295
Le Voleur 136
Lemberg 313, 319–20, 455
Lemnarchus 299, 335
Leonardo 96
Light Brocade 242
Lights o'London 143
Literato 341
Livernon 341
Lord Bill 234
Lorenzaccio 330
Louise 310
Lucky Patch 244–5, 382–3

The MacNab 297
Mah Iran 107, 260
Mah Mahal 107
Maharajah 127
Mahmoud: Frank Butters on
    246; and Freddie Fox 310;
    pedigree of 107, 201–2;
    races won 150, 245, 249;
    retirement of 203; sale
    of 148, 156–7, 211, 215,
    245–6, 330
Maintenon 202
Maltravers 307, 356, 371, 376
Malva 323
Mambaka 155
Manacor 341
Manna 112, 124
Maori Venture 329
Mario 127
Marmaduke Jinks 365, 367,
    390
Marsa 166
Masai King 173
Masaka 263, 271–2
Masala 98
Masked Light 274
Master Boatman 167–8
Mate 305–6, 308
Meena 126
Mehrali 158
Mid-day Sun 219, 222
Midlothian 229
Midstream 330
Migoli 107, 270–2
Military Court 179

Mill Reef 448, 453
Minoru 86, 87
Mir Zadeh 158
Mirawala 115
Mirza 106, 152–3, 252
Miss Erene 308
Mistress Ford 328–9
Mkata 155
Moemen 158
Mokan 221
Montjeu 442
Moondust 169, 275–6
Morals of Marcus 335
Morning Dew 330
Morning Madam 330
Morning Wings 330
Morogoro 159
Moti Begum 158, 239, 240
Moti Mahal 125
Motivator 200
Mr Jinks 229
Mrs Rustom 98, 147, 242, 244,
    304, 326
Mulji 158
Mumtaz Begum 107, 330
Mumtaz Mahal 100–8, 113,
    119, 178
Muzloom 157, 158, 340
My Love 166, 193
Myrobella 470–2
Myron 339

Nahar 148–9, 177
Naishapur 268
Nansen 114
Nashwan 443
Nasrullah 107, 159, 194, 213,
    261–4, 481
Nassovian 220
Nathoo 271–2, 273
Near Relation 244–5
Nearco 453
Nearctic 205–6
Neemah 172
Neocracy 270
Neron 179
Newminster 204
Niceas 110, 113
Nijinsky 442, 443–4, 448
Niloufer 339
Nimbus 442
Nizami 106–7
Noble Star 301
Noor 148–9, 167, 271, 273
Northern Dancer 199, 205
Nuccio 170, 175
Nunnykirk 204

Nun's Veil 335
Nureyev 330
Nushirawan 126
Nymph Errant 350–1

Obash 155
Ocean Swell 265, 267–8
Omaha 255, 435
Open Champion 158
Orban 341
Orby 404
Orchestration 335
Ormonde 222, 417
Orpen 236, 300
Orwell 238
Ouija Board 201

Palariva 177–8
Palestine 168–9, 213–14, 241,
    273–4
Palotta 100
Pampas Grass 346
Paola 93, 110, 113
Papyrus 94–5, 96
Parsan 339
Parwiz 126, 130, 132
Pasch 329
Passing Shot 341
Pay Up 246
Peaceful Walter 412–14
Pearl Diver 272
Pernod 341
Persian Gulf 266, 480–4
Persimmon 336
Petite Etoile 107, 178, 193–4,
    203, 272, 275
Petition 270–2
Phalaris 194, 201
Phanarite 114–15
Pharacre 302–3
Pharamond 225
Pharos 194
The Phoenix 340
Piachay 341
Pigling Brand 330
Pinza 172
Pioneerof the Nile 200
Plack 105
Plassy 365, 367, 426–8, 430–1,
    435
Plucky Liege 335
Plymouth Sound 387, 390
Poisoned Arrow 289–90
Polette 357
Polyphontes 120
Pomare 123
Pomme au Four 303

Pomme d'Api 144
Pommern 423–4
Pont l'Eveque 259, 467
Portfolio 384, 419, 435
Pot- Au-Feu 109, 119, 121
Powerful Prince 384, 390
Precipitation 480
Press Gang 295–6, 298
Prestige 202
Pretty Polly 121, 202, 277, 455
Primero 329, 330
Prince Firouze 127
Prince Palatine 86, 430
Prince Plunkett 126
Prince Simon 168
Prince Taj 181
Propaganda 303
Proud Chieftain 342
Pry II 403, 412–15, 426, 428,
    430–1
Purdysburn 285
Purslet 285

Quadrille Boy 359–60
Quakeress 103
Quashed 309, 435, 446
Queen of Baghdad 148–9
Queen of Bombay 155
Queen of Scots 148
Queen of Simla 148, 256
Qurrat-al-Ain 127, 131–2, 140

Radamedes 347, 357–8
Radiancy 286
Rajput Princess 341
Ramtapa 152
Ranjit Singh 127, 128
Red Biddy 351–2
Regal Exception 341
Regal Light 342
Reichenau 219
Reine Isaure 330
Research 335
Ribbon 292, 481
Ribot 448, 453
Right Win 341
Rigolo 272
Rivalry 296
Rivaz 263
Robber Chief 302, 404
Robin Goodfellow: other races
    419, 435; Ascot (1934):
    New Stakes 347; Derby
    (1935): *Breeders St Leger*
    425; Epsom (1935): *Derby*
    411–14; Liverpool (1935):
    St Leger 435; Newmarket

(1935): *Two Thousand
    Guineas* 387, 389–91; York
    (1935): *Great Yorkshire
    Stakes* 425
Rock Sand 423–4
Roi de Paris 305
Rooz 143
Rosa Bonheur 162
Rose of England 228
Rose Royale II 180–1
Rosecrag 419
Roseland 335
Rosewell 335
Roshun 116
Royal Drake 166
Royal Minstrel 147, 295
Royal Palace 442
Russian Pearl 341
Rustom Mahal 107
Rustom Pasha 98, 132, 136–9,
    153

Sadler's Wells 199, 330, 442
Sadri 339
Sadruddin 339
Saint Crespin III 270–1, 329
Saint Illiers 110
Sakura Chiyono-O 341
Sakura Hokuto-O 341
Saleve 126
Salmon-Trout 100, 119–20
Saltash 321–2
Samanga 155
Samos 94
Samson 342
Samya 94
San Gennaro 221
Sandals 303
Sansofine 357–8
Sansovino 321
Santeve 286
Santorin 435
Sapience 94
Saraikala 150
Sardanapale 202
Satyr 349
Saucer 99
Saucy Sue 321
Scamp 323–4
Scapa Flow 338
Sceptre 202
Screamer 361–2, 387, 390–1,
    403, 412–14
Sea Bequest: other races 385;
    Epsom (1935): *Derby* 398,
    400, 403, 407, 412–14;
    Newmarket (1935): *Two*

Thousand Guineas 387, 389–91
Sea Bird 448
Sea The Stars 440, 443, 448
Secretariat 213
Seistan 108
Selim Hassan 155
Seminole 303
Sendawar 210
Sensualita 181
Sequalo 351
Shadai Kagura 341
Shah Rookh 157, 158
Shahali 97, 346, 363, 371, 376, 400
Shahpoor 97, 158
Shami 135, 147
Shamsuddin 111, 302
Sheldrake 310
Shere Ali 160
Shergar 182, 448, 456
Sibell 305
Sica Boy 340
Signorina 198
Signorinetta 198
Silver Hussar 116
Singida 155
Sir Dane 342
Sir Gallahad III 335
Sir Ivor 442
Sirdar Singh 127
Sister Clover 228
Sky High 268–9
Slieve Gallion 404
Soga 155
Solar Ray 426–7, 430–3, 435
Solario 112–13, 124, 329
Soldado 329
Solenoid 303
Solicitor General 330
Southern 289
Spearmint 202
Spike Island 324
St Botolph 412, 414
St Germans 119–20, 291, 321–2
St Simon 185–6, 330, 333, 335
Stafaralla 115, 152, 256
Stamford 125
Star of Gujrath 162
Star of Iran 107
Stardust 153, 212, 257, 259, 469
Steady Aim 269
Straight Deal 480–1
Straitlace 105
Sultan Mahomed 255

Sun Cap 340
Sun Chariot 475–6, 478
Sun Stream 268, 322
Sunday Silence 206, 447
Sunny Boy 340
Sunstar 202, 391
Swaps 212
Swynford 286, 313, 318–22

Tabriz 169, 275
Tahir 152–3, 256
Tahiri 342
Taj Akbar 249–50, 255
Taj Kasra 145
Taj Mah 109, 118–19, 133
Taj Mahal 109
Tamar 321–2
Tambara 169, 275
Tant Mieux 465–6
Tantieme 116
Tatra 291
Tayeh 169
Teacup 132–3
Teasel 467
Teheran 108
Tehran 115, 152, 185–6, 194, 265, 267–8
Teresina 95–7, 158, 204
Tereson (Alykhan) 347
Tetracaun 126
The Tetrarch 201–2
Tetratema 289, 326
Thatch 330
Thatching 330
Theft: compared to Bahram 447; handicap 370–1; pedigree of 99; Ascot (1934): *Windsor Castle Stakes* 347–8, 355–6; Ascot (1935): *Jersey Stakes* 418, 447; Epsom (1935): *Coronation Cup* 447; *Derby* 398, 400, 403, 405, 407, 412–16, 447; Goodwood (1934): *Ham Produce Stakes* 352, 355; Newbury (1934): *Greenham Plate* 384, 447; Newmarket (1934): *Buckenham (Post Produce) Stakes* 352; Newmarket (1935): *Two Thousand Guineas* 387, 390–2, 408, 447; Sandown Park (1934): *National Breeders Produce Stakes* 348–9, 351–2, 454; Sandown Park (1935): *Eclipse Stakes* 447

Theresina 97, 139, 142, 158, 480
Tiara 98
Tiderace 384
Tiffin 131, 295
Time Charter 329
Toboggan 225, 227, 280
Topsider 330
Torchere 228
Toro 181
Tororo 158
Totalisator 117
Toubo 155
Trade Wind 348, 355, 362–3, 384
Tramaway 382–3, 400
Tranquil 96, 98, 321
Trelawny 293
Treve 200
Tricky Aunt 98, 110
Trigo 133, 325
True Tilda 357
Tudor Minstrel 270, 271, 453
Tulyar 170–2, 174–5, 215, 270, 329, 459
Turkhan 97, 257, 259, 465–70
Turtle Soup 142, 158
Twenty Grand 321

Udaipur 123, 202, 236–8, 326
Uganda 123
Ujiji 97, 158, 264, 478
Ukrania 118–19, 123
Umiddad: pedigree of 123, 330; races of 263–4, 265–6, 480–1, 482–3; successes 159
Umidwar: pedigree of 202; races of 242, 243–4, 304–5, 307–8, 326; at stud 329
Una 158, 241
Up Rivers 308
Usenge 155
Ut Majeur 140–1, 298
Uvira 155

Vaguely Noble 448
Valhalla 108
Vallema 345–6
Vayrann 210
Veldschoen 361–2
Velvet 110
Vermeil II 399
Vermillion Pencil 111–12
Via Media 158
Voleuse 99, 247

Walter Gay 295
Waterval 335
Watling Street 474–8
Whirlaway 330
White Eagle 323
Why Hurry 330
Wild Violet 330
William the Third 335
Winandermere 346
Windsail 245
Windsor Lad: and Blandford
    326, 328–30; compared to
    Bahram 414, 422–3, 453;
    Chester (1934): *Chester*

Vase 304–5; Epsom (1934):
    Derby 244, 305; Epsom
    (1935): *Coronation Cup*
    413; Newmarket (1933):
    Criterion Stakes 456;
    Sandown Park (1934):
    Eclipse Stakes 244, 307;
    Sandown Park (1935):
    Eclipse Stakes 447; York
    (1934): *Great Yorkshire
    Stakes* 360
Windybrae 299
Wool Winder 404
Workforce 209

Wychwood Abbot 435, 446

Yakimour 256
Yasmin 180
Yentoi 286
Young Lover 240–1

Zambo 110, 112, 124
Zarkava 448
Zingaro 384, 419
Zionist 111, 112, 120–1,
    123–4, 147
Zoroastra 110
Zug 341

Index of Races

Alexandra Park
Enfield Plate: (1923) Friar's
Daughter 336
Ascot
Bessborough Handicap: (1929)
Parwiz 132
Cesarewitch Handicap: (1943)
Bright Lady 266
Chesham Stakes: (1928)
Costaki Pasha 98, 130–1;
(1929) Rustom Pasha 132;
(1934) Shahali 346, 376;
(1937) Tahir 256; (1938)
Dhoti 99, 256; (1955)
Palariva 177
Churchill Stakes: (1932) Orpen
236; (1934) Felicitation
240, 306
Cork, Orrery Stakes: (1930)
Costaki Pasha 98
Coronation Stakes: (1923)
Paola, Teresina 93, 96;
(1924) Mumtaz Mahal 105;
(1925) Fironze Mahal 111;
(1926) Moti Mahal 125;
(1928) Toboggan 227;
(1930) Qurrat-al-Ain 127,
140; (1932) Udaipur 236–7;
(1935) Ankaret 309; (1948)
Masaka 272–3; (1950)
Tambara 169; (1957) Toro
181
Coventry Stakes: (1914) Lady
Josephine 101; (1921)
Drake's Drum 323; (1924)
Nansen 114; (1925)
Colorado 224; (1927)
Fairway 225; (1929) Diolite
297; (1934) Hairan etc. 346;
(1937) Mirza 106; (1939)
Hippius, Turkhan 257,
465–6; (1942) Nasrullah
262; (1945) Khaled 268–9;
(1949) Palestine 273
Errol Stakes: (1950) Fraise du
Bois 179
Fern Hill Stakes: (1923) Cos
98; (1929) Tiffin 295;
(1930) Diolite 297; (1933)
Myrobella 471; (1934)

Knighted 346; (1938) Mirza
106
Gold Cup: (1909) Bomba 286;
(1910) Bayardo 454–5;
(1912) Prince Palatine 86;
(1913) Prince Palatine 86;
(1927) Dark Japan 129;
(1930) Bosworth 230;
(1932) Ut Majeur 141;
(1933) Orpen 236; (1934)
Felicitation, Hyperion 159,
240–1; (1935) Brantôme
328; (1936) Omaha,
Quashed 435; (1943) Ujiji
264; (1945) Tehran 267
Gold Vase: (1926) Bongrace
292; (1927) Beam 225;
(1931) Pomme d'Api 144;
(1935) Flash Bye 428;
(1938) Foxglove II 154
Hardwicke Stakes: (1910)
Swynford 319; (1911)
Swynford 320; (1926)
Lancegaye 321
Jersey Stakes: (1935) Theft
418, 447
King Edward VII Stakes: (1929)
Bosworth 229; (1931)
Khorsheed 131; (1932)
Dastur 238; (1935) Field
Trial, Plassy, Solar Ray
427; (1947) Migoli 271
King George VI Stakes: (1952)
Tulyar 171
King's Stand Stakes: (1956)
Palariva 178
New Stakes: (1921) Scamp
324; (1927) Hakim 129;
(1929) Blenheim 132–3;
(1932) Ramtapa 152;
(1934) Robin Goodfellow,
Radamedes 347, 358;
(1935) Mahmoud 310;
(1936) Le Grand Duc 255;
(1946) Petition 270
Prince of Wales's Stakes:
(1925) Zionist 124; (1928)
Hunter's Moon 229; (1930)
Ut Majeur 140; (2000)
Sendawar 210

Princess Elizabeth Stakes:
(1946) Neocracy 270
Princess Margaret Stakes:
(1949) Tambara 275
Queen Alexandra Stakes:
(1926) Vermillion Pencil
111–12
Queen Anne Stakes: (1951)
Neron 179
Queen Elizabeth II Stakes:
(1955) Hafiz 176
Queen Mary Stakes: (1922) Cos
97, 109–10; (1923) Mumtaz
Mahal 104; (1924) Fironze
Mahal 111; (1925) Moti
Mahal 125; (1929) Qurrat-
al-Ain 127, 132, 140;
(1934) Caretta, Highland
Lament, Red Biddy 352–3,
375; (1937) Queen of Simla
148, 256; (1938) Belle
Travers 256–7; (1941) Mah
Iran 260; (1945) Rivaz
263; (1947) Masaka 271;
(1949) Diableretta 274
Rous Memorial Stakes: (1934)
Alishah 244; (1948)
Petition 272
Royal Hunt Cup: (1919) Arion,
Irish Elegance 288; (1930)
Diolite 297
Royal Lodge Stakes: (1949)
Tabriz 275; (1950) Fraise
du Bois 179; (1952)
Neemah 172
St. James's Palace Stakes:
(1905) Cherry Lass 322;
(1910) Swynford 319;
(1922) Captain Cuttle 324;
(1925) Zambo 110, 124;
(1928) Royal Minstrel 147;
(1930) Rustom Pasha 98;
(1931) Cameronian 300;
(1935) Bahram etc. 309,
419, 448–9, 454; (1946)
Khaled 269; (1950)
Palestine 169
Victoria Cup: (1948) Petition
272
Waterford Stakes: (1934)

Badruddin 242; (1935)
Fairbairn 427
Windsor Castle Stakes: (1921)
   Blandford 323; (1922)
   Tricky Aunt 110; (1922)
   Tricky Aunt, Voleuse 98–9;
   (1930) Tea Cup 132; (1931)
   Taj Kasra 145; (1934)
   Bobsleigh, Theft, Maltravers
   347, 355–6, 376; (1949)
   Tabriz 275
Austrian Derby
(1917) San Gennaro 221
(1918) Reichenau 219
Austrian Two Thousand
   Guineas
(1912) Mokan 221
(1913) Blondel 221
(1917) San Gennaro 221

Baltimore
Preakness Stakes: (1978)
   Affirmed, Alydar 446–7
Belmont Park
Belmont Stakes: (1931)
   Twenty Grand 321; (1978)
   Affirmed, Alydar 446–7

Calcutta, India
Viceroy Cup: (1928) Astre d'Or
   130
Chantilly
Prix de Diane (French Oaks):
   (1929) Ukrania 118
Prix du Dangu: (1935)
   Brantôme 328
Prix du Jockey Club (Derby):
   (1906) Maintenon 202;
   (1923) Le Capuchin, Niceas
   113; (1924) Pot-Au-Feu
   109, 119, 121
Chepstow
Welsh Oaks: (1928) Toboggan
   227
Chester
Chester Cup: (1927) Dark
   Japan 129; (1932) Ut
   Majeur 141; (1934)
   Blue Vision 305; (1956)
   Golovine 179–80
Chester Vase: (1925)
   Vermillion Pencil 111–12;
   (1932) Bulandshar 239,
   302; (1933) Hyperion,
   Shamsuddin 302; (1934)
   Windsor Lad 304–5; (1936)
   Taj Akbar 249

Dee Stakes: (1950) Khorassan
   169; (1951) Fraise du Bois
   179
Ormonde Stakes: (1952) Tulyar
   171
Curragh
Anglesey Stakes: (1904) Cherry
   Lass 322
Irish Derby: (1922) Spike
   Island 324; (1925) Zionist
   123–4; (1928) Baytown
   294; (1932) Dastur 237–8;
   (1940) Turkhan etc. 257,
   467; (1943) The Phoenix
   340; (1946) Caro 269;
   (1951) Fraise du Bois
   179
Irish Oaks: (1930) Theresina
   97, 139, 142; (1948) Masaka
   273
Irish Two Thousand Guineas:
   (1928) Baytown 294;
   (1943) The Phoenix 340;
   (1946) Caro 269
Phoenix Plate: (1907)
   Americus Girl 100
St Leger: (1949) Moondust
   276; (1951) Do Well 170

Deauville
Grand Prix: (1955) Rose
   Bonheur 162
Prix Jacques le Marois: (1973)
   Kalamoun 178
Prix Morny: (1933) Brantôme
   327; (1934) Mistress Ford
   329
Derby
Breeders St Leger: (1935)
   Robin Goodfellow 425
Derby Cup: (1931) Ut Majeur
   141
Doncaster
Champagne Stakes: (1919)
   Southern 289; (1921)
   Golden Corn 324; (1923)
   Mumtaz Mahal 104; (1927)
   Fairway 225; (1929)
   Blenheim, Fair Diana 133,
   296; (1930) Turtle Soup
   142; (1932) Myrobella 471;
   (1933) Alishah 242; (1934)
   Consequential, Hairan,
   Kingsem 360, 361–2, 375,
   377; (1935) Mahmoud 245,
   310; (1936) Le Grand Duc
   255; (1937) Mirza 106;

(1946) Petition 270; (1949)
   Palestine 273
Doncaster Cup: (1912)
   Prince Palatine 86; (1926)
   Bongrace 292; (1927) Dark
   Japan 129
Lincoln Handicap: (1926)
   Zionist 124; (1927) Priory
   Park 293; (1931) Knight
   Error 298; (1955) Military
   Court 179
Park Hill Stakes: (1924)
   Charley's Mount 108;
   (1954) Bara Bibi 173
Portland Handicap: (1919)
   Irish Elegance 288
Portland Plate: (1909)
   Americus Girl 100
Prince of Wales Nursery:
   (1933) Pomme au Four 303
Rous Memorial Stakes: (1949)
   Kisaki 275
Scarborough Stakes: (1926)
   Bongrace, Glommen 292
St Leger Stakes: (1905) Cherry
   Lass 322; (1909) Bayardo
   455; (1909) Prince Palatine
   430; (1910) Bronzino,
   Lemberg, Swynford 286,
   313, 319; (1911) Prince
   Palatine 86, 430; (1919)
   Keysoe 321; (1923)
   Teresina, Tranquil 96,
   321; (1924) Salmon-Trout
   119–20; (1925) Zambo 110,
   112, 124; (1926) Coronach
   456; (1928) Fairway 227;
   (1929) Bosworth 229;
   (1930) Rustom Pasha,
   Ut Majeur 98, 138, 140;
   (1931) Cameronian, Orpen
   236, 300; (1932) Dastur,
   Firdaussi etc. 137, 236–8,
   302; (1933) Felicitation
   240; (1934) Umidwar 307;
   (1934) Umidwar, Windsor
   Lad 244, 456; (1935)
   Bahram etc. 426–33, 449;
   (1936) Boswell, Fearless
   Fox, Mahmoud 246; (1943)
   Nasrullah, Umiddad 262,
   264; (1944) Tehran 115;
   (1945) Naishapur 268;
   (1946) Anwar 251; (1947)
   Migoli 271; (1948) My
   Love 166; (1949) Dust
   Devil 276; (1951) Fraise

du Bois 179; (1952) Tulyar
171; (1977) Alleged,
Dunfermline 444
Tattersall Sale Stakes: (1934)
Bunker 361–2; (1937)
Stafaralla 152

Epsom
Acorn Plate: (1932) Una 241;
(1949) Diableretta 274
City and Suburban Handicap:
(1929) Parwiz 132
Coronation Cup: (1911)
Lemberg, Swynford 320;
(1913) Prince Palatine 86;
(1922) Franklin 324; (1924)
Solario 112; (1933) Dastur
238; (1934) Mate 305–6;
(1935) Theft, Windsor Lad
413, 447; (1948) Migoli
272; (1952) Nuccio 175
Derby: (1886) Ormonde 417;
(1893) Isinglass 417;
(1897) Galtee More 403–4;
(1898) Jeddah 84; (1907)
Orby etc. 403–4; (1908)
Signorinetta 198; (1909)
Minoru 86, 87; (1911)
Atmah 286; (1922) Captain
Cuttle 324; (1923) Papyrus
95; (1924) Salmon-Trout
119; (1924) Sansovino
321; (1925) Zionist 112,
123–4; (1926) Colorado,
Coronach 224; (1928)
Fairway 226, 279; (1929)
Kopi, Trigo, Walter Gay
133, 295; (1930) Blenheim,
Diolite, Rustom Pasha 126,
135, 136–7, 297; (1931)
Cameronian, Orpen 236,
300; (1932) April the Fifth,
Dastur 237–8; (1934)
Colombo, Umidwar,
Windsor Lad 244, 305, 313;
(1935) Bahram etc. 309,
398–417; (1936) Mahmoud
etc. 107, 150, 249–50;
(1937) Mid-day Sun, Le
Grand Duc 219, 222, 256;
(1938) Bois Roussel, Mirza
106, 154; (1941) Morogoro
159; (1943) Umiddad
264; (1944) Tehran 265,
267; (1946) Khaled 269;
(1947) Migoli 271; (1948)
My Love, Noor, Royal

Drake 166–7, 273; (1950)
Khorassan 169; (1951)
Fraise du Bois 179; (1952)
Tulyar 171; (1955) Hafiz
176; (1956) Buisson Ardent
180; (1957) Prince Taj 181;
(1958) Hard Ridden 188
Diomed Stakes: (1949)
Moondust 276
Great Surrey Foal Stakes:
(1912) Friar Marcus 334;
(1924) Phanarite 114–15;
(1955) Palariva 177
Lonsdale Stakes: (1946)
Neocracy 270
Nonesuch Plate: (1936) Taj
Akbar 249
Nonesuch Stakes: (1931)
Lemnarchus 299
Oaks Stakes: (1905) Cherry
Lass 322; (1908)
Signorinetta 198; (1923)
Teresina 96; (1925) Saucy
Sue 321; (1927) Beam
224–5; (1928) Toboggan
227; (1930) Fair Isle, Rose
of England 228; (1932)
Udaipur 236–7; (1934)
Light Brocade 242; (1935)
Ankaret, Quashed 309;
(1946) Steady Aim 269;
(1948) Masaka 272; (1954)
Sun Cap 340; (1956)
Yasmin; (1957) Rose Royale
II 180–1
Princess Elizabeth Stakes:
(1954) Bara Bibi 173
Woodcote Stakes: (1931) Dastur
145; (1934) Bagman 346

Goodwood
Chesterfield Cup: (1929)
Double Life 480; (1930)
The MacNab 298; (1931)
Lord Bill 234
Goodwood Cup: (1924)
Teresina 96; (1927) Dark
Japan 129; (1928) Bois
Josselyn, Kinchinjunga
313; (1932) Ut Majeur
141
Gordon Stakes: (1930) Press
Gang, Ut Majeur 140, 298;
(1932) Firdaussi 239
Gratwicke Stakes: (1928)
Parwiz 130; (1929)
Hunter's Moon 229; (1934)

Umidwar 244, 307; (1935)
Flash Bye, Louise 310, 428
Ham Produce Stakes: (1925)
Moti Mahal 125; (1930)
Ann Gudman 133; (1932)
Moti Begum 239; (1933)
Mrs Rustom 98, 242;
(1934) Theft 352, 355;
(1937) Tahir 256; (1939)
Turkhan 466
King George Stakes: (1924)
Mumtaz Mahal 105; (1929)
Tiffin 295; (1930) Fair
Isle 228; (1933) Concerto,
Myrobella 472; (1956)
Palariva 178
Lavant Stakes: (1923) Diophon
113; (1927) Hakim 129;
(1933) Propaganda 303;
(1934) Maltravers 356, 376;
(1937) Mirza 106
March Stakes: (1934)
Felicitation, Hyperion 304
Molecomb Stakes: (1923)
Mumtaz Mahal 104; (1929)
Diolite 297; (1933) Light
Brocade 242; (1934) La
Gaiete 356; (1937) Ann
of Austria, Stafaralla 256;
(1941) Mah Iran 260;
(1949) Diableretta 274;
(1951) Tayeh 169; (1955)
Palariva 177
Nassau Stakes: (1905) Cherry
Lass 322
Prince of Wales's Stakes:
(1912) Friar Marcus 334
Richmond Stakes: (1922)
Bombay Duck 93; (1934)
Bobsleigh 352, 355, 376;
(1935) Mahmoud 310;
(1946) Petition 270; (1949)
Palestine 273
Rous Memorial Stakes: (1929)
Press Gang 296; (1934)
Bahram etc. 307, 357–8,
454
Stewards Cup: (1919) Irish
Elegance 288; (1930) Le
Phare 136, 140, 141–2;
(1933) Pharacre, Solenoid
302–3
Sussex Stakes: (1932) Dastur
238; (1933) Gino 240;
(1934) Badruddin 242;
(1935) Fairbairn, Hairan
427; (1936) Taj Akbar 255;

(1947) Petition 271; (1950)
Palestine 169
Trundle Stakes: (1933)
    Seminole 303

Hungarian St. Leger
(1917) San Gennaro 221
Hurst Park
Derby Trial: (1940) Tant
    Mieux, Turkhan 466
Duchess of York Plate: (1905)
    Cherry Lass 322
Great Two-year-old Stakes:
    (1924) Zionist 121; (1929)
    Press Gang 296; (1931)
    Firdaussi 236; (1933)
    Umidwar 242
Hyperion Stakes: (1935) Solar
    Ray 427
Paradise Stakes: (1922)
    Blandford etc. 324
Victoria Cup: (1932) Knight
    Error 302

Kempton Park
Classic Trial: (1950) Khorassan
    169
Duke of York Handicap: (1929)
    Double Life 480
Duke of York Stakes: (1922)
    Poisoned Arrow 290;
    (1932) Firdaussi 239
Imperial Produce Stakes:
    (1922) Cos 97–8; (1923)
    Mumtaz Mahal 104; (1927)
    Buland 129; (1932) Gino
    239; (1934) Shahali 363,
    376; (1949) Éclat, Kisaki
    275
One Thousand Guineas Trial:
    (1948) Masaka 272
Rosebery Handicap: (1936)
    Theft 447
Kentucky
Derby: (1978) Affirmed, Alydar
    446–7

Leicester
Astley Stakes: (1923) Friar's
    Daughter 337
Lincoln
Lincolnshire Handicap: (1953-
    4) Nahar 177
Lingfield
Derby Trial: (1935) Bahram
    etc. 400; (1952) Tulyar
    171

Oaks Trial: Astrakhan 166
Liverpool
Aintree Derby: (1938)
    Foxglove II 154
Atlantic Cup: (1925) Diophon
    124–5; (1930) Bosworth
    230; (1934) Alishah 244
Autumn Cup: (1908-09)
    Santeve 286; (1925)
    Donzelon 291
*Lancashire Breeders' Produce
    Stakes*: (1919) Southern
    289; (1934) Kingsem 361
St George Stakes: (1928)
    Toboggan 227; (1929)
    Bosworth 229; (1931)
    Khorsheed 131; (1934)
    Adept 307; (1935) Plassy
    428
St Leger: (1910) Swynford
    319; (1930) Ut Majeur 141
Summer Cup: (1910) Swynford
    319
Union Jack Stakes: (1929)
    Hunter's Moon 229; (1932)
    Bulandshar 239; (1935)
    Cyrus, Godolphin, Trade
    Wind 348
Longchamp
Grand Critérium: (1933)
    Brantôme 327; (1934)
    Mistress Ford 329
Grand Prix de Paris: (1906)
    Maintenon, Spearmint 202;
    (1930) Ut Majeur 140;
    (1947) Avenger II 162;
    (1948) My Love 166
Poule d'Essai des Poulains:
    (1934) Brantôme 327;
    (1973) Kalamoun 178
Poule d'Essai des Pouliches:
    (1957) Toro 181
Prix d'Arenberg: (1955)
    Palariva 177–8
Prix de Diane (French Oaks):
    (1936) Mistress Ford 329
Prix de l'Arc de Triomphe:
    (1934) Brantôme,
    Felicitation 241, 327;
    (1935) Samos 94; (1948)
    Migoli etc. 272; (1952)
    Nuccio 170, 175; (1954)
    Sica Boy 340; (1970)
    Nijinsky 443–4; (1977)
    Alleged, Dunfermline 444
Prix du Cadran: (1935)
    Brantôme 327

Prix du Prince d'Orange:
    (1935) Brantôme 328
Prix Lupin: (1934) Brantôme
    327; (1973) Kalamoun 178
Prix Royal Oak: (1934)
    Brantôme 327; (1947)
    Imphal 251
Louisville, Kentucky
Kentucky Derby: (1931)
    Twenty Grand 321; (1934)
    Cavalcade 321; (1936) Bold
    Venture 321

Maisons-Laffitte
Prix Robert Papin: (1933)
    Brantôme 327; (1934)
    Mistress Ford 328
Manchester
Autumn Breeders Plate: (1934)
    Radamedes 358
Manchester Cup: (1923)
    Bhuidhaonach 290; (1932)
    Ut Majeur 141; (1933)
    Robber Chief 302
Manchester Handicap: (1927)
    Dark Japan 129
Red Rose Stakes: (1950)
    Palestine 169
Royal Standard Stakes:
    (1925) Zambo 124; (1927)
    Trelawny 293; (1929)
    Bosworth 229; (1935)
    Plymouth Sound 387;
    (1947) Migoli 271
Musselborough
Edinburgh Cup: (1936) Near
    Relation 245

Newbury
Autumn Cup: (1931) Isfandiar
    143
Autumn Plate: (1931) Firdaussi
    143
Beckhampton Plate: (1934)
    Consequential 360
Champagne Stakes: (1941) Big
    Game etc. 474–5
Greenham Plate: (1924)
    Amilcar, Phanarite 114–15;
    (1929) Costaki Pasha 139;
    (1935) Theft 384, 447;
    (1937) Mirza 106; (1938)
    Mirza 252
John Porter Stakes: (1929)
    Silver Hussar 116; (1933)
    Firdaussi 239; (1934)
    Felicitation 241

Kennet Stakes: (1921)
Blandford 323
King George Stakes: (2005)
Azamour 210
Manton Plate: (1929) Blenheim
132
Midsummer Stakes: (1930) Fair
Isle 228
Reading Nursery Handicap:
(1923) Friar's Daughter
337
United Services Cup: (1931)
Lights o'London 143
Newcastle
Northumberland Plate: (1931)
Blue Vision 305
Newmarket
April Stakes: (1944) Persian
Gulf 482
Boscawen (Post) Stakes: (1934)
Bahram etc. 308, 362–3,
454
Bretby Handicap: (1914) Friar
Marcus 334
*Buckenham (Post Produce)
Stakes*: (1932) Gino 239;
(1933) Alishah 242; (1934)
Theft 352
Burwell Stakes: (1930)
Bosworth 230
Cambridgeshire Handicap:
(1918) Irish Elegance 288;
(1919) Brigand 285; (1929)
Double Life 480; (1933)
Gino 240; (1945) Esquire
340; (1946) Caro 269;
(1956) Hafiz 177
Cesarewitch Handicap: (1908)
Yentoi 286; (1923) Teresina
96; (1924) Charley's Mount
108; (1928) Baytown 294;
(1930) Ut Majeur 140–1;
(1931) Khorsheed, Noble
Star 143, 301; (1932)
Blue Vision 305; (1933)
Seminole 303; (1935)
Lucky Patch, Near Relation
244–5; (1936) Near Relation
245
Challenge Stakes: (1933)
Heronslea, Myrobella 472;
(1934) Mate 308
Champion Stakes: (1917)
Gay Crusader 220; (1928)
Baytown, Fairway 227,
294; (1930) Fair Isle,
Rustom Pasha 98, 138,

139–40, 228; (1932)
Cameronian, Dastur 237–8,
301; (1933) Dastur 238;
(1934) Umidwar 244, 308;
(1935) Alcazar, Buckleigh,
Wychwood Abbot 435–6;
(1940) Hippius, Stardust
257, 466; (1942) Big Game
etc. 478; (1943) Umiddad
264; (1946) Caro 269;
(1947) Migoli 271; (1952)
prize money 175; (1955)
Hafiz 176; (1957) Rose
Royale II 181
Cherry Hinton: (1949)
Diableretta 274
Chesterfield Handicap: (1914)
Friar Marcus 334
Chesterfield Stakes: (1923)
Diophon 113; (1927)
Hakim 129; (1934)
Alykhan, Maltravers 307,
347, 376; (1937) Mirza
106; (1941) Mah Iran,
Watling Street 260, 475;
(1948) Moondust 275–6
Cheveley Park Stakes: (1922)
Paola 93; (1933) Light
Brocade 242; (1934)
Caretta 375; (1937)
Stafaralla 115, 152, 256;
(1949) Corejada, Diableretta
274
Chippenham Stakes: (1911)
Swynford 320; (1935)
Felicitation 309; (1936)
Bobsleigh 404
Clearwell Stakes: (1933)
Badruddin 242; (1949)
Tambara 275
Column Produce Stakes: (1935)
Portfolio, Tiderace, Trade
Wind 384; (1946) Khaled
269
Coronation Cup: (1944)
Persian Gulf, Umiddad 266,
483
Coventry Stakes: (1941) Big
Game, Watling Street 474
Craven Stakes: (1928) Royal
Minstrel 140; (1930)
Ut Majeur 140; (1931)
Cameronian 299; (1935)
Buckleigh, Hindoo Holiday,
Zingaro 384; (1936) Bala
Hissar 249; (1940) British
Empire, Turkhan 257, 466;

(1947) Migoli 271; (1949)
Moondust 276
Crawfurd Plate: (1914) Friar
Marcus 334
Criterion Stakes: (1933)
Windsor Lad 456; (1934)
Shahali 376
Culford Stakes: (1944) Tehran
265
Dalham Stakes: (1948) Dust
Devil 276
Derby: (1940) Pont l'Eveque,
Turkhan 259
Dewhurst Stakes: (1919)
Southern 289; (1923)
Salmon-Trout 120–1;
(1927) Toboggan 225;
(1931) Firdaussi 145,
236; (1932) Ramtapa 152;
(1933) Mrs Rustom 98;
(1934) Hairan 309, 375;
(1935) Bala Hissar 247;
(1936) Sultan Mahomed
255; (1942) Umiddad 264;
(1946) Migoli 270; (1949)
Kisaki 275; (1952) Pinza
172
Dullingham Stakes: (1936)
Bobsleigh 404; (1946)
Caro 269
Exeter Stakes: (1934) Alykhan
347–8; (1935) Mahmoud
310
Falmouth Stakes: (1930)
Theresina 97, 139, 142;
(1945) Naishapur 268
Fen Ditton Stakes: (1944)
Persian Gulf 483
Free Handicap: (1904) Cherry
Lass 322; (1928) Baytown
294
Gold Cup: (1942) Afterthought
478; (1944) Umiddad 266
Granby Stakes: (1938) Dhoti
256
Great Bradley Stakes: (1942)
Nasrullah 262
Great Foal Stakes: (1935) Solar
Ray 435; (1945) Naishapur
268; (1946) Caro 269
Histon Stakes: (1953) Bara
Bibi 173
Hopeful Stakes: (1923)
Diophon 113; (1928)
Costaki Pasha 98, 131;
(1929) Blenheim 133;
(1931) Dastur 236; (1932)

Myrobella 471; (1934)
Radamedes 358; (1949)
Diableretta 274
Houghton Stakes: (1926) Beam
225; (1930) Khorsheed 131;
(1949) Tabriz 275
Jockey Club Cup: (1926)
Bongrace, Glommen 292;
(1930) Baytown 294;
(1931) Khorsheed, Ut
Majeur 131, 141; (1934)
Felicitation 241; (1935)
Alcazar, Quashed 446;
(1938) Foxglove II 154;
(1943) Bright Lady,
Shahpour 158, 266
Jockey Club Stakes: (1892)
Isinglass 308; (1912)
Prince Palatine 86; (1922)
Lady Juror 101; (1924)
Teresina 96; (1925)
Tatra etc. 291; (1928)
Toboggan 227; (1929)
Bosworth 229; (1931) Ut
Majeur, Khorsheed 141,
143; (1932) Firdaussi 237;
(1934) Umidwar 244, 308;
(1935) Plassy 435; (1949)
Dust Devil 276; (1950)
Holmbush 170
July Cup: (1918) Irish Elegance
287; (1929) Le Phare, Royal
Minstrel, Tiffin 147, 295;
(1933) Concerto, Myrobella
471–2
July Stakes: (1923) Diophon
113; (1927) Fairway, Hakim
129, 225; (1929) Teacup
132–3; (1933) Alishah 242;
(1934) Hilla 347; (1937)
Mirza 106; (1941) Ujiji
158; (1945) Rivaz 263;
(1946) Neocracy 270;
(1947) Masaka 271; (1949)
Diableretta 274
Limekiln Stakes: (1935)
Alcazar, Bobsleigh 404,
446
Linton Stakes: (1944) High
Chancellor, Persian Gulf
482
May Stakes: (1923) Friar's
Daughter 336–7
Middle Park Stakes: (1908)
Bayardo 455; (1912)
Friar Marcus 334; (1919)
Southern 289; (1921)

Golden Corn 324; (1922)
Paola 93; (1923) Diophon
113; (1925) Coronach 457;
(1927) Parwiz, Pharamond
130, 225; (1928) Costaki
Pasha 98, 130–1; (1929)
Press Gang 296; (1930)
Blenheim, Khorsheed 131,
133; (1932) Felicitation
239; (1933) Mrs Rustom
98; (1934) Bahram etc. 308,
360, 365–7, 454–5; (1937)
Mirza 106; (1939) Djebel,
Turkhan 466; (1941) Sun
Chariot, Watling Street
475–6; (1942) Nasrullah,
Ribon 262, 292; (1945)
Khaled 268; (1949) Masked
Light, Palestine 273
Midsummer Stakes: (1934)
Badruddin 307
New Derby: (1916) Fifinella,
Kwang-Su, Nassovian
220; (1940) Pont l'Eveque,
Turkhan 466–7; (1942)
Big Game etc. 477; (1943)
Nasrullah, Persian Gulf
263, 480
New Oaks: (1942)
Afterthought, Sun Chariot
478
Newmarket Stakes: (1923)
Teresina 96; (1925) Zionist
124; (1928) Fairway 225–6;
(1929) Hunter's Moon,
Mr. Jinks 229; (1930)
Ut Majeur 140; (1932)
Bulandshar 239; (1933)
Young Lover 241; (1935)
Bobsleigh, Flash Bye,
Hairan 396–7, 428; (1940)
Turkhan 466
Norfolk Two-year-old Stakes:
(1939) Turkhan 465
Oaks Stakes: (1905) Cherry
Lass 322; (1932) Udaipur
237; (1934) Miss Erene
308; (1945) Naishapur, Sun
Stream 268, 322
One Thousand Guineas: (1905)
Cherry Lass 322; (1911)
Atmah, Radiancy 286;
(1918) Ferry 321; (1921)
Bettina 321; (1923) Cos,
Tranquil 98, 321; (1924)
Mumtaz Mahal 105; (1925)
Fironze Mahal, Saucy Sue

111, 321; (1927) Beam
225; (1928) Toboggan 227;
(1929) Taj Mah 109, 118,
133; (1930) Fair Isle 228;
(1931) Four Course etc 299;
(1932) Udaipur 237; (1933)
Myrobella, Una 241, 471;
(1934) Light Brocade, Mrs
Rustom 242; (1936) Tide-
Way 322; (1942) Mah Iran
260; (1945) Sun Stream
322; (1947) Neocracy 270;
(1948) Masaka 272; (1950)
Diableretta 274; (1957)
Rose Royale II, Sensualita
180–1
Prendergast Stakes: (1923)
Salmon-Trout 120; (1932)
Myrobella 471; (1949)
Éclat 275
Princess of Wales's Stakes:
(1894) Isinglass 381; (1911)
Swynford 320; (1916)
Nassovian 220; (1922)
Blandford 324–5; (1924)
Salmon-Trout 120; (1927)
Colorado 224; (1930)
Bosworth, Press Gang 230,
298; (1935) Fairbairn, Flash
Bye 427–8; (1934) Bright
Bird 306; (1936) Taj Akbar
255
Queen Mary Stakes: (1941) Sun
Chariot 476
Rous Memorial Stakes: (1912)
Friar Marcus 334; (1934)
Maltravers 376; (1949)
Tambara 275
Rutland Stakes: (1945)
Naishapur 268
Select Stakes: (1919) Irish
Elegance 289
Severals Stakes: (1933)
Myrobella 471
St Leger: (1930) Ut Majeur
140, 141; (1935) Buckleigh
435; (1942) Sun Chariot,
Watling Street 478; (1943)
Persian Gulf etc. 481;
(1944) Tehran 265
Thorney Stakes: (1944) Persian
Gulf, Umiddad 266, 482
Two Thousand Guineas:
(1911) Sunstar 391; (1913)
Friar Marcus 334; (1914)
Kennymore 319; (1916)
Clarissimus, Kwang-Su,

Nassovian 220; (1922)
Captain Cuttle 324; (1924)
Diophon 119; (1925)
Manna 112, 124; (1926)
Colorado, Coronach 224,
456–7; (1928) Royal
Minstrel 147; (1929)
Hunter's Moon 229; (1930)
Blenheim, Diolite 136–7,
297; (1931) Cameronian,
Lemnarchus, Orpen 236,
299; (1932) Dastur, Orwell
237–8; (1933) Gino 97,
240; (1934) Badruddin,
Colombo, Umidwar 106,
242–3, 304; (1935) Bahram
etc. 308, 386–93, 396,
447; (1936) Bala Hissar,
Payup 246, 248; (1937)
Mirza 106; (1940) Djebel,
Turkhan, Stardust 257,
259, 466; (1941) Morogoro
159; (1942) Big Game,
Watling Street 476–7;
(1943) Nasrullah 262;
(1944) Tehran 152, 265,
267; (1946) Happy Knight,
Khaled 269; (1947) Tudor
Minstrel 271; (1950)
Palestine, Prince Simon
168; (1956) Buisson Ardent
180
Wood Ditton Stakes: (1922)
Captain Cuttle 324; (1928)
Baytown 294
Nottingham
Great Midlands Breeders Plate:
(1936) Taj Akbar 255
New Jockey Club Cup: (1940)
Turkhan 468
*Nottinghamshire Breeders Foal
Plate*: (1934) Theft 352,
375

Redcar
*Great National Breeders Foal
Plate*: (1935) Fairbairn 427

Salisbury
Champagne Stakes: (1934)
Quadrille Boy 360
Cranbourne Stakes: (1941) Big
Game 473
Hurstbourne Plate: (1941) Big
Game 473

Salisbury Maiden Plate: (1932)
Myrobella 470
Salisbury Plate: (1941) Big
Game 473–4
Salisbury Stakes: (1932)
Myrobella 470; (1942) Big
Game 476
Sandown Park
Eclipse Stakes: (1911)
Lemberg, Swynford 320;
(1912) Prince Palatine 86;
(1923) Teresina 96; (1924)
Salmon-Trout 119; (1925)
Zambo 110, 124; (1927)
Colorado, Coronach 224;
(1928) Fairway, Royal
Minstrel 147, 226; (1929)
Parwiz, Royal Minstrel
132, 147; (1930) Rustom
Pasha 98, 138; (1931)
Carleon 232; (1933)
Firdaussi, Gino 239, 240;
(1934) King Salmon etc.
244, 307; (1935) Theft,
Windsor Lad 447; (1946)
Khaled 269; (1947) Migoli
271; (1948) Migoli, Noor,
Petition 272–3; (1950)
Éclat, Palestine 169; (1952)
Tulyar, Fraise du Bois
171
Great Kingston Plate: (1923)
Friar's Daughter 337
*National Breeders Produce
Stakes*: (1908) Bayardo
455; (1922) Cos 98; (1923)
Mumtaz Mahal 104; (1924)
Mirawala 115; (1932)
Myrobella 470; (1934)
Bahram etc. 348–52, 454–5;
(1937) Tahir 256; (1939)
British Empire, Stardust
257; (1949) Palestine 273;
(1952) Masai King 173;
(1955) Palariva 177
Sandringham Foal Plate:
(1935) Solar Ray 427
Stud Produce Stakes: (1934)
Vallema 345; (1949)
Palestine 273

Thirsk
St Leger Stakes: (1940)
Turkhan, Stardust 97, 257,
259

Yorkshire St Leger: (1940)
Turkhan etc. 468–9

Windsor
Speedy Plate: (1923) Friar's
Daughter 337
Wolverhampton
Shrewsbury Selling Plate:
(1934) Double Event, Up
Rivers 308

York
Duke of York Plate: (1935)
Plassy 428
Ebor Handicap: (1938)
Foxglove II 154
Gimcrack Stakes: (1919)
Southern 289; (1921)
Scamp 324; (1928)
Hunter's Moon 229;
(1932) Young Lover 240;
(1933) Mrs Rustom 98,
147; (1934) Bahram,
Consequential 358–9,
366, 454; (1937) Tahir
256; (1946) Petition 270;
(1947) Masaka 271; (1949)
Palestine 273
Great Yorkshire Stakes: (1923)
Teresina 96; (1925) Zambo
124; (1934) Windsor Lad
360; (1935) Fairbairn, Robin
Goodfellow 425, 427
Lowther Stakes: (1938) Sultan
Mahomed 255; (1955)
Palariva 177–8
Malton Plate: (1934)
Maltravers 376
Nunthorpe Stakes: (1924)
Mumtaz Mahal 105; (1933)
Concerto, Myrobella 472
Prince of Wales's Stakes:
(1934) Maltravers 376;
(2005) Azamour 210
Yorkshire Cup: (1933) Orpen
236; (1934) Blue Vision
305; (1935) Felicitation
241
Yorkshire Stakes: (1935)
Felicitation 308